SYNTHESIS

Legal Reading, Reasoning, and Communication

ASPEN COURSEBOOK SERIES

SYNTHESIS

Legal Reading, Reasoning, and Communication

FIFTH EDITION

Deborah A. Schmedemann
Professor of Law Emerita

Christina L. Kunz
Professor of Law Emerita

*both of William Mitchell College of Law
(now Mitchell Hamline School of Law)*

Published by Wolters Kluwer in New York.

Wolters Kluwer Legal & Regulatory U.S. serves customers worldwide with CCH, Aspen Publishers, and Kluwer Law International products. (www.WKLegaledu.com)

To contact Customer Service, e-mail customer.service@wolterskluwer.com, call 1-800-234-1660, fax 1-800-901-9075, or mail correspondence to:

Wolters Kluwer

Attn: Order Department

PO Box 990

Frederick, MD 21705

Printed in the United States of America.

1 2 3 4 5 6 7 8 9 0

ISBN 9-781-4548-8650-1

Library of Congress Cataloging-in-Publication Data

Names: Schmedemann, Deborah A., 1956- author. | Kunz, Christina L., author.
Title: Synthesis : legal reading, reasoning, and communication / Deborah A. Schmedemann, Professor of Law Emerita, Christina L. Kunz, Professor of Law Emerita, both of William Mitchell College of Law (now Mitchell Hamline School of Law).
Description: Fifth edition. | New York : Wolters Kluwer, 2017. | Series: Aspen coursebook series | Includes bibliographical references and index.
Identifiers: LCCN 2017000475 | ISBN 9781454886501
Subjects: LCSH: Legal composition. | Law—United States—Interpretation and construction. | Forensic oratory. | LCGFT: Textbooks.
Classification: LCC KF250 .S36 2017 | DDC 808.06/634—dc23 LC record available at https://lccn.loc.gov/2017000475

About Wolters Kluwer Legal & Regulatory U.S.

Wolters Kluwer Legal & Regulatory U.S. delivers expert content and solutions in the areas of law, corporate compliance, health compliance, reimbursement, and legal education. Its practical solutions help customers successfully navigate the demands of a changing environment to drive their daily activities, enhance decision quality and inspire confident outcomes.

Serving customers worldwide, its legal and regulatory portfolio includes products under the Aspen Publishers, CCH Incorporated, Kluwer Law International, ftwilliam.com and MediRegs names. They are regarded as exceptional and trusted resources for general legal and practice-specific knowledge, compliance and risk management, dynamic workflow solutions, and expert commentary.

This edition is dedicated to the thousands of students we have taught in our careers, many of whom have become lawyers who have served—and continue to serve—their clients, their communities, and the law with great distinction.

SUMMARY OF CONTENTS

CONTENTS

CHAPTER 4

Reading Codes   73

CHAPTER 19

Oral Advocacy   441

LIST OF BOXES

LIST OF EXHIBITS

PREFACE

If you are reading this book, you are engaged in some way in legal education. That means you have chosen to learn something truly significant: for yourself, for your future clients, for your community, for our system of government (especially now, it would seem). This is a good thing to do.

Yet it is not an easy thing to do. Thus, this book is aimed at helping you learn the core skills to carry out those significant roles excellently, efficiently, and ethically. Some of those skills are "in-your-head" skills: reading legal texts, many of which are complicated, and reasoning in various ways about the facts of your client's situations. Some of those skills are "on-paper" skills: writing in various legal formats, from office memos to contracts to appellate briefs. Other skills are "people" skills: interviewing and counseling your client, negotiating with opposing counsel, arguing before a court.

All of these skills intertwine; to be good at one is to be good at the others. That is why the first word in the title of the book is "synthesis." Another reason is that as you build excellence in these skills, you will also build efficiency and ethical practice—these standards are all intertwined as well.

This is the fifth edition of this book. Over the years, it has been "co-written" by the dozens and dozens of practicing lawyers who have taught in the skills courses at William Mitchell College of Law[1] every year, who have informed us on the content of the chapters. Our other "co-writers" are the hundreds of students who have taken those courses each year, who have provided invaluable insights into the teaching choices reflected here:

- The various chapters provide essential background for each topic, discuss the skills in general terms, provide steps to follow, and explain applicable ethical principles. Some chapters include empirical studies as well.
- Skills are best learned through concrete examples, so the chapters provide examples drawing on four client situations, each arising in an area of law commonly taught in the first year of law school, each arising in a different practice context. As the client situations repeat, you will see how the various skills intertwine.
- The chapters feature various visual elements, including opening diagrams and charts, for visually oriented learners.
- Each chapter ends in a set of questions and answers, under the label Test Your Understanding, which you may use to prime your reading and then verify what you have learned.
- The book also features an extended set of exercises through which you may practice the various skills. These exercises are set in yet another area of law, draw on two client situations, and provide step-by-step guidance

---

1. William Mitchell is now a part of Mitchell Hamline School of Law.

for critiquing sample drafts, planning your own projects, or indeed writing your own text.

All in all, the book is designed to move you through a spiral of activities that will not only introduce you to the skills discussed here but also help you to solidify your competence.

***

Finally a word for professors: If you are familiar with the fourth edition of this book, I trust you will be pleased to note the following major changes:

- This book covers three new conversations: interviewing the client, counseling the client, and negotiating with opposing counsel. All may be taught from a dispute or transactional standpoint and are supported by extensive teaching materials in the teacher's manual.
- The four example cases that now thread throughout the book arise in contracts, torts, criminal law, and constitutional law. The exercises draw on a torts law topic. (These various cases overlap with the new ninth edition of *The Process of Legal Research*, to permit tightly coordinated teaching.)
- The appellate brief chapter features real briefs written for a real case, which was decided en banc by the Third Circuit Court of Appeals.
- The chapters are supplemented by Test Your Understanding questions and answers, to assist students in focusing on and reinforcing key concepts.

As always, I welcome your questions and comments.
Deborah A. Schmedemann
Minneapolis/January 2017

ACKNOWLEDGMENTS

Over the years, we have had the good fortune to write and revise this book in a perfect environment—with the careful eye and constructive suggestions of thousands of readers: thousands of students at William Mitchell College of Law (now Mitchell Hamline School of Law); hundreds of adjunct writing professors; and fellow course co-coordinators Ken Kirwin, Mehmet Konar-Steenberg, Dean Raths, and Gregory Duhl. Every administration has provided whole-hearted support. Cal Bonde, Darlene Finch, and Lynette Fraction of the College's staff have provided excellent administrative and production support.

This edition includes documents written by two students when they were students at William Mitchell College of Law—Annalise Backstrom and Christopher Ziolkowski; I am grateful to them for granting permission to use their work in this text. Similarly, this edition includes for the first time two briefs written by practicing lawyers in a real case—Mary Catherine Roper and John E. Freund, III. Their generosity in granting permission to use their work for these educational purposes is truly notable and greatly appreciated.

This is the fifth edition of this text. It has been a blessing to work with such a skilled—and in some cases familiar, understanding, and trusted—team: Sarah Hains, production editor; Susan McClung, copyeditor; and Kathy Langone, developmental editor, all of The Froebe Group.

I also acknowledge the publishers who have granted permission to reproduce the following works:

- ABA Model Rules of Professional Conduct §§ 1.6 and 4.1. © 2016 by the American Bar Association. Reprinted with permission. All rights reserved. This information or any portion thereof may not be copied or disseminated in any form or by any means or stored in an electronic database or retrieval system without the express written consent of the American Bar Association.
- Attorney fee retainer letter, West's Legal Forms, *Domestic Relations* § 2:15 (3d ed.). Copyright © 2016 by Thomson Reuters. Reprinted by permission.
- Annalise Backstrom, *Lynn and Brandon Brown on behalf of their minor child, Caleb Brown, Plaintiffs, vs. Perkinsberg School District, Defendant.* Reprinted by permission.
- Dan B. Dobbs, Paul T. Hayden & Ellen M. Bublick, *The Law of Torts* § 519 (2d ed.). Copyright © 2011 by Thomson Reuters. Reproduced with permission of Thomson Reuters.
- John E. Freund, Appellant's Brief in *B.H. v. Easton Area School District.* Reprinted by permission.

- *Luttrell v. United Telephone System*, Inc. July 19, 1984. Copyright © 2016 by Thomson Reuters. Reproduced with permission of Thomson Reuters.
- Thomas B. Merritt, *Connecticut Practice Series TM Elements of an Action,* § 5:8 October 2016 Update. Copyright © 2016 by Thomson Reuters. Reproduced with permission of Thomson Reuters.
- *Milton Moore, Administrator (Estate of John H. Moore) v. Bradford E. Bunk et al.* March 23, 1967. Copyright © 2016 by Thomson Reuters. Reproduced with permission of Thomson Reuters.
- Restatement of the Law Second, Contracts § 188 copyright © 1981 by The American Law Institute. Reproduced with permission. All rights reserved.
- Restatement of the Law, Third, Torts: Liability for Physical and Emotional Harm § 7 copyright © 2009 by The American Law Institute. Reproduced with permission of The American Law Institute and Thomson Reuters. All rights reserved.
- Mary Catherine Roper, Appellees' Brief in *B.H. v. Easton Area School District*. Reprinted by permission.
- Christopher Ziolkowski, *Lynn and Brandon Brown on behalf of their minor child, Caleb Brown, Plaintiffs, v. Perkinsberg School District, Defendant.* Reprinted by permission.

Finally, as always, I thank Craig Bower for his never-ending support.

SYNTHESIS

Legal Reading, Reasoning, and Communication

INTRODUCTION:

THE LAWYER'S ROLES

AND THE LEGAL SYSTEM

```
                    Representative
                      of Clients

                    THE ROLES OF
                     THE LAWYER

      Officer of the      Public Citizen
      Legal System     with Responsibility
                           for Justice
```

Every calling is great when greatly pursued.
—Oliver Wendell Holmes
"The Law," *Speeches* (1913)

A. INTRODUCTION

In the not-so-distant future, you likely will be a lawyer.[1] This means that you will find yourself helping people or entities (such as companies, nonprofit

---

1. The primary audience of this book is law students. If you are reading this book in some other capacity (such as a student in a legal assistant program), nearly all of what is stated here will apply to you too.

organizations, or government units) achieve their goals as they work through situations with legal dimensions. Your ability to perform legal reading, reasoning, and communication well will be critical to their success—and to your career success as well.

This book will teach you, first, how to read and reason in the law; a lawyer's unique service to a client is to provide legal analysis. This book will also teach you to write a range of common legal documents: the analytical office memo, the advice letter to the client, the demand letter to opposing counsel, contracts, pleadings, memoranda to district courts, and briefs to appellate courts. Furthermore, this book will help you learn how to converse with others: your client in interviewing and counseling, opposing counsel in negotiation, and the court in oral argument.

Skills cannot be learned in a vacuum. So this book discusses them in the context of a set of client situations:

- All-Day Wellness Minnesota provides workplace wellness services. This is a highly competitive industry, so All-Day Wellness would like to keep its employees from working for its competitors when they leave the company.[2]
- A Kansas grocery store, Bower's Bounty, has been charged with defamation by a recently terminated employee. Defamation involves making a damaging, false statement to one or more third persons.[3]
- Cassie Collins was ticketed in California for driving while using her cell phone after she was involved in a car accident while pulling out of a parking lot into traffic.[4]
- A student, Daniel de la Cruz, was suspended from public middle school for making statements in support of a breast cancer awareness group, raising an issue of federal constitutional law.[5]

As you will see, the various client matters arise in different legal contexts and different areas of law. They are set in different states as well. Many law firms handle client situations arising in various contexts and under various rules of law, but most firms focus on the laws of one location. This book uses the laws of various states for teaching purposes.

B. THE LAWYER'S ROLES

"A lawyer, as a member of the legal profession, is a representative of clients, an officer of the legal system, and a public citizen having special responsibility for the quality of justice," according to the Preamble to the *Model Rules of Professional Conduct* for lawyers, drafted by the *American Bar Association*

---

2. This situation is used as an example in Chapters 3, 5, 6, 8-11, 13, and 15.
3. This situation is used as an example in Chapters 3, 5-12, 14, and 15.
4. This situation is used as an example in Chapters 2, 4, 6, 7, and 8.
5. This situation is used as an example in Chapters 16-19.

(ABA).[6] In fulfilling these roles, what do lawyers actually do? And how do legal reading, reasoning, and communicating fit in?

1. Representing Clients

Whether law practice is a calling, an art, a science, or a business, *client representation* entails helping clients achieve their goals in legal situations. The practice of law encompasses a wide range of settings and tasks. In broad strokes, most practices can be categorized as transactional practice or dispute resolution.

As a *transactional lawyer*, a lawyer acts prospectively, counseling the client about the law that governs actions that the client may take in the future. The lawyer identifies options, assesses their legal implications, and often executes the option selected by the client. For example, transactional lawyers draft contracts and wills, write employee handbooks, prepare stock prospectuses, and complete license applications.

Lawyers who resolve disputes have traditionally operated in the court system and thus are known as *litigators*. A litigator acts primarily retrospectively, pleading the client's case before a decision-making tribunal so as to obtain a fair and favorable resolution of an existing dispute between the client and the opponent. The lawyer constructs legal arguments based on the facts and the law and presents them, generally in writing, sometimes orally, or sometimes both. For example, litigators prosecute or defend an individual charged with a crime, represent an employer in labor arbitration, present a landowner's argument before a zoning commission, or argue before an appeals court on behalf of a patent-holder.

In both the transaction and dispute settings, most lawyers spend much of their time negotiating favorable legal outcomes for their clients. The transactional lawyer seeks to secure a deal that provides favorable terms for his or her client within the parameters set by the law. Most disputes are resolved through negotiation that is informed by the law. For example, one side may assert that a jury would award substantial damages; the other may argue that the case would not even get to the jury because the judge would quickly dismiss the case. Most likely, the negotiated outcome would be somewhere between the parties' valuations of the case, reflecting not only the parties' legal positions but also other factors, such as their attitudes toward risk and economic situations.

In all of these instances, one of the lawyer's fundamental contributions is to develop and present a *legal analysis* of the client's situation. The lawyer places the facts of the client's experience within applicable legal rules and assigns to the client's experience the legal significance suggested by the rules.

> [I]n the law: we convert immediate experience into the subject of thought of a particular kind, which has at its center the question of meaning: *what this event means, and should mean, in the language of the law*; and what that language itself means, as a way in which we articulate our deepest values and attain collective being.[7]

---

6. The ABA is the leading national organization of lawyers. Among other functions, it plays a leading role in promulgating legal ethics codes and regulating legal education.

7. James Boyd White, *Meaning in the Life of the Lawyer*, 26 Cumb. L. Rev. 763, 770 (1996) (emphasis added).

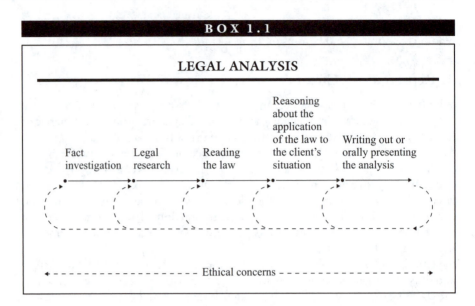

BOX 1.1

LEGAL ANALYSIS

This assignment of legal meaning, or legal analysis, occurs through several steps, as depicted in Box 1.1. Although the diagram shows an orderly sequence of steps, legal analysis is not entirely linear, as signified by the arrows looping back to earlier steps. Furthermore, as is discussed throughout this book, a lawyer faces ethical concerns at every step.

Ultimately, the client controls the case, whether it is a transaction or dispute. And the client may rely not only on the lawyer's expertise, but also on the counsel of other professionals, as well as on the client's own experience and values. There is no such thing as a purely legal problem.

Nor is legal analysis radically different from the types of analysis performed by other professionals. Rather, sound legal analysis resembles other forms of rigorous problem solving. Legal analysis requires the engineer's precision, the minister's close attention to text, the business manager's focus on strategy, the physician's openness to alternatives, and the social worker's concern for social good and individual well-being. Thus, no matter what background you bring to the law, your skills will be useful in the study and practice of law.

2. Serving the Legal System and Justice

As lawyers help clients achieve their goals, they also serve the public. In the words of the ABA Preamble, a lawyer acts as an "officer of the legal system" and as a "public citizen having special responsibility for the quality of justice."

As an *officer of the legal system*, a transactional lawyer aids in the implementation of the law. The lawyer advises the client on how to conform his or her conduct to the law and implements a legally permitted solution. The public benefits from the client's law-abiding conduct.

In that same role, a litigator, as a gatekeeper for the legal system, screens out frivolous claims and guides real disputes into litigation or less formal and less costly forms of dispute resolution. There the lawyer accurately depicts the facts and the law and utilizes the specified procedures fairly. The public benefits from fair and efficient resolution of disputes.

Furthermore, lawyers participate in the lawmaking process. Law is a reiterative system of legal issues and legal rules. Lawmakers create legal rules in response to issues brought to their attention, typically by lawyers. The new rule then applies to other people or entities involved in similar situations. When the application of an existing rule proves problematic, lawmakers may revise the rule—again with the guidance of lawyers. Thus, when a lawyer represents a client, the lawyer also influences the direction of the law for the future. As you will see, this is most obvious as to case law, where courts make law in the context of litigation, but lawyers also play key roles in other contexts as well.

Fulfilling these various roles often entails difficult judgment calls. For example, the lawyer must decide how to protect client confidences, how to present testimony in court, and whether to facilitate transactions that push the boundaries of the law. In making these decisions, a lawyer is guided by his or her own personal values, as well as by codes of professional ethics, which set the standards by which lawyers are judged.

In addition to serving clients and the legal system, lawyers are *public citizens* called upon to serve justice. Phrased in the terms of professional ethics codes, lawyers have a professional responsibility to engage in *pro bono publico*, which means "for the public good." Model Rule 6.1 recognizes that many activities serve the public good. Representing people of limited means for free and representing organizations that aim to serve people of limited means for free are emphasized in the ABA rule; these activities are for many lawyers the essence of pro bono. Other options include working for civil or public rights, representing community organizations, and participating in activities to improve the law or legal system. Failing to perform pro bono is unlikely to lead to professional discipline, yet many lawyers perform pro bono and find it highly meaningful and deeply rewarding.

3. Some Descriptions of Lawyer's Activities

To provide you with insights into law practice, we asked practicing attorneys from a range of settings to describe their day-to-day activities. Here are several responses from litigators in private law firms:

> I am on the phone five hours a day talking to clients and other lawyers. I listen sympathetically to everything they say, guide them, and lay the foundation for future calls when bad news may come. Talking to plaintiffs [i.e., the party that sues] is a matter of providing reassurance, much like in the ministry, but you need to be efficient. I also go to hearings, write briefs, take clients to lunch.
>
> I write—research and write. I'm usually part of a team. We spend lots of time developing a strategy, constructing arguments, figuring out what will happen down the road. I spend some time in client contact, advising them. Sometimes I go to [district or appellate] court (motion practice and appellate work). I take depositions and spend a lot of time

working with documents. [A deposition is a recorded pretrial interview of a witness or a party to a lawsuit.]

Currently I am setting up mediation for a large piece of litigation. [Mediation is a negotiation process aided by a third-party neutral.] So I talk on the phone with ten other attorneys. I keep in mind what the client wants, what the issues are, what procedures to follow. At the same time, I'm preparing for trial, in case mediation doesn't work: preparing a chronology of the facts, deciding which witnesses to call, analyzing evidentiary issues. I try mediation to avoid the time and expenses of trial for everyone yet prepare for trial so I know the case well and can anticipate what the other side will do.

Here are two responses from transactional lawyers in private firms:

I talk on the phone a lot of the day. I attend periodic day-long board meetings of my clients. The week before, I prepare opinions on new issues and status reports on pending matters. During the meetings, I advise on matters that were referred earlier, answer questions that come up. When I leave the meeting, I have a list of things to do for the next meeting. I consult with the client's in-house staff often, indeed on a daily basis.

I work for government entities or private individuals that want to build and need funding. I write documents that run over 100 pages to accomplish the deal and draft opinions about the deal. These must be written by an attorney in the red book, a guild-like system.

Other lawyers work as employees of clients, such as corporations or a government unit. Here are excerpts from an in-house corporate lawyer and a state assistant attorney general:

We handle every day-to-day problem that comes in the door. For example, how do we fire an employee, accept service of process on an employee who is hiding from it, draft articles of incorporation, manage litigation, pay off a mortgage, arrange executive compensation, modify an employee handbook? I do whatever I can to comply with the law and get the project off my desk: research, draft a letter or call someone, talk to the other side, talk to the client (the corporation's officers) or employees. I try to see what the problem is and what I can do to fix it, by contract, or phone call, or letter, or getting people to work together to work it out, or by paying a little money.

I do a lot of litigation—courtroom work—and heavy-duty brief writing. I research the applicable law, both sides of it; synthesize the cases; write the brief in support of the client's position. I write it to win, by making all arguments within the bounds of ethical conduct. Then I review it, file it, prepare for oral argument. I also advise the department I work for, when the department wants to do something new. So I research, brainstorm, think about it, give the best opinion as to whether the new action will withstand legal action. When there is a pervasive problem, I advise on initiating legislative action and consider: What is the evil to remedy? What is the solution? How can we write up the solution so it will be understandable to many people?

The following two excerpts are from lawyers on either side of the criminal justice system, a prosecutor (representing the government) and a public defender (representing the accused):

> I review police reports and decide what offense to charge. I advise police officers in ongoing investigations by answering the question on the other end of a ringing phone. I try cases: plan out the presentation of the evidence, meet with witnesses, prepare exhibits. I negotiate out most cases, since ninety-eight percent settle, which entails offering a plea to the defense attorney and agreeing to the sentence. I also research, write, and argue cases on appeal.

> My time is spent in client interviews, brief writing, oral arguments, as well as some trial court hearings. Because our clients have an absolute right to an appeal, we are not bound by professional responsibility rules on frivolous appeals, but we do retain the right to choose issues. It takes creativity to find colorable issues sometimes, although some cases do have real appealable issues.

Finally, the following excerpt describes a lawyer's pro bono representation of a man seeking asylum in the United States, based on his well-founded fear of persecution in his own country:

> At our first meeting—I'll never forget—he said to me, "If you can do this thing for me, you will be my brother." This sticks in your mind and is considerable motivation.
>
> I knew very little about the Oromo people. So I did research on the Internet and traditional library research, gathered material from Amnesty International and the State Department, and learned from my client. I came to know his story by sitting with him and talking to him; over six months, we met maybe twenty times for about an hour. We'd just talk about the asylum case—we didn't socialize. I wanted to keep this clinical, so I could remain dispassionate and objective. The first meeting, I got maybe five or ten percent of the story; he didn't open up with gruesome details until the third or fourth or fifth meeting. I needed to get him ready to talk about his situation before the asylum officer—he had to have some sort of interior distance from it.
>
> So then I wrote a letter, explaining why my client should get asylum and going through the three or four factors in the rule about well-founded fear. And I went with him to the interview with the asylum officer. The lawyer doesn't say anything until the end of the interview, when you bring your client back to inconsistencies or other troublesome parts of the interview.
>
> Happily, my client was granted asylum.[8]

As these excerpts demonstrate, the day-to-day activities of law practice vary depending on the lawyer's setting. Yet all lawyers aim to help their clients achieve their goals in a legal setting, by assigning a legal meaning to the situation and by using legal processes to advance the situation.

---

8. For additional accounts of lawyers' pro bono work, see Deborah A. Schmedemann, *Thorns and Roses: Lawyers Tell Their Pro Bono Stories* (2010).

BOX 1.2

HOW IMPORTANT ARE COMMUNICATION SKILLS?

Recent studies document the importance of communication skills. In one study:[9]

- 66 percent of litigation attorneys rated writing and drafting skills highly important among new associates.
- 74 percent of transactional attorneys rated drafting simple contracts and agreements as highly important.

In a forced-choice study of the most important skill sets for recent graduates, 41 percent of attorneys selected writing skills, and almost a quarter chose interpersonal skills.[10]

C. THE LEGAL SYSTEM

The U.S. legal system is complex, reflecting the intricate structure of the U.S. government. Box 1.3 presents the major institutions of our government and the forms of law each creates.

The *three levels* of government are *federal, state, and local*. The federal government generally occupies the highest position in a hierarchy, with state government in the middle and local government in the lowest position. In some areas of law, the federal government is the primary lawmaker, with state and local governments either supplementing the federal law or being precluded from lawmaking. In other fields, state or local law is the traditional and dominant source of law.

Under our tripartite system of government, the *three branches* of government are the legislature, the judiciary, and the executive. In the classic conception, each branch has its specific function in the legal system: the *legislature* making the law, the *judiciary* interpreting and applying the law to resolve specific disputes, and the *executive* implementing the law. The actual practice is more complex. Legislatures indeed make law through enacting statutes, but the judiciary also makes law via the *common law* (cases decided when there is no pertinent statute), the interpretation of statutes, and *rules of procedure*. *Administrative agencies* in the executive branch resolve specific disputes, issuing *decisions*, much as courts do, and promulgate *regulations* with the force of law, similar to the statutes that legislatures enact.

The genius of the tripartite system lies not only in the allocation of functions to each branch, but also in the *checks and balances* among the branches. For example, the judiciary may overturn legislation or agency actions that exceed

---

9. LexisNexis, *White Paper: Hiring partners reveal new attorney readiness for real world practice* (2015).
10. BARBRI, *State of the Legal Field Survey* (2015).

U.S. LEGAL SYSTEM: LEVELS AND BRANCHES OF GOVERNMENT, TYPES OF LAW

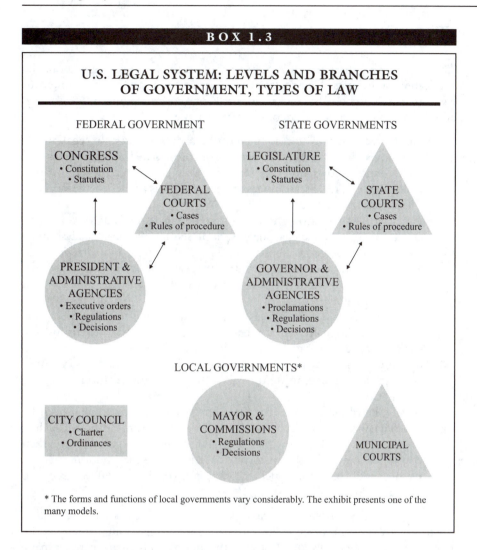

* The forms and functions of local governments vary considerably. The exhibit presents one of the many models.

the legislature's or agency's power. Through legislation, the legislature may respond to decisions of the courts interpreting its statutes.

These relationships among lawmaking bodies (as well as other key matters, such as the rights of citizens against the government) are stated in the *constitution* for each level of government. The U.S. Constitution is considered the supreme law of the land because it governs state and local governments, as well as the federal government. Constitutions are created through legislative processes and interpreted and applied by the courts.

The three branches and three levels of government engage in a continual process of lawmaking that can yield complex results. Thus, it is not surprising that a substantial body of legal scholarship, or *commentary*, explains the law and, in some cases, proposes reforms. Because these materials are written by lawyers, law professors, law students, or lawmakers not acting as lawmakers, they are not law. Yet they can be very helpful aids to you as you develop your legal analysis of a client's situation.

D. About This Book

This book covers three linked processes: reading the law, reasoning about the application of the rules of law to your client's situation, and communicating your legal analysis. This book has four major parts: one covers reading and reasoning, and the remaining three cover communication in each of three settings.

- Part One covers how to read the most basic of legal texts: the legal rule. It then covers how to read the two major formats of U.S. law—cases and codes—and follows up with reading commentary on the law. Part I concludes with legal reasoning, in which the law is applied to the facts of a client's situation.
- Part Two discusses how the work examined in Part I is used to advise a client: in writing up a legal analysis, in presenting that legal analysis in an analytical office memo about the client's situation, and in writing an advice letter to the client. Part II also discusses the two foundational conversations on which legal practice is built: the client interview and client counseling.
- Part Three discusses three facets of persuasion, the process by which one lawyer seeks to convince another party to take action benefitting the client, through informal means. One process is writing an analytical document: the demand letter. Another is drafting documents, whether contracts or pleadings. And the third is conversation—that is, negotiation.
- Finally, Part Four discusses the formal process of advocacy, the process by which a lawyer seeks a favorable ruling for a client from a tribunal, such as a court. This part begins with a general discussion of legal advocacy; then covers two main written forms of advocacy—the motion practice memorandum and the appellate brief; and concludes with a discussion of oral advocacy.

Each chapter offers various presentations of each skill. Each skill is discussed in the text, with key concepts in italics and diagrams and charts supplementing the text. The topics and skills are illustrated through various client matters; many chapters have sample documents in the text or in exhibits at the end of the chapter. Some of these documents are analyzed in the text; others are left for your analysis. Throughout, the book emphasizes four criteria by which to judge all your work: (1) completeness, (2) correctness, (3) coherence, and (4) comprehensibility. In addition, advisory work is judged by its creativity, and persuasive and advocacy work are judged by how convincing they are.

To help you test your understanding, each chapter ends with a set of questions and answers. Reading the questions before you read the chapter should help you sharpen your focus. After reading the chapter, try to fully answer the questions yourself before turning to the provided answers. This process will help you build your detailed reading skills—one of the critical skills that you will need to excel as a lawyer.

To further your understanding, following the chapter is a set of exercises affording you the opportunity to engage in the skills discussed in these chapters. The exercises provide you with client situations and a law library and then walk you through the steps to generate analyses and drafts of the various types of communications discussed in the chapters.

Three appendices (at the back of the book) cover facets of writing that are critical to any document that you may write as a lawyer: the writing process (Appendix I); paragraph, sentences, punctuation, and words (Appendix II); and citation, which is the practice of providing references to your sources (Appendix III). We encourage you to consult these appendices from time to time as you refine your written work.

One. Reading and Reasoning	
Chapter 2 Reading Legal Rules Chapter 3 Reading Cases Chapter 4 Reading Codes Chapter 5 Reading Commentary Chapter 6 Legal Reasoning	
Two. Advisory Communication	
Written Work	**Conversation**
Chapter 7 Writing Legal Analysis Chapter 8 The Analytical Office Memo Chapter 9 The Advice Letter	Chapter 10 Interviewing the Client Chapter 11 Counseling the Client
Three. Persuasive Communication	
Written Work	**Conversation**
Chapter 12 The Demand Letter Chapter 13 Contracts Chapter 14 Pleadings	Chapter 15 Negotiating with Opposing Counsel
Four. Advocacy Communication	
Written Work	**Conversation**
Chapter 16 Legal Advocacy Chapter 17 The Motion Practice Memorandum Chapter 18 The Appellate Brief	Chapter 19 Oral Argument in Court

TEST YOUR UNDERSTANDING

1. Read the statements of the All-Day Wellness, Bower's Bounty, Cassie Collins, and Daniel de la Cruz situations (on page 2). In which situations would the lawyer provide predominantly dispute resolution services, and in which would the lawyer provide predominantly transactional services?

2. If you were to represent one of these four clients on a pro bono basis, which is it most likely to be, and why?

3. As you will see, the All-Day Wellness and Bower's Bounty situations are governed by the common law. What is the common law?

4. On the other hand, the Cassie Collins situation is governed by a statute. What is a statute?

5. Finally, the Daniel de la Cruz situation in governed by the U.S. Constitution. What is the U.S. Constitution, and why would it apply to the de la Cruz situation?

6. To get an idea of which type of law governs your client's situation (and indeed what the law says), what type of legal materials do lawyers read?

7. Give two examples of checks and balances (that is, the interactions among the branches of government).

8. Name the three levels of government.

TEST YOUR UNDERSTANDING ANSWERS

1. All-Day Wellness calls for transactional services, whereas Bower's Bounty, Cassie Collins, and Daniel de la Cruz all call for dispute resolution services.

2. Daniel de la Cruz is the most likely pro bono client. The case involves free speech rights, and most parents would lack the resources for this type of litigation.

3. The common law is the law made through cases decided by courts in the absence of statutes.

4. A statute is a law enacted by a legislature.

5. The U.S. Constitution is considered the supreme law of the land, governs state governments, and addresses the rights of citizens against the government, which is the issue in the de la Cruz situation.

6. To get an idea of which type of law governs your client's situation and what the law says, lawyers read commentary.

7. The judiciary may overturn unconstitutional legislation, and the legislature may revise legislation in response to judicial opinions.

8. The three levels of government are federal, state, and local.

PART ONE

READING AND REASONING

In this part, you will study the reading and reasoning processes that precede the communications discussed in the three other parts of the book. Before you can write about a client's situation or converse with anyone about it, you must read the law and reason through the client's situation in light of the law.

Legal texts come in various forms and require a range of reading skills. Thus, the first four chapters in this part discuss reading the law, as follows:

- Chapter 2 discusses how to read legal rules—the core units of a legal text. You will learn what it means to create an if/then statement out of a legal rule.
- Chapter 3 discusses how to read cases—one of the two standard formats for legal authority in the U.S. legal system. You will learn how to deeply read and brief a single case and how to fuse a set of related cases.
- Chapter 4 discusses how to read codes—the other standard format for legal authority. In particular, you will learn how to parse and brief a statute and how to interpret it when it is ambiguous as applied to your client's situation.
- Chapter 5 discusses how to read various types of legal commentary—that is, material that is not itself law, but helps you to understand the law.

Finally, Chapter 6 covers the process of legal reasoning, in which you apply the law to a client's situation to yield a predicted legal outcome. You will learn about three related forms of legal reasoning, all of which depend on a careful reading of the law governing the client's situation.

READING LEGAL RULES

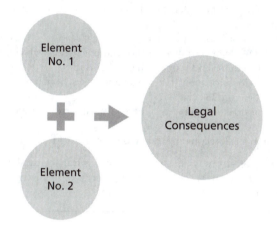

The prophecies of what the courts will do in fact, and nothing more pretentious, are what I mean by the law.
  —Oliver Wendell Holmes
    The Path of the Law, 10 Harv. L. Rev. 457, 461 (1897)

A. INTRODUCTION

The law is formed of rules. A *rule of law* is a general statement of what the law permits or requires of people or entities in certain situations. Rules of law appear in many legal authorities, such as cases, statutes, regulations, and rules of procedure. They all have the same function: to identify the legal consequences that follow when certain facts happen.

Rules of law benefit society. They specify predictable legal consequences of particular actions, so that people, companies, nonprofit organizations, and government units know how to conduct their activities legally. Rules of law also guide disputants and judges as they resolve disputes, so that similarly situated disputants obtain similar outcomes.

How does a lawyer draw guidance from a legal rule? In what can feel like a seamless process, a lawyer parses, or carefully reads through, the rule to discern its content and structure and then links the rule's requirements to key facts of the

---

BOX 2.1

CELL-PHONE DRIVING STATUTE

23123. (a) A person shall not drive a motor vehicle while using a wireless telephone unless that telephone is specifically designed and configured to allow hands-free listening and talking, and is used in that manner while driving.

(b) A violation of this section is an infraction punishable by a base fine of twenty dollars ($20) for a first offense and fifty dollars ($50) for each subsequent offense.

(c) This section does not apply to a person using a wireless telephone for emergency purposes, including, but not limited to, an emergency call to a law enforcement agency, health care provider, fire department, or other emergency services agency or entity.

(d) This section does not apply to an emergency services professional using a wireless telephone while operating an authorized emergency vehicle, as defined in Section 165, in the course and scope of his or her duties.

(e) This section does not apply to a person driving a school bus or transit vehicle that is subject to Section 23125.

(f) This section does not apply to a person while driving a motor vehicle on private property.

(g) This section shall become operative on July 1, 2011.

490. "Private road or driveway" is a way or place in private ownership and used for vehicular travel by the owner and those having express or implied permission from the owner but not by other members of the public.

---

client's situation. This chapter covers the first step, parsing the rule, and previews the second, deductive reasoning.

As you read this chapter, consider the situation of Cassie Collins, who was ticketed for using a standard hand-held cell phone while driving. She pulled out into traffic from the parking lot of a mini-mall while holding her cell phone and orally asking it to find the nearest Starbucks. She drove into the path of another car, and a minor crash occurred. The police came, and Ms. Collins was ticketed. Your research has led you to the law printed in Box 2.1, from California's Vehicle Code.

To parse this rule, or any other legal rule, you will engage in three steps:

(1) Frame the rule in an if/then form.
(2) Analyze its factual elements.
(3) Analyze its legal consequences.

B. FRAMING RULES IN IF/THEN FORM

Even though legal rules come in various legal authorities, they all can be framed, with a bit of work, in an *if/then statement* as follows:

IF the required factual conditions exist,
THEN the specified legal consequences follow.

The *if-clause* contains words or phrases describing a class of situations; these situations are *factual conditions* that must be met before the legal consequences in the rule follow. Typically, the if-clause refers to one or more actors (whether individuals or legal entities such as corporations), one or more actions, and circumstances under which the actions occur.

The *then-clause* identifies the *legal consequence* that follows when the factual conditions are met. The consequence may be a benefit to or burden on a specified party, and it may be multifaceted. Often, a benefit flows to one party and a burden is imposed on another, as when one party is ordered to pay monetary damages to the other.

The first step in working with a new rule, thus, is to identify and then separate the factual conditions from the legal consequences. This is a critical step in legal analysis. If you do not know what factual conditions are required, you could apply an inapplicable rule to your client's facts. If you do not discern the legal consequences, you could predict the wrong outcome for your client's situation.

Some rules consist of two or more sentences or clauses. If so, evaluate whether the factual conditions and legal consequences happen to appear in separate grammatical units. The words "where" and "when" often mean "if." If the rule is not so constructed, you will need to identify each concept in the rule as a factual condition or legal consequence and group them accordingly. Phrases that should appear in the if-clause relate to conduct undertaken by people or entities, albeit described in general, abstract, or even legalistic terms. Phrases that should appear in the then-clause relate to either a label that the law attaches to the conduct or the outcome that could follow through some legal process.

Some legal rules are stated in complex and wordy sentences. Thus, the next step often is to carefully paraphrase the rule, making sure that you do not remove meaning from the rule.[1] A legal dictionary can help you to determine which words carry particular legal meanings.

Our analysis of the rule in Box 2.1 proceeded as follows:

- Provision (a) of section 23123 states the main factual conditions, which we have slightly paraphrased: "if a person drives a motor vehicle and while driving uses a wireless telephone not configured for hands-free use and that phone is not used in a hands-free manner."
- Provisions (c) through (e) state additional factual conditions, but they are not pertinent to our client's situation. On the other hand, provision (f) states a factual condition that could well be pertinent: "a person while driving a motor vehicle on private property."
- Section 490 connects to this factual condition by defining a closely related term, "private road or driveway," as "a way or place in private ownership and used for vehicular travel by the owner and those having express or implied permission from the owner, but not by other members of the public."
- Provision (b) states the consequences: "an infraction punishable by a base fine of $20 for a first offense and $50 for each subsequent offense."

---

1. *See generally* Richard Wydick, *Plain English for Lawyers* (5th ed. 2005).

C. ANALYZING A RULE'S FACTUAL ELEMENTS

Most if-clauses contain several factual conditions; phrased another way, a rule states elements that must be met. An *element* is a factual condition that can be analyzed as a unit. Most elements can be stated in a simple clause, and some have sub-elements. Thus, once you have developed your if/then statement, your next goal is to restate the if-clause so that each element (with or without sub-elements) is stated separately.

The elements in a rule must be connected to each other in some discernible way. Virtually every rule follows one of four rule structures—conjunctive, disjunctive, aggregate, balancing—or is a mixture of these. Box 2.2 summarizes the four rule structures.

Some rules have multiple elements connected by the word "and." All elements of the if-clause must exist for the legal consequences of the then-clause to follow. This kind of rule is a *conjunctive* rule ("conjunctive" meaning joining or coming together). Conjunctive rules are fairly simple in structure and relatively predictable in application because courts have relatively little discretion in applying them.

A second type of rule contains multiple elements connected by the word "or." Thus, only one of the alternative elements of the if-clause must exist in order for the legal consequences of the then-clause to apply. This kind of rule is a *disjunctive* rule ("disjunctive" meaning separating or presenting alternatives). Disjunctive rules are fairly simple in structure and relatively predictable in application because courts have relatively little discretion in applying them. Few rules are completely disjunctive, but many are conjunctive as to the major elements and disjunctive as to one or more sub-elements.

The third and fourth types of rules are similar in that they state factors to consider; no specific factor is necessarily critical by itself. An *aggregate* rule requires a determination whether enough of the factors are present so as to justify the legal consequence. A *balancing* rule requires you to balance factors favoring one outcome and factors favoring the other outcome to determine whether the legal consequence will follow. A rule may be purely aggregate or balancing, or it may be a mix. For example, a rule may be conjunctive in overall design and contain one element that is aggregate.

Aggregate and balancing rules are difficult to apply. Courts may come to different results as they decide cases with similar facts. Parties seeking to order their behavior in reliance on these rules may have a difficult time predicting the rule's impact on their conduct. On the other hand, with these rules, courts have discretion to come to results called for by particular circumstances.

Finally, some rules state not only factual conditions necessary for the legal consequence to follow; they also include *exceptions*; that is, factual conditions that stave off the legal consequence. These rules take the following form:

> IF *some factual conditions exist,*
> THEN *the specified legal consequences follow,*
> UNLESS *other factual conditions exist.*

A rule in if/then/unless form can be restated as follows:

> IF *some factual conditions do exist and other factual conditions do not exist,*
> THEN *the specified legal consequences follow.*

> **BOX 2.2**
>
> ### RULE STRUCTURES
>
> | Rule Structure | Linguistic Concept | Applicability of Rule | Characteristics |
> |---|---|---|---|
> | **Conjunctive** | And | All elements must be met | Predictable, easy to apply, relative lack of discretion in application |
> | **Disjunctive** | Or | Only one of multiple elements must be met | Predictable, easy to apply, relative lack of discretion in application |
> | **Aggregate** | Some, but not all, of the listed factors | Depends on weight accorded to various factors | Unpredictable, difficult to apply, vests considerable discretion in the judge, potentially inconsistent application |
> | **Balancing** | If [x] outweighs [y], then . . . Balance [x]against [y] to determine whether . . . | Depends on weight accorded to each side | Unpredictable, difficult to apply, vests considerable discretion in the judge, potentially inconsistent application |

As an example, the rule derived from the pertinent provisions of Box 2.1 illustrates a conjunctive rule and an exception with a disjunctive sub-element, as follows:

- The conjunctive elements of the main rule are (1) a person driving a motor vehicle and (2) that person while driving uses a wireless phone not configured for hands-free use and used in a non-hands-free manner.
- The potentially applicable exception pertains to driving on private property, which (under section 490) has a disjunctive sub-element—people who have express or implied permission from the owner.

Consider the difference between the actual statute and this hypothetical rule: "To drive while talking or texting on a wireless telephone constitutes a misdemeanor depending on the presence and magnitude of the following risk factors: the configuration of the phone, traffic and road conditions, the experience level of the driver, the necessity of the call (including but not limited to calling for emergency services), and the harm posed to other drivers by the caller's lack of attention." This rule is an aggregate rule. Note that this rule lists factors that many would consider pertinent to assessing the wisdom of using a cell phone while driving. It would be much harder, however, to predict the outcome of a client's situation under this rule than under the actual California statute.

D. ANALYZING A RULE'S LEGAL CONSEQUENCES

Just as the if-clause merits careful analysis, so too should you carefully analyze the then-clause to discern the number and nature of the legal consequence(s). Box 2.3 summarizes the possibilities.

Many legal rules state a *single consequence* of conduct fitting within the if-clause. Others provide for *multiple consequences*, so you must discern the relationship between those consequences. Some rules provide for *cumulative consequences*; both (or all) consequences are to occur. Other rules provide for *alternative consequences*; only one of the stated consequences is to occur. Many legal rules use "or" in stating their consequences. Unfortunately, "or" can be understood several ways: A or B or both; A or B, but not both; if not A, then B. Generally, context will aid you in discerning which meaning is intended.

Some legal rules identify the *outcome* of conduct fitting within the if-clause; that is, they directly state the impact on the people or entities involved. For example, a rule may provide for a fine or state that damages may be recovered. Other rules only identify a *legal label* for conduct fitting within the if-clause, and you must consult an additional rule to determine the outcome. For example, if a rule has as its consequence that an individual is guilty of a misdemeanor, you would need to consult another rule on misdemeanors to discern what outcome (such as a fine) flows from that label.

As an example, provision (b) in Box 2.1 provides the legal consequence information, as follows:

- The rule provides a label: an infraction.
- It also provides the outcome: payment of fines in certain stated amounts.

BOX 2.3

THEN-CLAUSE ANALYSIS

Number of Consequences	How many consequences? If more than one, are they: • Cumulative → may the client experience more than one? • Alternatives → will the client experience only one?
Nature of Consequences	Is the consequence • The outcome? • The legal label? If the latter, what additional rule establishes the outcome of conduct fitting that legal label?

E. DEPICTING A RULE IN VARIOUS WAYS

Rules of law can be depicted in many ways. Your choice should be based on the nature of the rule and your needs in working with the rule. If the rule has a simple structure, it may be easily understood in sentence or paragraph form. Tabulation and enumeration can aid you in displaying the structure of more complex rules. Especially with complex rules, consider first stating the consequence, which typically is simpler, and then state the various elements.

Another way to depict rules is a chart. While the document containing your analysis will use not a chart but rather traditional text, a chart can provide a good sense of the rule's structure. Furthermore, its design can be tailored to the specific features of the rule.

We came up with three depictions of the rule from the cell-phone statute, as shown in Box 2.4.

BOX 2.4

SAMPLE RULES

IF   a person drives a motor vehicle
          and uses a non-hands-free wireless telephone in a non-hands-free manner
          and is *not* driving on private property, which is (interpreted under 490 to mean)
               in private ownership
               and used for vehicular travel by the owner and those having express or implied
               permission from the owner but not by other members of the public,
THEN   the person has committed an infraction with base fines of $20 for a first offense and $50
          for subsequent offenses.

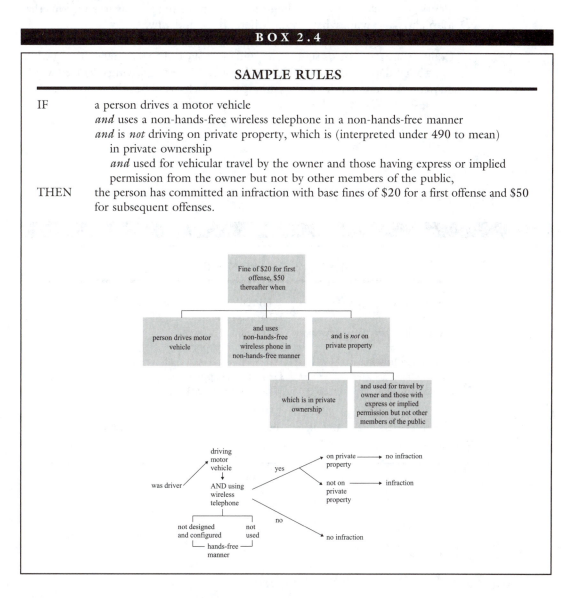

F. A PREVIEW OF DEDUCTIVE REASONING

Deductive reasoning, which is the basis of legal analysis, entails using a legal rule to predict the outcome of a client's situation. This process builds on a careful parsing of the rule, as discussed in this chapter. Once you have discerned the rule's elements, you have developed the framework of your analysis of your client's situation. The next step is to match each element to the relevant facts in your client's situation.

The type of rule under consideration is very important. For example, if the rule is conjunctive, all elements must be met for the consequence to follow, and your analysis should reflect this. If the rule is a balancing rule, your analysis would encompass the various factors in a less mechanical way.

It can be more or less challenging to discern which fact in your client's situation matches up with a rule's element, depending on the element and the client's situation. As suggested in Box 2.5, one way to approach this task is to identify each element as entailing one or more of the six classic questions that journalists ask: who, what, when, where, how, and why.

In the example for this chapter, connecting the elements of the statute to Ms. Collins's situation yields significant guidance. She did appear to be driving while using a standard (non-hands-free) cell phone. Where the driving occurred would matter—the car was both in the parking lot, which could be private property, and in the street. Can you think of any other point to pursue?

BOX 2.5

DEDUCTIVE REASONING

1. IF actor does X action ⟶ Who acted?
   What happened?
2. in Y location ⟶ Where did it happen?
3. at Z time ⟶ When did it happen?
4. under the following
   circumstances... ⟶ How did it happen?
5. for the following reasons... ⟶ Why did it happen?

THEN   THEN
the conduct is labeled _____ and the   these consequences do/do not follow.
outcome is _____.

G. REVIEW

This chapter has covered the following steps in stating rules of law as if/then statements with clearly identified elements and consequences:

(1) Frame the rule in an if/then form. Identify and separate the factual conditions and the legal consequences into if- and then-clauses. As needed, carefully paraphrase the rule for ease of use.

(2) Determine whether the rule is conjunctive, disjunctive, aggregate, balancing, or some combination. Identify any exceptions and consider rewording them as negative elements.

(3) Discern the number and nature of the legal consequences.

(4) Depict the rule in an accurate and useful way.

This approach works with rules derived from various authorities. Carefully following these steps should provide a sound basis for deductive reasoning, which in turn permits you to develop a sound prediction about the legal meaning of your client's situation.

TEST YOUR UNDERSTANDING

1. What is a rule of law, and how do rules of law benefit society?

2. A rule of law can be framed as an if/then statement. What does the if-clause contain? What does the then-clause contain?

3. Within the if-clause are elements. Define "element."

4. For each of the following if-clause structures, explain how the elements relate to each other:
   a. Conjunctive
   b. Disjunctive
   c. Aggregate
   d. Balancing
   e. Exceptions

5. What is the difference between a then-clause with cumulative multiple consequences and one with alternative multiple consequences?

6. What is the difference between a then-clause with a legal label and one with an outcome? Which is more useful?

7. To test not only your understanding but also your imagination, consider developing various rules to govern the Bower's Bounty situation, in which an employee claims that her employer defamed her by making damaging false statements about her as it terminated her employment.
   a. Think first about the factual circumstances in which an employer should be legally responsible to the employee. Aim to write two or three rules with various types of if-clauses (conjunctive, disjunctive, aggregate, balancing, or perhaps a mix) and label each if-clause.
   b. For each if-clause, write a then-clause with an outcome.

TEST YOUR UNDERSTANDING ANSWERS

1. A rule of law is a general statement of what the law permits or requires of people or entities in certain situations. Rules of law permit people to conduct their activities legally, guide disputants and judges in resolving disputes, and bring about similar outcomes in similar disputes.

2. The if-clause contains the required factual conditions. The then-clause contains the legal consequences that follow those factual conditions.

3. An element is a factual condition that can be analyzed as a unit.

4. The elements relate to each other in the various types of rules as follows:
   a. Conjunctive—all elements must be met.
   b. Disjunctive—only one of the alternatives must be met.
   c. Aggregate—the various factors are to be considered together.
   d. Balancing—factors favoring one outcome are to be balanced off against factors favoring the other outcome.
   e. Exceptions—an element that staves off the legal consequence is identified.

5. With cumulative multiple consequences, both (typically) would occur; with alternative multiple consequences, one or the other would occur.

6. A then-clause with a legal label identifies a legal category but not the impact of fitting within that category and so requires additional research. A then-clause stating the outcome of meeting the rule's elements, within the legal system, is more useful.

7. For an actual legal rule on the topic of defamation, see the case presented in Chapter 3.

READING CASES

Real-World Story
Legal-System Story
Legal-Analysis Story

[Common law] stands as a monument slowly raised, like a coral reef, from the minute accretions of past individuals, of whom each built upon the relics which his predecessors left, and in his turn left a foundation upon which his successors might work.
—Learned Hand
Book Review, 35 Harv. L. Rev. 479, 479 (1922) (reviewing Benjamin N. Cardozo's *The Nature of the Judicial Process*)

A. INTRODUCTION

For lawyers, the word "case" has several related meanings. Many lawyers use it to refer to a client's matter, of whatever sort. Once a dispute enters litigation, it becomes a case in a more formal sense and goes by the names of the litigants. The word "case" is also used to refer to the written decision issued by a court. This chapter discusses *case law*—that is, the law that derives from the decisions of courts on a topic.[1]

This chapter first covers the operation of cases in the U.S. legal system; then deconstructs cases so that you know how to read them; and then presents case briefing, a way to read and take notes on cases thoroughly and carefully. Most of the time, legal analysis involves more than one pertinent case; therefore, this chapter also covers fusing, or combining, several cases on the same topic.

The sample case used for most of this chapter is *Luttrell v. United Telephone System, Inc.*, the case printed as Exhibit 3A at the end of this chapter. It relates to this book's client situation involving Bower's Bounty, in Kansas. Bower's Bounty is a grocery store that has been charged with defamation by a recently terminated employee, Sarah Nicholson. She alleges that she was falsely accused of theft in a statement posted by management in the employee lounge, which her co-workers read. Please look over *Luttrell* now.

B. THE U.S. COMMON LAW SYSTEM

Understanding how cases work requires an understanding of the following elements of the U.S. legal system: court structures, jurisdiction, and stare decisis and precedent.

1. Court Structures

The United States has overlapping court systems with both federal and state courts. Although each court system has unique features, all court systems share certain fundamental features and procedures.

Every system has entry-level courts, often called *district or circuit courts*. Cases enter the legal system at this level when a *plaintiff* sues a *defendant* (in a civil case) or the government brings a criminal case against a defendant. Most cases conclude in district courts. Indeed, many cases are resolved by mutual agreement of the parties, typically through *negotiations* conducted by the parties' lawyers. Some systems require or encourage litigants to pursue informal means of resolving their disputes, such as mediation (negotiations aided by a neutral party).

If the case remains unresolved through negotiation, the district court resolves it one way or another. The district court resolves disputes about the facts, applies the law to the facts, and determines an outcome. Many cases are resolved by the judge through a *motion*; a motion is a request by one party that the judge take a specified action, which may entail deciding a case without trial. Alternatively, the case may be decided after a *trial*, at which witnesses testify and the decision-maker closely views objects and documents. Some cases are decided by juries; other cases are decided by a judge alone after a bench trial.

---

1. Other bodies resolve disputes as well, including administrative agencies and arbitrators (private decision-makers hired by the parties). Agency decisions constitute law; arbitrator awards do so only for the parties to the case. Much of what is said here about how to read a case applies to these bodies' adjudications as well.

Every court system also has one or more *appellate courts.*[2] A party that has suffered an adverse outcome in the district court, the *appellant,* brings the appeal, to which the other party, the *appellee or respondent,* responds. An appellate court reviews the district court's work for errors that are significant enough to have led to an improper result. These errors may include misunderstanding the law, failure to handle motions according to the rules of procedure, failure to conduct the trial according to the rules of evidence, and coming to a judgment contrary to the facts. Generally, an appellate court reviews a case only after all proceedings in the district court have occurred. Because the appellate court's function is to review the district court's work, not redo it, the appellate court does not conduct trials. Rather, the appellate court reviews the written record created at the district court and considers the written and oral arguments of the parties' attorneys.

As shown in Box 3.1, a three-tier court system has two tiers of appellate courts. In these systems, the intermediate court, typically called the *court of appeals,* handles virtually all cases coming out of the district courts. This court exercises *mandatory review* and focuses on *correction of error.* Some systems have multiple intermediate courts, each of which handles cases coming out of the district courts in its geographic region. Other systems have a single intermediate court that hears all cases from around the state.

The highest court in a three-tier appellate court system, typically called the *supreme court,* handles a fairly small percentage of the cases coming out of the intermediate court(s). The supreme court has the power to select most of its cases through *discretionary review.* The court selects cases with new or especially difficult legal questions or broad impact, because the supreme court's task is not so much to correct error as to *make law.* Some supreme courts also are required to handle certain limited categories of cases.

An alternative to a three-tier court system, which is uncommon today but was very common among the states for many years, is the two-tier court system. This system has a single appellate court, which handles all cases coming out of the trial courts, corrects error, and makes law.

The federal court system includes the U.S. Supreme Court; intermediate appellate courts for twelve regions;[3] and nearly a hundred federal district courts for the fifty states, the District of Columbia, and U.S. territories. Each federal district court covers either an entire state or a portion of a state.

As an example, *Luttrell,* the case in Exhibit 3A, was litigated in the state courts in Kansas, which has a three-tier court system. *Luttrell* involved an employee suing his employer for disparaging statements made about the employee by managers. The case was brought in the District Court for Johnson County, where the employee was the plaintiff and the employer the defendant. The trial judge dismissed the case upon the employer's motion. The employee appealed to the Court of Appeals of Kansas, where the employee was the appellant and the employer the appellee. In the decision discussed in this chapter, the

---

2. Table T.1 of *The Bluebook* and Appendix 1 of the *ALWD Citation Manual* provide basic information about the courts in each state.

3. There are eleven numbered circuits, as well as a circuit court for the District of Columbia. In addition, the Court of Appeals for the Federal Circuit hears appeals in specialized subject areas from around the country.

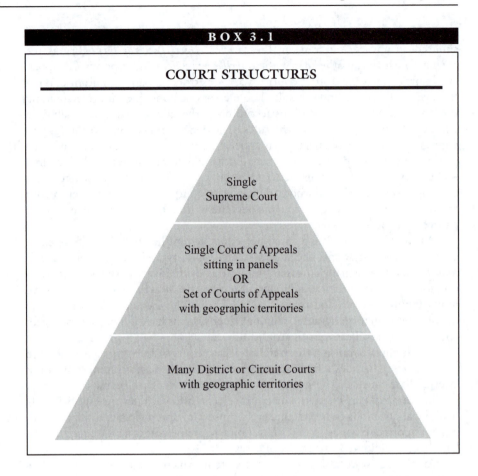

BOX 3.1

COURT STRUCTURES

Single
Supreme Court

Single Court of Appeals
sitting in panels
OR
Set of Courts of Appeals
with geographic territories

Many District or Circuit Courts
with geographic territories

court of appeals ruled in favor of the employee. The employer appealed to the
Kansas Supreme Court, and the employee prevailed, with the Kansas Supreme
Court adopting the decision discussed in this chapter.[4]

2. Jurisdiction

Every court has the power to decide only certain classes of cases.[5] Basically, to say
that a court has *jurisdiction* over a case is to say that it is empowered to decide the
case and enforce its decision. There are two types of jurisdiction, both being
necessary for a court to handle a case.

First, a court has *personal jurisdiction* over a party based on the party's contact with the state, based on such factors as the location of the events and the
party's citizenship. This type of jurisdiction is geographic in nature.

---

4. *Luttrell v. United Tel. System, Inc.*, 659 P.2d 1270 (Kan. 1985).
5. Jurisdiction is a complex topic. Indeed, the discussion of jurisdiction in the major treatise on
federal civil procedure—Charles Alan Wright, Arthur R. Miller, et al., *Federal Practice and
Procedure*—extends over seven volumes.

Second, a court has *subject matter jurisdiction* over a dispute when its legal issues fall within a category that the court has the power to decide. Most court systems have courts of general jurisdiction and courts of limited jurisdiction. Courts of *general jurisdiction* handle a wide range of cases. Courts of *limited jurisdiction,* on the other hand, have very specialized roles. For example, at the federal level, specialized courts handle military matters, bankruptcies, and patent cases. Many states have specialized courts for family, juvenile, and residential landlord-tenant cases.

As a general matter, the federal courts adjudicate cases raising issues of federal law, and state courts adjudicate cases raising issues of state law. However, in two fairly common situations, the federal courts handle issues of state law. First, in *diversity jurisdiction* cases, where citizens of two different states have a case with a significant amount at stake, a federal court may handle the case and decide state law claims. Second, where the case involves related federal and state claims and is brought in federal court, the federal court will consider the state claims under its *supplemental jurisdiction.* Similarly, in *concurrent jurisdiction* cases, state courts may consider federal claims when the U.S. Congress has chosen not to deny them jurisdiction over the claims.

Furthermore, from time to time, state courts handle issues that are governed by the law of sister states. For example, if a contract involving events taking place in more than one state indicates that the law of one of those states shall govern the contract, that law usually governs a dispute under the contract, even if the litigation occurs in a different state.

As an example, *Luttrell* arose in Kansas, involved residents of Kansas (one a person, another a company doing business in Kansas), and involved an issue of state law—the tort of defamation. Accordingly, the Kansas state courts had jurisdiction and handled the case.

3. Stare Decisis and Precedent

Judges write opinions explaining their decisions for several reasons. In difficult cases, the process of explaining the decision no doubt helps the judge actually come to the decision. In addition, the opinion justifies the result so that the parties (and, in some cases, the public) will accept it as just. Finally, in the U.S. common law system, the opinion operates as law, along with the other decisions on the same topic.

The Latin term underlying the common law is *stare decisis*; in full "stare decisis et non quieta movere" means "stand by decisions and not disturb settled matters." The term *precedent* refers to decisions in past cases that stand as law. Stare decisis is a doctrine based on consistency with the past; a court is to decide the present case in accord with decisions rendered in similar cases in the past.[6]

Stare decisis has several advantages. Litigants perceive that they are treated fairly because similarly situated persons receive the same outcomes. The doctrine creates predictability; a lawyer can predict the legal outcome of a present or future situation by examining the outcome in a case involving a similar situation.

---

6. For a more extended discussion, see Oliver Wendell Holmes, *The Common Law* (1881); Edward Levi, *An Introduction to Legal Reasoning* (1949).

By eliminating the need to reinvent solutions where one already has been developed, stare decisis preserves scarce judicial resources.

However, if stare decisis operated inflexibly, it would be counterproductive. As circumstances, information, and social values change, so too should the law. Fortunately, the common law system permits change. When the needed change is not dramatic, the courts modify the existing rule, typically by adding a new element or reframing an element of the existing rule. When the needed change is dramatic, the courts overrule the precedent and create a new rule in the new case.

As a general rule, judicial decisions are retroactive; they apply to a set of facts that arose in the past. The court applies the rule of law set out in the case to yield an outcome in the present dispute. Furthermore, the case governs the resolution of similar disputes currently in litigation.[7]

Stare decisis operates within a court system according to its internal hierarchy. Courts are bound by decisions of courts higher in the same court structure and are expected to decide cases consistently with their own decisions. When one court is applying the law of a different system, as in diversity jurisdiction, it follows that system's precedent. Decisions that a court must follow are *mandatory or binding precedents*.

In some situations, a court may choose to follow a decision that it is not bound to follow, such as a decision from the highest court in a neighboring state; such a decision is a *persuasive precedent*. Courts typically rely on persuasive precedent when there is no binding precedent or when the law is undergoing change in the direction set forth in the persuasive precedent.

Especially when a court is considering persuasive precedent, but also when a court is considering only binding precedent, there may be several applicable precedents from which to choose. Some decisions are more significant than others because they develop the law by creating a rule, explaining it, or applying it to a new situation. Courts reflect this distinction by designating a decision as *published or unpublished*. Typically, the court views an unpublished decision as not adding to the law, but rather applying settled law to unremarkable facts in a routine way. Indeed, some courts limit reliance on unpublished decisions.

Beyond this factor, as a general principle, the newer the precedent, the weightier it is. On the other hand, a longstanding precedent that has been followed in many recent decisions also carries significant weight; this is known as a *seminal case*. Unanimous decisions are weightier than split decisions (discussed below). The more thorough and cogent the court's reasoning, the weightier the case is. The greater the factual and legal similarities between the precedent and the client's case, the more useful the precedent is. Some courts command more respect than others because the general quality of their research and reasoning is high or because their decisions frequently constitute the cutting edge of an area of law. Many courts share similar orientations toward broad issues of public policy and thus often rely on each other's decisions.

As an example, the Court of Appeals of Kansas decision in *Luttrell* would be binding precedent for some courts deciding an issue involving defamation under

---

7. On rare occasions, when application of a new rule to a party that detrimentally and significantly relied on the old rule would be unjust, a court may modify its application or create new law prospectively. For more detail, see Edgar Bodenheimer et al., *An Introduction to the Anglo-American Legal System* (2d ed. 1988).

Kansas law. The decision would bind Kansas state district courts, as well as federal courts ruling on issues of state law. The Court of Appeals of Kansas would be expected to follow it or explain its divergence. The Kansas Supreme Court could follow it or not.

Another way to observe the operation of precedent is to examine the sources cited by the *Luttrell* court. In the paragraphs beginning "The tort of defamation . . ." and "Defendant argues . . . ," the court cited various Kansas cases (*Hein, Schulze, Gobin, Bourn, Dobbyn,* and *Scarpelli*). Yet the court also cited cases from other states in the paragraph beginning "There is considerable division. . . ." In that paragraph, the court was considering an issue not yet decided in Kansas and so looked to the decisions of other states, i.e., persuasive precedents. On this point, *Luttrell* made law (as explained below) and applied that law to the employer in this case.

C. Understanding Cases

Viewed as literature, judicial opinions can be complex, and some are quite long. Yet you must read and deeply analyze them if they govern your client's situation. How does a lawyer read a case with a client's situation in mind? Understanding the literary genre of the judicial opinion can help you see how to approach a case as a lawyer does.

1. Judicial Opinions as Entwined Narratives

A *judicial opinion* is written in response to a dispute brought before it. This dispute gives rise to the core narrative of the case. As with any good narrative, the parties' dispute has characters (not only the parties-protagonists, but generally also secondary characters), a setting, a series of events, and serious conflict. Many lawyers call this narrative the *real-world story* to distinguish it from the litigation (although litigation is certainly real too). Because the case has generated a judicial opinion, it is apparent that the parties did not resolve the conflict themselves.

So a case also has a second story—the *legal-system story*. Any litigation has its own narrative with characters (the lawyers, the parties, the judge(s), and sometimes a jury), a setting (the courts), events (such as the filing of the suit and motions), and conflict. A legal-system story can have many chapters as the case works its way through district and appellate courts, sometimes over a number of years.

Finally, the judge writes the opinion, which can be thought of as a *legal-analysis story*. Point of view is key to understanding the judicial opinion. The opinion is not written by any of the characters in the real-world story; each one no doubt would tell the story quite differently. Nor is the opinion written by the lawyers, who are the primary characters in the legal-system story. Rather, it is written by the judge, who sits at some distance from the real-world story, learns of it through the lawyers, and operates from a position of impartiality.

Furthermore, this writer, the judge, has several roles. First, the judge is charged with providing closure to the real-world dispute by facilitating a legal resolution. These are past-oriented and particularistic tasks. The judge is also charged with looking to the future, to the unknown similar situations not before the court that will be governed by the opinion—a much more abstract task.

In the legal-analysis story, the protagonists, so to speak, are the legal arguments presented by the lawyers. Given the prevalence of negotiation in U.S. litigation, a case demanding a judge's decision generally entails a conflict between legitimate arguments grounded in different understandings of the facts, different views of the law, or different beliefs about the intersection of the facts and the law. The judge must resolve this conflict—and in a manner that renders one party a winner and the other a loser.[8] A well-written opinion recounts the judge's thinking clearly and convincingly.

Thus, as depicted in the chapter-opening diagram, judicial opinions contain several narratives: the real-world story, reflecting the way in which the lawyers have presented it, given the present stage of litigation; the legal-system story, showing how the case came to the court; and the judicial-analysis story, explaining how the court came to its outcome in light of the applicable law.

2. Organization of a Case Report

Most published cases follow a standard organization with the components listed below. The *Luttrell* opinion at the end of this chapter has these components labeled; you may want to look at it as you read the following discussion. This particular version of *Luttrell* is from Westlaw, one of the major commercial online resources that provide cases. Many other resources exist, including court websites for newer cases.

Publication information: Located at the outset, the *publication information* identifies where the case is published, including the volume, reporter, and page number for print publications. Lawyers must provide citations to their sources, and most citation formats call for citation to some form of print publication (even though most case law research is done online). For *Luttrell*, the most useful publication information is 683 P.2d 1292: volume 683 of the second series of the *Pacific Reporter*[9] at page 1292.

Case name: The *case name* identifies the parties. The plaintiff generally is listed first, but some courts list the defendant first if it is the appellant. Some party designations are complicated; examples include cross-appeals, in which both sides won and lost in the district court so that both seek reversal of their losses, and litigation with more than two parties.

Court information: This information tells you the *deciding court*, the *date of decision*, and the *docket number* assigned to the case by the clerk of that court.

Publisher's editorial matter: The publisher's staff may insert some material, such as a summary of the case and *headnotes*, or short paragraphs summarizing the legal points made in the opinion. Although useful in legal research, this material is not part of the case, so you should not consider it as such.

---

8. In some areas of the law, there are middle grounds, such as degrees of crimes and percentages of liability in negligence, along with ranges in sentencing and amounts of damages.

9. The *Pacific Reporter* is one of the regional reporters of the West Reporter System, begun in the late 1800s. Although a private publication, it has dominated state and federal case reporting. See Appendix III for more detail.

Court's editorial matter: Some courts provide *synopses* of their opinions. Generally, these descriptions are written by the court's staff or designee, not by the judges themselves. If this is the case, you should not rely on them in lieu of the opinion itself.

Attorneys: Whether or not the attorneys like it, their involvement in the case is noted.

Authoring judge: Immediately before the opinion itself is the name of the *author of the opinion.* In appellate cases, which involve three or more judges, if the decision was not unanimous, you also will learn which other judges agreed with the lead opinion. Some brief opinions on which the judges were generally in agreement are not attributed to any judge but rather are labeled *per curiam.*

As a general rule, the judges of the highest court of a jurisdiction are referred to as *justices,* while others are referred to as *judges.*

Opinion(s): The lengthiest portion of a case report—and obviously the most important—is the *opinion* itself. There is no standard format for judicial opinions. However, generally the following appear at the beginning to orient the reader: the legal-system story, the legal issue(s) raised by the case, and the outcome(s). Typically, the next segment is a recitation of the real-world story. The bulk of the opinion is the legal-analysis story, which restates the legal issues raised by the parties and then states and explains their resolutions. The concluding paragraph presents the court's procedural outcome. A *district court* opinion indicates in whose favor the court rules. An appellate court outcome may be to *affirm* (uphold), *modify* (change in some respect), or *reverse* (overturn) the decision of the lower court; another possibility is to *remand* the case, that is, to send it back to the lower court with instructions as to how to proceed.

A case decided by an appellate court may yield more than one opinion when the *court splits* its vote. The opinion receiving over half the votes is the *majority opinion.* A judge *concurs* when he or she agrees with the result but chooses to state reasoning different than that of the majority. A judge *dissents* when he or she disagrees with the majority result. On occasion, a court splits so significantly that there is no majority opinion; the opinion drawing the largest number of votes is the *plurality* opinion and generally is viewed as the most influential of the opinions.

D. READING AND BRIEFING A CASE

1. Preparing the Case Brief

Given that a case is comprised of entwined narratives, an important analytical skill for a lawyer is the ability to disentangle these narratives, to pull the pieces apart, to divide the opinion into components that permit the lawyer to work with it to analyze a client's situation. This process is called *case briefing.* A case brief is a structured set of notes on a case; writing one is an excellent way to develop as well as to record your understanding of the case. Because the brief is written for the writer, formats vary from person to person. Nonetheless, most formats contain the components discussed here.

You most likely will find that you must read a case several times before you understand it fully. Do this in the following way:

(1) Scan the case first, without marking it or taking notes, to obtain an overview and general sense of the case.

(2) Then read it more carefully, highlighting important points and making marginal notes, such as key phrases or the components of the case brief (described below). Look up terms that you do not know in a legal dictionary.

(3) Then ponder the case for a few moments, asking yourself broad questions about each of the narratives: What was the dispute between the parties in the real world about? How did the legal system handle the case up to the point of the opinion at hand? What outcome does the opinion yield for these parties, and what is the significance of the case for future similar situations?

As you turn to writing the case brief, you may find it useful to ask journalist-style questions about the three narratives. As shown in Box 3.2, the answers to these questions appear in particular components of the case brief.

BOX 3.2

QUESTIONS AND CASE BRIEF COMPONENTS

Six Questions	Case Brief Components
Real-World Story	
• Who are the parties and other important people?	Heading, facts
• What happened between the parties?	Facts
• When did that happen?	Facts
• Where did that happen?	Facts
• Why did that happen?	Facts
Legal-System Story	
• Who sued whom for what?	Procedure
• If the opinion is an appellate opinion, what happened in the lower court(s)?	Procedure
Judicial-Analysis Story	
• Who (which court) wrote this opinion?	Heading
• When did this court rule?	Heading
• Where is this opinion published?	Heading
• What were the contending legal arguments? How did this court think about these arguments?	Issue, rule, reasoning, holding
• What has this court decided: who wins, and who loses?	Outcome

Your goal is to record the information you need to fully understand the case, but no more, and to do so efficiently. Use a standard set of abbreviations and contractions, omit minor words such as "the," and use a form tailored to your own preferences. You may find it easier to draft your briefs if you begin with the part of the case you generally understand the most readily.

Be sure to review your case brief carefully. Check the brief against itself, to be sure, for example, that the facts alluded to in the reasoning section are covered in the facts component. At least where the case is complicated or central to your analysis of your client's situation, skim the case after writing the brief, to check the brief against the case.

2. Components of the Case Brief

Before you read the discussion of the components below, you may want to read through Box 3.3, a sample brief of *Luttrell*.

BOX 3.3

SAMPLE CASE BRIEF

Luttrell v. United Telephone System, Inc., 683 P.2d 1292 (Kan. Ct. App. 1984), *aff'd*, 659 P.2d 1270 (Kan. 1985).

Facts: P (employee) alleges that another employee told his supervisor he was illegally taping phone conversations, was asked to stop, yet persisted despite being told not to. P's supervisor told another employee, who told yet another employee. P alleges statements were malicious and within scope of employment. Employees were supervisors apparently.

Procedure and outcome: P sued D (employer) for defamation. DC granted D's motion to dismiss for failure to state claim. P appealed. Here: reversed and remanded.

Issue: When defamatory words are exchanged by agents of same corporation about fellow employee's performance, is there publication required for tort of defamation?

Holding: Communication of remarks by one corporate employee to another concerning job performance of third employee is publication required for defamation action against employer.

Rules of law: (1) Defamation elements are: false & defamatory words communicated to third person, resulting in harm to reputation of person defamed. (2) Corporation is liable for defamation of agent made while acting within scope of employment. (3) Qualified privilege exists when good faith, interest to be upheld, statement limited in scope to interest, publication in proper manner to proper parties. Privilege is defeated if speaker acted with knowledge of falsity or reckless disregard for truth.

Reasoning: Issue of intracorporate communication was issue of first impression. Courts around country split on issue; *Prosser* [major torts treatise] favors view that such communications are publication. Focus should be on nature of injury in defamation—damage to reputation; this may be as devastating when communication is inside corporation as outside. Employer's need to evaluate and comment on employee work is protected by qualified privilege.

Pertinence: Strong factual parallel to our case, although there supervisors spoke to each other.

Heading: The *heading* includes the case's name, court, date, and publication information.

Facts: The *facts* components contains the real-world story. Generally you should condense the facts as stated in the opinion to some degree.

Present material that matters to the court's decision, and omit extraneous material. To sift through the facts effectively, first ask which facts you must know to understand the court's reasoning; these *relevant* facts belong in the case brief. Then ask which other facts provide important context for the relevant facts; these *background* facts also belong in the case brief. Extraneous facts failing these two tests should not be included.

State the facts you choose to present in a useful manner. Some writers prefer "plaintiff" and "defendant," while others prefer proper names or functional labels, such as "employee" and "employer." Present the facts in a logical order, which generally is chronological beginning with the first event. Indeed, where timing is critical and intricate, you may want to draw a timeline.

Procedure and outcome: This component chronicles the legal-system story predating the opinion being briefed. In the *procedure* part, first state who sued whom, on what type of claim, and what remedy was sought. Then, as applicable, state who won in the district court and how (by motion, judge trial, or jury verdict); then the decision of the intermediate appellate court, if any; and finally who has brought the current appeal. Finally, state the *outcome* rendered through the opinion you are briefing, that is, which party won and how. For example, a district court outcome may be "motion to dismiss granted," and an appellate outcome may be "reversed and remanded."

Issue: An *issue* is a question the court has to answer to decide the case. Because the court resolves specific disputes involving people or entities involved in real events by applying the law to these events, an issue refers to both a rule of law and real-world facts. In other words, issue = law + facts, in question form.

Issues vary on several dimensions. First, some issues are primarily questions about what the law is or should be, with the real-world facts in a secondary role. Other issues involve the application of settled law to facts, with the law in the secondary role and the facts in the primary role. Others involve evenly balanced interactions between law and facts.

Second, some issues involve primarily substantive legal topics, while others involve primarily procedural legal topics, and others are mixtures of the two. *Substantive rules* govern the conduct of people in the real world, while *procedural rules* govern the conduct of litigation.

Third, some issues are quite simple, dealing with a single legal concept. Others are more complex, involving several legal concepts that are sub-issues of a main issue.

You can deduce the issue(s) in a case in several ways. The court may expressly state the issue (although not necessarily artfully or completely). The court may summarize the arguments of the parties; often you can convert a party's argument into an issue. Alternatively, put yourself in the position of the court, and ask yourself what topics you need to address to decide the case. You may want to read the court's synopsis and the publisher's editorial matter to confirm your understanding.

Holding: The holding is the court's answer to the issue. Mirroring the issue, it connects the law to the facts of the case to reveal the legal significance of those facts. In other words, holding = law + facts, in statement form. As with issues, some holdings are more legal than factual or vice versa; some are substantive, whereas others are procedural; some are simple, whereas others are complex. If there are several decided issues, there will be several holdings.

A holding not only answers the issue for the parties in the current litigation; it also constitutes precedent. Under stare decisis, the deciding court and lower courts should come to a similar holding on similar facts in the future.

Discerning a holding can be difficult. Some judges pronounce holdings ("We therefore hold . . . ."); obviously, these statements are very helpful. Absent such a statement, think about which party won the case and use that information to answer the issue.[10]

The particular challenge in stating holdings is to decide how broadly or narrowly to phrase them. A narrow phrasing referring specifically to the facts before the court suggests that the case's impact does not extend much beyond the case before it. A broad phrasing stating the facts in more abstract terms suggests that the case's reach is expansive. If the court does not signal the breadth of its holding, your client's situation is likely to incline you in one direction. If your client's situation is very similar to the facts of the case, a narrowly phrased holding is appropriate. If your client's situation is similar only in a broad sense to the facts of the case, you may need to use a broadly phrased holding to draw out the case's significance for your client's situation.

For strategic reasons, you may be tempted to state a case with an unfavorable outcome narrowly or state a case with a favorable outcome broadly. However, you must be faithful to the decided case and mindful of your client's circumstances. In an advisory context, a neutral or cautious approach is preferable, to provide your client a margin of safety as he or she contemplates various possible options. When you are advocating for a client who has already taken action, you are more likely to read an unfavorable precedent narrowly and a favorable precedent broadly to persuade the tribunal to favor your client—so long as these readings are credible.

Rules of law: In reasoning to its holding, a court employs one or more rules of law. As discussed in Chapter 2, a rule of law states the legal consequences that flow from specified factual conditions. A case stands for the rules of law stated within it, as well as for its holdings. Indeed, a broadly stated holding resembles a rule of law.

To identify the rules of law in a case, look for a statement of legal consequences paired with a set of factual conditions. The factual conditions will be described in fairly general terms, so as to cover not only the circumstances of the particular case but also other similar cases. The legal consequences may be implied, rather than stated explicitly. In most cases, the rule of law applied by the court already exists; thus a citation to legal authority ordinarily follows the rule of law. However, in situations where the court has not yet addressed the issue or is

---

10. Some use "holding" to refer to the procedural outcome of a case, e.g., in *Luttrell*, "reversed and remanded." Others call for a single-word holding, e.g., in *Luttrell*, "yes." Because a case stands for its holding, it is most useful to frame a holding as a statement of law applied to facts.

turning in a new direction, the court creates a rule as it decides the case. In these situations, the court may well use a signal such as "we thus rule . . . ."

You may state the rules of law in a separate component of your case brief. Or you may state the rules, clearly labeled as such, within the reasoning component (discussed next). Either way, the rule is critical to your work on your client's case, so be sure that you have presented the rule carefully. You may follow the court's formulation or, as needed, rework the court's statement into an if/then statement, as discussed in Chapter 2.

Reasoning: The *reasoning* component presents the judicial-analysis narrative. It encompasses the rules of law stated in the case, if they are not stated in a separate component It links the rules to the real-world facts and thereby justifies the holding.[11] A case stands not only for its holding and rule, but also for its reasoning. When a lawyer reads a case, he or she tracks the court's reasoning, seeking parallels to the client's situation.

The court's reasoning may be quite lengthy. To keep your brief concise, focus on the following categories of material, which you may want to so label in your brief:

- State how the court applied the rule to the facts of the case, connecting the factual conditions of the if-clause to the specific facts of the case before the court.
- State the competing arguments of the parties (as to what rule of law is applicable or should be created or how the facts should be analyzed), along with the court's evaluation of the arguments.
- State the public policy or broad social goals the court relied upon.
- The court usually cites the major authorities it relied upon in reasoning to its holding. Include how the court relied on preexisting law.

Dictum: On occasion, courts remark upon matters not essential to any holding. No matter how clear and unequivocal such a remark may seem to be, it is considered *dictum*. This term derives from *obiter dictum*, which means "something said in passing." A dictum is not considered precedent because it is not necessary to the outcome of the case and may be less than fully considered.

Dicta typically arise in two situations. First, the court may rule on one of several issues in a case in such a way that it need not address the remaining issues, and yet the court may discuss the remaining issues. Second, to clarify its reasoning, the court may hypothesize about how it would handle a slightly or even radically different case.

You should note any pertinent dicta in your case brief because the statements do emanate from the court. In the future, dicta may become law, or the court may repudiate the dicta. In the meantime, dicta do provide insight into the court's thinking.

As an example, imagine that the *Luttrell* court discussed a scenario in which the subject of a defamatory statement went on to repeat the statement; this discussion would be dictum. Should you later have such a client situation, you

---

11. Some use a Latin term for the combination of rules and reasoning: *ratio decidendi*.

would consider the *Luttrell* discussion of the point if there is no other case on the topic. However, you could not rely on it as firmly as you could an actual holding.

Concurring and dissenting opinions: If an appellate court has split, you should note briefly who voted differently than the majority and how they would have decided the case. Also note who supported the outcome but would have reasoned differently. Dissents are not precedent. Concurrences only rarely are, in situations where the concurrence adds to a plurality to form a majority. Nonetheless, some of these opinions eventually do inspire the court to change the law in a future case, and all of them show the thinking of some members of the particular court.

As an example, although *Luttrell* did not draw a concurrence or dissent, it is possible to imagine them. A dissenting judge would have held that intracorporate communication would not constitute publication for purposes of defamation. A concurring judge could have written that addressing the issue of publication was premature on the slim basis of a motion to dismiss for failure to state a claim.

Cases with multiple issues: A case may well involve several distinct topics. For example, the plaintiff may have brought several claims against the defendant, or the defendant may have asserted several defenses, or a case may address both the claims and the remedy. You generally will not be concerned with all of the topics in a multi-topic case but instead will focus on topics pertinent to your client's situation. Read through the entire opinion at least once to be sure that a seemingly extraneous discussion really does not pertain to your client's situation.

If your brief covers more than one topic, you will write more than one of several components, generally the issue, holding, rule of law, and reasoning components. Most of the time, it makes the most sense to write one such sequence for the first issue, then turn to the second issue, and so on.

Questions: Here you may note any questions the court explicitly reserved for a future case or questions you had as you read the case.

Pertinence: When you are reading a case for a specific client's situation, you likely will draw connections as you go between the two. While it may be inefficient to write out an extended analysis of the client's situation as you read each case, noting some key ideas should help you when you turn to analyzing your client's situation.[12]

3. Review

Decided cases constitute legal authority and contain several entwined narratives. To read and understand the narratives and effectively brief a case:

(1) Read the case several times, and look up unfamiliar terms.
(2) Annotate the case by labeling the paragraphs according to the components of the case brief.

---

12. If you are writing your case brief as you research, you also may want to note any authorities cited within the case to consider consulting as you continue your research.

(3) Ponder the the real-world story, the legal-system story, and the judicial-analysis story.

(4) Write a case brief with the following components:
- Opening—heading, facts, procedure, and outcome;
- Core—issue, holding, rules of law, reasoning;
- Optional—dictum, dissent, concurrence, questions, pertinence.

(5) Review your brief against the case and itself.

As you evaluate your case brief, consider the following four criteria of sound legal writing:

- Completeness—Is everything present that is needed for a sound understanding of the case?
- Correctness—Are all points stated accurately?
- Coherence—Do all parts of the brief fit together?
- Comprehensibility—Can you readily understand the brief?

A well-written brief permits you to move on to use the case as precedent to analyze a client's situation. You may, however, first need to fuse several pertinent cases.

E. FUSING CASES

1. Introduction

Despite the enormous output of U.S. courts, a lawyer rarely finds a single mandatory precedent that so parallels the client's situation that the lawyer may stop researching. Much more often, a lawyer reads a good handful or even two of more or less pertinent cases.

What, then, does a lawyer do with a file of cases? It may be tempting to count favorable versus unfavorable outcomes and use the score as the basis of analysis, but counting is too blunt a tool. Rather, the lawyer uses *case fusion* to combine the cases to create a whole that is, indeed, more useful than the sum of its parts.

Case fusion is similar to analysis of multiple incidents that people do in fields outside of the law. Perhaps you have analyzed an employer's response to various employees' work in order to discern performance standards or tracked customer responses to new products in order to develop a marketing approach. The goal of the analysis is to discern an overall rule, pattern, or policy. This is also true of legal case fusion.

Occasionally the fusion process is easy because you can use a recent case or commentary source that summarizes the case law to date. However, this summary was not written with your client's situation in mind, so be sure to check and adapt it as needed. In the absence of such a summary, you will need to fuse the cases yourself, first by selecting and arraying the cases and then fusing them in various ways.

This part of the chapter shifts to a different client situation for its example. All-Day Wellness Minnesota operates in a highly competitive industry and does not want its employees to switch to working for the competition when they leave All-Day Wellness. Employers try to accomplish this business goal by entering into covenants not-to-compete with their employees. This part draws on the following three Minnesota cases in Exhibit 3B: *Davies & Davies Agency, Webb Publishing,* and *Overholt Crop Insurance.* Please look them over now.

2. Selecting and Arraying Cases

One consideration in *selecting cases* to fuse is jurisdiction. Cases from the same court system should, by virtue of stare decisis, be consistent with each other and thus amenable to fusion. Thus, cases decided within the same state court system should be incorporated in your fusion. Cases from other court systems need not be consistent with each other and thus should be left out. For example, a federal court may rule on an issue of state law, but this decision does not bind the state courts, so it may be excluded or given less weight than state court cases.

Fusing cases depends on your full understanding of each case. Be sure you have first read and briefed each case carefully. Verify that the cases you are fusing pertain to the same legal issue or very nearly the same legal issue. For example, a rule making certain conduct criminal may be quite different from a rule permitting a wronged person to sue the wrongdoer for damages. Furthermore, the more closely the facts of the cases resemble your client's situation, the better. At the same time, realize that an identical case is unlikely to exist.

As you read the cases that you select to fuse, follow a logical progression—for example, oldest to newest (or vice versa) or highest to lowest court. Focus on the relationship of each case to the other cases you read.

Two ways of *arraying cases,* shown in Box 3.4, can provide useful information at this early stage. First, array the cases hierarchically by level of court. If there is more than one case from a particular level, list those cases from top to bottom in reverse chronological order. This hierarchical array is especially useful when you have cases from multiple levels of the same court system.

Second, array your cases on a timeline from oldest to most recent cases, placing cases with one outcome above the line and cases with the other outcome below the line. For each case, sketch out the key facts and reasoning. Start looking for a pattern: what is true of all cases above the line and not true of cases below the line?

As you construct these arrays, keep in mind that cases from a given court are of varying weights. Cases from a higher court and recent are especially weighty, for example. In particular, watch out for older cases that may have been overruled.

3. Fusing Rule Language

There are various ways to fuse cases once you have arrayed them. One is *rule fusion,* which focuses on the rules stated in the cases.

You may wonder why the statement of a rule is not the same in every case. As the opening quote to this chapter notes, the common law is built by "minute accretions of past" cases, as each case builds upon past cases and adds to the foundation for future cases. Because a court can decide only the controversy presented to it, the court's opinion generally discusses only so much of a rule as is needed for that case. Other cases on the same general topic may entail other aspects of the rule. Another possibility is that the court may adjust the elements

BOX 3.4

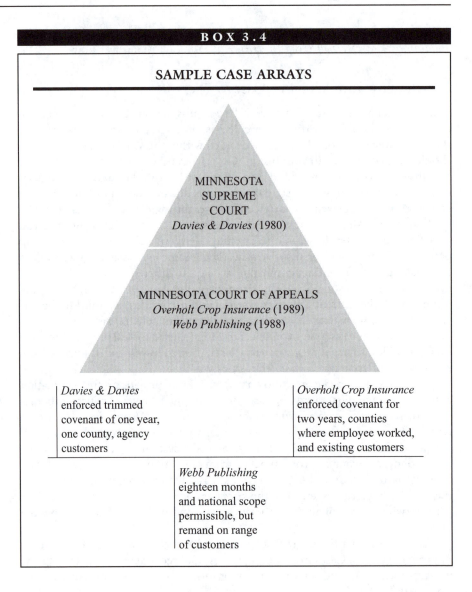

SAMPLE CASE ARRAYS

MINNESOTA
SUPREME
COURT
Davies & Davies (1980)

MINNESOTA COURT OF APPEALS
Overholt Crop Insurance (1989)
Webb Publishing (1988)

Davies & Davies
enforced trimmed
covenant of one year,
one county, agency
customers

Overholt Crop Insurance
enforced covenant for
two years, counties
where employee worked,
and existing customers

Webb Publishing
eighteen months
and national scope
permissible, but
remand on range
of customers

stated in previous cases to keep the rule current. Or the court may alter the phrasing of a rule, while not intending to change the meaning.

Rule fusion involves a word-by-word analysis of the similarities and differences in the rules drawn from the fused cases. First, compare each word and phrase of the various rules to be fused. Then separate the language into four categories, as follows:

(1) Begin to assemble the fused rule with the material that is identical in all rules.

(2) If similar material can be rephrased into a single broader term that still adequately describes the original material, use that new term in the fused rule. If it cannot, use one or more of the similar phrasings for this material.

(3) Add material appearing in only some cases to the fused rule, one item at a time. Test each new item by asking whether its addition would change the results of cases in which that item does not appear. If not, add the new item to the fused rule. If the addition would change any of the cases, try to adjust the new item by rewording it or by presenting the item as a disjunctive element (alternatives connected by "or").

(4) As for material that differs, consider the limits of case fusion, discussed below.

In the end, aim for a well-crafted if/then rule, perhaps with enumerated elements.

As you work with the cases, you no doubt will notice how the rule was applied to the facts of the various cases. Furthermore, in most cases, the court will discuss what one or more elements of the rule mean. This information, which exemplifies and elaborates upon the rule, can be very helpful to you as you seek to apply the rule to your client's situation, so noting it along with your statement of the rule is a good idea.

As an example, Box 3.5 presents a rule fusion of the three cases pertinent to the All-Day Wellness situation. This sample fusion focuses on the length of a time restraint on post-termination employment.

4. Discerning Patterns

Another fusion approach is to look for patterns in the various cases' facts, outcomes, and reasonings, including policies. This approach—*pattern fusion*—is especially effective where the court has not articulated the rule fully or clearly, perhaps because the area is new for the court or an old rule is losing support.

A features chart can help to capture the potentially significant features of the cases. In addition to the case name, court, year, and outcome, possible features include the real-world roles of the parties, the most significant relevant facts, and policies stated by the court. If the court stresses a specific feature, it should appear in your features chart. Be sure to list the cases in a logical order, such as oldest to most recent.

The next step is to look for patterns that explain the holdings:

- Does a particular outcome always follow from a particular fact or combination of facts?
- Does a particular policy consideration result in one holding or the other?
- Does one outcome occur until a certain date, and does another outcome occur thereafter?
- Has one fact or policy become more or less important over time?

These patterns may be cause/effect relationships, or they may be coincidences. A close reading of the cases should tell you which is true. If you cannot find a pattern that explains the holdings, reread the cases to find additional facts that may not have seemed significant on first reading, and revise your chart accordingly. If the cases truly conflict, concentrate on the later cases and the cases from the highest court.

BOX 3.5

SAMPLE RULE FUSION

The Three Cases

Davies & Davies Agency (Minn. Sup. Ct. 1980)

The court approved these two alternative standards used by the district court: "the length of time necessary to *obliterate the identification between employer and employee in the minds of the employer's customers* . . . and the length of time necessary for an *employee's replacement to obtain licenses and learn the fundamentals* of the business."

[Five years was pared to one and enforced.]

Webb Publishing Co. (Minn. Ct. App. 1988)

The temporal duration and geographic area of the restriction do not appear unreasonable, given . . . the *time required to establish a relationship between [the employee's] former customers and his replacement.*

[Eighteen months was permissible.]

Overholt Crop Insurance (Minn. Ct. App. 1989)

The test employed to determine the reasonableness of a temporal restriction examines *the nature of the employee's work, the time necessary for the employer to train a new employee, and the time necessary for the customers to become familiar with the new employee.*

[Two years was the permissible time period.]

Rule Fusion

The factors are:

(1) obliterating identification between employer and employee in the minds of customers (*Davies*) or time to establish the relationship between customers and the replacement (*Webb; Overholt*);

(2) time for the replacement to obtain a license and learn the business (*Davies*) or time needed to train the new employee (*Overholt*);

(3) nature of employee's work (a seemingly new, open-ended factor) (*Overholt*).

Finally, align the findings from your features chart with the rule from your rule fusion. The features that you have identified as important should be consistent with the elements of the rule.

As an example, Box 3.6 is a features chart for the three sample cases pertinent to the All-Day Wellness situation. The chart focuses on several factual features: the employee's position, the length of time the covenant would run, and its scope in terms of both region and work function.

BOX 3.6

SAMPLE FEATURES CHART

Case Name, Court, and Date	Outcome	Employee Position	Length of Time	Region and Function
Davies & Davies Agency (Sup. Ct. 1980)	Covenant enforced as trimmed, with a focus on agency clients	Sales agent of probate and court bonds	5 years, but district court reduced to 1 year	Engaging in insurance business within 50 miles of Minneapolis, St. Paul, or Duluth, but reduced to one county
Webb Publishing (Ct. App. 1988)	Remand on issue of overbreadth as to which customers	Account executive for custom publisher	18 months	Involvement in business that publishes or markets printed material for recent Webb customers (apparently nationally)
Overholt Crop Insurance (Ct. App. 1989)	Covenant enforced as written	Sales agent of crop insurance policies	2 years	Engaging in insurance business (contacting existing customers) in counties where he worked

5. The Limits of Fusion

On occasion, you may find yourself trying to fuse material that cannot be fused. For instance, your work with the rule language from the various cases might yield an element as to which the cases differ dramatically, in a way that cannot be accommodated by a disjunctive element or a wording change. In other situations, your features chart may not yield a pattern that explains all the cases' holdings. This typically arises in two situations.

First, the court may change the law over time. Generally, a court gradually modifies case law; these changes can be accommodated by weaving the new or different material into existing material. Other times, change is dramatic, and the court *overrules* existing law; then the line of cases begins anew. In these situations, it is not possible or desirable to fuse cases that are not meant to converge. A rare and vexing situation is when a court does not expressly overrule existing case law but nevertheless seems to be changing direction. A useful way to test whether there is an implicit overruling is to analyze new cases under the old rule and vice versa.

Second, you may have an *anomalous case* in an otherwise fusible set of cases. While anomalous cases frustrate lawyers seeking to understand an area of case law, they do not surprise most experienced lawyers. Recall that courts not only make precedent but also resolve real-world disputes. Some litigants have facts sympathetic enough to persuade a court, despite the legal weaknesses of their cases. If you have discovered a truly anomalous case, consider omitting it from your fusion. This omission is especially justifiable if later cases discount the anomalous case or do not take note of it.

6. Review

The purpose of case fusion is to generate a rule or pattern that encompasses the content of a set of cases. The steps of fusion are as follows:

(1) Select the cases to fuse.
(2) Prepare hierarchical and chronological arrays to help you understand the precedential and outcome relationships among the cases.
(3) Create case fusions as follows:
   (a) Fuse the rules stated in the cases, with examples and elaborations noted.
   (b) Seek a pattern in the cases by constructing a features chart.

Finally, check your fusion for completeness, correctness, coherence, and comprehensibility:

- Completeness—Are all cases, elements, and consequences included?
- Correctness—Have you accurately reflected the cases? Have you attended closely to the courts' language? Have you accurately represented the holdings, facts, and policies?
- Coherence—Are the elements consistent with each other?
- Comprehensibility—Can you understand the fusion?

Fusing cases in this way before you apply them to your client's situation will strengthen your understanding of the law and your analysis of your client's legal position.

EXHIBIT 3A LUTTRELL V. UNITED TELEPHONE SYSTEM, INC.

Publication Information	Luttrell v. United Telephone System, Inc., 9 Kan.App.2d 620 (1984)
	683 P.2d 1292, 47 A.L.R.4th 669

Court

9 Kan.App.2d 620
Court of Appeals of Kansas.

Case Name

Marvin G. LUTTRELL, Appellant,
v.
UNITED TELEPHONE SYSTEM, INC., Appellee.

Docket and Date

No. 56031. | July 19, 1984. | Review Granted Sept. 6, 1984.

Publisher's Summary

Employee brought action against employer alleging that statements by managerial employees concerning employee's job performance constituted defamation. The District Court, Johnson County, Phillip L. Woodworth, J., granted employer's motion to dismiss for failure to state claim upon which relief may be granted, and employee appealed. The Court of Appeals, Parks, J., held that remarks communicated by one corporate employee to another concerning job performance of third employee are publication for purposes of defamation against employer; thus, claim was improperly dismissed.

Reversed and remanded.

West Headnotes (8)

Headnotes

[1] Libel and Slander
☞— Nature and elements of defamation in general

Tort of defamation includes both libel and slander.

8 Cases that cite this headnote

[2] Libel and Slander
☞— Nature and elements of defamation in general

Elements of defamation include false and defamatory words communicated to a third person which result in harm to the reputation of the person defamed.

23 Cases that cite this headnote

[3] Corporations and Business Organizations
☞— Defamation

Corporation may be liable for defamatory utterances of its agent which are made while acting within scope of his authority.

2 Cases that cite this headnote

EXHIBIT 3A (cont.)

[4] **Libel and Slander**
⭕— Injury to reputation

Laws of libel and slander protect reputation.

Cases that cite this headnote

[5] **Libel and Slander**
⭕— Common business interest

Communication made within work situation is qualifiedly privileged if it is made in good faith on any subject matter in which person communicating has an interest, or in reference to which he has a duty, if it is made to a person having corresponding interest or duty.

11 Cases that cite this headnote

[6] **Libel and Slander**
⭕— As to character of employee

Employer who is evaluating or investigating employee in good faith and within bounds of employment relationship is protected from threat of defamation suits by requirement that employee prove that employer acted with knowledge of falsity or reckless disregard for the truth.

14 Cases that cite this headnote

[7] **Libel and Slander**
⭕— Publication

Remarks made in course and scope of employment by one corporate employee and communicated to second corporate employee concerning job performance of third employee are publication for purposes of defamation action against corporate employer. K.S.A. 60–212(b)(6).

13 Cases that cite this headnote

[8] **Libel and Slander**
⭕— Form and requisites in general

Allegation by employee that managerial employees of corporate employer had made false statements about his job performance was sufficient to state defamation action.

3 Cases that cite this headnote

*620 **1293 *Syllabus by the Court*

Court's
Synopsis

Remarks made in the course and scope of employment by one corporate employee and communicated to a second corporate employee concerning the

EXHIBIT 3A (cont.)

job performance of a third employee constitute publication for the purposes of a defamation action against the corporate employer.

Attorneys and Law Firms

Attorneys

Richard M. Smith of Smith & Winter-Smith, Mound City, for appellant.

Paul Hasty, Jr. of Wallace, Saunders, Austin, Brown & Enochs, Chartered, Overland Park, for appellee.

Before FOTH, C.J., and PARKS and SWINEHART, JJ.

Opinion

Authoring Judge

PARKS, Judge:

OPINION

Plaintiff Marvin G. Luttrell appeals the dismissal of his defamation action against the defendant, United Telephone System, Inc.

Facts

Plaintiff alleges in his petition that several managerial employees of defendant maliciously communicated defamatory remarks about him between themselves while acting within the scope of their employment. Particularly, he alleges that on or about April 6 or 7 of 1982, Mr. R.H. Baranek, an employee of defendant, stated to Mr. R.L. Flint, plaintiff's supervisor, that plaintiff was illegally taping telephone conversations on April 1 and that Baranek had requested him to stop but plaintiff persisted in this illegal activity the rest of the afternoon despite the direct order given him to stop by his supervisor. He further alleged that the communication of the same defamatory information was made by Mr. Flint to Mr. T.V. Tregenza and by Mr. Tregenza to Mr. W. Soble, all while acting within

Procedure

the scope of their employment. Defendant filed a motion to dismiss pursuant to K.S.A. 60–212(b)(6) on the grounds that intracorporate communications did not constitute "publication." The trial court sustained the motion to dismiss for failure to state a claim upon which relief may be granted.

Rules of Law

[1] [2] [3] The tort of defamation includes both libel and slander. The elements of the wrong include false and defamatory words (*Hein v. Lacy,* 228 KAN. 249, 259, 616 P.2d 277 [1980]) communicated ***621** to a third person (*Schulze v. Coykendall,* 218 Kan. 653, 657, 545 P.2d 392 [1976] which result in harm to the reputation of the person defamed. *Gobin v. Globe Publishing Co.,* 232 Kan. 1, 6, 649 P.2d 1239 (1982) (*Gobin III*). A corporation may be liable for the defamatory utterances of its agent which are made while acting within the scope of his authority. *Bourn v. State Bank,* 116 Kan. 231, 235, 226 P. 769 (1924).

Issue

In this case, the defendant argued and the district court agreed that there can be no communication to a third person, or "publication," when the defamatory words are exchanged by agents of a single corporate defendant. This issue of first impression is more precisely whether interoffice communications between supervisory employees of a corporation, acting within the scope and course of

EXHIBIT 3A (cont.)

their employment, regarding the work of another employee of the corporation, constitute publication to a third person sufficient for a defamation action.

Reasoning
• law
  elsewhere

There is a considerable division of authority concerning this issue. For example, courts recently considering the laws of Nevada, Missouri, Arkansas, Georgia and Louisiana have all accepted the assertion that intracorporate defamation is simply the corporation talking to itself and not publication. See *e.g., Jones v. Golden Spike Corp.,* 97 Nev. 24, 623 P.2d 970 (1981); *Ellis v. Jewish Hospital of St. Louis,* 581 S.W.2d 850 (Mo.App.1979); *Halsell v. Kimberly-Clark Corp.,* 683 F.2d 285 (8th Cir.1982); *Monahan v. Sims,* 163 Ga.App. 354, 294 S.E.2d 548 (1982); *Commercial Union Ins. Co. v. Melikyan,* 424 So.2d 1114 (La. App.1982). The contrary conclusion has been reached in courts applying the laws of Kentucky, Massachusetts, New ****1294** York and California. See *e.g., Brewer v. American Nat. Ins. Co.,* 636 F.2d 150 (6th Cir.1980); *Arsenault v. Allegheny Airlines, Inc.,* 485 F.Supp. 1373 (D.Mass.), *aff'd* 636 F.2d 1199 (1st Cir.1980); *Pirre v. Printing Developments, Inc.,* 468 F.Supp. 1028 (S.D.N.Y.), *aff'd* 614 F.2d 1290 (2d Cir.1979); *Kelly v. General Telephone Co.,* 136 Cal. App.3d 278, 186 Cal.Rptr. 184 (1982). The latter opinions have held that while communications between supervisory employees of a corporation concerning a third employee may be qualifiedly privileged, they are still publication. Prosser also favors the view that such communications are publication and dismisses those cases holding otherwise as confusing ***622** publication with privilege. Prosser, Law of Torts § 113, p. 767 n. 70 (4th ed. 1971).

• policy

[4] Undeniably, the district court's holding in this case is not without support or technical appeal; however, we believe it ignores the nature of the civil injury sought to be protected in a defamation action. Damage to one's reputation is the essence and gravamen of an action for defamation. It is reputation which is defamed, reputation which is injured, reputation which is protected by the laws of libel and slander. *Gobin III,* 232 Kan. at 6, 649 P.2d 1239. Certainly, damage to one's reputation within a corporate community may be just as devastating as that effected by defamation spread to the outside. Thus, the injury caused by intracorporate defamation should not be disregarded simply because the corporation can be sued as an individual entity.

• party's
  argument

• related rules

[5] Defendant argues that corporate employers must be free to evaluate and comment on their employees' work performance and that this freedom will be unduly restrained if they are liable for intracorporate defamation. However, the law in this state has already extended protection to comments made within a work situation by means of a qualified privilege. A communication is qualifiedly privileged if it is made in good faith on any subject matter in which the person communicating has an interest, or in reference to which he has a duty, if it is made to a person having a corresponding interest or duty. The essential elements of a qualifiedly privileged communication are good faith, an interest to be upheld, a statement limited in its scope to the upholding of such interest and publication in a proper manner only to proper parties. *Gobbyn v. Nelson,* 2 Kan.

EXHIBIT 3A (cont.)

App.2d 358, 360, 579 P.2d 721, *aff'd* 225 Kan. 56, 587 P.2d 315 (1978). Thus, in *Dobbyn* the Court held that a letter written by an employee of the Kansas State University library concerning the conduct of another employee and transmitted to the second employee's superior was qualifiedly privileged. *Dobbyn,* 2 Kan. App.2d at 361, 579 P.2d 721. As a result, the plaintiff was required to prove that the defendants acted with knowledge of falsity or reckless disregard for the truth before the privilege could be overcome. See also *Scarpelli v. Jones,* 229 Kan. 210, 216, 626 P.2d 785 (1981).

[6] By virtue of the qualified privilege, the employer who is evaluating or investigating an employee in good faith and within the bounds of the employment relationship is protected from the threat of defamation suits by the enhanced burden of proof *623 which the plaintiff would have to bear. We see no reason for greater freedom from liability for defamation to be accorded the corporate employer than that already available to all employers through the qualified privilege.

• holding

[7] [8] We conclude that remarks communicated by one corporate employee to another concerning the job performance of a third employee are publication for the purposes of a defamation action against the employer. Since the dismissal motion was granted in this case prior to the commencement of any discovery, we make no findings concerning the possible application of qualified privilege to the communications alleged.

• outcome

The dismissal for failure to state a claim upon which relief may be granted is reversed and the case is remanded for further proceedings.

All Citations

9 Kan.App.2d 620, 683 P.2d 1292, 47 A.L.R.4th 669

EXHIBIT 3B EXCERPTS FROM THREE CASES ON COVENANTS NOT-TO-COMPETE

298 N.W.2d 127

Supreme Court of Minnesota.

DAVIES & DAVIES AGENCY, INC., Appellant,

v.

Richard H. DAVIES, Respondent,

and

Richard H. DAVIES, Plaintiff,

v.

DAVIES & DAVIES AGENCY, INC. and

Everett W. Davies, Defendants,

and

DAVIES & DAVIES AGENCY, INC., et al., Appellants,

v.

Robert J. BUCKINGHAM, et al., Respondents.

Nos. 49594, 50016.

|

Oct. 17, 1980.

* * *

Opinion

WAHL, Justice.

* * *

Davies & Davies Agency is an insurance agency whose stock is owned solely by Everett W. Davies, its president. Richard Davies, the eldest son of Everett Davies, began working for the agency in June 1967. He was 20 years old at the time and had completed three years of study at the University of Minnesota. Everett Davies hoped at the time that Richard, and possibly his younger brothers, would eventually take over the agency. At the outset of his employment, Richard did general office and clerical work. On October 24, 1967, approximately four months after he began work and six days before his 21st birthday, he was presented with and executed an employment and noncompetition agreement. The agreement precluded Richard, upon termination of his employment with the agency for any reason, from engaging in the insurance business for a period of five years within a 50-mile radius of Minneapolis, St. Paul, or Duluth. All employees of the agency were required to sign a similar agreement.

Richard had not been required to sign the noncompetition agreement at an earlier date because Everett Davies was under the mistaken impression that an agreement signed by a minor is void. Everett Davies stated that Richard would not have been allowed to expand his duties at the agency and would not have been supported in his applications for insurance licensing if he had not signed the agreement.

EXHIBIT 3B (cont.)

Over a period of years, Richard was trained and acquired expertise in the sale of probate and court bonds, a specialty which comprised a significant portion of the agency's business. As Richard was entrusted with greater responsibility for the agency's clients concerning bounds, Everett Davies phased himself out of that part of the business. By 1972, Richard was in charge of the agency's bond business and was often the exclusive contact between the agency and its bond customers.

Conflict between Everett and Richard Davies concerning the agency's operations and their respective positions within the agency began and steadily increased in the last few years of Richard's employment. On Richard's behalf, it was asserted that morale was poor among all the employees, that Everett Davies generally ran the business as an autocrat, that there was disputes between Everett and employees about credit for production and compensation, and that Richard Davies was often put in the position of an intermediary between his father and other employees. At one point, Everett changed the locks to the office and did not provide keys to his employees.

On the other side, there was testimony from Richard himself that he used various kinds of threats to manipulate his father. He announced that he was quitting on several occasions, but then continued working. On one occasion, Richard smashed equipment in his office. He removed a file containing information about the agency's customers for over a week. According to Everett's testimony, Richard stated at a meeting in October 1977 that unless his compensation and other demands were met by the agency, he would be the most vindictive person in the city of Minneapolis.

The mutual mistrust between Everett and Richard and the continuing deterioration of their working relationship led Richard to announce his intention of resigning from the agency. Everett reminded Richard of his obligations under the noncompetition agreement but was unable to obtain from Richard any information about his future plans. On January 13, 1978, Richard **130** notified Everett that he was leaving the agency on January 31. Everett replied that Richard was relieved of his duties as of January 15.

After he was relieved of his duties, Richard contacted many of the attorneys who had been his clients. He was in the Hennepin County Government Center on January 16 talking to attorneys. There is conflicting testimony as to whether Richard systematically steered customers he had serviced at the agency to the Pat Thomas Agency, a competitor, or whether Richard merely explained his situation to attorneys who were also personal friends, and occasionally suggested the Thomas Agency to attorneys who contacted him personally for bonds and did not wish to obtain bonds through Davies & Davies. At the time of trial, Richard had not accepted employment with any other insurance agency.

The following issues are presented for our determination in the Richard Davies case:

1. Is the noncompetition agreement between the agency and defendant Davies valid?

2. If the noncompetition agreement is a valid contract, are the restraints imposed by the agreement reasonable?

EXHIBIT 3B (cont.)

3. If the noncompetition agreement is enforceable, is plaintiff entitled to monetary damages?

1. Richard Davies neither signed nor was shown the noncompetition agreement before commencing employment. Richard Davies was presented with the covenant four months after he began work, and was told to sign by his father. The implications of the agreement were not discussed. Richard testified that his father assured him that it was a formality. Defendant Davies argues that a noncompetition agreement entered into after an employee has already begun work for an employer, and for which no additional consideration other than continued employment is given, is void. This issue has not yet been addressed by this court. The trial court held that, under the circumstances, there was sufficient consideration, including continued employment, for Richard Davies' promise.

Decisions in other jurisdictions on this issue are quite evenly divided. Those cases which have held that continued employment is not a sufficient consideration stress the fact that an employee frequently has no bargaining power once he is employed and can easily be coerced. By signing a noncompetition agreement, the employee gets no more from his employer than he already has, and in such cases there is a danger that an employer does not need protection for his investment in the employee but instead seeks to impose barriers to prevent an employee from securing a better job elsewhere. See, e. g., James C. Greene Co. v. Kelley, 261 N.C. 166, 134 S.E.2d 166 (1964); Worth Chemical Corp. v. Freeman, 261 N.C. 780, 136 S.E.2d 118 (1964); George W. Kistler, Inc., v. O'Brien, 464 Pa. 475, 347 A.2d 311 (1975); Morgan Lumber Sales Co. v. Toth, 41 Ohio Misc. 17, 321 N.E.2d 907 (1974). Decisions in which continued employment has been deemed a sufficient consideration for a noncompetition agreement have focused on a variety of factors, including the possibility that the employee would otherwise have been discharged, the employee was actually employed for a substantial time after executing the contract, or the employee received additional compensation or training or was given confidential information after he signed the agreement. Daughtry v. Capital Gas Co., 285 Ala. 89, 229 So.2d 480 (1969); Faw, Casson & Co. v. Cranston, 375 A.2d 463 (Del.Ch.1977); M. S. Jacobs & Associates v. Duffley, 452 Pa. 143, 303 A.2d 921 (1973). The Iowa Supreme Court has held more generally that continued employment alone, without other circumstances, is sufficient consideration. Ehlers v. Iowa Warehouse Co., 188 N.W.2d 368 (Iowa 1971); Farm Bureau Service Co. v. Kohls, 203 N.W.2d 209 (Iowa 1972).

[1][2] The adequacy of consideration for a noncompetition contract or clause in an ongoing employment relationship should depend on the facts of each case. Mere continuation of employment as consideration could be used to uphold coercive agreements. *131 Yet, in cases such as these presently before the court, the agreement may be bargained for and provide the employee with real advantages. In the Richard Davies case, Richard derived substantial economic and professional benefits from the agency after signing the contract: He continued his employment for 10 years and advanced to a selling position within the agency which would not have been open to him

EXHIBIT 3B (cont.)

if he had not signed the contract. He received informal training from Everett Davies, was supported by the agency in his license applications, and had sole responsibility for many of the agency's customers. Richard's brother, John, who refused to sign an agreement, was limited to a largely clerical position during his tenure with the agency. We therefore agree with the trial court that there was adequate consideration to support the noncompetition agreement.

2. In the Richard Davies case, the trial court further held that although the agreement was a validly executed contract, its terms were overbroad and unreasonable. The test of reasonableness of a noncompetition contract was well stated in Bennett v. Storz Broadcasting Co., 270 Minn. 525, 534, 535-36, 134 N.W.2d 892, 899-900 (1965):

> The test applied is whether or not the restraint is necessary for the protection of the business or good will of the employer, and if so, whether the stipulation has imposed upon the employee any greater restraint than is reasonably necessary to protect the employer's business, regard being had to the nature and character of the employment, the time for which the restriction is imposed, and the territorial extent of the locality to which the prohibition extends.

> The validity of the contract in each case must be determined on its own facts and a reasonable balance must be maintained between the interests of the employer and the employee.

[3] The trial court found that the agency had a protectable interest in its client relationships but that the scope of the agreement was overly broad. The agency did little bond work outside Hennepin County; therefore, a prohibition against employment in the insurance business within 50 miles of Minneapolis, St. Paul or Duluth was unreasonable. On the duration question, the trial curt evaluated the five-year period under two alternative standards: the length of time necessary to obliterate the identification between employer and employee in the minds of the employer's customers (adopted by the Wisconsin Supreme Court in Lakeside Oil Co. v. Slutsky, 8 Wis.2d 157, 98 N.W.2d 415 (1959)) and the length of time necessary for an employee's replacement to obtain licenses and learn the fundamentals of the business. The trial court concluded that one year would be a proper length of time in this case under either standard, and modified the agreement to prohibit Richard Davies from engaging in the sale of bonds within Hennepin County for one year from the date of his last active employment.[1]

It appears that the agency's actual need for protection is limited to prohibiting its former employees from actively soliciting business from agency customers. A broader restriction than this could not enhance the agency's business: If a former employee were prohibited from selling any insurance in the area, the customers not served by him would not necessarily choose the Davies agency from all other insurance agencies. Instead, a blanket prohibition would only hurt the former employee's livelihood. Such restrictions have been expressly disapproved by this court. Bennett v. Storz Broadcasting Co., 270

EXHIBIT 3B (cont.)

Minn. 525, 134 N.W.2d 892;*132 Combined Insurance Co. of America v. Bode, 247 Minn. 458, 77 N.W.2d 533 (1956); Standard Oil Co. v. Bertelson, 186 Minn. 483, 243 N.W. 701 (1932). Everett Davies himself implied that this would be the general effect of enforcing the terms of the noncompetition agreement. He gave as a reason for not enforcing it, "We had an agency policy that recognized that people in the insurance industry had the right and the necessity to make a living ***" and "*** I recognize the fact that they have to have a right to make a living. The insurance industry is what they are involved in, where their experience is, they can go and work for an insurance company or another agency if they just leave us alone."

[4] Thus, based upon this practice of the agency, a prohibition against active solicitation of agency clients by a former employee is all that is reasonably necessary to protect the agency's interest in the insurance area. The two alternative standards used here by the trial court to determine appropriate duration for the agreement would appear to provide effective protection for an employer's interests without imposing unnecessary hardship on an employee's livelihood. Therefore, we hold that this modification, along with the trial court's "blue pencil" revisions made under the reasonableness test, are applicable in the Richard Davies case.

* * *

Footnote

  1. Minnesota adopted the "blue pencil doctrine," which allows a court to modify an unreasonable noncompetition agreement and enforce it only to the extent that it is reasonable, in the context of a sale of a business, in Bess v. Bothman, 257 N.W.2d 791 (Minn.1977). The reasons for permitting modification in that context are equally applicable to the employment context. Therefore, in employment cases, a court should be permitted to make changes such as those made by the trial court in this case rather than be compelled to strike down the entire agreement as unreasonable.

EXHIBIT 3B (cont.)

426 N.W.2d 445

Court of Appeals of Minnesota.

WEBB PUBLISHING COMPANY, Respondent,

v.

Neal T. FOSSHAGE, Appellant.

No. C1–87–2444.

|

June 21, 1988.

OPINION

LANSING, Judge.

After terminating appellant Neal Fosshage's employment as an account executive, respondent Webb Publishing Co. brought suit for damages and an injunction to enforce a noncompetition agreement allegedly signed by Fosshage. The trial court entered an ex parte temporary restraining order and, after a hearing attended by counsel for both parties, ordered a temporary injunction. Fosshage appeals.

FACTS

Webb's custom publishing division creates, designs, prints and distributes custom magazines for companies across the United States. Webb is one of approximately 12 major national custom publishers, although there are several smaller operations.

*447 In January 1980 Webb hired Neal Fosshage, who had 27 years of experience in marketing, as an account executive. His duties were not specified, but Fosshage's affidavit states that he solicited business and assisted Webb's clients in developing marketing strategies. Fosshage was the primary contact between Webb and four of its clients: Mobil, Melroe Company, American Cyanamid, and Valmont Industries. Those four clients produced $1.7 million of Webb's annual $3.8 million in custom publishing revenue.

On September 28, 1987, Webb terminated Fosshage's employment, allegedly because his aggressive style conflicted with corporate policy. In October 1987 Fosshage formed his own custom publishing corporation and solicited the business of American Cyanamid and Valmont Industries, both of which notified Webb of their intent to cancel their contracts with Webb. Webb brought this action seeking injunctive relief and damages based on Fosshage's noncompetition agreement.

Before the hearing on the temporary restraining order, Fosshage's counsel received Webb's motion papers and the name of the judge assigned to hear the motion. Fosshage's counsel did not appear at the hearing, and they dispute that they received notice of the time and place. Webb supported its TRO motion with affidavits alleging that in April

EXHIBIT 3B (cont.)

1986, in consideration for an increase in annual salary to $40,000 and an increased rate of commission, Fosshage signed the following noncompetition agreement:

> For a period of 18 months from termination of employment, I shall not, directly or indirectly, engage in or solicit or have any interest in any person, firm, corporation, or business that engages in or solicits, the publication or marketing of any custom publication, promotion piece, catalog, calendar, or any other printed material for any customer that has done business with the custom publishing division of Webb within the period of one year immediately prior to my termination of employment.

The notation "40M" appeared under Fosshage's signature on the agreement.

Webb's affidavits say that Fosshage was reminded of the noncompetition agreement the day after his termination, but said that he would not be stopped from talking to his friends. When told that his severance pay was conditioned on not contacting customers, Fosshage replied that they might as well not pay him.

Webb alleged that Fosshage had solicited the business of American Cyanamid and Valmont Industries, and if he successfully solicited the other two of his major clients, Webb's custom publishing division would lose approximately 45 percent of its revenue. Webb further alleged that the permanent loss of the business would affect Webb's business reputation and revenue, resulting in future indeterminable loss.

The trial court, without specific findings or conclusions, granted the temporary restraining order prohibiting Fosshage until further order from soliciting any customers with which Webb had done business since September 1986. Bond was set at $2,000, and a hearing on the request for a temporary injunction was set for December 3, 1987.

Fosshage made no motion to dissolve the TRO for procedural defects, but did submit an affidavit and memorandum in opposition to the temporary injunction. His affidavit states that although his signature on the noncompetition agreement appeared to be genuine, he did not recall having seen it before, had twice since April 1986 refused Webb's requests to sign noncompetition agreements, and did not learn they were claiming that he had signed one until October 1987. He stated that the salary and commission increases were not consideration for signing the agreement and that he did not have access to any confidential or proprietary information on custom publication. Finally, Fosshage asserted that his termination was contrary to his understanding that he would not be terminated without cause; he was never reminded of the noncompetition agreement; Webb had failed to pay commissions on sales which were not billed until after termination; and ***448** he would be forced to file for bankruptcy if Webb's motion were granted.

The trial court granted a temporary injunction barring Fosshage for 18 months from soliciting any customer with which Webb had done business for a year prior to termination. The $2,000 bond was continued as security. In its memorandum the trial court found that Fosshage had entered into the noncompetition agreement for

EXHIBIT 3B (cont.)

consideration which included an increase in annual salary and increased commissions; that Fosshage had solicited customers in violation of the agreement; that the agreement was individually negotiated by Fosshage; that Fosshage could still earn a living in custom publishing if he refrained from contacting Webb's customers; that if the temporary injunction were denied Webb would suffer irreparable harm to its current customers and its reputation; and that Fosshage had produced no persuasive evidence justifying his breach and it was likely Webb would succeed on the merits. The court concluded that Webb was entitled to injunctive relief, and Fosshage appeals.

* * *

[4]c. *Lack of Consideration.* Fosshage claims that the noncompetition agreement ***450** was unsupported by consideration because his pay increase was part of an annual performance review and account executives who did not sign noncompetition agreements were allowed to participate in increased commissions. Webb's affidavits say that the increase in pay occurred just six months after Fosshage's last annual review, and consideration for the agreements was negotiated with each account executive individually. Fosshage's argument is weakened by the notation "40M" under his signature. "The adequacy of consideration for a noncompetition contract or clause in an ongoing employment relationship should depend on the facts of each case."*Davies & Davies Agency, Inc. v. Davies,* 298 N.W.2d 127, 130 (Minn.1980). Although there are fact issues, the trial court did not err in concluding that Webb was likely to succeed on this issue.

[5]d. *Unreasonableness.* Because restrictive covenants are agreements in restraint of trade, they are enforced only to the extent reasonably necessary to protect a legitimate business interest. *Bennett v. Storz Broadcasting Co.,* 270 Minn. 525, 534, 134 N.W.2d 892, 899–900 (1965). Fosshage argues that the noncompetition agreement does not protect any legitimate interest of Webb's and that it is unreasonable in scope and duration.

1) Legitimacy of Interest. Employers have a legitimate interest in protecting themselves against "the deflection of trade or customers by the employee by means of the opportunity which the employment has given him."*Id.* at 533, 134 N.W.2d at 898. Although Fosshage disavows any "sensitive relationship" with his customers, their decision to remain with him indicates the strength of the relationship. *Compare Continental Car–Na–Var Corp. v. Moseley,* 24 Cal.2d 104, 107, 148 P.2d 9, 12 (1944) (no ongoing relationship with purchasers of floor cleaners where "[e]ach sale is a distinct transaction, not necessarily implying that another will follow.")

Fosshage argues that the client relationship is "largely the product of his own labors," and Webb cannot preclude him from continuing a business relationship. His reliance on *Sanitary Farm Dairies, Inc. v. Wolf,* 261 Minn. 166, 112 N.W.2d 42 (1961), is misplaced; the case did not involve a restrictive covenant, as the court expressly noted in its holding. *Id.* at 174–75, 112 N.W.2d at 48. Nor do Fosshage's other cited cases support his

EXHIBIT 3B (cont.)

---

argument. *See Klick v. Crosstown Bank of Ham Lake, Inc., 372 N.W.2d 85, 88 (Minn.Ct.App.1985)* (evidence showed that employee did not develop *any* special relationships with customers); *Granger* 159 Minn. at 302–03, 199 N.W. at 12 (enforcement of a restrictive covenant permitted because a substantial part of the employer's practice would otherwise leave with the employee.)

Fosshage's relationship with Webb customers was sufficiently close to give Webb a legitimate interest in protecting itself against Fosshage's solicitation of those customers.

2) Reasonableness of restriction. The temporal duration and geographic area of the restriction do not appear unreasonable, given the national character of Webb's business and the time required to establish a relationship between Fosshage's former customers and his replacement. *See Klick, 372 N.W.2d at 88.*

[6] However, the scope of the restriction suggests overbreadth in light of its purpose. Webb's only asserted interest is to protect itself from Fosshage's solicitation of his former customers. If Fosshage had access to information on other Webb customers which would aid him in soliciting their business, then restricting him from doing so would not be unreasonable. However, the record does not indicate such access but, rather, that clients are the responsibility of individual account executives without overlap.

Because the trial court did not address this issue, we remand for consideration of the appropriate scope of the restraint. In view of the harsh effect of the injunction on Fosshage's ability to earn a living, the trial court should also consider expediting trial pursuant to Minn.R.Civ.P. 65.02.

* * *

EXHIBIT 3B (cont.)

437 N.W.2d 698
Court of Appeals of Minnesota.

OVERHOLT CROP INSURANCE SERVICE COMPANY, INC., Respondent,

v.

Scott L. BREDESON, Appellant.

No. C5–88–1761.

|

March 28, 1989.

OPINION

RANDALL, Judge.

This is an appeal from an order enjoining appellant Scott L. Bredeson from any further breach of a noncompetition agreement contained in the employment contract he executed with respondent Overholt Crop Insurance Company. We affirm.

FACTS

Appellant Scott L. Bredeson executed an employment contract with respondent Overholt Crop Insurance Service Company on October 25, 1981. The employment contract contained a restrictive covenant that prohibited appellant from soliciting any business from customers he personally serviced while employed with respondent. The restriction covers the two-year period immediately following the termination of the employment relationship. The covenant also prohibited appellant from competing with respondent in any territory in which appellant worked.

When appellant started working for respondent, respondent sold only crop-hail insurance policies. In 1985, respondent began selling multi-peril crop insurance (MPCI). Appellant chose to sell the MPCI as well as the crop-hail insurance. Appellant received additional commissions for the MPCI he sold.

When appellant's contract commenced, he was assigned four counties to cover for respondent. Subsequently, appellant received an assignment for two more counties. Appellant earned commissions for insurance he sold in these additional counties.

Between 1985 and 1988, appellant executed addenda to the employment contract. The addenda dealt with commissions on both crop-hail insurance and MPCI. The addenda did not alter the terms of the noncompetition agreement.

The parties agree that from the time respondent started marketing MPCI, respondent employed independent agents as well as special representatives like appellant. These independent agents sold MPCI within areas serviced by respondent's employees, including the areas in which appellant worked.

Appellant resigned from respondent on February 13, 1988. Then, appellant starting contacting his former customers and offered to obtain competing MPCI and crop-hail coverage for them. Appellant admits to having signed new MPCI contracts with more than 50 of respondent's former customers. Appellant has also signed contracts with six or seven of respondent's crop-hail customers. These customers cancelled the coverage they had with respondent to sign new contracts with appellant.

According to one of respondent's officers, respondent lost over $100,000 in MPCI premiums in 1988 due to appellant's dealings with respondent's customers. With regard to MPCI insurance, federal regulations permit a commission to be awarded on only one transfer per year; thus, respondent has to now wait a minimum of one year before attempting to resell its former customers.

*701 Following an evidentiary hearing, the trial court found that appellant breached his noncompetition agreement with respondent and issued a temporary injunction prohibiting appellant from any further breach pending trial. Respondent was required to maintain a $10,000 bond as security for any damage to appellant. Appellant did not claim that the amount of the bond was inadequate. This appeal challenges the propriety of the trial court's granting the temporary injunction.

* * *

1. Consideration

[7] The Minnesota Supreme Court has ruled that the adequacy of the consideration for a noncompetition agreement in an employment contract depends upon the facts of each case. *Davies & Davies Agency, Inc. v. Davies*, 298 N.W.2d 127, 130–31 (Minn.1980). *Davies* involved a noncompetition agreement signed *after* the employment relationship started. *Id.* at 130. Only noncompetition agreements entered into subsequent to the initial employment contract require independent consideration. *See National Recruiters, Inc. v. Cashman, 323 N.W.2d 736, 740 (Minn.1982).* Since appellant and respondent entered into this noncompetition agreement at the inception of the employment relationship, no independent consideration is necessary to support the agreement.

* * *

2. Reasonableness

Appellant argues that the restrictive covenant is unreasonable because it is overbroad as to subject matter, geographic scope, and length (two years). With regard to the overbreadth problem, appellant claims that the term "insurance business" contained in the covenant is not defined and is not limited to insureds or customers. Appellant also contends that the geographical scope of the covenant includes more than just the territory assigned to appellant; he argues it includes any territory in which the appellant may have worked.

[10] Appellant correctly points out that covenants not to compete are agreements in partial restraint of trade and are looked upon with disfavor. *See Bennett v. Storz Broadcasting Co., 270 Minn. 525, 533, 134 N.W.2d 892, 898 (1965)*. However, courts

EXHIBIT 3B (cont.)

uphold such covenants when they are designed to protect the employer against the deflection of trade or customers by the employee. *Id.* at 533, 134 N.W.2d at 898.

[11] Testimony at the hearing indicated that the parties understood the provision to prevent contact by former employees with existing policyholders. Such an understanding is consistent with the term "insurance business," and is limited to protect legitimate interests of respondent. We find the noncompetition agreement was not overbroad as to subject matter.

[12] With regard to the reasonableness of the geographical scope of the restriction, the temporary injunction applies only to those counties in which appellant worked for respondent. Courts generally uphold geographic limitations when they are limited to areas necessary to protect the employer's interest. *See, e.g., Davies, 298 N.W.2d at 131* (prohibition on competition with employer in employer's principal business area is reasonable); *Klick v. Crosstown State Bank of Ham Lake Inc.,* 372 N.W.2d 85, 88 (Minn.Ct.App.1985) (noncompetition clause which extends beyond employer's reasonable trade area is invalid). Since the geographical scope of this covenant is limited to the areas in which appellant actually worked for respondent, we find the restriction is not overbroad when examined in light of its purpose.

[13] Appellant next contends that the length of temporary injunction, two years, is unreasonable and claims no evidence was presented to justify that limitation. The trial court concluded the two-year limitation served the legitimate business needs of respondent.

The test employed to determine the reasonableness of a temporal restriction examines the nature of the employee's work, the time necessary for the employer to train a new employee, and the time necessary for the customers to become familiar with the new employee. Note, *Employment Contracts: Covenants Not to Compete in Minnesota,* 9 Wm. Mitchell L.Rev. 388, 404 (1984). The record contains evidence that appellant received training from respondent on marketing and service techniques for both MPCI and crop-hail insurance. *704 The record supports the conclusion that appellant established a good relationship with respondent's customers during his five years with respondent. Furthermore, the nature of appellant's work for respondent required close contact with customers. Based on this evidence, we hold the trial court properly found a two-year restriction on direct competition was reasonable.

TEST YOUR UNDERSTANDING

1. Assume that you are counseling Bower's Bounty, which may be facing a lawsuit by its former employee alleging defamation under the *Luttrell* case. Explain the following matters:
   a. Who would be the plaintiff, and who would be the defendant?
   b. In which level of state court would the lawsuit begin, and how might it conclude there?
   c. How many levels of state appellate courts could consider the case, and what is the role of each?
   d. Is it possible that the case would be set in federal court? If so, under what circumstances?

2. Assume that you succeeded in securing a favorable ruling for Bower's Bounty at the district court, and the employee has appealed. Which of the following appellate outcomes would you most hope for on appeal: affirm, modify, remand, or reverse? Which would you least desire? Explain.

3. What does "stare decisis" mean, and why would a legal system follow this principle?

4. You have continued to research the Bower's Bouty situation and found cases from the following courts decided in the following years. How weighty are each of them, and why?
   a. Kansas Supreme Court 1950
   b. Kansas Court of Appeals 2015, unpublished
   c. Nebraska Supreme Court 2010
   d. U.S. Court of Appeals for the Tenth Circuit 2007, construing Kansas law
   e. Kansas Court of Appeals 1990
   f. Kansas Court of Appeals 2005, reversed on appeal by the Kansas Supreme Court
   g. Sedgwick County (Kansas) District Court 2016

5. A judicial opinion includes the real-world facts of the litigants' dispute, as should your case brief. Why are these facts important to both documents?

6. How do the issues and holding in a judicial opinion relate to each other?

7. How do the holding, rule of law, and reasoning in a judicial opinion relate to each other? When you look to a case as precedent, for which of these does the case stand?

8. If you found a case in your research in which the court strayed from the actual dispute to make a related point that is favorable for Bower's Bounty, may you use this portion of the opinion? Explain.

9. Assume that you found a case in your research in which the Kansas Supreme Court split. Four of the seven justices agreed on one opinion; two on another favoring the same outcome, but for a different reason; and the final justice would have come to a different decision. What are the

correct labels for each opinion? When you brief this case, on which opinion(s) should you focus?

10. How do arraying cases and fusing cases relate to each other?

11. How are rule fusion and pattern fusion similar? How do they differ?

12. Return to question 4. Assume that all the listed cases are factually and legally pertinent to the Bower's Bounty situation. Which of those cases would you include in a case fusion?

13. If you fused the cases that you selected for question 12 and found that the Kansas Court of Appeals 2015 unpublished decision simply did not fit, what might be the explanation?

14. Assume that you are counseling Daniel de la Cruz, who is considering bringing a claim against the public school district that has suspended him, based on his rights under the U.S. Constitution. Explain the following matters:
   a. How many levels of federal courts might hear his claim, and what are they?
   b. Is it possible that a state court would hear his case? If so, under what circumstances?

TEST YOUR UNDERSTANDING ANSWERS

1. For the Bower's Bounty litigation:
   a. The employee, as the party suing, would be the plaintiff. Bower's Bounty, as the party sued, would be the defendant.
   b. The suit would begin in the district court, where it could conclude through negotiation, by motion, or at trial.
   c. Kansas has an appeals court, which focuses on correction of error, and a supreme court, which focuses on making law.
   d. The case could be set in federal court, most likely through diversity jurisdiction if the parties are citizens of different states. Another possibility is that the employee would bring a federal claim.

2. A successful party would prefer that the appeals court affirm (the result stands as is) or even modify (the result mostly stands). Remanding (the case goes back with instructions for change) probably would be preferable to outright reversal, which would be the worst outcome.

3. "Stare decisis" means to stand by decisions and not disturb settled matters. This principle promotes predictability and fairness.

4. The weightiness of the decisions are as follows:
   a. Kansas Supreme Court 1950—very weighty, as a decision of the highest court
   b. Kansas Court of Appeals 2015, unpublished—not very weighty, because it is unpublished
   c. Nebraska Supreme Court 2010—only persuasive, because it is from a different state
   d. U.S. Court of Appeals for the Tenth Circuit 2007, construing Kansas law—only persuasive, because it is not from the Kansas state court system
   e. Kansas Court of Appeals 1990—weighty, as a Kansas appellate decision
   f. Kansas Court of Appeals 2005, reversed on appeal by the Kansas Supreme Court—not to be used because it has been overturned
   g. Sedgwick County (Kansas) District Court 2016—not weighty, because it is only a district court opinion

5. The facts are important because the court rules only on the dispute presented to it and because the parallel between the facts of the case and the client's situation help to determine how closely the holding can connect to the client's situation.

6. The issues are the fact + law questions that the court must answer to reach an outcome in the case, and the holdings are the facts + law answers to those questions.

7. The holding represents the outcome in the case, combining the facts of the case with the rule of law. The rule of law is broader, connecting factual conditions (more broadly stated) with legal consequences. In the reasoning, the court sets out rules of law, connects them to the facts, and provides additional points such as policy and its evaluation of the parties' arguments, along with citations to legal authorities. The case stands for the holdings, rules of law, and reasoning.

8. A statement that strays from the actual dispute is dictum. It may be used because the court wrote it, but it is less reliable than the material required to decide the case.

9. The opinion of four justices is the majority opinion and must be briefed. The opinion of two justices is a concurring opinion, and the opinion of the final justice is a dissenting opinion. It is a good idea to note the points in the non-majority opinions, although they are not the governing opinion.

10. Arraying cases entails presenting cases so as to show their basic relationships in court hierarchy and over time. Fusing cases entails deriving the rules and pattern of decisions from the cases.

11. Rule fusion and pattern fusion both entail discerning what a set of cases teaches about the law. Rule fusion focuses on the language that each case uses to state the rule of law. Pattern fusion focuses on the outcomes of the cases and features of the cases that explain those outcomes.

12. The following cases would be included in a fusion: definitely a and e; b if unpublished cases are usable; d (especially if the federal courts generally align with the state courts); not g because it is a non-precedential decision; not f because it is an invalid decision; not c because it is a case arising under a different state's law.

13. The case that does not fit may be an anomalous case (which could explain why it was designated as unpublished).

14. For the Daniel de la Cruz litigation:
    a. There are three levels of federal courts: district courts, circuit courts of appeals, and the U.S. Supreme Court.
    b. A state court could hear his claim under concurrent jurisdiction.

READING CODES

Scope and Definitions ▶ General Rules and Exceptions ▶ Consequences and Enforcement

The law is a living growth, not a changeless code.
—Inscription carved over the entrance to the Yale Law School,
1929-1931

A. INTRODUCTION

This chapter focuses on the law found in a *code*: a set of rules of general applicability. The discussion focuses on statutes, the codes enacted by legislatures. There are other types of codified law: legislatures (and voters) create constitutions, administrative agencies create rules and regulations, and courts create rules of procedure to govern litigation. These forms of law stand in a hierarchical relationship: constitutions at the top, statutes and court rules in the middle, and administrative regulations at the bottom. Thus, statutes must accord with constitutional requirements, and regulations must accord with statutes. These various types of codes exist at the federal, state, and local levels.

Statutes and other forms of codified law read quite differently than cases. Cases have three entwined narratives (the real-world, legal-system, and judicial-analysis stories) and include legal rules. Codified law consists virtually entirely of legal rules. Most readers find them abstract, technical in tone, and sometimes complex in structure. These features reflect the deliberative processes by which they are created. Yet a codified law can be understood as encompassing a set of stories; viewed in this way, the law becomes more accessible and the challenge of reading it more interesting.

This chapter uses the Cassie Collins situation as its example. Ms. Collins, who is thirty-three, was ticketed for using a cell phone as she was pulling out into traffic from the parking lot of a mini-mall. She was talking into her standard, hand-held cell phone, asking a search program to find the nearest Starbucks, at which point an accident occurred. Exhibit 4A contains pertinent portions of the California Vehicle Code, and Exhibit 4B is a leading case, *People v. Spriggs*, that interprets the statute. Please read Exhibit 4A now; read Exhibit 4B when instructed later in the chapter.

B. LEGISLATIVE PROCESS

1. Enactment of a Law

The legislative process is a highly collaborative and somewhat structured process, in which legislators, the executive, and interested members of the public participate.[1] Proposals for new legislation come from many sources: legislators, the executive branch, individual citizens, organizations such as industry associations and public interest groups, and law reform commissions. Ultimately, for a proposal to receive the legislature's official attention, it must become a *bill*, or draft law, introduced by one or more legislators.

Most legislatures, including the federal Congress, are *bicameral*, consisting of both a house of representatives and a senate. For a bill to become law, it must be passed in identical form by both chambers. It then must be signed or permitted to become law by the executive. See Box 4.1.

Both chambers typically consider bills in several stages: (1) A *subcommittee* specializing in the general area of the bill's topic considers the bill. The subcommittee may hold a public *hearing* and receive testimony from interested individuals and groups. In the later stages, lobbyists may be involved, speaking to legislators on behalf of their clients. (2) The *committee deliberates* on the bill and then either *reports* it favorably to the full chamber (generally along with a report) or tables it, precluding further action on the bill. (3) The *full chamber debates* the bill. The debate may actually be a true airing of competing views involving most members of the chamber, or it may be a series of speeches by the bill's supporters that go unheard by most other legislators. Ultimately, the legislators *vote* on the bill. Either concurrently or after the consideration by the first chamber, the other chamber follows a similar process (4-6).

If both chambers have passed identical bills (7A), that bill goes to the executive (president or governor). If the two chambers considered nonidentical bills and the differences are minor (7B), one chamber may accede to the other's changes; then the bill clears the legislature. If the differences are major (7C), a *conference committee*, with members from both chambers, resolves the differences and reports a consensus bill back to the two chambers, which may then pass the consensus bill.

Once both chambers pass the same bill, it proceeds to the executive for signature (8). The executive may disagree with the bill and veto it, subject to override by the legislature. On the other hand, if the *executive signs* it, or in some systems neither signs nor vetoes it, the bill becomes law and turns into a statute.

In some respects, the legislative process is similar to the judicial process. For example, both are lawmaking processes, both involve participation by those governed, and both have mechanisms for adjusting the law. However, the two processes also differ in important ways. The courts are reactive, considering only

---

1. For further detail, *see* Jack Davies, *Legislative Law and Process in a Nutshell* (2d ed. 1986).

BOX 4.1

THE LEGISLATIVE PROCESS

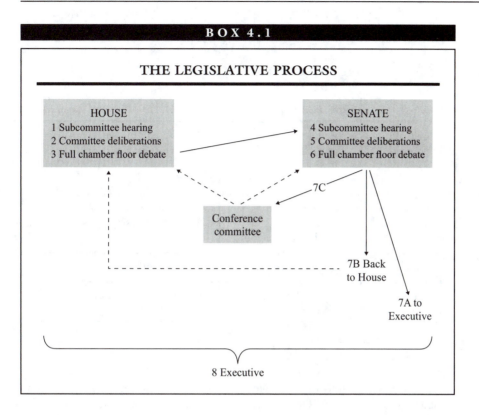

cases brought to their attention by the parties; the legislature acts both reactively and proactively, taking on topics brought forth by the public, as well as those identified by the legislators themselves. The courts take the issues as they are framed by the parties' dispute; the legislature defines its own issues. A small segment of the public participates in judicial lawmaking through litigation, which is a very formal process defined by rules of procedure; a wider segment participates in legislative lawmaking through lobbying, a less formal and defined process. The judicial process is intended to be nonpolitical; conversely, the legislative process is intended to be highly political. See Box 4.2.

As an example, the sample statute for this chapter, section 23123, was originally enacted by the California legislature in 2006 as part of the California Wireless Telephone Safety Act. As you might surmise, the legislature had become concerned with the safety risks posed by distracted drivers using cell phones; adding a new statute to its existing Vehicle Code was its response.

2. Legislative Intent and Word Choice

The product of the legislative process is a collection of words that differs significantly in form from cases. Again, see Box 4.2. As discussed in Chapter 3, judges write most directly to the parties to the case, explaining the outcome of the litigation for them. Certain portions of an opinion, chiefly the rules of law and the holding, are written with an eye toward unknown participants in future disputes, and these portions are very carefully worded. In comparison, the

BOX 4.2

COMPARISON OF CASES AND STATUTES

	Cases	Statutes
Lawmaking Process	• Reactive • Parties frame issues • Litigation • Nonpolitical	• Reactive and proactive • Legislature frames issues • Lobbying • Political
Focus	• Facts of current litigation • Case before the court	• Future situations • Broad class of situations
Effect	• Generally retroactive	• Generally prospective
Form	• Entwined narratives • Embedded rule	• Rule with encompassed stories • Rules of game

legislature writes entirely to unknown persons whose future activities are encompassed within the statute. Thus, every word in a statute carries the impact of the rule of law and the holding from a case.

Statutes are to be read so as to give effect to *legislative intent*. To a significant extent, legislative intent is a legal fiction. As to any statutory provision, some legislators probably intended to state one idea, others intended another, and yet others did not think seriously enough about it to have a clear intent. Although there may be individual legislators' intentions, rarely is there a single legislative intent. Furthermore, a particular factual situation may pose a question that the legislature never even contemplated. Nonetheless, the premise of legislative intent is powerful. Thus, the precise language in the statute—each word, each phrase, each punctuation mark—commands respect.

As an example, the California legislature undertook a challenging task when it undertook to address cell-phone use while driving. The legislature chose the word "using" to describe the activity and the phone as one that is not configured for "hands-free listening and talking." Consider for a moment how many different uses of such a phone you would place within this language. Then think about what a state legislature may have meant in 2006.

3. Effective Periods of Statutes and Their Evolution

Unlike case law, which typically is retroactive, a statute typically has *prospective effect*,[2] that is, covering conduct occurring on or after the statute's effective date.

---

2. On occasion, a statute may have retroactive effect, but this is rare and typically involves matters of procedure, not substantive legal rights.

Some statutes take effect on the date of enactment, which generally is the date of signature by the executive. Others do not take effect until a date specified in the statute, which is usually some months after the date of enactment. Others take effect on the legislature's default effective date, for statutes with no stated effective date.[3] Thus, determining which language was in effect at the time of the events that you are analyzing is critical.

The legislature may *amend* the statute at a later time. The legislature may not be satisfied with the way that the statute has worked out and may modify problematic language to more closely reflect what the legislature intended. Or the legislature may become aware of facts that it did not initially have and revise the statute to reflect that new knowledge. Or the legislature may change its collective mind about what the law should be and alter the statute accordingly. In these situations, you must carefully track the effective dates of the various versions relative to the timing of your client's events.

On rare occasions, a statute ceases to be in effect at all. This may occur by legislative action when the legislature *repeals* the statute. Alternatively, the statute may reach its *sunset date* set in the original legislation, specifying the statute becomes ineffective unless reenacted. In addition, a court may *declare a statute unconstitutional*, as when a legislature exceeds its granted powers or a statute abridges the rights of citizens.

As an example, cell-phone use while driving has proven to be a moving legislative target. Thus, in major revisions, the California legislature has added section 23124, which further restricts cell-phone use by drivers under eighteen to include phones equipped with hands-free devices. In addition, the legislature has added section 23123.5, prohibiting text messaging.

4. Federalism

One of the most complex facets of U.S. law is *federalism*—the interplay between federal law and state and local law. Statutes exist at multiple levels of government. Federal law governs matters that Congress has perceived to be of national interest, such as air and water pollution, the operation of the securities market, and union-management relations. The U.S. Constitution reserves to the states matters of primarily local interest, such as property, contract, and tort issues.

Most areas of law are governed by some statute—indeed sometimes more than one. Where both federal and state statutes exist, the federal statute typically identifies the permissible role of state law. In some areas, Congress has sought to control a field with federal law, so state statutes cannot also exist. In other areas, Congress has sought to ensure minimum standards while permitting the states to provide similar or additional protection. In yet other areas, Congress has created a federal model that the states may opt into or out of; states opting out may be required to enact comparable state statutes. One of the first topics that a lawyer learns when entering a new area of law is this interplay of federal, state, and local law.

---

3. For federal statutes, the presumed effective date is the date they are signed by the president.

As an example, the cell-phone driving statute falls within traffic regulation, an area of law traditionally left to the states.

C. UNDERSTANDING STATUTES

1. An Analogy: Rules of the Game

How does a lawyer read a statute or other code to discern its impact on a client's situation? Just as cases can be seen as entwined narratives, statutes resemble a particular type of literature: the rules of a game. Note that, in a way, the rules of a game tell a story: how a game is meant to be played.

Sometimes the game covered by a statute is straightforward, and the statute is short and simple. Other statutes encompass a wide range of complicated versions of the game; such a statute runs many pages and includes hundreds of interconnected sections. Whatever the length and intricacy of the statute under consideration, approaching it with the following game-based questions can help you to decipher it:

- What is the name of the game?
- What is its purpose?
- Who can play?
- What kind of conduct is generally encouraged or prohibited?
- Are there any exceptions to these general rules?
- What are the consequences of playing or not playing the game as described?

2. Organization of a Statute

Although each statute is unique, many statutes have standard components, which may or may not be so labeled. Furthermore, these components generally appear in a fairly standard sequence. Section 23123 in Exhibit 4A, the key section for Ms. Collins's situation, is labeled by these components.

Name: Legislatures occasionally *name* major statutes. Named statutes often are referred to by their names or acronyms for their names.

Purpose statement: Sometimes a legislature includes a *purpose statement* in enacting the statute, which may be framed as the problems that the legislature sought to address, the interests that the legislature sought to serve, or the results that the legislature desired. Although this language does not itself constitute the rule of law created by the statute, it can provide very helpful insight into the legislature's intent.

Scope: Some statutes contain *scope* sections, near the beginning, that define which situations are within the reach of the statute and which are not. A statute's scope section generally has three dimensions: actors (people or entities), actions, and circumstances.

Definitions: Many statutes employ particular meanings for words that appear in them, and some definitions may be different than what the word might mean in everyday parlance. These *definitions* generally appear at the beginning of the statute or in the scope section. Regardless of their location, they are critical.

Three types of sections determine the operation of the statute, i.e., the effect that it is meant to have on the situations within its scope. Together, they constitute the statute's *operative provisions*. All statutes contain general rules, many contain exceptions, and most contain consequences and enforcement sections.

General rule: As the core of the statute, the *general rule* describes the conduct that the legislature has chosen to encourage (by providing for some type of benefit) or prohibit (by providing for some type of penalty). Many statutes state several or more general rules that are related to each other in some way.

Exceptions: In the *exceptions*, the legislature carves out situations that otherwise would be covered by the general rule and provides a different outcome for them. Frequently, a legislature grapples with competing interests and policies as it enacts a statute. One way to reflect various concerns is to favor one policy in the general rule and acknowledge a different one to a lesser extent in an exception.

Consequences and enforcement: As a legal rule, the purpose of a statute is to connect the factual conditions specified in the general rule to certain *consequences*. The legislature may encourage conduct by making a transaction legally enforceable, for example. More statutes prohibit conduct; penalties include criminal sanctions (fines and imprisonment), civil fines, and payment of damages to the harmed party. Furthermore, the statute may also specify some *enforcement* method, such as a government action or a claim brought by a harmed party.

Unfortunately, some statutes do not clearly state their consequences or enforcement methods. Of these, a good number provide a label for conduct violating the statute. From this statement, further research into related statutes generally reveals the appropriate method of enforcement.

Additional clauses: Some statutes state their effective dates or include sunset provisions, as discussed previously. In addition, some include a *severability provision*, which indicates that should any sections be deemed unconstitutional, the other sections are intended to remain in effect.

D. READING AND BRIEFING A STATUTE

1. Preparing the Statute Brief

A key skill for lawyers is *parsing a statute,* that is, identifying and analyzing the sections that govern the game (situation) in which the client is involved. This involves reading the statute carefully and briefing it. *Briefing a statute* entails writing a summary that both prompts you to work carefully through the statute and records your analysis of it.

To parse a statute, you should always read through it several times, as follows:

(1) First, look over the list of sections within the statute to discern its organization and which sections might be most pertinent.

(2) Next, read all sections that you have identified as even remotely pertinent; err on the side of over-inclusiveness at this stage.

(3) If a pertinent section has a *cross-reference* to some other statute, read that statute as well.

(4) Then allocate the pertinent language according to the questions set forth above, with a focus on who is covered, what kind of conduct is encouraged or prohibited, whether there are any exceptions, and what the consequences are.

For some people, this may be a tedious exercise, compared to reading the stories in a case. One way to make it more interesting is to consider the statute's *paradigm case,* which is the real-world story that most clearly fits within the language of the statute. You can figure it out in various ways: What story might have inspired a legislator to propose the bill that became the statute? If I were counseling a client based on this statute, what would I tell my client to do or not do? If one were to film an instance of the situation covered by the statute, what would it look like?

As you write the brief, realize that you are writing a legal rule aimed at your client's situation. You can start in various places, so long as all pieces are included in the end. For some people, starting with the definitions makes the most sense because they are integral to everything else. Others start with the general rule because that is the major point of the statute.

As you prepare your brief, balance the obligation to respect the statute's exact phrasing with the need to be efficient. Paraphrasing is less appropriate in a statutory brief than in a case brief. On the other hand, abbreviations that you create to reflect statutory language are appropriate, as is omitting language that does not affect the meaning of the pertinent language that you keep. Pay very close attention to details; for example, "or" is very different from "and" in a statute, the placement of a modifying clause is always important, and a comma can convey important meaning.

Especially if a statute is long or complex, including references to sections and subdivisions where you found the various phrases that you include is wise; it may save you considerable time later when you are writing your analysis of the statute.

Be sure to review the draft of your statutory brief carefully. At least where the statute is complicated, skim the statute after writing the brief to be sure that your brief indeed aligns with the statutory language. Also, make sure that the components of the brief, as described below, align with each other; be sure, for example, that you have properly linked an exception to its general rule.

2. Formats of a Statutory Brief

The purpose of any statutory brief is to accurately and concisely state the legal rule from the statute that applies to the client's situation. One option is to brief the statute by the typical components of statutes. See Box 4.3.

Better yet, create a brief that operates like an if/then rule, albeit long and elaborate if there is significant language to incorporate. This approach captures all language that contributes to the rule's factual conditions in one clause, wherever it may appear in the statute, and the legal consequences in another clause. The following formula equates components of a statute to places in an if/then statement:

BOX 4.3

SAMPLE COMPONENTS-BASED STATUTORY BRIEF

Scope (implied): Person 18 or older driving motor vehicle while using non-hands-free wireless telephone. 23124 covers persons under 18.

Definition: "Private road or driveway" is "way or place in private ownership and used for vehicular travel by owner and those having express or implied permission from owner but not by other members of public." 490.

General rule: Person shall not drive motor vehicle while using wireless telephone unless telephone is specifically designed and configured for hands-free listening and talking and is used in that manner while driving. 23123(a).

Exception: Does not apply to person while driving motor vehicle on private property. 23123(f).

Consequences and enforcement: Infraction; base fine of $20 for first offense, $50 for each subsequent offense. 23123(b).

IF the client's situation meets the statute's definitions,
 falls within the scope,
 meets the requirements of the general rule, and
 does not meet the requirements of any exception—
THEN the consequences follow through the specified enforcement system.

This type of brief may be presented in an outline or a flowchart. See Box 4.4.

3. Review

Statutes, as well as other codes, constitute law and resemble the rules of a game. To parse and brief a statute:

(1) Read it several times, both to identify pertinent sections and to discern what those sections say. Pursue the cross-references.
(2) Allocate pertinent language to the questions that need to be answered, such as the conduct prohibited by the statute and any exceptions.
(3) Carefully convert the language into a statutory brief, which may take the form of a components-based brief or an if/then statement.
(4) Review your brief against the statute and itself.

Evaluate your statute briefs according to the following four criteria of sound legal writing:

- Completeness—Is everything present that is needed for a thorough presentation of the statute?
- Correctness—Is all language captured accurately?
- Coherence—Do all parts of the brief fit together?

B O X   4 . 4

BRIEFS

IF   person drives motor vehicle
         and uses non-hands-free wireless telephone in non-hands-free
         manner
         and is *not* driving on private property, interpreted under 490 to mean
             in private ownership
             and used for vehicular travel by owner and those having express or
             implied permission from owner but not by other members of the
             public,
THEN   person has committed infraction with base fines of $20 for first
         offense and $50 for subsequent offenses.

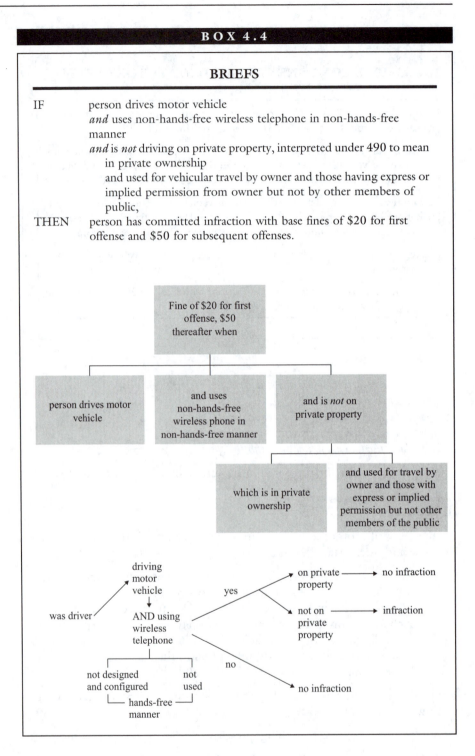

■ Comprehensibility—Given the complexity of the statutory language, can you understand the brief reasonably well?

A well-written brief permits you to move on to interpret the statute, which is discussed next.

E. INTERPRETING A STATUTE

1. Statutory Ambiguity

Once a lawyer briefs a pertinent statute, it may seem that the analysis of the client's situation is nearly done. However, as you turn to connecting the language of the statute to your client's facts, you may discover ambiguity. Statutory language is *ambiguous* when more than one meaning is possible. Statutes are ambiguous because the language is vague, key language could be read more than one way, or a point logically related to the statute's topic is omitted. The language may be ambiguous about any of various topics, including which actors or actions or circumstances fall within the statute, what the statute's general rule requires or permits, what the exceptions cover, or how the statute is enforced.

Statutory ambiguity has several causes. The legislature may have intentionally chosen ambiguous language because legislators were unable to agree on clearer language and were willing to defer to the courts or a later session of the legislature. Or the legislators may have tried but been unable to write less ambiguous language. Or the legislature may not have perceived an ambiguity in its choice of words. Or new situations may have arisen since the statute's enactment, turning language that once was clear into ambiguous language.

How does a lawyer bring clarity to ambiguous statutory language? Mindful of the importance of legislative intent, he or she employs a variety of *statutory interpretation tools*.[4] Some of these are more powerful than others. Some involve reasoning from the statute itself; others involve considering other materials. Not infrequently, different tools lead to different conclusions. Informed judgment and careful thought are critical in statutory interpretation. These tools of statutory interpretation are depicted in Box 4.5.

As an example, section 23123 contains ambiguous language: the verb "using" along with "telephone . . . configured to allow hands-free listening and talking, and is used in that manner." The paradigm case is a driver engaged in conversation—listening and talking—with another person on a hand-held cell phone. What is not clearly within or outside the statute is when a driver uses a cell phone for other purposes, such as reading an online map or asking for and receiving information.

Section 23123 was interpreted by the Court of Appeals of California in *People v. Spriggs*, found in Exhibit 4B. There, a driver was ticketed for checking a map application on his cell phone while driving, and the lower courts agreed with the citation. However, the court of appeals ruled that the language does not prohibit all hand-held cell-phone uses; rather it prohibits "listening and talking." In so doing, the court relied on many of the approaches discussed in this part.

---

4. *See generally* William N. Eskridge, Jr., et al., *Legislation and Statutory Interpretation* (2d ed. 2006).

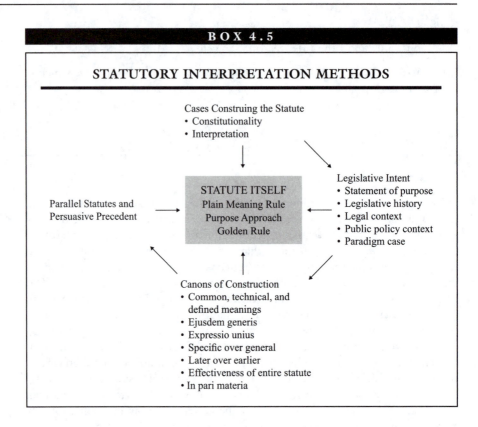

BOX 4.5

STATUTORY INTERPRETATION METHODS

Cases Construing the Statute
• Constitutionality
• Interpretation

STATUTE ITSELF
Plain Meaning Rule
Purpose Approach
Golden Rule

Legislative Intent
• Statement of purpose
• Legislative history
• Legal context
• Public policy context
• Paradigm case

Parallel Statutes and
Persuasive Precedent

Canons of Construction
• Common, technical, and
  defined meanings
• Ejusdem generis
• Expressio unius
• Specific over general
• Later over earlier
• Effectiveness of entire statute
• In pari materia

Please read the opening and Facts and Procedural Background of the opinion now. This part describes the court's reasoning, which you should read yourself after you finish reading this part.

2. Employing the Plain Meaning Rule, Purpose Approach, and Golden Rule

The focus of statutory interpretation is the language that the legislature chose. Thus, analysis begins with the *plain meaning rule*: to follow the letter of the law. When the statute's meaning is plain, one need not use the methods of interpretation discussed in this part.

A second approach is the *purpose approach*. According to the purpose approach, the lawyer's task is to ascertain and then give meaning to the legislature's purpose in enacting the statute—that is, to respect legislative intent.

In many situations, these two approaches converge because the legislature's purpose is articulated well in the statute's language. But the two approaches diverge when the statutory language leads to a result probably not intended by the legislature. The bridge between the plain meaning rule and the purpose approach is the *golden rule*, which instructs lawyers not to honor the wording of a statute when it produces an absurd or unreasonable result, calls for an impossible outcome, or yields an unconstitutional result. The meshing of the purpose approach and plain meaning rule is thus left to the sound discretion of the lawyer interpreting the statute.

As an example, the *Spriggs* court cited the plain meaning rule early on, yet it also noted that the statute must be interpreted to obtain reasonable results and avoid unjust or absurd results. Later in the opinion, the court focused on the absurdity of too broad a reading of the "using" language.

3. Relying on Cases Construing Statutes

In many situations, the lawyer's choice among various statutory meanings is firmly guided by *construing cases*. When a dispute is governed by a statute and the parties are unable to settle the dispute themselves, they bring the dispute to the courts (not the legislature) for resolution. In addition to resolving the dispute for the parties, the court undertakes two important tasks in relation to the statute.

First, the court assesses the *constitutionality of the statute*. The court will attempt to read the statute to render it constitutional, if possible. If it cannot do that, the statute is declared unconstitutional in whole or in part, and the unconstitutional portion or statute has no further legal effect.

Second, courts provide authoritative *interpretation of a statute*, or judicial gloss, thereby reducing the ambiguity in the legislature's language. The statute provides the rule of law by which the case is decided. The court may elaborate on this rule, give definition to unclear language, or fill gaps in the statute. It then links the abstract language of the statute to the facts of a specific dispute. The rule of law, holding, and reasoning in the case have precedential effect.

The lawmaking process can also work in the opposite direction. When the court deems a statute unconstitutional, the legislature may enact a revised statute. On occasion, when the court interprets a statute, the legislature registers its objection to the court's interpretation by amending the statute. Where the law consists of dialogue between the legislature and courts, you must trace what the law is at various points in time; creating a timeline can be helpful in doing this. Box 4.6 is an example.

BOX 4.6

STATUTORY TIMELINE

Common law rule	Original statute	*Andrews:* statute is unconstitutional	Amended statute	*Burton:* new statute is constitutional	*Coffman:* application of statute
Common law governs.	Original statute governs.	Common law governs.	Amended statute governs.	Amended statute governs.	*Coffman* interpretation of statute governs.

4. Incorporating Legislative Intent

As already noted, the touchstone of statutory interpretation is to respect legislative intent. Although the most straightforward indication of legislative intent is a statement of purpose in the statute itself, few statutes contain this statement. Generally, you must rely on a statute's legislative history, legal and public policy context, and paradigm case.

First, you might turn to *legislative history*: the record developed during the legislature's consideration of the bill and enactment of the statute. Some legislative history materials are more authoritative than others. For example, the committee report is highly authoritative because it is a formal document prepared by the legislators most involved in the statute's enactment. The comments of legislators during the debates vary in significance, with the sponsor's comments generally viewed as the most authoritative.

In most situations, there are practical obstacles to using legislative history. Legislative history can be difficult to research, especially for older statutes and state statutes. Furthermore, there may be nothing pertinent on a given point or conflicting statements by different legislators.

Second, you may turn to the statute's *legal context*. Most statutes join an existing body of law of which the legislature presumably is aware when it enacts a statute. A statute's common law, statutory, and constitutional context can provide helpful background information about the legislature's intent.

Statutes relate to *preexisting common law* in several ways. In some areas, the legislature acts to codify or clarify the common law. In other areas, the legislature acts to overturn or substantially modify the common law. In yet other areas, the common law and statutory law operate in tandem, each addressing an aspect of the behavior that they regulate.

Similarly, a new law may affect *preexisting statutory law* in several ways. The new law may cover a topic not yet addressed by existing statutes. Amendments clarify or add to existing statutes. Repealers delete existing statutes and thus signify a dramatic change in the law. When the legislature has revisited an area, it may be possible to make inferences about the legislative intent behind a particular version of the statute by examining its previous and subsequent forms.

Lawyers presume that the legislature acted with knowledge of and in accordance with constitutional provisions. Thus, statutes are interpreted so as to *avoid unconstitutionality*.

Third, you may be able to deduce the legislature's intent from the *public policy* issues at the time of enactment. Sometimes the statutory language itself suggests what these issues were. In other situations, you may be able to find evidence of these issues outside of the statute.

Fourth, as already noted, although a statute does not state a specific story as a case does, there may be one or more situations that clearly would bring the statute into play. This paradigm case encompasses the actors, actions, and circumstances that fall squarely within the statute. One value of the paradigm case is that it permits inferences about legislative intent. If you can assume that the legislature was concerned with the paradigm case, then you can ask what broader concerns underlie it. A second value is that you may compare your client's situation to the paradigm case.

As an example, *Spriggs* explores legislative intent through various sources. It quotes the legislative findings (akin to a purpose statement), which reveal the public policies underlying the statute. It surveys documents created during the section's legislative consideration, as well as the governor's statement. Its discussion of conversing on a cell phone reflects consideration of the statute's paradigm case.

5. Applying Canons of Construction

Canons of construction are maxims for reading—and writing—statutes. Each is based on a psychological principle of language use. Because some have Latin names, they appear more mystical than they really are. Seven of the more commonly used canons are:

Defined, common, and technical meanings: Some terms are defined in the statute itself. Otherwise, according to this canon, which reflects the importance of context in word choice, terms should be understood in their everyday sense or, where the context suggests it, in a technical sense.

Ejusdem generis: The phrase means "of the same class," and the canon applies where the legislature has created a list and included a general term as a catch-all. The catch-all term then refers to items of the same class as the specific items in the list.

Expressio unius: The full phrase, "expressio unius est exclusio alterius," means "expression of one excludes others." According to this canon, where the legislature created a list with specific items but did not mention others or include a catch-all term, unmentioned items are not included.

Specific prevails over general: Where there is a conflict between two sections, the more specific section should take precedence over the more general section. This is because specific information is more salient than general. In essence, all exceptions to general rules rest on this principle.

Later prevails over earlier: Later-enacted sections prevail over earlier sections when there is a conflict because recent information is more reliable than older information.

Effectiveness of the entire statute: This canon assumes that all statutory language is meant to communicate some meaning. Hence, language that could be construed to add nothing should, if possible, be construed to add something.

In pari materia: This phrase means "of the same matter," and the canon comes into play when two or more sections or statutes relate to the same topic. The statutes must be construed together; consistency is assumed. One application of this canon is that a word should carry over its meaning from one statute to a related statute.

Other canons: Finally, some canons pertain to particular types of statutes. For example, penal (criminal) statutes are to be construed narrowly to avoid criminal sanctions where conduct was not clearly forbidden.

You may well find that different canons of construction point in different directions. If so, consider the application of these canons in the context of the other methods described in this part.

As an example, *Spriggs* concludes by construing statutes in light of each other.[5] The court reasoned that there would be no need for a section prohibiting text messaging if section 23123 already prohibited all uses of cell phones.

6. Looking to Parallel Laws and Persuasive Precedent

When the methods described above do not adequately reduce a statute's ambiguity, an option is to look to *persuasive precedents interpreting parallel laws.* Reliance on persuasive precedent for statutory interpretation occurs most regularly in two situations. First, some state statutes are based on a *model law* promulgated by a law reform organization.[6] Use of persuasive precedent to interpret these statutes is common because the language is nearly identical from state to state and the origins of the statutes are the same. Second, state courts sometimes—but not always—interpret *state statutes based on federal statutes* similarly to how federal courts interpret the federal statutes.

7. Incorporating Interpretation into a Statutory Brief

Once you have finished the analysis of interpreting a statute, whether through reading construing cases or doing it on your own, consider incorporating the points that you have developed into your statutory brief. For example, although inserting a full case brief into a statutory brief may be too much, inserting the main points can be helpful. This incorporation is most easily done with a textual statutory brief. See Box 4.7.

BOX 4.7

SAMPLE STATUTORY BRIEF WITH INTERPRETATIONS

If   person drives a motor vehicle
            and uses non-hands-free wireless telephone in non-hands-free
            manner
                Spriggs: "uses" means talking and listening, not looking at map
            and is *not* driving on private property, interpreted under 490 to
            mean
                in private ownership
                and used for vehicular travel by owner and those having express
                or implied permission from owner but not by other members of
                public
THEN   person has committed infraction with base fines of $20 for first
            offense and $50 for subsequent offenses.

---

5. The case also has an interesting example of reverse legislative history—using a later-enacted statute to explain an earlier-enacted one.
6. The most widely used example is the Uniform Commercial Code.

8. Review

You can use various methods to reduce ambiguity in statutory language, all aimed at deducing the legislature's intent and giving meaning to the words that the legislators chose. This chapter has set out these methods as follows:

(1) First consider application of the plain meaning rule, purpose approach, and golden rule.

(2) Seek an authoritative interpretation in a case construing the statute.

(3) As needed, pursue other modes of interpretation:
  • Seek information about the legislature's intent in the statute's purpose statement, its legislative history, the legal context of the statute, its public policy context, or its paradigm case.
  • Apply canons of construction to the statute's language.
  • Seek guidance in cases from other jurisdictions that interpret parallel laws.

(4) Incorporate the main points into your statutory brief.

All these methods require you to exercise judgment to reach an appropriate result. The proper use of these options reduces statutory ambiguity and prepares you to reason about your client's situation in light of the statute as interpreted.

EXHIBIT 4A CALIFORNIA MOTOR VEHICLE CODE SECTIONS

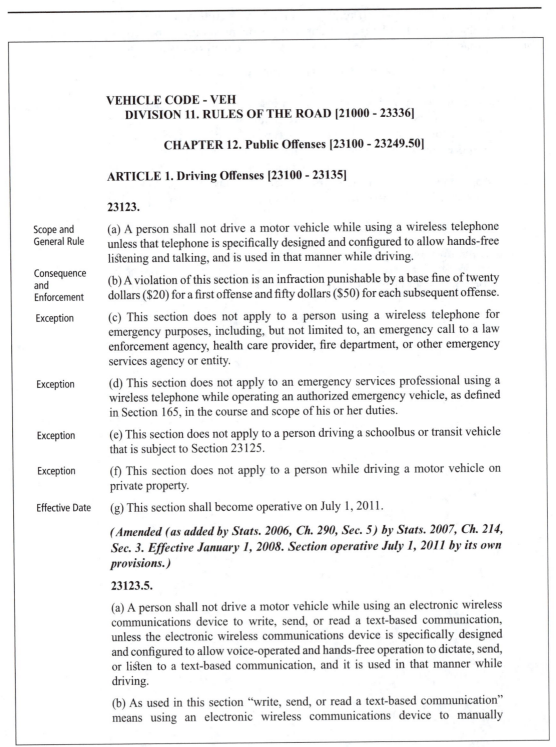

VEHICLE CODE - VEH
DIVISION 11. RULES OF THE ROAD [21000 - 23336]

CHAPTER 12. Public Offenses [23100 - 23249.50]

ARTICLE 1. Driving Offenses [23100 - 23135]

23123.

Scope and General Rule

(a) A person shall not drive a motor vehicle while using a wireless telephone unless that telephone is specifically designed and configured to allow hands-free listening and talking, and is used in that manner while driving.

Consequence and Enforcement

(b) A violation of this section is an infraction punishable by a base fine of twenty dollars ($20) for a first offense and fifty dollars ($50) for each subsequent offense.

Exception

(c) This section does not apply to a person using a wireless telephone for emergency purposes, including, but not limited to, an emergency call to a law enforcement agency, health care provider, fire department, or other emergency services agency or entity.

Exception

(d) This section does not apply to an emergency services professional using a wireless telephone while operating an authorized emergency vehicle, as defined in Section 165, in the course and scope of his or her duties.

Exception

(e) This section does not apply to a person driving a schoolbus or transit vehicle that is subject to Section 23125.

Exception

(f) This section does not apply to a person while driving a motor vehicle on private property.

Effective Date

(g) This section shall become operative on July 1, 2011.

(Amended (as added by Stats. 2006, Ch. 290, Sec. 5) by Stats. 2007, Ch. 214, Sec. 3. Effective January 1, 2008. Section operative July 1, 2011 by its own provisions.)

23123.5.

(a) A person shall not drive a motor vehicle while using an electronic wireless communications device to write, send, or read a text-based communication, unless the electronic wireless communications device is specifically designed and configured to allow voice-operated and hands-free operation to dictate, send, or listen to a text-based communication, and it is used in that manner while driving.

(b) As used in this section "write, send, or read a text-based communication" means using an electronic wireless communications device to manually

EXHIBIT 4A (cont.)

communicate with any person using a text-based communication, including, but not limited to, communications referred to as a text message, instant message, or electronic mail.

(c) For purposes of this section, a person shall not be deemed to be writing, reading, or sending a text-based communication if the person reads, selects, or enters a telephone number or name in an electronic wireless communications device for the purpose of making or receiving a telephone call or if a person otherwise activates or deactivates a feature or function on an electronic wireless communications device.

(d) A violation of this section is an infraction punishable by a base fine of twenty dollars ($20) for a first offense and fifty dollars ($50) for each subsequent offense.

(e) This section does not apply to an emergency services professional using an electronic wireless communications device while operating an authorized emergency vehicle, as defined in Section 165, in the course and scope of his or her duties.

(Amended by Stats. 2012, Ch. 92, Sec. 1. Effective January 1, 2013.)

23124.

(a) This section applies to a person under the age of 18 years.

(b) Notwithstanding Sections 23123 and 23123.5, a person described in subdivision (a) shall not drive a motor vehicle while using a wireless telephone or an electronic wireless communications device, even if equipped with a hands-free device.

(c) A violation of this section is an infraction punishable by a base fine of twenty dollars ($20) for a first offense and fifty dollars ($50) for each subsequent offense.

(d) A law enforcement officer shall not stop a vehicle for the sole purpose of determining whether the driver is violating subdivision (b).

(e) Subdivision (d) does not prohibit a law enforcement officer from stopping a vehicle for a violation of Section 23123 or 23123.5.

(f) This section does not apply to a person using a wireless telephone or a mobile service device for emergency purposes, including, but not limited to, an emergency call to a law enforcement agency, health care provider, fire department, or other emergency services agency or entity.

(g) For the purposes of this section, "electronic wireless communications device" includes, but is not limited to, a broadband personal communication device, specialized mobile radio device, handheld device or laptop computer with mobile data access, pager, and two-way messaging device.

(Amended by Stats. 2013, Ch. 754, Sec. 1. Effective January 1, 2014.)

EXHIBIT 4A (cont.)

VEHICLE CODE - VEH
   DIVISION 1. WORDS AND PHRASES DEFINED [100 - 680]

490.

"Private road or driveway" is a way or place in private ownership and used for vehicular travel by the owner and those having express or implied permission from the owner but not by other members of the public.

(Enacted by Stats. 1959, Ch. 3.)

EXHIBIT 4B PEOPLE V. SPRIGGS

No. F066927.

224 Cal.App.4th 150 (2014)

168 Cal. Rptr. 3d 347

THE PEOPLE, Plaintiff and Respondent, v. STEVEN R. SPRIGGS, Defendant and Appellant.

Court of Appeals of California, Fifth District.

February 27, 2014.

Attorney(s) appearing for the Case

McCormick, Barstow, Sheppard, Wayte & Carruth, Scott M. Reddie and Todd W. Baxter for Defendant and Appellant.

Kamala D. Harris, Attorney General, Dane R. Gillette, Chief Assistant Attorney General, Michael P. Farrell, Assistant Attorney General, Daniel B. Bernstein and Doris A. Calandra, Deputy Attorneys General, for Plaintiff and Respondent.

OPINION

LEVY, Acting P. J.—

While stopped in heavy traffic, Steven R. Spriggs pulled out his wireless telephone to check a map application for a way around the congestion. A California Highway Patrol officer spotted him holding his telephone, pulled him over, and issued him a traffic citation for violating Vehicle Code section 23123, subdivision (a), which prohibits drivers from "using a wireless telephone unless that telephone is specifically designed and configured to allow hands-free listening and talking, and is used in that manner while driving." Spriggs contends he did not violate the statute because he was not talking on the telephone. We agree. Based on the statute's language, its legislative history, and subsequent legislative enactments, we conclude that the statute means what it says—it prohibits a driver only from holding a wireless telephone while conversing on it. Consequently, we reverse his conviction.

FACTUAL AND PROCEDURAL BACKGROUND

After Spriggs was cited for violating Vehicle Code section 23123, subdivision (a) (hereafter section 23123(a)),[1] he contested the citation. At the trial held before a Fresno County Superior Court traffic commissioner, both Spriggs and the California Highway Patrol officer who issued the citation testified that Spriggs was cited for looking at a map on his cellular telephone while holding the telephone in his hand and driving. The traffic court commissioner subsequently found Spriggs guilty of violating section 23123(a) and ordered him to pay a $165 fine.

EXHIBIT 4B (cont.)

Spriggs appealed his conviction to the appellate division of the superior court. There he argued the only use of a wireless telephone section 23123(a) prohibits is listening and talking on the telephone if the telephone is being used in a manner that requires the driver to hold the telephone in his or her hand. Spriggs asserted the conduct for which he was cited was not a violation of section 23123(a) because he was not listening and talking on the telephone. The People did not file a brief or otherwise appear in connection with the appeal.

The appellate division affirmed Spriggs's conviction in *People v. Spriggs* (2013) 215 Cal.App.4th Supp. 1 [154 Cal.Rptr.3d 883].[*] The appellate division concluded, after reviewing the statute's plain language as well as its legislative history, that the statute was not "designed to prohibit hands-on use of a wireless telephone for conversation only," but instead was "specifically designed to prevent a driver from using a wireless telephone while driving unless the device is being used in a hands-free manner," and "outlawed all 'hands-on' use of a wireless telephone while driving." (*People v. Spriggs, supra,* 215 Cal.App.4th at pp. Supp. 5, 6, italics omitted.)

We subsequently granted review of the matter after the appellate division granted Spriggs's request for transfer certification to this court. We specifically asked the parties to address the following issue: "whether a person driving a motor vehicle, while holding a wireless telephone and looking at or checking a map application on the wireless telephone, violates Vehicle Code section 23123."

On appeal, Spriggs asserts the answer is no, as he was not "using" the wireless telephone within the meaning of the statute because the statute applies only if a driver is listening and talking on a wireless telephone that is not being used in a hands-free mode. The People contend the statute is much broader and applies to all uses of a wireless telephone unless the telephone is used in a hands-free manner.

We agree with Spriggs and conclude, pursuant to the rules of statutory interpretation, including our review of the language and legislative history of section 23123(a), that the Legislature intended the statute to only prohibit the use of a wireless telephone to engage in a conversation while driving unless the telephone is used in a hands-free manner. Therefore, we hold that Spriggs did not violate section 23123(a) and reverse the judgment.

DISCUSSION

1. **The applicable principles of statutory construction are well settled.**

The question we must decide, as an issue of first impression, is whether a person violates section 23123(a) by holding a wireless telephone in his or her hand and looking at a map application while driving.[2] This involves statutory interpretation, which we review de novo. (*Bruns v. E-Commerce Exchange, Inc.* (2011) 51 Cal.4th 717, 724 [122 Cal.Rptr.3d 331, 248 P.3d 1185]; *California Chamber of Commerce v. Brown*(2011) 196 Cal.App.4th 233, 248 [126 Cal.Rptr.3d 214].)

EXHIBIT 4B (cont.)

(1) The principles of statutory construction are clearly established. "Our task is to discern the Legislature's intent. The statutory language itself is the most reliable indicator, so we start with the statute's words, assigning them their usual and ordinary meanings, and construing them in context. If the words themselves are not ambiguous, we presume the Legislature meant what it said, and the statute's plain meaning governs. On the other hand, if the language allows more than one reasonable construction, we may look to such aids as the legislative history of the measure and maxims of statutory construction. In cases of uncertain meaning, we may also consider the consequences of a particular interpretation, including its impact on public policy." (*Wells v. One2One Learning Foundation* (2006) 39 Cal.4th 1164, 1190 [48 Cal.Rptr.3d 108, 141 P.3d 225]; see *People v. Smith* (2004) 32 Cal.4th 792, 797-798 [11 Cal.Rptr.3d 290, 86 P.3d 348].) Moreover, "[r]eviewing courts may turn to the legislative history behind even unambiguous statutes when it confirms or bolsters their interpretation ...." (*In re Gilbert R.* (2012) 211 Cal.App.4th 514, 519 [149 Cal.Rptr.3d 608].)

(2) "'To resolve [an] ambiguity, we rely upon well-settled rules. "The meaning of a statute may not be determined from a single word or sentence; the words must be construed in context, and provisions relating to the same subject matter must be harmonized to the extent possible. [Citation.] Literal construction should not prevail if it is contrary to the legislative intent apparent in the statute.... An interpretation that renders related provisions nugatory must be avoided [citation]; each sentence must be read not in isolation but in light of the statutory scheme [citation]; and if a statute is amenable to two alternative interpretations, the one that leads to the more reasonable result will be followed [citation]."[Citations.]' (*People v. Shabazz* (2006)38 Cal.4th 55, 67-68 [40 Cal.Rptr.3d 750, 130 P.3d 519]; see also *Robert L. v. Superior Court* (2003) 30 Cal.4th 894, 903 [135 Cal.Rptr.2d 30, 69 P.3d 951] [statutory language should not be interpreted in isolation, but must be construed in the context of the entire statute of which it is a part, in order to achieve harmony among the parts].) We must interpret a statute in accord with its legislative intent and where the Legislature expressly declares its intent, we must accept that declaration. (*Tyrone v. Kelley* (1973) 9 Cal.3d 1, 10-11 [106 Cal.Rptr. 761, 507 P.2d 65].) Absurd or unjust results will never be ascribed to the Legislature, and a literal construction of a statute will not be followed if it is opposed to its legislative intent. (*Webster v. Superior Court* (1988) 46 Cal.3d 338, 344 [250 Cal.Rptr. 268, 758 P.2d 596]; *Lungren v. Deukmejian* [(1988)] 45 Cal.3d [727], 735 [248 Cal.Rptr. 115, 755 P.2d 299].)" (*In re J.B.* (2009) 178 Cal.App.4th 751, 756 [100 Cal.Rptr.3d 679].)

2. Section 23123(a) is reasonably construed as only prohibiting a driver from holding a wireless telephone while conversing on it.

a. **Statutory language**

Section 23123(a) provides: "A person shall not drive a motor vehicle while using a wireless telephone unless that telephone is specifically designed and configured to allow hands-free listening and talking, and is used in that manner while driving." The statute does not define the word "using" or any other term contained therein.

EXHIBIT 4B (cont.)

Spriggs contends the statute is clear: "It applies if a person is listening or talking on a wireless telephone while driving and while the wireless telephone is not being used in hands-free mode." He asserts this interpretation is bolstered by the words "telephone" and "hands-free listening and talking," which demonstrate the focus of the statute is on talking on the wireless telephone and not some other use of the telephone, such as looking at a map application.

The People, however, assert the statute clearly prohibits the act of "using a wireless telephone" while driving and, since the word "using" is not ambiguous, it encompasses all uses of the telephone. According to the People, the statute "allows 'using' a wireless 'telephone while driving if the telephone is specifically designed and configured to allow hands-free listening and talking, and is used in that manner while driving.' Otherwise, using a wireless telephone while driving is prohibited." The People reason that, because under section 23123(a) a "driver may not *use* a cell phone unless it is used in a hands-free manner," that section is violated when a driver holds a wireless telephone and looks at a map application while driving.

(3) While the statute may be interpreted, on its face, as the People assert, we agree with Spriggs that the statute is reasonably construed as only prohibiting engaging in a conversation on a wireless telephone while driving and holding the telephone in one's hand. This is because the statute specifically states the telephone must be used in a manner that allows for "hands-free listening and talking." (§23123(a).) It does not state that it must be used in a manner that allows for hands-free looking, hands-free operation or hands-free use, or for anything other than listening and talking. Had the Legislature intended to prohibit drivers from holding the telephone and using it for all purposes, it would not have limited the telephone's required design and configuration to "hands-free listening and talking," but would have used broader language, such as "hands-free operation" or "hands-free use." To interpret section 23123(a) as applying to any use of a wireless telephone renders the "listening and talking" element nonsensical, as not all uses of a wireless telephone involve listening and talking, including looking at a map application.

The appellate division interpreted section 23123(a) as prohibiting all "hands-on use" of a wireless telephone based on its finding that the statute's plain language showed the "primary evil" the Legislature sought to avoid was "the distraction the driver faces when using his or her hands to operate the phone," and "if the Legislature had intended to limit the application of the statute to 'conversing' or 'listening and talking,' as [Spriggs] maintains, it could have done so." (*People v. Spriggs, supra,* 215 Cal.App.4th at pp. Supp. 5, 4.) While the statute certainly could have been written more clearly, we believe the inclusion of the phrase "hands-free listening and talking" does in fact limit the statute's prohibition to engaging in a conversation while holding a wireless telephone.

b. **Legislative history**

The legislative history of section 23123(a) supports our interpretation.[3] Section 23123 was enacted through Senate Bill No. 1613 (2005-2006 Reg. Sess.) as part of the

EXHIBIT 4B (cont.)

California Wireless Telephone Automobile Safety Act of 2006 (the Act). (Stats. 2006, ch. 290, §1, p. 2366.) A review of the legislative history of Senate Bill No. 1613 reveals that, while the Legislature was concerned about hand-held use of wireless telephones, this concern was addressed by prohibiting drivers from engaging in conversations while holding the telephone in one's hand rather than prohibiting all hand-held uses of the telephone.

As explained in both the Senate and Assembly analyses of the bill, two distractions arise when one uses a cell phone while driving: (1) "the physical distraction a motorist encounters when either picking up the phone, punching the number keypad, holding the phone up to his or her ear to converse, or pushing a button to end a call," and (2) "the mental distraction which results from the ongoing conversation carried on between the motorist and the person on the other end of the line." (Sen. Com. on Transportation and Housing, Analysis of Sen. Bill No. 1613 (2005-2006 Reg. Sess.) Feb. 24, 2006, p. 2; Assem.Com. on Transportation, Analysis of Sen. Bill No. 1613 (2005-2006 Reg. Sess.) as amended June 20, 2006, pp. 2-3.)[4]

According to these analyses, the bill addresses the first distraction, i.e., the physical distraction of placing a telephone call and holding the phone to one's ear to converse. (Sen. Com. on Transportation and Housing, Analysis of Sen. Bill No. 1613 (2005-2006 Reg. Sess.) Feb. 24, 2006, pp. 1-2; Assem.Com. on Transportation, Analysis of Sen. Bill No. 1613 (2005-2006 Reg. Sess.) as amended June 20, 2006, p. 2.)[5] There is no mention in the legislative history of trying to prevent distractions that arise from other uses of a wireless telephone when driving, such as looking at a map application while holding the telephone.

As explained in the legislative analyses, to address the physical distraction arising from the use of cell phones to place calls and carry on conversations, the bill's author, Senator Joseph Simitian, proposed what he believed to be a "minimal restriction on the use of cellular telephones in automobiles," namely the hands-free requirement. (Assem.Com. on Transportation, Analysis of Sen. Bill No. 1613 (2005-2006 Reg. Sess.) as amended June 20, 2006, p. 4.) To minimize the burden imposed by this restriction, the author pointed out that "[h]ands-free cellular telephone equipment, or kits, are either given away with telephones or can be acquired as an after-market purchase for under $20. Such equipment could be an earpiece, headset, speaker phone, or even Bluetooth technology." (Assem. Com. on Transportation, Analysis of Sen. Bill No. 1613 (2005-2006 Reg. Sess.) as amended June 20, 2006, p. 4; see Sen. Com. on Transportation and Housing, Analysis of Sen. Bill No. 1613 (2005-2006 Reg. Sess.) Feb. 24, 2006, p. 2.)

These excerpts show that, while the Legislature was concerned about hand-held use of wireless telephones, that concern arose only with respect to holding the telephone while engaging in a conversation. The Legislature's focus was on preventing drivers from holding a wireless telephone while speaking on it so the driver would have both hands free during the conversation. This is demonstrated by a reference in the Assembly

EXHIBIT 4B **(cont.)**

Committee on Transportation's legislative analysis to the methods by which the hands-free requirement could be fulfilled, namely using an earpiece, headset, speaker phone or Bluetooth, all of which can be used only for hands-free listening and talking. (Assem.Com. on Transportation, Analysis of Sen. Bill No. 1613 (2005-2006 Reg. Sess.) as amended June 20, 2006, p. 4.)

That the Legislature's focus was on holding a wireless telephone during a conversation is buttressed by the concerns raised in the Legislature about the bill, which pertain only to the mental distraction of talking on the telephone while driving rather than distractions that may arise from other uses of the telephone. As explained in the Senate Transportation and Housing Committee analysis, "The majority of evidence concerning distractedness and the use of cell phones indicates that the mental activity of holding a conversation, rather than the type of phone used for the conversation, leads to distractedness. The author contends that requiring motorists to use a hands-free phone while driving allows them to have two hands on the steering wheel, however, this bill does not require that two hands actually be placed on the wheel at any time while the driver is operating the car." (Sen. Com. on Transportation and Housing, Analysis of Sen. Bill No. 1613 (2005-2006 Reg. Sess.) Feb. 24, 2006, p. 5.) As commented in several analyses, "[a] central question posed by this bill is whether or not its enactment would significantly reduce the risk of distracted driving on our roadways. A driver's ability to maintain both hands on the steering wheel and eyes on the road while engaged in a phone conversation may or may not necessarily preclude a collision. But using a hand-held phone guarantees only one hand will be on the wheel." (Assem. Com. on Transportation, Analysis of Sen. Bill No. 1613 (2005-2006 Reg. Sess.) as amended June 20, 2006, p. 6; see Sen. Rules Com., Off. of Sen. Floor Analyses, 3d reading analysis of Sen. Bill No. 1613 (2005-2006 Reg. Sess.) as amended Aug. 21, 2006, p. 5.)

Notably, many analyses of the bill contain reviews of studies on driving and wireless telephone use, all of which concern the distractedness created when conversing on the telephone while driving. These analyses note that the studies and data "indicate that drivers can lose substantial cognitive awareness with the situation on the road when they are concentrating on a cell phone conversation. This is true whether or not the motorist is holding the phone up to his or her ear or is using a hands-free system." (Sen. Com. on Transportation and Housing, Analysis of Sen. Bill No. 1613 (2005-2006 Reg. Sess.) Feb. 24, 2006, p. 3; Sen. Rules Com., Off. of Sen. Floor Analyses, 3d reading analysis of Sen. Bill No. 1613 (2005-2006 Reg. Sess.) as amended Aug. 21, 2006, p. 3; Sen. Rules Com., Off. of Sen. Floor Analyses, Unfinished Business Analysis of Sen. Bill No. 1613 (2005-2006 Reg. Sess.) as amended Aug. 29, 2006, p. 4.) Significantly, no concerns were raised as to mental distractions that may arise from other uses of the wireless telephone while driving.

c. **Executive branch actions**

Finally, statements from the executive branch, while not controlling, further confirm the law was intended to only prohibit holding wireless telephones during conversations.

(*Elsner v. Uveges* (2004) 34 Cal.4th 915, 934 & fn. 19 [22 Cal.Rptr.3d 530, 102 P.3d 915][finding enrolled bill reports prepared after a bill's passage instructive on matters of legislative intent]; *People v. Tanner* (1979) 24 Cal.3d 514, 520 [156 Cal.Rptr. 450, 596 P.2d 328] [finding governor's press release on signing a bill instructive on matter of legislative intent].) As stated in the Department of Finance's analysis of the enrolled bill, the intent behind the law was to "improve traffic safety by eliminating the distraction of holding a cellular phone and engaging in a conversation while driving." (Dept. of Finance, Bill Analysis of Sen. Bill No. 1613 (2005-2006 Reg. Sess.) as amended Aug. 9, 2006, p. 2.) Moreover, in Governor Schwarzenegger's press release upon signing the bill, the Governor stated the "'simple fact is it's dangerous to talk on your cell phone while driving.'" The press release further commented: "Using a hands-free device while driving does not eliminate the distraction that comes with cell phones. Talking on the phone and dialing and hanging up the phone create a distraction. However, requiring drivers to use hands-free devices better ensures that drivers have two hands free to place on the wheel while driving." (Off. of the Governor, press release, Sept. 15, 2006.)

3. The People's interpretation of section 23123(a) is not supported by the legislative history and would lead to absurd results.

The appellate division found the legislative history did not support the conclusion that section 23123(a) was intended to only prohibit holding a wireless telephone during a conversation. This finding was based on legislative statements that the bill's focus was on the distraction of using one's hands to operate a wireless telephone. From this, the appellate division reasoned that this distraction was present "whether the phone is used for carrying on a conversation or for some other purpose." (*People v. Spriggs, supra,* 215 Cal.App.4th at pp. Supp. 4-5.) But as we have explained, although the Legislature was concerned about the distraction caused by operating a wireless telephone while holding it, the Legislature's focus was on prohibiting holding the telephone only while carrying on a conversation, not while using it for any other purpose. This is not surprising, given that when the statute was enacted in 2006, most wireless telephones were just that—a telephone—rather than an electronic device with multiple functions.

While the People acknowledge statements in the legislative history regarding the concern about talking on wireless telephones, they assert the bill in its final form was intended to prohibit all hand-held telephone use. The People cite to the Legislature's findings and declarations that accompanied the bill's enactment, one of which states that "(d) there is a growing public concern regarding the safety implications of the widespread practice of using hand-held wireless telephones while operating motor vehicles." (Stats. 2006, ch. 290, §2, p. 2366.) But the Legislature's other findings and declarations refer to the benefits of wireless telephone use, which involve, directly or indirectly, using such telephones for talking, not other uses.[6] Moreover, the legislative analyses cited above consistently discuss, throughout the bill's history, the concern of distractedness resulting from talking on a wireless telephone. There is no indication in any legislative analysis that the Legislature intended to broaden the prohibition of hand-held use to all uses of a wireless telephone.

The People's interpretation of section 23123(a)—that the statute bans all hand-held use of wireless telephones—would lead to absurd results and is opposed to the legislative intent. (*In re J.B., supra,* 178 Cal.App.4th at p. 756 ["Absurd or unjust results will never be ascribed to the Legislature, and a literal construction of a statute will not be followed if it is opposed to its legislative intent."].) If the phrase "using a wireless telephone" includes all conceivable uses, then it would be a statutory violation for a driver to merely look at the telephone's display if the telephone was not designed and configured to allow hands-free listening and talking. It would also be a violation to hold the telephone in one's hand, even if configured for hands-free listening and talking, and look at the time or even merely move it for use as a paperweight. The People do not point to anything in the legislative history to suggest the Legislature intended such a broad prohibition. The People assert the statute would not be violated if a driver looked at a map application as long as the wireless telephone was mounted and the application was "activated using the phone'shand[s]-free capability." However, as Spriggs points out, under this scenario the statute could still be violated merely by looking at the map application on the wireless telephone if the telephone was not designed and configured to allow hands-free listening and talking.

(4) When the legislative history of section 23123 is considered in conjunction with section 23123(a)'s language, it is apparent that the Legislature both understood and intended the statute be limited to only prohibit a driver from holding a wireless telephone while conversing on it. It did not intend to extend the prohibition to other uses of a wireless telephone and most certainly did not intend to prohibit the use at issue here, namely looking at a map application while holding the telephone and driving.

4. The Legislature's subsequent enactments of sections 23124 and 23123.5 confirm it intended section 23123(a) to only prohibit a driver from holding a wireless telephone while conversing on it.

The Legislature's subsequent enactments pertaining to the use of wireless telephones and other electronic devices while driving confirm our conclusion. In 2007, the Legislature passed Senate Bill No. 33 (2007-2008 Reg. Sess.), which added section 23124 to the Vehicle Code. As explained in an analysis of the later-enacted adult text messaging ban (section 23123.5), section 23124 prohibits drivers under the age of 18 "from using a wireless telephone or other mobile service device even if used in a hands-free manner while operating a motor vehicle," including "talking, writing, sending, reading or using the internet, or any other function such a device may enable." (Sen. Com. on Transportation and Housing, Analysis of Sen. Bill No. 28 (2007-2008 Reg. Sess.) Aug. 4, 2008, p. 1.)[7]

Thereafter, Senator Simitian, the author of Senate Bill Nos. 1613 (2005-2006 Reg. Sess.) and 33 (2007-2008 Reg. Sess.), introduced Senate Bill No. 28 (2008-2009 Reg. Sess.).

EXHIBIT 4B   (cont.)

(Sen. Com. on Transportation and Housing, Analysis of Sen. Bill No. 28 (2007-2008 Reg. Sess.) Aug. 4, 2008, pp. 1-2.) The bill as passed in 2008 added section 23123.5 to the Vehicle Code, which prohibited driving "while using an electronic wireless communications device to write, send, or read a text-based communication." (Former §23123.5, subd. (a); Stats. 2008, ch. 270, §2, p. 2254.) Section 23123.5, subdivision (b) provides that, as used in that section, "'write, send, or read a text-based communication' means using an electronic wireless communications device to manually communicate with any person using a text-based communication, including, but not limited to, communications referred to as a text message, instant message, or electronic mail." The statute does not define the term "electronic wireless communication device." When enacted, section 23123.5 further provided that, for purposes of that section, "a person shall not be deemed to be writing, reading, or sending a text-based communication if the person reads, selects, or enters a telephone number or name in an electronic wireless communications device for the purpose of making or receiving a telephone call." (Former §23123.5, subd. (c).)

It was explained in one legislative analysis that Senate Bill No. 28 (2007-2008 Reg. Sess.) went "one step further" than section 23123(a), by "[p]rohibit[ing] a driver from using an electronic wireless communications device to write, send, or read a text-based communication," and "essentially extends the teen ban on text messaging to all drivers, regardless of age." (Sen. Com. on Transportation and Housing, Analysis of Sen. Bill No. 28 (2007-2008 Reg. Sess.) Aug. 4, 2008, pp. 2, 1, 3.) As explained in one legislative document, "Drivers over the age of 18 are allowed to read, compose, and send text messages while driving. This has been called a 'loophole' in the body of laws dealing with cell phone use while driving. The intent of this bill is to make text messaging a primary offense for all drivers." (Assem. Com. on Transportation, Background Information Request, Sen. Bill No. 28 (2007-2008 Reg. Sess.) p. 1.) There would be no "loophole" for text messaging in section 23123(a), or need to extend the teen ban on text messaging, if section 23123(a) prohibited all hand-held use of wireless telephones. As noted in the Senate Transportation and Housing Committee's analysis of Senate Bill No. 28 (2007-2008 Reg. Sess.), the bill "addresses an *additional* form of distracted driving." (Sen. Com. on Transportation and Housing, Analysis of Sen. Bill No. 28 (2007-2008 Reg. Sess.) Aug. 4, 2008, p. 2, italics added.)

* * *

(5) In sum, based on the legislative history of section 23123 and the statute's language, as well as the Legislature's subsequent enactments of sections 23123.5 and 23124, we conclude that section 23123(a) does not prohibit all hand-held uses of a wireless telephone. Instead, it prohibits "listening and talking" on the wireless telephone unless the telephone is used in a hands-free mode. Accordingly, Spriggs did not violate the statute when he held his cellular telephone in his hand and looked at a map application while driving and his conviction must be reversed.

EXHIBIT 4B **(cont.)**

DISPOSITION

The judgment is reversed.

Kane, J., and Detjen, J., concurred.

Footnotes

1. Undesignated statutory references are to the Vehicle Code.
* Reporter's Note: Appeal transferred by Court of Appeal, Fifth Appellate District, on April 30, 2013, F066927. Superseded by this opinion.

2. The only published case concerning the scope of section 23123(a) is *People v. Nelson* (2011)200 Cal.App.4th 1083 [132 Cal.Rptr.3d 856] (*Nelson*). That case addressed the issue of whether a driver's use of a wireless telephone while stopped at a red traffic light constitutes use while driving within the meaning of the statute. (*Id.* at p. 1087.) The appellate court rejected the defendant's argument that he was not driving because his car was stopped during his phone use and concluded the Legislature intended section 23123(a) "to apply to persons driving on our public roadways who, like defendant, may pause momentarily while doing so in order to comply with the rules of the road." (*Nelson, supra,* 200 Cal.App.4th at p. 1087.)

3. On May 22, 2013, Spriggs filed a motion to take judicial notice of the legislative history of sections 23123(a) and 23123.5, as well as 23123.5's subsequent amendment, prepared by Legislative Intent Service, Inc., which he supplied with the motion. We deferred ruling on the motion. The People have not objected to the request, which we now grant. (Evid. Code, §§452, subd. (c), 459; *Doe v. City of Los Angeles* (2007) 42 Cal.4th 531, 544 & fn. 4 [67 Cal.Rptr.3d 330, 169 P.3d 559]; *Intel Corp. v. Hamidi* (2003) 30 Cal.4th 1342, 1350, fn. 3 [1 Cal.Rptr.3d 32, 71 P.3d 296].)

4. See Senate Rules Committee, Office of Senate Floor Analyses, third reading analysis of Senate Bill No. 1613 (2005-2006 Reg. Sess.) as amended August 21, 2006, page 3, and Senate Rules Committee, Office of Senate Floor Analyses, Unfinished Business Analysis of Senate Bill No. 1613 (2005-2006 Reg. Sess.) as amended August 29, 2006, pages 6-7.

5. See Senate Rules Committee, Office of Senate Floor Analyses, third reading analysis of Senate Bill No. 1613 (2005-2006 Reg. Sess.) as amended August 21, 2006, page 3, and Senate Rules Committee, Office of Senate Floor Analyses, Unfinished Business Analysis of Senate Bill No. 1613 (2005-2006 Reg. Sess.) as amended August 29, 2006, pages 6-7.

6. Section 2 of Senate Bill No. 1613 (2005-2006 Reg. Sess.) states in its entirety: "The Legislature finds and declares all of the following:

"(a) There are significant safety benefits associated with the availability of wireless communication technologies, including, but not limited to, providing assistance that helps save lives and minimizes property damage.

"(b) On a daily basis, California drivers make thousands of wireless telephone emergency 911 calls.

"(c) The availability of wireless telephones in motor vehicles allows motorists to report accidents, fires, naturally occurring life-threatening situations, including, but not limited to, rock slides and fallen trees, other dangerous road conditions, road rage, dangerous driving, criminal behavior, including drunk driving, and stranded motorist situations.

"(d) There is growing public concern regarding the safety implications of the widespread practice of using hand-held wireless telephones while operating motor vehicles.

"(e) It is in the best interests of the health and welfare of the citizens of the state to enact one uniform motor vehicle wireless telephone use law that establishes statewide safety guidelines for use of wireless telephones while operating a motor vehicle." (Stats. 2006, ch 290 §2, p. 2366.)

EXHIBIT 4B (cont.)

7. When enacted, section 23124 prohibited minors from driving a motor vehicle "while using a wireless telephone, even if equipped with a hands-free device, or while using a mobile service device." (Former §23124, subds. (a) & (b).) The statute defined a "mobile service device" as including, but not limited to, "a broadband personal communication device, specialized mobile radio device, handheld device or laptop computer with mobile data access, pager, and two-way messaging device." (Former §23124, subd. (g).) The section became operative on July 1, 2008—the same operative date as section 23123. (Former §23124, subd. (h); former §23123, subd. (h).)

In 2013, subdivision (b) of section 23124 was amended to prohibit minors from driving "while using a wireless telephone or an electronic wireless communications device, even if equipped with a hands-free device," and replaced the phrase "'mobile service device'" in subdivision (g) with the term "'electronic wireless communications device,'" but left the definition of such devices identical with the prior version. (Stats. 2013, ch. 754, §1.)

TEST YOUR UNDERSTANDING

1. This chapter focuses on a state statute addressing the use of cell phones while driving. If the U.S. Congress decided to enact a statute prohibiting various types of distracted driving on interstate highways, answer the following questions:
   a. What are the steps that the bill would go through to become law?
   b. Would it be unusual to have both federal and state law on a similar topic?
   c. If you had a client who has been charged with violating this very new statute, how would you figure out when the law became effective?
   d. Your client believes that the law abridges his right to free speech, given the nature of the conversation that he was having. Which branch of government would consider this argument?

2. If you were drafting a distracted driving statute for Congress, what are the typical types of sections that you could include, in the order they generally appear? For each one, state its main purpose.

3. If you were representing a client governed by the distracted driving statute and briefed it, which statutory components would align with the if-clause, and which would align with the then-clause?

4. As you consider the statute's application to your client's situation, you discern ambiguity. What is statutory ambiguity? List several ways in which statutory language can be ambiguous.

5. Explain the plain meaning rule, purpose approach, and golden rule.

6. If a key principle in working with statutes is to honor legislative intent:
   a. What is the main practical import of this principle?
   b. Why is there often no actual legislative intent as a matter of fact?
   c. What are sources (other than the statute itself) that provide indications of legislative intent?

7. Assume that the ambiguity you discerned in the distracted driving statute is in the intricate description of the prohibited conduct. List some canons of construction that you would consider using to work through the language.

8. If the statute that you are interpreting is not a federal statute but rather a state statute based on a model law, what might you look for to aid you in interpreting it?

TEST YOUR UNDERSTANDING ANSWERS

1. As to the federal statute on distracted driving:
   a. The typical steps that the bill would go through to become law are a subcommittee hearing, committee deliberation and report, chamber debate and vote in one house, the same process in the other house, conference committee consideration as needed, and signature by the president.
   b. It is not unusual to have both federal and state law on similar topics, especially because this law would cover interstate highways.
   c. Statutes have prospective effects, with either the effective date specified in the laws or some other presumed date; for federal statutes, the presumed effective date is the date of presidential approval.
   d. Courts (i.e., the judicial branch) would determine whether the statute is unconstitutional.

2. The typical components of a statute are:
   a. Name—identifies the topic of the statute
   b. Purpose statement—specifies why the legislature enacted the statute
   c. Scope—frames the situations covered by the statute
   d. Definitions—provides particular meanings for words used in the statute
   e. General rule—describes the conduct that the legislature is encouraging or prohibiting
   f. Exceptions—carves out situations that will not have the same outcome as the general rule
   g. Consequences and enforcement—provides at least a label and perhaps also specific outcomes and legal methods by which those outcomes occur
   h. Additional clauses—effective date, sunset provision, and severability

3. The if-clause contains the definitions, scope, general rule, and exceptions. The then-clause contains the consequences and enforcement.

4. Statutory ambiguity occurs when more than one meaning of the language is possible as it is applied to a situation. Language may be vague, it could be read in two ways, or a point may be omitted.

5. The plain meaning rule calls for following the letter of the law (and not using interpretive tools when the meaning of the words is plain). The purpose approach calls for determining and following legislative intent. The golden rule indicates that when the actual words of a statute would yield an absurd, unreasonable, or unconstitutional result, the wording should not be followed to the letter.

6. As for legislative intent:
   a. The main import is that every word in a statute is to be considered and respected.
   b. There rarely is actual legislative intent, because the legislature is a collection of people who may have had different opinions or may not have considered the issue.
   c. Sources of legislative intent are the statute's purpose statement, legislative history documents, the statute's legal context, public policy, and the statute's paradigm case.

7. Canons of construction used to untangle complex language include defined, technical, and common meanings; ejusdem generis and expressio unius (as to lists); specific prevails over general; effectiveness of entire statute; and in pari materia.

8. To interpret a state statute based on a model statute, you could read construing cases from other states that also have enacted the model statute.

READING COMMENTARY

Delusive exactness is a source of fallacy throughout the law.
—Oliver Wendell Holmes
Truax v. Corrigan, 257 U.S. 312, 342 (1921)

A. UNDERSTANDING COMMENTARY

In many areas, the law is complex, controversial, or both. Furthermore, the law changes over time. It can be hard to understand fully how the law has evolved, what the law is, or what the law should be.

How does a lawyer make sense out of a difficult area of law?[1] One option is to read legal scholarship, or *commentary*. Commentary can be written by persons without lawmaking authority (professors, lawyers, and indeed students) or persons with lawmaking authority (such as judges and legislators) acting in other than a lawmaking capacity. In most situations, you are likely to use commentary that falls into one of these six categories: treatises, encyclopedias, legal periodicals, Restatements of the Law, jury instruction guides, or *American Law Report* (ALR) annotations.

All forms of commentary consist of some form of discussion of the law, along with references to legal authorities. Box 5.1 provides brief information about the particular features—purpose, authoritativeness, format, and coverage—of each type.

Commentary is also called "secondary authority" to distinguish it from the law itself, which is called "primary authority." This lesser status does not mean that it is unimportant. First, most commentary presents general principles on a legal topic. Some commentary (such as treatises and encyclopedias) may provide a big picture overview of the area of law encompassing your topic. Other commentary (such as ALR annotations) may provide clarification where the law is murky, complex, or fragmented.

Second, some commentary (such as treatises) may provide background information not stated in the law itself. The most common type of information is historical, such as the background of a case or the history of a statute.

Third, some commentary (such as legal periodical articles) may present perspectives on the law (from such diverse intellectual schools as feminist jurisprudence and law and economics) and critique existing law, thus providing insight into the policies underlying the law. You are most likely to look to the discussion of policy in commentary in several situations: when you need additional support for the argument that you are making on a client's behalf in an advocacy setting or when you are seeking to change the law.

Although you have little discretion in selecting which primary authority to analyze, you do have considerable discretion in choosing commentary. Obviously, the more pertinent the commentary, the better. Additional factors weighing in favor of a particular source are its credibility (generally a function of the author), comprehensiveness, and quality of analysis. Also important is how current the commentary is; be sure to consult any updating materials in addition to the original publication.

One type of commentary, the Restatements of the Law, is particularly authoritative. The Restatements are created by the American Law Institute (ALI), a national organization of elite lawyers who engage in an extensive deliberative process to create each Restatement. Courts not infrequently follow the Restatements in formulating their own rules. Similarly, a jury instruction guide is created through a deliberative process by a panel of experts within a particular jurisdiction and is particularly authoritative within that jurisdiction.

As examples of commentary, Exhibit 5A contains an excerpt from a torts treatise pertinent to the Bower's Bounty client situation, and Exhibit 5B contains a Restatement rule and explanatory material pertinent to the All-Day Wellness client situation. Please read those materials now.

---

1. Indeed, commentary is one of the best means of identifying which legal authorities to read in the early stages of legal research.

BOX 5.1

TYPES OF COMMENTARY

Type	Purpose	Authoritativeness	Authors	Format	Coverage and Updating
Treatises	Primarily to describe and explain rules of law	Varies according to author's prestige	Professors, attorneys	Textual discussion supplemented with fairly extensive footnotes	Each covers a specific broad or narrow topic in some depth; may or may not be updated
Encyclopedias	To summarize law	Depends on credibility of particular encyclopedia	Attorneys, editors	Overview of rules, supported by footnotes	Very wide range of topics described in general terms; updated
Legal Periodical Articles (also known as law reviews)	To describe and explain rules of law; advocate for change	Varies depending on author: highly authoritative if well-regarded judge or professor, less so if student	Attorneys, judges, legislators, professors, students	Essay with extensive supporting footnotes	Selected narrow topics discussed in great detail; not updated
Restatements of the Law	To "restate" the law, although some state what law should be in drafters' views	Generally highly authoritative, with some sections adopted by courts	American Law Institute (attorneys, professors)	Rule statement followed by explanations (comments) and examples (illustrations)	Broad statement of selected general areas of law; some Restatements are infrequently updated; recent cases citing to Restatement are listed
Jury Instruction Guides	To state law of specific jurisdiction	Highly authoritative within its jurisdiction	Panel of experts	Rule statement followed by explanation	Concise statements of jurisdiction's law in certain areas; generally updated
American Law Reports (ALR) **Annotations**	To summarize case law, especially splits among jurisdictions	Minimal, except to document jurisdictional splits	Attorneys, editors	Overview; then series of case descriptions, grouped by holdings	Selected topics discussed in considerable depth; updated

B. READING COMMENTARY

When you read commentary, you typically are doing so for several reasons: to obtain the description of the law; to acquire additional information; and to find references to other sources, such as cases or statutes, to read. You should look for points that connect to the facts of the client's situation. At the same time, you should be open to legal topics that the commentary raises that you may not yet have thought of yourself. The points you will draw from any particular commentary will vary depending on the type of commentary and what it happens to contain.

As one example, Box 5.2 is a set of notes for the treatise excerpt in Exhibit 5A, written with the Bower's Bounty situation as the focus.

As a second example, Box 5.3 is a set of notes for the Restatement material in Exhibit 5B, written with the All-Day Wellness situation as the focus. Section 188 covers various types of contracts that restrain competition, so the notes focus only on what is stated about the employment setting. The notes differentiate between the rule, which is what courts adopt most often, and the explanatory material in the comments and illustrations, which are less often adopted.

BOX 5.2

SAMPLE NOTES ON TREATISE

Dan. B. Dobbs, Paul T. Hayden, & Ellen M. Bublick, *The Law of Torts* (2d ed. 2011; updated June 2015, Westlaw)

Rules
Defamation by writing = libel (oral = slander).
Recovery of substantial damages for libel requires defendant's publication of defamatory material of and concerning plaintiff to third person. Furthermore, some courts say plaintiff must prove fault equivalent to negligence or something greater, publication was false, and plaintiff suffered actual damages. But with constitutional decisions, states may now presume damages and provide recovery based on strict liability. Opinion statements cannot be basis of liability.

References
No Kansas cases, but Restatement (Second) of Torts § 558

BOX 5.3

SAMPLE NOTES ON RESTATEMENT

Restatement (Second) of Contracts § 188

Rule in (1) states:
Promise to refrain from competition that imposes restraint that is ancillary to otherwise valid transaction or relation is unreasonably in restraint of trade if (a) restraint is greater than needed to protect promisee's legitimate interest or (b) promisee's need is outweighed by hardship to promisor and likely injury to public.
(2)(b) states that rule (1) includes promise by employee not to compete with employer.

Comment g states:
Employer's interest is usually confidential trade information or means to attract customers away from employer. Whether this risk is enough to justify promise depends on facts. These restraints are especially scrutinized due to unequal bargaining power and employee inattention to hardship, especially where employer uses standardized printed form. Line is drawn between general skill and knowledge peculiar to this employer. Public has interest in workable employment relationships, slowing down dissemination of ideas, impairing moves of manpower to areas of greatest productivity. As for ability to attract customers, nature, extent, locale of customers are relevant; restraint is more justifiable if linked to one field of activity and to taking of former customers (versus all competition).

Illustration 6 states:
Covenant applying to fitter of contact lenses (who has worked for employer for five years) that runs for three years, same town, fitting contact lenses is permissible; employee's customer contacts are such that they would attract customers away from employer.

EXHIBIT 5A TREATISE EXCERPT

§ 519.Elements of defamation—Common law and constitution, Dan B. Dobbs, Paul T....

Dan B. Dobbs, Paul T. Hayden and Ellen M. Bublick, The Law of Torts § 519 (2d ed.)

Dobbs' Law of Torts
Database updated June 2015
Dan B. Dobbs, Paul T. Hayden, and Ellen M. Bublick
Part VII. Dignitary and Economic Torts
Subpart B. Dignitary Torts
Chapter 44. Defamation
Topic B. Common Law Requirements

§ 519. Elements of defamation—Common law and constitution

The Common Law
Traditional common law elements—libel. Defamation by writing and by contemporary means analogous to writing is libel. Defamation communicated orally is slander. Communication in any form can be defamatory, but defamation is most commonly communicated in words, pictorial elements, acts or some combination of these methods. This chapter often uses the term defamation to include any form of communication. In claims for libel, once the plaintiff showed a publication of defamatory material about the plaintiff, the traditional rule permitted courts to presume that the publication was made with malice,[1] that the words were false,[2] and that the plaintiff suffered damages.[3] The upshot was that the plaintiff could recover substantial damages for libel upon proof of three elements: (1) defendant's publication of defamatory material (2) of and concerning the plaintiff (3) to a third person. These rules created a regime of prima facie strict liability, because no proof of the defendant's fault was required. As usual with such extremes, courts then created a limited number of affirmative defenses with the burden on the defendant.[4]
Additional elements required in contemporary law. Many contemporary cases have announced that three non-traditional requirements are now necessary to sustain a libel claim. These cases tend to say the plaintiff must prove, besides the elements listed above, that (4) the defendant was guilty of fault equivalent to negligence or something greater in all cases,[5] (5) the publication was false,[6] and (6) the plaintiff suffered actual damages.[7] Others list only some of these added elements.[8] These added elements came about as courts attempted to integrate federal Constitutional rules of free-speech[9] into the common law of libel. When the Restatement first introduced these additional requirements in 1977,[10] they appeared to reflect the Constitutional requirements. A later Supreme Court decision, however, suggests that the Constitution does not require these added elements where the defendant defames a purely private person on an issue that is not of public concern.[11] Nevertheless, states apparently continue to state these added elements of proof for all cases, not merely those involving public figures or issues of public concern.[12]
Slander, special requirements. In the case of slander, the plaintiff must also prove either (a) special (pecuniary) harm *or* (b) a publication meaning that the plaintiff has committed a serious crime, or that the plaintiff has a character trait or a practice incompatible with her trade, business, or profession, or that the plaintiff suffers an incurable and communicable disease.[13] The requirement of pecuniary harm is significantly more demanding than the requirement of actual harm or damages.[14]
The Constitution
Since 1964, the structure of the common law defamation case has been radically altered by constitutional rulings based upon defendants' rights to free speech. All three of the common law presumptions—fault, falsity, and damages—have been reversed by constitutional decisions governing a substantial number of cases.[15] Although some issues remain undecided, the constitutional rules probably cover the following territory:
    (1) If the plaintiff is a public official or a public figure, she must now prove that the defendant published a knowing or reckless falsehood, but states are free to permit recovery of presumed damages if they choose to do so.[16]
    (2) If the plaintiff is a private person but the issue involved in the publication is one of public concern, the plaintiff is required to prove falsity of the publication, some fault on the part of the defendant (usually negligence), plus actual injury or damages. Upon such proof, she cannot recover punitive damages, and without such proof she cannot

EXHIBIT 5A (cont.)

recover anything.[17]

(3) If the plaintiff is a private person and the alleged defamation is of no public concern, the states are free to permit recovery of presumed damages; probably the states are free to invoke common law strict liability rules as well.[18] Where falsity is required, the effect is to protect opinion statements that cannot be said to be either true or false.[19] Even where the constitutional limitations may not apply, some states have now adopted some of these constitutional limitations as a part of their common law.[20] The constitutional rules increased the rationality of defamation law, but they have also added their own complexity to the existing intricacies of defamation.

Westlaw. © 2015 Thomson Reuters. No Claim to Orig. U.S. Govt. Works.

Footnotes

[1] See, e.g., Senna v. Florimont, 196 N.J. 469, 958 A.2d 427 (2008) (but holding that fault is now required when the publication touches on an issue of public concern); Doss v. Jones, 5 Howard 158 (Miss. 1840) ("the law imputes malice or an evil intention in all cases, when words actionable in themselves are spoken")

[2] See Hepps v. Philadelphia Newspapers, Inc.506 Pa. 304, 485 A.2d 374, 379 (1984) ("falsity of the defamatory words is presumed," truth is an affirmative defense, rev'd, Philadelphia Newspapers, Inc. v. Hepps, 475 U.S. 767, 106 S.Ct. 1558, 89 L.Ed.2d 783 (1986) (Constitutional rules require the plaintiff to prove falsity, at least in certain cases).

[3] See Greenmoss Builders, Inc. v. Dun & Bradstreet, Inc., 143 Vt. 66, 76, 461 A.2d 414, 419 (1983), aff'd, Dun & Bradstreet, Inc. v. Greenmoss Builders, Inc., 472 U.S. 749, 105 S. Ct. 2939, 86 L. Ed. 2d 593 (1985) ("When the defamation is actionable per se the plaintiff can recover general damages without proof of loss or injury, which is conclusively presumed to result from the defamation") (Constitutional rules permit presumption of damages in libel cases where the plaintiff is a private person and the defamation does not touch issues of public concern); In re Storms v. Action Wisconsin Inc., 309 Wis.2d 704, 748, 750 N.W.2d 739, 761 (2008) ("Damages are presumed from proof of the defamation by libel"; but holding that Constitutional fault levels were required when a public figure sues).

[4] See generally § 538.

[5] See Seaton v. TripAdvisor LLC, 728 F.3d 592 (6th Cir. 2013) (applying Tennessee law, defamation requires proof that a party published a statement with knowledge that it is false, or with a reckless disregard for the truth of the statement, or with negligence in failing to ascertain its truth); Blodgett v. University Club, 930 A.2d 210 (D.C. 2007); Costello v. Hardy, 864 So.2d 129 (La. 2004); Morgan v. Kooistra, 941 A.2d 447 (Me. 2008); Higginbotham v. Public Service Com'n of Maryland, 412 Md. 112, 985 A.2d 1183 (2009) ("There can 'be no recovery without fault in any defamation action'"); Smith v. Anonymous Joint Enterprise, 487 Mich. 102, 793 N.W.2d 533 (Mich. 2010); Boone v. Sunbelt Newspapers, Inc., 347 S.C. 571, 556 S.E.2d 732 (2001); Sullivan v. Baptist Mem. Hosp., 995 S.W.2d 569 (Tenn. 1999); Belcher v. Wal-Mart Stores, Inc., 211 W.Va. 712, 568 S.E.2d 19 (2002).

[6] Eckman v. Cooper Tire & Rubber Co., 893 So.2d 1049 (Miss. 2005); Mark v. Seattle Times, 96 Wash.2d 473, 635 P.2d 1081 (1981).

[7] Nazeri v. Missouri Valley College, 860 S.W.2d 303 (Mo. 1993). Traditionally, slander claims required proof of *pecuniary* damages while libel cases presumed damages. Under a rule developed in some 19th Century American cases, pecuniary damages must be proved in certain libel cases, but not all. See § 535.

[8] E.g., Hopkins v. O'Connor, 282 Conn. 821, 925 A.2d 1030 (2007) (adding to the traditional common law elements only that the plaintiff must show reputational injury resulting from the defendant's publication).

[9] § 554.

[10] Restatement Second of Torts § 558 (1977).

[11] See § 557.

EXHIBIT 5B   **RESTATEMENT RULE AND EXPLANATORY MATERIAL**

Restat 2d of Contracts, § 188

Restatement 2d, Contracts - Rule Sections > *Chapter 8- Unenforceability on Grounds of Public Policy* > *Topic 2- Restraint of Trade*

§ 188 Ancillary Restraints on Competition

(1) A promise to refrain from competition that imposes a restraint that is ancillary to an otherwise valid transaction or relationship is unreasonably in restraint of trade if

(a) the restraint is greater than is needed to protect the promisee's legitimate interest, or

(b) the promisee's need is outweighed by the hardship to the promisor and the likely injury to the public.

(2) Promises imposing restraints that are ancillary to a valid transaction or relationship include the following:

(a) a promise by the seller of a business not to compete with the buyer in such a way as to injure the value of the business sold;

(b) a promise by an employee or other agent not to compete with his employer or other principal;

(c) a promise by a partner not to compete with the partnership.

COMMENTS & ILLUSTRATIONS

Comment:

a. Rule of reason. The rules stated in this Section apply to promises not to compete that, because they impose ancillary restraints, are not necessarily invalid. Subsection (1) restates in more detail the general rule of reason of § 186 as it applies to such promises. Under this formulation the restraint may be unreasonable in either of two situations. The first occurs when the restraint is greater than necessary to protect the legitimate interests of the promisee. The second occurs when, even though the restraint is not greater than necessary to protect those interests, the promisee's need for protection is outweighed by the hardship to the promisor and the likely injury to the public. In the second situation the court may be faced with a particularly difficult task of balancing competing interests. No mathematical formula can be offered for this process.

b. Need of the promisee. If a restraint is not ancillary to some transaction or relationship that gives rise to an interest worthy of protection, the promise is necessarily unreasonable under the rule stated in the preceding Section. In some instances, however, a promise to refrain from competition is a natural and reasonable means of protecting a legitimate interest of the promisee arising out of the transaction to which the restraint is ancillary. In those instances the same reasons argue for its enforceability as in the case of any other promise. For example, competitors who are combining their efforts in a partnership may promise as part of the transaction not to compete with the partnership. Assuming that the combination is not monopolistic, such promises, reasonable in scope, will be upheld in view of the interest of each party as promisee. See Subsection (2)(c) and Comment *h*. (It is assumed in the Illustrations to this Section that the arrangements are not objectionable on grounds other than those that come within its scope.) The extent to which the restraint is needed to protect the promisee's interests will vary with the nature of the transaction. Where a sale of good will is involved, for example, the buyer's interest in what he has acquired cannot be effectively realized unless the seller engages not to act so as unreasonably to diminish the value of what he has sold. The same is true of any other property interest of which exclusive use is part of the value. See Subsection (2)(a) and Comment *f*. In the case of a post-employment restraint, however, the promisee's interest is less clear. Such a restraint, in contrast to one accompanying a sale of good will, is not necessary in order for the employer to get the full value of what he has acquired. Instead, it must usually be justified on the ground that the employer has a legitimate interest in restraining the employee from appropriating valuable trade information and customer relationships to which he has had access in the course of his employment. Arguably the employer

EXHIBIT 5B (cont.)

Restat 2d of Contracts, § 188

2. The facts being otherwise as stated in Illustration 1, neither A's nor B's business extends to a radius of a hundred miles. The area fixed is more extensive than is necessary for B's protection. A's promise is unreasonably in restraint of trade and is unenforceable on grounds of public policy. As to the possibility of refusal to enforce limited to part of the promise, see § 184(2).

3. A sells his grocery business to B and as part of the agreement promises not to engage in business of any kind within the city for three years. The activity proscribed is more extensive than is necessary for B's protection. A's promise is unreasonably in restraint of trade and is unenforceable on grounds of public policy. As to the possibility of refusal to enforce only part of the promise, see § 184(2).

4. A sells his grocery business to B and as part of the agreement promises not to engage in a business of the same kind within the city for twenty-five years, although B has ample opportunity to make A's former good will his own in a much shorter period of time. The time fixed is longer than is necessary for A's protection. A's promise is unreasonably in restraint of trade and is unenforceable on grounds of public policy. As to the possibility of refusal to enforce only part of the promise, see § 184(2).

5. A, a corporation, sells its business to B. As part of the agreement, C and D, officers and large shareholders of A, promise not to compete with B within the territory in which A did business for three years. Their promises are not unreasonably in restraint of trade and enforcement is not precluded on grounds of public policy.

g. Promise by employee or agent. The employer's interest in exacting from his employee a promise not to compete after termination of the employment is usually explained on the ground that the employee has acquired either confidential trade information relating to some process or method or the means to attract customers away from the employer. Whether the risk that the employee may do injury to the employer is sufficient to justify a promise to refrain from competition after the termination of the employment will depend on the facts of the particular case. Post-employment restraints are scrutinized with particular care because they are often the product of unequal bargaining power and because the employee is likely to give scant attention to the hardship he may later suffer through loss of his livelihood. This is especially so where the restraint is imposed by the employer's standardized printed form. Cf. § 208. A line must be drawn between the general skills and knowledge of the trade and information that is peculiar to the employer's business. If the employer seeks to justify the restraint on the ground of the employee's knowledge of a process or method, the confidentiality of that process or method and its technological life may be critical. The public interest in workable employer-employee relationships with an efficient use of employees must be balanced against the interest in individual economic freedom. The court will take account of any diminution in competition likely to result from slowing down the dissemination of ideas and of any impairment of the function of the market in shifting manpower to areas of greatest productivity. If the employer seeks to justify the restraint on the ground of the employee's ability to attract customers, the nature, extent and locale of the employee's contacts with customers are relevant. A restraint is easier to justify if it is limited to one field of activity among many that are available to the employee. The same is true if the restraint is limited to the taking of his former employer's customers as contrasted with competition in general. A restraint may be ancillary to a relationship although, as in the case of an employment at will, no contract of employment is involved. Analogous rules apply to restraints imposed on agents by their principals. As to the duty of an agent not to compete with his principal during the agency relationship, see *Restatement, Second, Agency §§ 393*, 394.

Illustrations:

6. A employs B as a fitter of contact lenses under a one-year employment contract. As part of the employment agreement, B promises not to work as a fitter of contact lenses in the same town for three years after the termination of his employment. B works for A for five years, during which time he has close relationships with A's customers, who come to rely upon him. B's contacts with A's customers are such as to attract them away from A. B's promise is not unreasonably in restraint of trade and enforcement is not precluded on grounds of public policy.

TEST YOUR UNDERSTANDING

1. Assume that you have been assigned to work on the Daniel de la Cruz situation. He was suspended from public middle school for making statements in support of a breast cancer awareness group, and his case could involve complicated constitutional litigation in federal court. If commentary is not the law, why bother reading it?

2. As you consider which type of commentary to read, what are the specific strengths of each of the following types of commentary?
   a. Treatise
   b. Encyclopedia
   c. Legal periodical article
   d. ALR annotation

3. Two others types of commentary—the Restatements of the Law and jury instruction guides—are less likely choices for this project because of their limited coverage. In what ways are these two similar?

4. If you found a commentary pertinent to the Daniel de la Cruz situation, what would you focus on in your reading and note-taking?

TEST YOUR UNDERSTANDING ANSWERS

1. Reading commentary can help you identify which types of primary authority apply (e.g., federal or state law), give you an understanding of what the rules of law are, and provide you with a set of references.

2. Specific strengths of each of the following types of commentary include:
   a. Treatise—depth of coverage, extensiveness of references, potential credibility, updating
   b. Encyclopedia—wide range of topics, overview of law, updating
   c. Legal periodical article—extensive detail on narrow topic, advocacy for change, potential authoritativeness
   d. ALR annotation—summary of case law in considerable depth, coverage of jurisdictional splits, updated

3. The Restatements of the Law and jury instruction guides are similar in that they are created through deliberative processes by groups of elite lawyers and are thus highly authoritative. (The Restatements have a national scope, whereas jury instruction guides are written for specific jurisdictions.)

4. In reading and note-taking, you should focus on the facts of your client's situation, as to both the facts and the law. Be open to topics that you may not have thought of initially. Take down the legal rules, additional points about the law, and references to additional authorities you may want to read.

LEGAL REASONING

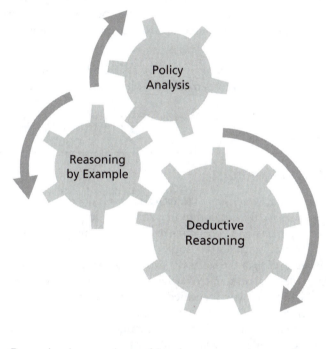

Reasoning is an ancient subject but an everyday practice.
—David A. Conway & Ronald Munson
The Elements of Reasoning (1990)

A. INTRODUCTION

Lawyers read the law not only because it is interesting but also, primarily, because they seek to derive the legal meaning of a client's situation. In moving into *legal reasoning*, a lawyer acts much as a judge does in deciding a case (as discussed in Chapter 3). The client's situation is parallel to the real-world story in a judicial opinion, and the lawyer develops a legal analysis: applying the law to the facts of the client's situation to yield a predicted legal outcome. Based on this analysis, the lawyer can provide the needed legal services, such as negotiating a transaction, settling a dispute, or presenting a client's case in court.

Legal reasoning is structured but not mechanical, technically demanding yet also creative. Legal reasoning requires considerable precision and judgment. There are three primary forms of legal reasoning:

- In deductive reasoning, you apply elements of a rule from a case, statute, or other authority to the facts of a client's situation in order to predict the legal outcome of the client's situation. Deductive reasoning is a necessary step in legal reasoning.
- In policy analysis, you consider the purposes of the law and discern how potential outcomes would or would not serve those purposes. Policy analysis is frequently helpful but not necessary.
- In reasoning by example, you compare the facts of a client's situation, which has no known legal outcome, to the facts of a similar decided case that has a known legal outcome. Reasoning by example is frequently helpful but not necessary.

As examples, this chapter returns to the Cassie Collins, Bower's Bounty, and All-Day Wellness situations to demonstrate different facets of legal reasoning.

B. DEDUCTIVE REASONING

1. Introduction

Deductive reasoning, which involves using known general principles to solve a specific unknown situation, is common outside the law. For instance, a mathematician uses theorems and corollaries to solve a geometric proof, and a physician uses diagnostic principles to diagnose a patient's disease.

Deductive reasoning in the law is the process of using rules from legal authorities to predict the legal outcome of a client's situation. It is grounded in stating the rule in if/then form, with identified elements and legal consequences. Legal reasoning involves matching the rule's elements to your client's facts and then making a judgment about whether the elements of the rule are present, so that the rule's legal consequences will or will not follow.

As an example for this part, consider the Cassie Collins situation. She was ticketed for driving while speaking into her cell phone in an attempt to locate a nearby Starbucks as she pulled out of a mini-mall's parking lot. The California Vehicle Code governing this situation is briefed in Box 6.1.

2. Matching Elements to Client Facts

Deductive reasoning is structured: the rule's elements frame the analysis; each element directs you to some aspect of the client's situation, and relevant facts pertain to that aspect.

Most elements of a rule focus your attention on one, or perhaps two, of the six classic questions that journalists ask; that is, who, what, when, where, why, and how elements. An element describing an actor focuses on the who aspect of the situation, and an element focusing on the action taken is a what element. An element focusing on the circumstances may be a when, where, why, or how

> ### BOX 6.1
>
> ### SAMPLE STATUTORY BRIEF
>
> | | |
> |---|---|
> | If | person drives motor vehicle |
> | | *and* uses non-hands-free wireless telephone in non-hands-free manner |
> | | *Spriggs:* "uses" means talking and listening, not looking at map |
> | | *and* is *not* driving on private property, interpreted under 490 to mean |
> | | in private ownership |
> | | and used for vehicular travel by owner and those having express or implied permission from owner but not by other members of public |
> | THEN | person has committed infraction with base fines of $20 for first offense and $50 for subsequent offenses. |

element. If you are unsure of the factual focus of a case law element, reread the case and study the facts that the court discussed in writing about that element. Similarly, if you are unsure of the factual focus of a statutory element, examine a case interpreting the statute or consider the statute's paradigm case.

The *relevant facts* in your client's situation are those that answer the related journalist question for the element, and they meet the element's requirements or not. Thus, for a who element, consider whether the identity of a person in your client's situation meets the rule's description of a person.

Discerning the relevant facts in your client's situation may be straightforward. In some situations, it is difficult. The facts may be complicated; if so, consider creating a timeline or dividing the facts into logical clusters (e.g., people involved, events). The difficulty may arise because you are missing key facts or you have conflicting information on a fact from different sources. In these situations, note the omission or conflict, make one or more sensible assumptions, and proceed on your assumptions.

As an example, in the Cassie Collins situation, the relevant fact for the who element is Ms. Collins, a person.[1] The facts for the action elements (what and how) entail Collins's driving and speaking into her standard cell phone to ask it for directions (which connects to "use"). The facts for the where element are partly in a mini-mall's parking lot (which connects to "private property") and partly on a city street.

3. Making the Judgment About the Legal Consequences

The rule's structure determines the significance of the various elements. If the rule is conjunctive, all elements must be present for the rule's legal consequence to follow; the absence of one element means that the rule does not apply. If the

---

1. Because section 23124 covers drivers under the age of eighteen, this section implicitly covers adults. Ms. Collins is thirty-three and within this section.

rule has disjunctive elements, the absence of one of them does not matter if another is present. In aggregate and balancing rules, it is the relative strength of the various factors that determines whether the legal consequence follows.

As an example, the statute in Box 6.1 is primarily conjunctive: there must be a person driving a motor vehicle, that person must be using a non-hands-free cell phone in a certain way, and that activity must occur other than on private property. Thus, all these elements must be present for there to be an infraction. Note that the location element has a disjunctive piece; the permission to be on private property may be express or implied.

An important note: the conclusion that the rule's elements are not met does not necessarily conclude your analysis. More than one rule may apply to a situation, and the failure to meet all requirements of one rule does not necessarily foreclose meeting the requirements of a different rule. For example, conduct may not be a federal crime but may be a state crime, conduct may not be criminal but may be tortious, and conduct may not be a tort but may be a breach of contract.

4. Depicting Deductive Reasoning

As you work through your analysis, you may depict deductive reasoning in various ways. Any depiction must use a rule of law as its point of departure and reflect the structure of the if-clause of the rule.

In addition to traditional sentences and paragraphs, you may want to use a column chart, as in Box 6.2. The elements of the rule in the left column line up with the relevant facts of your client's situation in the middle column; the right column is space for indicating the element's presence or absence. For conjunctive rules, "yes" and "no" indicate an element's presence or absence; with aggregate or balancing rules, plus and minus marks represent the strength of the various factors.

5. Review

Deductive reasoning—applying a rule to the facts of the client's situation to predict the legal outcome for the client—is the fundamental form of legal reasoning. Based on a careful reading of the law, deductive reasoning involves moving through the following sequence:

(1) Analyze each element of the if/then rule; focus on who, what, when, where, why, or how questions.
(2) Identify the facts in the client's situation that are relevant to each element.
(3) Analyze whether each element is met by the facts of the client's situation.
(4) Conclude either that the necessary elements are not met, so the legal consequence does not result under this rule, or that the elements are met, so the legal consequence of the rule does follow.

The deductive reasoning process sometimes leaves unanswered questions. You may be able to answer those questions with policy analysis or reasoning by example. Both derive from legal authorities. Both are less structured than deductive reasoning and require good judgment. Policy analysis is more abstract than deductive reasoning, and reasoning by example is more concrete.

BOX 6.2

SAMPLE DEDUCTIVE REASONING COLUMN CHART

Element	Client Situation	Element Present
IF person drives motor vehicle ————————▶	Collins drove car	YES
uses non-hands-free wireless telephone in non-hands-free manner ————————▶	Her phone was standard cell phone	YES
"use" means talking and listening ————————▶	Collins spoke into phone to ask for directions	UNCLEAR
and is *not* driving on private property ————————▶	Was pulling into street from parking lot for mini-mall	MAYBE
interpreted under 490 to mean: in private ownership and used for vehicular travel by owner and those having express or implied permission from owner, but not by other members of public	Lot is likely privately owned, with users being patrons of stores	PROBABLY
THEN person has committed infraction—base fines follow.		UNCLEAR

C. POLICY ANALYSIS

1. Introduction

Policy analysis involves discerning and relying on the goal to be served in a situation when making a decision. You no doubt use policy analysis in nonlegal contexts. For example, policies that impose a penalty for turning in a paper late are teaching the importance of timeliness and being fair to students who turn their work in on time. A policy supporting merit pay is promoting excellent work by all employees.

In the context of legal reasoning, policy analysis entails using the broad principle or social goal to be achieved by applying a legal rule to inform the analysis of a client situation. Policy considerations drive the creation of legal rules. Legislators enact statutes based on their conceptions of the social good. Judges too, especially in the highest court, develop rules in particular cases based in part on their judgment of how to further society's interests, beyond those of the specific parties to the case.

In many areas of law, society has more than one competing interest. Very often, lawmakers seek to serve more than one interest, which makes for a complex and nuanced rule. Competition among policies also causes jurisdictions to diverge in the rules that they make on the same subject. These jurisdictional splits occur in both the judicial and legislative branches.

Legal policy often is informed by other disciplines that also address how to achieve the public good. For example, legal rules about who should bear the risk of loss in accidents are informed by philosophical conceptions of fault and responsibility. As another example, economic principles about efficient markets underlie many rules of contract law.

As an example, this part continues with the Cassie Collins situation and the statute governing cell-phone use while driving.

2. Deriving and Applying Policy

To apply policy to a client's situation, you first must discern the policy underlying the law. In some situations, the court or legislature states its policy in so many words in the reasoning portion of a judicial opinion or in the purpose section of a statute. Commentary writers often discuss the underlying policy of a rule in the process of describing and critiquing it.

When your research has not yielded a statement of policy, you may find *stakeholder analysis* useful. In business settings, stakeholder analysis is a method of discerning the ethical implications of a situation; it entails identifying the stakeholders in a situation, discerning their respective interests, and assessing possible resolutions to serve those interests.

In the legal context, stakeholder analysis focuses on inferring the policy or policies that the law is intended to serve from the interests of stakeholders affected by a legal rule. Begin by identifying the immediate participants in the situation (the parties), as well as persons who are less immediately involved but nonetheless affected by the law. Then identify what stake, or interest, each stakeholder has in the rule of law and how each would want the rule to read. Finally, match these preferences to the way that the rule does read.

You may find that more than one policy is inherent in a complex rule. To decide which policy to favor, ask two questions. First, is either policy preferred over the other by lawmakers? For example, has the court cited or relied on one policy more than the other recently? Second, which policy is more clearly served by the possible outcomes in the client's situation? If one outcome would clearly serve one policy while the other outcome would only somewhat serve the competing policy, the former outcome might be favored by the courts.

As an example, Box 6.3 depicts a stakeholder analysis of the statute governing cell-phone use while driving in a hub-and-spokes diagram.[2] The driver wants to be able to act and communicate as she wishes—yet also to be safe, presumably. Bystanders, such as passengers, people in other cars, and people on the street are most interested in safety, which would be served by a law prohibiting an act that may cause distracted driving. Less obviously, cell phones can be used to assist safety through calling 911, for example. These various interests are apparent in the statute in various ways. The statute prohibits the most problematic use of cell

---

2. The California legislature passed a statement of findings, set out in footnote 6 of *People v. Spriggs*, in Exhibit 4B of Chapter 4. This statement parallels the text's stakeholder analysis to a significant degree.

BOX 6.3

SAMPLE STAKEHOLDER ANALYSIS

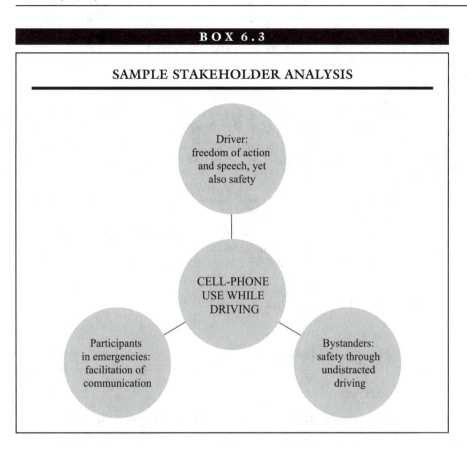

phones: non-hands-free conversations while driving on public roads. On the other hand, some uses (chiefly calling for emergency assistance) are still permitted, and the penalty is not substantial.

Once you have discerned the policy underlying a legal rule, you can incorporate this information into your reasoning about your client's situation. Policy analysis is often used in two situations. First, if you are not certain how to read a rule, you can select the interpretation that best serves the rule's policy. Second, if you have identified an element of the rule, matched it to your client's facts, and are uncertain whether your client's facts meet the requirements of the rule, you can test your conclusion by how well it serves the rule's policy. In both situations, ask how well each potential outcome in your client's situation would serve the policy that you have identified.

As an example, Ms. Collins's situation raises an issue about the meaning of "uses," which, according to the *Spriggs* case, means listening and talking but does not encompass looking at a map. Ms. Collins's activity falls between these two scenarios. As a second example, Ms. Collins's situation raises an issue about whether her facts fall within the exception for driving on private property because she was partly in a parking lot and partly on a city street. The statutory policy is related to the safety of the driving public, which became an issue due to her activity and location. This policy analysis suggests that "use" should be interpreted to include her activity (especially if the program "spoke" back to her), and that the exception should not apply to her situation.

3. Review

Policy analysis can supplement deductive reasoning in order to reduce uncertainty in the rule or its application to the client's situation. It entails the application of broad principles to your client's situation. The broad principle is the purpose of the legal rule—the goal sought by lawmakers. Policy analysis entails the following actions:

(1) Discern the policies from a statement in the law itself or from commentary on the law.
(2) Alternatively, if there is no satisfactory statement of policy, conduct a stakeholder analysis to figure out the policies.
(3) Apply the policy or policies to your client's situation.

In addition, or as an alternative, strengthen your legal analysis by engaging in the third form of legal reasoning: reasoning by example.

D. REASONING BY EXAMPLE

1. Introduction

Reasoning by example involves using the known outcome(s) of one or more resolved situations to draw a conclusion about a current situation with an unknown outcome. It, too, is common outside the law. For instance, a student who turns in a paper late expects that he or she will be treated similarly to other students who have turned in late papers. An employee who performs an employment obligation poorly or well expects to be treated like other similarly performing employees.

In law in particular, *reasoning by example*, or analogical reasoning, focuses on the comparison of the client's situation to precedent. It is based on a principle of justice—namely, that similar facts should be treated similarly. Not insignificantly, the use of precedent as an example adds a human side to the law and demonstrates how the rule has affected the lives of others.

As an example for the first half of this part, consider the Bower's Bounty situation. Bower's Bounty has been charged with defamation by a recently terminated employee who alleges that she was falsely accused of theft in a posting by management that co-workers read. The *Luttrell* case governing this situation is briefed in Box 6.4.

2. Reasoning Based on a Single Decided Case

To reason by example, you must first select the case to work with, then compare the decided case to your client's situation, and finally conclude whether that case and your client's situation are analogous or distinguishable. All three steps require you to exercise considerable judgment.

BOX 6.4

SAMPLE CASE BRIEF

Luttrell v. United Telephone System, Inc., 683 P.2d 1292 (Kan. Ct. App. 1984), *aff'd,* 659 P.2d 1270 (Kan. 1985).

Facts: P (employee) alleges that another employee told his supervisor he was illegally taping phone conversations, was asked to stop, yet persisted despite being told not to. P's supervisor told another employee, who told yet another employee. P alleges statements were malicious and within scope of employment. Employees were supervisors apparently.

Procedure and outcome: P sued D (employer) for defamation. DC granted D's motion to dismiss for failure to state claim. P appealed. Here: reversed and remanded.

Issue: When defamatory words are exchanged by agents of same corporation about fellow employee's performance, is there publication required for tort of defamation?

Holding: Communication of remarks by one corporate employee to another concerning job performance of third employee is publication required for defamation action against employer.

Rules of law: (1) Defamation elements are: false & defamatory words communicated to third person, resulting in harm to reputation of person defamed. (2) Corporation is liable for defamation of agent made while acting within scope of employment. (3) Qualified privilege exists when good faith, interest to be upheld, statement limited in scope to interest, publication in proper manner to proper parties. Privilege is defeated if speaker acted with knowledge of falsity or reckless disregard for truth.

Reasoning: Issue of intracorporate communication was issue of first impression. Courts around country split on issue; *Prosser* [major torts treatise] favors view that such communications are publication. Focus should be on nature of injury in defamation—damage to reputation; this may be as devastating when communication is inside corporation as outside. Employer's need to evaluate and comment on employee work is protected by qualified privilege.

Pertinence: Strong factual parallel to our case, although there, supervisors spoke to each other.

As for *case selection*, a decided case is a candidate for reasoning by example if it meets two criteria. First, it must address the same, or very nearly the same, legal rule or element that arises in your client's situation. Second, the facts pertaining to that rule or element should be similar to your client's facts, although they almost certainly will not be identical, or even nearly so. You should focus on the client's facts that are relevant to the rule or element that you are analyzing and select a decided case with relevant facts similar to those client facts.

The second step is *comparison of the cases*, in which you line up the facts of the decided case against those of your client's situation, focusing on the facts relevant to the rule or element under consideration. Initially, simply note how the facts match, and be sure that you have drawn out all relevant facts for all elements.

Then ascertain whether each pair is similar or different; there likely will be both similarities and differences. Deciding whether a client's fact is similar to or different from its parallel fact in the decided case requires careful thought. If your focus is too narrow, the decided case will appear utterly different from your client's situation; on the other hand, if your focus is too broad, every decided case will begin to look similar to your client's situation. To judge how much *elasticity* is justifiable, look at how broadly or narrowly the court discussed the facts and law in the decided case. Other authorities discussing the decided case also may help you decide how elastic it is. Avoid the temptation to stretch or constrict a comparison to bring your client's situation within a favorable decided case or to avoid the impact of an unfavorable decided case.

The third and final step is to come to the *conclusion of analogy or distinction*. If your client's situation is *analogous* to the decided case, the outcome of the decided case should follow if your client's situation were to be litigated. If your client's situation is *distinguishable* from the decided case, the decided case's outcome should not follow. Note the use of the word "should"; there always is some uncertainty in reasoning by example. Inexactitude is inherent in the process of judging how much and what kind of similarity are needed for an analogy or how much and what kind of difference are needed to distinguish a case.

To come to the conclusion of analogy or distinction requires careful reading of the court's reasoning, especially the court's discussion of how the law applies to the facts. One strategy is to rank those facts from most to least weighty; with this list in mind, study your list of similar and different facts. Sometimes you will decide that your client's situation is analogous because there are more similar than different facts, or vice versa. Or a single key comparison may prompt you to draw an analogy or a distinction.

3. Depicting Reasoning by Example

Just as with the other forms of reasoning, you can depict reasoning by example in various ways. In addition to sentences and paragraphs, you may want to consider diagrams.

One option is a Venn diagram. The purpose of a Venn diagram is to illustrate the areas of similarity and difference between two sets of items. The areas of similarity appear in the center, the areas of difference at the sides. The Venn diagram is most useful in helping you tease out both the similarities and differences between the facts of the decided case and your client's situation. See Box 6.5.

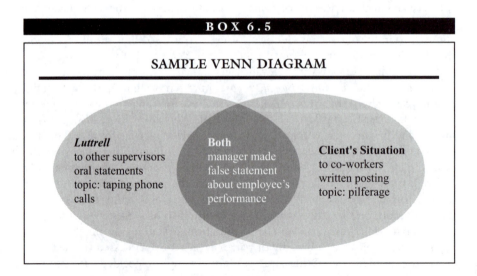

BOX 6.5

SAMPLE VENN DIAGRAM

Luttrell
to other supervisors
oral statements
topic: taping phone
calls

Both
manager made
false statement
about employee's
performance

Client's Situation
to co-workers
written posting
topic: pilferage

BOX 6.6

SAMPLE CHECKERBOARD CHART

Luttrell	Client's Situation	Comparison
Issue: Is there publication for purposes of a defamation claim?	Same	Same
Fact 1: Several supervisors talked to each other, i.e., within company.	Manager posted sign that co-workers read.	Not identical, but differences favor employee because wider and more fixed publication.
Fact 2: Topic was plaintiff-employee's job performance.	Topic was his performance.	Same
Outcome: Yes; there was publication.		Same outcome here; analogy.

Another option is a checkerboard chart, as in Box 6.6, that lines up the decided case's issue, facts, and holding with the client situation's issue, facts, and predicted outcome. This chart guides you in thinking through not only the fact parallels, but also the parallels in the legal facets of the cases.

As an example, reasoning by example from *Luttrell* to the Bower's Bounty situation leads to the conclusion that there was publication for defamation purposes, as shown in Boxes 6.5 and 6.6. In both cases, a managerial employee spoke falsely about an employee's performance. The two cases do differ, though. The topics of the statements vary, which does not seem significant to the publication topic. On the topic of publication, the *Luttrell* speakers were supervisors who spoke among themselves, whereas the Bower's Bounty manager posted a written statement read by co-workers. If the former counted as a publication, the latter, which is more widespread and fixed in form, should be as well. Therefore, the two cases are analogous.

As an example of distinguishing a case, consider this variation: In *Luttrell*, the court decided instead that there was no publication because supervisors should be able to discuss employee performance issues among themselves, given their shared job duties. Bower's Bounty would be distinguishable from this decision because manager-to-co-worker communications would not fall within this reasoning of the court.

4. Reasoning Based on Multiple Cases

Reasoning by example from a single case may not provide as much certainty as desired, and you may have a set of cases to work with. You could engage in a series of comparisons, working with one case at a time. The better approach, however, is to work off of your pattern fusion, as discussed in Chapter 3, and reason from that pattern to the client's situation. This process, *inductive generalization*, entails reasoning from the specific (the decided cases) to a generalization (their pattern) to the specific (the client's situation).

The strongest basis for an inductive generalization is a fact that differentiates the decided cases—cases with different versions of the key fact come out differently. Once you have identified the cases with the split in facts and outcomes, you can compare your client's facts to the two examples in the decided cases.

As an example for this section, consider the All-Day Wellness situation. All-Day Wellness would like to enter into covenants not-to-compete with its employees, to keep them from competing with it when they depart. Three cases pertinent to this topic revealed the pattern excerpted in Box 6.7.

In advising All-Day Wellness, one could report that the information in the first column provides a time range (one to two years) that the courts have considered permissible. The information in the second column is at first glance more puzzling, with the geographic range extending from one county to the entire nation; the unifying principle is the nature of the employee's job and the employer's business. Thus, the proper scope of the All-Day Wellness covenant would depend: it should be local or regional if these factors are local or regional, national if these factors are national.

5. Review

Reasoning by example can supplement deductive reasoning in order to reduce uncertainty in the rule or its application to the client's situation. The process of reasoning by example entails the following sequence of events:

(1) Select a decided case involving the same legal rule and element that you are analyzing in your client's situation and similar facts.
(2) Evaluate the similarities and differences between the relevant facts in the client's situation and those of the decided case.

BOX 6.7

EXCERPTED SAMPLE PATTERN FEATURES CHART

Case	Length of Time	Region
Davies & Davies	5 years, reduced to 1 year	Within 50 miles of 3 cities, reduced to 1 county
Webb Publishing	18 months	Apparently national
Overholt Crop Insurance	2 years	Counties where he worked

(3) Determine whether the client's situation and the decided case are overall analogous or distinguishable.

(4) As an alternative, use inductive generalization when you have a set of cases; reason from the pattern of decisions to the probable outcome of your client's situation.

Once you have read the law and reasoned carefully about your client's situation, through at least deductive reasoning, and also possibly policy analysis and reasoning by example, you should have a thorough analysis of the legal meaning of your client's situation. You are now ready to communicate your analysis in writing.

TEST YOUR UNDERSTANDING

1. Assume that you have been assigned to work on the Daniel de la Cruz situation. He was suspended from public middle school for certain statements he made. As you move from the law that you have found into legal reasoning, you might want to think of yourself as a judge deciding his case. Explain this analogy.

2. Define each of the following forms of legal reasoning you may use:
   a. Deductive reasoning
   b. Policy analysis
   c. Reasoning by example
   d. Inductive generalization

3. You have found a pertinent rule (whether in a statute or a case). To engage in deductive reasoning:
   a. How can you label each element of the rule?
   b. What does it mean to look for relevant facts in the Daniel de la Cruz situation?
   c. Why should you analyze the relationship between the elements of the rule?

4. To employ policy analysis to deepen your legal reasoning of the Daniel de la Cruz situation:
   a. What are two standard situations for using policy analysis?
   b. What sources could provide indications of the policy underlying your rule?
   c. If you do not have any such source and decide to use stakeholder analysis, what steps would you follow?

5. Fortunately, you have found cases involving suspension of students for misconduct, so to use reasoning by example:
   a. What factors should you consider in selecting a case to use?
   b. Once you select a case, how do you know which facts in the decided case to compare to which facts in the de la Cruz situation?
   c. What does it mean to say that a decided case and a client's case are analogous? Distinguishable?
   d. If the case that you selected comes out favorably for de la Cruz, how do you know whether you may conclude that they are indeed analogous? What does elasticity have to do with this?

6. To proceed one step further, you have three cases applying the same rule, so you may want to engage in inductive generalization. How does inductive generalization differ from reasoning by example three times in a row?

TEST YOUR UNDERSTANDING ANSWERS

1. In legal reasoning, the client's situation parallels the real-world story of a judicial opinion, and the lawyer develops a legal-analysis story to predict a legal outcome.

2. The various forms of legal reasoning are:
   a. Deductive reasoning—applying elements of a rule to the facts of the client's situation to predict the legal outcome
   b. Policy analysis—considering the purposes of the law and how possible outcomes would serve those purposes
   c. Reasoning by example—comparing the facts of the client's situation to the facts of a decided case to yield a conclusion of analogy or distinction
   d. Inductive generalization—reasoning from the pattern of decided cases to the client's situation

3. As for deductive reasoning:
   a. Each element of the rule can be labeled as a who, what, when, where, why, or how element.
   b. Relevant client facts are those that answer a question connected to an element.
   c. You must know what the rule requires in terms of the elements to know whether or not the legal consequence in the then-clause of the rule will follow, once you have decided whether the client's situation meets the requirements of the elements.

4. As for policy analysis:
   a. Policy analysis can be used to decide which way to read a rule and whether a client's situation fits within a rule.
   b. Sources of policy include the reasoning portion of an opinion, the purpose section of a statute, and commentary.
   c. Stakeholder analysis entails identifying participants and other interested persons, identifying their interests and preferred rules, and matching these to the actual rule.

5. As for reasoning by example:
   a. The case to use should address the same legal rule or element and have facts similar to the client's situation.
   b. The facts to compare are the facts that the elements make relevant.
   c. If the two are analogous, the outcome in the decided case should follow in the client's situation. If they are distinguishable, the decided case outcome would not follow in the client's situation as to this rule.
   d. The decision should be based on how broadly or narrowly the court wrote the opinion as to law and facts—this is the concept of elasticity. It should not depend on whether the outcome of the decided case is favorable for the client.

6. Inductive generalization entails reasoning from a pattern of cases to the client's situation, rather than proceeding case by case.

PART TWO

ADVISORY COMMUNICATION

In this part, you will study the communications that form the foundation of all types of client representation. These communications rely on the work discussed in Part I on reading and reasoning and generally precede the work discussed in Parts III and IV on persuasive and advocacy communication.

The first three chapters in this part cover writing topics:

- Chapter 7 examines the template in which lawyers write legal analysis, commonly known by the acronym IRAC. You will learn what it means to write an introduction + a rule + its application + the conclusion.
- Chapter 8 discusses the analytical office memo, in which a lawyer presents an objective analysis of a client's situation. You will learn about the various components that combine with IRACs to constitute an office memo and the contribution that each makes to a thorough understanding of the client's legal position.
- Chapter 9 discusses the advice letter, in which the lawyer communicates the analysis of the client's situation to the client. You will learn how to translate a legal analysis into a document that speaks effectively to a client.

The final two chapters in this part cover two key related conversations in which lawyers engage:

- Chapter 10 examines the client interview, when the lawyer and client first explore the client's situation and the possibility that the lawyer will represent the client. You will learn ways to establish trust with a client and elicit information from a client.
- Chapter 11 examines client counseling, when the lawyer explains the legal significance of the client's situation and the lawyer and client develop strategies for actions to be taken on the client's behalf. You will learn ways to assist a client in exploring various options and selecting the most promising course of action.

WRITING LEGAL ANALYSIS

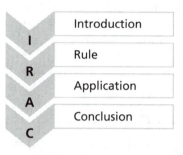

Words after all are symbols, and the significance of the symbols varies with the knowledge and experience of the mind receiving them.
—Benjamin N. Cardozo
Cooper v. Dasher, 290 U.S. 106 (1933)

A. INTRODUCTION

The processes of reading the law and reasoning about a client's situation in light of the law can take quite a bit of time and energy. The next step, generally, is to capture your thoughts in writing.

How does a lawyer express legal analysis in writing? Legal writing, like other disciplines, has a standard template: *introduction + rule + application + conclusion = IRAC*. The deconstruction of this template is as follows:[1]

(1) Readers need an introduction to the topic.
(2) They need to know the rules that apply to the topic.
(3) They want to see your application of those rules to the facts of the client's situation.
(4) They seek your conclusion about the client's predicted legal outcome.

Thus, IRAC resembles the classic expository writing template TEC: topic (the introduction) + explanation (the rule and the application) + conclusion.

---

1. There are variations on this theme. For example, some prefer to see I as meaning "issue"; others supplant I with C for "conclusion."

IRAC is used in many types of analytical papers written by lawyers. It appears in memos written in law offices, advice letters to clients, demand letters to opposing counsel, memoranda submitted to a district court, and appellate briefs. IRAC looks a bit different in various genres, but the analyses amount to either IRAC or variations on IRAC.

IRAC is the standard tool of legal writing for several reasons. It is highly adaptable: it works for different types of legal rules and many factual situations. Because of its prevalence, it promotes efficiency, both for the writer (at least once you master it) and the reader.

This chapter focuses on IRAC's use in an objective memo discussing the client's situation at the outset of the representation. Box 7.1 is an IRAC on the Cassie Collins situation involving driving while using a cell phone. Please read it now. Exhibit 7 contains another IRAC on the Bower's Bounty situation, to be read after you have finished reading this chapter.

B. UNDERSTANDING IRAC

As noted above, each of the four components of IRAC—introduction, rule, application, conclusion—has a key role to play. Each also has particular features to be mastered.

1. Introduction

Providing an introduction is important in legal writing for several reasons. Legal writing can involve complicated material, so orienting the reader is crucial. The introduction should help the reader focus on the topic at hand. Furthermore, writing the introduction helps you focus as well.

The *introduction* is typically one sentence long and may take any of the following forms:

- A topic is a reference to the subject of the upcoming IRAC.
- An issue is a question, linking law to facts, that you are about to address.
- A conclusion is a statement, linking law to facts, about your client's legal position.
- A transition is a sentence linking the previous topic to the upcoming topic.

The topic option is shorter than the others. The issue and conclusion options tend to be longer than the others and thus work best at the start of a lengthy IRAC. The transition option is a good choice if consecutive IRACs have important links that the reader may miss unless they are pointed out. Consider using the same option for a series of IRACs, for stylistic coherence.

As an example, the overall introduction is an issue in the IRAC in Box 7.1. Each of the IRACs on particular elements uses a transition or a topic for an introduction.

BOX 7.1

SIMPLE IRAC

Overall issue and rule	Can a driver be ticketed for driving while speaking into a cell phone to get directions as she was pulling out of a mini-mall's parking lot into traffic? In general, "[a] person shall not drive a motor vehicle while using a wireless telephone unless that telephone is specifically designed and configured to allow hands-free listening and talking, and is used in that manner while driving." Cal. Vehicle Code § 23123(a) (West Supp. 2015). A violation is punishable by a base fine of $20 for the first offense and $50 thereafter. *Id.* (b).
Entire IRAC for easy elements	Several elements are easily resolved. Ms. Collins (a person) was driving a car, and the phone that she was using was a non-hands-free cell phone. These elements of this rule are met.
Major element: transition, rule, application, conclusion	A less clear element is the statutory requirement that the person drive "while using" a cell phone along with the reference to "listening and talking." In *People v. Spriggs*, 168 Cal. Rptr. 3d 347 (Ct. App. 2014), the California Court of Appeals interpreted this language to not encompass reading a map but rather stated, "it prohibits a driver only from holding a wireless telephone while conversing on it." *Id.* at 348. The court did note the policy of promoting safe driving. *Id.* at 351. Here, Ms. Collins did more than read a map; she did talk, albeit not to another person. Particularly if the program could provide information in spoken words, the *Spriggs* listening facet would be met. The policy of promoting safe driving favors this outcome, given the collision that occurred as Ms. Collins was driving and using her cell phone in this manner. Thus, this element likely is met.
Exception: transition, rule	However, subsection (f) provides an exception when a person drives a motor vehicle "on private property." While section 23123 does not define "on private property," a different section of the Vehicle Code defines "private road or driveway" as "a way or place in private ownership and used for vehicular travel by the owner and those having express or implied permission from the owner but not by other members of the public." *Id.* § 490. Although the terms are not exactly the same, this definition can be used by analogy, as it appears within the same portion of the code.
Application, conclusion	Presumably, the mini-mall's lot is privately owned, and the patrons have implied permission to come onto it. The more challenging question is whether Ms. Collins was *on* private property if her car was partly in the lot and partly in the street. The state would argue that some part—enough—was in the street to cause a problem due to her distracted driving. Ms. Collins could argue that the better approach is to determine where most of the car was, which would involve more fact investigation. Given the statutory policy of ensuring safety, the first view is more sound, and the exception would not apply here.
Overall conclusion	In conclusion, although there is some possible debate as to the interpretation of "using" and the private-property exception, on balance, Ms. Collins's conduct likely did amount to an infraction under California Vehicle Code section 23123.

2. Rule

Your legal reasoning appears in the rule and application components; thus, the *rule* is one of the two major elements. The rule precedes the application because, as discussed in Chapter 6, the legal rule informs the legal analysis of a client's situation. Without the rule, readers would not know what to make of the facts discussed in the application component. The length and content of the rule component vary.

- At a minimum, the rule component consists of the rule of law, as when the rule derives from a statute or rule of procedure.
- If your rule is derived from a single case, you will present the court's statement of the rule from the case, along with a summary of the facts and holding if the facts are similar enough to merit a comparison to your client's situation.
- If your rule is derived from a set of cases, you will state the rule fused from those cases and refer to the set of cases. You also may present the pattern of the holdings, summarize the case that most closely resembles your client's situation, or briefly present two cases with different facts and outcomes.
- If your rule is derived from a statute or rule supplemented by case law or other materials, you will first quote the statute or rule and then present the supplementary material.
- Whether your rule is from a statute or case law, if readers would benefit from knowledge of the rule's underlying policy at this point, you could state that policy as well.

In some situations, the rule may not be clear. For example, a statute could be read two ways, or an issue may not have been addressed by the court. In these situations, the rule component has two versions. State that the rule is not settled; then present what you believe to be the better supported version, followed by the other version.

Each legal proposition that you present must be supported by a citation to one or more authorities. Citation is covered in Appendix III.

As an example, in the sample IRAC in Box 7.1, the first paragraph presents the statute. The statute serves as the umbrella rule for most of the IRAC, in that it provides some of the elements and the consequence. The IRAC on the easy elements uses that statutory quotation for its rule. The IRAC discussing the major element ("using" the cell phone) is the most complicated, re-presenting the key statutory language and then a case, including its holding, facts, and reasoning in compact form. The discussion of the "on private property" exception introduces new statutory language.

3. Application

The *application*, the other major component, presents your reasoning about the client's facts in light of the law. Your goal is not simply to restate the facts but rather to show whether the various elements of the rule are met or not.

As discussed in Chapter 2, nearly all rules have more than one element. A complete IRAC must cover all of the required elements. One option is to proceed through the elements in the order that they appear in the rule. Another option is first to cover the easily discussed elements, i.e., the ones that are clearly met. Unless a necessary element is unequivocally not met, you must discuss all the elements.

The application of an element closely reflects the type of reasoning that you are presenting:

- Sometimes the reasoning process involves only deductive reasoning. Connect the relevant facts of your client's situation to the element, and tell the reader whether the element is met or not.
- As you reason by example, identify the similarity or difference between the facts of the decided case and the client's situation, and then tell the reader the significance of the comparison, i.e., analogy or distinction.
- If you have several cases to work with, present reasoning by inductive generalization. To strengthen your analysis if the outcome is less than clear, show that your client's situation is analogous to one case and distinguishable from another.
- As you deal with policy, spell out for readers how the various possible outcomes would or would not serve the policy you have identified.

Deductive reasoning usually comes first, followed by reasoning by example. Policy analysis is located after the material it pertains to, e.g., after a rule that could be read various ways.

If the application of the law to the facts could yield more than one outcome, you must consider the different possibilities. The traditional way of framing competing points is as the *arguments and counter-arguments* that the parties in the situation would make. The more conventional approach is to lead with the better argument (whether it favors the client or not), follow it with the weaker one, and then explain why you favor the first. Often, policy forms the basis for the choice among competing arguments and thus is discussed near the end.

Although the application relies to a great extent on the development of the law in the rule component, the application may refer to and cite legal authorities to expand upon the opening statement of the rule.

As an example, the IRAC in Box 7.1 displays deductive reasoning in the various application paragraphs. Brief reasoning by example appears in the discussion of "using," as does policy analysis. The discussion of the private-property exception includes argument and counter-argument.

4. Conclusion

The IRAC discussion closes with a statement of your *conclusion*—that is, whether the elements of the rule are met or not. The conclusion is important in legal writing because the point of legal analysis is to predict the probable legal meaning of the client's situation. The conclusion in an IRAC discussion, however, does not address the actions that the client should take; that topic appears elsewhere in the document.

As an example, the IRAC in Box 7.1 has a single-sentence conclusion that both notes the possibility of debate on two points and states the ultimate conclusion that a violation of the statute has occurred.

C. WRITING IRACs

The length and design of an IRAC vary depending on the complexity of the analysis. If a simple rule applies to the client's situation in a quite obvious way, IRAC may run only one paragraph, with the first sentence stating the introduction, several sentences stating the rule and its application, and the final sentence stating the conclusion. An alternative is to write two paragraphs, with the paragraph break occurring between the rule and the application.

On the other hand, IRAC likely will run pages when the rule is more complex. Several elements of a rule may each merit extended discussion. Then an *IRAC series* is needed. As shown in Box 7.2, a roadmap introduces the topic and rule, and each element receives its own IRAC. Each element IRAC ends with a *mini-conclusion*; the summary states the *overall conclusion,* explaining whether all elements are met. In this situation, transitions are important to keep the reader on track.

Another situation calling for a number of paragraphs is when a particular element requires significant discussion. This occurs when, for example, a statute and case law are involved, an extended comparison to a decided case or lengthy policy analysis would be instructive, or there are good arguments on both sides of the application. In these situations, IRAC takes the form of an *IRAC paragraph bloc.* As shown in Box 7.3, the key to a successful bloc is to break at appropriate spots and to include transitions, such as "Our client's situation is similar to the *Johnson* case."

BOX 7.2

IRAC SERIES

Roadmap

Introduction + rule + mini-application + mini-conclusion for element #1
Introduction (with transition) + rule + application + mini-conclusion for element #2
Introduction (with transition) + rule + application + mini-conclusion for element #3
Summary, with overall conclusion

BOX 7.3

IRAC PARAGRAPH BLOC

Para. 1: Introduction (issue) and rule from the statute
Para. 2: Rule/major case interpreting the statute
Para. 3: Application/parallel between the case and the client situation
Para. 4: Application/contrast between the case and the client situation
Para. 5: Application/policy analysis
Para. 6: Conclusion

As examples, the IRAC in Box 7.1 is an IRAC series with three IRACs: one IRAC for the first set of elements, one for the "using" element, and one for the "on private property" exception. The discussion of the exception is a two-paragraph IRAC bloc, with the break occurring between the rule and the application.

D. REVIEW

IRAC is the building block of legal writing. In following the IRAC template, you present your legal analysis in a way that reflects legal reasoning and, thus, your readers' expectations. IRAC is structured but not rigid:

- The introduction may be a topic, issue, conclusion, or transition.
- The rule may involve statutes, cases, other authorities, or indeed a combination.
- The application always involves deductive reasoning and may involve reasoning by example and policy analysis.
- The conclusion presents your view of the legal meaning of the client's situation.

As you complete an IRAC, check whether it meets the criteria for all legal writing:

- Completeness—Have you included the pertinent law and the relevant facts? Have you discussed both sides of a debatable element?
- Correctness—Have you stated both the law and the facts accurately?
- Coherence—If your topic involves more than one legal authority, do they fit together? Does the application clearly connect the rule and the facts? Does the conclusion follow from the application?
- Comprehensibility—Will your reader be able to understand your IRAC in one careful reading?

Exhibit 7 is an IRAC on the Bower's Bounty situation, which is longer and more complex that the Cassie Collins IRAC. It is followed by questions to assist you in labeling it. To reinforce your understanding of IRAC, please read through Exhibit 7, and consider those questions now.

EXHIBIT 7 **MORE COMPLEX IRAC**

INTRODUCTION

This IRAC relies on the following facts asserted by the employee, Sarah Nicholson, in her claim against Bower's Bounty:

- She supervised the fresh produce department and was supervised by new store manager Dan Molinaro.
- As approved by the previous store manager, Ms. Nicholson donated outdated produce to a nearby food shelf; a friend of hers picked it up in his truck.
- Sam Olson, an employee she supervised and disciplined, told Mr. Molinaro that she was stealing produce.
- Based on this report, but without talking to Ms. Nicholson, Mr. Molinaro terminated her employment.
- He also posted a notice on the bulletin board in the employee lounge. It stated: "Due to pilferage on her part in violation of company policy, Sarah Nicholson is no longer with Bower's Bounty. We do take these rules seriously!"
- A number of co-workers read and believed this statement.

To keep this IRAC simple for the purposes of demonstrating IRAC structure, this IRAC works with just one case. If you were analyzing this situation in actual practice, you would incorporate more recent cases, and the analysis would be more complex.

QUESTIONS TO CONSIDER AS YOU READ THIS IRAC

1. How many IRACs are there?
2. What types of introductions does the IRAC use?
3. How many legal rules are stated, and where are they?
4. Where does deductive reasoning appear?
5. Does reasoning by example appear at any point?
6. What about policy analysis?
7. If there is a debatable issue, how does the IRAC handle it?
8. Do you see an IRAC series or IRAC paragraph blocs in this sample?

IRAC

Is an employer liable for defamation when a manager posts a false statement in the employee lounge that the employee was terminated for committing pilferage and the employee's co-workers read and believed that statement? This topic has three main issues: publication of a defamatory statement, scope of employment, and qualified privilege.

First, the elements of defamation are false and defamatory words, communication to a third party, and resulting harm to the reputation of the person defamed. *Luttrell v. United Tele. Sys., Inc.*, 683 P.2d 1292, 1293 (Kan. Ct. App. 1984), *aff'd*, 659 P.2d 1270 (Kan. 1985). For purposes of this analysis, we accept the assertions of the employee that she

Exhibit 7   145

EXHIBIT 7 (cont.)

donated the discarded food with permission to a food shelf, so that the charge of pilferage was indeed false. A charge of theft would be defamatory and harm the reputation of a grocery store manager, and her co-workers read and believed the statement. Thus, the first and third elements are met.

As for communication to a third party, *Luttrell* holds that communication between corporate co-workers counts as publication. *Id.* at 1294. There, supervisors discussed an employee's workplace conduct among themselves. The employer argued that the discussion amounted to the corporation talking to itself. The court disagreed and ruled that the conversations constituted communication to a third party. *Id.* Here, too, the manager communicated with employees about the employee's workplace conduct. Unlike *Luttrell*, the recipients of the message were not other supervisors but rather a group of lower-level employees, and the message was written, not oral. These contrasts favor the employee. Thus, communication under *Luttrell* occurred. Accordingly, all elements of the claim of defamation are present.

Second, if defamation is established, the issue of holding the employer liable arises. The defamatory utterances must have been made while the speaker was acting within the scope of employment for the employer to be held liable. *Id.* at 1293. In *Luttrell*, the discussion involved an employee's performance and discipline by supervisors. The same is true here; the manager was responsible for enforcing company policy as well as the evaluation and discipline of the employee. Thus, he acted within his scope of employment.

Third, if defamation has occurred within the speaker's scope of employment, the employer may raise the defense of qualified privilege. "A communication is qualifiedly privileged if it is made in good faith on any subject matter in which the person communicating has an interest, or in reference to which he has a duty, if it is made to a person having a corresponding interest or duty." *Id.* at 1294. Once a privilege is established, the plaintiff may overcome it by showing that "the defendants acted with knowledge of falsity or reckless disregard for the truth." *Id.*

The application of these rules to the client's situation yields a close call. On the one hand, the manager had a duty to evaluate store employees as well as a duty to enforce store policies. Informing employees why the employee was terminated had the dual benefits of deflecting speculation and reinforcing the anti-pilferage rule. On the other hand, informing employees exactly why a specific employee was terminated is unusual, and there are other ways to reinforce workplace rules. The employee also can argue that the manager acted recklessly in determining that pilferage had occurred; relying on the statement of one co-worker whom she had disciplined was reckless. Consulting with Ms. Nicholson, or with other company officials, before terminating her would have yielded a more complete view of the situation.

The policy underlying this area of law proves useful at this point. The qualified privilege exists to protect the employer "who is evaluating or investigating an employee in good faith" from the threat of a defamation suit. *Id.* This policy would protect earlier

EXHIBIT 7   (cont.)

statements in the disciplinary process but should not protect the statement to co-workers. On balance, Bower's Bounty may not be protected by the qualified privilege.

In summary, the elements of defamation are present, and the manager was acting within the scope of employment. Bower's Bounty can claim a qualified privilege, but it may well be defeated by the employee.

TEST YOUR UNDERSTANDING

1. What does IRAC stand for, and how does it parallel the TEC template?

2. Assume that you have been assigned to work on the Daniel de la Cruz situation. He was suspended from public middle school for certain statements he made. You are ready to write your analysis of the situation. As for the I component:
   a. What are your four options?
   b. If the IRAC is going to be long and complex, which would you likely choose?

3. Assume that you found the following authorities pertinent to the Daniel de la Cruz situation: a statute, a case interpreting the statute, and a legal periodical article discussing the purpose of the statute. As for the R component:
   a. Which of these would you present during the R component?
   b. How would you present them, e.g., in what order?

4. As for the A component:
   a. As a general matter, how many of the elements of the rule do you need to cover, and how do you determine the sequence in which to cover them?
   b. Given the authorities stated in question 3, what types of legal reasoning would you likely include?
   c. If you see one element as highly debatable, what is a traditional way of presenting the discussion of that element?

5. What does the C component include, and what does it *not* include?

6. What is the difference between an IRAC series and an IRAC paragraph bloc?

TEST YOUR UNDERSTANDING ANSWERS

1. IRAC stands for introduction + rule + application + conclusion. Introduction parallels topic, rule and application parallel explanation, and conclusion parallels conclusion.

2. As for the I component:
   a. Four options for the I component are topic, issue, conclusion, and transition.
   b. Good choices for a long and complex IRAC are issue and conclusion.

3. For the R component:
   a. The statute and case definitely would be presented in the rule, and the article could be included.
   b. The statute would lead off, and the others would follow. Statutory language should be quoted. If there is only one case, it should be summarized. Important points from commentary are presented briefly.

4. As for the A component:
   a. You should almost always cover all elements of the rule. The order depends on how they apply to the facts. Possibilities include the order that they appear in the rule and the easiest to the most difficult to analyze.
   b. The likely forms of legal reasoning are deductive reasoning, reasoning by example, and policy analysis.
   c. The traditional approach is to present one party's argument, state the other party's counter-argument, and then identify the better view.

5. The C component states the conclusion about how the law applies to the client's situation, but it does not make recommendations.

6. An IRAC series encompasses several IRACs on the various elements of a rule. An IRAC paragraph bloc is a series of paragraphs, all constituting one IRAC.

THE ANALYTICAL OFFICE MEMO

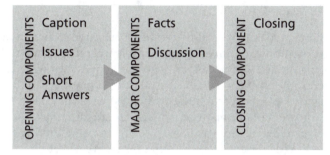

You may write for the joy of it, but the act of writing is not complete in itself. It has its end in its audience.
　　　—Flannery O'Connor
　　　　　The Habit of Being (Sally Fitzgerald ed., 1979)

A. INTRODUCTION

1. Audience and Purpose

Memos are written in law offices for various purposes. Some simply record conversations with the client or opposing counsel, information recently obtained from other sources, or ideas generated in discussions among lawyers working on the matter. The *analytical office memo* discussed in this chapter plays a particularly significant role. It records the facts of the client's situation as currently known; documents the research conducted on the matter, along with citations to the sources; presents the writer's reading of the pertinent legal authorities and legal analysis of the client's situation; and sets out the predicted outcome and recommendations for appropriate action. It precedes various other documents written on behalf of the client and various important conversations, such as client counseling and negotiations. Indeed, it is the basis of these diverse communications.

So how does a lawyer write an effective analytical office memo? In addition to carefully and fully performing background work (factual and legal research, reading the law, legal reasoning, etc.), the lawyer should keep in mind the seven principles of effective communication set out in Box 8.1.

BOX 8.1

PRINCIPLES OF EFFECTIVE COMMUNICATION

Take the reader's characteristics into account.
Convey the truth as you see it.
Give neither too much nor too little information.
Keep to relevant points.
Produce a paper that is appropriate to the context and circumstances.
Produce a message that is appropriate to your purpose.
Try to be understood; write coherently and comprehensibly.[1]

In law, these seven principles distill first to a focus on the paper's audience and purpose. The most obvious *audience* for the analytical office memo is the named recipient—typically the senior lawyer, who has requested the memo from a junior lawyer. Other lawyers working on the case in question also may read it. The writer also is a member of the audience because he or she is likely to return to the memo as the work on the matter continues. Some matters take months, some years to resolve, and a memo may be reviewed many times during that period. Furthermore, lawyers in the office working on different matters involving the same legal topics may read the memo as well.

The *purpose* of the analytical office memo is to state the writer's best analysis of the client's situation. The memo serves as the basis of advice to the client, which in turn leads to steps taken on the client's behalf, such as the structuring of a transaction, discussions to settle the dispute, or arguments made to courts or other tribunals.

To accomplish this purpose, a lawyer, even though acting on behalf of the client, must write with *objectivity*. A lawyer must assess both the strengths and weaknesses of the client's legal position in accord with the lawyer's role as an officer of the legal system. The requirement of objectivity also stems from considerations of practicality and trust. A lawyer best serves a client contemplating a legally risky transaction by telling the client the risks and how to avoid them, rather than permitting the transaction to go forward and hoping that liability will not follow. For a client in a difficult position in litigation, a lawyer's most valuable service is to alert the client to the problems and to help the client obtain a realistic outcome, rather than to pursue a losing position until the case is lost at great expense.

Focusing on these audiences and this purpose means that the office memo is a form of *reader-centered writing*. It may then seem that your voice, as a writer, is muffled. Admittedly, your aim in legal writing is not primarily self-expression, and your personal preferences may differ from the language and conventions of legal writing. Nonetheless, it is your analysis that is presented within the conventional form. Your analysis reflects your creative way of thinking about

---

1. *See generally* C. Douglas McCann & E. Tory Higgins, Personal and Contextual Factors in Communication: A Review of the "Communication Game," in *Language, Interaction, and Social Cognition* 144 (Gun R. Semin & Klaus Fiedler eds., 1992).

problems and your choice of phrasing. No two lawyers, writing about the same client's situation, would generate the same memo.

Many lawyers have been trained never to use the first person ("I think . . .") in legal writing. A typical explanation is that the reader does not care what you think but is concerned only with what the law is; without the first person, your analysis will seem more objective and hence more credible. A better explanation is that the reader does in fact care what you think, but the reader also realizes full well, without a reminder, that your memo reflects your thinking. In choosing whether to use the first person, consider the preferences of your specific reader on this topic. In any event, your memo will bear your name because most memo formats include the writer's name.

2. Overview of the Analytical Office Memo

To a significant extent, to write effectively to the readers of the analytical office memo and to accomplish its purposes are accomplished by writing within the conventional format of the memo. Legal writing conventions closely reflect the ways that lawyers approach and solve problems. IRAC (discussed in Chapter 7) is the major convention; this chapter introduces more of them. If you follow the profession's conventions, other lawyers will proceed quickly through your memos and they will view your work as credible. As you learn these conventions, think about how they respond to these concerns:

- What will the reader already know? What does the reader still need to know?
- How can the information be presented so as to maximize understanding?
- How will the reader best grasp the big picture and still see the nuances?

There is no single format for the analytical office memo on which lawyers everywhere agree. On the other hand, several components are common to almost every format. The components are preceded by prominent labels set out by white space. These common components are, in brief:

Caption: A typical *caption* consists of the recipient's name, the writer's name, the date, and the subject. The date is important because every office memo is time-bound, reflecting only what the writer knew and thought about the client's situation and the law as of the date the memo was written. The subject of the memo usually consists of the client's name and file number, along with a brief description of the topic of the memo.

Issue(s): The issues orient the reader to the legal questions arising in the client's situation and to the organization of the memo. They appear in the same order as the main topics appear in the discussion.

Short answer(s): The short answers further orient the reader and provide the reader with the writer's position on the issues, permitting the reader to read the rest of the memo in light of the writer's position. They parallel the issues in number and sequence. Taken together, the issues and short answers constitute the executive summary of the memo.

Facts: The facts statement informs the reader about the client's situation. If the client has sought advice before taking action, the facts statement refers to present facts and future possibilities.

BOX 8.2

FACTS AND LAW IN OFFICE MEMOS

Components	Facts	Law
Issues	Brief	Brief
Short answers	Brief	Brief
Facts	Thorough	—
Discussion	Selected	Thorough
Closing	Selected	Selected

Discussion: The bulk of the office memo is the discussion, in which the writer systematically analyzes each issue and justifies each short answer for the reader. The discussion consists of one or more IRACs.

Closing: The closing both summarizes the preceding material for the reader and recommends actions to be taken for or by the client. The recommendations should flow from the legal analysis in the discussion and also may be based on nonlegal factors, which should be clearly stated.

It may seem that the office memo presents the same information over and over again. As Box 8.2 shows, this is in some sense true; the facts appear in every major component, the law in five out of six components. It is the way the facts and law are handled—the depth of treatment and manner of presentation—that varies from component to component.

In some ways, office memos parallel judicial opinions. See Box 8.3. A lawyer writing an office memo is, in essence, seeking to anticipate what a court would do when faced with the client's case. Indeed, one way to maintain objectivity is to imagine that you are the judge deciding your client's case.

Finally, some office memos contain appendices: key authorities, such as a key statute or new case, especially if the authority is not well known to the recipient of the memo; an important contract, map, or other document; or a timeline if there are many specific events and their precise timing is crucial.

As examples, this chapter draws on three sample analytical office memos. Exhibit 8A is a memo discussing the Bower's Bounty situation, in which the client is facing a claim of defamation by a recently terminated employee. This memo is discussed throughout the chapter; please read it now. Exhibit 8B contains a memo discussing All-Day Wellness's proposal to enter into covenants not-to-compete with its employees, and Exhibit 8C is a memo discussing Cassie Collins's ticket for driving while using a cell phone. These two memos pertain to later parts of the chapter.

COMPARISON OF JUDICIAL OPINION
TO ANALYTICAL OFFICE MEMO

Judicial Opinion	Office Memo
Case name, court, date, docket number	Caption (client's name, writer's name, date, file number)
Issues	Issues
Holdings	Short answers
Facts statement	Facts
Reasoning	Discussion
Concluding paragraph with procedural outcome	Closing

B. ISSUES AND SHORT ANSWERS

The analytical office memo typically opens with two closely linked sections: issues and short answers.

1. Issues

In general, questions attract and focus a reader's attention. Thus, the *issues* in an office memo focus the reader's attention on the legal topics and key facts addressed in the memo.[2] If there is more than one issue, as is typically the case, the issues also show the reader how the memo is organized, alerting the reader to the number and order of major topics and to the relationships among them.

The format of an issue is to present law and facts in question form. In most situations, the issue links a major legal concept to the most important relevant facts of the client's case. To maximize your reader's understanding, you generally should present the legal concept at one end of the issue and the factual material at the other rather than interweaving the two. You can lead with the law and proceed to the facts or vice versa:

- *Is [law] when [facts]?*
- *Do [facts] result in [law]?*

---

2. In some formats, this component is labeled "questions presented."

When fitting important material into one sentence proves too bulky, an option is an opening sentence followed by short questions. The opening sentence typically states the key facts of the client's situation, and the questions tie in the legal concepts. For example:

> An employee with X trait was terminated, allegedly for Y reasons, where the employee handbook provided Z.

(1) Is there a claim for breach of contract?
(2) Is there a claim of discrimination based on X?
(3) Is there a claim for wrongful termination based on Y conduct?

On occasion, your issue will be almost purely legal or factual. For example, when the rules of law are unsettled and your primary task is to determine what the rule is, with the application to your client's situation following as a matter of course, your issue will be primarily legal in content. On the other hand, when your task is to assess the facts under a straightforward rule, the issue will be primarily factual.

Many memos cover more than one topic. Generally, you should write an issue for each topic that you cover in the discussion. The issues should signal the relationships among the topics through transitional phrases or cross-references. For example, where one topic follows from another, the second issue could begin with "if so" or "as a result." In some situations, you may want to reflect sub-topics as well. The classic approach is to present an introductory segment or question referring to the main topic, followed by specific questions referring to the sub-topics.

In all these situations, your goal is to state the topics of the discussion clearly and in the form of questions that are informative and fully readable the first time through. Chart a middle course between generality and specificity. Present only the most important legal concepts and facts, not every detail. Refer to the concepts in the pertinent rule, rather than such general terms as "liability" or "illegality" or only citations. Refer to roles under the rule rather than such abstract references as "person" or proper names (except perhaps for the client).

Furthermore, because the analytical office memo should be objective, the issue should be phrased objectively. Avoid slanted language that plays on the reader's emotions; rather use language that a neutral observer, such as a court, would use. Present the most important facts and legal concepts, whether they are favorable or unfavorable to your client.

Most lawyers present each issue in its own paragraph and number them. Finally, although some writers introduce an issue with "whether," this construction is undesirable because the items are not complete sentences.

As an example, in Exhibit 8A, the memo about the Bower's Bounty situation on the defamation topic, the first issue begins with the facts and moves to the first legal topic (the claim). The second and third issues use a transitional phrase for brevity ("under these circumstances"), then raise the second and third legal issues (employer liability and the defense of privilege).

2. Short Answers

In most memo formats, the issues are followed by *short answers*.[3] Short answers continue to orient the reader to the memo; they also tell the reader the legal meaning that you would ascribe to the client's situation. Knowing your answers to the issues at the outset permits the reader to examine along the way how well the analysis supports the answers.

Short answers are very similar to issues, but they contain more content and take the form of statements such as the following ones:

- *[Law]* + *[facts] because [a reason]*.
- *[Facts]* + *[law] because [a reason]*.

Short answers are more extensive than issues because they include brief statements of your reasoning. Take care not to synopsize all the steps of your reasoning, or the answer will no longer be short. Rather, you should state, in simple and concise terms, the main reason for each answer. Ordinarily, you will not include citations to your authorities in your short answers.

Not surprisingly, many of the principles of writing issues apply as well to the writing of short answers. There should be an answer for every issue. Short answers should read well the first time through and be phrased objectively. You should use transitional phrases, cross-references, and formatting to convey the relationships among the answers.

A particular challenge in writing short answers is to convey the degree of certainty of your answer. Sometimes you will be certain how the law applies to your client's situation, but other times you will be quite unsure. The way that many lawyers think about framing short answers is to imagine a court deciding a case involving the client's situation, even if litigation is not likely. Whatever your uncertainty, you should state your best prediction as to the outcome. You may phrase your short answer to reflect your uncertainty, possibly by using a hedging phrase, such as "probably." Indeed, some lawyers include probabilities in their predictions, e.g., there is a seventy-five percent chance that a court will rule in favor of the client. (Your instincts for predicting legal outcomes will develop along with your expertise in a particular area of law.)

As an example, in Exhibit 8A, the first and second answers are short and certain because the law and facts are straightforward. The third answer is long and less certain because there are two sub-topics and the application of the law to the facts is debatable.

C. FACTS STATEMENT

1. Introduction

The statement of *facts* is precisely what the name suggests: a recounting of the important facts of the client's situation. The facts statement does not duplicate the coverage of the facts in the other components of the memo, where they are

---

3. In some memo formats, this component is labeled "brief answers."

interspersed among legal rules and elements. Here the client's situation is presented as a story, not merely as bits of factual material tied to legal rules.

Some readers of an analytical office memo may not be familiar with the client's situation, so they will learn of it through the facts. Some may have already worked on the matter; for them, the facts statement serves as a coherent story. For the writer of the memo, writing the facts statement requires you to revisit and work through the facts carefully. It is easy to lose track of the facts as you research the law, read it, and reason about the client's situation. Indeed, the importance of a particular fact may become clear for the first time during the writing of the facts statement.

In addition, the facts statement serves as a record of the facts as of the date the memo is written. Often you will learn facts gradually, over days, weeks, or even months. You must take stock periodically to determine which facts are fully known, which facts are not known, and which are disputed. The legal analysis in the memo is tied to the facts known when the memo was written. When new facts come to light, not only the facts statement, but also portions of the analysis, may need revision.

How does a lawyer assemble the facts, decide which to include and exclude, and present them in a coherent, objective narrative?

2. Assembling the Facts

Facts rarely come in a single, tidy statement. Rather, you gather facts by talking to your client and other participants, reading documents, examining other items, perhaps visiting the location of the events, and so on. Then you must *assemble the facts* from these sources of information.

Of course, the first step is to review and take notes on each source so that you have a very good idea of the information that it provides. As you work through the sources one by one, start a list of topics and sub-topics. These topics may be relationships, communications, events, locations, and so on. Once you know the territory covered in your sources, you should have an idea of the big picture. To systematically capture and organize what you are learning, you may want to develop codes for each topic and annotate your notes or the sources with the codes.

As a next step, you may develop a matrix chart, as shown in Box 8.4. The boxes contain the information from each source or references to pages within a source.

Another classic way to organize factual information is the timeline, as shown in Box 8.5. The line itself contains key dates; the material above and below the line consists of date-specific information. You can use the timeline as a dividing line by recording information from one source above the line and information from another below the line, or you can record information about one of two simultaneous events above the line and information about the other below the line.

As you assemble your facts, you may well discover not only overlap, but also *discrepancies* in information from various sources. Experienced lawyers expect this discrepancy. Participants or observers of an event often differ in their recollections of what they have experienced or perceived. They vary in their abilities to perceive, understand, and recall situations, as well as their perspectives and interests. Over time, memories of an event change. Your task is to reconcile these

BOX 8.4

FACT MATRIX CHART

	Participant X	Participant Y	Document A	Document B
Description of Location				
Background of X-Y Relationship				
Event #1				
Event #2				
etc.				

BOX 8.5

TIMELINES

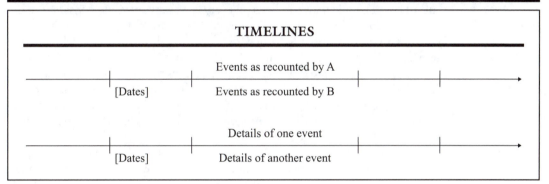

discrepancies, as best you can, to permit you to analyze the situation. You can do this as follows:

- You may discern a core area of agreement and leave the details in dispute, so long as the details are not crucial.
- If the discrepancy is minor, you may be able to cover both versions with a somewhat broadly phrased fact, such as a numerical range rather than a precise number.
- If one source has greater credibility, a clearer perspective, or less self-interest than the other, you could choose the version provided by that source and state the reason for your selection.
- If these methods fail, you may need to state both versions and their sources—in which case, as discussed later in this chapter, the discussion may come to a branchpoint and proceed along two paths.

Assembling the facts is an early step in the writing process. Indeed, for many writers, it precedes legal analysis, if not legal research. Once you have progressed into your research and analysis, you may find that you need to return to your sources of information to confirm some facts or to seek additional information as you learn of new points that are legally important.

As an example, the facts statement in Exhibit 8A draws on four sources: the letter received from the employee, the employee handbook, the employee's personnel file, and the vice-president of operations. At this point, when the claim is being assessed for its legal validity, the facts as presented in the letter are being taken as true. Should the claim proceed, additional investigation would occur.

3. Sorting the Facts

Once you have assembled the information from the various sources, you need to choose which facts to include in the fact statement by *sorting the facts*. Facts fall into three categories: legally relevant facts, background facts, and residual facts. You should include the first and second, but not the third.

Legally relevant facts pertain directly to the elements in the legal rules; they are used in your deductive reasoning, reasoning by example, or policy analysis. As a court, legislature, or other lawmaker creates law, it sets the factual focus of the rule of law. The rule may not focus on every fact that you would consider important, but you are bound by the lawmaker's selection of which facts to focus on (although you may argue for a new or revised legal rule in a compelling situation). All facts appearing in your discussion should appear in the fact statement.

Background facts are facts that the reader needs to know to make sense of the client's situation, even though they do not pertain directly to the elements of the rule. To identify the background facts, ask: what does the reader need to know to fit the relevant facts into a coherent narrative? Focus on what the reader needs to know, not on what might be interesting to know.

Residual facts are neither legally relevant nor background. You should exclude these facts because they clutter the narrative and distract the reader. Some residual facts are emotionally charged, causing one to feel sympathy or distaste for your client or some other participant. You should take particular care to exclude these residual facts, which may cloud the reader's ability to assess the client's situation objectively.

Of course, you will be quite aware that some facts are particularly *favorable* or *unfavorable* to your client. This distinction is not an appropriate basis on which to include or exclude facts. Both favorable and unfavorable facts belong in the fact statement, just as they do in the discussion, if they are legally relevant or needed for background.

Although you likely will assemble your facts early on, sorting of the facts must occur later. You should not sort your facts until you have analyzed the situation in light of the law, because only at that point will you appreciate the legal significance of the various facts.

As an example, the legally relevant facts for the Bower's Bounty situation include whether Ms. Nicholson took produce, what the posting said, and how the manager investigated before making the statement. Ms. Nicholson's employment relationship with Bower's Bounty is a background fact. As is required, the facts statement in Exhibit 8A includes unfavorable facts, such as the cursory nature of the manager's investigation.

4. Presenting the Facts

Proper *presentation* of the facts depends first on how you structure the facts statement and then on how you state each fact.

The *structure* of your facts statement should contribute greatly to making the story coherent. The classic organization entails an introductory paragraph, several paragraphs or pages of development, and a wrap-up paragraph as needed.

The *introductory paragraph* sets the stage and orients the reader. It should identify the client and other important people or entities and briefly summarize the client's situation.

The *body* of the fact statement should be a well-organized telling of the client's story. The most common organizational scheme is *chronological*, in which the fact statement begins with the first important event and moves forward in time to the most recent. Also very common is *topical* organization, in which each paragraph or paragraph block covers a facet of the situation, such as relationships among people or features of transactions. Least common is *perceptual* organization, in which an event is presented first from one person's perspective, then from another's. A mixed organization may work well; for example, several topical paragraphs may be used to set the scene for a series of chronologically ordered paragraphs.

The final, *wrap-up paragraph* typically draws a link between the facts and the upcoming discussion of their legal meaning. This paragraph should describe the client's current legal situation, e.g., the stage of litigation, the reason the client is seeking legal advice. The last paragraph may also note the client's nonlegal concerns.

Whatever sequence you select, first and foremost, you must take care in *stating* the facts. Above all else, state the facts *accurately*. Checking what you have written against the sources themselves is very advisable.

Similarly, you must state the facts *objectively*. Indeed, the harder you work on writing an objective fact statement, the more likely it is that other components will be objective as well. Following these standard practices will help you meet this key criterion:

- Refer to the individuals in the situation in a respectful way; use their names or the roles that they play in the situation.
- Use verbs with straightforward meanings. Avoid adverbs and adjectives.
- Avoid words that have legal connotations, such as "negligently."
- Use a detail from the story in lieu of words that carry some judgment on your part, e.g., numbers rather than "large" or "small," "fast" or "slow."

Tell the story *completely*. As the narrator, you have the advantage of an omniscient third-person point of view; you know whatever there is to be known. Show how one event led to another, why a participant selected the course of conduct that he or she engaged in, and how an event affected each participant. In other words, link the events to each other and the participants to each other. At the same time, decide how much detail the reader needs on each topic, and condense the facts to provide only needed details. Consider attaching material that otherwise would require a lengthy explanation, such as a contract or map.

Even so, a facts statement is not meant to have the flair or drama of a prize-winning short story. Some of the tools that a short-story writer would use are inappropriate to memo writing, such as first-person point of view, shifts in time, symbolism, and ambiguity. Nonetheless, your fact statement need not be clinical or wooden either; you are, after all, telling an important story.

At various points, provide *attributions* to your sources. Although you need not provide formal citations, you should inform the reader whose statement or which document yielded your information, for instance, "according to Ms. Smith," or "as indicated in the contract."

As an example, in Exhibit 8A, the first paragraph serves as an introduction. The second and third paragraphs each cover a necessary background topic, and the following paragraphs set out the relevant facts in essentially chronological order. The final paragraph sets out the client's concerns and goals. All sentences are objective in phrasing, and the links between events are made clear by transitions. The sources of the facts are noted.

D. DISCUSSION

1. Introduction

The core, as well as the bulk, of the analytical office memo is the discussion component. The *discussion* presents a thorough legal analysis of each issue, applying the law to the facts of the client's situation so as to justify each short answer.

The discussion is somewhat akin to an essay, an expository discussion of a topic. You should not write an encyclopedia, providing more detail than your reader really needs. Nor should you write an epitaph, a cursory statement without an explanation. Nor should you write an editorial that aims to persuade your reader of the wisdom of your personal point of view.

To accomplish its purpose, the discussion must be both effective and efficient, especially if it is lengthy and the analysis is complex. *Effectiveness* is a function of how well the reader understands the analysis, and *efficiency* is a function of how easily the reader processes the text. So how does a lawyer write an effective and efficient discussion? Effectiveness is accomplished through logical organization, and efficiency is accomplished through clarity of presentation.

2. Developing a Logical Organization

Analysis and organization are intertwined. Therefore, the *organization* should directly reflect the rule of law, or rules of law, pertinent to the client's situation.

Many office memos cover several issues. Thus, the discussion proceeds in parts, each covering a topic and containing one or more IRACs, as discussed in Chapter 7. You should order the parts of the discussion according to either the logic of the law or the factual logic of the client's situation. It is more common to follow legal logic, but factual logic may be used if there is no clear legal logic to follow.

One option for discerning the legal logic of your discussion is to examine the legal authorities that you have read, such as the leading case or a commentary

BOX 8.6

STANDARD LEGAL CONVENTIONS

- *Claim/defense/remedy:* Many memos start with the rules applicable to the plaintiff's claim, proceed to the rules governing the defendant's defense, and then discuss any rules pertaining to remedies.
- *Pivotal rule first:* A pivotal rule comes first because the conclusion from that discussion sets up the analysis of related rules.
- *Threshold rule first:* A threshold rule nearly always appears first because its application dictates whether analysis of the other rules is necessary, e.g., a rule of jurisdiction precedes rules about liability.
- *General to specific:* Generally, discussion of a broad rule precedes discussion of a narrower rule, such as an exception.
- *More to less important alternatives:* When conduct is covered by more than one rule, e.g., overlapping common law and statutory rules, begin with the rule that is more clearly applicable, better established, or more significant in consequence.
- *Procedural/substantive or substantive/procedural:* Procedural rules often appear together, and substantive rules often appear together.
- *Chronology:* Begin with the first rule to arise in time and follow the progression; for example, contract law parallels the unfolding of the transaction (formation, terms, performance, breach, remedies).
- *Actors:* The discussion focuses first on all rules pertaining to a particular actor, then proceeds to the rules pertaining to another actor, and so on.
- *Easy to difficult:* This approach is not based on logic but rather on helping the reader; the reader eases into the discussion with an easy topic before turning to more difficult material.

source. Of course, you should be sure that the borrowed organization is indeed logical and fits your client's situation.

Another option is to use one of the *standard legal conventions* set out in Box 8.6. Even in a simple memo, you may employ two or more of these conventions. For instance, you may proceed through procedural rules chronologically and then move to substantive rules by claim/defense/remedy.

Organizing a discussion is especially challenging in two legal settings. First, some complex discussions entail *overlapping legal rules*. For example, the same rule may apply to two different sets of parties involved in closely related transactions:

- One option is to discuss all claims involving one set of parties and then all claims involving the other set: A and B—claim 1, claim 2; then A and C—claim 1, claim 2.
- Another option is to discuss all instances of one claim and then all instances of the other claim: Claim 1—as between A and B, as between A and C; then Claim 2—as between A and B, as between A and C.
- A third option is a hybrid—for example, to discuss first the topics on which there is no difference across the parties and then the topics that are unique to each party.

All options involve some repetition, but that is inherent in the situation. Whatever organization you choose, use shortened discussions and cross-references in the later portions of the discussion to reduce repetition.

TYPES OF BRANCHPOINTS

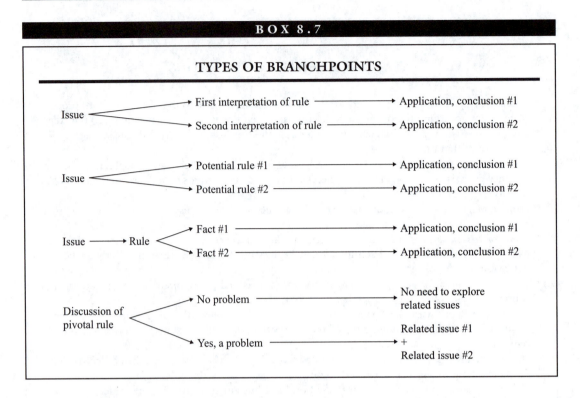

Second, some complex discussions entail *branchpoints.* Branchpoints occur when an analysis can proceed down one of two roads, each with its own analysis and implications. Branchpoints commonly occur in four situations, depicted in Box 8.7. First, an ambiguous rule requires you to apply more than one interpretation of the law. Second, the rule is unsettled in your jurisdiction, so you have to consider more than one rule. Third, unknown facts, disputed facts, or facts that have yet to occur because the client has sought advice before acting require you to apply the law to alternative versions of the facts. Fourth, rules interlock, so the debatable outcome of the pivotal rule requires progressing to analysis of the other rules.

Regardless of the type of branchpoint, you must not only proceed down the first road, but also loop back to proceed down the second. Otherwise, the analysis will not be complete. Generally, the most straightforward approach is to provide an initial roadmap, complete one path of the analysis, indicate that the discussion is about to loop back to an earlier point where the analyses diverge, pursue the second path, and conclude with a summary.

There are many ways to create a well-organized discussion. Some prefer to create the organization first and write within it. Others prefer a more organic approach, writing small pieces that they eventually assemble into an organized discussion. Either way can work, so long as you build on the IRAC template as you fill in your outline or write your small pieces.

Furthermore, there are various ways to depict your organization. The classic depiction is an outline. See Box 8.8. A quite different alternative is a flowchart in

BOX 8.8

SAMPLE OUTLINE

I. Defamation Claim

A. False and defamatory words; harm to reputation

- No pilferage; harm to reputation for honesty

B. Communication to third party—can be co-workers

- Posting in employee lounge

II. Employer Liability

Acting within scope of employment

- Manager engaging in disciplinary function

III. Qualified Privilege

A. Speaker and listener have corresponding interests

- Employment arena—but listeners are co-workers, and statement is post-discipline

B. Speaking with knowledge of falsity or reckless disregard for truth

- Reliance on only one co-worker; no discussion with Nicholson or others

which the rules occupy large boxes, the elements middle-sized boxes, and so on. See Box 8.9. The key point is to create some depiction of your discussion at some point. Doing so is an important way of ensuring that you have created a well-organized (and hence effective) discussion for your reader.

As an example, Boxes 8.8 and 8.9 both pertain to the discussion in Exhibit 8A about the Bower's Bounty situation. That memo covers three topics. The first is the claim of defamation, the second is Bower's Bounty's liability for that claim, and the third is Bower's Bounty's defense; these topics are covered in their most logical order. Furthermore, within the discussion of the claim of defamation, two easy topics are discussed before the more significant topic of publication.

3. Writing a Clear Discussion

Clarity in presentation ensures that a reader processes the discussion efficiently, at least to the extent that the content permits.

In part, clarity is accomplished by controlling the *amount of information* that you provide on each topic. Avoid overly long discussions of straightforward material and overly compact discussions of complex material. For your memo

BOX 8.9

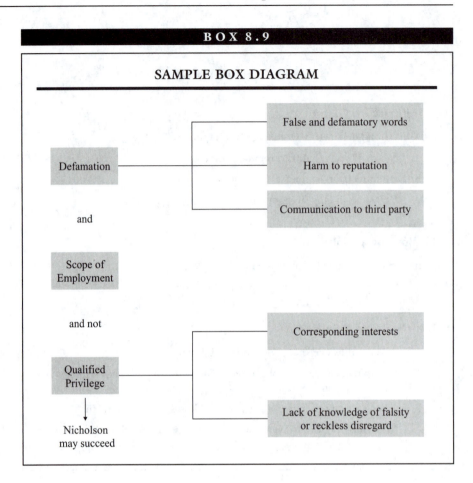

SAMPLE BOX DIAGRAM

to be efficient, each sentence must convey its fair share of the information to be communicated.

In addition, clarity is accomplished by using *signaling passages*, which help the reader both know in advance what is coming and track the organization as the discussion unfolds. Signaling passages include paragraphs, sentences, phrases, and even single words that appear throughout the discussion.

- Within the discussion, *headings* announce the topics and (in a long and complicated memo) sub-topics. Topic headings typically are words or phrases, not full sentences.
- A *roadmap* briefly states the points in the order they will appear in the following text. It may preview the entire discussion or the elements of a complex rule and run a paragraph or sentence.
- Similarly, a *summary* reviews the material just presented.
- Scattered throughout the discussion, *transitions* link segments, alerting the reader that one segment has finished and the next is starting. As shown in Box 8.10, a transition can be a mere word, a phrase, a sentence,

BOX 8.10

TRANSITIONAL WORDS AND PHRASES*

Introducing	Exemplifying	Adding or Amplifying
first	for example	again
initial	for instance	furthermore
to begin	to illustrate	moreover
the first reason	in particular	additionally
primarily	namely	similarly
in general		also
	Emphasizing	alternatively
Sequencing	indeed	a further reason
first, second, third	certainly	
finally	above all	*Connecting Logically*
initially	especially	thereby
next	not only . . . but also	therefore
then		thus
last	*Contrasting*	as a result
before	however	hence
	but	accordingly
Restating	on the other hand	consequently
that is	yet	because
in other words	unlike *x*	
more simply	in contrast	*Concluding*
in brief	nevertheless	to conclude
as noted	nonetheless	in summary
	rather	to review
	although	finally
	despite	as a result
		as we have seen

---

*Adapted from Lynn B. Squires et al., Legal Writing in a Nutshell 95-98 (2d ed. 1996).

or even a paragraph, depending on the complexity of the material and the size of the units being linked.

As you write your transitions, take care to select words that truly convey the connection between the segments that you are linking.

As an example, signaling passages appear throughout Exhibit 8A. A roadmap opens the discussion, and a summary closes it. The three main topics are introduced by "first," "second," and "third." Before the second and third topics are discussed, a transitional phrase ties the upcoming discussion to the preceding discussion. The discussion of the qualified privilege uses these phrases: "on the one hand," "on the other hand," and "on balance."

E. CLOSING

At the end of the analytical office memo comes the *closing*, which has two purposes.[4] The closing prompts the reader to make a final judgment about whether he or she accepts the writer's answers to the issues. In addition, the closing presents the writer's recommendations as to how the situation should be handled, so as to achieve the best possible results for the client.

The closing begins with a brief *restatement of the answers* to the issues. Unless the memo is quite long, you need not restate the reasoning, and it is rare to include citations. This restatement should be no more than a paragraph long and may run no more than a sentence.

The bulk of the closing should be devoted to a discussion of the client's *options*. For example, in a litigation context, the closing may discuss settling, employing an alternative to litigation such as mediation, or filing a lawsuit. The option that the client identified, if any, should be discussed. The probable outcome of each option should be noted.

As you write the closing, keep in mind *ABA Model Rule of Professional Conduct 2.1*: "In representing a client, a lawyer shall exercise independent professional judgment and render candid advice. In rendering advice, a lawyer may refer not only to law but to other considerations as well, such as moral, economic, social, and political factors, that may be relevant to the client's situation."

Note, first, that legal advice is to be "candid" and based on "independent professional judgment." The lawyer's job is to inform the client about how the law governs the client's case, not only when the law favors the client's plans, but especially when the law constrains the client. Lawyers must know how to say "no" effectively. Of course, to the extent possible, the lawyer should also provide the client with alternatives that avoid or minimize the legal problems.

---

4. In some formats, this component is labeled "summary," "conclusion," or "recommendations."

Note, second, that, although legal advice is grounded in the law, it also may incorporate nonlegal factors. Many cases call for consideration of other disciplines: engineering for patent law, finance for corporate law, psychology for criminal law, and so on. Lawyers do give advice mixing law and nonlegal factors, especially when the lawyer has training in another relevant discipline and the client has come to value the lawyer's counsel over time. The comments to the Model Rule also state that a lawyer should recommend that a client consult a professional in a different discipline if the situation calls for that expertise.

As an example, in Exhibit 8A, the closing first synthesizes the three legal conclusions into one legal position. The next paragraph explores the current dynamics of the client's situation and possible grounds for resolution. The final paragraph recommends two courses of action for this early stage in the matter.

F. THE TRANSACTIONAL MEMO

Many lawyers do not work to resolve disputes about past events; rather, they focus on creating desirable future legal positions for their clients through documents such as contracts, wills and trusts, and incorporation documents. These documents draw on the legal analysis presented in the *transactional analytical office memo*, which has some distinctive features.

The purpose of the transactional memo is to present a *legal evaluation of options* that the client could take, with a focus on the comparative benefits and drawbacks of each. In considering a specific option, the transactional lawyer does think somewhat like a litigator: if the client takes this option and it is challenged in court, what would be the outcome? A useful way of depicting the options available to a client is a *decision tree*. A decision tree charts the client's options, linking each to the most likely legal outcome and nonlegal outcomes. See Box 8.11.

The various components of the transactional office memo reflect this focus. The issues and short answers generally are framed in terms of options, rather than past facts, or in terms of options combined with legal concerns.

When you write the facts statement for a transactional memo, you write both about fixed past or present facts and about future possibilities. The *fixed facts* are the client and its situation, the other participants to the possible deal, and the context in which they all operate. Writing about these facts is very similar to writing about the facts in a dispute-oriented memo. This information generally appears in the beginning of the facts statement.

A transactional memo's facts statement also covers *future possibilities*. One challenge is selecting which possibilities to cover. You should cover at least the specific proposal that the client has framed. Whether to cover more depends on whether the client's proposal is permissible and how clearly worth considering the other options are. Cover each option in as much detail as the reader needs to understand the proposal, and follow the analysis presented in the discussion.

As for presentation, a facts statement in a transactional memo generally follows a topical organization, with the fixed facts stated first and the client's proposal following. To distinguish what is fixed and what may or may not come to

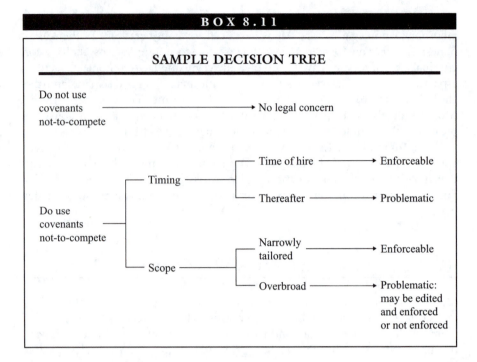

BOX 8.11

SAMPLE DECISION TREE

[Decision tree:]

Do not use covenants not-to-compete ——————→ No legal concern

Do use covenants not-to-compete
— Timing
— Time of hire ——————→ Enforceable
— Thereafter ——————→ Problematic
— Scope
— Narrowly tailored ——————→ Enforceable
— Overbroad ——————→ Problematic: may be edited and enforced or not enforced

be, use the subjunctive mood ("client would do . . .") in your discussion of options. The final paragraph should focus on what has prompted the client to seek counsel. If you have specific information about the client's goals, stating them in the last paragraph can be an excellent transition to the discussion.

The discussion in a transactional memo may be organized around legal concerns, paralleling the litigator's issue-oriented approach, or it may be *organized around options*. Another approach is to blend these two. For example, if an employer is concerned about protecting inventions on which its employees have worked, it may use several different options: a non-disclosure agreement, a covenant not-to-compete, or trade secret protection. The main parts of the discussion would be these two options, and the legal issues that each raises would be discussed within these main parts.

The difference in context between disputes and transactions is especially pronounced in the closing component. In a transactional context, the client's situation is less fixed, so the closing should be especially wide-ranging. Good legal advice entails creative and expansive thinking, similar to that used in other forms of problem-solving. Although you should start with the client's proposal, you should generate *alternative possibilities* that have the potential of serving the client's interests. Once you have generated a list of possibilities, you should assess each and select those that best serve the interests of the client and conform to the law.

As an example, Exhibit 8B discusses the All-Day Wellness situation, in which the client is considering the use of a covenant not-to-compete to protect its competitive position in its employment market. The questions preceding it should help you analyze this transactional memo according to the points stated here.

G. THE SHORT-FORM MEMO

Some situations do not call for an analytical office memo, with all of the components described in this chapter. The law and facts may be straightforward. The facts may be little developed so that what is needed is a basic summary of the law. Timing or resource constraints may call for a brief memo, to be followed by a more extensive memo when circumstances permit. In these situations, you may write a *short-form memo*.

Some attribute the development of the short-form memo to recent changes in the practice of law. Because research and communications[5] technology have reduced the time needed for those phases of the process, clients may expect results more quickly. Furthermore, clients have become more sensitive to the costs of legal counsel, so some seek a less elaborate and less expensive work product. It is beyond the scope of this book to present these developments in depth, other than to note a key principle of legal ethics. As stated in *ABA Model Rule of Professional Conduct 1.1*, "A lawyer shall provide competent representation to a client." According to comment 5, "Competent handling of a particular matter includes inquiry into and analysis of the factual and legal elements of the problem, and use of methods and procedures meeting the standards of competent practitioners. It also includes adequate preparation." In other words, there are ethical limits to how little effort can be devoted to a matter.

The content and organization of short-form memos depend on the reason for writing a less complete memo. Often, a single opening component is used. Facts may be omitted or merged into the opening component if few facts are known or the facts are straightforward. The closing may be only a restatement of the legal conclusion.

By contrast, the discussion should be as complete as the situation permits; the purpose of the memo—to fully inform the reader of the meaning of the client's legal situation—applies however long or short a memo is. Thus, the pertinent legal authorities should be cited, the pertinent rules stated, your legal reasoning set out, and your conclusions indicated. In other words, the IRAC that is the core of a longer analytical office memo is also the core of the short-form memo.

As an example, Exhibit 8C discusses the Cassie Collins situation, in which the client was ticketed for driving while using her cell phone. The questions preceding it should help you analyze this short-form memo according to the points stated here.

---

5. The issue of communicating with clients by e-mail is covered in the Chapter 9 on advice letters.

H. REVIEW

A common question is in which order to draft the various components of the office memo. A classic sequence is: discussion, issues, short answers, closing, and facts. The discussion flows most directly from your reasoning; the issues, short answers, and closing derive from the discussion; and the facts must support the rest of the memo. However, if you are a big-picture thinker, you might begin with the issues and short answers. If you are more oriented toward the facts, you might draft them first. No matter what order you choose, you should assemble the memo components in the order set out in this chapter: issues, short answers, facts, discussion, and closing.

And you should revise your entire memo once it is assembled, as discussed in Appendix I. The Writing Process, to ensure that it works well as a whole. As you do, examine your work against these four criteria for sound legal writing:

- Completeness—Have you covered the material completely?
- Correctness—Have you stated both the law and the facts accurately?
- Coherence—Does each component make sense unto itself? Does each component align with the others?
- Comprehensibility—Will your reader be able to understand your work in one careful reading?

Also, take care to present an objective analysis with sufficient breadth and depth to fully inform, but not overwhelm, your reader. In assessing your advice to your client, consider whether you have approached your client's situation candidly and creatively.

EXHIBIT 8A DISPUTE MEMO

TO: Partner[6]
FROM: Associate
RE: Bower's Bounty: defamation claim
DATE: Dec. 1, 2016

ISSUES

A) When a manager posts a memo stating that an employee was terminated for theft that the employee did not commit—a statement that co-workers read and believed—does the employee have a claim for defamation?

B) Under these circumstances, is the employer vicariously liable for the manager's defamation?

C) Under these circumstances, is the communication covered by the defense of qualified privilege?

SHORT ANSWERS

A) Yes. A false statement about an employee's performance made within the workplace constitutes defamation.

B) Yes. Liability extends to the employer because the manager acted within the scope of employment.

C) Possibly. The employer may argue that the posting was privileged as a communication between people with corresponding interests, but the privilege may not extend as far as this posting and arguably was lost at any rate when the manager acted with reckless disregard for the truth.

FACTS

Until three months ago, our client Bower's Bounty, a grocery store, employed Sarah Nicholson. Bower's Bounty has received a letter indicating that Nicholson is considering bringing a lawsuit claiming defamation against Bower's Bounty.

According to the employee handbook, Bower's Bounty employees may be terminated at any time, for any reason. In addition, the handbook prohibits the pilferage of food or other products; this policy extends to the employee herself, as well as friends and family. According to our contact, Sheryl Grant (vice-president of operations), notwithstanding this prohibition, pilferage continues to occur.

---

6. For purposes of illustration, this analytical office memo works with only one case. If you were analyzing this situation in actual practice, you would incorporate more recent cases, and the analysis would be more complex.

EXHIBIT 8A   (cont.)

According to Nicholson's personnel file, she worked at Bower's Bounty for seven years. She rose through the ranks to supervisor of the fresh produce department. She has been successful in that role. Her most recent direct supervisor was the new store manager, Dan Molinaro. The last entry (by Molinaro) indicates that Nicholson was terminated for violation of the pilferage policy.

At this point, we are accepting the assertions in the letter from Nicholson's lawyer. The letter states that one of the recent hires she supervised, Sam Olson, became resentful of the discipline that he had received from Nicholson. Nicholson wrote up Olson for tardiness and arriving at work under the influence of alcohol.

Some time before she was terminated, Nicholson arranged for the contribution of outdated produce to a local food shelf. This donation was consistent with the practice approved by the previous store manager. At the end of her shift, Nicholson went to the loading dock and helped load the available produce onto a truck. Olson observed this activity.

The day her employment was terminated, Molinaro called Nicholson to his office and terminated her employment. He did not explain the reasons for this action.

When Nicholson went to clear out her locker, she saw a posting on the employee bulletin board stating, "Due to pilferage on her part in violation of company policy, Sarah Nicholson is no longer with Bower's Bounty. We do take these rules seriously!"

Nicholson further states in her letter that she has never engaged in pilferage. Olson must have fabricated a false report, which Molinaro believed without investigation. Furthermore, Molinaro could have learned the facts of the donation with minimal investigation. Co-workers have read and believed the posting, which has led to significant damage to Nicholson's personal and professional reputation.

Grant expressed considerable concern over the situation. Bower's Bounty does not have significant sums to spend on this matter and is seeking a prompt and amicable resolution.

DISCUSSION

Is an employer liable for defamation when a manager posts a false statement in the employee lounge that the employee was terminated for committing pilferage and the employee's co-workers read and believed that statement? This topic has three main issues: publication of a defamatory statement, scope of employment, and qualified privilege.

First, the elements of defamation are false and defamatory words, communication to a third party, and resulting harm to the reputation of the person defamed. *Luttrell v. United Tele. Sys., Inc.*, 683 P.2d 1292, 1293 (Kan. Ct. App. 1984), *aff'd*, 659 P.2d 1270 (Kan. 1985). For purposes of this analysis, we accept the assertions of the employee that she

EXHIBIT 8A   (cont.)

donated the discarded food with permission to a food shelf, so the charge of pilferage was indeed false. A charge of theft would be defamatory and harm the reputation of a grocery store manager, and her co-workers read and believed the statement. Thus, the first and third elements are met.

As for the second element, communication to a third party, *Luttrell* holds that communication between corporate co-workers counts as publication. *Id.* at 1294. There, supervisors discussed an employee's workplace conduct among themselves. The employer argued that the discussion amounted to the corporation talking to itself. The court disagreed and ruled that the conversations constituted communication to a third party. *Id.* Here, too, the manager also communicated with employees about the employee's workplace conduct. Unlike *Luttrell*, the recipients of the message were not other supervisors but rather a group of lower-level employees, and the message was written, not oral. These contrasts favor the employee. Thus, communication under *Luttrell* occurred. Accordingly, all elements of the claim of defamation are present.

Second, if defamation is established, the issue of holding the employer liable arises. The defamatory utterances must have been made while the speaker was acting within the scope of employment for the employer to be held liable. *Id.* at 1293. In *Luttrell*, the discussion involved an employee's performance and discipline by supervisors. The same is true here; the manager was responsible for enforcing company policy as well as the evaluation and discipline of the employee. Thus, he acted within his scope of employment.

Third, if defamation has occurred within the speaker's scope of employment, the employer likely will raise the defense of qualified privilege. "A communication is qualifiedly privileged if it is made in good faith on any subject matter in which the person communicating has an interest, or in reference to which he has a duty, if it is made to a person having a corresponding interest or duty." *Id.* at 1294. Once a privilege is established, the plaintiff may overcome it by showing that "the defendants acted with knowledge of falsity or reckless disregard for the truth." *Id.*

The application of these rules to the client's situation yields a close call. On the one hand, the manager had a duty to evaluate store employees as well as a duty to enforce store policies. Informing employees why the employee was terminated had the dual benefits of deflecting speculation and reinforcing the anti-pilferage rule. On the other hand, informing department employees exactly why a specific employee was terminated is unusual, and there are other ways to reinforce workplace rules. The employee can also argue that the manager acted recklessly in determining that pilferage had occurred; relying on the statement of one co-worker whom she had disciplined was reckless. Consulting with Nicholson before terminating her, or with other company officials, would have yielded a more complete view of the situation.

The policy underlying this area of law proves useful at this point. The qualified privilege exists to protect the employer "who is evaluating or investigating an employee

EXHIBIT 8A (cont.)

in good faith" from the threat of a defamation suit. *Id.* This policy would protect earlier statements in the disciplinary process but should not protect the statement to co-workers. On balance, Bower's Bounty may not be protected by the qualified privilege.

In summary, the elements of defamation are present, and the manager was acting within the scope of employment. Bower's Bounty can claim a qualified privilege, but it may well be defeated by the employee.

CLOSING

In brief, Bower's Bounty's legal position is not strong: Nicholson has a viable claim of defamation and can hold the company liable for the store manager's actions. It is debatable whether the statement would be covered by a qualified privilege, and Nicholson may well be able to overcome the privilege, based on the facts asserted in the letter.

Fortunately, Nicholson has contacted Bower's Bounty promptly. Her economic losses should be minimal, and her willingness to settle may be high at this point. Bower's Bounty may be interested in not just a reasonable monetary settlement, but also other assistance, such as a positive reference and, perhaps, reinstatement in one of the company's other stores in the area.

From a process standpoint, we should proceed on two fronts. We should do our own factual investigation, in particular to determine whether the manager's investigation was indeed as cursory as alleged in the letter. And prompt contact with Nicholson's lawyer is in order. Managing this dispute through negotiation rather than litigation will keep it quiet. In the consumer business of grocery stores, Bower's Bounty has little to gain by media attention. Furthermore, negotiation will be less costly and burdensome for all involved.

EXHIBIT 8B TRANSACTIONAL MEMO

QUESTIONS TO CONSIDER AS YOU READ THIS MEMO

(1) How do the issues and short answers signal that this is a transactional memo?
(2) Which facts are fixed? What is not yet known?
(3) How is the discussion organized? How do the legal issues and options intertwine?
(4) How many options are discussed? How many are recommended?

MEMO

TO: Partner
FROM: Associate
RE: All-Day Wellness: covenant not-to-compete
DATE: Dec. 1, 2016

ISSUE

Under what circumstances, if any, may a company that provides employee wellness consultants to organizations enforce a covenant not-to-compete with its employees who work in that role?

SHORT ANSWER

The covenants will be enforceable if they are included in the original hire agreement, protect a legitimate interest on the part of the company, and are only as broad as needed to protect that interest.

FACTS

All-Day Wellness (our client) began operations in Washington State some years ago. It plans to open for business in Minnesota in two months.

All-Day Wellness provides wellness consultants to organizations, such as companies and nonprofit organizations, to assist their employees in improving their overall health. All-Day Wellness consultants perform an assessment of the health status of the client's workforce, suggest programs tailored to the particular workforce, and implement the programs desired by the client, whether through direct service or contracting with another provider. As an example, a consultant may conduct a nutrition assessment of food available on site, make arrangements for regular yoga classes, and conduct smoking-cessation classes.

One of the advantages of the services provided by All-Day Wellness is the wide range of the consultant's expertise. All consultants have degrees and work experience in health-related occupations. In addition, they undergo a month of training and an additional three months of shadowing experienced consultants before working on their own.

The experience in Washington indicates that most clients form close relationships with their consultants. Furthermore, most new business comes from word-of-mouth referrals.

EXHIBIT 8B   (cont.)

Several years after the business opened in Washington, competitors began to open in the state. Several consultants moved to the competitors, and some clients followed the consultants to the competitors. Thus, All-Day Wellness is interested in including covenants not-to-compete in its employment agreements here in Minnesota. The assumption is that the covenants would be part of each consultant's individual employment agreement, signed at the time of hire. That agreement would also state the employee's salary, benefits, and other conditions of employment.

DISCUSSION

Covenants not-to-compete that restrict an employee from working for a competitor after he or she leaves the first employer are enforceable if three conditions are met: consideration, a legitimate employer interest, and reasonableness in terms.

First, as to consideration, when the covenant is signed at the inception of the employment, the requirement of consideration is met. *Overholt Crop Insur. Serv. Co. v. Bredeson*, 437 N.W.2d 698, 702 (Minn. Ct. App. 1989). Failure to include the covenant in the original hire agreement makes enforcement much more problematic on this score. *See Davies & Davies Agency, Inc., v. Davies,* 298 N.W.2d 127, 130-31 (Minn. 1980) (requiring some form of benefit to employee in exchange for covenant). All-Day Wellness plans to include the covenant in the original hire agreements. Thus, this condition would be met.

Second, as to the employer's legitimate interest, although covenants not-to-compete are disfavored as restraints of trade, they are enforced when they protect the employer against deflection of trade or customers. *Id.* at 703 (*citing Bennett v. Storz Broad. Co.,* 143 N.W.2d 892, 898 (Minn. 1965)). The requisite employer interest is present when the employee has close contact with the employer's customers so that the employee personifies the employer. *See Davies & Davies Agency* (insurance agency); *Overholt* (also insurance agency); *Webb Pub. Co. v. Fosshage,* 426 N.W.2d 445 (Minn. Ct. App. 1988) (custom magazine publishing). The All-Day Wellness business model calls for precisely this close connection between individual consultants and clients. Furthermore, the experience in Washington shows that clients may follow consultants who leave All-Day Wellness. Thus, this condition also would be met.

The third condition, reasonableness of terms, is the most difficult to call. The test is vague: "whether the stipulation has imposed upon the employee any greater restraint than is reasonably necessary to protect the employer's business." *Davies & Davies Agency,* 298 N.W.2d at 131. Three dimensions are typically involved: geographic range, length of time, and job function. The geographic range should reflect the area in which the employee works. *Id.* at 131. The length of time should reflect the time needed to obliterate the identification between the employee and the customers, train a replacement, and establish a relationship between the replacement and customers. *See id.; Overholt,* 437 N.W.2d at 703; *Webb Pub. Co.,* 426 N.W.2d at 450. For example, the covenant in *Overholt Crop Insurance* covered solicitation of customers whom the employee personally served and working in the counties where he had worked for two years; the court approved this clause. 437 N.W.2d at 703-04.

EXHIBIT 8B (cont.)

To add to the complexity, a court faced with an overbroad covenant may "blue-pencil" it, i.e., pare it to a reasonable scope. Thus, in *Davies & Davies Agency*, the original covenant applicable to an insurance agent who sold bonds in one county covered employment in the insurance business within fifty miles of three cities for five years. *Id.* at 131. The Minnesota Supreme Court upheld a blue-penciled covenant drafted by the trial court confined to one county and one year, along with a prohibition on active solicitation of agency clients. *Id.*

These cases provide guidance, but not a single course to follow. One option is for All-Day Wellness to craft a covenant that would clearly be enforced. This covenant would confine the restraint to the precise job functions of the consultants; the customers whom they have served, the territory of their service, or both; and a reasonable time period. The latter should be based on the time needed to break the relationship between the departing consultant, train a new one, and establish a new relationship; we do not yet have the facts needed to suggest what this time would be.

A second option is to craft a broader covenant. This option is based on a two-fold legal strategy: the court would either enforce the covenant as written or blue-pencil it to a more moderate covenant.

CLOSING

From a legal standpoint, All-Day Wellness is in a good position to create enforceable covenants. Including them in the original hire agreement provides consideration, All-Day Wellness has a legitimate interest in avoiding the loss of clients, and the covenant will be enforced if the terms are reasonable.

Although the client did not mention this, one option is not to use covenants at all. This option is grounded mostly on nonlegal factors, such as employees' resistance to them versus the losses to be suffered from competition. The experience in Washington suggests that All-Day Wellness will reject this option.

Intentionally using an overbroad clause is problematic. If it were to be reviewed in court, it could be pared back and revised. In the meantime, however, an uninformed employee would not know that the clause may not be enforceable as written and thus may stay with All-Day Wellness. So this approach raises ethical issues for All-Day Wellness, as well as this firm. *See* Greg Duhl, *The Ethics of Contract Drafting*, 14 Lewis & Clark L. Rev. 989 (2010).

The best option is to use a carefully tailored covenant based on the actual facts of All-Day Wellness's situation here in Minnesota. This covenant should, as planned, be included in original hire agreements. All-Day Wellness should alert the employees to the covenants and explain the reasons for them. This approach will not only secure the desired legal advantages; it should also prove minimally objectionable to new employees while protecting the company's legitimate interests.

EXHIBIT 8C SHORT-FORM MEMO

QUESTIONS TO CONSIDER AS YOU READ THIS MEMO

(1) Why might this client situation be discussed in a short-form memo?
(2) Which components of the analytical office memo appear in full here?
(3) How is this memo briefer than the other two sample memos?

MEMO

TO: Partner
FROM: Associate
RE: Cassie Collins: cell-phone use while driving
DATE: Dec. 1, 2016

While talking into her handheld cell phone to ask directions to the nearest Starbucks, Ms. Collins drove partway out of the parking lot of a mini-mall into traffic. A minor crash occurred. The responding officer issued her a ticket for driving while using a cell phone.

In general, "[a] person shall not drive a motor vehicle while using a wireless telephone unless that telephone is specifically designed and configured to allow hands-free listening and talking, and is used in that manner while driving." Cal. Vehicle Code § 23123(a) (West Supp. 2015). A violation is punishable by a base fine of $20 for the first offense and $50 thereafter. *Id.* (b).

Several elements are easily resolved. Ms. Collins (a person) was driving a car, and the phone that she was using was a non-hands-free cell phone. These elements of this rule are met.

A less clear element is the statutory requirement that the person drive "while using" a cell phone, along with the reference to "listening and talking." In *People v. Spriggs,* 168 Cal. Rptr. 3d 347 (Ct. App. 2014), the California Court of Appeals interpreted this language to not encompass reading a map but rather stated, "it prohibits a driver only from holding a wireless telephone while conversing on it." *Id.* at 348. The court did note the policy of promoting safe driving. *Id.* at 351. Here, Ms. Collins did more than read a map; she did talk, albeit not to another person. Particularly if the program could provide information in spoken words, the *Spriggs* listening facet would be met. The policy of promoting safe driving favors this outcome, given the collision that occurred as Ms. Collins was driving and using her cell phone in this manner. Thus, this element likely is met.

However, subsection (f) provides an exception when a person drives a motor vehicle "on private property." While section 23123 does not define "on private property," a different section of the Vehicle Code defines "private road or driveway" as "a way or place in private ownership and used for vehicular travel by the owner and those having express or implied permission from the owner but not by other members of the public." *Id.* § 490. Although the terms are not exactly the same, this definition can be used by analogy, as it appears within the same portion of the code.

EXHIBIT 8C (cont.)

Presumably, the mini-mall's lot is privately owned, and the patrons have implied permission to come onto it. The more challenging question is whether Ms. Collins was *on* private property if her car was partly in the lot and partly in the street. The state would argue that some part—enough—was in the street to cause a problem due to her distracted driving. Ms. Collins could argue that the better approach is to determine where most of the car was, which would involve more fact investigation. Given the statutory policy of ensuring safety, the first view is more sound, and the exception would not apply here.

In conclusion, although there is some possible debate as to the interpretation of "using" and the private-property exception, on balance, Ms. Collins's conduct likely did amount to an infraction under California Vehicle Code section 23123.

TEST YOUR UNDERSTANDING

1. Assume that you have been assigned to work on the Daniel de la Cruz situation. He was suspended from public middle school for certain statements that he made. You have been asked to write an analytical office memo on potential litigation in federal court. You have researched his rights under federal constitutional law and state statutory law, as well as the pertinent rules of federal procedure. You have read notes of the client interviews and the documents between the parents and the officials from the school district.
   a. Who is the audience for your memo?
   b. What is the purpose of your memo?
   c. What does it mean to write an objective memo?
   d. What does it mean to write a reader-centered memo?

2. List four items to include in the caption.

3. As for the issues:
   a. What is the purpose of stating issues at the beginning of the memo?
   b. How do you determine how many issues to state?
   c. State two formulas for effective issues.

4. As for the short answers:
   a. What is the purpose of stating short answers near the beginning of the memo?
   b. How do you determine how many short answers to state?
   c. Why are short answers longer than issues?

5. As for the facts:
   a. What are some strategies for dealing with discrepancies in facts?
   b. Should you include or omit each of the following types of facts, and why: background, favorable, relevant, residual, and unfavorable?
   c. Your facts statement should begin with an introduction and end with a wrap-up; what should each cover?
   d. List three organizational schemes for the body of your facts statement.
   e. List three standards by which to assess your presentation of the facts, and identify a technique for assuring that you meet each standard.

6. As for the discussion:
   a. What is the difference between effectiveness and efficiency?
   b. If you were to organize the topics in the Daniel de la Cruz memo, what standard convention or conventions might you use?
   c. Assume that the test for examining the school district's actions under the federal constitution is not clear; there are two different possible approaches. What is this organizational challenge called, and how should you handle it?
   d. List four categories of signaling material, and for each, indicate where in the discussion you would use them.

7. As for the closing:
   a. What are the two requirements for your advice under ABA Model Rule 2.1?
   b. Do nonlegal concerns (such as the impact of litigation on a teenager) fall within the potential topics for a closing?
   c. What are the two components of the closing?

8. As for the transactional memo:
   a. Because events have not yet occurred, what does the memo focus on?
   b. How is a decision tree used in the preparation of this memo?
   c. What are the two types of facts set out in the facts statement?
   d. What is a distinctive organizational design possibility for the discussion?
   e. What is the transactional lawyer's contribution to the client's future plans?

9. As for the short-form memo:
   a. What is the minimum requirement set by ABA Model Rule 1.1?
   b. For what reasons might you write a short-form memo?
   c. How is a short-form memo shorter than a full-length analytical office memo?
   d. Which part of the office memo should not be truncated in a short-form memo?

TEST YOUR UNDERSTANDING ANSWERS

1. If you were writing an analytical office memo on the Daniel de la Cruz situation:
   a. Your audience would be other people in the office working on that matter, yourself, and people in the office working on similar future matters.
   b. The purpose of the memo would be to set out your best legal analysis of the matter (based on your factual and legal research, reading, and reasoning) to permit informed judgment by your readers and advice to the client.
   c. Objectivity means that both the strengths and weaknesses of the client's legal position are assessed.
   d. Focusing on the audience and purpose leads to a reader-centered memo, in which the memo is written to maximize the effectiveness and efficiency for the reader rather than to reflect the preferences of the writer.

2. Four items to include in the caption are the recipient's and writer's names, the date, and the subject; the latter includes the client's name, file number, and topic.

3. As for the issues:
   a. They are stated at the beginning to focus the reader's attention on the key legal topics and facts, as well as to preview the organization.
   b. There should be as many issues as there are topics in the discussion.
   c. The two classic formulas are: Is [law] when [facts]? Do [facts] result in [law]?

4. As for the short answers:
   a. They are stated near the beginning to orient the reader and to permit the reader to examine along the way how strong the analysis is.
   b. There should be as many short answers as there are issues.
   c. Short answers are longer than issues because they include brief reasons.

5. As for the facts:
   a. To deal with discrepancies, you can state facts in general terms, state the more credible view, or state both versions and analyze both branches.
   b. Relevant and background facts should be included because they are needed for the analysis and to understand the situation; residual facts should be omitted because they do not fit either of those criteria; favorable and unfavorable facts should be included or not, depending on which of the previous three categories they fall into.
   c. The introduction identifies the client and other important players and summarizes the client's situation; the wrap-up describes the client's current legal situation and nonlegal concerns.

     d. Three organizational schemes for the body of the facts statement are chronological, topical, and perceptual.

     e. To ensure accuracy, review your sources. To ensure objectivity, use straightforward verbs and avoid words that carry judgments. To tell the story completely, show how the events lead to each other through linking phrasing.

6. As for the discussion:

     a. Effectiveness is a function of how well the reader understands the discussion, and efficiency is a function of how easily the reader processes the text.

     b. Pertinent standard conventions are substantive/procedural, claims/remedy, and more to less important.

     c. When there are two different possible approaches, there is a rule branchpoint. You must analyze one branchpoint through to its conclusion, loop back, and analyze the other through to its conclusion.

     d. Headings appear at the start of topics; roadmaps announce topics; summaries conclude topics; and transitions appear throughout the text.

7. As for the closing:

     a. ABA Model Rule 2.1 requires advice to be independent and candid.

     b. You may include considerations other than law, although a referral to another professional is also recommended.

     c. The two components of the closing are a brief restatement of the answers to the issues and a discussion of the client's options.

8. As for the transactional memo:

     a. The memo focuses on providing a legal evaluation of options.

     b. A decision tree can be used to depict options available to the client.

     c. The facts statement covers fixed facts and future possibilities.

     d. The distinctive organizational design is to organize the discussion around options.

     e. The lawyer should not only assess the client's proposal but also generate sound legal alternatives.

9. As for the short-form memo:

     a. ABA Model Rule 1.1 requires competent representation and adequate preparation.

     b. Reasons for writing a short-form memo include straightforward law and facts, as well as timing and resource constraints.

     c. The typical short-form memo has a compact opening with facts merged into it, and the closing may only state the legal conclusion.

     d. The discussion should not be truncated in a short-form memo.

THE ADVICE LETTER

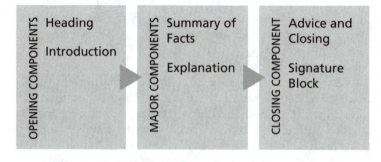

Letters are expectation packed in an envelope.
—Shana Alexander
"The Surprises of the Mail," *Life* (1967)

A. INTRODUCTION

1. Audience and Purpose

As important as the analytical office memo is, it rarely serves as the final expression of the lawyer's analysis. The lawyer still must take the next critical step: sharing the lawyer's analysis and conclusions with the client. How does a lawyer explain the legal meaning of a client's situation and suggest steps to take on the client's behalf? Client counseling almost always involves a conversation and often also involves a written document—the *advice letter*.

The advice letter is only one of many types of letters that lawyers write.[1] They also write letters to clients to ask for information, inform the client of new developments, enclose documents related to the matter, seek payment, and so on. Lawyers write letters on behalf of clients to other people, demanding payment or other relief from opposing parties, seeking records or information from third parties, making arrangements with opposing counsel, enclosing briefs sent to courts, and similar matters. Some lawyers specialize in writing formal opinion

---

1. For a discussion of various letters, see Elizabeth Fajans, Mary Falk & Helene S. Shapo, *Writing for Law Practice* 229-63 (3d ed. 2015).

letters; an opinion letter discusses the client's compliance with a particular rule and is used to induce others to transact business with the client.

This chapter focuses on advice letters because of their importance to the lawyer-client relationship. Moreover, the advice letter is a challenging letter to write well. If you can master the advice letter, most other types of client letters should come relatively easily.

If the client is an individual, the primary *audience* of the advice letter is that individual, of course. If the client is an organization, such as a corporation or government agency, the primary reader is the person empowered to act for the client in the matter. Some advice letters will be read by more than one person. For example, a letter advising a corporation may be read by its in-house counsel and president, board members, or key managers. Sometimes it is possible for a single letter to address both primary and secondary readers. In other instances, you may need to write to the primary reader and cover the different needs of the secondary reader another way (for example, by providing a more detailed memo for a more sophisticated secondary reader).

Every reader has preferences to be taken into account to the extent possible. Some readers prefer considerable detail about legal authorities; for others, summary information suffices. Some readers prefer extensive discussion of the nonlegal dimensions of the case; others view such analysis as overstepping by the lawyer. Some readers prefer a no-nonsense approach; others prefer a more empathetic style. These preferences reflect the reader's personal attributes and the client's situation. For example, a reader with legal training may prefer a detailed legal analysis. A reader who has suffered a personal injury or lost a loved one typically looks for empathy as well as legal analysis. Thus, an important step in writing an advice letter is to think about your reader's preferences. Take care not to act on stereotypes; for instance, the elderly widow with little formal education or work experience may be a savvy reader due to her volunteer work.

Regardless of who your reader is, your letter has two main *purposes*. First, the letter informs the reader of the lawyer's legal analysis of the client's situation. Second, the letter persuades the client to take action that has sound legal support, whether resolving an existing dispute or framing an upcoming transaction. Subsidiary purposes include establishing rapport with the client and verifying the facts and tasks that the client has presented to the lawyer. On occasion, these purposes may conflict. For example, it may be difficult to establish rapport with a client who strongly desires to engage in behavior that is illegal or legally risky. When a conflict among purposes arises, aim to serve the main purposes of informing the client and persuading the client to take legally sound actions.

2. The Advisor's Ethics

Not surprisingly, various ethics rules address the matter of advising the client. *ABA Model Rule of Professional Conduct 1.2* makes a key distinction. It states: "[A] lawyer shall abide by a client's decisions concerning the objectives of representation and . . . shall consult with the client as to the means by which they are to be pursued." The client's matter is just that—the client's dispute or transaction. The client sets the objectives of the representation, subject to legal constraints and the lawyer's professional obligations. According to the comment to Rule 1.2, the lawyer is to consult with the client about the means for obtaining the client's objectives; the lawyer leads the way as to technical, legal, and tactical matters; the client leads the way as to expenses to be incurred and the impact on third parties. In practice, lawyers and clients jointly delineate their respective roles, reflecting the client's desire for control or involvement, the degree of trust between client and lawyer, the lawyer's experience with the type of situation at hand, and similar factors.

In addition, as discussed in Chapter 8, *Rule 2.1* makes two important points. First, "[i]n representing a client, a lawyer shall exercise independent professional judgment and render candid advice." Second, a lawyer may refer to moral, social, and economic considerations as well as to the law.

Finally, *Rule 1.4* requires a lawyer to "promptly inform the client" of key decisions, "reasonably consult with the client about the means" of the representation, "keep the client reasonably informed about the status" of the case, and "promptly comply with reasonable requests for information." In other words, communication with clients is critical to the ethical practice of law. The rule sets this standard for lawyer-client communication: "A lawyer shall explain a matter to the extent reasonably necessary to permit the client to make informed decisions regarding the representation." The case in Box 9.1 illustrates these principles.

In living out these ethical standards, lawyers and clients relate to each other in various ways. Thomas Shaffer and Robert Cochran have posited four models:[2]

- The hired gun acts as directed by the client, without regard for the impact of the client's actions on others; the autonomy of the client is the key value.
- The godfather, focusing on client victory, makes choices with fairly little client involvement, so as to produce victory for the client.
- The guru, focusing on client rectitude, makes choices with fairly little client involvement, so as to prompt the client to do what the lawyer sees as the right thing.
- The friend, focusing on client goodness, engages the client in a discussion of what is good for the client and others affected by the case.

A lawyer often uses a blend of these models, switching from one to another, depending on the client and the situation. As you learn more about being a lawyer, you may want to consider which models are true to practice, professional principles, and your own values.

---

2. Thomas L. Shaffer & Robert F. Cochran, Jr., *Lawyers, Clients, and Moral Responsibility* (2d ed. 2009).

BOX 9.1

WHAT HAPPENS WHEN YOU FAIL TO FULLY INFORM YOUR CLIENT?

As you read the following case, think about these questions:

(1) *Why (do you think) did the lawyer choose not to fully inform his client about the state of the law governing his case?*

(2) *What would you do to avoid this situation?*

(3) *Is the penalty here appropriate? Would you have issued a different penalty?*

In re Thonert,
733 N.E.2d 932 (Ind. 2000).

. . .

The parties agree that the respondent represented a client charged with operating a motor vehicle while intoxicated. Prior to the client's initial hearing and before the client met with or hired the respondent, the client was advised by videotape of his rights. He pleaded guilty to the charge, and the matter was set for sentencing hearing. Prior to that hearing, the client met with the respondent to discuss the possibility of withdrawing his guilty plea. During their meeting, the respondent told the client of another criminal case, *Snowe v. State*, 533 N.E.2d 613 (Ind. Ct. App. 1989), in which the respondent had prevailed on appeal for the defendant. He provided a copy of the Indiana Court of Appeals decision to his new client. The respondent agreed to represent the client for $5,000, which the client paid.

Snowe also involved a prerecorded videotaped televised advisement of rights, but the record in that case failed to indicate whether the defendant had ever viewed the tape advising him of his rights. Further, the opinion held that a trial court judge cannot rely solely on displaying a videotape advisement of rights, but instead must also determine whether the defendant knows of and understands his rights, the nature of the charge or charges against him, the full import of the rights waiver in his guilty plea, and the sentencing possibilities for the charges against him. *Snowe*, 533 N.E.2d at 617.

At the client's initial hearing, it was established that he had viewed the videotape, that the videotape advised him of his rights and the sentencing possibilities under the charges filed against him, that he understood the charge against him and his rights as explained in the videotape, and that he voluntarily waived those rights and pleaded guilty.

On May 30, 1996, the respondent entered an appearance on behalf of the client and filed a motion to withdraw the guilty plea. The trial court denied the motion without hearing. The respondent appealed that ruling, alleging that his client had a right to withdraw the plea because, due to the absence of counsel at the time he entered it and the fact that the record did not reflect that the trial court property examined the client as to waiver of his rights, the client had not made it knowingly, intelligently, or voluntarily. The respondent further argued that the client had a right to a hearing on his motion to withdraw the plea.

The respondent represented the defendant in *Fletcher v. State*, 649 N.E.2d 1022 (Ind. 1995). In that case, this Court addressed the questions that the respondent raised in his client's case. The ruling in *Fletcher* was adverse to the arguments that the respondent offered on appeal of his client's case. [footnote omitted] The respondent had served as counsel of record for defendant Fletcher in the appeal before this Court. This Court's ruling in *Fletcher* was issued on May 1, 1995, over one year before the respondent filed his appeal on behalf of the client. In his appellate brief filed on behalf of the client, the respondent failed to cite to *Fletcher* or argue that its holding was not controlling authority in the client's case. The respondent also failed to argue that the holding in *Fletcher* should be changed or extended. Although he advised his client of the *Snowe* case, he failed to advise him of *Fletcher* or explain any impact *Fletcher* might have on his case. Opposing counsel had not previously disclosed *Fletcher* to the Court of Appeals . . . .

BOX 9.1 (Cont.)

Professional Conduct Rule 1.4(b) provides that a lawyer shall explain a matter to the extent reasonably necessary to permit a client to make informed decisions regarding a representation. A client should have sufficient information to participate intelligently in decisions concerning the objectives of the representation. *Comment* to Prof. Cond. R 1.4. By failing to advise his client of a ruling in the controlling jurisdiction that was adverse to the legal arguments contemplated for his client's case on appeal, and instead choosing only to advise the client of an earlier appellate decision favorable to his position, the respondent effectively divested his client of the opportunity to assess intelligently the legal environment in which his case would be argued and to make informed decisions regarding whether to go forward with it. Accordingly, we find that the respondent violated Prof. Cond. R 1.4(b) . . . .

The parties agree that the respondent should be publicly reprimanded for his misconduct. We agree that a public admonishment is appropriate in this case, given the negative impact on the efficient resolution of the client's appeal occasioned by the respondent's lack of disclosure and its attendant deception of the client as to the viability of any efforts to withdraw the guilty plea. Accordingly, we accept the parties' agreement and the discipline called for therein.

B. THE FORMAT OF THE ADVICE LETTER

The format of the advice letter is governed not by rule, but by convention, and it differs from law office to law office and across client situations. The format of the advice letter roughly parallels the analytical office memo, as shown in Box 9.2. In a long letter, headings may set off some of these components; in short letters, transitions are used instead.

BOX 9.2

COMPARISON OF ADVICE LETTER AND ANALYTICAL OFFICE MEMO

Advice Letter	Analytical Office Memo
Heading	Caption
Introduction	Issues and short answers
Summary of facts	Facts
Explanation	Discussion
Advice and closing	Closing

As examples, this chapter draws on two sample advice letters. Exhibit 9A discusses the Bower's Bounty situation, in which the client faces a claim of defamation. This letter is discussed throughout the chapter; please read it now.

Exhibit 9B discusses All-Day Wellness's proposal to enter into covenants not-to-compete; it pertains to a later part of the chapter.

Heading: As with any business letter, the *heading* includes the sender's letterhead followed by the date of the letter; the name, position, and address of the recipient or recipients; and the salutation. The heading also may include a one-line reference to the topic of the letter; this feature is most common when the letter is sent to a client with multiple pending matters.

Introduction: This first part should establish *rapport* with the reader and generally refers to the previous contact with the client. To personalize this opening, avoid a sentence such as "This letter is in response to yours of October 14th."

The second part of the introduction provides the *overview* of the legal points covered in the letter. Often, the reader will have asked an open-ended, bottom-line question; the overview helps the reader see how the law frames that concern. Your options are to state the conclusions that you have come to, the topics that you have analyzed, the issues that you have addressed, or some combination. Generally, stating your conclusions at the outset will benefit the reader. However, if the conclusions are complex or significantly adverse, it may be wiser to identify the topics or issues instead. This overview is not stated as completely or technically as the issues and short answers in an office memo. See Box 9.3. Even so, it should be carefully phrased. The reader should be clear what is covered in the letter and how certain or uncertain any stated conclusions are.

Some lawyers include a third part in the introduction: a brief paragraph stating the *ground rules* of a legal advice letter:

- In most situations, you should advise the reader to keep the letter confidential.
- You may want to note that the letter states the facts of the client's situation, identify the source, and ask the client to verify those facts.
- You also may note that the conclusions are based on the facts currently known or assumed as well as on current law, so that the conclusions could change with changes in the facts or law.
- If you are concerned that you have not addressed all your client's issues, you could urge the client to contact you if there are omissions.

These points may be omitted if it is likely the reader is well aware of them.

As an example, the introduction in Exhibit 9A, discussing the Bower's Bounty situation, takes this tripartite approach. The first paragraph seeks to establish rapport with the reader, the second provides an overview of the topics, and the third alerts her to the ground rules of the letter.

Summary of facts: As with the facts statement in the analytical office memo, the *summary of facts* recounts the facts of the client's situation. The summary of facts serves several critical purposes: it shows the reader that you have carefully listened to the client's story, it permits the reader to verify your account, and it helps the reader to see the facts objectively and from a legal perspective.

The *scope* of the facts summary is nearly parallel to that of the office memo. You must include legally relevant facts and important background facts, whether favorable or unfavorable. You also may want to include residual facts that are significant to the client; do so sparingly, however, so as not to blur your focus on what is legally relevant. The sources of the facts should be noted informally.

BOX 9.3

SAMPLE ANALYTICAL OFFICE MEMO SHORT ANSWERS VERSUS ADVICE LETTER INTRODUCTION

Short Answers from the Analytical Office Memo

(A)   Yes. A false statement about an employee's performance made within the workplace constitutes defamation.

(B)   Yes. Liability extends to the employer because the manager acted within the scope of employment.

(C)   Possibly. The employer may argue that the statement is privileged as a communication between people with corresponding interests, but the privilege may not extend as far as this posting and arguably was lost at any rate when the manager acted with reckless disregard for the truth.

Introduction from the Advice Letter

In this letter, I have addressed the single concern that we discussed last week: whether the defamation claim asserted against Bower's Bounty in the employee's letter is viable under Kansas law. As you will see, my conclusion is that the claim likely is viable if the facts prove to be as stated in the letter. However, Bower's Bounty may assert a defense called "qualified privilege," but its success will depend on facts yet to be developed.

In some ways, the summary of facts reads similarly to the facts statement of the analytical office memo. The *organization* should be clear and logical; chronological and topical approaches typically work well. When you know the differing perspectives of two or more people regarding the situation, you may employ perceptual organization. In addition, the *presentation* should be accurate and objective, as with the office memo.

There are some additional dimensions to consider as you write the advice letter. The phrasing should be *diplomatic;* remember that your reader experienced the events, directly or indirectly, and may view the situation with some mix of negative emotions. In addition, you may need to include *caveats* about the facts: that you have not yourself investigated the facts (especially if you have doubts about them or believe that your client may assume that you have investigated them) or that you have concerns about establishing an important fact at trial.

As an example, the organization of the summary of facts in Exhibit 9A is topical and roughly chronological (the parties, the prohibition of pilferage, the facts surrounding the alleged pilferage and termination, the posting, and the unclear nature of the investigation). Throughout, the letter notes what is known and what is not, as well as where the information came from. Unfavorable facts are included, phrased in a diplomatic manner ("Ms. Nicholson's letter asserts that those grounds are factually incorrect.").

Explanation: The *explanation* sets out your objective legal analysis of the client's situation. It should proceed in a logical way through the issues, as to each presenting the legal rules, linking them to the relevant facts, and indicating your best prediction as to the legal outcome. The explanation should in general terms explore both sides of issues as to which there is a reasonable debate, and your statement of the outcome should reflect your degree of certainty. The organization should be made clear through transitions, especially if there are branchpoints in the analysis. If the explanation covers several topics, a brief roadmap at the beginning or a summary at the end may be needed to knit the topics together.

The explanation differs from the discussion in an analytical office memo primarily in how it presents the law. The explanation focuses not so much on the legal authorities or fully stated legal rules; rather, it presents key *legal concepts*. Those concepts typically are stated in concrete terms paralleling the client's situation. Indeed, where the legal concept is fairly straightforward and its link to the facts is obvious, you may merge the law and relevant facts into a single statement. On the other hand, if similar situations may arise in the future for the same client or if the law is complex, you should state the law as a rule and then link it to the facts. Unless the reader is a lawyer or otherwise sophisticated in the law, the explanation does not include citations.

As an example, the explanation in Exhibit 9A covers the three topics in a logical order (viability of the claim, legal responsibility of the client for its employee's actions, and the defense). It uses legal concepts rather than full rules for the first two topics because those two topics are not debatable (at least at this point). See Box 9.4, showing the contrast in the phrasing between the analytical office memo passage and the advice letter passage on the defamation claim. The final topic is developed further, with the rule more fully stated, because this topic is likely to be the focus of further investigation and the client's best argument. Each rule is applied in a precise manner to the client's facts. At the end of each topic, the reader can see whether the analysis is favorable or not. A summary paragraph combines all three conclusions.

Advice: The purpose of the *advice* component is to link the legal analysis presented in the letter to concrete actions to be taken by or on behalf of the client. Most clients have more than one option. For example, a potential claim may be abandoned, presented to the wrongdoer for informal resolution, or filed as a complaint. A client charged with wrongdoing may opt to settle or litigate.

The client may have suggested one or more options. Given your expertise, in most situations, you should be able to generate others. Your conclusion should present the relative legal advantages and disadvantages of each option. If you know of nonlegal concerns that the client has, you may bring these into the mix as well.

Whether to advance a particular option as the best is a matter of considerable judgment. On occasion, the law may decide for you; there may be only one legal course of action. Where various options are legally sound, in deciding whether to indicate your preference, you should think about your relationship with the client: Do you know all the facts regarding the client's financial situation? Do you know for sure how the client weighs various nonlegal factors? Do you have an established relationship of trust with the client? If you do indicate your preference, you should take care to convey that the choice is ultimately the client's.

As an example, the advice component in Exhibit 9A first calls for a necessary course of action (learning more about the facts) and then discusses how to approach the other side. It covers two options and recommends the classic first step (meeting with counsel). This discussion reflects the nonlegal concerns

BOX 9.4

SAMPLE ANALYTICAL OFFICE MEMO DISCUSSION VERSUS ADVICE LETTER EXPLANATION

Discussion in Office Memo

First, the elements of defamation are false and defamatory words, communication to a third party, and resulting harm to the reputation of the person defamed. *Luttrell v. United Tele. Sys., Inc.*, 683 P.2d 1292, 1293 (Kan. Ct. App. 1984), *aff'd*, 659 P.2d 1270 (Kan. 1985). For purposes of this analysis, we accept the assertions of the employee that she donated the discarded food with permission to a food shelf, so the charge of pilferage was indeed false. A charge of theft would harm the reputation of a grocery store manager, and her co-workers read and believed the statement. Thus, the first and third elements are met.

As for the second element, communication to a third party, *Luttrell* holds that communication between corporate co-workers counts as publication. *Id.* at 1294. There, supervisors discussed an employee's workplace conduct among themselves. The employer argued that the discussion amounted to the corporation talking to itself. The court disagreed and ruled that the conversations constituted communication to a third party. *Id.* Here, too, the manager communicated with lower-level employees about the employee's workplace conduct. Unlike *Luttrell*, however, the recipients of the message were not other supervisors, but rather a group of employees, and the message was written, not oral. These contrasts favor the employee. Thus, communication under *Luttrell* occurred. Accordingly, all elements of the claim of defamation are present.

Explanation in Advice Letter

To prove defamation under Kansas law, Ms. Nicholson must show that false and defamatory words about her were communicated to a third party, resulting in harm to her reputation. For purposes of this letter, we assume that Mr. Molinaro's posting inaccurately stated that Ms. Nicholson engaged in pilfering and that this posting damaged her reputation for honesty in her profession. Although the posting was made within Bower's Bounty, this type of intracompany statement is considered communication to a third party because co-workers read it. Thus, the claim is viable.

---

that the client has raised and encourages the client to think about key elements of how the dispute may be resolved.

Closing: The *closing* is not simply the end of the letter but also the basis of the *continuation of the representation*. It has three parts: an indication of what you plan to do next, instructions as to what the client should do next, and the signature block. Generally, your next step should be to contact the client so you are sure that the client fully understands the letter. Various further actions follow an advice letter, such as suing or pursuing settlement—or, indeed, doing nothing. Depending on the situation, the advice letter also may set out tasks for the client to accomplish in preparation for the upcoming meeting.

As an example, the closing in Exhibit 9A concisely refers both to an upcoming meeting and actions for the client to take in the meantime.

C. The Transactional Advice Letter

The *transactional advice letter* differs somewhat from an advice letter focused on the resolution of a past dispute. As with the case of the analytical office memo written in the transactional context, the transactional advice letter is *contingent* in information, structure, and tone. The introduction refers to the legal consequences of a future transaction. The summary of facts includes those that are known, those that are projected to occur, and the client's present goals and intentions. In setting out the law, the explanation focuses on how key legal concepts apply to the client's proposed course of conduct, if any, as well as other related options that you develop, if any. The advice component presents options that fit within the law; this component is especially important if the client's proposal does not do this. The letter uses verb structures such as "may," "might," "could," and "would."

As an example, Exhibit 9B discusses the All-Day Wellness situation, in which the client is considering the use of a covenant not-to-compete. The questions preceding this transactional advice letter should help you analyze it according to the points stated here.

D. Additional Considerations

The artistry of an advice letter derives from its *tone*. Tone conveys a great deal about the lawyer as a person and influences the relationship between the lawyer and the client. The letter should convey that the lawyer is professional: thorough, objective, careful, creative, and cooperative. Other impressions, such as that the lawyer is assertive or sympathetic, may be more or less appropriate in particular settings.

These impressions are created through subtle stylistic choices. Consider, for example, how to use personal pronouns. A certain intimacy results when the letter uses the first person ("I recommend . . ."), perhaps even drawing the client into the first-person plural ("We could contact their lawyer . . ."). Distance results when an organizational client is referred to by name ("Bower's Bounty could take the following actions . . ."), rather than the second-person pronoun ("You could take the following actions . . .").

As a second example, consider the use of active versus passive voice. The active voice has a harder edge to it than the passive voice. Active voice ("We will defend against this claim") may be appropriate if the lawyer wants to appear emphatic, whereas passive voice may be appropriate if the lawyer wants to appear compassionate ("Unfortunately, suit has been brought against Bower's Bounty").

E. Review

The advice letter is an important document because it communicates your legal advice to your client and forms a basis for your client's future actions. To write it successfully, you should follow these steps:

(1) Respect the relative roles of yourself and your client.
(2) Carefully consider how best to communicate with the probable reader or readers of the letter.
(3) Present the information in the following components: heading, introduction, summary of facts, explanation, advice, and closing.
(4) Bring creativity to your advice; develop various options for the client and assess their wisdom in light of the law and nonlegal factors.

Be sure that the letter fulfills the following four criteria:

■ Completeness—Does the letter address all topics brought to you by the client? Have you covered the pertinent legal rules and incorporated all relevant facts?
■ Correctness—Have you accurately stated the client's facts? Do your statements of the law fairly reflect the key legal concepts?
■ Coherence—Do the various components mesh well? Do the conclusions fit the rules and facts, and do they fit with each other?
■ Comprehensibility—Will your specific reader probably be able to understand the letter in one careful reading?

Following these steps should enable you to meet your professional obligation to communicate with your client so that the client can make well-informed decisions about its situation.

F. A FEW WORDS ABOUT E-MAIL

E-mail has become a common means of sending an advice letter to a client. E-mail affords various advantages, especially speed. At the same time, it requires some care. First, take care in choosing to whom to send the letter; avoid a group or reply-to-all message. Second, include a clear subject in the subject line. Third, include an indication that the message is confidential. Fourth, as appropriate, indicate that the message is urgent.

Finally, include a transmittal message, which is itself a letter. It should include the addressee's information, a sentence or two indicating that you have attached a letter discussing the specified topic, and a closing block. The closing block should include a word such as "Sincerely," your name, and your contact information. Many lawyers also include a statement that the attachment is to be read only by the intended addressee, that it is an attorney-client communication, and that it should be destroyed if someone else comes across it.

Furthermore, electronic communication raises risks that other forms of communication do not to the same extent. For example, access by a third party may impair the confidentiality of the communication. Thus, you are ethically bound to ascertain and guard against these risks if you choose to use e-mail when communicating with clients.[3]

---

3. For an extensive discussion, see ABA Comm. on Ethics & Prof'l Responsibility, Formal Op. 11-459 (2011).

EXHIBIT 9A DISPUTE ADVICE LETTER

Bowmann & Selleck[4]

123 Fifth Ave.
Suite 600

Lawrence, KS 60000
December 10, 2016

Ms. Sheryl Grant
Bower's Bounty Groceries
456 Main St.
Lawrence, KS 60000

Dear Ms. Grant:

It was good to catch up with you during our meeting last week, although I wish the circumstances were different. Receiving a letter threatening a lawsuit is jarring, I am sure. As I mentioned on the phone on Friday, your insurer has indeed decided to have me work on your behalf in this matter.

In this letter, I have addressed the single concern that we discussed last week: whether the defamation claim asserted against Bower's Bounty in the employee's letter is viable under Kansas law. As you will see, my conclusion is that the claim likely is viable if the facts prove to be as asserted in the letter. However, Bower's Bounty may assert a defense called "qualified privilege," but its success will depend on facts yet to be developed.

Please note that I have based my analysis and conclusions on the facts stated below. Please correct any errors that you see. Furthermore, as we discussed, I have accepted the facts as stated in the letter and plan to investigate some matters further. From the legal standpoint, my research is current to today, and the law does change from time to time. If I have failed to address any of your concerns in my analysis, please contact me. Finally, please keep this letter confidential.

Summary of Facts

According to our conversation and her personnel file, Sarah Nicholson supervised the fresh produce department at a Bower's Bounty grocery store in Lawrence. Ms. Nicholson started at Bower's Bounty seven years ago and has a strong record of employment until her termination about three months ago by store manager Dan Molinaro. As you indicated, Mr. Molinaro began work about a month before Ms. Nicholson's termination.

---

4. For purposes of illustration, this advice letter works with only one case. In actual practice, you would incorporate more recent cases, and the analysis would be more complex.

EXHIBIT 9A (cont.)

The stated grounds for termination were that Ms. Nicholson had been pilfering produce. This is against store policy, as stated in the employee handbook. You indicated that pilferage has been an ongoing issue for Bower's Bounty.

Ms. Nicholson's letter asserts that those grounds are factually incorrect. She asserts—and for the purposes of this letter we will accept her assertion as true—that she had received permission from the regional manager to provide outdated produce to a local food shelf. Sam Olson, a recent hire whom she supervised and had disciplined, saw Ms. Nicholson loading the produce into a truck. Ms. Nicholson believes that Mr. Olson reported what he saw to Mr. Molinaro, who then not only went on to terminate Ms. Nicholson for pilferage but also to post a statement to that effect in the employee lounge.

It is the posting that forms the basis of Ms. Nicholson's claim. It read: "Due to pilferage on her part in violation of company policy, Sarah Nicholson is no longer with Bower's Bounty. We do take these rules seriously!" Ms. Nicholson's letter states that some co-workers read and believed this statement, which has damaged her reputation.

At this preliminary stage, I have not yet discussed this situation with Mr. Molinaro. I assume, for now, the following: he was not aware of the permission given to Ms. Nicholson to donate produce, he relied on the information provided by Mr. Olson, and he did not contact Ms. Nicholson. It may be that he did consider other sources before terminating Ms. Nicholson; this point merits investigation as this matter proceeds.

Explanation

To prove defamation under Kansas law, Ms. Nicholson must show that false and defamatory words about her were communicated to a third party, resulting in harm to her reputation. For the purposes of this letter, we assume that Mr. Molinaro's posting inaccurately stated that Ms. Nicholson engaged in pilfering and that this posting damaged her reputation for honesty in her profession. Although the posting was made within Bower's Bounty, this type of intracompany statement is considered communication to a third party because co-workers read it. Thus, the claim is viable.

To hold an employer legally responsible for the defamation of its employee, the employee must have spoken within the scope of his employment. Mr. Molinaro was doing his job when he posted the memo in the lounge, as he was addressing discipline and workplace rules. Thus, Ms. Nicholson may hold Bower's Bounty responsible for his actions.

The best news for Bower's Bounty is the potential defense known as "qualified privilege." This defense has a two-step analysis. First, if the statement is made in good faith on a matter as to which the speaker and listeners have corresponding interests, the communication may be protected. This privilege is often recognized in employment situations. We can argue that Mr. Molinaro had a duty to evaluate employees and enforce workplace rules; employees had a corresponding interest in knowing about these matters.

However, under current case law, the privilege clearly protects communications with co-managers during investigations, not so clearly communications with other employees post-termination.

Furthermore, if the speaker acts with knowledge that the statement is false or with reckless disregard for the truth, the privilege does not apply. Here is where more investigation is needed. It does not appear that Mr. Molinaro knew that the statement was false. A closer question is whether he acted recklessly in discerning the truth of the situation before he spoke. He had firsthand information from Mr. Olson, but I note, with some concern, that he apparently did not interview Ms. Nicholson. It will be important to find out why Mr. Molinaro believed that Ms. Nicholson had indeed engaged in pilferage before he posted the statement.

In summary, based on what the letter asserts, the claim of defamation may indeed be viable, and Bower's Bounty likely is responsible for Mr. Molinaro's actions. Bower's Bounty's best means of avoiding liability is through the defense of qualified privilege, although success will depend on extending the case law and establishing that Mr. Molinaro did not act recklessly.

Advice

As suggested above, the claim has enough merit that some factual investigation is needed, in particular an interview with Mr. Molinaro.

As for our response to Ms. Nicholson's lawyer, I see several options. One is to wait for further contact, but I fear that inaction will only prompt a formal complaint. Rather, I suggest that we formulate a response and that I then meet with her lawyer. To formulate our response, it would be helpful for you to reflect on the facts involved, Bower's Bounty's interests in resolving this dispute, and the process that you would prefer to employ. Many cases settle well and without litigation if the lawyers meet and both clients are open to a middle-ground solution. In this situation, for example, I suspect that much of Ms. Nicholson's concern is her ability to find work soon; I imagine that Bower's Bounty could be very helpful to her in that regard.

I hope that this letter is helpful to you. I look forward to our meeting next week to discuss its contents and our next steps. In the meantime, I would appreciate your considering possible terms of settlement with Ms. Nicholson and providing my office with Mr. Molinaro's contact information.

Sincerely,

Karen Bowmann

EXHIBIT 9B TRANSACTIONAL ADVICE LETTER

QUESTIONS TO CONSIDER AS YOU READ THIS LETTER

(1) Label the components of the letter.

(2) In the summary of facts, which facts are fixed? Which are projected to occur?

(3) In the explanation, how many options are discussed? How many legal topics are there, and which is the least certain?

(4) In the advice component, how many options are discussed, and how many are recommended? Does the advice rely on nonlegal factors?

Michaels & Arents
123 Fifth Ave.
Suite 600
Minneapolis, MN 50000
December 10, 2012

LETTER

Ms. Ella Dionne
All-Day Wellness Minnesota
456 Great Wood Lane
Eden Prairie, MN 50000

Dear Ms. Korynta:

I enjoyed talking with you last week and learning about your business. Until our conversation, I had not heard of businesses such as yours. I can see why yours is a growth industry.

In this letter, I have addressed the single issue that we discussed last week: whether All-Day Wellness may preclude its employees from working for a competitor upon leaving the company. As you will see, my conclusion is that All-Day Wellness may enter into a reasonable covenant not-to-compete with the employees that likely will be enforced by Minnesota courts.

Please note that I have based my analysis and conclusions on the facts stated below; please correct me if you see any errors. Furthermore, my analysis is current to today, and the law does change from time to time. If I have failed to address any of your concerns in my analysis, please contact me. Finally, please keep this letter confidential.

Summary of Facts

According to our conversation, having worked for All-Day Wellness in Washington, you are now the manager of All-Day Wellness Minnesota. You plan to open for business in two months.

All-Day Wellness employees work as consultants to organizations, such as companies and nonprofit organizations, to assist their employees in improving their overall health.

EXHIBIT 9B (cont.)

All-Day Wellness consultants perform an assessment of the client's workforce, suggest programs tailored to the particular workforce, and implement the programs desired by the client, whether through direct service or contracting with another provider. As an example, you noted that a consultant may conduct a nutrition assessment of food available on site, make arrangements for regular yoga classes, and conduct smoking-cessation classes.

One of the advantages of the services provided by All-Day Wellness is the wide range of the consultant's expertise. You hire only individuals with degrees and work experience in health-related occupations. Once at the company, they undergo a month of training and an additional three months of shadowing experienced employees before working on their own.

Your experience in Washington is that most clients form close relationships with their consultants. Furthermore, most new business comes from word-of-mouth referrals.

Several years after All-Day Wellness opened in Washington, competitors began to open shop. Several of your employees moved to your competitors, which the employment agreements did not preclude. Unfortunately, some clients followed the employees to your competitors.

Thus, you are interested in including covenants not-to-compete in the employment agreements here in Minnesota, if possible. Your plan is to include the covenants in the employment agreements, which are signed at the time of hire and cover such terms as salary and benefits.

Explanation

Under Minnesota law, a covenant not-to-compete must meet several requirements to be enforced by the courts. First, the employee must receive something of value in exchange for agreeing to the covenant. You plan to include the covenant in the employment agreements with the employees, so this requirement is met.

Second, the covenant not-to-compete must protect a legitimate interest of the employer. One such interest is the loss of customers who follow the departing employee, when the employer has created the connection between the employee and the customers. In your situation, the experience in Washington demonstrates the risk of loss of customers. Thus, a court asked to enforce a covenant likely would find this requirement met.

Third, and most significant as you look towards drafting the covenant, is the requirement that the covenant not-to-compete be reasonable in scope. A covenant not-to-compete may be only as broad as needed to protect the employer and not so broad that it unduly restrict the employees. Courts look at the geographic, temporal, and functional scope of the covenant. Thus, the All-Day Wellness covenant should (a) be confined to the geographic region where the employee has worked or where his or her clients are located, (b) last for as long as it will take for the company to train a replacement and for that replacement to establish a relationship with the clients, and (c) encompass the type of

EXHIBIT 9B (cont.)

work the employee does. If the covenant is written too broadly, the court may either fail to enforce it or pare it back and enforce the diminished covenant.

With this legal framework in mind, I see several options for All-Day Wellness. One is not to include a covenant not-to-compete in the employee agreements. The main reason for taking this approach is that these covenants typically are viewed negatively by employees; you may be able to hire more easily without such a covenant in place.

A second option is to include a properly drafted covenant in the original employment agreements. You may want to link it to a hiring bonus so that the covenant is more palatable to the employees.

I do not recommend either of two other options but should note them here. One is to use a covenant with broad constraints. Some employers may theorize that a broad covenant may deter a prized employee from leaving, and if the covenant comes to be litigated, the court may enforce it in part anyway. However, this practice is not certain from a legal standpoint and problematic from an ethical perspective, in my view, because the employees perceive themselves more bound than they may in fact be.

The final option is to wait until later to introduce the covenant. The enforceability of such a covenant is possible but less certain. Your current plan, to introduce the covenants when employees are hired, is wise.

I hope that this letter is helpful to you. I look forward to our meeting next week to discuss its contents. At that time, should you decide to include a covenant not-to-compete in the employee agreements, we can discuss the details of its phrasing. Furthermore, I would be happy to advise you on other aspects of your contracts with your employees under Minnesota law.

Sincerely,

Luke Michaels

TEST YOUR UNDERSTANDING

1. Assume that you have been assigned to write the draft of the advice letter to the parents of Daniel de la Cruz. He was suspended from his public middle school for certain statements that he made. The firm has decided that there are grounds to pursue a claim against his school district for violating his free speech rights and that this matter would justify a lawsuit in federal court if the school district does not agree to return Daniel to class.
   a. Who is the audience for your letter?
   b. What are the two main purposes of your letter?
   c. What are its subsidiary purposes?
   d. What is the distinction in areas of responsibility, as between lawyer and client, made in ABA Model Rule 1.2?
   e. How does Rule 2.1 describe the advice you should provide to your client?
   f. What requirements as to client contact does Rule 1.4 impose?

2. List the items you would include in the heading of your letter.

3. As for the introduction:
   a. What is the purpose of the first part?
   b. What are the options for stating the overview?
   c. List three ground rules of an advice letter that could be included in the introduction, and indicate whether you likely would include them in this letter.

4. As for the summary of facts:
   a. Should you include or omit each of the following types of facts, and why: background, favorable, relevant, residual, and unfavorable?
   b. List two organizational schemes that you would consider using.
   c. In addition to accurately and objectively, how should you phrase your facts?
   d. Why might you include some caveats in your summary? Provide an example.

5. As for the explanation:
   a. What means should you use to present a clearly organized explanation?
   b. How does presentation of the law in an advice letter differ from its presentation in an analytical office memo?
   c. Does presentation of your predicted legal outcome differ from the analytical office memo to the advice letter?

6. As for the advice:
   a. In what ways does the advice extend beyond the legal analysis presented in the explanation?
   b. Under what circumstances would you indicate which option you consider the best for the client to pursue?

7. What are the three parts of the closing?

8. If you were writing an advice letter to the school district as it considered creating a student appearance code, you would be writing a transactional advice letter. This letter would be contingent in nature; provide four examples of what this means.

9. If you decide to use e-mail to send your advice letter to a client, state five protocols you should follow to do so in a professional manner.

TEST YOUR UNDERSTANDING ANSWERS

1. If you were writing an advice letter for the Daniel de la Cruz situation:
   a. Your audience is the client, most likely his parents.
   b. The two main purposes of your letter are to inform the clients of your legal analysis and to persuade them to take action with sound legal support.
   c. Its subsidiary purposes are to establish rapport and verify the facts and your tasks.
   d. Rule 1.2 provides that the client sets the objectives of the representation and that the lawyer decides the means by which to pursue them.
   e. Rule 2.1 describes your advice as independent and candid; it may include moral, social, and economic considerations.
   f. Rule 1.4 requires you to promptly inform the client of key decisions, reasonably consult about the means of representation, keep the client reasonably informed about the status of the case, and promptly comply with requests for information.

2. The heading includes your letterhead and date; the recipient's name, position, and address; the salutation; and sometimes the topic of the letter.

3. As for the introduction:
   a. The purpose of the first part is to establish rapport with the reader.
   b. In the overview, you may state the conclusion, the topics, the issues, or some combination.
   c. Three ground-rule topics are confidentiality, a request for verification of facts, and a note that conclusions may change. Given that this is a new client, stating these points would be wise.

4. As for the summary of facts:
   a. Relevant and background facts must be included because they are needed for the analysis and for the story to make sense; residual facts that are important to the client may be included within limits; favorable and unfavorable facts are included depending on the preceding analyses.
   b. The most likely organizational schemes are chronological and topical.
   c. Facts should be phrased diplomatically, as well as accurately and objectively.
   d. Caveats refer to the manner in which facts are known or could be proven and should be included if the situation calls for them. An example is that you have not investigated the facts; it could be useful to state this point in the de la Cruz situation.

5. As for the explanation:
   a. A clearly organized discussion is accomplished through a logical order, transitions, a roadmap, and a summary.
   b. The law is presented less in the form of fully stated rules and legal authorities and more in the form of key legal concepts.
   c. No, the legal outcome should be your best prediction of the legal outcome and reflect your degree of certainty.

6. As for the advice:
   a. The advice looks to concrete actions to be taken by or on behalf of the client and may incorporate nonlegal concerns.
   b. You would cover only one option if the law afforded only one option, and you would support a specific option among several if you have a strong client relationship based on trust and knowledge.

7. The three parts of the closing are an indication of your next steps, instructions for the client, and your signature.

8. A transactional advice letter is contingent in nature, which means;
   a. The introduction refers to the legal consequences of a future transaction.
   b. The summary of facts includes events that are projected to occur.
   c. The explanation focuses on the application of legal concepts to proposed conduct.
   d. The advice presents options that would fit within the law.

9. Five protocols for using e-mail professionally are:
   a. Send a targeted message, not a group or reply-to-all message, so that your message is received by the right recipient(s).
   b. Include a clear subject.
   c. Indicate that the message is confidential.
   d. As needed, indicate that the message is urgent.
   e. Include a transmittal letter.

INTERVIEWING THE CLIENT

I learned that I never really know the true story of my guests' lives, that I have to content myself with knowing that when I'm interviewing somebody, I'm getting a combination of fact and truth and self-mythology and self-delusion and selective memory and faulty memory.
    —Terry Gross (host of *Fresh Air*)

A. INTRODUCTION

Most lawyers spend a lot of time talking. Their most important conversations are with their clients. Of these, the foundational conversations are the initial ones: the client interview and the first client counseling session. Although the distinction is somewhat artificial, in the *client interview*, the lawyer and potential client[1]

---

1. For ease of expression, this chapter generally uses "client" rather than "potential client."

explore the client's situation and whether the lawyer will represent the client. In client counseling, the lawyer advises the client about the legal significance of her[2] situation, and they develop strategies for actions to be taken on the client's behalf. This chapter discusses client interviewing, and Chapter 11 discusses client counseling.

The client interview is a complex conversation. It has three interlocking *purposes*: to establish personal and professional rapport between the lawyer and the client, to permit the lawyer to learn enough about the client's situation to decide whether to represent the client, and to help the client decide whether to hire the lawyer. To a certain extent, these purposes align with the three main stages of the interview: establishing rapport, learning the client's situation, and discussing next steps. Accordingly, the chapter is organized around these three stages. It closes with a discussion of professional practices in interviewing.

As examples, this chapter refers, for a dispute example, to the Bower's Bounty situation, with a shift: here, the client is the recently terminated employee considering whether to bring a claim of defamation against Bower's Bounty. For a transactional example, this chapter refers to the All-Day Wellness situation, in which the client seeks to prevent its employees from working for the competition when they leave the company.

B. ESTABLISHING RAPPORT

In many law offices, your client will have spoken to a member of your office staff before meeting you. Thus, you will have some preliminary information, such as her name and her concerns, before you meet. It may be tempting to jump right into asking questions about her situation, but doing so would undermine your chances of establishing a personal connection. The key to a strong lawyer-client relationship is *mutual trust*, and the interview is the occasion for beginning to build that trust. Only if that trust is established will the client tell you what you need to know, and only with that trust will you gain her full support for actions that you take on her behalf.

Thus, the initial minutes of the interview should be spent introducing yourself, welcoming the client to your office, and engaging in idle conversation. Aim to find a non-legal topic of mutual interest, and consider sharing something personal about yourself. Refer to your client by name. Establish an engaging style of *non-verbal communication* through eye contact, facial expressions, nodding and other body language, and active listening. *Active listening* consists of waiting until the client has finished speaking before you chime in and reflecting her comments in what you say next. If possible, arrange to sit with the client at a table rather than sitting across a desk from the client.

Once you have established some comfort with the client, you are ready to move into the body of the interview. Make a transition by providing an agenda of

---

2. For ease of expression, this chapter uses feminine pronouns for the client. Many clients are, of course, male. Furthermore, many clients are entities, such as companies, government units, or nonprofit organizations, but individuals speak for them.

what is to come, encouraging the client to ask questions or make comments at any time, and providing the client a means of taking notes if she so desires.

C. LEARNING THE CLIENT'S SITUATION

Most of the time in any client interview is spent learning the client's situation, which can be much harder than you would think. This part discusses this stage of the interview in four sections:

- Facing the challenge, which discusses the dynamics surrounding the revelation of the client's situation;
- Learning the client's factual context, which covers the objective dimensions of the client's situation;
- Learning the client's interests and goals, which covers the subjective dimensions of the client's situation; and
- Working with challenging clients, which discusses strategies for handling overly emotional, forgetful, and misrepresenting clients.

1. Facing the Challenge

You would think that a client would be willing, if not happy, to tell her lawyer the whole, unvarnished truth about her situation. Experienced lawyers will tell you that this is often not the case. Many potential clients are reticent around lawyers. *Negative emotions* such as embarrassment, sorrow, or trauma may keep clients from wanting to talk fully about their situations. Some clients do not want to undermine their situations by revealing what they think are adverse facts. Other clients are intimidated by lawyers.

Furthermore, clients may be *cognitively impeded* from fully or accurately telling their stories. People vary in their abilities to observe an event based on such factors as the time they are exposed to the event, how noteworthy the event was, how observant they are in a general sense, how stressed they were at the time of the event, and how much self-interest they have in the event. Furthermore, even an accurately observed event may not be recalled accurately. Memory is not fixed; rather, it is highly malleable. An accurate memory of an event can be undermined by the passage of time, its blending into the memories of other events, the individual's own processing of the memory, and the conduct of other people in discussing the event—including how the individual has been questioned about it.[3]

These emotional and cognitive factors may or may not operate during any particular client interview, but you should always be alert for them. One strategy for increasing a client's willingness to tell a complete and truthful story is to explain the *duty of attorney confidentiality*. In general, a lawyer is ethically obligated not to reveal information related to the representation of a client, other than

---

3. A classic example is when the police provide a set of photographs suggesting that the perpetrator of a crime is among those shown. *See* Stefan H. Krieger & Richard K. Neumann, Jr., *Essential Lawyering Skills: Interviewing, Counseling, Negotiation, and Persuasive Fact Analysis* 83-87 (5th ed. 2015).

BOX 10.1

ABA MODEL RULE 1.6 CONFIDENTIALITY OF INFORMATION

(a) A lawyer shall not reveal information relating to the representation of a client unless the client gives informed consent, the disclosure is impliedly authorized in order to carry out the representation or the disclosure is permitted by paragraph (b).

(b) A lawyer may reveal information relating to the representation of a client to the extent the lawyer reasonably believes it necessary: (1) to prevent reasonably certain death or substantial bodily harm; (2) to prevent the client from committing a crime or fraud that is reasonably certain to result in substantial injury to the financial interests or property of another [and will entail the lawyer's services]; (3) to prevent, rectify, or mitigate [a similar crime or fraud]; (4) to secure legal advice about the lawyer's compliance with these Rules; (5) to establish a claim or defense on behalf of the lawyer [in various legal proceedings arising out of the representation]; (6) to comply with law or other court order; or (7) to detect and resolve conflicts of interest arising from the lawyer's change of employment or from changes in the composition or ownership of a firm [only if doing so would not harm the client].

(c) A lawyer shall make reasonable efforts to prevent the inadvertent or unauthorized disclosure of, or unauthorized access to, information relating to the representation of a client.

---

to carry out the representation or with client consent. Box 10.1 sets out the formulation provided in *ABA Model Rule of Professional Conduct 1.6*; furthermore, *Model Rule 3.3* may require disclosure of client fraudulent conduct under certain circumstances in litigation. The details of these rules are complicated and vary from state to state.[4] A full recitation of the confidentiality rule would overwhelm any client, but a statement of the main idea should be a part of every interview. Stating it when you begin to discuss the client's situation is one option.

Another topic to cover before beginning to discuss the client's situation is your note-taking. You may be tempted to take as many notes on your computer as you can during the interview. However, this approach would be counterproductive: not only would it undermine the eye contact and body language that you need to establish rapport with your client,[5] it also would keep you from fully processing what you are hearing and being ready to continue the interview. The better approach is to jot down key points on a notepad and record your extensive notes immediately after the interview.

---

4. A parallel area of law, the evidence rule of attorney-client privilege, prohibits a lawyer from testifying to what a client has stated to her lawyer unless the client has waived the privilege.

5. An often-cited study in the field of non-verbal communication is that only 7 percent of the impact of some messages derives from the words themselves, whereas 55 percent derives from the speaker's body language and 38 percent from the tone of voice. See the work of social psychologist Albert Mehrabian, *Silent Messages* (1971), and the various types of non-verbal communications discussed at the website creducation.org.

2. Learning the Factual Context

As you talk with your client about her situation, keep in mind that your purpose is to learn enough about it to decide whether to represent the client in resolving her dispute or arranging her transaction. This decision may come at the end of the interview, if you are sufficiently confident of the facts, the applicable law, and your read of the client. Or you may decide to hold off to engage in some further investigation before deciding.

Either way, though, you need to obtain an accurate and deep understanding of the client's *objective situation*—the events that led her to visit your office. They may be past events that gave rise to a dispute that now needs resolution, or they may be present events that could give rise to a transaction and the events that the client would like to see occur. You need to know not just what happened, is happening, or may happen; you also need to know how the client thinks about the facts and how the facts can be shown. And you should learn these facts in a way that fosters rapport between you and your client. A classic approach to this stage of the interview is a three-round interviewing cycle: narration, exposition, and reiteration.[6]

First, in the *narration cycle,* the client tells you about her situation, as unimpeded as possible by your questions. Through this narration, you receive not only an overview of the situation, but also a sense of what is most important to the client, based on how she chooses to frame her narrative. A good way to begin this cycle is by asking an *open-ended question,* such as "What brings you here today?" To keep the narration going if the client tails off, ask *prompting questions,* such as "What happened next?" and "How did you react to that?"

Second, in the *exposition cycle,* you take more control to obtain information you consider useful in light of the probably applicable law and the client's situation. In this cycle, you ask *probing questions* for the purposes of clarifying confusing points, such as unclear chronology or roles; obtaining additional details; and indeed exploring new topics. The client may feel interrogated, so to minimize this awkward feeling, begin by explaining why you need additional information to look into her matter, and encourage the client to tell you everything that she can remember. In addition, ask your questions in logical packages of related questions and preface each topic with a statement recalling briefly what the client has stated to date. The categories of questions differ somewhat from the dispute setting to the transactional setting; Box 10.2 contains sample questions for the Bower's Bounty dispute situation and the All-Day Wellness transactional situation. Here are questioning strategies to employ and not employ during this cycle:

- Ask only one question at a time, and give your client time to think before she answers. If you ask two questions, you may get only one answer, and you may not know which question was answered.
- To obtain a full understanding of a key event, cover the full set of journalist's questions: who, what, when, where, why, and how? For some people, it is difficult to explain why they did some things; an easier question to answer is "How did you come to do that?"

---

6. You might think of these three cycles in laundry terms: the first as pre-wash (the client tells the story), the second as wash (you seek out the facts through your questions), and the third as rinse (you seek verification of what you believe to be the facts).

BOX 10.2

SAMPLE INTERVIEW QUESTIONS AS TO FACTUAL CONTEXT

DISPUTE SETTING

Bower's Bounty terminated Ms. Nicholson's employment and stated in a posting on a bulletin board that she engaged in pilferage. The following questions could be asked of Sarah Nicholson.

Narration Cycle

What brings you here today?
What happened after you talked to your manager?
What was your reaction when you read the posting?

Exposition Cycle

What time of day was it when you read the posting?
Where was the posting on the bulletin board?
What is generally posted on that part of the bulletin board?
Who generally reads that part of the bulletin board?
Was anyone else in the room when you read the posting?
Did he or she say anything to you about the posting?
What, as best you recall, did the posting say?
Did you write down the words or take a picture?
Please make a chart of the people to whom you report.
Did you receive any written statement regarding your termination?
I can be a good advocate for you only if I can think about this from Bower's Bounty's point of view. Do you have thoughts about why Mr. Molinaro would have posted this statement?

TRANSACTION SETTING

The following questions could be asked of Ella Dionne, the president of All-Day Wellness, who is seeking a means of preventing her employees from working for the competition when they leave the company.

Narration Cycle

What brings you here today?
What services does your business provide to its clients?
What are the competitive pressures facing your company?

Exposition Cycle

In Washington, how many employees have left your company over the past few years?
Of those, how many went to work for competitors?
(After explaining what a covenant not-to-compete is) Have you ever tried using covenants not-to-compete with your employees?
What are the precise tasks that your consultants do for your clients?
How many clients does each consultant generally work with?
How wide a geographic territory does each consultant cover?
What terms do the employment agreements cover now?
What is the process you use for entering into the agreements?
How do you think employees will react to having a covenant not-to-compete in their agreements?
Have you thought about what you would do if a prospective employee refused to sign one?

- For important matters, press for hard facts rather than soft descriptions. For example, it may matter that "five people" were present rather than just "a group."

- Consider asking for a visual aid to support an answer relating to topics such as locations (a map) or groups of people (a family tree or organizational chart).

- Ask about documents or papers that the client has received, created, or signed that relate to the matter.

- Similarly, ask about people who know about the matter, whether they are participants in the events or people with whom the client has talked about the event.

- Do not ask *leading questions*. A leading question implies an answer, and the client may agree with that answer because she believes that you know it to be true or wants to please you. (Many clients view their lawyers as authority figures.) An example of a leading question is "I imagine that would be very stressful; how did you feel then?"

- Do not use *loaded language*. A loaded word contains a judgment and can thus prompt a skewed answer. An example of a loaded question is: "Were you speeding as you approached the intersection?" A non-loaded question on the same topic is: "What was your approximate speed as you drove up to the intersection?"

- Avoid, to the extent possible, the use of *legal language* as you ask questions.[7] First, the client may not understand the terminology. Second, the client may assume that you have made some legal conclusions about the situation when she hears you use these words.

Third, in the *reiteration cycle*, you restate the main points of the client's situation. This restatement confirms to the client that she has been heard, which reinforces your rapport, and it highlights for her the most important facts of her situation from a legal standpoint. It also affords the client the opportunity to correct any errors and to add any omitted points. Thus you should preface your restatement with perhaps the most important "questions": "I am now going to briefly summarize what I've heard. Please let me know if I have anything wrong, and please let me know if there is anything else I need to know."

As you proceed through these cycles, take care not to let your mind shift into legal analysis and narrow your interview accordingly. It is natural to categorize client situations by legal topics within a few minutes, but doing so may obscure your openness to facets of the situation that do not fit your initial legal analysis. Until you have heard your client's full story—and indeed, until you have researched the law—you will not fully know what is legally significant.

---

7. This point is less important when dealing with sophisticated clients, as well as in transactional settings, where the names of the options may themselves be legal terms.

3. Learning the Client's Interests and Goals

Your client's situation is not comprised only of objective facts; it also has a *subjective dimension*. Your client's emotional responses to the facts of her situation form part of this dimension. These responses, along with your client's setting, life experiences, personality, and values, fuel your client's interests and goals as to the result of the representation. An *interest* is an abstraction that is of value to the client; a *goal* is a concrete result that the client would like to see when the representation concludes. Goals serve interests. For example, in a dispute setting, an interest in financial security leads to a goal of recovering money damages. As another example, in a transactional setting, an interest in avoiding publicity leads to a clause that provides private means of resolving disputes arising under the contract. Two clients in an identical situation would not necessarily have the same sets of interests and goals, and neither may have the interests and goals that you would have if you were in that situation. Thus, you should never assume that you know your client's interests and goals.

Some clients may be very adept in discussing interests and goals; others may not. Again, asking an open-ended initial question about the results of the representation can be a good way to start: "What would you like to see as the result of my work on your behalf?" Comparable questions can begin the discussion of the client's interests: "Why is that result important to you?" If these questions do not work, or in order to obtain additional insight, consider asking about adverse results and their impacts. Probing questions should explore matters such as timing, expense, reputation, and concern for third parties. Box 10.3 contains sample questions for the Bower's Bounty dispute situation and the All-Day Wellness transactional situation.

You may well uncover a conflict in interests, as when a client in a dispute setting seeks vindication but at little expense, or a client in a transaction setting seeks an elaborate document in a short period of time. In general, noting rather than resolving the conflict is the best approach at the interview stage.

You may experience the rare occasion that a client at this point states that she seeks a clearly illegal result. Depending on the seriousness of this statement, you may need to decline taking on the client to avoid facilitating the illegal conduct.

4. Working with Challenging Clients

As you listen to and question some clients, you may find that they pose particular challenges, from the standpoint both of forming a relationship of trust and of learning about their situations. Although there are many variations, three categories merit mention: the highly emotional client, the forgetful client, and the misrepresenting client.

The *highly emotional client*: You should expect a client to express emotion, depending on the nature of her situation. Indeed, these expressions can provide valuable insights. As a caring person, you should express genuine empathy; however, avoid hollow platitudes (such as "I know how you feel"). However, because you are licensed as a lawyer, it is not appropriate to slip into the role of psychologist or therapist.[8] And you still need to obtain all the information about

---

8. Comment 4 to ABA Model Rule of Professional Conduct 2.1 encourages recommending consultation with professionals in related fields when a lawyer encounters issues within those fields.

BOX 10.3

SAMPLE INTERVIEW QUESTIONS
AS TO INTERESTS AND GOALS

DISPUTE SETTING

What results would you like to see from my work on your behalf?

How do you see a reference letter from Bower's Bounty helping you move forward?

How soon would you like to resolve this situation?

TRANSACTION SETTING

What results would you like to see from my work on your behalf?

How much do your employees' attitudes toward the covenant not-to-compete matter to you?

If an employee did leave and go to work for a competitor, would you be willing to litigate to enforce the covenant?

---

the client's situation, even if her strong emotions are posing an obstacle. Several useful techniques are to explain clearly how knowing sensitive information will help you help the client, to reiterate your duty of confidentiality, to discuss less sensitive facets of the situation first, to come at the sensitive topics through narrow questions, and to take breaks to permit your client to recover emotionally.

The *forgetful client*: It is possible, of course, that your client never knew or will never remember the facts as well as you would like. On the other hand, some techniques can help people remember facts that they do know. One simple technique is to encourage the client to tell you everything, in order to loosen up a client who is engaging in self-editing. A second technique is to ask the client to describe the setting of the event by asking her to "set the scene," e.g., recall the time of the day, the weather, the other people present, her clothing. A third technique is to disrupt the chronology; asking about a later event in detail can sometimes trigger a clearer memory of an earlier event because the later event sheds light on what must have happened before it. Finally, provide time for a client to think; some clients need some time to think and formulate their thoughts before speaking.

The *misrepresenting client*: You may detect factual misrepresentations on the part of your client in an initial interview, or you may become aware of a misrepresentation after you have done some investigation. Keep in mind that the client may be acting more or less innocently or intentionally. Simply accepting the misrepresentation raises ethical issues, of course.[9] While it may be tempting to

---

9. For three pertinent ethics rules, see ABA Model Rules of Professional Conduct 3.3 Candor Toward the Tribunal; 3.4 Fairness to Opposing Party and Counsel; and 4.1 Truthfulness in Statements to Others.

call out the lie, other techniques may be more effective in preserving rapport with the client, making the point about the need for accuracy, and leading to the truth. These techniques include reiterating your duty of confidentiality; explaining the necessity of knowing the whole truth—including unfavorable facts—if you are to represent the client effectively; telling a story in which facts learned too late undermined effective representation; asking probing questions about what others in the situation would say about the situation; and asking a series of leading questions that align with the truth.[10] Of course, if the would-be client is recalcitrant, the relationship may lack the trust necessary for you to take on the matter.

D. DISCUSSING NEXT STEPS

The concluding stage of the client interview is discussing next steps. One possibility, of course, is that you will decide not to represent the individual, in which case you should communicate this decision courteously and clearly.[11] Another possibility is that the individual will not be interested in hiring you.

On the other hand, if things have gone well, you may be willing to either agree to represent the client at this point or to do so if your factual investigation, legal research, or both yield positive results. In this instance, you and the client would proceed to discuss your next steps. At some point, whether at the end of the interview or at a later meeting if the representation decision is deferred, you and your client should discuss your terms of engagement. These terms are stated in the *retainer letter*, by which the lawyer and client formally enter into their contractual relationship. The retainer letter should cover such matters as the scope of the matter to be handled, the respective responsibilities of the lawyer and client, and the termination of the relationship. For an example, see the form retainer letter in Exhibit 10.[12]

One major topic to be covered in the letter and discussed thoroughly with the client is, of course, the matter of *attorney fees* and costs to be paid during the representation. The fee structure for legal representation varies, depending mostly on the type of matter as well as the financial capacity of the client and the negotiations between the lawyer and the client. See Box 10.4. The amount of the fee must be reasonable, according to ethics rules.[13] Often, no fee is specifically charged for the interview.

---

10. You may use some of these techniques in a follow-up interview based on your factual investigation.

11. In this instance, good practice calls for follow-up written communication to make clear that you have not been hired and that the client should act promptly if any rights may be in jeopardy, such as promptly filing a claim to avoid the running of a statute of limitations.

12. That form is recommended for us in domestic relations practice involving matters such as pre-marital agreements. Some technical clauses have been deleted.

13. Under ABA Model Rule of Professional Conduct 1.5, factors include the time and labor required, the difficulty of the matter, the skill required, the standards of the community, the length of the lawyer-client relationship, and the experience of the lawyer.

BOX 10.4

TYPICAL FEE STRUCTURES

- *Hourly rate:* The client pays a set fee (which depends on the status and experience of the lawyer) per increment of each hour that the lawyer works on the matter. Bower's Bounty likely would pay its lawyer an hourly rate.
- *Flat fee:* The client pays a specified amount for the project, regardless of how much time it takes. For an example, All-Day Wellness might pay a flat fee for the covenant not-to-compete.
- *Contingent fee:* The client pays a percentage of the amount recovered on behalf of the client, if any, in the litigation. This is not permitted in criminal and domestic cases, according to Model Rule 1.5(d). Sarah Nicholson likely would pay her lawyer on a contingent fee basis in the Bower's Bounty situation.
- *Pro bono representation:* The client does not pay a fee, generally because she does not have the means to pay. Daniel de la Cruz may be represented on a pro bono basis if his parents are of limited means, given the free speech nature of his claim.
- Under the *American Rule*, parties in litigation generally pay their own attorney fees; exceptions include contract agreements and statutes providing for recovery of fees by the prevailing parties.

Some clients will press for a prediction of the result at the end of an interview, even though you may not be ready to provide one because you need to research the law or look into the facts or both. Unless the client's situation is clear-cut on the facts and the law, avoid providing a prediction. Rather, provide some closure by explaining the importance of careful analysis and indicating that you will be undertaking the steps that will lead to a prediction.

The closing stage also should cover what the client will do next. In general, you should instruct the client to not impair her situation, such as by talking to the opposing party in a dispute; to gather her papers that pertain to the matter; and to record any thoughts or questions that she has until your next contact. You should set a date and method for your next contact, and be sure that the client who hires you knows how to contact you.

Of course, as the client leaves, you should engage in common courtesies: thank her for her time and for the opportunity to (potentially) work on her matter; and wish her a good day.

E. PROFESSIONAL PRACTICES

For your potential client to be willing to hire you—and furthermore to build the trust that will sustain your relationship—you must conduct the interview in a professional manner. Certainly. every lawyer has his or her own style. Norms do vary from somewhat setting to setting; what is expected in a firm that represents large corporations may not be expected in a legal aid office that works with people of limited financial means. Regardless of your personal style and setting, certain practices will convey professionalism to any potential client:

- Your communication should be correct. Be sure, for example, that you are pronouncing your client's name right.
- Your communication should be clear. In particular, avoid unnecessary legalese. Far from impressing the client, such language only confounds and annoys most clients. Overuse of legalese suggests disrespect.
- Your communication should be articulate. Most of us have oral tics—phrases that we say without thinking. Avoid the use of phrases such as "you know what I mean?" In particular, aim to avoid saying "okay," because this may convey to the client that you approve what has been said. On the other hand, occasional "hmms" and "ohs" or "I see" are not an issue.
- Signal your competence. This is why lawyers post their diplomas and bar certificates on their office walls. It is also appropriate to explain that you have experience in matters similar to what your client is facing.
- Present yourself as organized and prepared. Be ready with whatever materials you need to take notes; have a copy of your retainer letter at hand.
- Convey that you are focused on her specific matter. Start when scheduled, and block out enough time for a decent discussion. Do not accept interruptions during the interview absent a true emergency. Turn off your electronic devices.
- Your personal appearance, attire, and office should be well-maintained and suitable to your practice setting. If you or your office appears disorganized or messy, you will cast doubt on your ability to manage your client's matter in an orderly fashion.

Finally, heed the newest *ABA Model Rule of Professional Conduct 8.4(g)*, which states that it is professional misconduct to "engage in conduct that the lawyer knows or reasonably should know is harassment or discrimination on the basis of race, sex, religion, national origin, ethnicity, disability, age, sexual orientation, gender identity, marital status, or socioeconomic status in conduct related to the practice of law."[14] Ours is a diverse country, and the chances are high that you will have the opportunity and privilege to represent people who differ from you. It is a measure of your professionalism to not only tolerate these differences but also to convey genuine respect for these differences.

---

14. This amendment was adopted on August 8, 2016; twenty-five jurisdictions already had such rules. For discussion of the rule, see Peter Geraghty, *ABA adopts new anti-discrimination Rule 8.4(g)*, YOUR ABA e-news for members (Sept. 2016) (available at www.americanbar.org/youraba).

Exhibit 10   219

EXHIBIT 10   SAMPLE RETAINER LETTER[15]

Dear *[Client]*:

Please let this letter confirm that you have requested my firm ("the Firm") to represent you in connection with the negotiation and entry into of a *[specify type]* agreement. In order to avoid any confusion with respect to the Firm's fee structure for services to be rendered, the Court Rules require this engagement letter, which serves to outline and explain our agreement. It is important that you read this letter carefully inasmuch as after you sign the acknowledgment on the last page hereof, it will constitute a legal and binding contract between you and the Firm. Please also refer to the Statement of Client's Rights and Responsibilities, which is annexed to this agreement.

I. INITIAL RETAINER AND REPLENISHMENTS

Before commencing any work, the Firm requires an initial fee retainer in the sum of $*[dollar amount]* on account of services to be rendered in connection with your matter. This retainer is not a minimum non-refundable amount and any part of same that remains unearned at such time as the Firm's representation terminates will be refunded to you.

The attorney and staff time, and disbursements incurred, all as more particularly set forth in the following paragraphs, will be applied against your retainer. At such time as there exists a balance of $*[dollar amount]*, or less, in your retainer account, you agree to immediately replenish same with an additional $*[dollar amount]* retainer (or other reasonable amount dictated by the circumstances then existing), and so on, so that there will always be sufficient funds in your retainer account to cover services rendered and disbursements incurred on a going forward basis. If you do not replenish your retainer, or if your bill is not paid in full within 30 days of receipt, the Firm has the right to, on reasonable notice to you, immediately terminate its representation.

II. HOURLY RATES AND ATTORNEY PRIMARILY RESPONSIBLE FOR CASE

You will be billed at the following hourly rates for the following attorneys, paralegals and in-house investigator:

Attorney	Hourly Rate
[Name]	*[Rate]*
Paralegals	
[Name]	*[Rate]*

---

15. Source: 7 West's Legal Forms, *Domestic Relations* § 2:15 (3d ed. 2016).

EXHIBIT 10 (**cont.**)

Junior Paralegal
[Name]   _[Rate]_
In-House Investigator
[Name]   _[Rate]_

. . .

At this time I will be the attorney primarily responsible for the handling of your case. However, unless you specifically direct me otherwise, in my discretion I may utilize the services of other attorneys and staff in order to provide you with the best possible representation and to keep your fees to a minimum.

It is the Firm's policy to bill all time at a daily minimum of two-tenths (.2) of an hour per day on those days when work is performed on your matter. All billing rates are subject to change in accordance with the Firm's policy and you will be notified accordingly.

Services shall include, but not necessarily be limited to, any and all time spent on investigation, research, preparation of pleadings, memoranda, correspondence or similar documentation, telephone communications, travel time to and from and attendance at related conferences, depositions and court proceedings, together with any and all other attorney and indicated staff time spent on your case.

Although the Firm has a general policy of not charging for the first hour of time in connection with an initial consultation, in the event more than one hour is spent at the initial consultation, any time in excess of the first hour will be billed to you. **Additionally**, in the event that you elect to retain the Firm after the initial consultation, since the information gathered at the initial consultation will be used by the Firm for your representation, **all time will be billed, including the time spent at the initial consultation**.

III. **PAYMENT OF DISBURSEMENTS**

In addition to attorney and indicated staff time, you agree to pay any and all disbursements incurred in connection with your matter, including, but not necessarily limited to, the following:

Computerized legal research (e.g., Westlaw, Lexis, etc.);

Copy costs (presently _____¢ per copy);

Courier costs;

Exhibit 10   221

EXHIBIT 10 (cont.)

Court filing fees and costs;

Court transcript fees;

Deposition costs (e.g., stenographer and transcript fees);

Fax charges;

Lay and expert witness fees;

Meal costs incurred in connection with attendance at court/case-related proceedings;

Postage and overnight mailing fees;

Telephone (incl. pro-rated monthly cellular charges);

Travel costs (generally, tolls and, presently, _____¢ per mile).

. . .

VI. **WITHDRAWAL/DISCHARGE OF COUNSEL**

Please be advised, that in the event the Firm believes that you are not in compliance with any term of this engagement letter, or if you should fail to timely cooperate with the Firm's representation, you agree that the Firm can decline, on reasonable notice to you, continuing representation in this matter — without refund of the cost of time spent or disbursements and costs incurred through the date of termination of the representation. Of course, if you are dissatisfied with the Firm's services, you are free to discharge the Firm at any time.

VII. **NO PREDICTION OR GUARANTEE OF COST OF REPRESENTATION**

At this time, the Firm cannot accurately predict or guarantee how much your representation will ultimately cost. This is due to various factors, including the level of reasonableness, compromise and/or cooperation between you and the other party involved, the complexity of the issues presented, and, of course, the amount of time it actually takes to bring this matter to a satisfactory conclusion. However, the Firm will make every reasonable effort to keep fees to a minimum and assures you that only services deemed reasonable and necessary to satisfactorily represent you will be performed.

. . .

EXHIBIT 10   (cont.)

IX. NO PREDICTION OR GUARANTEE OF SUCCESS/RESULTS

Of course, given the inherent uncertainty of legal proceedings, the interpretation of and changes in the law, and myriad unpredictable variables, the Firm cannot predict and, therefore, does not guarantee a particular result or absolute success on any issue in your case. This notwithstanding, the Firm, with your cooperation, agrees to represent your interests conscientiously, diligently, within the bounds of ethical propriety and with the purpose of accomplishing your desired objectives.

X. SCOPE OF THE FIRM'S REPRESENTATION

As we discussed, the Firm's representation of your interests at this time is limited solely to services relating to the negotiation and entry into of a *[specify type]* agreement. Unless otherwise indicated herein, our representation according to the terms of this agreement specifically does not include representing you in any other legal proceedings such as, without limitation, the following:

1. Commencing any litigation in any court.
2. Handling a real estate transaction.
3. Preparing a Last Will and Testament or performing any trust and estate planning matters.

Should you desire the Firm to perform any services pertaining to matters other than that specifically described herein, we will be pleased to discuss an appropriate additional fee arrangement with you. However, if the Firm undertakes to represent you in any other matter with your implied and/or express understanding, knowledge and consent, without first discussing such other appropriate additional fee arrangement, the fee structure, terms and conditions of this engagement letter shall apply.

XI. POTENTIAL CONFLICT

Prior to commencing your representation, the Firm has performed an internal conflict check to determine whether or not there exists any restriction on the Firm's ability to represent you. Although at this time the Firm does not believe there is any conflict in its representation of your interests, a presently unknown conflict may arise in the future. In that event, the Firm will discuss with you all available representation options, which may include, without limitation, the Firm's voluntary withdrawal from any further representation on your behalf, or litigating the potential conflict such that a court will determine the extent of any possible conflict. In the event the Firm must withdraw as your counsel, at your request, the Firm will assist you to the best of its ability insofar as your retaining substitute counsel. Notwithstanding any possible future restriction on the Firm's ability to represent your interests in this matter, all fees for services and disbursements theretofore due and owing shall be paid by you.

. . .

Exhibit 10

223

EXHIBIT 10 (cont.)

XIII. **ACKNOWLEDGMENT**

If you understand and agree to the foregoing engagement arrangement, please sign and date the acknowledgment, below, on the accompanying copy of this correspondence, and promptly return the executed copy to my attention in the return envelope provided. The firm requires the receipt of your signed acknowledgment and initial fee retainer in order to commence work on your behalf.

Please feel free to contact me with any questions you may have concerning this agreement.

Very truly yours,

[Attorney's name]

ACKNOWLEDGMENT

The undersigned hereby acknowledges having read and fully understood the terms and conditions set forth in the foregoing engagement agreement. The undersigned further acknowledges having had any and all questions concerning the instant engagement agreement satisfactorily answered and that this agreement is entered freely and voluntarily without any compulsion or duress in so doing. The undersigned agrees to comply with the terms and conditions stated therein.

_____

[Client's name]

DATED:

EXHIBIT 10 (cont.)

STATEMENT OF CLIENT'S RIGHTS AND RESPONSIBILITIES

The client has the right:

1. To have their attorneys diligently advocate their interest within the bounds of the law and legal ethics.
2. To have the fee arrangement fully and completely explained prior to entering into any agreement for services.
3. To have a written retainer agreement describing the financial terms of their relationship between the client and the attorney.
4. To refuse to enter into an unacceptable fee arrangement or modification of a fee arrangement.
5. To be provided information as to the attorney(s) who will be primarily responsible for their matter and all other legal staff who will be working on the matter as well as information as to the costs for those individuals.
6. To be provided bills on a regular basis, itemized as to the charges and time spent on each activity.
7. To be informed of and be present at any court proceeding involving their case unless otherwise ordered by the court.
8. To be provided copies of all documents presented to the court by any party in their matter unless otherwise ordered by the court.
9. To be afforded reasonable access to their attorneys.
10. To make the final decision as to whether, when, and how to settle their case and as to economic and other positions to be taken with respect to issues in the case.

The client is responsible to:

1. Provide full and accurate information to their attorneys regarding their matter.
2. Be available to participate in a timely fashion regarding their matter and respond reasonably to request[s] from their attorneys.
3. Advise their attorneys promptly of any change[s] in their lives that might reasonably be expected to affect the handling of their matter.
4. Pay for the legal services rendered on their behalf within the time period set forth in the retainer agreement.
5. Diligently review all bills submitted by their attorneys and raise any objections regarding billing within a reasonable time.
6. Not take any position in the matter for any improper purpose, such as intentionally delaying the proceeding to increase the cost to other litigants.
7. Not seek to use their attorneys for any improper means.
8. Recognize and be responsible for the costs associated with any action initiated or requested by the client.
9. Provide sufficient time for their attorneys to explain the financial costs and other ramifications of a potential action in the matter and reasonably consider the advice of their attorneys.

TEST YOUR UNDERSTANDING

1. Assume that you have been assigned to participate in the interview of the parents of Daniel de la Cruz. The firm's legal assistant has informed you that he was suspended from his public middle school for shaving a message into his hair in support of his sister, who has breast cancer, and the firm is considering taking on his case as a possible pro bono matter. How does the upcoming interview differ from client counseling?

2. Why is trust central to the lawyer-client relationship, and how can you foster it as you begin your interview?

3. Although what you say matters, so do other forms of communication:
   a. Give several examples of non-verbal communication.
   b. Explain active listening.

4. Even though you have not yet met any of the de la Cruzes, you should anticipate that it may be difficult to learn the precise details of their factual context from them.
   a. Why may they be reluctant to explain their situation to you?
   b. Why might they be unable to describe their situation accurately for you?

5. State the general principle of the lawyer's duty of confidentiality, and three exceptions that you may note during the interview.

6. What are the objective and subjective dimensions of the client's situation?

7. When you learn about the client's factual context:
   a. How do the three cycles of interviewing a client about her factual context differ from each other?
   b. Describe the following types of questions, and indicate in which cycle you would use each: open-ended, prompting, and probing.
   c. Explain why each of the following types of questions are problematic: leading questions, questions using loaded language, and questions using legal language.
   d. What are key questions to ask as you conclude your discussion of the client's factual context?

8. What is the distinction between your client's interests and your client's goals? How do they relate to each other?

9. If by chance the de la Cruzes happen to be challenging for the following reasons, what are some strategies you could employ? For each situation, list three strategies.
   a. Mr. de la Cruz is very emotional.
   b. Mrs. De la Cruz is very forgetful.
   c. Daniel appears to be misrepresenting a key fact.

10. One key topic to discuss as the interview ends is attorney fees. If the firm were not going to handle the case pro bono:
    a. What are fee structures that could be considered?
    b. What is the legal standard for measuring the propriety of how much an attorney charges?

11. List several topics that you would include in your retainer letter with your client.

12. List at least five categories of discrimination proscribed in the practice of law by ABA Model Rule of Professional Conduct 8.4(g).

TEST YOUR UNDERSTANDING ANSWERS

1. In client interviewing, the lawyer and client explore the client's situation and whether the lawyer will represent the client. In client counseling, the lawyer advises the client about her situation, and they develop actions to be taken.

2. With mutual trust, the client will tell the lawyer what he needs to know, and the client will support what the lawyer does on her behalf. At the beginning of the interview, you may begin to establish trust by creating a personal connection.

3. As for types of communication:
   a. Non-verbal communication includes eye contact, facial expressions, nodding, and other body language.
   b. Active listening entails waiting until the client has finished speaking before you chime in and reflecting on what the client has said when you speak next.

4. It may be difficult to learn the precise details for the following reasons:
   a. Clients may be intimidated, impeded by emotion, or concerned about revealing adverse facts.
   b. Inaccuracy in describing a situation may be due to weaknesses in observation (due to, e.g., stress, self-interest, or brevity of exposure) or weaknesses in recall (due to, e.g., passage of time, blending into other memories, processing of the memory, or discussion with other people).

5. A lawyer is ethically obligated not to reveal information related to the representation other than to carry out the representation, with client consent, or to comply with a court order.

6. The objective dimensions are the events that led the client to seek legal advice, and the subjective dimensions are the client's response to those events, along with her interests and goals.

7. When you learn about the client's factual context:
   a. In narration, the client tells you her story, little impeded by your questions. In exposition, you ask the client questions to develop the story told during narration. In reiteration, you restate the key facts to confirm them.
   b. Open-ended questions are used in narration and simply ask the client to tell her story. Prompting questions also are asked in narration and ask the client to continue her story. Probing questions focus on some part of the story and are used in exposition.
   c. Leading questions are problematic because they assume an answer that may not be true. Loaded questions contain a judgment and can prompt a skewed answer. Questions using legal language can be confusing and suggest that you have drawn a legal conclusion.

      d. As you conclude your discussion of the client's factual context, you should ask for correction of your restatement and any additional information.

8. Interests are abstractions that are of value; goals are concrete results a client desires. Interests are served by goals.

9. Three strategies for the following clients are:
   a. An emotional client—re-explain the duty of confidentiality, explain why the sensitive information is needed, use narrow questions.
   b. A forgetful client—set the scene, disrupt the chronology, provide some time to think.
   c. A misrepresenting client—reiterate the duty of confidentiality, explain the importance of accuracy to your representation, ask probing questions about what others would say.

10. As for attorney fees:
    a. The basic fee structures are hourly, flat, and contingency.
    b. Fees must be reasonable.

11. Topics to include in a retainer letter include the matter to be handled, the responsibilities of the two parties, termination of the relationship, and fees.

12. Proscribed categories of discrimination in the practice of law are race, sex, religion, national origin, ethnicity, disability, age, sexual orientation, gender identity, marital status, and socioeconomic status.

COUNSELING THE CLIENT

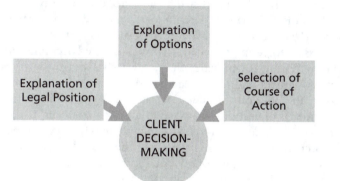

How true Daddy's words were when he said: all children must look
after their own upbringing. Parents can only give good advice or put
them on the right paths, but the final forming of a person's character
lies in their own hands.
—Anne Frank

A. INTRODUCTION

As noted in Chapter 10, the most important conversations that lawyers have are
with their clients, and the foundational conversations are the initial ones: the
client interview and the first counseling session. In *client counseling*, the lawyer
advises the client about the legal significance of his[1] situation, and together they
develop strategies for actions to be taken on the client's behalf. Some client
matters are complicated enough that they will require multiple counseling sessions; others will require only one session, with updating conversations from
time to time as the matter progresses.

---

1. For ease of expression, this chapter uses masculine pronouns for the client. Many clients are,
of course, female. Furthermore, many clients are legal entities, such as companies, government
units, or nonprofit organizations, but individuals speak for them.

You and your client contribute different elements to your counseling session. Your client brings a situation needing action, deep knowledge of the non-legal dimensions of the situation, and probably some ideas about what to do. You contribute legal expertise, the ability to take action within the legal system, and your own ideas about what to do. So when you counsel your client, the two of you engage in a particular form of *professional collaboration*. The word "collaboration" comes from the Latin term meaning "working together." Counseling entails hard work in the form of rigorous legal analysis and creative problem-solving. It also involves close engagement between lawyer and client through communications that you should strive to make as clear as possible.

Various ethics rules frame your role in client counseling. *ABA Model Rule of Professional Conduct 1.2* states that the client decides the "objectives of representation," although the lawyer determines the means by which these objectives are pursued. *Rule 1.4* requires a lawyer to "explain a matter to the extent reasonably necessary to permit the client to make informed decisions regarding the representation." Rule *2.1* provides that a lawyer must provide "independent, professional judgment and render candid advice" and may refer to economic, social, moral, and political considerations as well as the law in doing so.

A classic means of ensuring that your counseling conforms to this model of professional collaboration is to follow a four-stage sequence. In the short first stage, you prepare for the coming stages. In the second stage, you explain the client's legal position to set the foundation for the rest of the session. In the third stage, you and the client explore options; this stage looks quite different depending on whether the client's matter is a dispute to be resolved or a transaction. In the fourth stage, you assist the client in selecting a course of action. Throughout this sequence, your approach to the conversation should accord with the principles of professional practice.

For a dispute example, the chapter refers to the Bower's Bounty situation, involving a claim of defamation by a terminated employee against her former employer. For a transactional example, this chapter refers to the All-Day Wellness situation, in which the client seeks to prevent its employees from working for the competition when they leave the company.

B. PREPARING

A counseling session should not begin not by getting down to business right away but rather start with a *preparation stage*. First, get reacquainted: welcome your client again to your office, engage in some idle conversation, and find out how he is doing. Then present the agenda for the session; encourage the client to ask questions or insert comments as you go; and provide a means for note-taking, if he so desires.

As a transition to the next stage, ask whether there are any new developments in the client's factual context or evolution in his interests and goals. If there happen to be any changes, they could alter your legal analysis. Asking this question also reinforces your expectation that your client keep you informed.

C. Explaining the Client's Legal Position

The *explanation of the client's legal position*, the second stage, entails setting out the client's position with sufficient clarity so he can make decisions with some confidence. This stage will vary in length and nature, depending on both the situation and the client. For a sophisticated client about to become engaged in major litigation or a complex transaction, this stage will take some time. For a client with less education and a simpler situation from a legal standpoint, this stage will be briefer.

Present your legal analysis by stating legal concepts in terms that are accessible to the client and linking those concepts to the most important relevant facts in the client's situation. Clearly delineate the various topics and explain how they relate to each other. Note, for example, when you are switching from a substantive point to a procedural point, from a claim to a remedy, from one claim to another. If you must use a distinctively legal term, define it. As you proceed through this explanation, you are helping the client see what is covered—and not covered—by your legal advice.

Take special care in *framing the conclusions* that you present. Lawyers vary in how they prefer to state predicted legal outcomes. Language such as "chances are good that the court would rule for you" can mean very different things to different people. This is why many lawyers prefer to use phrases such as "our odds are three in four" or "fifty/fifty." A good approach is to state your conclusion, along with your reason for any lack of certainty, such as "We are likely to win, but only if the court agrees with our reading of the statutory language." An approach to consider using with visually oriented clients is to present a spectrum on which you place the situation. In any event, avoid waffling (stating one conclusion and then another). See Box 11.1. However you state your legal conclusions, ask your client if he has any questions and provide any necessary clarification before moving to the third stage.

D. Exploring Options

Clients come to lawyers not just to learn what the law is and how it applies to their situations; they also seek legal services. So the third stage of the counseling session is the *exploration of options*, in which both lawyer and client actively

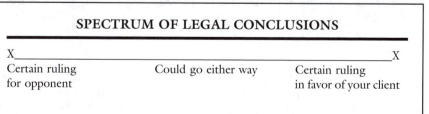

BOX 11.1

SPECTRUM OF LEGAL CONCLUSIONS

X_____X
Certain ruling   Could go either way   Certain ruling
for opponent   in favor of your client

participate. You and your client both participate, for several reasons. Two heads can come up with more good ideas than one. You bring your legal expertise, but the client also is an expert—in his factual context, interests, and goals.

The purpose of this stage is to examine each realistic option by devising *an equation* for each option: its legal factor plus its non-legal advantages minus its non-legal disadvantages. A challenge when discussing options is to conduct a sufficiently wide-ranging, yet also focused, discussion. One strategy is to preface the discussion by confirming the client's interests, goals, and major concerns before working through the various options. A second strategy is to briefly preview the options that you have developed before you discuss any of them in depth; then add others that the client has brought forth. A third strategy is to consistently use distinctive labels for each option. A fourth strategy is to use some standard tools of problem-solving, as discussed below.

When you are *counseling a client in the context of resolving a dispute*, a logical approach is to proceed by discussing pursuing or defending a potential claim, depending on the client's role in the dispute. One key topic of counseling in this setting is the *value of the claim* that either could be brought by the client or has been brought against the client—a sophisticated topic that can be addressed only briefly here. The value of a claim is fixed by various factors: the application of the law to the facts; the ability of each party to establish what it must establish in litigation, which is a function of rules of procedure and other factors, such as the credibility of witnesses and the generosity of local juries; and monetary elements, including the losses the plaintiff has suffered, the types of remedies the law affords, the availability of attorney fees, and the expenses of litigation. For example, a claim that is very sound on the law may not be worth much if the key witness is not credible or the plaintiff's damages are minimal.

A tool that can organize your thinking about the value of a claim is a *probability tree*. In devising this tree, you begin by charting the legal/factual points that must be established in the case. For each, you assign a probability (between 0% and 100%) that the point would be established. At each terminus is a potential legal outcome, along with a percentage chance of its occurrence. To provide a value to the case, you incorporate an estimate of the monetary worth of the case based on your analysis of the case itself, a study of local verdicts in comparable cases, ideas of colleagues, or some combination of these. See Box 11.2 for a sample probability tree[2] for the Bower's Bounty situation, in which the projected verdict amount was $300,000.

Once you have a sense of the value of a claim, you may then consider with your client what legal actions to take. This decision differs depending on whether your client is the potential claimant or respondent. A claimant may decide not to go forward with his case; a respondent must respond somehow to the move taken by the claimant. In either situation, your counseling will incorporate the available *methods for dispute resolution*—another sophisticated topic that can be addressed only briefly here.

---

2. This sample tree is based on the decision tree and process set out in Richard Birke, *Decision Trees—Made Easy* (2004), as synopsized in Stefan H. Krieger & Richard K. Neumann, Jr., *Essential Lawyering Skills: Interviewing, Counseling, Negotiation, and Persuasive Fact Analysis* 268-72 (2015).

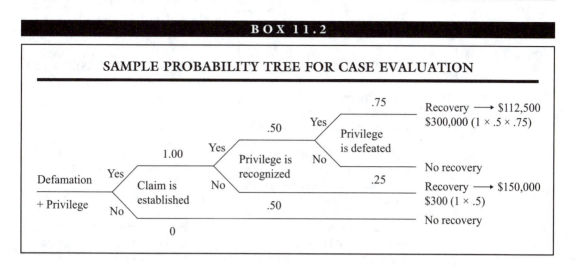

BOX 11.2

SAMPLE PROBABILITY TREE FOR CASE EVALUATION

Depending on the dispute, a process may be foreordained, such as *criminal prosecution* or a particular *administrative proceeding*, in which the government initiates the action, generally against a private party. Other disputes fall within the realm of *civil litigation*. The vast majority of civil disputes settle through early and effective *settlement negotiations* between the parties' lawyers. Unsettled disputes proceed to some other forum, which may be the formal process provided by the courts or an alternative process, whether arranged by the parties acting on their own or under the auspices of the courts.[3] As an example, see Box 11.3 for a listing of the options available to litigants in the Minnesota state court system. Of these many processes, the most commonly used are *arbitration and mediation*.

Discussing the methods to use to resolve the dispute requires that you teach your client about the main options. Most people in the United States have a very skewed idea about how our court system works. So your client needs to have some practical information about what the litigation experience would actually entail for him, including such matters as what happens during discovery, whether trial is even a realistic possibility, and how long each litigation stage typically takes. Similarly, review the nature and practical dimensions of the alternative processes that are workable options for his matter.

Then work with your client on understanding his *process preferences*: how much money, time, effort, and emotion he is willing to devote to the case; whether he seeks privacy or publicity; how willing he is to enmesh others in the case; how much risk the client is willing or able to tolerate; and how much delay is tolerable. Discuss as well the client's stake in the case: is this a matter of recovering damages, changing his situation, proving a principle, or altering a relationship? Your client needs to know that legal disputing is rarely enjoyable and often draining; although lawyers can buffer their clients somewhat, they cannot carry all the burden. In this discussion, make clear that the method of dispute resolution is not a decision that one party can

---

3. Indeed, where the dispute arises under a contract, the parties may have agreed in advance to arbitrate the dispute rather than proceed in court.

BOX 11.3

ALTERNATIVE DISPUTE RESOLUTION PROCESSES

(a) ADR Processes
Adjudicative Processes

(1) *Arbitration.* A forum in which a neutral third party renders a specific award after presiding over an adversarial hearing at which each party and its counsel present its position. If the parties stipulate in writing that the arbitration will be binding, then the proceeding will be conducted pursuant to the Uniform Arbitration Act (Minn. Stat. §§ 572.08-.30). If the parties do not stipulate that the arbitration will be binding, then the award is non-binding and will be conducted pursuant to Rule 114.09.

(2) *Consensual Special Magistrate.* A forum in which the parties present their positions to a neutral in the same manner as a civil lawsuit is presented to a judge. This process is binding and includes the right of appeal to the Minnesota Court of Appeals.

(3) *Summary Jury Trial.* A forum in which each party and their counsel present a summary of their position before a panel of jurors. The number of jurors on the panel is six unless the parties agree otherwise. The panel may issue a non-binding advisory opinion regarding liability, damages, or both.

Evaluative Processes

(4) *Early Neutral Evaluation (ENE).* A forum in which attorneys present the core of the dispute to a neutral evaluator in the presence of the parties. This occurs after the case is filed but before discovery is conducted. The neutral then gives an assessment of the strengths and weaknesses of the case. If settlement does not result, the neutral helps narrow the dispute and suggests guidelines for managing discovery.

(5) *Non-Binding Advisory Opinion.* A forum in which the parties and their counsel present their position before one or more neutral(s). The neutral(s) then issue(s) a non-binding advisory opinion regarding liability, damages or both.

(6) *Neutral Fact Finding.* A forum in which a neutral investigates and analyzes a factual dispute and issues findings. The findings are non-binding unless the parties agree to be bound by them.

Facilitative Processes

(7) *Mediation.* A forum in which a neutral third party facilitates communication between parties to promote settlement. A mediator may not impose his or her own judgment on the issues for that of the parties.

Hybrid Processes

(8) *Mini-Trial.* A forum in which each party and their counsel present its position before a selected representative for each party, a neutral third party, or both, to develop a basis for settlement negotiations. A neutral may issue an advisory opinion regarding the merits of the case. The advisory opinion is not binding unless the parties agree that it is binding and enter into a written settlement agreement.

(9) *Mediation-Arbitration (Med-Arb).* A hybrid of mediation and arbitration in which the parties initially mediate their disputes; but if they reach impasse, they arbitrate any deadlocked issues.

(10) *Other.* Parties may by agreement create an ADR process. They shall explain their process in the civil cover sheet.

Source: Minnesota General Rule of Practice 114.02(a).

make alone; indeed, collaborating successfully on that decision may be one of the first major steps that the lawyers will take in resolving the dispute.

When you are *counseling a client in the context of a transaction*, a logical approach is to proceed by discussing various ways to *structure the transaction* that are viable from a legal standpoint. In discussing each such option with your client, you could work through a *pro/con chart*, in which you list for each option the advantages and disadvantages based on business factors, such as financial costs, other costs, impact on reputation, alignment with company culture, and other matters. See Box 11.4 for two pro/con charts discussing two of the options available to All-Day Wellness, as it considers whether to use a covenant not-to-compete to constrain employees from competing with it upon their departure.

An often-overlooked point, in both the dispute and transactional resolution settings, is that a good option may be to do nothing or to do nothing for the time being. A would-be claimant in a dispute setting may decline to pursue a case that is legally weak or has only a minimal remedy. A client may forego a transaction because it is too risky legally or insufficiently advantageous financially. Thus, the do-nothing and pause options should often be included in your discussions.

BOX 11.4

SAMPLE PRO/CON CHARTS

Option 1: Do *not* include covenants not-to-compete in employment agreements.

PRO	CON
No legal concerns at all. Would not deter strong applicants from wanting to work for All-Day Wellness. Would not require potential monetary payments for covenant. Promotes pro-employee culture and reputation.	Secures no legally enforceable restraint against employees' competing. Risks harm to the company's competitive position through loss of clients.

Option 2: Include clearly *reasonable* covenants not-to-compete in employment agreements.

PRO	CON
Likely to be legally enforced. Would provide protection against employees' competing with All-Day Wellness upon departure.	Could deter some potential applicants. Could require some hiring payments to obtain agreement. Could entail some undermining of pro-employee culture and reputation. Could entail litigation if enforcement dispute arises.

E. SELECTING OF COURSE OF ACTION

The exploration of options is not an academic exercise but rather a prelude to the *selection of a course of action*, the fourth stage of the counseling session. For most clients, this is the most challenging stage because now some type of legal action is looming on the horizon. You may need to exercise some skill in guiding your client through the decision-making process and take care to avoid some potential boundary issues.

Your client may become emotional; hence, you may need to convey empathy through reassuring verbal comments and non-verbal communication, such as nodding and eye contact. In addition, be alert to your client's potential shortcuts in thinking. Psychologists have documented various *cognitive biases* that influence our thinking and distort rational decision making, as noted in Box 11.5. If you perceive that your client is rushing to make a decision, it may be because one of these is operating. For example, a would-be claimant may be overly optimistic due to news reports that he has read of a major recovery in a similar case, even though many other plaintiffs were less successful (the availability heuristic). As another example, a client planning a transaction may be overly confident about his product or company and thus uninterested in clauses that protect the company against risks (overconfidence).

Furthermore, be mindful of your client's *orientation towards risk*. Every individual has a baseline orientation towards risk, and his circumstances (such as the amount of wealth he has) influence his risk tolerance as well. As the stakes in a situation increase, aversion to taking risks generally increases too. Thus, it is important to address risk by offering options with varying degrees of risk, by discussing risk, by noting what most people would choose to do in his circumstances, and ultimately by respecting your client's approach.[4]

To achieve a properly paced and orderly decision-making process, work through the options in a systematic fashion. To decide whether to put an option on the table for possible selection, consider how well it aligns with the client's major goals. If you have several options that would serve the client's goals, you will need some means of deciding which to pursue. One method is to rate each option by how well it serves your client's goals; this rating works best if you first prioritize and weight the goals. A somewhat more complicated approach is to construct various pairs of options and ask the client which of each pair is preferable; out of these choices should come insight into the client's preferred option, as well as his underlying reasoning. Often, the selection of a course of action entails not a single option but a sequence of options: first and second choices as to methods of resolving a dispute or the structure of a transaction, depending on the reactions of the other side.

To be clear, in this discussion, the client is choosing the "objectives of representation," within the language of Rule 1.2, and also likely providing some broad guidance on means of carrying out the representation. Exactly how much guidance varies not only from lawyer to lawyer, but also from client to client and matter to matter. An unsophisticated client may cede more control

---

4. *See* Stefan H. Krieger & Richard K. Neumann, Jr., *Essential Lawyering Skills: Interviewing, Counseling, Negotiation, and Persuasive Fact Analysis* 272-73 (2015).

BOX 11.5

COGNITIVE BIASES THAT AFFECT DECISION-MAKING[5]

- *Anchoring bias:* I overrely on the first piece of information that I receive on the topic.
- *Availability heuristic:* I overestimate the importance of information readily available to me.
- *Bandwagon:* The probability of a belief increases based on the number of people I know who hold it.
- *Choice-supportive bias:* Once I choose something, I feel positive about it, even if it has flaws.
- *Clustering illusions:* I see patterns in random events.
- *Confirmation bias:* I tend to listen only to information that confirms my preconceptions.
- *Conservation bias:* I prefer prior evidence over new evidence or information that has recently emerged.
- *Overconfidence:* I am too confident about my ability and take great risks.
- *Survivorship bias:* I focus only on successful examples, forgetting examples that have failed.
- *Zero-risk bias:* I love certainty, even when it's counterproductive.

over the means to the lawyer; a client who has worked with a lawyer many times also may cede more control over the means to the lawyer. Some dividing lines are fairly standard. As an example, in the Bower's Bounty situation, both Ms. Nicholson and Bower's Bounty would make the decision whether to settle the dispute or to litigate, but neither would decide on details of the discovery process should litigation occur. As another example, the client in the All-Day Wellness situation would decide whether to include a covenant not-to-compete but would leave the precise language up to the lawyer to write.

In some situations, your client or you may struggle with this *decision-making boundary*. One possibility is that your client may want you to decide the objectives of representation. Such a client may find his situation overwhelming, think of you as far more expert than he is, want to avoid the responsibility of making a bad choice, or simply not want to bother with the hard work of decision-making. But the ethics rules—and the dynamics of the lawyer-client relationship as well— dictate that you not take on the decision-making role for the client. Good strategies in this situation are to explore why the client finds it hard to decide what to do, to re-explain any areas of confusion, to encourage the client to consult other advisors, and to meet again when the client has had more time for reflection.

A second boundary issue arises when the client seeks to use the lawyer's services for improper purposes. A lawyer's duty is to represent a client, but not to the undue detriment of a third party. As *Rule 4.4* states, "[a] lawyer shall not use means that have no substantial purpose other than to embarrass, delay, or burden a third person." You may discover during a counseling session that your client expects you to act in just this manner. If so, cutting off this expectation before

---

5. http://www.businessinsider.com/cognitive-biases-that-affect-decisions-2015-8.

the relationship begins—or even deciding to forego the representation altogether—is wise.

A final boundary issue is that you may develop a strong view about what your client should do, which does not accord with your client's selected course of action. Ideally, you will represent clients with situations that interest you; you will come to know their situations; you may come to care about them as people or entities. Indeed, you may decide what you would do if you were in your client's place. Furthermore, in many situations, your own interests as a lawyer are implicated in the course of action that a client chooses: you may stand to earn more money or acclaim if a client decides to pursue a transaction or a case. The wise lawyer maintains a certain degree of detachment. See Box 11.6.

BOX 11.6

ONE LAWYER'S STORY

In 1997-1998, I had the privilege of spending a year volunteering with the Appalachian Research and Defense Fund, a legal services organization serving the civil legal needs of low-income residents of eastern Kentucky. During that year, the office secured a major federal court ruling that certain loans, which had become very common in that part of the state, were indeed regulated under various state and federal statutes. These loans entailed little explanation of their terms, imposed exorbitant interest rates, and in some cases contained threats of bad-check prosecution for failure to repay the loan. The applicable statutes entitled customers to recover significant monetary penalties. For a detailed discussion, see Deborah A. Schmedemann, *Time and Money: One State's Regulation of Check-Based Loans*, 27 Wm. Mitchell L. Rev. 973 (2000).

Once the ruling became known, the office counseled many individuals who had entered into such loans. My view was that the law entitled our clients to significant monetary recoveries, which they should receive given the abusiveness of the loans. This view was, of course, influenced by my lawyer's pride in the federal court ruling, my desire to make that ruling mean something for the people of the region, and my belief that the legal process would come through eventually with a full-blown legal remedy for our clients.

I was humbled to find that our clients had other views. Some sought only a promise that they would not be prosecuted. Others sought to set up terms to repay all or some of the amounts owed or to be excused from paying further on their loans. What they did not want, by and large, was to litigate or to engage in lengthy negotiations to obtain the monetary penalties. In part, the clients were risk-averse: the lesser forms of relief, which could be obtained quickly, were more desirable than the greater benefits that might be obtainable later but less certainly. This was understandable, given their circumstances. But their views were grounded in something deeper too: the clients did not want to posit themselves as victims or as people who did not make good on their contracts.

As you close the selection stage, clarity of communication becomes especially critical. Recount the decisions that you and your client have come to. You may have decided on a single action or on a series of actions to be taken. For example, in a dispute setting, you may decide to attempt settlement first and then suggest mediation should settlement discussions fail; in a transaction setting, you may decide on your most desired clause to include in a contract and on a fallback position if the other party to the transaction resists that option. You may come to tentative decisions for the client to contemplate for a set period of time and confirm through some form of specified communications.

After you recount your decisions, take note of the actions that you will take next and those that your client will take next. Provide a time frame for the first steps that will occur, to your best estimation.

F. PROFESSIONAL PRACTICE

To sustain the *mutual trust* that is key to a strong lawyer-client relationship, you should conduct the counseling session in a professional manner. While there will be variations depending on what your practice setting is, who your client is, and what your personal style is, the following dimensions of professionalism always matter:

- Your communication should be complete, correct, clear, and comprehensible. For example, pronounce your client's name correctly, and know the key dates of his situation. Avoid legalisms that confound your client and causal phrases that clutter your speech. Use concise sentences, especially when discussing complex topics, and pause to let your client ask questions.
- Engage in active listening during the collaborative stages. You need to hear what your client says, and your client needs to perceive that he has been heard. So wait until your client has finished before you talk, and reflect his comments in what you say. Use encouraging non-verbal communication such as eye contact, nodding, and facial expressions.
- Always respect your client's dignity, mindful rather than dismissive of any differences there may be between you. Keep in mind the lawyer's professional obligation not to engage in harassment or discrimination, discussed in Chapter 10.
- Present as organized and prepared. Have the client's file and copies of materials that you need for the client available. Make an outline of the session if it will be extended or complicated.
- To convey that you are focused on the client's matter, start the meeting on schedule, block out enough time, and avoid all but truly necessary interruptions.
- Your personal appearance, attire, and office should be well-maintained and suitable to your practice setting. Otherwise, your client may doubt your ability to manage his matter in an orderly fashion.

TEST YOUR UNDERSTANDING

1. Assume that you have been assigned to participate in counseling the parents of Daniel de la Cruz. He was suspended from his public middle school for shaving a message into his hair in support of his sister who has breast cancer, and the firm has decided that Daniel has a credible claim that the school violated his constitutional right of free speech.
   a. What is the purpose of a client counseling session?
   b. What does a lawyer contribute to the session?
   c. What do the parents, speaking on behalf of Daniel, contribute to the session?

2. What do the following ABA Model Rules of Professional Conduct say about your conduct in carrying out the counseling session?
   a. Rule 1.2
   b. Rule 1.4
   c. Rule 2.1
   d. Rule 4.4

3. During the preparation stage, you should ask the de la Cruzes two questions. What are they, and why are they important to ask?

4. During the stage in which you explain the client's legal position, what are several strategies that you may use to accomplish each of the two key tasks?
   a. Presenting your legal analysis
   b. Framing your conclusions

5. During the stage in which you explore options:
   a. What is the equation that a lawyer and client should develop for each option?
   b. Given that de la Cruz situation involves a dispute to be resolved, what are two main topics to be discussed?
   c. List three common methods through which civil disputes are often resolved, other than litigation in court.
   d. What is the logical approach for this stage for a client situation involving a transaction?

6. During the stage in which a course of action is selected:
   a. What is the scope of the decision that the client is to make? Provide an example based on the de la Cruz situation.
   b. List and explain several cognitive biases that you might foresee operating in the de la Cruz situation.
   c. What are some strategies that you might use if the de la Cruzes seem to want you to decide whether to pursue the case?

TEST YOUR UNDERSTANDING ANSWERS

1. As for counseling the parents of Daniel de la Cruz:
   a. The purpose of the counseling session is to advise them of the legal significance of their situation and to develop strategies to pursue on their behalf.
   b. A lawyer contributes legal expertise, the ability to take certain actions, and ideas about what to do.
   c. The parents contribute the situation itself, knowledge about its non-legal dimensions, and ideas about what to do.

2. The ABA Model Rules of Professional Conduct provide as follows:
   a. Rule 1.2—that the client decides the objectives of representation and the lawyer determines the means by which the objectives are pursued.
   b. Rule 1.4—that a lawyer must explain a matter to the extent reasonably necessary to permit the client to make informed decisions regarding the representation.
   c. Rule 2.1—that a lawyer must provide independent, professional judgment and render candid advice; that a lawyer may refer to economic, social, moral, and political considerations.
   d. Rule 4.4—that a lawyer shall not use means that have no purpose other than to embarrass, delay, or burden a third person.

3. During the preparation stage, you should ask the de la Cruzes about changes in the facts and changes in their interests or goals. These changes may alter the legal analysis, and asking these questions reinforces the expectation that a client keep you informed.

4. As for the explanation of the client's legal position:
   a. In presenting a legal analysis, use accessible language, delineate the topics, and define distinctively legal terms.
   b. In framing legal conclusions, use numerical formulas or a visual aid, and incorporate key reasons. Avoid waffling.

5. As for the exploration of options:
   a. A lawyer and client should develop this equation for each option: legal factor plus non-legal advantages minus non-legal disadvantages.
   b. For the de la Cruzes' dispute, the two main topics are the value of the claim and methods of resolving the claim.
   c. Three common methods through which civil disputes are often resolved are settlement negotiation, mediation, and arbitration.
   d. For a transaction, a logical approach is to discuss various ways to structure the transaction that are legally viable.

6. As for the selection of a course of action:
   a. The client decides the objective of representation, such as recovery of damages or reinstatement in school.

b. Possibilities include confirmation bias (listening only to information that confirms one's preconceptions) and zero-risk bias (favoring certainty even if it's not in your best interests).

c. To avoid deciding what to do for a client, explore what is causing the indecision, re-explain areas of confusion, and arrange a later meeting.

PART THREE

PERSUASIVE COMMUNICATION

In this part, you will study the communications used when a lawyer seeks to persuade another lawyer to act favorably toward his or her client. These communications rely on the work discussed in Part I, on reading and reasoning, as well as on the work discussed in Part II, on advisory communication.

Chapter 12 discusses the writing of a demand letter, which is an analytical type of writing through which a lawyer sets out the client's situation, legal position, and demand for action by the other side in a dispute or transaction. You will learn how to write about a client's situation in an ethical and persuasive manner to a reader who has at least somewhat opposing interests.

The next two chapters both involve a different type of writing—drafting—which involves describing situations and corresponding actions:

- Chapter 13 covers the drafting of a contract, a key transactional document. You will learn ten tenets that make for a contract that both covers the necessary content and reads well.
- Chapter 14 covers the drafting of pleadings, which are key litigation documents. You will learn how procedural rules govern the drafting of these documents and how the two main pleadings (complaints and answers) interact with each other.

Finally, Chapter 15 examines negotiation, the improvisational conversation between opposing counsel through which much of legal representation occurs. You will learn about the importance of preparation, a standard sequence of scenes, and strategies for each scene.

THE DEMAND LETTER

OPENING COMPONENTS	MAJOR COMPONENTS	CLOSING COMPONENT
Heading Introduction	Client's Situation Client's Legal Position Demand	Closing Signature Block

And do as adversaries do in law—Strive mightily, but eat and drink as
friends.
    —William Shakespeare
      The Taming of the Shrew I, 2

A. INTRODUCTION

1. Audience and Purpose

Lawyers communicate not only with their clients, of course, but also with other
people on behalf of their clients.[1] Generally, the goal is to persuade those people
to act so as to benefit the client. Litigators seek to convince the other party to
settle or seek a favorable outcome from a judge, a jury, or an arbitrator.
A transactional lawyer seeks agreement to favorable terms from the other side
to the transaction. Each of these situations entails written communications; the
content and format of the documents vary by context.

How does a lawyer begin the process of persuasion? Often the first step is to
send a seemingly basic yet highly sophisticated document: the demand letter.
A demand letter apprises the recipient of the client's factual situation, legal positions, and proposed outcome. The recipient may send back a letter in response.
Ideally, and frequently, these letters lead to amicable negotiations and a prompt
and fair solution.

---

1. For a wide-ranging discussion of various types of correspondence, *see* Mary Barnard Ray &
Barbara J. Cox, *Beyond the Basics: A Text for Advanced Legal Writing* 364-416 (3d ed. 2013).

This exchange of letters occurs in various practice settings. This chapter focuses on the context of resolving a dispute and more specifically on the letter sent by the claimant. Much of what is said here applies as well to other letters.

A demand letter has two *audiences*. The less obvious audience is the client, who will be looking to the letter to see how her lawyer depicts her situation.[2] The more obvious audience is the opponent, including opposing counsel and people who can approve settlement of claims against the opponent (such as its insurer). If you do not know the opponent or know whether the opponent has a lawyer, the issue of audience is complicated. For example, figuring out how much detail to provide in the statement of the client's legal position can be challenging. Asking what the client knows about the opponent is one way to minimize this uncertainty. Writing a standard letter for the particular area of practice (such as personal injury or construction litigation) is another. Another option is preparing more than one letter: an initial letter directed to the opponent and a second letter directed to the opponent's lawyer (if you know that the opponent has a lawyer).

However the letter is directed, it has three main *purposes*: to introduce yourself, your client, and the dispute; to inform the opponent of your client's factual situation and legal position; and to persuade the opponent to accede to your client's demand for a remedy. In addition, a demand letter begins a conversation with the opponent or opposing counsel. Thus, the letter elicits the opponent's factual information, view of the law, and initial thoughts about acceptable resolutions to the dispute.

2. The Advocate's Ethics

When most people think about lawyers, they perceive them as zealous advocates for their clients. This is indeed one role of a lawyer, but there are limits. Several legal ethics rules address demand letters, all reflecting the risk that a demand letter could prove unduly coercive.

First, *ABA Model Rule of Professional Conduct 4.2* provides that if the lawyer knows that the opponent is represented by a lawyer, the demand letter (indeed, all communications) must be sent to that lawyer, not the opponent. *Rule 4.3* provides that when a lawyer does communicate with an unrepresented opponent, the letter must identify the lawyer's role in the dispute and avoid giving legal advice, other than suggesting that the opponent seek representation.

Second, a demand letter must be truthful, under *Rule 4.1*. In communicating with a third party, a lawyer "shall not knowingly . . . make a false statement of material fact or law." Misrepresentation can occur by incorporating someone else's false statement or in some situations by failing to make a statement. Some points that may be covered in a letter—including a party's intentions as to settlement—are not deemed "material facts" and thus are not held to as high a standard of truthfulness, as noted in comment 1. As a practical matter, shading the truth in a demand letter may cause the opponent and opposing counsel to distrust you, which may prove troublesome in the negotiations that follow the demand letter.

---

2. This chapter uses feminine pronouns for the client; the client in the sample situation is female.

BOX 12.1

WHAT ARE THE BOUNDS OF ZEALOUS ADVOCACY IN A DEMAND LETTER?

As you read the following case, think about these questions:

1. *Why (do you think) did the lawyer write the letter the way he did?*
2. *What would you do instead?*
3. *Is the penalty here appropriate? Would you have issued a different penalty?*

In re Glavin,
484 N.Y.S.2d 933 (N.Y. App. Div. 1985).

[An attorney sent a letter to an individual who had apparently done some unsatisfactory repair work at the home of one of his clients. The letter sought to obtain a refund of money the client had paid.]

Following the filing of respondent's answer, we vacated his demand for a bill of particulars and denied petitioner's motion for a reference noting that respondent did not deny sending the letter and no other factual issues of any substance were presented. In accordance with 22 NYCRR 806.5 of our rules, respondent was permitted to appear and be heard in mitigation.

Respondent's one-page letter, written on behalf of his client, charges the recipient with having "conned her out of $1,000 before you did a lick of work." The letter further informs the recipient, *inter alia*, that "you will return the money or go to jail," "you will be arrested," and "I will have a warrant issued for your arrest." In addition, the letter advises the recipient that "If you return her money and just don't do any work, *then I will tell the City not to punish you*" (emphasis added). We conclude that these statements, read together, could be construed as suggesting that respondent possessed authority to impose or withhold criminal sanctions and thus constituted misrepresentation in violation of the Code of Professional Responsibility, DR 1-102(A)(4). We also find respondent's letter to be improper in that it threatens to use the criminal process to coerce the adjustment of a private civil claim (see Code of Professional Responsibility, DR 7-105, EC 7-21; *Matter of Beachboard*, 263 N.Y.S. 492; *Matter of Gelman*, 230 App. Div. 524, 245 N.Y.S. 416; *Matter of Hyman*, 226 App. Div. 468, 235 N.Y.S. 622).

Although respondent believed he was justified in sending the correspondence in question, his behavior constituted unprofessional conduct for which, considering all of the circumstances, censure is the appropriate sanction.

Respondent censured.

Under some state ethics codes, a demand letter may not threaten to instigate a criminal case or similar proceedings, such as a disciplinary action before a licensing board or an investigation of a business for consumer fraud, except in fairly narrow situations.[3] See box 12.1 for an illustration of this rule.

Finally, some bar associations have created guidelines that are not legally binding but aspirational standards. For example, the 1996 Guidelines for Conduct

---

3. *See* Margaret Z. Johns & Clayton S. Tanaka, *Professional Writing for Lawyers: Skills and Responsibilities*, 70 (2d ed. 2012).

of the American Bar Association Section of Litigation state: "We will treat all other counsel, parties, and witnesses in a civil and courteous manner, not only in court, but also in all other written and oral communications." A lawyer who seeks to resolve a client's dispute is entering a conflict that may already be bitter and protracted. The lawyer should not only avoid exacerbating the conflict, but also, through his or her integrity and moderation, decrease the level of animosity.

B. THE FORMAT OF THE DEMAND LETTER

There is no fixed format for demand letters. On the other hand, the sequence discussed in this chapter is fairly standard. Note that it tracks, to a certain extent, the sequence of components in the analytical office memo and the advice letter. See Box 12.2. It is the content within the various components that differentiates the demand letter from objective analytical writing. If the letter is lengthy, you may want to label the main components of the letter.

As an example, this chapter draws on a sample demand letter written for the Bower's Bounty situation, in which a terminated employee is considering bringing a claim of defamation against her former employer; in this chapter, the client is the employee. That sample letter appears as Exhibit 12. Please read it now.

Heading: As with any business letter, the heading includes your letterhead and the date; the name, position, and address of the recipient; and a respectful salutation.

Introduction: Unless the recipient has reason to expect the demand letter and knows that you represent your client, the letter may be something of a surprise. So the *introduction* should clearly identify who you are, who your client is, what is in dispute, and very generally what you are seeking on behalf of your client. Although other parts of the letter make assertions adverse to the opponent and thus will read as adversarial, the introduction should be measured in tone so as to begin to develop the working relationship needed to resolve the dispute with a minimum of rancor and energy. If the letter is long, the introduction may also provide a roadmap of the rest of the letter.

BOX 12.2

COMPARISON OF DEMAND LETTER TO ANALYTICAL OFFICE MEMO AND ADVICE LETTER

Demand Letter	Analytical Office Memo	Advice Letter
Heading	Caption	Heading
Introduction	Issues and short answers	Introduction
Client's situation	Facts	Summary of facts
Client's legal position	Discussion	Explanation
Demand and closing	Closing	Advice and closing

If you are writing directly to your client's opponent, you should include a statement that you are representing your client, not the opponent, and that the opponent should consider hiring a lawyer to assist with resolving this dispute.

As an example, the introduction in Exhibit 12, the demand letter for the Bower's Bounty situation, follows this format in introducing the writer and Ms. Nicholson, identifying her claim against Bower's Bounty, expressing a hope for prompt and amicable settlement, encouraging the recipient to contact counsel, and providing a brief roadmap.

Client's factual situation: For the opponent to be willing to provide a remedy to your client, you must convey that there is a wrong to be remedied. The first step in this process is for your opponent to see your *client's factual situation* from her perspective.

When you recount your client's situation, organize it logically (e.g., chronologically). Furthermore, tell the story persuasively and credibly. Note how the problem that led to the dispute has affected and continues to affect your client. Include facts from sources other than your client that support your client's position. Avoid melodramatic language; let the story itself make your client's case. You need not include unfavorable facts. However, you may do so; noting and defusing unfavorable facts in the demand letter may prompt an early and favorable settlement. The length and level of detail of the story should be determined by how many facts you know with confidence and how much of the story is favorable to your client. See the contrasting passages in Box 12.3, which are from an analytical office memo and the sample demand letter.

BOX 12.3

ANALYTICAL OFFICE MEMO FACTS VERSUS DEMAND LETTER'S FACTUAL SITUATION

Facts from the Analytical Office Memo

According to Nicholson's personnel file, she worked at Bower's Bounty for seven years. She rose through the ranks to supervisor of the fresh produce department. She has been successful in that role. Her most recent direct supervisor was the new store manager, Dan Molinaro. The last entry (by Molinaro) indicates that she was terminated for violation of the pilferage policy.

Client's Factual Situation from the Demand Letter

Ms. Nicholson was a strong employee of seven years' standing; she rose through the ranks to become supervisor of the fresh produce department. In that position, she brought in more local produce, enhanced its display, and increased sales. Furthermore, as a public service, Ms. Nicholson arranged for outdated produce to be provided to an area food shelf periodically. This arrangement was approved by the regional manager.

Nonetheless, Ms. Nicholson was discharged by new store manager Dan Molinaro, which came as a complete surprise to Ms. Nicholson. Apparently, Mr. Molinaro believed that Ms. Nicholson was pilfering food.

As an example, the statement of the client's factual situation in Exhibit 12 begins by painting Ms. Nicholson in a favorable light as a valued employee, so that her termination comes as a surprising and puzzling event. It cites other employees in support of her claim. It concludes with the effects of the opponent's actions on her. It uses simple sentences and crisp transitional phrases to keep the story moving.

Client's legal position: The second step in conveying that there is a wrong to be remedied is showing your opponent that the law favors your client. When you present your *client's legal position*, frame it persuasively.

First, the legal position should be *logically organized*; it is hard to persuade someone who is puzzled. If there is more than one logical organization, consider the following strategies:

- Start with the major basis for your client's claim.
- Start with points that are indisputable or tilted in your client's favor.
- Start with points that are not as critical of the opponent as others.
- Start with points that are easily understood, especially if you are writing to an opponent, not a lawyer.

If your client has a number of potential claims against the opponent so that the letter would be unduly lengthy if all were discussed in depth, consider presenting one or two in full and briefly referring to the rest.

Second, carefully *pitch your statement* of your client's legal position. If you know that you are writing to a lawyer, the statement may be technical and lengthy, and you should include citations for major propositions. If you are writing to the opponent, not a lawyer, the statement should be less technical and extensive. As with the facts, you need not include unfavorable legal points, but doing so and defusing them may be a good strategy, especially if you are writing to a lawyer.

As to both facts and law, take care not to inadvertently undermine your case. Check for statements that are inaccurate, ambiguous, overly revealing, or too conciliatory, as well as statements that could be viewed as admissions of fault by your client.

As an example, the presentation of the law in Exhibit 12 runs only one paragraph because there is only one claim. The points proceed in a logical order and begin and end on strong points for Ms. Nicholson. The writer has chosen to avoid the intricacies of the debatable legal rules involving qualified privilege, in part because the defense of privilege is for the employer (the opponent) to establish.

Demand: Ideally, by the time your reader gets to your *demand*—that is, your statement of the actions that you seek from your opponent—he or she should feel that some remedy is in order. Setting out your demand as an *appealing option*, rather than off-putting demand, is not easy. Consider the following strategies:

- Frame your demand in terms of common goals; show that the opponent will benefit along with the client.
- Frame your demand as a fair solution to a problem that both sides are facing and will continue to face unless they settle.
- Frame the opponent's situation as an opportunity to benefit because the opponent will be better off with others positioned similarly to your client, such as future customers.
- Offer various ways that the opponent can meet the demand.

■ Pair the demand with an incentive.

■ Pair the demand with warnings—within reason and ethical constraints, of course—of what will occur if the demand is not met.

The demand itself should be defined well and expressed in a straightforward way.

Often, the client seeks *damages*. You may want to set a high but tenable figure (the maximum that the client could recover). Or you may want to focus on the items for which your client will be seeking compensation, especially if the losses are ongoing. Breaking down a monetary demand into components provided for by the applicable law may induce a higher settlement because the demand is objective. Keep in mind that courts may follow formulas for setting damages, but the parties may settle for a sum that reflects their compromise rather than a strictly legal formula.

The demand may be for *non-monetary relief* as well. Parties may fashion remedies that a court cannot order; indeed, this is a major advantage of settling disputes. Examples of non-monetary relief are rewriting the parties' contract, erasing an adverse performance evaluation, alterations in the opponent's business practices, a training program for the opponent's employees, and creation of a fund for aiding others who may be in the same situation as your client.

As an example, the demand in Exhibit 12 includes both damages and non-monetary relief. The letter does not specify an amount of damages because the losses are ongoing, but the letter does specify the categories for which compensation is sought. The letter also leaves somewhat open how Bower's Bounty could assist Ms. Nicholson—a specific strategy that appeals to Bower's Bounty for ideas. The demand notes how settlement would assist Ms. Nicholson, how the reputation of Bower's Bounty would be improved, and how a prompt resolution could yield more favorable settlement terms.

Closing: You should include a date by which the opponent needs to contact you and indicate what action you will take if there is no contact. An option is to indicate that you will call the opponent, if the opponent does not have a lawyer, or opposing counsel on a specific date in the not-too-distant future. State your optimism that the dispute can be resolved satisfactorily and soon, and conclude with a courteous signature block.

The sample demand letter in Exhibit 12 follows this formula.

Responding to a demand letter: When your client receives a demand letter, you may choose to respond. At the least, the *responsive letter* informs the opponent's lawyer that you are representing your client, so all future communications should come to you. You also may choose to state your client's perspective on the factual and legal points stated in the opponent's demand letter, along with your client's reaction to the demand itself. Rarely does a client assent to the full relief specified in the demand letter. More likely, your client may want to make a counterproposal to begin the process of negotiation.

C. ADDITIONAL CONSIDERATIONS

Achieving the proper *styles and tone* in a demand letter can be challenging. You want the opponent to understand the claim, so you should avoid legal jargon and unnecessary complexity. You want the opponent to realize that your client's demand is serious and you are confident about the claim, so your tone should be direct and firm. You want the opponent to see that working with you to resolve the claim will be productive, so you want to appear professional and reasonable. You want the opponent to feel respected, so you should avoid condescension and irritation.

To achieve these goals, generally use short affirmative sentences with strong verbs; use adverbs and adjectives sparingly. You should write the demand diplomatically; use indirect phrasing, such as passive voice and the subjunctive mood. A demand letter is a formal letter, so you should use titles and last names, and avoid colloquialisms and shorthand references.

Finally, keep in mind that you are voicing your client's claim. You should definitely confer with your client about the content of the letter and may find it helpful to confer about the letter's tone as well.

D. REVIEW

The demand letter is a significant document because it states your client's claim against your client's opponent and because it begins the process of resolving that claim. To write an effective demand letter:

(1) Conform to the ethical principles governing communication on behalf of a client.
(2) Discern whatever you can about the likely readers of the letter, and pitch the letter accordingly.
(3) Organize the letter by these components: heading, introduction, your client's factual situation and legal position, the demand, and closing with a signature block.
(4) Write the letter so that the opponent will want to work with you to settle the dispute, by conveying that you are professional, reasonable, and respectful.

A well-written demand letter fulfills the criteria for all good legal writing:

- Completeness—Although it does not purport to cover all of the facts or present your full legal analysis, does it cover enough to inform the opponent of the client's situation and support the demand?
- Correctness—Are the facts and the law stated accurately, albeit favorably?
- Coherence—Do the various components (the client's factual situation, legal position, and demand) fit together? Does the demand flow naturally from the preceding material?
- Comprehensibility—Can the probable reader, whether the opponent or the opponent's lawyer, understand it in one careful reading?

Furthermore, write your demand letter in a style that conveys confidence and reads convincingly.

Exhibit 12   253

EXHIBIT 12   DEMAND LETTER

Owen & McKenna[4]
987 Oak St.
Suite 200
Lawrence, KS 60000
November 1, 2016

Ms. Sheryl Grant
Bower's Bounty Groceries
456 Main St.
Lawrence, KS 60000

Dear Ms. Grant:

I am a lawyer here in Lawrence with the firm of Owen & McKenna, and I have been retained by Ms. Sarah Nicholson to represent her in her claim against Bower's Bounty Groceries. Her claim arises out of her discharge almost three months ago and a false statement made at that time. Ms. Nicholson and I both hope that this situation can be resolved promptly, amicably, and fairly.

An important note: I represent Ms. Nicholson. I strongly suggest that you contact Bower's Bounty's insurer or counsel.

To speed the resolution of Ms. Nicholson's claim, I have stated here the events that she experienced, the legal basis of her claim in basic terms, and the remedy she seeks.

Ms. Nicholson was a strong employee of seven years' standing; she rose through the ranks to become supervisor of the fresh produce department. In that position, she brought in more local produce, enhanced its display, and increased sales. Furthermore, as a public service, Ms. Nicholson arranged for outdated produce to be provided to an area food shelf periodically. This arrangement was approved by the regional manager.

Nonetheless, Ms. Nicholson was discharged by new store manager Dan Molinaro, which came as a complete surprise to Ms. Nicholson. Apparently, Mr. Molinaro believed that Ms. Nicholson was pilfering food. The best Ms. Nicholson can figure out is that this erroneous belief was based on a conversation with a single employee (Sam Olson), who had been properly disciplined by Ms. Nicholson and may have fabricated a story about pilferage after seeing Ms. Nicholson assist in the loading of produce into the food shelf truck one day. But at no time did Mr. Molinaro talk to Ms. Nicholson about any alleged pilferage before discharging her. Nor did he explain his basis for believing that she engaged in pilferage. Ms. Nicholson has never engaged in pilferage.

Mr. Molinaro proceeded to post a message on the bulletin board in the employee lounge, for all employees to see. It stated: "Due to pilferage on her part in violation of company policy, Sarah Nicholson is no longer with Bower's Bounty." Ms. Nicholson's co-workers have told her that they read and believed this statement, and her previously strong reputation for honesty has been damaged.

---

4. For purposes of illustration, this demand letter works with only one case. In actual practice, you would incorporate more recent cases, and the analysis would be more complex.

EXHIBIT 12   (cont.)

Not surprisingly, Ms. Nicholson has been unable to secure a comparable job since she was terminated by Bower's Bounty, as she has had to operate in the shadow of the false pilferage charge. The stresses of unemployment, loss of income, and damage to her reputation are taking a significant toll on her.

Under Kansas law, when Mr. Molinaro posted this statement for other employees to read, he defamed Ms. Nicholson. He stated that Ms. Nicholson engaged in pilferage, which was not true. The false statement was communicated to her co-workers and has harmed her professional reputation for honesty. Furthermore, Mr. Molinaro acted at best recklessly in failing to discern the facts before he posted the statement. Because he made the statement in his role as a manager, Bower's Bounty is legally responsible for his actions.

Ms. Nicholson's concerns are her economic losses and security, her reputation, and her emotional well-being. She has been out of work and thus has lost wages and benefits for several months already. She will continue in this predicament until she is re-employed. Furthermore, this situation has caused Ms. Nicholson considerable documentable distress. For these losses, she seeks full monetary compensation.

Furthermore, Bower's Bounty has the capacity to assist Ms. Nicholson in securing employment in the grocery business. Indeed, it is in the company's best interest to assist her, so as to reduce any doubts among its current employees and in the community about the fairness of its employment practices.

We believe that it is in our mutual interests to resolve this matter promptly, when the losses are still fairly minimal. Thus, if I have not heard from you within two weeks, I will give you a call. We look forward to working with you or your counsel.

Sincerely,

Kyle McKenna

Attorney for Sarah Nicholson

TEST YOUR UNDERSTANDING

1. Assume that you have been assigned to write the demand letter to the school district that has suspended Daniel de la Cruz from public middle school for certain statements that he made. The firm has decided that there are grounds to pursue a claim for violating his free speech rights and will bring a lawsuit in federal district court if the school district does not agree to return Daniel to class.
   a. Who is the audience for your letter?
   b. What are the three purposes of your letter?
   c. If you know that the district has a lawyer, to whom should you send the letter?
   d. If you are sending the letter to a non-lawyer individual within the district, what information must you include?
   e. What major requirements does ABA Model Rule 4.1 impose as to truthfulness?

2. As for the introduction:
   a. What information should you include?
   b. What tone should you aim to strike?

3. As for your statement of your client's factual situation:
   a. What is your goal in writing this component?
   b. List several specific strategies to use to accomplish this goal.

4. As for your statement of your client's legal position:
   a. State several points to keep in mind when organizing this component.
   b. State several points to keep in mind when pitching this component.

5. As for the demand:
   a. What are two categories of remedies that your client may seek?
   b. List several ways that you can make your demand appealing to the opponent.

6. What should you include in the closing of the demand letter?

TEST YOUR UNDERSTANDING ANSWERS

1. If you were writing a demand letter for the Daniel de la Cruz situation:
   a. Your audiences are your clients (his parents) and your opponent (the representative of or lawyer for the district).
   b. Its purposes are to introduce yourself, your client, and the dispute; to inform the opponent of your client's factual situation and legal position; and to persuade your opponent to accede to the demand.
   c. If you know that the district has a lawyer, you should send the letter to the lawyer.
   d. If you send a letter to a non-lawyer individual, you must identify your role in the dispute, not give legal advice, and suggest that the individual seek counsel.
   e. Rule 4.1 requires that a lawyer not knowingly make a false statement of material fact or law, which can include incorporating another's statements and non-disclosure.

2. As for the introduction:
   a. The introduction should identify the lawyer, the client, the dispute, and the desired remedy or remedies.
   b. The tone should be measured so as to establish a good working relationship.

3. As for your statement of your client's factual situation:
   a. The goal is that the opponent see the facts from the client's perspective.
   b. Strategies include telling the story chronologically, showing how the client has been affected, including sources other than the client, and defusing unfavorable facts.

4. As for your statement of your client's legal position:
   a. Organizational principles include logic and leading with points that are strong, important, or not as critical of the opponent.
   b. Points to keep in mind are matching the technical ability of the reader, judging whether to include unfavorable points, and guarding against undermining the legal arguments.

5. As for the demand:
   a. The two categories of remedies are damages and non-monetary relief.
   b. To make a demand appealing to the opponent, frame it in term of common goals or a fair solution; note various ways that the demand can be met; or pair the demand with an incentive or a legitimate warning.

6. The closing should include the timing of the next contact, an optimistic closing line, and a signature block.

CONTRACTS

Lawfulness, Accuracy, Balance, Comprehensiveness, Foresight, Practicality

Precision, Comprehensibility, Style and Tone, Aesthetics

> A contract is an ask game, and if it asks for an hour, and I submit to an hour, then it's an hour. When I look at the contract, I look at the obligation—where, when, how long, the compensation. If I agree to it, that's the way it is. I have an obligation. They have an obligation.
> —Chuck Berry

A. INTRODUCTION

Lawyers engage in two main types of writing: analytical writing and drafting. In *analytical writing,* the writer states facts and rules, explains their connection, and posits a legal meaning for the client's situation. Analytical office memos, advice letters, demand letters, and memoranda and briefs written to courts are all types of analytical writing.

By contrast, *drafting* entails describing situations and setting out what is to happen. Lawyers draft documents in a wide range of settings. As discussed in Chapter 14, litigators draft many types of documents as they process a lawsuit. Transactional lawyers draft contracts, wills, estates, articles of incorporation, by-laws, deeds, benefit plans, and many other categories of documents.[1] This chapter discusses the drafting of contracts,[2] although much of what is said here applies to other transactional drafting as well.

---

1. Government lawyers also draft statutes and regulations.
2. For additional detail, see Kenneth A. Adams, *A Manual of Style for Contract Drafting* (3d ed. 2013); Scott J. Burnham, *Drafting and Analyzing Contracts: A Guide to the Practical*

It is a privilege to write a contract for your client. In doing so, you give written expression to the client's agreement with the other party to the contract and guide the future conduct of both parties. If you do your job well, their relationship should be harmonious and productive. If you do not do your job well, their relationship may be marred by inefficiency, conflict, and litigation.

The parties to a contract govern themselves—hence the classic image of a contract as private law. Another way to see a contract is as the rules of a game. The various provisions tell the parties what to do as their agreement plays out. Some provisions, such as performance and payment, cover moves that are certain to occur. Others deal with moves that may not occur but should be anticipated because events do not always occur as clients intend.

Every client's game is unique because it reflects your client's situation, the situation of the other party, and the agreement they have forged. Thus, when you draft a contract for your client, you should start by learning about the deal, and you should expect to consult your client from time to time as you go along.

This chapter sets out ten tenets for drafting a contract and its various clauses. Six of the ten pertain to the content of the clauses; four pertain to their composition. Each tenet is stated in general terms and then demonstrated in the context of the employment agreement between All-Day Wellness and its employees. All-Day Wellness is in the business of providing health care consulting services to employers (a very competitive industry).

B. CONTENT TENETS

1. Lawfulness

A well-written contract is *lawful*. Although contracts reflect private choices, they are nonetheless regulated in various ways: Some legal rules, typically statutes, prohibit certain clauses, while others require certain clauses. Other rules operate more subtly, by discouraging or encouraging certain clauses or providing parameters within which the parties may contract. Court opinions construe particular language, so that the parties can predict how a court might view their contract should they incorporate that language. Still other legal rules affect the process of contracting, addressing, for example, capacity to contract or the requirement of a writing. Some contract rules govern nearly all contracts, others contracts of a particular sort.

A contract is not written well unless it complies with all pertinent legal requirements. Less obviously, a contract should secure the legal position desired by your client and minimize your client's risk, consistent with the deal struck by the parties. For example, if a buyer and seller have discretion as to a particular term and have decided to favor the buyer over the seller on that term, the contract should use language that courts have construed to favor buyers.

As you draft contract language, a good way to think through its legal significance is to imagine that a contract dispute has arisen. Ask yourself: What would I

Application of the Principles of Contract Law (4th ed. 2016); Tina L. Stark, *Drafting Contracts: How and Why Lawyers Do What They Do* (2d ed. 2013).

argue on behalf of my client? What could a lawyer for the other party argue based on this language? How would a court decide the dispute?

Conforming to the law is a point that is obvious to most clients. However, for business reasons, some clients may want to overreach by including an overly one-sided clause in a contract with a less powerful partner, on the premise that the partner will comply with it rather than litigate it. An important ethical issue is whether a lawyer can draft such a clause; one factor is whether the other party or lawyer knows that the clause is problematic.[3]

Finally, a word or two about sample forms: In your legal research, you may well come across sample language in commentary, such as form books. You may get some good ideas from such a source. But you should never adopt the language of a sample form without careful consideration of its suitability for your client's situation. The form may be based on the law of another jurisdiction, it may not be written well, and it certainly does not reflect the specific situation of your client.

As an example of legal issues related to the All-Day Wellness situation, the law provides that if the employment agreement includes a covenant not-to-compete restricting the employee's post-employment competition with All-Day Wellness, those restrictions (temporal, geographic, and functional) must be reasonable for the covenant to be enforced. This is an example of a rule that provides parameters but not specific language.

2. Accuracy

A well-written contract is *accurate* in reflecting the facts of your client's situation. Although a contract is oriented toward the future, it does rest on some present facts—the parties' identities, locations, and operations—that the contract must state accurately. Some contracts include recitals that state the parties' purpose in contracting. Furthermore, the contract must accurately state the parties' agreement.

As an example, the All-Day Wellness covenant not-to-compete should correctly specify the time frame, geographic scope, and type of work it encompasses. For example, if the covenant is intended to prohibit only the type of work that the employee performed while at All-Day Wellness, the covenant should not include the phrase "in any capacity" or similarly broad language.

3. Balance

A well-written contract is *balanced* in that it is fair and realistic. To some extent, the contract's *fairness* is a product of the parties' negotiations: the contract is fair because they consider it fair. Each party may, of course, consider some terms one-sided, but presumably the overall agreement is acceptable to both.

In most situations, lawyers write not only fully negotiated terms but also *undickered terms*; these are terms that the parties have not explicitly discussed. If you are the lawyer primarily responsible for drafting the contract, you may be

---

3. *See* Christina L. Kunz, *The Ethics of Iffy and Invalid Contract Clauses.* 40 Loy. L.A. L. Rev. 487 (2006).

tempted to write clauses on undickered terms so as to protect your client to the detriment of the other party. However, this strategy often backfires when the other party either resists signing the contract as written or signs the contract but carries mistrust into the contractual relationship.

Additionally, lawyers often draft *form contracts* for a party that are signed by the other party to the agreement without negotiation. Form contracts are used when one party provides goods or services to many users and are typical in consumer transactions. If those contracts are significantly adverse to the other party, there is a risk that a court would not enforce it or one of its provisions.

Closely related to fairness is the notion that contract terms be *realistic*. A contract may state high aspirations, but ordinarily the aspirations should also be reasonably attainable (or the contract should otherwise reflect the inherent riskiness of the deal). In particular, you should guard against unduly high performance standards and very tight time frames.

Furthermore, most contracts affect not only the contracting parties but also *third part*ies. As you assess the contract for balance, be sure to consider these third parties' interests, the extent to which they correspond to or diverge from those of your client, and your client's view of how to accommodate those interests.

As an example, All-Day Wellness likely would provide its employees with a form contract with certain spaces (for the name of the employee, the employee's salary, and the employee's start date and duties) to be filled in after discussion with a new employee. Through this process, the two parties presumably would come to a mutually fair agreement on terms that they discuss. The contract probably would have clauses on undickered terms too, such as a dispute resolution clause. All-Day Wellness could favor its interests to the detriment of the employee (e.g., by compelling arbitration and requiring the employee to pay an unreasonable percentage of an arbitrator's fee), but doing so would be unwise. Neither party should promise more than it can deliver, such as lifetime employment for the employee or the employee never competing with All-Day Wellness.

As for the interests of third parties, the covenant not-to-compete clause is an example of the law requiring the parties to take the interests of third parties into account. The rule requiring reasonableness not only strikes a balance between the parties' interests but also serves society's interest in free trade in the labor market.

4. Comprehensiveness

A well-written contract provides *comprehensive coverage of intended events*. To discern what needs to be covered in the contract's major clauses, consider what the parties intend to have happen during the term of the contract. Ask yourself as to each such event: who, what, when, where, and how? Unless an answer is obvious, the contract should state all these dimensions of an intended event. Especially important is the matter of identifying who is to undertake a particular task; few contract provisions should be written in truncated passive voice (lacking the actor). As you describe intended events, write flexibly enough to cover standard changes in the parties' circumstances, such as changes in personnel.

As to some matters, the law provides *default rules*; a default rule is a standard approach that is implied unless the contract provides otherwise. Although a contract need not state a default rule for it to operate, you may want to do so in some situations, so that the parties know what the default rule is. If the parties do not want to use the default rule, the contract should state their preferred rule.

As an example, standard matters that would be covered in the All-Day Wellness employment agreement are the employee's start date, job duties, compensation, benefits, and time off. The default rule is that employment is at will, that is, either the employer or employee may terminate the relationship without notice or a reason.[4] If, by contrast, All-Day Wellness sought to employ the employee for a fixed term, the employment agreement should so state.

5. Foresight

A well-written contract operates with *foresight as to important unintended events*. Especially when a contract covers a long time, calls for many exchanges, or involves circumstances with some risk or volatility, events are unlikely to go exactly as planned.

Consider what could happen to derail the intended course of events, both to the advantage and disadvantage of your client. As to each such unintended event, determine its probability and significance. Plan to cover the most probable and significant events. No contract covers everything; to write a truly exhaustive contract would be unduly time-consuming and expensive, and the contract would be too unwieldy for the parties. Furthermore, contract law provides sound default rules for common situations.

Once you have decided which unintended events are worth covering, consider your options. To a certain extent, the contract can make some events more or less likely. The contract can create a stick: that is, an adverse consequence when one party fails to meet expectations, such as an adjustment in the price or cancellation of the contract. Another option is a carrot: that is, a favorable consequence when high expectations are met, such as a bonus payment for performance in the face of adversity. Some events will be outside the parties' control; in that case, the contract should identify an outcome that is fair to both.

As an example, in the All-Day Wellness situation, one unintended but predictable event is that the company will go out of business. This situation is covered well by a default rule that accords with the parties' expectations, so it need not be covered. Another unintended but predictable event is that the employee will not successfully complete the training requirement. Different consequences (re-training, probation, termination of employment) could follow this failure, so this event merits coverage.

6. Practicality

A well-written contract is *practical*: it is easy to follow as events unfold. Most contracts involve concepts that can be formulated in various ways. Consider, for example, the notion of timeliness. Timeliness could be defined by reference to an

---

4. This rule does not permit termination for a legally proscribed reason, however.

abstract and general standard ("within a reasonable time"), a specific and concrete standard ("by 1:00 p.m. on July 4th"), or a process ("as determined by the
buyer's general manager").

You should choose a formulation that is as precise and as flexible as the parties
need it to be and that will be practical for them to implement during the contract
term. Again, think of your contract as a game, and ask whether the parties will be
able to figure out how to make their moves as the game unfolds.

As an example, in the All-Day Wellness situation, a clause covering the duty of
the employee to obtain re-training would need to include an expression of the
idea of "periodically." That word would be very difficult to implement. A better
approach would be to state a formula, for example, "once per quarter for the first
year following completion of the probation period and annually thereafter."
Another approach would be to provide for re-training "as called for by a
supervisor."

C. Composition Tenets

7. Precision

A well-written contract is phrased with *precision*: every clause says what it means
to say. Each concept should have one word or phrase, and each significant word
or phrase should stand for one concept. Choose words and phrases that make
sense in terms of common parlance, the language of the pertinent trade, and the
language of applicable legal rules.

Definitions: As with statutes, contracts often include *definitions*. You should
establish a definition when you have created a term without a readily discernible
dictionary definition or when you are using a familiar word in a different way than
its standard meaning. If a concept appears throughout the contract, its definition
should appear in a definitions section at the beginning of the contract; if the
concept appears only within a particular part, it should be defined within that
part.

Incorporate terms of art from the law or the trade (the client's area of business) if they are indeed what you mean and are well understood. Some concepts
are amenable to definition via a list. Be sure to note whether the items listed are
exhaustive (a closed-ended list) or illustrative (an open-ended list); in the latter
situation, be sure you have chosen representative examples. Avoid circular and
overly complex definitions, especially nested definitions in which one definition
incorporates another, which in turn incorporates a third, and so on.

As an example, in the All-Day Wellness contract, the concept of "health consultant's services" most likely would appear in various places throughout the
contract and would merit a definition because it is not a commonly used
term. One option would be to include a non-exhaustive list: "the term 'health
consultant's services' includes services such as conducting a nutrition assessment
of available food, arranging for regular yoga classes, and planning smoking-cessation classes." Another option would be to explain a process for giving meaning
to the term: "the services selected by the client in discussion with the consultant." A concept in the contract that could be defined by reference to the law (if it
were to appear in the contract at all) is "employment at will."

Verbs: *Verbs* are especially important in contracts because they create legal consequences:

- Most contract provisions state *promises* by one party to act in a particular way; promises create duties on the part of the promisor and rights on the part of the promisee. A straightforward way to state a promise is: "Party A shall do X."
- Often a *promise is conditional* on the occurrence of some event. This situation is expressed as follows: "If condition C occurs, then Party A shall do X."
- A *privilege* is a discretionary authority to act without creation of a right on the part of the other party, expressed as follows: "Party A may do Y."

As an example, consider the verbs in the following contract term about training in the All-Day Wellness employment agreement:

(1) All-Day Wellness shall provide the Employee with extensive training during the Employee's first four months. (2) If the Employee satisfactorily completes the extensive four-month training and documents an area of needed additional training, All-Day Wellness shall provide additional training. (3) All-Day Wellness may require the Employee to undertake further training at any other time.

Clause 1 states a promise. The first half of clause 2 states a condition to the promise in the second half of clause 2. Clause 3 states a privilege.

Ambiguity: To the extent feasible, avoid *ambiguity,* that is, language that conveys two distinct yet inconsistent meanings. Ambiguity typically arises in the following linguistic settings:

- Two passages carry conflicting meanings.
- Some information is omitted (for example, the actor is missing in a passive-voice sentence).
- A sentence is awkwardly constructed (for example, a modifier is misplaced, a pronoun has two possible antecedents, or the import of a negative construction is unclear).
- An ambiguous word is used without clarification.

To detect and remove ambiguity, check for the potential trouble-spots listed above, and make corrections accordingly. For example, check the draft for passive voice; in those cases, clarify who the actor is. Check for plural constructions; switch to the singular to avoid the question whether the plural applies to the singular.

Ambiguous words can be quite short. For example, "or" has several meanings: A or B but not both; A or B or both; A, but if not A, then B. The words "from," "to," and "by" can be ambiguous when used in timing clauses. For example, does "by September 6th" mean before 12:00 a.m. or by 11:59 p.m. of that date?

As an example, consider the following All-Day Wellness covenant not-to-compete:

The Employee may not compete with All-Day Wellness by performing similar services within the Midwest for a reasonable period of time after the Employee ends her employment with All-Day Wellness.

This passage raises numerous questions: What do the following words mean: "similar services," "Midwest," "reasonable period of time"? Does "compete" include working directly for a company who was an All-Day Wellness client, as well as working as a consultant? What if All-Day Wellness terminates the employee, for cause or without cause?

8. Comprehensibility

A well-written contract is easily *comprehended by the parties* to the contract.

Comprehensibility is in part a function of the *sequence* in which information is presented; it is hard to comprehend a document in which first things are presented fifth or eighth. You should employ logical principles when ordering the main topics and when ordering the points within each main topic. Some classic choices are:

- Present the topics in chronological order, i.e., the order in which they will arise as the contract plays out.
- Present the clauses covering the most likely situations to arise at the beginning of the contract and the clauses covering the least likely situations toward the end.
- Present general points before more specific points.
- Similarly, present general rules before exceptions.

To make your organization readily apparent, develop a set of headings and sub-headings that do not overlap and that precisely state the scope of the following material.

As an example, one possible organization for the All-Day Wellness contract is as follows: preliminary matter (the parties and the purpose of the contract); definitions; job duties; training; compensation and benefits; time off; process for resolving disputes; job security; the covenant not-to-compete; and boilerplate clauses (typically such matters as arbitration, assignment, choice of law, and modification).

Comprehensibility also is a function of *sentence design*. Some contracts are required by law to be written in plain English; many should be. In Minnesota, for instance, consumer contracts must be written "in a clear and coherent manner using words with common and everyday meanings [and must be] appropriately divided and captioned."[5] Use short, simple sentences, framed affirmatively. Avoid the following usages, which add words, confusion, or both:

- *Legalese* is a word that you would not use in everyday speech (e.g., "aforesaid").
- A *redundant synonym*, or couplet, is a pair of words in which both mean much the same thing (e.g., "covenant and agree").
- *Compound prepositional phrases* arise when two or more such phrases pile up on each other (e.g., "in the city of Minneapolis in the county of Hennepin in the state of Minnesota").
- *Nominalization* entails converting a verb into a noun and pairing another verb with it (e.g., "making an agreement" versus "agreeing").

---

5. Minn. Stat. § 325G.31 (2014).

- *Passive voice* entails the subject of the sentence being acted upon, rather than acting, and is constructed by some version of "to be" and the past participle of the main verb (e.g., "the contract was negotiated by the parties" versus "the parties negotiated the contract").
- *Expletives* are unneeded filler phrases (e.g., "it is agreed that").
- *Lapses in parallel structure* occur when the sentence contains a series of elements, typically verb phrases or modifying phrases, that should be grammatically the same but are not (e.g., "the Employee is prohibited from performing health consultant services within fifty miles of Minneapolis, may not contact customers of All-Day Wellness, or recruit co-workers of Employer").

A particularly troublesome legalism is the *proviso*—"provided that . . ."—typically appended to a lengthy sentence. This phrase has been interpreted to mean "if," "except," and "in addition." Furthermore, most sentences with provisos are too long and complicated.

Comprehensibility is also a function of *conciseness*. Avoid stating a point twice. Although this practice is common in other forms of legal writing, it can lead to confusion in a contract, which is an economically written document in which each statement is deemed to have meaning not conveyed elsewhere within it.

Do, however, provide clear *signals* throughout the contract. Some links are semantic, such as transitional words and repeated references. Other links are structural, such as an introductory phrase or clause followed by a list of related phrases or clauses in parallel structure.

As an example of a sentence that scores low on comprehensibility, consider the following sentence that one could find in the All-Day Wellness employment agreement:

> In the event that any dispute, controversy, or disagreement arising hereunder shall proceed to litigation, it is the parties' agreement that it shall be the law of the jurisdiction of Minnesota that shall be utilized by the court called upon to adjudicate such dispute, controversy, or disagreement.

This sentence of forty-seven words contains nearly all of the writing problems listed above; its meaning can be conveyed in fewer than a dozen words: "Minnesota law governs the resolution of disputes under this contract." Compare the training clause stated above under tenet 7. Note that each sentence makes its own discrete point, the points proceed chronologically, there are semantic links (the types of training), and the clauses are written in parallel structure.

9. Style and Tone

A well-written contract has a *style and tone* that is suitable to the parties' relationship. Generally, contracting parties want a contract that conveys that the parties have entered voluntarily into a mutually advantageous agreement between equals. The contract should read as though they wrote it for each other, not as though a lawyer wrote it for a judge forced to adjudicate a dispute. This is especially true when a contract has been fully negotiated by the parties.

Some contracts fit into a different paradigm, in which a large company presents a standard form contract to many consumers. Some large companies opt for a legalistic and tough tone; others opt for contracts that are conversational and friendly. In these situations, in choosing a tone, you should consider the contract from your client's perspective, of course. But also consider it from the perspective of the typical consumer (who may well be less sophisticated in the transaction) as well as the perspective of a judge.

As an example, compare the training clause under tenet 7 with the choice-of-law clause under tenet 9. The two clauses differ in tone. The choice-of-law clause is abstract and technical. The additional training clause is more personal and direct. One obvious and significant difference is their means of referring to the contracting parties: "the parties" in the choice-of-law clause versus "All-Day Wellness" and "the Employee" in the training clause.

10. Aesthetics

Finally, a well-written contract has sound *aesthetics*: it is, if not pretty, at least relatively pleasant to peruse. Few people read contracts for fun; rather, they read them to find pertinent information. You may use the following tools to make the contract easy to peruse:

- fairly small blocks of text;
- clear headings and sub-headings, cleanly formatted;
- a simple numbering and lettering system;
- tabulation and enumeration for lists of related items;
- easily readable type and font; and
- plenty of white space.

TEST YOUR UNDERSTANDING

1. Explain how drafting differs from analytical legal writing.

2. Provide three examples of different ways in which the law regulates contracts.

3. Which categories of information must a contract state accurately?

4. As for balance in a contract:
    a. Explain how fairness is achieved when terms are negotiated, when terms are undickered, and when a contract is a form contract.
    b. Explain the concept of realistic contract terms.

5. As for comprehensive coverage:
    a. How can you ensure that you fully cover intended events?
    b. What is a default rule, and how should you rely on such a rule?

6. As for foresight as to unintended events, how would you determine which events to cover in the contract?

7. What makes a contract term practical?

8. As for precision:
    a. Identify two ways to develop a definition for a contract term.
    b. Explain the differences among these ideas that pertain to the verbs used in contracts: promise, condition, and privilege.
    c. Explain what contractual ambiguity is, and state three different linguistic settings in which it often arises.

9. As for comprehensibility:
    a. List three sound principles for organizing the topics in a contract.
    b. List at least four common issues that make for confusing and overly long sentences in contracts.
    c. Explain why provisos are problematic in contracts.
    d. Identify the two types of signals you may use in a contract.

10. What makes the style and tone of a contract suitable?

11. List at least four tools that make a contract pleasant to peruse.

TEST YOUR UNDERSTANDING ANSWERS

1. Drafting entails describing situations and setting out what is to happen, whereas analytical legal writing entails explaining the legal meaning of a situation.

2. Some rules prohibit or require certain clauses, others provide parameters within which parties may contract, cases interpret contract language, and some rules affect the contracting process.

3. A contract must accurately state the parties' factual situation and the terms of their agreement.

4. As for balance in a contract:
   a. Fairness is achieved when terms are negotiated because the parties have agreed on the terms. When terms are undickered and when a contract is a form contract, the drafting lawyer bears significant responsibility for the contract's fairness.
   b. The terms should be reasonably attainable; e.g., they should not set unduly high performance standards.

5. As for comprehensive coverage:
   a. To fully cover intended events, address its who, what, when, where, and how dimensions.
   b. A default rule is a standard approach that the law provides if the parties do not contract otherwise. It should be used if the parties intend to use it; it need not be stated in the contract but may be for clarity.

6. As for unintended events, you should cover the most probable and most significant ones.

7. A contract term is practical if it is easily followed; it is as precise and flexible as the parties need it to be.

8. As for precision:
   a. Ways to develop a definition include using a legal definition or term from the trade and creating a list.
   b. A promise creates a duty by one party; a condition is an event that must occur before a party has a duty; a privilege is discretionary authority.
   c. Contractual ambiguity arises when language conveys two distinct yet inconsistent meanings. It may arise between two passages, when information is omitted, when a sentence is awkwardly constructed, and when an ambiguous word is used.

9. As for comprehensibility:
   a. Three sound organizing principles are chronology, most likely before least likely events, and general rules before exceptions.

   b. Common issues are legalese, redundant synonyms, compound prepositional phrases, nominalizations, passive voice, expletives, and lapses in parallel structure.
   c. Provisos are problematic because they have many different meanings.
   d. The two types of signals are semantic and structural.

10. A contract is suitable in style and tone when it fits the parties' relationship.

11. Tools that make a contract pleasant to peruse include small blocks of text, headings, a numbering and lettering system, lists, readable type, and white space.

PLEADINGS

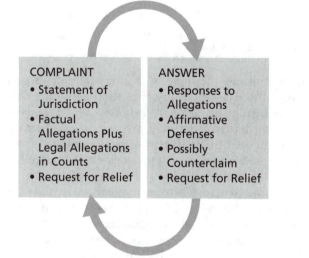

Litigation is the pursuit of practical ends, not a game of chess.
—Felix Frankfurter

A. INTRODUCTION

Lawyers engage in two main types of writing: analytical writing and drafting. In analytical writing, the writer states facts and rules, explains their connection, and posits a legal meaning for the client's situation. By contrast, drafting entails describing situations and setting out what is to happen.

Litigators draft many types of documents as they process a lawsuit. Each has a particular purpose and follows a fairly standard formula:

- *Pleadings* frame litigation by setting out a party's factual allegations, legal claims, and requested relief. The main pleadings are the plaintiff's complaint and the defendant's answer. In complex litigation, there may be additional pleadings, such as cross-complaints and counterclaims.

■ *Discovery documents* facilitate the process of exchange of information between the parties. For example, an interrogatory poses questions for the other party to answer.

■ *Motions* request the court to take the stated action, e.g., to dismiss a complaint because it lacks a sound legal basis or to compel a party to answer interrogatories.

This chapter discusses the drafting of the complaint and answer. It first covers the ethical standards applicable to both documents and then discusses commonly used formats and formulations for complaints and answers. The example for this chapter is the Bower's Bounty situation, in which a terminated employee claims defamation based on a statement about her that other employees read.

B. ETHICAL CONSIDERATIONS

Various sources constrain the lawyer's drafting of pleadings, so that the lawyer not only represents the client zealously but also fulfills the role of officer of the legal system. According to *ABA Model Rule of Professional Conduct 3.1*, "A lawyer shall not bring or defend a proceeding, or assert or controvert an issue therein, unless there is a basis in law or fact for doing so that is not frivolous, which includes a good faith argument for an extension, modification, or reversal of existing law."[1]

This standard may require less certainty than you would expect. It does not require that the lawyer be convinced of the facts of the client's case before bringing suit. As the comments note, the standard is not violated if the facts are not yet fully substantiated and are to be developed through litigation, so long as the lawyer is informed about the facts and can make a good faith argument in support of the client's position. Similarly, the lawyer need not believe that the client's legal position ultimately will win in court, so long as there is a good faith argument for change in the law.

Furthermore, rules of procedure supplement ethics rules. These rules not only set standards of conduct but also provide for sanctions that operate within the litigation, such as payment of the aggrieved party's attorney's fees and expenses resulting from the violation. For an example of such a rule, see Federal Rule of Civil Procedure, excerpted in Box 14.1.

C. COMPLAINT

A *complaint* is the document by which the plaintiff begins the lawsuit. On its face, a well-written complaint seems to be a simple document. But actually, a complaint is a complex document: it must properly allege the facts and all pertinent legal points; it must comply with pleading standards; it must conform to many detailed requirements, such as specific information to provide and formats to

---

1. The standard for the lawyer for a criminal defendant is formulated differently.

BOX 14.1

FEDERAL RULE 11. REPRESENTATIONS TO THE COURT

As you read the following rule, think about these questions:

1. *In the context of writing complaints and answers, what do you think would constitute "an inquiry reasonable under the circumstances"?*
2. *Before you could bring a motion to the court to sanction opposing counsel under this rule, what must you do? (Note: Service is delivery upon the other party, and filing is delivery to the court.)*
3. *What types of sanctions may the court impose, and what is the purpose of any such sanction?*

(b) REPRESENTATIONS TO THE COURT. By presenting to the court a pleading, written motion, or other paper—whether by signing, filing, submitting, or later advocating it—an attorney or unrepresented party certifies that to the best of the person's knowledge, information, and belief, formed after an inquiry reasonable under the circumstances:

(1) it is not being presented for any improper purpose, such as to harass, cause unnecessary delay, or needlessly increase the cost of litigation;

(2) the claims, defenses, and other legal contentions are warranted by existing law or by a nonfrivolous argument for extending, modifying, or reversing existing law or for establishing new law;

(3) the factual contentions have evidentiary support or, if specifically so identified, will likely have evidentiary support after a reasonable opportunity for further investigation or discovery; and

(4) the denials of factual contentions are warranted on the evidence or, if specifically so identified, are reasonably based on belief or a lack of information.

(c) SANCTIONS.

(1) *In General.* If, after notice and a reasonable opportunity to respond, the court determines that Rule 11(b) has been violated, the court may impose an appropriate sanction on any attorney, law firm, or party that violated the rule or is responsible for the violation. Absent exceptional circumstances, a law firm must be held jointly responsible for a violation committed by its partner, associate, or employee.

(2) *Motion for Sanctions.* A motion for sanctions must be made separately from any other motion and must describe the specific conduct that allegedly violates Rule 11(b). The motion must be served under Rule 5, but it must not be filed or be presented to the court if the challenged paper, claim, defense, contention, or denial is withdrawn or appropriately corrected within 21 days after service or within another time the court sets. If warranted, the court may award to the prevailing party the reasonable expenses, including attorney's fees, incurred for the motion.

(3) *On the Court's Initiative.* On its own, the court may order an attorney, law firm, or party to show cause why conduct specifically described in the order has not violated Rule 11(b).

(4) *Nature of a Sanction.* A sanction imposed under this rule must be limited to what suffices to deter repetition of the conduct or comparable conduct by others similarly situated. The sanction may include nonmonetary directives; an order to pay a penalty into court; or, if imposed on motion and warranted for effective deterrence, an order directing payment to the movant of part or all of the reasonable attorney's fees and other expenses directly resulting from the violation.

(5) *Limitations on Monetary Sanctions.* The court must not impose a monetary sanction:

(A) against a represented party for violating Rule 11(b)(2); or

(B) on its own, unless it issued the show-cause order under Rule 11(c)(3) before voluntary dismissal or settlement of the claims made by or against the party that is, or whose attorneys are, to be sanctioned.

(6) *Requirements for an Order.* An order imposing a sanction must describe the sanctioned conduct and explain the basis for the sanction.

follow. Every complaint is closely scrutinized by the defendant to determine whether it is subject to dismissal. Furthermore, it should be a persuasive document that prompts the readers to see the case from the plaintiff's perspective.

Exhibit 14A is a complaint written for the Bower's Bounty situation. Please read through it now.

The complaint begins with technical components, which vary by court system. The complaint opens with the *caption*, which typically identifies the court, the parties, the nature of the action, and the title of the document.[2] The text of the complaint may begin with a prefatory phrase (such as "Plaintiff [name] for her Complaint hereby alleges as follows:"). The next section may be a statement of the court's *jurisdiction*—that is, the court's power to hear the case. In federal court, for example, the jurisdictional statement may cover the facts establishing diversity of the parties, along with a citation to the diversity jurisdiction statute.

The bulk of the complaint consists of the *allegations*, or statements that the plaintiff asserts to be true. The allegations encompass both the facts and the law supporting the plaintiff's claims. Thoroughness is critical when stating the allegations: failure to allege a fact satisfying a necessary element or to assert an element of a claim provides the basis for the court to dismiss that claim.[3] As noted above, the facts must be supported to a certain degree and the legal claims must be warranted to a certain degree. To account for a less-than-high degree of factual certainty, an allegation of fact may be preceded by "upon information and belief."

The organization of a complaint varies substantially according to the protocols of the court and the complexity of the case. It is common to begin with *factual allegations*, starting with an introduction to the parties and the location of the events, then the events giving rise to the dispute (in chronological order), the dispute itself, and the harm suffered by the plaintiff. Each fact or set of very closely related facts is set out in its own numbered paragraph.[4] Paragraphs may be clumped under topical headings if the recitation of facts is lengthy.

How specifically to allege the facts varies by jurisdiction and claim and is based on *pleading requirements*. Traditionally and in many states, fairly general statements suffice because the purpose of pleading is to give fair notice of the incident to the opponent.[5] Under more rigorous U.S. Supreme Court precedents, a complaint in federal court must contain enough facts to "state a claim to relief that is plausible on its face."[6] Some types of cases, such as fraud, must be pled with a high degree of factual specificity.[7]

Following the factual allegations are the allegations of *legal claims* framed in *counts*.[8] Many complaints have more than one claim, or count, because the same

---

2. Once a case is filed with the court, it acquires a docket number, which appears on all documents.

3. *See, e.g.*, Fed. R. Civ. P. 12(b)(6).

4. *See, e.g.*, Fed. R. Civ. P. 10(b).

5. For example, see the Minnesota Supreme Court decision in *Walsh v. U.S. Bank, N.A.*, 851 N.W.2d 598, 602 (relief is "possible on any evidence which might be produced consistent with the pleader's theory"). In this case, the court declined to follow the federal *Twombly-Iqbal* standard.

6. *Bell Atlantic Corp. v. Twombly*, 550 U.S. 544 (2007); *Ashcroft v. Iqbal*, 556 U.S. 662 (2009).

7. *E.g.*, Fed. R. Civ. P. 9.

8. If there is only one simply stated count, the factual allegations and legal claims may be merged.

events may give rise to more than one cause of action under different rules in the complex U.S. legal system, e.g., a tort and breach of contract, a tort and a violation of statute, and violations of state and federal statutes. A lengthy complaint with multiple counts typically presents each count in a separately numbered part, each beginning with a statement re-alleging the factual allegations.

The style of a complaint varies according to court protocols. In the past, complaints had to be written in stylized language to fit within very specific pleading requirements, but this is generally no longer the case. Nonetheless, some lawyers still write rather ornate complaints; however, many jurisdictions call for direct and concise language.[9] Furthermore, the style of a complaint may influence its persuasiveness. As a simple example, using an injured plaintiff's name humanizes her, as compared to referring to her as "Plaintiff." The complaint is not only the document that serves to begin litigation in the court system; it also presents the claim to the defendant, who may opt to settle rather than litigate.

The complaint ends with a *request for relief* sought by the plaintiff; this statement may be dictated by rules related to the claim or rules related to pleadings. The *signature* of the attorney follows, with certain identifying and contact information.[10]

In your legal research, you may come across sample complaints. If the sample is an authoritative one, written under the auspices of the court in which you are filing your case, it merits much greater consideration than one that you may find in general commentary sources. If the sample is not from your specific jurisdiction, take great care in scrutinizing whether the legal points match the law of your jurisdiction. In all events, your complaint must state the facts and law of your client's unique claims accurately and fully, so it is best to use a sample for ideas, not as a model to be followed too closely.

As an example, Exhibit 14A, the sample complaint for the Bower's Bounty situation, begins with the caption in the Kansas state forms. The complaint does not have a jurisdictional statement because none is required. It proceeds directly into the first part of the complaint, which recounts the facts of the plaintiff's situation, organized around the participants in the story and their relationships and focused on the erosion of the plaintiff's reputation. The second part states the elements of the claim of defamation after setting out the legal rule connecting Bower's Bounty to the acts of Dan Molinaro, the manager. Finally, the "wherefore" clause sets out the requested relief using the language provided for in Kansas rules and forms.

D. Answer

A defendant may respond to a complaint in various ways, including negotiating a settlement and making certain motions. The standard response is to write an *answer*. In the answer, the defendant must respond to the allegations of the

---

9. *E.g.*, Fed. R. Civ. P. 8(d)(1) ("simple, concise, and direct").
10. In some jurisdictions, a signed statement attesting to conformity to ethical standards follows the main signature block.

complaint. Some answers include affirmative defenses. The defendant may also bring a counterclaim against the plaintiff.

Exhibit 14B is a sample answer, responding to Exhibit 14A, written for the Bower's Bounty situation. Please read through it now.

As with the complaint, the answer opens with a caption and an appropriate prefatory phrase. The major part of all answers is the *response*[11] in which the defendant addresses the allegations in the complaint. The defendant has three choices: to *admit* what it agrees with, *deny* what it does not agree with, or indicate that it *lacks knowledge or information* sufficient to form a belief about an allegation. The latter option requires the plaintiff to prove the allegation and thus operates as a denial. If the defendant considers its response to the points in a specific paragraph in the complaint to be a mix of these options, it must set out this mix of responses. The defendant may proceed paragraph by paragraph, or the defendant may list the paragraphs that it admits, then list those that it denies, then list those as to which it lacks information, and finally present its mixed responses.

The second major part of many answers is the assertion of *affirmative defenses*,[12] in which the defendant goes beyond countering the points in the complaint. The defendant alleges facts and a corresponding legal basis for succeeding in the lawsuit on some other ground. That ground may be substantive, such as immunity from suit, or procedural, such as the plaintiff's failure to sue promptly enough given the statute of limitations for the claims brought.

Finally, a defendant may bring a *counterclaim* against the plaintiff for losses that it suffered due to actions of the plaintiff.[13] This portion of the answer resembles the complaint, although the factual allegations may be somewhat truncated.

As with the complaint, the answer closes with the defendant's request for relief and a signature block.

As an example, Exhibit 14B, the sample answer for the Bower's Bounty situation, begins with the caption in the Kansas state forms. It consolidates the responses to the various paragraphs in the complaint by category of response: admissions, lack of knowledge, denials, and mixed answers. Some factual allegations are admitted, but almost all the legal allegations are denied. The answer includes the affirmative defense of qualified privilege, but it does not include a counterclaim. The requested relief thus is confined to, essentially, denying relief to the plaintiff.

---

11. *See, e.g.,* Fed. R. Civ. P. 8(b)(1)-(6).
12. *See, e.g.,* Fed. R. Civ. P. 8(c).
13. *See, e.g.,* Fed. R. Civ. P. 13(a)-(c).

IN THE SEVENTH JUDICIAL DISTRICT[14]
DISTRICT COURT OF DOUGLAS COUNTY, KANSAS

Sarah Nicholson,
  Plaintiff,
v.   Case No. _____
Bower's Bounty Groceries, Inc.
  Defendant.
Proceeding Pursuant to K.S.A. Chapter 60

COMPLAINT

Plaintiff Sarah Nicholson states the following claim for relief against the Defendant, Bower's Bounty Groceries, Inc.:

FACTS

1. From August 1, 2009 until August 8, 2016, Plaintiff Sarah Nicholson was employed by Defendant Bower's Bounty Groceries, Inc. in its store in Lawrence, Kansas, most recently serving as supervisor of the fresh produce department.
2. Ms. Nicholson enjoyed a reputation for honesty and integrity in her professional and personal life before and while working at Bower's Bounty.
3. At no time did Ms. Nicholson take any goods of value from Bower's Bounty.
4. The business community in general, and the grocery store community in particular, in Lawrence, Kansas, is a small and close-knit community.
5. Dan Molinaro was hired as the manager of the Lawrence Bower's Bounty store on July 1, 2016.
6. Dan Molinaro terminated Ms. Nicholson's employment without advance warning or discussion on August 8, 2016.
7. On August 8, 2016, Dan Molinaro posted a notice in the employee lounge stating that Ms. Nicholson had engaged in pilferage, leading to termination of her employment for violation of company policy.
8. This statement was read and believed by employees of Bower's Bounty.
9. Ms. Nicholson has suffered damage to her reputation, unemployment, and documented emotional distress as a result of the communication of the posted statement.

---

14. This sample more or less follows the protocols of the Kansas state courts (although Kansas uses "petition" in lieu of "complaint"). For simplicity, it uses the law of only one case, *Luttrell v. United Telephone System, Inc.*, 683 P.2d 1292 (Kan. Ct. App. 1984), *aff'd*, 659 P.2d 1270 (Kan. 1985).

CLAIM FOR DEFAMATION

10. The actions of Dan Molinaro on August 8, 2016, relative to the statement posted in the employee lounge were within the scope of his employment by Defendant Bower's Bounty Groceries, Inc.

11. Defendant posted a statement containing words about Plaintiff that were false and defamatory in accusing her of dishonest conduct in her workplace that she did not in fact undertake.

12. Defendant published the statement to third parties by posting the statement in the employee lounge, where employees did read and believe the statement.

13. In posting this statement, Defendant acted without regard to any legitimate interest and, at best, with reckless disregard for the truth of the statement.

14. Because of this statement, Plaintiff's professional reputation for honesty and integrity has been harmed.

15. As a consequence of the damage to her reputation, Plaintiff has suffered a lengthy period of unemployment, with consequent economic losses and documentable emotional distress.

Wherefore, Plaintiff demands judgment against Defendant in an amount in excess of $75,000, together with interests, costs of this action, and other appropriate relief.

Kyle McKenna

Kyle McKenna
Attorney for Sarah Nicholson
Atty # 020687
Owen & McKenna
987 Oak St.
Suite 200
Lawrence KS 60000
(123) 456-7890
kmk@owen&mckenna.com

EXHIBIT 14B ANSWER

**IN THE SEVENTH JUDICIAL DISTRICT
DISTRICT COURT OF DOUGLAS COUNTY, KANSAS**

Sarah Nicholson,
  Plaintiff,
v.   Case No. _____
Bower's Bounty Groceries, Inc.
  Defendant.
Proceeding Pursuant to K.S.A. Chapter 60

ANSWER

Defendant Bower's Bounty Groceries, Inc. answers the Complaint as follows:

1. Defendant admits the allegations stated in the Complaint in paragraphs 1, 5, and 10.
2. Defendant is without knowledge or information sufficient to form a belief as to the truth of the allegations stated in the Complaint in paragraphs 2, 4, 8, and 9, and therefore denies those allegations.
3. Defendant denies the allegations stated in the Complaint in paragraphs 3, 11, 12, 13, 14, and 15.
4. Defendant admits the allegations stated in the Complaint in paragraph 6, except that Mr. Molinaro did meet with Plaintiff to inform her of her termination.
5. Defendant admits the allegation in the Complaint in paragraph 7 that a statement was posted in the employee lounge on August 8, 2016, which statement speaks for itself.

AFFIRMATIVE DEFENSE

6. Further, Defendant alleges Plaintiff's claim for relief should be denied by reason of qualified privilege.

   Wherefore, Defendant prays that Plaintiff be denied relief and that Defendant have judgment for costs and other relief as the Court deems just and proper.

Karen Bowmann

Karen Bowmann
Attorney for Bower's Bounty Groceries, Inc.
Atty # 090687
Bowmann & Selleck
123 Fifth Ave.
Suite 600
Lawrence KS 60000
(123) 456-9870
ksb@bowmann&selleck.com

TEST YOUR UNDERSTANDING

1. Explain how the following three categories of drafted litigation documents differ from each other: pleadings, discovery documents, and motions.

2. In terms of ethical standards guiding pleading:
   a. What are the two standards articulated in ABA Model Rule 3.1 and Federal Rule of Civil Procedure 11?
   b. In what setting is Rule 11 enforced, and what is the purpose of the sanctions?

3. What are the two basic pleadings in civil litigation, and which party drafts which one?

4. What information appears in a typical caption?

5. As for the complaint:
   a. What is included in a jurisdictional statement?
   b. What two types of material appear in the allegations?
   c. What is a pleading requirement, and on what bases does it vary?
   d. May a complaint have more than one count? Explain.
   e. What areas of law determine how to draft the request for relief?

6. Regarding the answer:
   a. Is writing an answer the only option available to the defendant?
   b. What are the three main options that the defendant may select when responding to each allegation of the complaint?
   c. What is an affirmative defense, and do all complaints include them?
   d. What is a counterclaim, and do all complaints include them?
   e. Do answers include requests for relief?

TEST YOUR UNDERSTANDING ANSWERS

1. Pleadings frame the litigation by setting out factual allegations, legal claims, and requests for relief. Discovery documents are used to facilitate the exchange of information. Motions request the court to take certain actions.

2. As for ethical standards guiding pleading:
   a. ABA Model Rule 3.1 uses the "not frivolous" and "good faith" standards. Rule 11 requires, as to the law, at least a "nonfrivolous argument" for changing the law and, as to facts, at least evidentiary support after investigation or discovery—both based on reasonable inquiry.
   b. Rule 11 is enforced within litigation of a case, and sanctions are intended to deter repetition of the conduct or comparable conduct.

3. The plaintiff drafts the complaint, and the defendant drafts the answer.

4. A typical caption includes the court, the parties, the nature of the action, the title of the document, and eventually the docket number.

5. As for the complaint:
   a. A jurisdictional statement includes the facts related to jurisdiction and the basis for jurisdiction, including the citation.
   b. The two types of allegations are factual events and legal claims.
   c. A pleading requirement sets out how rigorously facts must be pleaded, and they vary based on jurisdiction and claim.
   d. Many complaints have more than one count, drawing on various sources of law or on both state and federal law.
   e. The law related to the claim and the rules related to pleadings may determine the framing of the request for relief.

6. As for the answer:
   a. A defendant may settle, make a motion, or answer.
   b. A defendant may respond to each allegation by admitting it, denying it, or indicating that it is without knowledge or information sufficient to form a belief about it.
   c. An affirmative defense is a point that goes beyond those made in the complaint; not all answers include them.
   d. A counterclaim is a claim brought against the plaintiff for losses that the defendant has suffered due to actions of the plaintiff; not all complaints include them.
   e. Yes, answers include requests for relief.

NEGOTIATING WITH
OPPOSING COUNSEL

The best move you can make in negotiation is to think of an incentive
the other person hasn't even thought of—and then meet it.
  —Eli Broad

A. INTRODUCTION

Notwithstanding common depictions of the legal profession, lawyers accomplish
most of their work on behalf of clients not by arguing in court; rather they negotiate with other lawyers. This is true for transactional lawyers and also for litigators because a high percentage of disputes in the United States are resolved

through negotiated settlements.[1] Thus, to be an effective lawyer, you must excel in negotiating.

You have already negotiated thousands of times on your own behalf for purposes large and small (with varying degrees of success, no doubt). Even so, negotiating on behalf of a client to secure the best possible legal outcome will be a new challenge. *Legal negotiation* is a form of improvisation between lawyers: a protracted conversation in which each lawyer seeks to obtain a strong outcome for his or her client that is also acceptable to the other party. In legal negotiation, the facts of the two parties' situations, the applicable legal rules, their broader contexts, the psychological dimensions of negotiation, and rules of legal ethics are all in play at the same time.

Most productive negotiations broadly follow a four-scene sequence. In the first scene, the lawyers set the stage for the improvisation to follow. In the second scene, the lawyers exchange information they need for fruitful conversation. In the third scene, the lawyers engage in what you most likely think of as negotiating—that is, they bargain back and forth. In the final scene, if all has gone well, they come to an agreement. Preceding these interactions with opposing counsel is the indispensable process of preparation for the negotiation. This chapter proceeds by discussing each scene in turn.

This chapter refers, for a dispute example, to the Bower's Bounty situation involving a claim of defamation by a terminated employee against her former employer. For a transactional example, the chapter refers to the negotiation of an employment agreement between All-Day Wellness, a new company in the health care consulting field, and a key new hire.

B. PREPARING

Lawyers who excel in negotiation will tell you that negotiation begins with thorough *preparation*. One facet of preparation is obtaining your *authority*: in your role as a lawyer, you may agree only to those terms your client has authorized you to agree to. As framed in *ABA Model Rule of Professional Conduct 1.2(a)*, "a lawyer shall abide by a client's decisions concerning the scope of representation." Thus, a key step in preparing for any negotiation is detailed consultation with your client about the scope of your authority.

Simply knowing your authority is insufficient preparation, however. You must also know, in depth, the *facts of your client's situation* that is the subject of the negotiation. In a dispute negotiation, you must know about the dispute and its past, present, and probable future impacts on your client. In a transactional negotiation, you must know the general nature of the transaction, its purpose, your client's circumstances that relate to the transaction (such as financial status and production capacity), and any existing agreements between the parties.

1. *See* Theodore Eisenberg & Charlotte Lanvers, *What Is the Settlement Rate and Why Should We Care?* 6 J. Leg. Studies 111 (2009).

Furthermore, you must also know the applicable *legal rules* and apply them to your client's situation. Although negotiation outcomes are not fixed by the application of legal rules, they are influenced by legal arguments; in other words, lawyers "bargain in the shadow of the law."[2] Thus, you should carefully analyze why your client would prevail in litigation or is entitled to a particular clause in a contract.

Negotiation is about more than legal analysis, however. Thus, you must take into account the *broader context* of your client's situation. Various factors in the parties' contexts influence a negotiation, in part by giving each party negotiating power or taking away power. In dispute negotiations, economics, the desire for publicity or confidentiality, the timing of the settlement, the potential for similar claims, and risk tolerance generally are important context factors. In transactional negotiations, the availability of other contracting partners, timing, financing options, and security of information are generally important context factors.

Two key dimensions of your preparation are your *client's interests and goals* related to the negotiation. As discussed in Chapter 10, an *interest* is an abstraction that is of value to the client; a *goal* is a concrete feature of an agreement that serves an interest. In both dispute and transactional negotiations, you should approach your client's interests and goals in both monetary and non-monetary terms. While the standard terms of a contract or other document generally provide a helpful framework for doing this in the transactional setting, sometimes the non-monetary facets of a dispute negotiation may be less obvious. Furthermore, goals need not be items that a court would order. For an example of the employee's analysis for the Bower's Bounty dispute, see Box 15.1.

Furthermore, to the extent possible, you should think through these same matters—the factual situation, legal analysis, broader context, interests, and goals—from the standpoint of the other party to the negotiation. Seeing the negotiation from the other party's point of view makes you a more perceptive negotiator.

On the basis of this analysis, you may develop your *list of terms* to include in the agreement. In both the dispute and transactional settings, some items are so standard that they are not typically negotiated; you should make a list of these terms. For terms that you anticipate negotiating, you should develop a *set of positions*.

The first position to identify is your *BATNA position*. BATNA stands for "best alternative to a negotiated agreement," and it amounts to your walk-away position, or the point at which you would not enter into an agreement. The idea behind BATNA is that you should identify your best alternative to coming to agreement during the present negotiation and not agree to terms that are less favorable than that alternative. In a dispute setting, BATNA reflects the value that you place on continuing to litigate.[3] In a transactional setting, your BATNA position reflects the opportunities that you could obtain with a different

---

2. *See* Robert D. Cooter, Stephen Marks, & Robert Mnookin, *Bargaining in the Shadow of the Law: A Testable Model of Strategic Behavior*, 11 J. Legal Studies 225 (1982).
3. See the probability tree in Box 11.2 and its discussion on page 232.

BOX 15.1

SAMPLE INTERESTS AND GOALS ANALYSIS FOR DISPUTE NEGOTIATION

Out of work/lost job Nicholson loved

- Company reinstates her (but what about issues she might have with employee who may have falsely accused her, or what about issues with her manager?)
- Company places her in different job
- Company assists her in getting job elsewhere

Loss of income and benefits

- Money damages
- Reinstating various benefits until she gets another job (if not reinstated)

Damaged reputation

- Retract posting in same way that it was initially made
- Correct Nicholson's personnel file
- Strong reference letter and favorable response to calls

Emotional distress

- Company apologizes
- Company pays for counseling

Concern about employment practices at Bower's Bounty

- Company agrees to change its termination practices

party. For an example of the analysis for the All-Day Wellness contract, see Box 15.2.

The second position to identify is your *aspirational position*: the most favorable, realistically attainable position, given the law and your client's facts and broader practical context. The aspirational position should not be so generous to the client that it will offend the other party or suggest bad faith. You should be able to justify it with points grounded in the facts, law, and broader context.

Finally, you should identify *probable settlement positions,* terms that you can envision the other party agreeing to. You should be ready to fully state and explain these terms during the negotiation so that it is easy for opposing counsel to understand and consent to them. Furthermore, as discussed below, negotiating about several topics together is advisable, so you should be able to tie various terms together into logical, desirable combinations.

SAMPLE OPPORTUNITY COST ANALYSIS FOR TRANSACTIONAL NEGOTIATION

Salaries likely to be paid other candidates $\times$ probability of hiring each (if we do not hire current candidate):

Candidate A: $120,000 $\times$ .20 = 24,000
Candidate B: $150,000 $\times$ .50 = 75,000
Candidate C: $100,000 $\times$ .30 = 33,000

Expected value of other opportunities is = $132,000 (24,000 + 75,000 + 33,000), so hiring current candidate for up to $132,000 would be wise, based on this factor.

Finally, based on this preparation, a *theory of the negotiation* should evolve. Because negotiation happens in the moment, is wide-ranging, and can cover many complicated topics, it helps to have a central idea as a touchstone to emphasize throughout the negotiation. In a dispute negotiation, it may be the major loss that the client experienced, the principle at issue, or the future that the client seeks to experience. In a transactional negotiation, it may be the shared advantage the two parties would gain from the transaction.

C. SETTING THE STAGE

The first scene in a negotiation is crucial, although it may seem that very little progress is being made. This is because the first scene *sets the stage*, in terms of both tone and structure, for what is to follow. The first scene has three purposes: developing personal rapport, creating a positive atmosphere, and establishing a working agenda.

The early moments in the negotiation session should be spent developing rapport with opposing counsel; a positive relationship between negotiators leads to more effective negotiation. Aim to find common interests or experiences to chat about, such as law school, community activities, or sports. Use warm communication methods, such as eye contact, a friendly tone of voice, and pleasant demeanor.

As you make the transition into discussing business, seek to create a positive atmosphere. While the precise phrasing will vary depending on the context, the main point to convey is that your client is interested in obtaining a resolution and looks forward to working with the other party to that end.

The next task is to establish a working agenda. The general framework of the negotiation is likely to follow the sequence of exchanging information, bargaining, and coming to agreement. The agenda to be discussed is the set of topics to be negotiated, although not yet the specific terms. Thus, for example, agenda items for the Bower's Bounty negotiation would be monetary compensation and assistance in helping Sarah Nicholson in gaining employment, not a specific dollar amount or action to be taken by Bower's Bounty. Both parties should identify agenda items, and the attitude should be one of openness. Ideally, this discussion yields consensus on topics to at least put on the table—the first agreement of the negotiation.

D. EXCHANGING INFORMATION

In the second scene, the lawyers *exchange information* that permits them to bargain fruitfully during the third and fourth scenes. This information is important because the strongest agreements are those that serve the shared interests of both parties or, where they share few interests, as many of their separate interests as possible. Without exchanging information about their factual situations, broader contexts, and interests and goals, these agreements are unlikely to come about.

In this exchange of information, lawyers operate within ethical parameters. First, information that falls within the bounds of lawyer-client confidentiality may indeed be revealed with client consent or to carry out the representation.[4] Second, *ABA Model Rule of Professional Conduct 4.1(a)* states, "In the course of representing a client a lawyer shall not knowingly . . . make a false statement of material fact or law to a third person." The comments provide important nuance as to negotiation, as excerpted in Box 15.3. According to these comments, some matters fall within the realm of "puffing" and are not within the false statement rule. But matters of fact are subject to the prohibition on false statements, and that rule encompasses more than outright lies. As one expert has written, "When negotiators are asked about delicate issues or decide to raise those matters on their own, their statements should be phrased in a manner that conveys—both explicitly and implicitly—truthful information. They should not use half-truths they know are likely to induce listeners to misunderstand the actual circumstances. If they are not sure what to say, they may remain silent. If they choose to speak, however, they must do so in a way that is not misleading."[5] This rule requiring candor is a lesson to the wise: candor promotes trust between the negotiators, which can lead to better outcomes.[6]

On the one hand, you should strategically *reveal information*. Identify information that strongly supports your theory of the negotiation. You may want to volunteer some information in a prepared oral or written statement (a settlement brochure for a dispute negotiation or a prospectus for a transaction negotiation). You may decide to wait to provide other information in response to questions. See Box 15.4 for several areas to reveal in the sample dispute and transactional situations.

---

4. *See* Model Rules of Prof'l Conduct 1.6(a) (Am. Bar Ass'n 2013).
5. Charles B. Craver, *Skills and Values: Legal Negotiating* 219-20 (2d ed. 2012).
6. *See* Deborah Schmedemann, *Navigating the Murky Waters of Untruth in Negotiation: Lessons for Ethical Lawyers*, 12 Cardozo J. Conflict Reso. 83 (2010).

BOX 15.3

TRUTHFULNESS IN NEGOTIATION

ABA Model Rule of Professional Conduct 4.1 Comment 1

A lawyer is required to be truthful when dealing with others on a client's behalf, but generally has no affirmative duty to inform an opposing party of relevant facts. A misrepresentation can occur if the lawyer incorporates or affirms a statement of another person that the lawyers knows is false. Misrepresentations can also occur by partially true but misleading statements or omissions that are the equivalent of affirmative false statements.

Comment 2

This Rule refers to statements of fact. Whether a particular statement should be regarded as one of fact can depend on the circumstances. Under generally accepted conventions in negotiation, certain types of statements ordinarily are not taken as statements of material fact. Estimates of price or value placed on the subject of a transaction and a party's intentions as to an acceptable settlement of a claim are ordinarily in this category. . . .

No doubt opposing counsel will ask you questions. Avoid defensiveness when *answering questions*, keep in mind that exchanging information facilitates negotiation. However, you are not obligated to answer every question simply because it is asked. You may deflect a question, e.g., by talking about a related topic or by asking a question in return. A more straightforward approach is to decline to answer, coupled with an appropriate explanation, e.g., that the question touches on information that a client has asked not to have revealed.

On the other hand, you should *seek information* from opposing counsel. Consider these categories discussed earlier in this chapter: the facts of the party's situation, its broader context, and its interests and goals. Decide which points in each of these categories you know the least about and would consider the most influential if you were forming negotiation positions on behalf of the other party; ask about these points.[7] A mix of questions can work best, with open-ended questions followed by closed-ended questions. Use supportive non-verbal communication and active listening (waiting until opposing counsel has concluded speaking and reflecting understanding of what has been said in your comments) to encourage complete disclosure. As to key information and any answers that you doubt, consider asking for the source of information or documentation. For sample topics to inquire about in the sample dispute and transaction negotiations, again see Box 15.4.

---

7. While you could ask about the party's positions on the various terms, the chances of receiving useful information is low, and most lawyers would view these questions as naïve.

BOX 15.4

SAMPLE TOPICS FOR INFORMATION EXCHANGE

DISPUTE NEGOTIATION

Topics that Bower's Bounty would reveal

- Evidence of real pilferage concerns when Nicholson was terminated
- Bower's Bounty's silence re situation since her termination
- Bower's Bounty's general practices re employment references

Topics that Bower's Bounty would ask about

- Nicholson's employment since leaving Bower's Bounty
- Documented evidence of Nicholson's emotional distress
- Evidence that Nicholson has reflecting her diminished reputation

TRANSACTIONAL NEGOTIATION

Topics that All-Day Wellness would reveal

- Competition issues when it did not have covenants not-to-compete
- Benefits package and values
- Salary survey data

Topics that All-Day Wellness would ask about

- Candidate's salary history
- Candidate's tenure in previous jobs
- Candidate's experience with covenants-not-to-compete

The second scene may also entail some *discussion of the legal positions* of the parties, which must be handled with finesse. In negotiation, you are not making an argument to a court in order to win a case; rather, you are seeking to establish some bargaining power for your client, without undermining your commitment to coming to an agreement. To achieve this balance, deliver a concise statement that frames the pertinent legal rules, highlights your client's favorable facts, acknowledges any strengths in the other party's position, and returns to your client's strong points. Acknowledging the other party's strengths demonstrates your preparation and reasonableness and subtly reduces the other party's power. In response to points made by opposing counsel, be ready with additional points, including probing questions and fresh angles on your own position. To keep the legal discussion from dominating the negotiation, make the point that the parties have come to seek a negotiated agreement and may need to "agree to disagree" on their legal positions.

E. BARGAINING

In most negotiations, the longest, most challenging, and fastest-paced scene is the third, in which the lawyers *bargain*: they discuss potential terms that could appear in the agreement, seeking to find and identify ones on which they can agree. Ethics rules do not say much about the practices to use during this scene.[8] Every lawyer has his or her own style of negotiating, and each negotiation takes its unique course. Even so, the considerable research into negotiation in recent decades has yielded useful guidance.

In broad strokes, one could come at negotiation through an adversarial or problem-solving approach. The *adversarial negotiator* focuses on her own party, positions, the law, and winning. By contrast, the *problem-solving negotiator* focuses on both parties, underlying interests and needs, various factors in addition to the law, and obtaining mutually beneficial outcomes. See Box 15.5. The significance of these two categories is that problem-solvers have been shown to be more effective negotiators. In one study of lawyers as negotiators, for example, less than one-tenth of the adversarial lawyers were rated as effective negotiators by their peers, whereas over half of the problem-solvers were. Of the lawyers identified as effective negotiators, over ninety percent were categorized as problem-solving in approach, less than ten percent as adversarial in approach.[9]

The problem-solving approach involves various strategies. General strategies include indicating an interest in using a problem-solving approach early in the negotiation, frequently mentioning the interests of both parties, presenting solutions that tie into those interests, and inviting opposing counsel to develop other similar solutions. Brainstorming is a common strategy in problem-solving. Problem-solvers do not see topics as "fixed pies" to be divided between the parties; rather, they redefine them so that both parties gain as much as possible. Another strategy is to incorporate elements of both parties' ideas into a term. Finally, if opposing counsel seems reluctant to engage in problem-solving, one strategy is to use questions to open up the discussion, asking for the reasoning behind the positions offered and for reactions to a proposal.[10]

Regardless of approach, as to some topics, the parties will state opening positions that are some distance apart and then, through a series of large and small concessions, move toward a middle point. For these terms, coming to agreement depends on *bargaining range*. Each party has its BATNA and aspirational positions, which together establish a *settlement zone*. For there to be a positive

---

8. ABA Model Rule 4.4, however, does state that "a lawyer shall not use means that have no substantial purpose other than to . . . embarrass . . . or burden a third person." Comment 1 to Rule 1.3 precludes the use of "offensive tactics" and calls for "treating . . . all persons . . . with courtesy and respect."

9. Andrea Kupfer Schneider, *Shattering Negotiation Myths: Empirical Evidence on the Effectiveness of Negotiation Style*, 7 Harv. Negot. L. Rev. 143 (2002).

10. *See* Stefan H. Krieger & Richard K. Neumann, Jr., *Essential Lawyering Skills: Interviewing, Counseling, Negotiation, and Persuasive Fact Analysis* 370-76 (5th ed. 2015).

BOX 15.5	

PROBLEM-SOLVERS AND ADVERSARIES AS NEGOTIATORS[11]

Problem-Solvers	Adversaries
Demonstrate accurate understanding of my client's underlying interests	Did not demonstrate accurate understanding of my client's underlying interests
View negotiation as process with possibly mutually beneficial outcome	View negotiation as process with winners and losers
Conceptualize problems in terms of underlying interests, motivations, and needs	Conceptualize problem in terms of bargaining between positions
Use legal entitlements as one of several factors in determining solution	Conceptualize problem solely in terms of legal entitlements
Have broad view of case	Have narrow view of case

bargaining range and hence grounds for agreement,[12] the settlement zones of the two parties must overlap. See Box 15.6.

A key issue in the bargaining scene is whether to make the *initial offer* on a topic. In some negotiations, the standard practice is for one party to take that step (e.g., the seller of a business, the plaintiff in a lawsuit). Standard practice aside, there are sound strategic reasons to make the first offer—and also sound reasons not to do so. The argument for making the first offer is that it serves as the *anchor* for that term; that is, the discussion proceeds from that value. On the other hand, going first entails the risk that the offer is far off of the value envisioned by the other party; the best safeguard against this risk is thorough preparation. In any event, you should rarely accept an opening offer from the other party but rather engage in some give and take, so that both sides believe that they made a good deal.

As you engage in the give-and-take about potential terms for the agreement, certain basic strategies should serve you well:

   ■ All else being equal, first discuss topics on which agreement should come easily, to build momentum; then work on the more challenging topics in the middle; turn to routine topics at the end.

---

11. Andrea Kupfer Schneider, *Shattering Negotiation Myths: Empirical Evidence on the Effectiveness of Negotiation Style*, 7 Harv. Negot. L. Rev. 143 (2002).
12. An alternative term is "zone of possible agreement (ZOPA)."

BOX 15.6

BARGAINING ZONE AND SETTLEMENT RANGES

EXAMPLE 1

Buyer's settlement zone

* Buyer's aspiration is to pay only $100,000.
* Buyer would walk away (BATNA) if price exceeds $140,000.

Seller's settlement zone

* Seller's aspiration is to receive $160,000.
* Seller would walk away (BATNA) if price is less than $125,000.

There is a positive bargaining zone: $125,000 – 140,000.

EXAMPLE 2

Buyer's settlement zone

* Buyer's aspiration is to pay only $100,000.
* Buyer would walk away (BATNA) if price exceeds $130,000.

Seller's settlement zone

* Seller's aspiration is to receive $170,000.
* Seller would walk away if price (BATNA) is less than $140,000.

There is no bargaining zone.

- Tie topics together as you bargain. This avoids the zero-sum problem inherent in bargaining on only one topic at a time, in which one party's gain inevitably entails loss by the other party.
- As you bargain, keep your mind attuned to your aspirational positions rather than your BATNA positions. This orientation should help you obtain a favorable, rather than acceptable, overall outcome for your client.
- As you make each proposal, provide a supporting rationale. These rationales may be grounded in the facts of the parties' situations, their broader contexts, their interests and goals, or the law, depending on what the topic is and which type of point favors your client.
- Frame each proposal in a manner that is appealing to the other party. Most people react to proposals according to various mindsets set out in Box 15.7, so careful phrasing can make the same idea appealing or not appealing.
- When you concede, i.e., adjust your position in favor of the other party, provide a rationale for doing so. Also signal that reciprocity is expected.
- When you concede, do so after the other party has done so—not after a concession of your own. Otherwise, opposing counsel will continue to expect you to bargain against yourself.

BOX 15.7

PSYCHOLOGICAL MINDSETS INVOLVED IN NEGOTIATING[13]

- *Attribution bias:* People attribute beneficial outcomes to their own efforts and adverse outcomes to situational factors. Application: A defendant in a dispute negotiation may be reluctant to accept responsibility for the incident causing loss.
- *Endowment effect:* People value a thing more highly when they already possess it than when they do not yet have it. Application: A buyer in a transaction negotiation tends to value the item at a lower value than the seller.
- *Entrapment:* People who have put considerable time into a negotiation become anxious to get a deal and may agree to deals that are not necessarily beneficial. Application: Take care not to make unwise concessions simply because you have invested considerable time in the negotiation.
- *Gain-loss framing:* People who are given a choice between (a) a sure gain and (b) obtaining either a larger gain or no gain choose (a); that is, they act in a risk-averse way. However, if they are in the position of having to make a payment or taking a loss, they act in a risk-taking manner. Application: Framing negotiation moves in terms of gains that the other party may make versus losses that they may avoid can alter the party's risk assessment.
- *Optimistic overconfidence:* People evaluate outcomes from their own perspective. Application: Plaintiffs evaluate the probability of a plaintiff verdict and size of a jury verdict as higher than do defendants.
- *Reactive devaluation:* People react negatively to an idea that comes from an antagonist, as compared to someone else.[14] Application: To persuade opposing counsel of an idea, present it through a neutral source.
- *Regret aversion:* People act so as to avoid the chances of later discovering that they made the wrong choice. Application: A plaintiff may decide to settle to avoid learning after trial that she should have accepted the settlement offer.

- As apparent agreements are made, unless you are certain that you would agree to them regardless of what else eventuates, note that they are contingent on success in negotiating the remaining topics.
- As apparent agreements are made, restate and record them. Generally, do not aim for precise language; drafting the agreement is a separate process.

At times, legal negotiations can become heated. This is more likely if the lawyers approach the session adversarially than in a problem-solving way. If, for example, the lawyers forget that the purpose of the negotiation is to seek agreement rather than to prove who is right on the law, emotions are likely to get heated. Rarely do overheated negotiators perform well. If you find yourself getting angry, take a break to calm down and think through the situation. If you are confronted with counsel who is engaging in unprofessional conduct or becoming overheated, consider these strategies: ignoring the challenging

---

13. Charles B. Craver, *Skills and Values: Legal Negotiating* 135-39 (2d ed. 2012).
14. *See* Lee Ross & Constance Stillinger, *Barriers to Conflict Resolution*, 7 Negot. J. 389 (1991).

behavior and continuing on calmly, waiting silently until the storm blows over, redirecting the discussion to a different topic that may be less troublesome, blandly describing the challenging behavior and indicating that it is impeding the negotiation, or taking a break. The least useful and most unprofessional response is, of course, to respond in like measure.

F. COMING TO AGREEMENT

It may be that, notwithstanding the best efforts of both counsel, *agreement is elusive*. It may not be possible to find agreement because, as noted above, a positive bargaining zone does not exist on some important topic. The main option then is for one or both lawyers to seek additional authority; failing that, the parties proceed to other courses of action.

A second less-than-successful ending of negotiation is that one party succumbs to an agreement that is less beneficial than it should be. The entrapment mindset may set in, especially after lengthy or challenging negotiations. See Box 15.7. Preparing well for a negotiation can help you avoid this situation, as can taking breaks and holding a lengthy negotiation over several sessions.

Ideally, a negotiation ends in an agreement that meets the interests and goals of both parties as completely as possible. The last point that the lawyers typically negotiate is which of the lawyers will begin the drafting process. Often there is a standard practice governing this matter, or one party has a document to start with. In general, it benefits your client if you are working from your document, rather than the other way around. In any event, most negotiations are followed by several rounds of document review.

G. PROFESSIONAL PRACTICE

When you first speak on behalf of a client, you generally will say, "I represent (client's name.)." This representation is multifaceted. You will not only state points on behalf of your client. You also will—for better or worse, presumably better—make some impression about your client through the way you present yourself. In this way, the idea of representation traces back to the origins of the word "represent": "making present." For you to make a good impression of yourself and of your client, follow these professional practices:

- Your communication should be correct, complete, comprehensible, and coherent. Negotiation is challenging enough without having to deal with obfuscating language.
- Convey respect to opposing counsel. This includes not only avoidance of any form of discriminatory or disrespectful conduct (such as name-calling, pejorative language, and belittling gestures) but also professional conduct, such as active listening and use of appropriate names for the other party.

- Present yourself as organized and prepared, with detailed analyses already worked out, sources gathered, and copies of useful materials available for opposing counsel.
- Maintain your focus on the negotiations by arriving on time, blocking out enough time, and avoiding all but truly necessary interruptions.
- Your personal appearance, attire, and office should be well-maintained and suitable to your practice setting.

BOX 15.8

SHOULD YOU NEGOTIATE ELECTRONICALLY?[15]

Lawyers have long used telephones (and more recently videophones) to negotiate. E-mail and text messaging have introduced a new wrinkle, in that these forms of communication are so thin: they consist only of words, lacking the intonations of the human voice, facial expressions, and gestures. Furthermore, given their social distance, users tend to create more negative messages and interpret electronic messages more negatively than they do other forms of communication. Thus, electronic messaging poses significant challenges to the creation of rapport and to nuance in the expression of ideas throughout bargaining. On the other hand, e-mail has logistical advantages, permits lengthy and carefully written responses, and can work well in multi-party negotiations. Thus, best practice is to not negotiate solely through electronic messaging; rather mix modes of communication.

---

15. *See* Stefan H. Krieger & Richard K. Neumann, Jr., *Essential Lawyering Skills: Interviewing, Counseling, Negotiation, and Persuasive Fact Analysis* 350-51 (5th ed. 2015).

TEST YOUR UNDERSTANDING

1. Assume that you have been assigned to participate in the negotiation of a dispute between Daniel de la Cruz, who was suspended from public middle school for shaving a message in his hair in support of his sister with breast cancer, and the school district. The firm, representing Daniel's parents acting on his behalf, has decided Daniel has a credible claim that the school violated his constitutional rights of free speech.
   a. Describe legal negotiation.
   b. Who decides what the terms of the settlement may be?

2. What do the following ABA Model Rules of Professional Conduct say about your conduct in the negotiation?
   a. Rule 1.6(a)
   b. Rule 4.1(a) and comments
   c. Rule 4.4

3. As you prepare for the negotiation:
   a. What are the various topics that you should learn about?
   b. What positions should you develop for the key potential terms of the agreement, and what does each signify?
   c. What might your theory of the negotiation draw on?

4. As the negotiation enters its first scene (setting the stage), what are your three goals?

5. During the second scene (exchanging information):
   a. What types of information would you reveal to opposing counsel, and why?
   b. What types of information should you seek from opposing counsel, and why?
   c. Are you obligated to answer all questions asked by opposing counsel?
   d. What is the purpose of discussing legal positions?

6. During the third scene (bargaining):
   a. What are the two main approaches to bargaining, and how do they differ?
   b. Which has been shown to be more effective as a general matter?
   c. What is important about the settlement zones and bargaining range on a topic?
   d. As you work your way through the various topics, does it matter:
      i.   Whether you handle topics individually or in clusters?
      ii. Whether you provide explanations or merely exchange proposals?
      iii. How you frame a proposal?
      iv. In what order the parties make concessions?
   e. What are strategies you can use to defuse overheated negotiations?

7. During the fourth scene (coming to agreement):
   a. If agreement is elusive, what might you do as a final option?
   b. As a general matter, would your client be better served if you or the opposing party drafted the document containing the negotiated agreement?

Test Your Understanding Answers

1. With regard to negotiating on behalf of the parents of Daniel de la Cruz:
   a. Legal negotiation is a long, improvised conversation in which the two lawyers seek to obtain outcomes for their own clients that are also acceptable to the other party.
   b. Clients give their lawyers authority to settle on specified terms in a negotiation.

2. The ABA Model Rules of Professional Conduct provide:
   a. Rule 1.6(a)—that information falling within the duty of lawyer-client confidentiality may be revealed with client consent or to carry out the representation.
   b. Rule 4.1(a) and comments—that a lawyer shall not knowingly make a false statement of material fact or law; that this prohibition extends beyond outright lies to encompass partially true but misleading statements and omissions; that some topics (such as estimates of value and intentions as to settlement) are not considered material facts.
   c. Rule 4.4—that a lawyer shall not use tactics that have no purpose other than to burden a third person.

3. As you prepare for the negotiation:
   a. You should learn the facts of your client's situation, the applicable legal rules, the broader context, and the client's interests and goals.
   b. A BATNA is the best alternative to a negotiated agreement (the walk-away point). An aspirational position is the most favorable, reasonably attainable position given the client's facts, the law, and the broader context. Probable settlement positions are terms that you can envision the other party agreeing to.
   c. A theory of the negotiation could draw on the effects of the school district's actions, the outcome that the parents or Daniel are seeking, or the principle that they are pursuing.

4. In the first scene (setting the stage), the three goals are establishing rapport, creating a positive atmosphere, and establishing a working agenda.

5. During the second scene (exchanging information):
   a. You should reveal some information about your client's situation, broader context, and interests and goals because this information is needed to help the parties find the most mutually beneficial agreement.
   b. You should seek reveal similar information, to help you understand the positions of the other party.
   c. No; indeed, some information may be subject to the duty of confidentiality.
   d. You would discuss legal positions to establish bargaining power within the negotiation, not to prove who is right.

6. During the third scene (bargaining):
   a. The adversarial negotiator focuses on her own party, her positions, the law, and winning. The problem-solving negotiator focuses on both parties, underlying interests, various factors, and obtaining mutually beneficial outcomes.
   b. In general, the problem-solving negotiator has been shown to be more effective.
   c. The two parties' settlement zones must overlap for there to be a positive bargaining range, so as to make agreement on a topic possible.
   d. As you bargain:
      i. It is preferable to take topics in clusters.
      ii. It is preferable to provide explanations.
      iii. It is desirable to frame a proposal so as to take into account the other party's possible mindset.
      iv. You should alternate with your opponent in making concessions.
   e. To defuse overheated negotiations, you could ignore the behavior, shift to a different topic, describe it and explain that it is impeding the negotiation, or take a break.

7. During the fourth scene (coming to agreement):
   a. If agreement is elusive, you could seek additional authority from your client.
   b. As a general matter, it is desirable for you to draft the document.

PART FOUR

ADVOCACY COMMUNICATION

In this part, you will study how a lawyer communicates with a tribunal on behalf of a client to obtain a favorable resolution of a dispute. These communications rely on the work discussed in Part I on reading and reasoning as well as on the work discussed in Part II on advisory communication.

This part begins with Chapter 16, which discusses general principles of legal advocacy. You will learn how to craft a theory of your case out of its various elements, how to operate well within the constraints of legal ethics, and how to use rhetorical tools to convey your theory of the case effectively.

The next two chapters examine written legal advocacy in two different settings. Chapter 17 covers the motion practice memorandum written for the district court, and Chapter 18 covers the appellate brief written for an appellate court. As you read these chapters, you will learn about the litigation setting for these documents, the strategies underlying the documents, and the components of the documents as seen from the two sides of a case.

Finally, Chapter 19 examines the conversation featured in advocacy: the oral argument, in which a lawyer presents his or her case to the court and answers the court's questions. You will learn about the necessity of preparation, ways to manage questions, and practices to ensure that you make the best impression for yourself and your client.

LEGAL ADVOCACY

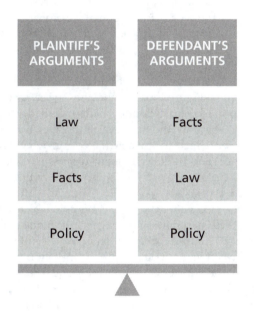

Tell all the Truth but tell it slant—
Success in Circuit lies—
—Emily Dickinson

A. INTRODUCTION

1. Perspectives on Legal Advocacy

Most of the time, when a case is brought to a tribunal for decision, whether a court, arbitrator, or administrative agency, both sides have good arguments. So how does a lawyer convince the tribunal to decide in the client's favor? This is the realm of legal advocacy or "making the case" for the client.

According to the principles of *Aristotelian rhetoric*, advocacy is a function of three elements: logos, pathos, and ethos. In simple translation, these three elements are an appeal to logic or proof, an appeal to emotion, and reliance on the writer's good character. An argument must be logically sound, it must appeal to the reader's sense of what is right on the facts, and the advocate must appear credible and trustworthy.[1]

Similarly, Karl Llewellyn, a prominent legal scholar in the first half of the twentieth century, wrote that a successful lawyer must "bring in a technically perfect case on the law" and "make the facts talk" to be persuasive.[2] If the tribunal is to adopt an advocate's view of the legal meaning to be assigned to the case, the advocate must present the facts and the law in a compelling and credible combination.

Legal advocacy is similar to photography. Photographers and lawyers share this task: to present what exists or has happened in a way that informs the observer about the subject and generates a particular response. For the photographer, the subject is the scene, and the goal is to produce a reaction—be it curiosity, sorrow, amusement—in the viewer. For the lawyer, the subject is the case, and the goal is to convince the reader to assign to the case the legal meaning the client desires.

Both the photographer and the lawyer must take their subjects as they find them. However, both the photographer and the lawyer have the opportunity, within limits, to set boundaries, to decide what is included in the photograph or memorandum and what is not. And both can choose which aspects of the subject to bring into focus and which to leave in the background. Photographers use lenses, camera settings, and the development process in various ways to make their photographs distinctive. Lawyers use only words, but words are remarkably powerful and flexible tools.

The points in this chapter apply to all documents in which legal arguments are made to a tribunal, including motion practice memoranda written for a district court (see Chapter 17) and appellate briefs (see Chapter 18). For ease of reference, the chapter refers to "court" and "memorandum" throughout.

For its examples, the chapter draws on the client situation of Daniel de la Cruz, a public middle school student. He was suspended because he had the phrase "I ♥ boobies" shaved into his hair as a sign of solidarity with his sister, who was undergoing treatment for breast cancer.[3] The legal issue is whether the school district's action violated Daniel's right to free speech. The examples are drawn without regard to a specific advocacy setting. As you will see, this basic scenario carries through Chapters 17 through 19.

2. The Advocate's Ethics

According to the preamble to the ABA Model Rules of Professional Conduct, the lawyer who serves as a client's zealous advocate also serves as an officer of the legal system. At times, you may perceive conflict, or at least tension, between these roles. But they are intended to be complementary; clients should be interested in fair process as well as favorable results.

---

1. *See generally* Louis J. Sirico, Jr. & Nancy L. Schultz, *Persuasive Writing for Lawyers and the Legal Profession* 1-20 (2d ed. 2001).
2. Karl N. Llewellyn, *The Modern Approach to Counseling and Advocacy*, 46 Colum. L. Rev. 167, 182-83 (1946).
3. This saying is part of the Keep a Breast Foundation's campaign for breast health among young people.

A lawyer, as an officer of the legal system, may pursue only non-frivolous claims and defenses. *Model Rule 3.1* states: "A lawyer shall not bring or defend a proceeding, or assert or controvert an issue therein, unless there is a basis in law and fact for doing so that is not frivolous, which includes a good faith argument for an extension, modification or reversal of existing law." A lawyer who violates this rule faces professional sanctions such as reprimand and disbarment. Similarly, *Federal Rule of Civil Procedure 11* provides for sanctions when a lawyer signs a document that is not, according to the lawyer's informed belief, "warranted by existing law or by a non-frivolous argument" for a change in the law or that contains factual contentions with insufficient "evidentiary support." Many states have similar rules.

A lawyer must be candid with the court. According to *Model Rule 3.3*, it is a violation of professional ethics to knowingly make a false statement of fact, fail to correct a previous false statement of material fact, or offer evidence that the lawyer knows to be false. Similarly, it is a violation to knowingly fail to disclose known and adverse legal authority not disclosed by opposing counsel. See Box 16.1 for two cases illustrating these rules.

Finally, a lawyer must expedite litigation and refrain from engaging in unduly burdensome, harassing, or delaying tactics. Examples of the latter under *Model Rule 3.4* include obstructing access to potentially relevant material and resisting proper requests for information from opposing counsel.

For many lawyers, these formal ethics rules serve as minimum standards of conduct. Their personal values prompt them to act according to even more stringent standards of respect for the law, candor, and civility. Furthermore, as a practical matter, unethical conduct is likely to be counterproductive. If you engage in misrepresentation, opposing counsel is likely to discover it and point it out to the court. If you are obstreperous, you are likely to encounter resistance. In these situations, your desire to act zealously may be sated but at the expense of undermining your client's cause and damaging your reputation.

B. ANALYZING THE ELEMENTS OF YOUR CLIENT'S CASE

As just noted, each case presented to a court weaves together several elements. To construct an effective whole, each element must first be thought through on its own.

1. Recounting Your Client's Story

Rarely are the facts of a case truly fixed. Rather, most litigation records consist of bits of information from various sources that suggest a set of relationships and series of events. Thus, the information requires interpretation. Judges look to you to *recount your client's story*.

You must, of course, *fully and fairly inform the court*. The court needs to be apprised of all relevant facts and necessary background facts. Ethics rules require you to present unfavorable as well as favorable facts that are relevant. You may include persuasive residual facts, so long as you do so judiciously.

BOX 16.1

WHAT HAPPENS WHEN YOU FAIL TO FULFILL THE OBLIGATION OF CANDOR TOWARD THE COURT?

As you read the following cases, think about these questions:

1. *Why (do you think) did the lawyer in* Thonert *chose not to disclose the legal authority to the court? And why did the lawyer for Capital Management Consultants (CMC) make the statements that the court discussed?*
2. *What can you do to avoid such situations?*
3. *Which of the sanctions—a public reprimand (*Thonert*) or a $5,000 fine (*Sobol*) is more appropriate for such conduct? Would you recommend a different remedy?*

In re Thonert,
733 N.E.2d 923 (Ind. 2000).

[Review the facts of this case in Chapter 9, page 188.]

Indiana Professional Conduct Rule 3.3(a)(3) provides that a lawyer shall not knowingly fail to disclose to a tribunal legal authority in the controlling jurisdiction known to the lawyer to be directly adverse to the position of the client and not disclosed by opposing counsel. The concept underlying this requirement of disclosure is that legal argument is a discussion seeking to determine the legal premises property applicable to the case. *Comment* to Ind. Professional Conduct Rule 3.3. The respondent's intimate familiarity with *Fletcher* is established by his having served as counsel to the defendant. Accordingly, we find that the respondent violated the rule by failing to disclose *Fletcher* to the Court of Appeals in his legal arguments on behalf of the client.

. . .

[The court accepted the parties' agreement that the respondent be publicly reprimanded.]

Sobol v. Capital Management Consultants, Inc.,
726 P.2d 335 (Nev. 1986).

[Saul Sobol developed a medical practice under the name Physicians Medical Center. Capital Management Consultants, a competitor, sought to use the name Physician's Medical Center. Sobol sued and sought a preliminary injunction. The Nevada Supreme Court reversed the trial court's denial of the injunction.]

[S]ome discussion of the brief submitted by respondents is in order. This court recently warned the bar that "[w]e expect and require that *all* appeals brought in this court . . . will be pursued in a manner meeting high standards of diligence, professionalism, and competence." *State, Emp. Sec. Dep't v. Weber,* 100 Nev. 121, 123, 676 P.2d 1318, 1319 (1984) (emphasis in original). In the answering brief, CMC strenuously argues that Sobol affirmatively admitted and acknowledged in a statement of stipulated facts issued prior to the preliminary hearing that the term "Physicians Medical Center" was "not capable of tradename [sic] or copyright registration and is in the public domain." This is a blatant misrepresentation of the stipulated facts. The supposed "admission" provides in pertinent part:

> 18. The sole and only basis upon which Defendants claim a legal right to the name "Physician's Medical Center" is by virtue of the filing of the fictitious name certificate in March of 1985, the issuance of a county business license in May of 1985 and that said name is not capable of trade name or copyright registration and is in the public domain.

CMC also quotes language from *Frederick Fash, Inc. v. Mayo Clinic,* 461 F.2d 1395 (C.C.P.A. 1972), as though it were holding on the case, when in fact the language comes from the dissent. While vigorous advocacy of a client's cause is expected and encouraged, these representations transcend the outer limits of zeal and become statements of guile and delusion. In light of CMC's disregard of the rules and professional standards established by this court, we have determined that the imposition of sanctions on respondents is warranted. *See* NRAP 38(b). Accordingly, CMC shall pay the sum of $5,000.00 to the Clark County Law Library Contribution Fund within thirty (30) days from the date of the issuance of this opinion, and shall promptly provide the clerk of this court with proof of such payment.

One situation requiring careful recounting is *inconsistency*, which may arise, for example, between the statements of two observers, between the early and later statements of the same observer, or between a document and a witness. Some inconsistencies are not significant because, for example, the fact is not relevant or the inconsistency relates to a meaningless detail. Other inconsistencies are significant and can be handled in various ways. You may be able to show that one source is more credible, based on capacity to perceive the events or lack of bias. A legal rule may dictate how to handle an inconsistency (e.g., taking the plaintiff's view of the facts on a motion to dismiss the complaint for failure to state a claim). Or you may have to discuss both versions of the fact in your analysis.

A second situation requiring careful recounting is the *drawing of inferences:* a fact is established by the evidence, and a second fact is inferred through reasoning from the first. Often, a fact can give rise to more than one inference depending on whose perspective is taken, and the inferences may be as important as the known fact itself. In such situations, you must take care to delineate what the record itself says, then present the inference favored by your client, and explain it well.

Finally, the *absence of evidence* of a specific fact may be significant. If this absence is to your advantage, you may want to note it and who could have testified to the fact, were that fact true. Of course, absent "facts" are not as weighty as facts that are stated in the record.

2. Developing Your Client's Legal Arguments

As you research and analyze your client's case, you may develop a long list of legal topics that could be discussed and points that could be made, and you may want to include them all, lest you omit the winning argument. But if you try to develop too many points, you are unlikely to develop any of them fully. As judges say, one convincing argument suffices; no number of unconvincing arguments can suffice.

To identify the topics you need to address, consider the *structure of the rules* involved in the case, for they both impose requirements on the memorandum and offer you options. For example, if the *substantive rule* governing the plaintiff's claim is conjunctive, as plaintiff's counsel, you must present an argument for each element; as defendant's counsel, you need only prevail on one element and could omit discussion of one or possibly more elements. As another example, if the situation is governed by an aggregate or balancing rule, both plaintiff and defendant may select the factors to be discussed.

In most tribunals, *procedural law* will be in play, along with the substantive law governing the claim. For example, the party opposing a motion for a temporary injunction need not necessarily demonstrate that the movant will lose on the merits but may be able to deflect the injunction by demonstrating that the balance of harms favors denial of the injunction. In appellate practice, the standard of review is critical (e.g., a de novo standard if the case involves interpretation of a statute).

Once you have selected the topics to cover, you should consider the *various arguments* to make on each topic. If you have more than one argument to make on a topic, think first about the relative power of each. A legal argument derives its power from the law, the facts, and the strength of the link between them. Ask yourself:

- Does the law unambiguously say what I am asserting, or is some interpretation necessary?
- Are my important facts uncontroverted and sympathetic?
- Is the link between the law and the facts obvious, or is there some murkiness?
- How well does this argument defeat my opponent's argument?
- Would I be convinced if I were the judge or opposing counsel?

As you prepare your memorandum, as at other times, you should consult with your client about the arguments to be made. While the client may not fully grasp the fine points of an argument, the client should be aware of and endorse the gist of the argument. The client may feel strongly about making some arguments or forgoing others, based on considerations other than the law.

Ideally your best arguments will form a coherent whole. Each legal argument will proceed logically from the previous one and lead logically to the next. Not infrequently, however, your best arguments will be disconnected. There may be a break between two arguments: "X is true. Whether X is true or not, Y is true." Or there may be a conflict: "X is true. Even if X is false, Y is true."

Making conflicting arguments—*arguing in the alternative*, as lawyers think of it—may seem intellectually dishonest. However, lawyers often argue in the alternative, as do judges when they write opinions. Often, facts and law are malleable enough that more than one legal meaning may reasonably be ascribed to a situation. For example, a statute may be amenable to two interpretations; a fact may be unknown or ambiguous. Nonetheless, arguing in the alternative does have its drawbacks. It entails complexity and risks confusing the reader. The alternative argument may suggest that the first argument is not all that strong. The key to a successful argument in the alternative is clarity of presentation. You should begin with a clear roadmap and introduce the second argument with a signpost calling attention to the alternative relationship.

BOX 16.2

SHORT AND SWEET, OR THE KITCHEN SINK?[4]

In the summer of 2000, Bryan Garner surveyed state and federal trial and appellate judges about their preferences as to motion practice memoranda and appellate briefs. He posited two options, and the nearly sixty judges voted as follows:

- "A brief should be an essay that advances two or three cohesive, well-supported arguments . . . while rebutting the opposition's counter-arguments" and run short if possible. Fifty judges chose this statement (86%).
- "A brief should be a repository of all the information that a curious judge might want to know about a case" and use all the allotted space. No judges chose this statement.
- "Neither view is quite right." Eight judges chose this statement (14%).

---

4. *Judges on Briefing: A National Survey* iii-iv (Bryan A. Garner comp., 2001).

3. Deflecting Your Opponent's Legal Arguments

Legal advocacy has both offensive and defensive aspects. Not only must you convince the court of the merits of your argument; you also must *deflect your opponent's argument.*

If your memorandum is the first to be written, you must anticipate your opponent's arguments. Ask yourself: What would I argue if I were representing my client's opponent? If I were the judge on this case, what points would I discuss if I ruled in favor of my client's opponent?

Compare your opponent's actual or probable arguments to your own. You very probably will discern both points of concurrence and points of clash. *Points of concurrence* are propositions on which you and your opponent agree; *points of clash* are propositions on which you and your opponent disagree. Both may involve various matters:

- You may agree or disagree about what the relevant facts are, especially inferences to be drawn from the facts.
- You may agree or disagree as to what the governing legal rule is on a topic (e.g., how to read a set of cases, how to interpret a statute).
- You may agree or disagree about how the rule applies to the facts, which party is favored by public policy, or whether a leading case is analogous or distinguishable.

Your memorandum should cover the points of concurrence enough to provide a full legal framework of the case. Your memorandum should focus on the points of clash, providing the court with compelling reasons to resolve them in your client's favor.

A useful tool for depicting this analysis is the *T-chart*, in which you state the main arguments and significant assertions of the two sides in juxtaposition. You can use boldface to highlight significant points of disagreement. See Box 16.3 for a sample T-chart for the Daniel de la Cruz case.

BOX 16.3

SAMPLE T-CHART

Daniel de la Cruz Arguments	School District Arguments
• First Amendment applies to school district	Agree
• Daniel as public school student has free speech rights	Agree
• District may regulate lewd/offensive speech	Agree
• **BUT this did not qualify as such.**	**Disagree**
• District may regulate speech that causes substantial disruption	Agree
• **BUT this did not qualify as such.**	**Disagree**

4. Framing Proposals for New Legal Rules

Some disputes enter litigation and persist because the parties disagree about what the law is or what it should be. When the law is uncertain, the lawyers have the privilege and responsibility of contributing to the development of the law by proposing a rule of law. Because courts adhere to stare decisis and are bound to follow statutory language in most situations, it is preferable to argue a case by showing how it fits within established law. Thus, you should engage in a discussion of what the rule should be only when your case does not fit an established rule or when an alternative to the established rule would provide a strong basis for your desired outcome. In these instances, you should keep four points in mind.

First, in general, the less radical your position, the more likely it is to be adopted by the court. Hence, an important step is to *connect your rule to existing law*. For example, show how your rule simply adds an element or defense to an existing common law claim or how your interpretation of a statute resolves ambiguity in an existing interpretation of the statute.

Second, to the extent possible, *rely on persuasive materials*, whether precedent or commentary. Select the strongest available persuasive material, based on its source, reasoning, factual parallels to your case, and currency. If there is an opposing strand of persuasive authority, you should acknowledge it and then show its weaknesses.

Third, the court is likely to be concerned about the wisdom of making new law in your particular case. You therefore must *apply the rule to the facts* of your case, yielding a clearly equitable result. Also, show that the existing rule improperly favors your client's opponent or the opponent does not deserve sympathy, given its actions.

Fourth, the court also is likely to be concerned about the rule's impact beyond your case—the proverbial "slippery slope." *Specify the parameters* of your proposed rule, so the court will be able to provide guidance for future situations and need not fear a rash of cases. You should show how the proposed rule yields sound results in the situations that it would govern.

Furthermore, disciplines other than law also examine issues of justice, and scholars in those disciplines may have insights that could be useful. Near the turn of the twentieth century, Louis Brandeis (later Justice Brandeis of the U.S. Supreme Court) submitted a brief that presented social science research on the detrimental effects of long work hours on the health of women.[5] Henceforth, a brief presenting non-legal information has been known as a "Brandeis brief."[6] Thus, in an appropriate situation, you may incorporate social science research or theoretical perspectives from other fields, such as psychology and economics.

---

5. The case was *Muller v. Oregon*, 208 U.S. 412 (1908), and the brief can be found at 16 *Landmark Briefs and Arguments of the Supreme Court of the United States: Constitutional Law* 63 (Philip B. Kurland & Gerhard Casper eds., 1975).

6. For further discussion, *see* Ellie Margolis, *Beyond Brandeis: Exploring the Uses of Non-Legal Materials in Appellate Briefs*, 34 U.S.F. L. Rev. 197 (2000).

C. CREATING A THEORY OF YOUR CASE

Once you have thought through the elements of your client's case, you are ready to develop a convincing *theory of your case*. The theory of a case is what the case is about, in simple (but not simplistic) terms. If you were to write a newspaper article about your case, the headline would state the theory of the case. If you were to make a movie about your case, the poster would present the theory of the case.

The theory of a case provides a theme for your entire memorandum. For you, the theory of the case provides a basis for deciding which points to make or emphasize and which to exclude or downplay, helps you unify what might otherwise seem to be disparate points, and suggests language to use throughout the memorandum. For the reader, a strong theory of the case is an idea that can be easily grasped and adopted, even in a complex memorandum.

Because a case meshes facts, substantive law, procedural law, and often policy, the ideal theory of the case partakes of all of these. One or the other may dominate, however. For example, your core concept may be a key factual detail or a phrase representing the pertinent legal rule. Less commonly, a public policy may be your core concept. Whatever your core concept, the court's acceptance of your theory should lead directly toward the outcome desired by your client and away from the outcome desired by your opponent.

One way to depict a theory of the case is a pie chart, divided into quarters, with key phrases allocated to facts, substantive law, procedure, and policy slices. As you assign each phrase to its appropriate slice, you should see concepts that parallel each other. See Box 16.4 for a sample theory of the Daniel de la Cruz case, from his perspective.

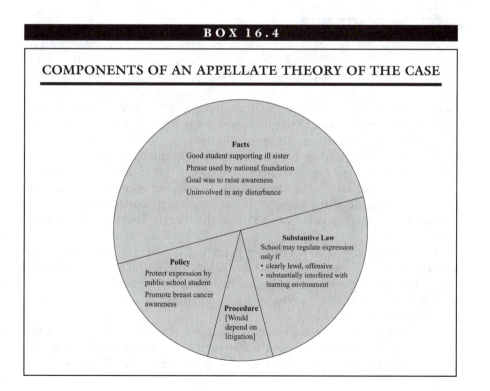

BOX 16.4

COMPONENTS OF AN APPELLATE THEORY OF THE CASE

Facts
Good student supporting ill sister
Phrase used by national foundation
Goal was to raise awareness
Uninvolved in any disturbance

Substantive Law
School may regulate expression only if
• clearly lewd, offensive
• substantially interfered with learning environment

Policy
Protect expression by public school student
Promote breast cancer awareness

Procedure
[Would depend on litigation]

D. STRESSING STRENGTHS AND WORKING AROUND WEAKNESSES

1. Introduction

Once you have analyzed the separate elements and developed the theory of your case, you are ready to work on conveying that theory to the court. A two-fold approach is to (1) stress the strengths of your case and (2) work around the weaknesses. Every case in litigation has its strengths and weaknesses; truly one-sided cases generally are resolved before litigation. Of course, one party's strength is usually the other party's weakness.

Some cases are strong on the law, while others are strong on the facts or strong on policy. A case is *strong on the law* when the rule is well established, clearly addresses the client's situation, and calls for the client's desired outcome. A case is *strong on the facts* or equities when a reasonable observer easily empathizes with the client and sees the client's desired outcome as sensible and fair. A case is *strong on policy* when the client's desired outcomes serves an important social interest. A case is *weak* on any of these dimensions when the other party is strong on that dimension. If the case raises multiple issues, the strengths and weaknesses of your client's case may vary across the issues. For example, the plaintiff may have the stronger legal position as to one claim, while the defendant has the stronger legal position as to another. Or the plaintiff's case may be strong on the facts as to liability but weak on the facts as to damages. Moreover, one party may have an advantage on the substantive law, while the other may have an advantage on the procedural law.

2. Stressing Strengths

As you draft your memorandum, you should, of course, *stress the strengths* highlighted in your theory of the case. If your case is strong on the law, fully develop the law. For a rule that emanates from a statute, quote and paraphrase the statute, discuss its underlying policy, and provide an illustrative case. For a rule that emanates from case law, present the rule itself, and also describe one or two cases in some depth, cite an early case to underscore the rule's long standing, and cite a recent case to underscore its continued authority.

If your case is strong on the facts, fully develop the facts: Quote from the record. Stack evidence on a key fact by showing that it appears in multiple sources. Note not only what the evidence shows, but also what it does not show. If possible, develop an extended comparison to a decided case, or present several case comparisons (but not so many that the reader loses sight of your client's case).

If your case is strong on policy, fully develop that policy: Quote from cases, a statutory purpose section, or commentary to establish the policy. Show how the policy plays out in the facts of your case. Refute any opposing policy statements by your opponent by citing authority that critiques that policy or demonstrating its irrelevance to the case.

To convey your case's strong suits effectively, you must *pitch* them at the proper level. By the time you write a memorandum, you are deeply immersed in the facts and law of the case, but these elements will be unfamiliar to the court.

BOX 16.5

SAMPLE PITCH ANALYSIS

Legal Principles	Degree of Coverage
First Amendment protects free speech	Could omit
First Amendment covers acts of state government	Could omit
Free speech rights attach to public school students	Undisputed; establish briefly
Under U.S. Supreme Court case law, those rights depend on the nature of speech and disruptions	Cover in detail

You should see yourself as writing for an educated and intelligent, but not-yet-informed, reader. A useful strategy is to ask yourself: What basic information did I need to know about the facts and law when I first took on this case? And what has been difficult for me to sort out as I have worked on this case? Your memorandum should include the former, in compact form, at the outset of a topic and then proceed to focus on the latter. See Box 16.5 for a pitch analysis of the law of the Daniel de la Cruz case.

3. Working Around Weaknesses

You cannot simply wish away the weaknesses in your client's case. Your duties of zealous advocacy and candor require you to grapple effectively with your case's weaknesses, and it is unwise to let your opponent's discussion of the weaknesses go unanswered. On the other hand, you should not dwell on the weaknesses. Rather, your goal is to dispel them as efficiently as possible.

Some cases are weak on the law. If the adverse authority is not mandatory, you should downplay it as merely persuasive and non-binding. You also should criticize any weaknesses in its reasoning or policy.

If the adverse authority is mandatory case law, you have a range of options: Distinguish the case by showing that the facts or issues differ from your case. Narrow the scope of the case by confining its holding to facts not present in your case. Show that the adverse statement is a dictum rather than a holding. Demonstrate that the case is inconsistent with other binding precedent and should be discounted. If needed, argue that the case should be overruled because it relies on weak reasoning, the trend of the law is against it, or the holding is contrary to public policy.

If the adverse mandatory authority is a statute or procedural rule or regulation, you have several options: Argue that your case falls outside its scope, based on definitions or other scope sections. Demonstrate that the law applies ambiguously given the facts of your case; then provide a favorable interpretation based on legislative history or intent, canons of construction, or policy. The most difficult option is to establish that the law is unconstitutional or outside the power of the lawmaking body; a less radical form of this option is to argue for a favorable interpretation that would avoid these concerns.

Some cases are weak on the facts, as to which you may have several options; if there is conflicting evidence on a fact, emphasize the helpful evidence. Discuss other facts that put the unfavorable fact in context. For example, if the client acted unwisely, show why the client did so. Show that the record does not present an even worse scenario.

Some cases are weak on policy, as to which you again have several options: show that your case does not truly implicate the policy. Show that the policy is outdated or needs reevaluation. Shift the focus to a competing policy that is served by the outcome that your client seeks. If the law is clear and favors your client, point out that the law must be followed, even if the court would favor a different policy.

4. Handling Concessions and Rebuttals

Many legal arguments entail two challenging rhetorical points: concessions and rebuttals. While both enable the court to fully understand the case, they also distract from your argument, because they entail allocating at least some space to your opponent's argument. Hence, both should be handled with care.

The need to present a *concession* arises when the two sides concur on a point and that point favors your client's opponent. Concessions may be handled several ways. First, and least obviously, you may *implicitly concede* the point through omission, neither stating it nor presenting an argument to the contrary. For example, you could note that the issue concerns a statute and begin your argument with a discussion of the exceptions, implicitly conceding that your client's case falls within the scope and general rule of the statute.

In an explicit concession, known as "confession and avoidance," you state the conceded point but move on to an argument that nullifies the harmful impact of the concession. For example, you could state that although the client's conduct falls within a statutory definition, the client's conduct is permitted by a statutory exception.

In another explicit concession, known as "assuming arguendo," you state the conceded point—but only for the purposes of the present argument. For example, you would argue first that your client's case is outside the scope of the statute, then assume arguendo that the client's case falls within the statute's general rule, and go on to show how its conduct is governed by a statutory exception.

Whenever you state a concession, you should minimize how much of the reader's attention is paid to the concession. For example, you could allocate little space to the concession or place it in a dependent clause. Allocate more space to your argument responding to the concession and place that argument in the main clause.

The second challenging rhetorical point is the *rebuttal*: your response to the argument of your opponent. As noted above, most of your argument should address the points of clash in the case, the topics on which the two sides disagree. As to many points of clash, you will find that stating your argument implicitly rebuts your opponent's argument and that little needs to be said about the opponent's argument.

In other situations, you will decide that your memorandum should refer to your opponent's argument so that the reader fully sees how your argument dispenses with your opponent's argument. Or your rebuttal to your opponent's argument may be understandable only as a negation of the opponent's argument. In either situation, an effective rebuttal will boost your credibility. Again, minimize the opponent's argument by merely referring to it, rather than completely stating it, allocating little space to it, or positioning it in a dependent clause. Even if you think the opponent's argument is very weak, take care to critique it in a professional tone, taking aim at the ideas rather than the author. Indeed the better approach is to state points favoring your client rather than only undermining your opponent's argument. For example, you should provide a preferred—i.e., better reasoned and favorable—interpretation of a statute in addition to criticizing the one offered by your opponent.

E. SLANTING YOUR PROSE

Once you have determined the strengths that you want to stress and the weaknesses to work around, you are ready to craft your prose. Often, the way that something is said determines its impact. In an advocacy setting, because your obligation is to incline the court to favor your client, you should *slant your prose*. This part discusses five writing techniques to make your prose persuasive— space allocation, sequence, syntax, semantics, and special sentences—and one that undermines its effectiveness.

1. Space Allocation

The more we read about a topic, the more we attend to it, the more we recall about it, and the greater the importance we attach to it. Hence you should *allocate space* strategically: more space to the material that you want the court to remember and less space to the material you need to include yet want to de-emphasize. For example, in a statement of facts, you could write several paragraphs on your client's circumstances and motivations and only a few on the opponent's actions. In the argument, you could present several paragraphs on a favorable element of the rule and only one paragraph on a more troublesome element.

One way to implement this strategy is to allocate target percentages to various topics before you write and then monitor how well your draft complies with your allocation. Or, after you have completed a draft, run a word count of your paragraphs, and compare the results to a desirable space allocation.

2. Sequence

As you frame your memorandum, you must, of course, follow format requirements, and you must organize the material within each component in a logical sequence. If several sequences are permissible and logical, you should devise a *sequence* reflecting the primacy and recency effects. According to the primacy effect, we process most thoroughly and remember best the information that appears at the start of a text. And according to the recency effect, we process and remember nearly as well the information that appears last. Information in the middle of a text recedes in memory. Thus, you should aim to lead and close with strong material and place weaker material in the middle. This approach can be used in various components, e.g., opening and closing a statement of facts, ordering the legal topics within an argument, and ordering the elements within a legal rule.

3. Syntax

Readers respond more to ideas presented in a strongly framed sentence than to ideas couched in an obscure manner. Careful use of *syntax* allows you to highlight material you want the reader to remember and downplay material you want to de-emphasize. As noted above, you should de-emphasize concessions and your statement of your opponent's arguments for rebuttal purposes. Here are some specific methods:

- State favorable material in short, simple sentences, and state unfavorable material in long, complex (but still understandable) sentences. Complex sentences draw attention to the structure of the sentence and away from the sentence's content.
- Place unfavorable material in dependent clauses and favorable material in main clauses. Main clauses demand more attention than dependent clauses.
- Use the active voice to convey favorable material, and use the passive voice to convey unfavorable material. Active voice demands more attention than passive voice. Also, with passive voice, you can obscure the actor; this strategy is appropriate where the actor is unknown or unimportant—or where you do want to de-emphasize who the actor is for some reason.
- Similarly, use nominalization, instead of a simple verb, for unfavorable information. Nominalization and passive voice have similar effects.

4. Semantics

Given the richness of the English language, you will have many *semantic choices* to make when writing a memorandum. Readers respond more to vividly stated concepts than to blandly stated concepts. Use vivid words for material that you want your reader to notice and recall, and use nondescript language for material that you want your reader to notice less.

Perhaps the most important semantic choice is how to label the parties, where court rules do not mandate or forbid certain labels. One option is to use procedural labels, such as "Plaintiff" and "Defendant"; the reader typically feels distanced from the situation when these terms are used. A middle ground is to use labels reflecting the parties' roles in the real-world situation, such as "student" and "school district." A third option is to use their proper names.

This option personalizes the parties the most, especially if they are individuals. Some writers prefer to use merely last names, which sounds matter-of-fact, while others prefer Mr. de la Cruz, for example, which sounds more respectful. You should use first names only if the individual is a child. If two or more individuals have the same last name, you should use differentiating words such as "Mr." and "Ms." or both the first and last names.

Less obvious but equally important are the labels that you use for the key legal concepts in the case. Most legal concepts can be referred to by more than one name, and some labels carry more serious connotations than others. Generally, you will want to use the serious label for a cause of action if your client is the wronged party and the milder label if your client is the defendant.

Finally, pay close attention to the verbs that you use to describe the actions of various parties. Some verbs are more vivid than others. Adding an adverb to a dull verb to make it stronger is less effective than using a more vivid verb.

5. Special Sentences

Some statements are more memorable than others due to their structure.[7] Within limits, it is appropriate to use rhetorical flourish in legal advocacy. Be sure to use it to make your most important points. Indeed, you may want to express your theory of the case through a special sentence and then return to a portion of that phrasing in key locations throughout the memorandum. Box 16.6 sets out several types of special sentences.

BOX 16.6

SPECIAL SENTENCES

- *Alliteration*: Repeated use of a starting letter, typically a consonant, in neighboring words to make a phrase stand out.
- *Allusion:* An implied or indirect reference to a commonly known situation, typically drawn from history or literature.
- *Anaphora and epistrophe:* The repeated use of a few words or a phrase at the outset (anaphora) or end (epistrophe) of several consecutive clauses or sentences, so as to underscore that phrase and strengthen the connection among the ideas.
- *Aphorism:* A terse statement of a point, designed to draw the reader's attention and linger in the reader's mind.
- *Juxtaposition:* A sharp contrast between two ideas presented one after another.
- *Rhetorical question:* Asking a question without answering it; the question may imply an answer, or it may have no good answer. Some lawyers avoid rhetorical questions on the grounds that they are too showy, so you should use this technique sparingly.

---

7. *See* Louis J. Sirico, Jr. & Nancy L. Schultz, *Persuasive Writing for Lawyers and the Legal Profession* App. A (2d ed. 2001) for many non-legal examples.

Virtually all memoranda involve *quotations* because some material must be presented verbatim. To some extent, you must quote the law, especially statutory material and key phrases from the common law. You also may quote portions of the record and nonessential passages from legal authorities, such as key portions of the reasoning in a case or helpful commentary. However, if you quote too frequently or your quotations run too long, the reader will not take special note of that material. Furthermore, your memorandum will not flow well because each quote breaks out of your writing style. On the other hand, if you quote sparingly, the quotes will stand out.

6. But Not Sarcasm

Tone is in part a matter of your personal style or voice as a writer and in part a reflection of the needs of the specific case. Within a range of reason, you may choose the tone for your memorandum, be it matter-of-fact, impassioned, or scholarly.

However, *sarcasm* is not acceptable. Especially in protracted and hard-fought litigation, you may be tempted to use sarcasm toward the opposing party, opposing counsel, or the lower court that ruled against your client. Do not succumb to this temptation. A sarcastic memorandum only irritates your target and causes the court to doubt your professionalism and the merits of your arguments.

To avoid sarcasm, focus your memorandum on the law and the facts of the case; do not write about opposing counsel. Focus on the ruling below, not the court that issued it. Read your memorandum with this question in mind: If I were opposing counsel or the lower court, would I find the tone of this memorandum to be respectful? See Box 16.7 for a case on this topic.

F. REVIEW

When lawyers write on behalf of their clients, they write as zealous advocates and also as officers of the legal system. Thus, ethical and effective advocacy requires careful crafting indeed. The approaches covered here are applicable in many settings:

(1) Thoroughly analyze the separate factual and various legal elements of your client's case.
(2) Develop a theory of the case that incorporates these elements.
(3) Discern how to stress the strengths of your client's case and work around its weaknesses.
(4) Use the tools of space allocation, sequence, syntax, semantics, and special sentences to slant your prose.

These points apply in various settings, including writing to a district court (covered in Chapter 17) and to an appellate court (covered in Chapter 18).

BOX 16.7

HOW DO COURTS RESPOND TO
INTEMPERATE LANGUAGE?

As you read the following case, think about these questions:

1. *Why (do you think) did the appellants use the language quoted in the opinion?*
2. *What can you do to avoid similar language?*
3. *Does the remedy here seem appropriate? Would you recommend a different penalty?*

Henry v. Eberhard,
832 S.W.2d 467 (Ark. 1992).

[Willene Henry and Richard Roth, employees of the Arkansas Department of Human Services, took a minor child into protective custody rather than permit supervised visitation with the child's father as ordered by the judge handling the parents' divorce. The trial court held Henry and Roth in contempt of court. The Arkansas attorney general was permitted to intervene in the appeal of the contempt orders.]

[A]ppellants make numerous accusations of the lower courts which are disrespectful. Appellants state that a concise picture of what happened in Benton County cannot be presented to this court because they "sincerely believe a spark was ignited that turned into a blaze for reasons other than the administration of justice." Appellants accuse the trial court of "pursuing an independent agenda" and characterize its conduct as "calculated to lead to the public humiliation of the officials of the Department of Human Services."

The above-quoted language from appellants' brief is so offensive that it prompted the intervenor, the Attorney General, to request that the language be stricken from the briefs. Pursuant to Ark.Sup.Ct.R. 6, and *McLemore v. Elliot,* 272 Ark. 306, 614 S.W.2d 226 (1981), we conclude the intervenor's motion is well-taken. In *McLemore,* as a sanction for violating Ark.Sup.Ct.R. 6, we struck the briefs containing the language that was disrespectful to the trial court from the records of this court. The language used in the present case is far more inflammatory and disrespectful than the language used in *McLemore.* Accordingly, we grant the intervenor's request to strike pages 462-67 of appellants' brief from our records.

Test Your Understanding

1. Assume that you are working on writing a persuasive document to a tribunal on behalf of Sarah Nicholson in her dispute with Bower's Bounty. According to Aristotelian rhetoric, what are the three elements of advocacy that you should keep in mind?

2. What do the following ABA Model Rules require of legal advocates?
    a. Rule 3.1
    b. Rule 3.3
    c. Rule 3.4

3. What does Federal Rule of Civil Procedure 11 require of lawyers representing clients in litigation, and how is it enforced?

4. As you recount her story, how would you handle the following:
    a. Inconsistencies
    b. Inferences
    c. Absent facts

5. As you develop legal arguments to be made:
    a. What would you think through as you decide which topics to cover?
    b. What would you think through as you decide which arguments to make on the topics you decide to cover?
    c. What is arguing in the alternative, and would you be willing to do so?
    d. What are points of concurrence and points of clash, and how much would you cover each?
    e. If you discern that you need to argue for a change in the law on behalf of Ms. Nicholson, what are key steps in doing so?
    f. What is a Brandeis brief, and under what circumstances would you write one?

6. As you develop a theory of the case for Ms. Nicholson, what are the slices of the pie that you should incorporate?

7. You might decide that Ms. Nicholson's case is one or more of the following. What does each mean, and what is a strategy to use for each one?
    a. Strong on the facts
    b. Strong on case law
    c. Strong on statutory law
    d. Strong on policy

8. How does pitch relate to writing a legal memorandum?

9. What are strategies that you would use if you considered Ms. Nicholson's case weak on each of the four dimensions listed in question 7?

10. What is the difference between implicit and explicit concessions?

11. What are some ways of effectively framing a rebuttal to an argument of your opponent?

12. Which of the following uses of language will—or will not—make key points more prominent?
    a. Allocating a large amount of space to it
    b. Presenting it in the middle of a component
    c. Presenting the point in a short sentence
    d. Using a complex verb phrase
    e. Using a lengthy quotation

TEST YOUR UNDERSTANDING ANSWERS

1. According to Aristotelian rhetoric, the three elements of advocacy are an appeal to logic (logos), an appeal to emotion (pathos), and reliance on the writer's good character (ethos).

2. ABA Model Rules require:
   a. Rule 3.1—that there be a basis in law and fact that is not frivolous for a proceeding.
   b. Rule 3.3—that lawyers not knowingly make misrepresentations of facts or fail to disclose known legal authority not disclosed by opposing counsel.
   c. Rule 3.4—that lawyers expedite litigation and not engage in unduly burdensome, harassing, or delaying tactics.

3. Federal Rule of Civil Procedure 11 provides for sanctions when lawyers sign litigation documents that are not warranted by existing law or non-frivolous arguments for changes in the law or that contain factual contentions without sufficient evidentiary support.

4. As you recount her story:
   a. Inconsistencies may be handled as a rule requires, may be discussed according to the credibility of witnesses, or may require discussion of both views.
   b. An inference requires discussion of the fact in the record and then an explanation of the inference being drawn.
   c. Absent facts may be noted, along with who would have testified to them, if beneficial to the client.

5. As you develop legal arguments to be made:
   a. The structures of the substantive and procedural rules fix the topics to be covered.
   b. The arguments to be made depend on the clarity of the law and the facts, the link between the law and the facts, and the strength of the argument in meeting the opponent's arguments.
   c. Arguing in the alternative is making conflicting arguments; although it is not as compelling as making consistent arguments, it is commonly done.
   d. Points of concurrence are propositions on which the parties agree, and points of clash are propositions on which the parties disagree. The former merit little coverage; the latter should be covered in detail.
   e. Key steps for arguing for a change in the law include connecting the new rule to existing law, relying on persuasive materials, applying the rule to your case, and specifying the parameters of the new rule.
   f. A Brandeis brief presents social science research and is written when such findings would help a court understand the import of a new rule of law.

6. The slices of the pie in a theory of the case are facts, substantive law, procedure, and policy.

7. As for strengths of a case:
   a. "Strong on the facts" means that the client's outcome seems sensible and fair. Quote from the record, including multiple sources on a key fact; use an extended case comparison.
   b. "Strong on case law" means that the case law is well established and calls for the client's desired outcome. Quote the rule, and describe one or two supporting cases in depth.
   c. "Strong on statutory law" means that a statute clearly calls for the client's desired outcome. Quote the statute, discuss its policy, and provide an illustrative case.
   d. "Strong on policy" means that the client's desired outcome serves an important social interest. Quote from cases, a statutory policy section, or commentary; apply the policy to the facts of the case.

8. Pitch entails covering information at the level at which the court needs it, i.e., basic information in compact form; more difficult information in detail.

9. As for weaknesses of a case:
   a. Weak on the facts—point out conflicting evidence or explain the context.
   b. Weak on case law—distinguish a case, identify a point as a dictum, argue that it is inconsistent with other cases, or argue that the case should be overruled.
   c. Weak on statutory law—argue that your case is outside the statute, that the statute applies ambiguously to your case, or that the statute is unconstitutional.
   d. Weak on policy—show the policy is outdated, present a different favorable policy, or stress a favorable rule.

10. An implicit concession entails not mentioning the point at all, whereas an explicit concession entails stating the conceded point (and then moving on to a positive point).

11. Effectively framing a rebuttal involves stating the opponent's argument briefly, critiquing it (as opposed to criticizing the person) in a professional tone, and providing points favoring the client.

12. As for uses of language that make key points, which of the following uses of language will make key points more prominent?
    a. Allocating a large amount of space to it—yes.
    b. Presenting it in the middle of a component—no; presenting information at the beginning or ending of a component makes it more prominent.
    c. Presenting the point in a short sentence—yes.
    d. Using a complex verb phrase—no; strong, simple verbs are more powerful.
    e. Using a lengthy quotation—no; short quotations are noticed more.

THE MOTION PRACTICE

MEMORANDUM

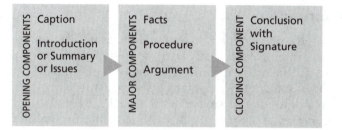

Of every hundred cases, ninety win themselves, three are won by advocacy, and seven are lost by advocacy.
　　—A. Fountain
　　　Wit of Wig, 1980

A. INTRODUCTION

Litigation—the process of resolving disputes, whether civil or criminal, within the courts—involves advocacy that is quite formal in nature. This is because specific rules control each step of litigation and define the protocols for making arguments at each step. How do lawyers, operating within these rules, advocate effectively for their clients?

They operate strategically: They know what is at stake for their clients and identify outcomes to be achieved. They understand the litigation process and devise plans to use that process to achieve their clients' goals; they think many steps ahead and re-evaluate often. They communicate with various audiences in mind: their clients, their opponents, and the court. They operate squarely within ethical constraints and use the model of legal advocacy discussed in Chapter 16.

This chapter thus begins with an overview of several topics that provide essential background for writing effectively to a district court. The discussion then describes the persuasive analytical document written to a district court: the motion practice memorandum.[1]

Two motion practice memoranda written by talented law students appear as Exhibits 17A and 17B. The memoranda discuss a fictional case parallel to the Daniel de la Cruz client situation, *Brown v. Perkinsberg School District*. In *Brown*, a public middle school student, suspended because he shaved a message in his hair, has brought a free speech claim against his school district. The case is set in the state courts of Minnesota. The chapter discusses Exhibit 17A; questions precede Exhibit 17B so that you can analyze it yourself. Please look over both before proceeding.

B. CIVIL LITIGATION AND MOTION PRACTICE

1. Civil Litigation

The main purpose of litigation is to resolve disputes through the application of legal rules to proven facts carried out by decision-makers empowered by the government. The following discussion presents a generic model of *civil litigation*, a very broad category encompassing litigation in which a government unit is not acting as a prosecutor seeking criminal penalties.

In broad strokes, as illustrated in Box 17.1, civil litigation entails framing the case, exchanging information through discovery, and obtaining a decision. At various points in the litigation, one side or the other may bring a *motion*, which is a request to the court to act as desired by the moving party, or *movant*, against the other party, or *non-movant*. The movant may seek to move the litigation along (a *non-dispositive motion*), or the movant may seek a resolution of the case in its favor (a *dispositive motion*). Courts either grant or deny motions; indeed, many more cases are resolved by motion than by trial.[2] Box 17.1 lists common motions.

In the first phase of litigation, the parties *frame the case* through the plaintiff's complaint and the defendant's answer. The two sides name the persons or entities involved, assert various facts to be true or deny the opponent's assertions, identify legal claims or defenses arising out of those facts, and state their desired outcomes. In complicated cases, there may be three or more parties, the defendant may sue the plaintiff as well as be sued, or a group of similarly situated individuals may sue as a class.

Motions are quite common at this initial stage of litigation. For example, the defendant may seek to dismiss the case on various grounds, such as the court's lack of jurisdiction (power to decide the case), the plaintiff's excessive delay in bringing the lawsuit, or inadequate legal support for the plaintiff's claim. The plaintiff may seek certification of a class (i.e., a large group of people represented in the case). Or the plaintiff may seek a temporary injunction to preserve the status quo during the litigation.

---

1. Chapter 18 covers the same topics in the appellate context.
2. One study of large counties found that an average of only three percent of cases go to trial. U.S. Dept. of Justice, Bureau of Justice Statistics, *Civil Trial Cases in State Courts, 2005*.

OUTLINE OF CIVIL LITIGATION

Phases of Litigation	Illustrative Motions
FRAMING THE CASE	
• Complaint • Answer • Joinder of parties • Counterclaims • Class certification	• Dismissal for lack of jurisdiction • Dismissal for failure to state a claim • Class certification • Temporary injunction
EXCHANGING INFORMATION	
• Admissions • Interrogatories • Production of documents • Depositions	• Compel discovery
OBTAINING A DECISION	
Pre-Trial • Settlement by parties • Mediation • Arbitration **Trial** • Selection of jury • Opening statements • Presentation of evidence • Closing arguments • Instruction of jury • Deliberations by jury and delivery of verdict • Entry of judgment	**Pre-Trial** • Summary judgment **Trial** • In limine • Judgment as matter of law • New trial
APPEAL (see Chapter 18)	

In *discovery*, the second phase of litigation (which may overlap somewhat with the first), the parties *exchange information* about the relevant facts through several methods: admissions (statements of agreement as to certain facts), answers to interrogatories (written questions), production of documents or other items, and depositions (interviews) of parties and witnesses.

Motions arise during discovery if the parties are unable to manage the process themselves. A party may resist discovery if it believes that the opponent is seeking irrelevant or protected information or is asking for discovery that is exceedingly burdensome. Then the party seeking discovery brings a motion to compel discovery.

Discovery concludes as the case nears the trial date, and the parties move on to *obtaining a decision*. The parties may avoid trial in various ways. They may *negotiate a settlement* themselves, or they may resolve the case with the assistance of a *third-party neutral*, through processes such as mediation and arbitration. If one party believes the key facts to be undisputed and its position to be supported by the law, it may ask the court to grant it summary judgment. *Summary judgment* is a decision by the court based on factual documents supporting the motion (such as depositions, affidavits, or a stipulated statement of facts) and arguments of counsel. Summary judgment may cover all claims or defenses in the case or only some portions of it. A grant of summary judgment obviates the need for trial on that portion of the case.

If the case has not been resolved during the pre-trial phase, it will proceed to *trial*. A jury trial consists of selection of a jury; opening statements by the lawyers; each side's presentation of evidence through witnesses, documents, and other items; closing arguments; the judge's instruction of the jury on the law; jury deliberations; and the verdict. The judge then reviews the jury's decision and decides whether to enter judgment on the verdict. Some cases are tried to a judge without a jury (which is known as a *bench trial*), in which case the judge determines what the facts are and applies the law to the facts.

Motions are common at various points in a trial. For example, one party may bring a motion in limine, to obtain a ruling on the admissibility of certain evidence. The defendant may bring a motion for judgment as a matter of law at the end of the plaintiff's case, seeking a ruling that the plaintiff failed to carry its burden of proof and that the defendant therefore wins. Alternatively, either party may move for judgment as a matter of law before or after the case goes to the jury. The party that lost before the jury may seek a new trial based on erroneous rulings by the judge on such matters as admissibility of evidence.

If a party that loses at the trial court is sufficiently disturbed by the loss and wants to pursue the case further, it may appeal. The appeals process is described in Chapter 18.

As an example, Exhibits 17A and 17B are summary judgment memoranda; the defendant is the moving party. The discovery preceding the motion included requests for admissions, a deposition, and production of a document. This is a small volume of discovery, but the facts were not seriously contested in this case.

2. Motion Practice

a. Procedures

Judges are assigned to hear motions under one of several systems. In a *block system*, each case is assigned to a judge from the very earliest stages through trial; that judge hears motions in the case. In a *calendar system*, each judge rotates through a schedule in which he or she hears all motions scheduled for a specific day. Furthermore, in *federal court*, judges typically hear and decide dispositive motions while magistrates (assistant judges, essentially) typically hear and decide non-dispositive motions.

Motion arguments can be made orally, in writing, or both. A few motions are made and argued only orally. For example, an evidentiary motion generally is made and argued orally while the trial is in progress.

More typically, the movant brings a motion by filing a notice of motion and then a motion. The *notice of motion* alerts the opponent to the motion and provides information about the time and location of the hearing. The *motion* requests the court to take the action desired by the movant. Generally, the movant also provides a *proposed order* for the court's consideration, should the court grant the motion.

The movant and non-movant typically write memoranda of law for and against the motion. The movant writes first, filing the *memorandum in support of the motion* with the court and serving it on opposing counsel. The non-movant writes the *memorandum in opposition to the motion*, in response to the movant's memorandum, and then serves and files it. The movant then may prepare, serve, and file a *reply memorandum* if the memorandum in opposition raises matters unaddressed by the movant's initial memorandum. Motion practice memoranda state the facts of the case, with citations to the record; set out the law governing the case, with citations; and apply that law to the facts of the case.

In addition to submitting written materials, the lawyers usually argue orally before the judge. These *oral arguments* may be very formal (in the courtroom, with the lawyers standing at a lectern and arguing in turns) or quite informal (with the lawyers seated around the judge's desk in his or her chambers or office). Oral argument is discussed in detail in Chapter 19.

b. Court Rules

Writing a motion practice memorandum is a rule-bound activity. Federal or state rules of procedure, depending on where the case is set, define the types of motions that can be made and state the standards for granting them. In addition, local court rules, which supplement the rules of procedure and are drafted by a single court or by a set of district courts, cover matters of detail. For example, in the state courts in Minnesota, memoranda can be no longer than thirty-five pages, exclusive of facts, absent court permission. The parties must file their memoranda at fixed intervals before the date of the hearing (e.g., the movant's initial memorandum is due twenty-eight days before the hearing on a dispositive motion). If the deadlines are not met, adverse consequences may follow, such as loss of the opportunity to argue orally or imposition of attorney fees.[3] See Box 17.2 for a case discussing failure to comply with format rules. The message here should be clear: know and comply with both the rules of procedure and the local rules in your jurisdiction.

c. Strategy

Bringing a motion should reflect a well-considered choice. The most obvious reason for bringing a motion is to obtain the relief sought, whether it be dismissal of the case, a temporary injunction, or a discovery order. In addition, if the case has been assigned to a specific judge, motions provide an opportunity to educate the judge about the case and, in turn, to see how the judge assesses the case. Furthermore, because the non-movant typically defends against the motion, motions provide an opportunity to learn the non-movant's strategy.

---

3. Minn. Gen. R. Prac. Dist. Ct. 115.03-.06.

BOX 17.2

HOW IMPORTANT ARE COURT RULES?

As you read the following case, think about these questions:

1. *Why (do you think) did the lawyer fail to follow the rules?*
2. *What would you do to avoid this situation?*
3. *Is the penalty appropriate here? Would you have issued a different penalty?*

Kano v. National Consumer Cooperative Bank,
22 F.3d 899 (9th Cir. 1994).

The opening brief filed on behalf of appellant violated Fed. R. App. P. 32(a) in that the lines were not double-spaced, but were spaced only one-and-one half spaces apart. Furthermore, the footnotes were of a typeface much smaller than that permitted by the rule, and contained approximately eight lines per inch, as opposed to six lines per inch in a normal single-spaced format. We estimate that the opening brief was the equivalent of at least sixty-five pages in length, far exceeding the fifty-page limit.

Counsel for appellant took full responsibility for the form of the brief. However, it is apparent from the reply brief filed by counsel that he knows what the spacing requirements are, even though the footnotes in the reply brief also do not comply with Rule 32. Consequently, we impose sanctions against counsel for the appellant in the amount of $1,500. *See Adriana Intern. Corp. v. Thoeren*, 913 F.2d 1406, 1417 (9th Cir. 1990), *cert. denied*, 498 U.S. 1109 . . . (1991) (imposing sanctions for failure to comply with Fed. R. App. P. 32(a)); *see also* 28 U.S.C. 1927 (authorizing sanctions for failure to comply with rules governing form of briefs. The court acknowledges payment of the sanction.

Nonetheless, there are distinct disadvantages to motions, especially ill-considered ones. Bringing a motion takes time and energy, and therefore money as well. A premature or weakly supported motion presents a poor impression of the case (and the lawyer) to the judge. Excessive use of motions can undermine the relationship between the lawyers, who must work together throughout the litigation.

The non-movant typically chooses to defend against the motion. Alternatively, the non-movant may offer to negotiate about the matter in dispute. For example, a party facing a summary judgment motion may offer to settle the case.

As an example, in the fictional *Brown* litigation, the issue was whether the school's actions were constitutional, an important issue of principle for both parties. Thus, they may not have perceived much middle ground, and money would not be a suitable remedy. The defendant school district brought the motion for summary judgment primarily to terminate the litigation in its favor; secondary reasons included obtaining clarity about the legal framework for the case (by prompting both sides to set out their arguments and the judge to write an opinion) and promoting settlement. The plaintiff had little option but to defend against the motion.

WHAT DO JUDGES SEEK IN MOTION PRACTICE MEMORANDA?[4]

A brief should be an essay with a clear train of thought, advancing only as many cohesive, well-supported arguments as necessary, that, taken together, make up a unified whole—while rebutting that opposition's counterarguments. The brief should marshal the relevant precedent but need not address irrelevant arguments. Also, it must include contrary authority that is on point and controlling.

. . .

Credibility is an extremely important component of a good brief. Misleading or incorrect citations, however unintentional, detract from the persuasiveness of the brief. The brief-writer should carefully draft and edit for correct citations, as well as for punctuation, grammar, and syntax . . . . Mark Twain once said, "Easy writing makes damned hard reading." How true this is in legal writing.

—Hon. Duross Fitzpatrick, United States District Court for the Middle District of Georgia

Memoranda of law are called *briefs* rather than *encyclopedias* for a reason. A brief presents the elements of an argument concisely with references to the sources of law and with descriptions of the particular facts that define the transaction . . . .

Briefs are a medium for articulation and presentation—goals assisted by clarity, precision, and *brevity*.

—Hon. Lynn N. Hughes, United States District Court for the Southern District of Texas

C. THE MOTION PRACTICE MEMORANDUM

1. Audience and Purpose

As you prepare your motion practice memorandum, keep in mind who comprises your *audience*: the judge and his or her law clerk, opposing counsel, and your client. Each reader has different reasons for reading the memorandum.

Judges, of course, are familiar with the law in general and the legal system. Every judge has a few areas of expertise and some areas that he or she has not studied since law school (if then). Law clerks typically are recent law school graduates who assist judges by researching cases and writing memos analyzing the cases; they too have only general knowledge of most issues that are presented to the court. To render a sound decision, the judge and clerk need to know the facts of the dispute, the applicable substantive and procedural law, and the application of the law to the facts of the case. To find in your favor, they need to be fully informed and find you and your client credible. And they need to understand the case with a minimum of time and effort; most judges and law clerks are pressed for time due to heavy caseloads.

---

4. *Judges on Briefing: A National Survey* 5, 7 (Bryan A. Garner comp., 2001).

As for opposing counsel, your primary purpose is to convince him or her of the merits of your position. If your opponent is at least somewhat convinced of your position, your opponent may settle or contest fewer points in pre-trial or at trial. Your secondary purpose is to develop a good working relationship; modern litigation requires considerable cooperation between the lawyers, even as they pursue their clients' divergent interests.

Your final purpose is to maintain your client's trust. Your client should see his or her story told effectively and see that you believe in his or her position and want the court to do so as well.

2. Format Choices

No single format for the motion practice memorandum is used in courts across the country. Some courts dictate a format, so you should check for—and scrupulously follow—any applicable local rules. You also should consult other attorneys about any informal local practices. As shown in Box 17.4, the typical motion practice memorandum is a variation on the analytical office memo.

The movant's initial memorandum begins with a caption. Most formats move into issues or an introduction or a summary. Virtually all formats include a fact statement. Some cover the procedural history of the case within the fact statement; others include a separate procedure statement. All formats include an argument—the most substantial component—and close with a conclusion, followed by a signature block.

The formats for the non-movant's memorandum in opposition to the motion are similar. The non-movant need not follow the format selected by the movant. The non-movant generally does not include a procedure statement. Also, the non-movant occasionally elects not to include a fact statement if the movant's statement is acceptable, as occurs when the parties are not disputing the facts and may even have an agreed-upon (stipulated) fact statement. More often, the non-movant tells its own story in a fact statement.

BOX 17.4

COMPARISON OF MOTION PRACTICE MEMORANDUM AND ANALYTICAL OFFICE MEMO

Motion Practice Memorandum	Analytical Office Memo
Caption	Caption
Introduction, summary, issues	Issues and short answers
Facts	Facts
Procedure	
Argument	Discussion
Conclusion with signature	Closing

The movant's reply memorandum is the most flexibly structured. Its purpose is to respond to points raised by the non-movant that are not addressed in the movant's initial memorandum. It is fairly common to include an introduction; address factual matters in a short fact statement, legal matters in a short argument, or both; and close with a conclusion and a signature.

3. Memorandum Components

This section discusses the various components of the memorandum in the order that the reader generally encounters them. However, you need not write the motion practice memorandum in this order. For example, you may write the argument before the facts, or you may write the introduction last.

Caption: The chief purpose of the *caption* is to permit easy recognition and accurate processing of the document. The caption lists the parties, the court in which the case is venued, the docket number of the case, and the title of the document. Local rules may require additional information, such as the type of case and the judge's name, and specify the layout of the caption.

As an example, note that the captions of Exhibits 17A and 17B both contain the information set out above and are nearly identical. Only the document titles differ.

Introduction, summary, or issues: Most memoranda have an introduction, a summary, or issues. All serve to frame the main point of the motion and orient the reader.

When written well, the *introduction* not only orients the reader to the motion, but also begins to persuade the reader to adopt the client's position. The introduction briefly identifies the parties, the nature of their dispute, and the result sought. It also presents a key point or two drawn from the theory of the case. A *summary* provides this information, as well as an overview of the legal arguments in the memorandum.

As an example, Exhibit 17A, which is the defendant's memorandum, opens with a summary. The first paragraph acquaints the reader with the factual dispute and introduces the main themes of the memorandum. The second paragraph provides an overview of the argument.

Alternatively, a statement of *issues* poses concise questions answered in the memorandum. It reveals the scope and sequence of the points covered in the memorandum. The issues should be accurately yet subtly phrased to suggest the answers desired by the client. Most issues link the law to key facts. Many issues refer both to the law of the motion (procedural law) and to the law governing the parties' claims or defenses (substantive law), although some issues involve only procedural law, as in a discovery motion. Some issues are purely legal, as in an argument that a jurisdiction does not recognize a cause of action. The classic approach is to frame an issue in a single sentence. However, if a single sentence would be unwieldy, you may write a two- or three-sentence issue: the law, the facts, and then a question about their link. You should write one issue for each major point in the argument and may flag minor points in the argument with sub-issues. Use outlining levels (I, II; A, B, C) and transitional words to convey the relationships among the issues and sub-issues. See Box 17.5 for two sets of issues.

BOX 17.5

SAMPLE ISSUES

Two Single-Sentence Issues

I. May a school district suspend a middle school student from displaying the phrase "I ♥ Boobies" in his hair on the grounds that it is, within that setting, lewd and offensive?

II. May a school district suspend a middle school student from displaying the phrase "I ♥ Boobies" in his hair on the grounds that it will substantially interfere with coursework?

Compound-Sentence Approach

The First Amendment permits public schools to limit student speech that is offensively lewd or likely to cause substantial disruption. A middle school student came to school with the phrase "I ♥ Boobies" shaved into his head, which did cause disruption. Did the school district act constitutionally in suspending the student until he changed his haircut?

Facts: The *facts* statement informs the reader of the events that gave rise to the litigation. Equally important, the facts statement recounts the story from the client's point of view, thus eliciting empathy for the client and setting the scene for the legal arguments.

The key to a successful facts statement is the careful selection of facts. Your two goals are that the reader understand the situation and that the reader see your client as having acted responsibly. As synopsized in Box 17.6, you should include legally relevant facts (related to the elements of the rule) and background facts (necessary for the reader to understand the story)—regardless of whether they are favorable or unfavorable to your client. As tempting as it may be to omit unfavorable facts, you must include them to fulfill your ethical responsibility to the court. Place unfavorable facts in the best light possible, e.g., show why your client acted in a way that harmed the other party. You need not include any residual facts, but you may want to include a few favorable residual facts.

As the case proceeds through the court system, the pleadings, discovery documents, transcripts of oral proceedings, and other material filed with the court become the *record* of the case. In the facts statement, you must cite to the pertinent portion of the record. You need not quote the record verbatim, although you may want to quote some material directly if the precise wording is important or persuasive. Your presentation must be faithful to the record. For example, inferences drawn from the facts should be clearly identified as inferences, lest they be taken to be stated facts.

The facts statement should have a clear beginning, body, and ending. The *opening paragraph* should identify the important participants in the situation and establish the labels used for them in the memorandum. If there is no introduction or summary, the opening paragraph also should present a very brief synopsis of the parties' dispute.

BOX 17.6

COVERAGE OF FACTS STATEMENT

Material	Coverage
Favorable relevant facts	Must include
Unfavorable relevant facts	Must include
Favorable background facts	Include to make sense of story
Unfavorable background facts	Include if needed to make sense of story
Favorable residual (emotional facts)	Limited
Unfavorable residual (emotional facts)	Exclude

The body of the facts statement chronicles what happened between these participants. The common *organizational schemes* are chronological, topical, and perceptual. The first two presentations are more strictly objective, while the third introduces an element of subjectivity. In a chronological presentation, events are told in the order that they occurred. A topical presentation proceeds from one aspect of the facts, such as location or relationships, to another. In the perceptual presentation, the events are presented as a key participant experienced or learned of them; then a competing perspective is presented. The perceptual presentation should be used when the participants' perspectives are critical and differ fundamentally. You should choose the organizational scheme that best permits you to tell your client's story, from your client's perspective, in a coherent and interesting narrative. Lengthy fact statements may have subject headings.

The *final paragraph* of the facts statement generally states the pertinent procedural history of the litigation up to the point at which the motion was made. There need not be much detail about unimportant procedural matters. If the memorandum includes a procedure component, the procedural history appears there instead.

As an example, Exhibit 17A provides some context in the summary. Thus, the facts statement uses a strictly chronological presentation: it begins with the action that caused the school's concern and ends with the deadlock between the school and the student. Facts that favor the other side, such as the reason for the boy's action, are acknowledged, but the focus remains on the school's concerns. The final paragraph covers procedure.

Procedure: The *procedure* component is most commonly used for cases with complex procedural histories and for motions that are predominantly procedural (such as a motion to compel discovery) rather than substantive (such as a motion to dismiss for failure to state a claim). This component sets out the history of the litigation up to the current motion. It identifies the main events, typically in chronological order, and provides citations to pertinent documents, such as the complaint or request for admissions.

Argument text: The *argument* is the longest component of most memoranda. Its purpose is to establish that the client is entitled to the outcome sought, by providing a legal rationale that is ideally compelling or at least more convincing than the opponent's argument. Indeed, the judge may use portions of a successful argument in writing his or her opinion.

To prove its points, the argument first must *fully state the law*, as synopsized in Box 17.7. Ethics rules require counsel to cover and cite the legal authorities that the court will deem important in deciding the motion—not only favorable authorities but also unfavorable authorities not covered by opposing counsel. The argument must present mandatory authority where it exists, of course; it also may present persuasive precedent and commentary that may be useful to the court and is favorable to the client. If no mandatory authority exists, the argument should demonstrate how to use persuasive authority and commentary to decide the case and how to consider unfavorable persuasive authority. The argument should present all analytical steps necessary to develop the applicable rule of law. Thus, as appropriate, it should show how to fuse several cases or interpret an ambiguous statute.

The argument should demonstrate the *interaction of substantive and procedural law*. Some procedural rules operate relatively independently of the substantive law governing the case; an example is a motion to compel discovery where the issue is burdensomeness. Other procedural rules are nearly entirely dependent on the substantive law; an example is a motion to dismiss for failure to state a claim recognized by the law. Still other procedural rules include elements that rely heavily on substantive law and also elements that operate independently of substantive law; an example is a motion for a temporary injunction, which includes the likelihood of success on the merits (fixed by substantive law) and the relative burdens on the parties (not so fixed).

Furthermore, the argument must tightly and convincingly *connect the law to the facts* of the case. The argument must discuss the relevant facts—both favorable and unfavorable—in depth and demonstrate why the court should draw the

---

B O X 1 7 . 7

LEGAL CONTENT OF ARGUMENT

Material	Coverage
Favorable mandatory authority	Required
Unfavorable mandatory authority	Required if opponent does not raise it; should be included
Persuasive precedent	May be used; no need to cite if unfavorable
Commentary	May be used; no need to cite if unfavorable

desired conclusion. This task requires clear deductive reasoning; in many cases, it also requires reasoning by example and policy analysis.

On debatable issues, your argument also should *address your opponent's arguments*. This discussion commonly arises in one of two postures. If the conflict relates to which rule to apply, you would focus on the favorable rule and briefly address the unfavorable rule. If the conflict relates to how the rule applies to the facts, you would focus on the favorable application and briefly address the unfavorable application.

Of course, you must fully and properly *cite* the law in your argument. In general, the citations to the record in the facts statement support references to the facts within the argument. However, you should provide record citations in the argument when you use a direct quote from the record or want the court to look at a key page.

As an example, in Exhibit 17A, the defendant, as the moving party, first states the two requirements of summary judgment: lack of a genuine issue of material fact and entitlement to judgment as a matter of law. The defendant concedes that the facts are to be viewed in the plaintiff's favor and then moves on to arguing that it is entitled to judgment as a matter of law. That argument begins with an overarching point: that the boy's behavior must be understood in the middle school educational context, which the school has the prerogative to safeguard; this is its theory of the case. The two specific legal arguments follow, both based on a line of Supreme Court cases: the school's capacity to prohibit offensively lewd speech and the school's right to stave off substantial interference with coursework. The argument uses deductive reasoning, case comparisons, and non-legal sources to make key policy arguments. It also rebuts several points likely to be made by the plaintiff by returning to the focus on the middle school context. The cases and facts in the defendant's memorandum and the plaintiff's memorandum (Exhibit 17B) are similar, although the two parties use these materials to contrasting ends.

Argument point headings: An argument cannot be persuasive if it cannot be followed. *Point headings* throughout the discussion reveal the structure of the arguments. Each point heading makes a full-sentence assertion; taken together, they state the handful of key assertions the court must accept (in total or in part) to rule in the client's favor.

In most situations, each major point heading ties together the substantive and procedural law and the key facts relevant to the assertion. Each point heading should be a single persuasively worded sentence. The sentence can be compound, but it should not be so complex that its readability suffers. For complicated or lengthy topics, the major point heading is a broad assertion, and minor point headings state the subsidiary assertions, which may combine law and facts, or refer only to the law, or refer only to the facts. If an argument is primarily legal or procedural, the point headings will be too.

Point headings should stand out from the text; use white space (open lines) above and below the heading and underlining, italics, boldface, or initial capital letters as well. Using all capital letters is also an option, but studies have shown that readers have to work harder and retain less information when reading sentences in all capital letters. Multiple headings and sub-headings should be numbered and lettered in outline form.

BOX 17.8

SAMPLE POINT HEADINGS

I. Brown's speech occurred in Perkinsberg Middle School and must be examined within that unique educational setting.

II. The Supreme Court grants schools the authority to limit certain student speech to ensure the proper administration of schools.

A. Within Perkinsberg Middle School, Brown's haircut was lewd and offensive.
B. Perkinsberg School District administrators had reason to believe that the haircut would substantially interfere with coursework and were therefore legally able to limit it.

As an example, the content of the argument in Exhibit 17A is apparent from its point headings, reprinted in Box 17.8. Each major heading makes a main assertion, and the minor headings elaborate on the points in the second major heading.

Point headings do not eliminate the need for signaling passages within your text. Roadmaps may appear in various places, such as between the argument heading and point heading I, or between point heading I and sub-heading A. You should use strong topic and transition sentences to guide the reader through your paragraphs.

Conclusion and signature: The purpose of the *conclusion* is to remind the reader of the outcome desired by the client. It typically follows a simple formula, in which the writer respectfully requests that the court act in the client's favor. Some writers also synopsize the argument.

The *signature block* begins with "Respectfully submitted," followed by the lawyer's signature, as an endorsement of the preceding material. The signature block also includes the lawyer's name, firm affiliation, client, contact information, attorney registration number, and the date.

As an example, Exhibit 17A has a lengthy conclusion, which reviews the main policy and legal arguments and then restates the relief sought.

D. REVIEW

In the setting of civil litigation, motion practice memoranda serve multiple audiences by seeking to persuade the judge, opposing counsel (and the client) that the client's position is the better one. A typical format for a motion practice memorandum is as follows:

(1) The caption provides identifying information.
(2) The introduction or summary orients the reader by providing basic information about the case and begins to persuade the reader by featuring a key point or two. Alternatively, the issues frame the legal/factual questions to be decided.

(3) The fact statement recounts the client's story and sets the scene for the legal argument.

(4) The procedure component (if included) sets out the important events in the litigation to date.

(5) The argument establishes a sound legal basis for the client's desired outcome, showing it to be the better one on the facts and the law.

(6) The conclusion states the relief desired by the client and is followed by a signature block.

The resulting memorandum should be complete, correct, coherent, comprehensible, and (if written according to the model of legal advocacy discussed in Chapter 16) convincing.

EXHIBIT 17A MOVANT'S MEMORANDUM

STATE OF MINNESOTA   DISTRICT COURT
COUNTY OF GOODHUE   FIRST JUDICIAL DISTRICT

Lynn and Brandon Brown   )   Court File No. 25-CV-12-0001
on behalf of their minor child,   )
Caleb Brown,   )
Plaintiffs,   )
)
            vs.   )   DEFENDANT'S MEMORANDUM
)   IN SUPPORT OF MOTION FOR
Perkinsberg School District,   )   SUMMARY JUDGMENT
Defendant   )

SUMMARY

In the context of Perkinsberg Middle School, the phrase "I ♥ boobies" is lewd and disruptive. When the Plaintiff, Caleb Brown, chose to shave this phrase into his hair and wear it to school, he did not raise breast cancer awareness as intended. Instead, the phrase provoked middle school students to grab the breasts of a female classmate. This incitement created a disruptive educational environment for all students. The school pursued all administrative remedies and ultimately chose to temporarily suspend Brown rather than tacitly encourage the sexual abuse of students.

The school district's limiting of Brown's lewd and disruptive haircut in this manner was lawful. Public schools are important public institutions; their special societal role gives administrators the responsibility and discretion to limit speech that disrupts the educational environment. The Supreme Court has held that there are two kinds of speech that can be limited to protect this mission: speech that is offensively lewd and speech that is materially disruptive. Brown's haircut fell into both of these categories. Therefore, when the district suspended Brown until he removed the offensive phrase, the school acted within its authority to maintain an appropriate educational environment. Because there is no genuine issue of material fact, this case should be decided in Perkinsberg School District's favor on summary judgment.

FACTS

On November 4th, 2011, Caleb Brown arrived at Perkinsberg Middle School with the phrase "I ♥ boobies" shaved into his hair. (Brown Dep. 100:1-20.) That day at lunch, some of Brown's male classmates repeatedly shouted "I love boobies" and grabbed a female student's breasts. (*Id.* at 101:1-7.) Word spread throughout the school, and other kids acted out this sexual assault. (*Id.* at 101:18-19.) Like other public middle schools, Perkinsberg Middle School takes these incidents seriously; it disciplines all students who grope female students or make sexual comments towards them. (Def.'s Resp. to Pl.'s Req. for Admis. No. 10.)

EXHIBIT 17A (cont.)

In response to these incidents, Principal Wilson met with Brown. (Brown Dep. 102:12-13.) Wilson learned that Brown's haircut was in response to his sister's breast cancer and that Brown thought it could raise awareness. (*Id.* at 102:13-14.) Wilson informed Brown that the phrase "I ♥ boobies" was inappropriate and disruptive. (Wilson Letter Ex. A ¶ 2.) He encouraged Brown to show support in a more organized and school-appropriate manner. (*Id.* ¶ 2.) Wilson warned Brown that if he continued to display the offending phrase, he could be suspended. (*Id.* ¶ 7.)

Despite this knowledge, Brown returned to school the next day without removing "I ♥ boobies" from his hair. (Brown Dep. 101:16-102:1.) As a result, Brown was sent home and told that he could not return until the words in his hair were removed. (Wilson Letter Ex. A ¶ 9.)

Soon after Brown's suspension, Perkinsberg School District convened a meeting of the school board. (*Id.* ¶ 10.) This board of Perkinsberg community members agreed that the phrase was inappropriate for Perkinsberg Middle School; it affirmed the suspension. (*Id.* ¶ 10.)

Principal Wilson then reached out to Brown's family and informed them of the situation. (*Id.* ¶ ¶ 1-10.) He expressed condolences for Brown's sister and encouraged the family to contact him if they had questions or concerns. (*Id.* ¶ 10.) Principal Wilson once again reminded Brown that he could return if he removed the offending speech; however, Brown was unwilling to have a haircut and decided not to raise breast cancer awareness in a manner appropriate for seventh- and eighth-graders. (*Id.*)

Unhappy with the decision of both Principal Wilson and the Perkinsberg school board, the Browns sued Perkinsberg School District. (Compl.) Brown is seeking to attend the school with the haircut, compensation for attendance at a private school, attorney's fees, and other relief. (*Id.*) The school district maintains that it acted within its rights as a school. (Answer.) Based upon the pleadings and the evidence produced in discovery, Perkinsberg School District moves for summary judgment. (Def.'s Mot. Summ. J.)

ARGUMENT

As the party seeking summary judgment, the school district must show that given the evidence, there is no genuine issue of material fact and that it is entitled to judgment as a matter of law. *Anderson v. Mikel Drilling Co.*, 102 N.W.2d 293, 297 (Minn. 1960). When determining the validity of the district's summary judgment motion, this Court views the facts in the light most favorable to Brown. *Id.* Even when doing so, this Court should find that Perkinsberg School District acted lawfully and is entitled to judgment as a matter of law.

I. Brown's speech occurred in Perkinsberg Middle School and must be examined within that unique educational setting.

Brown's speech must be viewed within the context of a public middle school's unique educational role. The Supreme Court has determined that the important duty of schools necessitates the curtailment of certain expression in order to ensure a proper learning environment, unlike speech in the public square. *Brown v. Bd. of Educ.*, 347 U.S. 483, 493 (1954); *New Jersey v. T.L.O.*, 469 U.S. 325, 340-42 (1985). While it is true that "the

EXHIBIT 17A (cont.)

vigilant protection of constitutional freedoms is nowhere more vital than in the community of American schools," when expressive speech occurs within a school environment, "nothing in the Constitution prohibits the states from insisting that certain modes of expression are inappropriate and subject to sanctions." *Epperson v. Arkansas*, 393 U.S. 97, 104 (1968) (quoting *Shelton v. Tucker*, 364 U.S. 479, 487 (1960)); *see also Bethel Sch. Dist. No. 403 v. Fraser*, 478 U.S. 675, 683 (1986). The context of speech is important when a court determines its appropriateness. *Epperson*, 393 U.S. at 106; *Quarterman v. Byrd*, 453 F.2d 54, 57 (4th Cir. 1971) (stating that the protection of free speech is not absolute and the extent of its application may properly consider the audience's age and maturity); *Mailloux v. Kiley*, 448 F.2d 1242, 1243 (1st Cir. 1971) (*per curiam*) (appropriateness of sanctions depends on the age and sophistication of the students).

The administrators of Perkinsberg School District are entrusted by their community to create an educational environment fit for all students. In creating and enforcing its policies, the school district must take into account the ages, maturity levels, and cultural values unique to Perkinsberg. These features define the Perkinsberg Middle School context. Because this mix is unique to the school, so too are the prescribed disciplinary measures.

Brown was not allowed to return to school until his sexually explicit haircut was changed. This disciplinary measure was necessitated by the unique circumstances of Perkinsberg Middle School. The school was working to discourage students from grabbing the breasts of female classmates. This goal was especially important to Perkinsberg given that sexual harassment has more adverse effects than bullying and that these effects are especially notable among girls. James Gruber, *Comparing the Impact of Bullying and Sexual Harassment Victimization on the Mental and Physical Health of Adolescents* 1 (2011). From this perspective and to preserve the educational environment for all students, Principal Wilson properly limited Brown's haircut.

Although Principal Wilson initiated the suspension of Brown, he did not act alone. The Perkinsberg School board "met and approved [Brown's] suspension." (Wilson Letter Ex. A ¶ 11.) The Perkinsberg School Board, representing the community, is in the best position to determine the appropriateness of student actions, and a court "ought not impose its own views in such matters where there is a rational basis for the decisions and actions of the school authorities." *Trachtman v. Anker*, 563 F.2d 512, 519 (2d Cir. 1977).

II. The Supreme Court grants schools the authority to limit certain student speech to ensure the proper administration of schools.

A. Within Perkinsberg Middle School, Brown's haircut was lewd and offensive.

The Supreme Court held in *Fraser* that school administrators have the authority to impose sanctions upon a student for "offensively lewd and indecent speech." 478 U.S. at 685. There, a high school student gave an innuendo-laden speech in front of the student body. The Court in *Fraser* found that the student could be disciplined for using such speech.

The circumstances within Perkinsberg Middle School are even riper for limiting speech than in *Fraser*. There, the speech was a one-time occurrence. *Id.* at 677.

EXHIBIT 17A (cont.)

By contrast, Brown's haircut was constantly visible to all students who saw him. Fraser's speech was not sexual on its face; the students and administration needed to read into the speech to know that it was lewd. *Id.* at 683. Brown's haircut used sexual language that middle school students use. The major difference between *Fraser* and Brown is that the school in *Fraser* was allowed to punish the student for a single act. *Id.* at 687. Perkinsberg School District did not suspend Brown to punish him but rather has acted to keep him from continuing to display the offending haircut.

The Court labeled Fraser's speech "plainly offensive" and did not go into further detail about the criteria. *Id.* at 683. Many courts have decided that the classification of speech as lewd is "best left to the locally elected school board." *E.g., Poling v. Murphy,* 872 F.2d 757, 761 (6th Cir. 1989); *Lopez v. Tulare Joint Union High Sch. Dist.,* 34 Cal. App. 4th 1302 (1995) (court defers to school board's standards of offensive language). The rationale is that the limits of speech are closely tied to the values of the school's community and the belief structures of its parents; these individuals are better suited to the management of community schools than are judges. *Pyle v. South Hadley Sch. Comm.,* 861 F. Supp. 157, 194 (D. Mass. 1994).

In light of these holdings, this Court should find the word "boobies" lewd and offensive in this context. The principal of Perkinsberg Middle School found the word to be offensive to the standards of its school community and disruptive to its school environment. The school board agreed with this assessment. Therefore, Brown's speech was deemed to be offensive by the standards and values of Perkinsberg and should be found offensive by this court.

Brown contends that the speech was not offensive but instead was designed to raise awareness of health issues. However, in suggesting that awareness raising was needed, Brown is admitting that his peers were unfamiliar with the issue of breast cancer. Thus, the phrase "I ♥ boobies" would not be interpreted by the students as a campaign to raise awareness; rather, they would view it as adolescents would view it—an explicitly sexual phrase.

Indeed, Brown's classmates associated the phrase with sexual assault. Incidents that happened not long after his haircut debuted underscore that in Perkinsberg Middle School "I ♥ boobies" is sexually explicit. In a crowded lunchroom, one of Brown's classmates groped a female student while shouting the phrase "I love boobies." (Brown Dep. 101:1-7.) After the lunchroom incident, "other kids acted out what happened . . . or at least they pretended to." (*Id.* at 101:18-19.) Such a connection would be especially traumatic to the girl who was groped in the lunch room; every time she saw that phrase shaved into her classmate's head, she would be forced to relive that traumatic experience. Despite Brown's best intentions, to the students of Perkinsberg Middle School, especially that girl, the phrase is about sex, not cancer.

The school was not opposed to Brown's goal of raising breast cancer awareness. Perkinsberg merely sought to change the form of Brown's speech from a lewd and disruptive manner to one more appropriate for its middle school. If Brown had provided some context, like the students did in the distinguishable case of *H. v. Easton Area School District,* 2011 WL 1376141 (E.D. Pa. 2011),[5] then the speech is more likely to have been

---

5. This memorandum was written before the district court decision was published at 827 F. Supp. 2d 392 and affirmed en banc by the Third Circuit in 2013 at 725 F.3d 293.

EXHIBIT 17A (cont.)

allowed by the school and legally protected. In *Easton*, the phrase "I ♥ boobies" appeared in the context of a larger breast cancer awareness campaign. 2011 WL 1376141, at *1. The word "boobies" and "I ♥ boobies" were deemed not to be lewd in the context of Easton Area Schools; however, the court held that "boobies" could be lewd under other circumstances because "context matters in interpreting the word [boobies]." *Id.* at *11.

Even when the phrase appears in a larger campaign, however, it can be offensive. *See, e.g.*, Tracy Clark-Flory, *Why I do not "(heart) boobies,"* Salon (Sept. 2, 2010), http://bit.ly/HFQ0my (last visited April 10, 2011) ("I'm offended by these [I ♥ boobies] bracelets, too . . . Not only are women reduced to their breasts, but men are reduced to their love for breasts."). Critics have described this method of awareness as "fetishizing of breasts . . . at the expense of the bodies, hearts, and minds attached to them." Peggy Orenstein, *Think About Pink*, The New York Times Magazine (Nov. 12, 2010), *http://nyti.ms/aIDIOI* (last visited April 10, 2011).

If even adults are offended by this phrase, imagine how caustic it can be in the context of a school full of impressionable adolescents confronting their sexuality for the first time. Brown's haircut did not appear in the context of a larger awareness campaign; it appeared in the context of a school where breast grabbing and sexual objectification already presented an issue for administrators. They interpreted "I ♥ boobies" within this particular context and found it offensive. The issue was taken to the Perkinsberg School Board, and Brown's suspension was upheld until he removed that specific phrase from his hair. Such an action should be permitted by this court as an appropriate use of a school district's authority to create an environment safe from lewd speech. Therefore, the school should not be found to have violated Brown's free speech rights.

B. Perkinsberg School District administrators had reason to believe the haircut would substantially interfere with coursework and were therefore legally able to limit it.

The Supreme Court has held that if student speech leads school authorities to reasonably forecast a substantial or material disruption of school activities, then correcting that speech is constitutional. *Tinker v. Des Moines Indep. Cmty. Sch. Dist.*, 393 U.S. 503, 513 (1969). This line of reasoning was continued in *Hazelwood School District v. Kuhlmeier*, 484 U.S. 260, 266 (1988), where the Court held that limiting speech is allowed when the administration "has reason to believe [the speech] will 'substantially interfere.'" The Eighth Circuit has followed and summarized these holdings, stating that "*Tinker* and its progeny allow a school to 'forecast' a disruption and take necessary precautions before [problems] escalate out of hand." *B.W.A v. Farmington R-7 Sch. Dist.*, 554 F.3d 734, 739 (8th Cir. 2009).

Perkinsberg Middle School had reason to believe that Brown's haircut would substantially interfere with coursework. The school had a history of incidents where female students were groped. Brown's haircut was an overt display of affection for "boobies." With this phrase connected to breast grabbing, the school had a reasonable fear that the haircut could inspire other incidents because students are influenced by speech that the school appears to tolerate. *See Bd. of Educ. v. Earls*, 536 U.S. 822, 840

EXHIBIT 17A (cont.)

(2002) (Breyer, J., concurring). Had the Perkinsberg Middle School not corrected the speech, it would have appeared to tolerate breast-grabbing.

Indeed, one student shouted "I love boobies" and grabbed a classmate's breast. Other students reenacted that incident after it occurred. This gave the school notice enough to worry that the haircut could continue to inspire others to substantially disrupt class. Without the intervention by the school, female students would have been forced to endure an educational environment where sexual assault was apparently tolerated by the administration and openly reenacted by other students. Such an environment would be especially disruptive and harmful to the young girl who was groped in the lunchroom.

An environment of sexual harassment has been found to be detrimental to psychological well-being. Catherine Hill, Am. Ass'n of Univ. Women Educ. Found., *Crossing the Line: Sexual Harassment at School* 1 (2011). Sexual harassment materially affects how students experience school; students report not wanting to go to school, feeling sick to their stomachs, and having difficulty studying. *Id.* at 22. Such an impact cannot possibly be anything but a materially disruptive learning environment for students. It certainly does not uphold the school district's important task of "training our children to be good citizens-to-be." *See Tinker*, 393 U.S. at 524. Had the school district not corrected Brown's speech, it would have failed its duty to the citizens of Perkinsberg by allowing speech that contributes to an ecosystem of sexual assault.

While Brown's haircut was not wholly responsible for the sexual assaults at the school, it contributed to the already volatile environment and inspired students to continue the cycle of assault. Apparent tolerance by the school would not only have a detrimental effect on female students; it would undermine the focus on learning that all students deserve. Thus, Brown's haircut was subject to regulation under *Tinker* and its progeny.

CONCLUSION

The school district did not censor Brown's ideas; indeed, Principal Wilson encouraged Brown to raise awareness for breast cancer. However, public middle schools are delicate ecosystems carefully tended by teachers tasked with keeping this environment safe for all students. Within this context, Brown's haircut harmed the educational environment both because it was offensively lewd and because it could cause further disruption. Thus, Perkinsberg School District acted responsibly and constitutionally when it suspended Brown until he changed his haircut.

Even when the facts are viewed in the light most favorable to the non-moving party, the district acted lawfully and is therefore entitled to judgment as a matter of law. For these reasons, the Court should grant this motion for summary judgment in favor of Perkinsberg School District.

Respectfully submitted,

Dated: March 28, 2012

B. John Schroeder[6]
B. John Schroeder (#195153)
400 Literary Way West
Perkinsberg, MN 55555
Phone: (507) 555-1000
Fax: (507) 555-1001
BJSchroeder@SBLaw.com
Attorney for Defendant

ACKNOWLEDGMENT

The undersigned hereby acknowledges that sanctions may be imposed if, after notice and a reasonable opportunity to respond, the Court determines that the undersigned has violated the provisions of Minnesota Statutes section 549.211 (2010).

Dated: March 28, 2012   B. John Schroeder

---

6. This paper was written by Christopher Ziolkowski while a first-year student at William Mitchell College of Law and has been only lightly edited. My thanks to Chris for permitting its use here.—DS

EXHIBIT 17B NON-MOVANT'S MEMORANDUM

QUESTIONS TO CONSIDER AS YOU READ THIS MEMORANDUM

1. Based on the first paragraph of the summary (and indeed the rest of the memorandum), what is the theory of the case for the plaintiff?
2. In terms of the facts statement:
   a. What is its organizational scheme?
   b. Which facts are emphasized? How so?
   c. Which facts are downplayed? How so?
3. In terms of the argument:
   a. How does the memorandum handle the two prongs of summary judgment? How does this compare to the defendant's memorandum?
   b. Why is this memorandum's argument organized as it is? How similar or dissimilar is it to the argument in the defendant's memorandum?
   c. Both memoranda address the two leading Supreme Court cases, *Tinker* and *Fraser*. How do the memoranda differ in how they use those cases?
   d. Both memoranda also discuss *Easton Area School District*, a district court decision with similar facts. How do the memoranda differ in how they discuss that case?
4. If you were the court, how would you rule on the motion for summary judgment?

MEMORANDUM

STATE OF MINNESOTA	DISTRICT COURT
COUNTY OF GOODHUE	FIRST JUDICIAL DISTRICT

Lynn and Brandon Brown	)	Court File No. 25-CV-12-0001
on behalf of their minor child,	)	
Caleb Brown,	)	
Plaintiffs,	)	
	)	
vs.	)	PLAINTIFF'S MEMORANDUM
	)	IN OPPOSITION TO DEFENDANT'S
Perkinsberg School District,	)	MOTION FOR SUMMARY
Defendant	)	JUDGMENT

SUMMARY

Caleb Brown is fourteen years old and in the eighth grade at Perkinsberg Middle School. Even at this age, Caleb has a First Amendment right to express himself. In support of his older sister's battle with breast cancer, Caleb got a haircut with the nationally recognized breast cancer awareness campaign slogan "I [heart] boobies." Although an incident occurred at school, Caleb did not have control over the other students' choices. Caleb was suspended; he is being punished more for the actions of other students than he is for his harmless, indeed praiseworthy, haircut.

EXHIBIT 17B   (cont.)

A public school student has First Amendment rights when he enters the school premises, and Caleb was exercising his rights in a reasonable manner. A public school may restrict a student's expression when the language is lewd or offensive and interferes with the school's educational mission. It also may act when the language creates a substantial disturbance. However, Caleb's expression meets neither of those tests, demonstrating that the school district violated Caleb's First Amendment right to free speech.

Because there is sufficient evidence that would allow a reasonable person to find that the school district violated Caleb's First Amendment rights, summary judgment is not warranted here. First, the phrase "I [heart] boobies" is not lewd or offensive. Second, the phrase in Caleb's haircut did not cause substantial disruption. Therefore, the school district violated Plaintiff's First Amendment right to free speech, and Defendant's Motion for Summary Judgment should be denied.

FACTS

When Caleb Brown's sister was diagnosed with breast cancer, Caleb immediately wanted to do something to support her. Brown Dep. 1:18-19. He came across the website for the Keep a Breast Foundation, which discussed spreading awareness about cancer and promoted the use of the phrase "I [heart] boobies" in support of those fighting breast cancer. *Id.* at 99:6-10. Caleb chose to have the phrase "I [heart] boobies" shaved into his hair as a way to show support for his sister, for cancer patients often lose their hair during treatment. *Id.* at 99:14-16.

Caleb respects authority and is not a troublemaker. He has never been disciplined by the school, aside from this incident, and he is a good student who is involved with school activities. Def.'s Resp. to Pls.' Rule 36 Req. for Admis. No. 8; *see also* Brown Dep. 1:11-16. He had parental permission to get his haircut; his father went with him to the barbershop and knew what Caleb planned to state via his hair. Brown Dep. 100:8-11. Caleb got his haircut with the honest intention of spreading awareness about breast cancer, while also supporting his sister, whom he loves very much. *Id.* at 102:2; 1:18.

When Caleb went to school after his haircut, he was willing to talk about it with anyone who asked, and he even explained the meaning behind it to his entire social studies class. *Id.* at 100:18-19; 102:1-3. However, not all students were aware of the meaning of the phrase or behaved in a mature manner when they saw the phrase in Caleb's hair. An incident occurred in the cafeteria at lunch, where some students yelled "I love boobies" and someone grabbed a female student's breast. *Id.* at 101:1-7. Caleb did not instigate the incident, and the boys who participated were not friends of his. *Id.* at 101:10-11. In addition, the boys who participated in the incident were disciplined by the school for their behavior. Def.'s Resp. to Pls.' Rule 36 Req. for Admis. No. 9. Caleb felt bad for the female student and did not condone the behavior of the students involved. Brown Dep. 101:8-9. Although there have been rumors of other possible disturbances stemming from the incident in the cafeteria, there is no direct evidence or confirmation. *Id.* at 101:17-19; *see also* Def.'s Resp. to Pls.' Rule 36 Req. for Admis. No. 7.

EXHIBIT 17B (cont.)

Caleb was called in to talk to the principal, Mr. Wilson, after the cafeteria incident. Mr. Wilson told Caleb that he could not come to school with his haircut because it was a violation of school policy. Brown Dep. 102:12-13; *see also* Def.'s Resp. to Pls.' Rule 36 Req. for Admis. Ex. A. The next day, Caleb wore a hat to school to cover up the words in his hair. Brown Dep. 102:16. Caleb did not want to disobey Mr. Wilson, but his sister was upset that he could not go to school with the haircut, so he tried to compromise by wearing a hat. The compromise of wearing the hat was not satisfactory, however, because it was also a violation of school policy. Def.'s Resp. to Pls.' Rule 36 Req. for Admis. Ex. A. Caleb was suspended from school for not changing his haircut. Brown Dep. 103:4-5.

Because of Caleb's suspension, his parents sent him to a private school, Hiawatha Academy, which allows his haircut as an acceptable form of expression. *Id.* at 103:11; 1:9. However, Caleb misses Perkinsberg Middle School, and the private school is expensive and far away from home. *Id.* at 1:9-10; 103:12.

Caleb had honest intentions when he got the phrase "I [heart] boobies" shaved into his hair and does not understand why he should have to change his hair when his sister cannot change the fact that she has cancer. *Id.* at 103:1-2. Since Caleb did not participate in the inappropriate behavior that occurred in the cafeteria, it is not clear why he is being punished for that incident. *Id.* at 103:16-18.

Primarily seeking Caleb's return to Perkinsberg Middle School—while wearing the haircut—and compensation for the costs of attending a private school, Plaintiffs sued Defendant for violation of Caleb's First Amendment right to free speech on November 23, 2011. Compl. Defendant denies that it violated Plaintiff's First Amendment right to free speech, claiming that it has the "right to regulate disruptive or offensive conduct." Answer ¶ 4. Defendant now moves this Court under Minnesota Rule of Civil Procedure 56 to grant summary judgment in its favor. Def.'s Mot. Summ. J.

ARGUMENT

The party seeking to defeat a motion for summary judgment must prove that there are genuine issues of material fact or that the moving party is not entitled to judgment as a matter of law. Minn. R. Civ. P. 56.01, 56.03; *DLH, Inc. v. Russ*, 56 N.W.2d 60, 71 (Minn. 1997). Thus, when there are no genuine issues of material fact, the case rests on how the law applies to the facts and whether the moving party is entitled to judgment as a matter of law.

In this case, the facts and the law—viewed in a light most favorable to the Plaintiff as the non-moving party—do not support a grant of summary judgment to Defendant. *See Bennett v. Storz Broad. Co.*, 134 N.W.2d 892, 897 (1965). Plaintiff, as a student in a public school, has a First Amendment right to express himself, and the phrase "I [heart] boobies" in his haircut neither was lewd or offensive nor caused substantial disturbance. The Defendant violated Plaintiff's First Amendment right to free speech by suspending him until he removed the expression. Therefore, this Court should deny the Defendant's Motion for Summary Judgment.

EXHIBIT 17B (cont.)

I. The Defendant violated Plaintiff's First Amendment right to free speech and is not entitled to summary judgment because "I [heart] boobies" is not lewd, vulgar, indecent, or offensive.

Public school students have a constitutionally protected right to free speech and freedom of expression, including the right to govern their personal appearance. *Tinker v. Des Moines Indep. Cmty. Sch. Dist.*, 393 U.S. 503, 513-14 (1969) (about the wearing of black armbands).

Under the standard set by the Court in *Bethel School District No. 403 v. Fraser*, 478 U.S. 675, 683 (1986), a school may prohibit speech that is considered "lewd, vulgar, indecent, or offensive." Lewd and offensive speech typically refers to words with inherent sexual association, words that are profane, and words that are contrary to the school's educational mission. *Id.* at 683-85.

A school cannot simply apply the *Fraser* standard every time it decides that a student's expression undermines its educational mission. *Guiles v. Marineau*, 461 F.3d 320, 330 (2d Cir. 2006). Although public schools do have narrow authority to decide what things are and are not appropriate in an educational environment, their authority to regulate student speech and expression is not absolute. *Tinker*, 393 U.S. at 511. In order for the *Fraser* standard to apply, it must be clear that the language in question has an inherent sexual association, is profane, or is plainly offensive. *Fraser*, 478 U.S. at 683-85.

In *Gillman v. School Board for Holmes County*, 567 F. Supp. 2d 1359, 1370 (N.D. Fla. 2008), the wearing or displaying of symbols or phrases that advocated tolerance and support of homosexuals was not found to undermine the school's educational mission, part of which was to promote tolerance, acceptance, fairness, and support of different groups. The court in *Gillman* overturned the school board's prohibition of such phrases or symbols. *Id.*

Similarly, Caleb's choice to display a phrase that is part of a national breast cancer awareness campaign in support of his sister's struggle with breast cancer is not contrary to a school's educational mission. The message of the phrase "I [heart] boobies" is a positive one, used to communicate the importance of breast cancer awareness to a target audience, specifically including young women. *H. v. Easton Area Sch. Dist.*, No. 10 6283, 2011 WL 1276141, at *11 (E.D. Pa. Apr. 12, 2011).[7] It would be contrary to public policy for a school to claim that advocating awareness and support for breast cancer among young public school students is contrary to its educational mission.

If a word or phrase could possibly have different meanings, it is important to analyze the context of the language to determine what meaning was intended. In *Fraser*, the student deliberately used sexual innuendo in his speech nominating a classmate for student elective office. He delivered the speech at a high school assembly that was part of a school-sponsored educational program in self-government. 478 U.S. at 677-78.

In the present case, the language was not used in any way that was meant to be sexual; rather, it was used to support Caleb's sister in her fight with breast cancer and to increase

---

7. This memorandum was written before the district court decision was published at 827 F. Supp. 2d 392 and affirmed en banc by the Third Circuit in 2013 at 725 F.3d 293.

EXHIBIT 17B (cont.)

awareness about breast cancer. Although not all middle school students may be aware that "I [heart] boobies" is a phrase related to a national breast cancer awareness movement, Caleb was willing to explain the phrase to everyone who asked. The breast cancer awareness bracelets are also becoming popular in schools now, so it would be reasonable to assume that a lot of middle school students have some idea about what the phrase is associated with. Additionally, the phrase "I [heart] boobies" should not be considered vulgar when it is used by the media in the context of a national breast cancer awareness campaign. *Easton*, 2011 WL 1276141 at *11.

The Defendant is unable to establish that the phrase "I [heart] boobies" is lewd, vulgar, indecent, plainly offensive, or that the phrase is contrary to the school's educational mission as a matter of law. Therefore, the school district is not entitled to summary judgment under *Fraser.*

II. The Defendant violated Plaintiff's First Amendment right to free speech and is not entitled to summary judgment because Plaintiff's haircut did not cause a substantial disturbance.

A. The incident in question was not intended by or caused by any conduct of the Plaintiff.

Given the inapplicability of the *Fraser* standard, the case is then properly analyzed under the standard set out in *Tinker v. Des Moines Independent Community School District*, 393 U.S. 503 (1969). In *Tinker*, three students wore black armbands to school as a symbolic expression publicizing their objections to the Vietnam War. The students were suspended for violating school policy. The Court overturned the policy and held that school officials could not ban the students' expression. *Id.* at 514.

To prohibit speech under *Tinker*, a school must show material and substantial interference with the operation of the school. *Id.* at 509. Additionally, *Tinker* requires that the school show "more than a mere desire to avoid the discomfort and unpleasantness that always accompany an unpopular viewpoint" to justify prohibition of student speech or expression. *Id.* "Undifferentiated fear or apprehension of disturbance is not enough to overcome the right to freedom of expression." *Id. Tinker* emphasizes the specific conduct of the student when determining whether his expression caused or could reasonably cause a material and substantial disruption of schoolwork or discipline. The actions and intentions of the student displaying the phrase or symbol are significantly more important to analyze than are the actions of the onlookers. *Id.* at 513.

When Caleb chose to display the phrase "I [heart] boobies" on the back of his head, he did not intend to cause any disturbance within the school. Similar to the students in *Tinker,* who wore the armbands to promote awareness of their views and to encourage others to adopt them, Caleb was trying to support his sister and raise awareness about breast cancer. Caleb explained that he chose to get his hair cut with that phrase, rather than wearing a bracelet or a t-shirt with the phrase on it, because cancer patients often lose their hair during their treatment. Additionally, Caleb gladly explained the meaning behind his haircut whenever he was asked. Thus, Caleb did not intend his haircut to cause any disturbance.

Caleb's case resembles others where students had no intent to cause a disturbance. For example, in *Bragg v. Swanson*, 371 F. Supp. 2d 814, 820 (S.D.W. Va. 2005), wearing

EXHIBIT 17B (cont.)

clothing with the Confederate flag on it was permissible because the student had no intent to cause a disruption. Here too, Caleb's haircut should also be permissible.

In addition, the incident in the cafeteria was not instigated by any conduct of Caleb's. He did not support the conduct of the other students and felt bad for the student who was touched. Brown Dep. 101:5-9. Although the incident in the cafeteria was influenced by Caleb's haircut, no conduct of Caleb's directly caused the occurrence.

Incidents happen in schools for a number of reasons, and it would be senseless to ban, punish, or prohibit every unintentional trigger of those incidents. It seems that Caleb is being punished more for the inappropriate behavior of the other students in the cafeteria than he is for the expression in his hair—an improper impingement on his First Amendment right to free speech.

B. The event in the cafeteria did not constitute a substantial and material interference with the school's learning environment.

Not only did Caleb not intend or instigate the event in the cafeteria, the fact that an incident did occur should not deprive him of his right to freedom of expression. Following the *Tinker* standard, the Defendant is required to prove that the incident in the cafeteria substantially and materially interfered with Perkinsberg Middle School's learning environment to justify the suspension and ban of Caleb's haircut. 393 U.S. at 509.

First, the incident occurred in the cafeteria, not in the classroom or in the hallway. The cafeteria is a place for students to socialize and take a break from schoolwork, so the incident did not interfere with the actual learning environment of the school.

Second, proof exists that similar incidents occurred at Perkinsberg before the Plaintiff's haircut. Defendant admitted that incidents involving male students touching female students and making inappropriate comments towards them have occurred at the school in the past. Such incidents are not uncommon and are actually expected from students in middle school, who have not yet reached maturity and who are just becoming aware of human sexuality. For that reason, isolated incidents such as the one in this case "are well within a school's ability to maintain discipline and order." *See Easton*, 2011 WL 1276141, at *14.

H. v. Easton Area School District, a recently decided case, addresses whether the suspension of middle school students for wearing "I [heart] boobies" bracelets was a violation of their First Amendment right to free speech. The court discussed two incidents that occurred: one in which boys were making inappropriate remarks about "boobies" and another in which a boy said "I want boobies" and made inappropriate gestures. *Id.* at *6. Under the *Tinker* standard, the court held that the incidents failed to create a substantial disruption of the magnitude required for justification of a ban of the bracelets. *Id.* at *14.

The incident in the cafeteria at Perkinsberg Middle School is comparable to those that occurred in *Easton*. The school handled the incident appropriately and was able to maintain discipline. The incident was not substantial enough to interfere with the school's learning environment: all students returned to class as usual after it occurred, and there is

EXHIBIT 17B (cont.)

no evidence that many students even knew of the incident. Although there was inappropriate physical contact in one case, the young man who behaved inappropriately should and did face punishment for that. A similar incident could have occurred if Caleb did not have the phrase "I [heart] boobies" in his hair, and a similar incident may not be prevented by suppressing Caleb's freedom of expression.

Students are considered people with rights under the Constitution. *Tinker*, 393 U.S. at 511. Public schools have only limited authority to regulate expression for reasons of disruption, and if there is no constitutionally valid reason to regulate a student's expression, the court must protect the student's rights. Under *Tinker,* the school district overstepped its bounds and should be denied summary judgment.

CONCLUSION

This case is primarily focused on how the law applies to these facts. The Defendant is not able to establish that "I [heart] boobies" is lewd or offensive or that Caleb's haircut interfered with the school's educational mission. Additionally, his haircut has not led to substantial and material interference with the learning environment or discipline of the school. Because there is sufficient evidence to allow a reasonable person to find for the Plaintiffs, Plaintiffs respectfully request that this Court deny Defendant's Motion for Summary Judgment.

Dated: <u>April 13, 2012</u>   VanPelt and Johnson, P.A.
                                      By: <u>Donna Johnson</u>[8]
                                      Donna Johnson (#100250)
                                      250 South Legionnaire Blvd
                                      Perkinsberg, MN 55555
                                      Phone: (507) 555-3333
                                      Fax: (507) 555-3334
                                      DJohnson@vpjlaw.com
                                      Attorneys for Plaintiffs
                                      Lynn, Brandon, & Caleb
                                      Brown

ACKNOWLEDGMENT

The undersigned acknowledges that sanctions may be imposed in the circumstances specified in Minnesota Statutes section 549.211 (2010).

Dated: <u>April 13, 2012</u>   <u>Donna Johnson</u>
                                      Donna Johnson (#100250)

---

8. This paper was written by Annalise Backstrom while a first-year student at William Mitchell College of Law and has been only lightly edited. My thanks to Annalise for permitting its use here.—DS

TEST YOUR UNDERSTANDING

1. Assume that you are representing Sarah Nicholson in her dispute with Bower's Bounty and that it is entering litigation. Define civil litigation.

2. What is a motion, and what is the difference between dispositive and non-dispositive motions?

3. For each of the three following phases of litigation, explain what would happen in Ms. Nicholson's case, and name a standard motion:
   a. Framing the case
   b. Exchanging information through discovery
   c. Obtaining a decision

4. Assume that Bower's Bounty has brought a motion for summary judgment.
   a. Who is the movant, and who is the non-movant?
   b. Who writes the following documents, and what is the purpose of each: notice of motion, motion, and proposed order?
   c. List the memoranda, and identify who writes which.
   d. What are the two possible systems for assigning the motion to a judge?
   e. Why would Bower's Bounty bring this motion, and why would Ms. Nicholson defend against this motion?

5. What are the two sets of rules applicable to a motion, and what are the different coverages of these rules?

6. Who is the audience for the memorandum that you will write on behalf of Ms. Nicholson?

7. For each of the following standard components of a motion practice memorandum, explain its purpose, and state a key point about writing it:
   a. Caption
   b. Summary and introduction
   c. Issues
   d. Facts
   e. Procedure
   f. Argument
   g. Point headings in the argument
   h. Conclusion with signature block

8. List the categories of facts that you could cover in your memorandum, and indicate which you must, may, and would not include.

9. List the categories of legal authorities that you could cover in your memorandum, and indicate which you must versus may include.

TEST YOUR UNDERSTANDING ANSWERS

1. Civil litigation is the process of resolving disputes through the application of legal rules to proven facts in court, where the government is not serving as a prosecutor.

2. A motion is a request that a court take the desired action. A dispositive motion seeks a resolution of the case; a non-dispositive motion does not seek a resolution of the case.

3. As for the three phases of litigation:
   a. Framing the case—The parties file the complaint and answer (and possibly other pleadings), and other parties may be brought in. A standard motion is dismissal for failure to state a claim.
   b. Exchanging information through discovery—The parties exchange information through admissions, interrogatories, production of documents, and depositions. A standard motion is to compel discovery.
   c. Obtaining a decision—The parties come to a resolution through settlement, by aid of a third-party neutral, by motion, or through trial. A standard motion is summary judgment.

4. As for Bower's Bounty motion for summary judgment.
   a. Bower's Bounty is the movant, and Ms. Nicholson is the non-movant.
   b. Bower's Bounty, as the movant, writes the documents. The notice of motion alerts the non-movant to the motion, the motion makes the request to the court, and the proposed order is a draft that the court may consider if it decides to grant the motion.
   c. The movant writes a memorandum in support of the motion, the non-movant writes a memorandum in opposition to the motion, and the movant may write a reply memorandum.
   d. The motions may be assigned to a judge by calendar or block system.
   e. Bower's Bounty would bring this motion primarily to win the case and secondarily to learn of Ms. Nicholson's strategies and the judge's view of the case, which could promote settlement. Ms. Nicholson would defend against this motion so as to avoid losing the case and to influence the judge in her favor.

5. The rules of procedure set the main standard, and local court rules cover such matters as timing and memorandum format.

6. The audiences for a memorandum are the judge and his or her clerk, the opponent and its counsel, and the client.

7. The purpose of and some key points about the following standard components of a motion practice memorandum are:
   a. Caption—The caption lists the parties, court, docket number, and document title. It is important to follow local rules concerning additional information and format.

b. Summary and introduction—These two items frame the dispute and the motion and begin to orient the reader, with the summary adding an overview of the argument. They should be written persuasively.

c. Issues—The issues pose concise questions answered in the memorandum in the sequence that they appear in the argument. They also should be written persuasively.

d. Facts—This statement recounts the events that gave rise to the litigation, including the relevant and background facts, both favorable and unfavorable. It should recount the story from the client's perspective and must include citations to the record.

e. Procedure—This statement sets out the history of the litigation up to the current motion. It proceeds in chronological order.

f. Argument—This longest component establishes why the client is entitled to the relief that she seeks, based on a legal analysis that ties together an accurate statement of the substantive and procedural law, thorough legal reasoning, and discussion of the opponent's argument on debatable points. It is important to confront adverse material and provide citations.

g. Point headings in the argument—These full-sentence assertions capture the main points that the court must accept to rule in the client's favor and appear in prominent type throughout the memorandum. They may include major and minor point headings.

h. Conclusion with signature block—The conclusion states the relief requested, and it is followed by a signature block with contact information. The conclusion may also include a brief synopsis of the argument.

8. Relevant facts must be included (whether favorable or unfavorable); background facts should be included to the extent needed for the story to make sense (whether favorable or unfavorable); limited favorable residual facts may be included, but unfavorable residual facts should not be included.

9. Favorable mandatory authority is required, as is unfavorable mandatory authority that the opponent does not raise. It is wise to discuss unfavorable mandatory authority in any event. Persuasive precedent and commentary may be used but need not be cited if unfavorable.

THE APPELLATE BRIEF

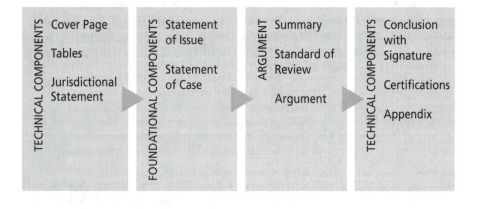

Be brief, be pointed, let your matter stand
Lucid in order, solid and at hand;
Spend not your words on trifles but condense;
Strike with the mass of thought, not drops of sense;
Press to the close with vigor, once begun,
And leave—how hard the task!—leave off when done.
—Joseph Story
Advice to a Young Lawyer

A. INTRODUCTION

Although the vast majority of legal disputes end in settlement or a district court judgment, some do not, for various reasons. A party may simply be unwilling to abide by the district court judgment for financial, emotional, or reputational reasons. Or a party may believe that the district court committed a serious error that affected the outcome. In other cases, the law governing the dispute may be uncertain, two public policies may conflict, or the issue may have very wide repercussions. *Appellate litigation* is the means of handling these cases.

How does a lawyer reverse a loss or defend a win in the district court? And, when the occasion arises, how does a lawyer participate in making law? The adept appellate lawyer knows how to operate in a procedurally and intellectually complex system, refines the theory of the case to incorporate its appellate posture, and delivers a nuanced argument. The appellate lawyer operates squarely within ethical constraints and uses the model of legal advocacy discussed in Chapter 16.

This chapter thus begins by providing an overview of several topics that are essential background for writing effectively to an appellate court. The chapter then proceeds to discuss the persuasive analytical document written to an appellate court: the appellate brief.

For examples, this chapter draws on two appellate briefs from a real case, shown in Exhibits 18A and 18B. The case is *B.H. v. Easton Area School District*, on appeal to the Third Circuit Court of Appeals from the United States District Court for the Eastern District of Pennsylvania. The district court ruled in favor of students who wore rubber bracelets with the slogan "I [heart-symbol] Boobies!," provided by the Keep a Breast Foundation, to their middle school,[1] and the school district appealed this ruling. The Third Circuit affirmed.[2] Please consult these briefs as you read this chapter.

B. THE APPELLATE SETTING

1. The Role of Appeals

Appeals provide important *benefits* to our legal system. Most obviously, an appeal serves as a check on the district court. The district court judge is engaged in a venture with some potential for error, which may be due to inadvertence, mistakes in judgment, or, less commonly, bias. Hence, the case may benefit from a second analysis by a removed observer, the appellate court.

Appeals also benefit the legal system by providing a mechanism for making law. Appellate courts are collegial bodies of experienced and respected judges who have gained broad perspective on legal issues from seeing a range of district court results. Thus, appellate courts have the authority to make precedent, promoting uniformity and the best public policy.

Yet the appellate system has several *disadvantages*. Appeals add delay to the judicial resolution of disputes and prolong the strain of litigation. They impose costs on the parties and society: salaries for the judges and court personnel, building and equipment costs, and additional attorney and filing fees for the parties.

To achieve these benefits and minimize these disadvantages, the appellate process differs markedly from the district court process. As discussed in Chapter 16, a district court is the court of first impression. In some cases, the district judge resolves the cases by motion. Alternatively, at trial, the case is presented through the parties, experts, other witnesses, documents, and other exhibits. District courts focus primarily on ascertaining the facts of the case and applying the law to the facts; they focus only secondarily on making law.

By comparison, appellate courts determine whether the district court properly ruled on motions, properly applied the substantive and procedural law; they

---

1. The district court ruling is reported at 827 F. Supp. 2d 392.
2. The Third Circuit decision is reported at 725 F.3d 293.

also examine the fact findings (whether by judge or jury) for support in the record. Cases arrive at the appellate court in file folders and boxes (or, increasingly, electronically submitted files) containing the transcript of the trial and hearings, the pleadings and other discovery, and the briefs of the parties. The only in-person contact is the oral argument and perhaps a pre-argument conference between the attorneys and a judge. The party bringing the appeal is the *appellant or petitioner;* the party against whom the appeal is brought is the *respondent or appellee.* The appellate court may *affirm, reverse, or modify* the district court judgment, or it may *remand* the case to the district court with instructions. See Box 18.1.

Most jurisdictions have *two levels of appellate courts.* The *judges* of the intermediate appellate court focuses on correcting errors. While the high court supervises the lower and intermediate courts, its *justices* focus on making law and its underlying policies. For brevity's sake, this chapter generally uses the term "judges" to include both judges of the intermediate court and justices of the high court.

At the intermediate appellate court, cases typically are heard by a *panel of judges;* three is the most common number. Intermediate courts hear only unusually important cases *en banc,* i.e., as a full court; sometimes after a panel hears a case initially, a full court may rehear the case if the losing party convinces the full court of its significance. As a general rule, the high court hears all cases en banc, which typically involves seven or nine justices. Whatever the number of judges hearing your case, they are likely to have a range of backgrounds, areas of expertise, worldviews, and preliminary leanings in cases like yours.

BOX 18.1

COMPARISON OF DISTRICT COURT PROCEEDINGS AND APPEALS

	District Court	Appeals Courts	
		Intermediate	High
Primary Role of Court	Initial determination through application of law to fact	Review of district court outcome and procedure	Policy and lawmaking
Decision-makers	Judge; sometimes jury	Usually a panel of judges	Usually entire court
Parties	Plaintiff and defendant	Appellant/petitioner and respondent/appellee	
Presentation of Case	Pleadings, motions, memoranda, witnesses, exhibits, oral arguments	Transcript of trial, pleadings, motions, memoranda, exhibits; lower court opinion(s); briefs and oral arguments	
Possible Outcomes	Dismissal, judgment for plaintiff, judgment for defendant	Affirm, reverse, modify, remand	

As an example, the Third Circuit decision in the *B.H.* case was rendered en banc, with fourteen judges participating. The court split, nine to five. This unusual decision pattern demonstrates the significance and difficulty of the constitutional issues in this case.

2. The Law of Appellate Review

A considerable body of appellate law operates to constrain what could otherwise be an enormous number of hasty and ill-considered appeals. This body of law has three categories of rules: the types of review that a court exercises, the types of district court rulings that are subject to review, and the degree of scrutiny to which a district court ruling is subjected.

a. Appeal as of Right and Discretionary Review

Some appeals arise as a *matter of right*. In almost every jurisdiction, the intermediate appellate court must take nearly every appeal because a constitution or statute guarantees the right to one appeal. In many jurisdictions, some very serious cases, such as capital punishment or life imprisonment cases, are granted appeal to the high court as a matter of right.

In a two-tier appellate system, as to most cases, the high court exercises *discretionary review*. The would-be appellant petitions to the high court for a writ of certiorari compelling a lower court to transfer the record to the high court; this writ is either granted or denied. The justices vote on which cases to hear.[3] The following factors favor grant of review: there are conflicting rulings among the intermediate courts of appeals, the case involves important or pressing questions, the lower court has ruled on the constitutionality of a statute, the lower court departed from established precedent, or the high court seeks to harmonize or rules across a set of cases.[4] Because the decision to deny review is not a decision on the merits of the case, there is no precedential value to the denial of review.

In recognition of our federal system of government, federal courts sometimes *abstain from reviewing* cases in a range of situations, thereby deferring to state courts. For example, the U.S. Supreme Court generally will not review a state supreme court decision that a government action violates both the state and federal constitutions because the violation of the state constitution as interpreted by the high court of that state is sufficient to uphold the judgment.

As an example, the school district's appeal in the *B.H.* case to the Third Circuit was an appeal as of right. The school district also petitioned for a writ of certiorari to the Supreme Court, which the Court in its discretion denied.[5]

b. The Scope of an Appeal

Usually one party is the winner in district court, the other is the loser, and the appeal is brought by the party that lost at the district court. The appellant may

---

3. For example, four or more of the nine members of the U.S. Supreme Court must vote in favor of review for the petitioner to obtain a writ of certiorari.

4. The factors prompting discretionary review may be published in the court's rules, provided for by a statute on the court's jurisdiction, developed on a case-by-case basis, or presented in articles written by the justices.

5. 134 S. Ct. 1515 (2014).

appeal all adverse rulings of the district court. However, sometimes the appellant appeals only a portion of the final judgment because there is no reversible error (explained below) in the unappealed portions of the case, a successful appeal as to certain matters would not have enough impact to be worth the cost, or a portion of the case is better left as is (because, for example, the factual record is weak).

A more complex case may lead to a *cross-appeal*. In these cases, both parties win and lose different rulings in the case. For example, the plaintiff may win on liability but lose on damages. If both parties are unhappy with the district court outcome, both parties may appeal. Thus, in a cross-appeal, both parties are simultaneously appellants and respondents.

Furthermore, three rules on the *scope of appellate review* define which district court rulings are properly before the appellate court. These rules preserve the proper roles of the district and appellate courts, set the timing of an appeal, and in effect reduce the likelihood of appeals.

First, most appeals must be taken from a *final judgment*, which means that the district court judgment was final as to the entire case (or perhaps as to a claim or a party). A final judgment may be, for example, a grant of a motion to dismiss the whole case or a jury verdict followed by a judgment entered on the verdict. Decisions that are not final include denial of a motion to dismiss and rulings on evidence to be admitted at trial. The final judgment rule gives the district court an opportunity to conclude the case before appeal.

Occasionally, however, a party will want to appeal a non-final ruling of the district court, i.e., an *interlocutory appeal*. Appellate courts routinely grant some interlocutory appeals, such as an appeal from an order granting, denying, or dissolving an injunction. Generally, however, appellate rules discourage interlocutory appeals because the would-be appellant could nonetheless go on to win the case and because a more completely adjudicated case will have a stronger factual record for the court to review on appeal.

A limited exception to the final judgment rule is when a district court *certifies a question* to an appellate court. When a trial court considers a major issue in the case to be unsettled by mandatory precedent, it may seek an appellate ruling early in the case. Certifying a question can occur within the federal court system, within the state court system, or from a federal district court to the high court of the state whose law governs the question. Rules of procedure vary as to when certified questions are allowed.

The second rule on scope of review is the *bar on new facts and legal issues* on appeal. The district court need not have been apprised of every case, argument, and alternative line of reasoning presented on appeal, but the district court must have had a chance to address the basic issues. This rule gives parties the incentive to present the case fully to the district court and maximizes the likelihood of a correct ruling in the first instance. For any issue that one may want to raise on appeal, there is a means of preserving the issue for appeal during the district court proceedings. These means include motions and objections to evidence during trial.

The third rule on scope of review is the *reversible error rule*. The appellate court is interested only in errors that are substantial enough to justify reversal (in whole or in part) of the district court judgment. An error meeting this test is labeled "reversible error," and an error not meeting this test is labeled "harmless error." An error is not reversible if the district court reached the right result, even if the decision was based on incorrect reasoning.

As an example, the appeal in *B.H.* is an interlocutory appeal, but it fits within the rule that permits appeals arising out of rulings involving preliminary injunctions.

c. Standards of Appellate Review

The *standard of review* applied to an appeal sets the degree of scrutiny that the appellate court applies to the decision of the district court; it is a key element of the appellate lawyer's argument. Stated another way, appellate courts defer to the district court decision to a greater or lesser degree based on the type of ruling or judgment under appeal. The wording varies from jurisdiction to jurisdiction; the following phrasings are typical:

- Rulings within the *discretion of the district court*, such as whether to allow the plaintiff to amend the complaint a second time, can be overturned only if the ruling was an abuse of discretion—that is, arbitrary or capricious.
- A *jury verdict* is upheld unless, as a matter *of law*, reasonable minds could not have reached the jury's conclusions.
- *Findings of fact by a trial judge* can be overturned if they are clearly erroneous or contrary to the manifest weight of evidence.
- A judge's rulings on *questions* of law are reviewed de novo and can be overturned if the lower court ruled incorrectly on the law.

As an example, the standard of appellate review for a preliminary injunction is a mixed standard because the district court engages in various types of rulings. Thus, the legal conclusions are reviewed de novo, the findings of fact for clear error, and the balancing of factors related to harm to the parties and the public for abuse of discretion.

3. Appellate Procedure

Although the details of appellate procedure differ among jurisdictions, the major steps are essentially the same from court to court. See Box 18.2.

The preparation for an appeal actually occurs during the *district court proceedings*. An appeal is grounded in the pleadings, discovery, motions, and trial, where the important facts and legal theories are first brought to the attention of the court and any errors are preserved for the appeal.

Within a specified time after the district court has ruled, the appellant must file a *notice of appeal* with the appellate court and serve it on the opponent. Shortly thereafter, if the respondent also wants to appeal some issues, it may initiate a cross-appeal.

Meanwhile, the appellant must arrange for *compilation of the record*. The typical record of a fully litigated case contains pleadings, motions, orders of the district court, exhibits, a transcript of the trial proceedings, the charge to the jury, the verdict, the judgment, and the notice of appeal. The respondent may identify additional portions to be included in the record.

Also during this time, the appellate court may require a *pre-hearing conference* between one of the appellate judges or the court's designee and the parties' counsel, to focus or narrow the issues and to discuss what material the court would like covered. During this period, as well as later, settlement talks may occur between counsel.

BOX 18.2

STAGES OF CIVIL APPELLATE LITIGATION

Preparing for Appeal at the District Court

- Drafting and amending pleadings
- Making all appropriate pre-trial motions
- Getting all needed facts into evidence or, if the judge rules a fact inadmissible, noted in the record
- Making needed objections and motions to preserve issues for appeal
- Briefing all issues thoroughly

Framing the Appeal

- Appellant files and serves the notice of appeal
- Appellant arranges for the compilation of the record
- Respondent may cross-appeal and add to the record
- An appellate court judge may hold a pre-hearing conference

Presenting the Argument

- Appellant files its initial brief
- Respondent files its brief
- Appellant may file its reply brief
- Amici may file briefs, if allowed by the court
- Counsel present oral arguments

The appeal moves into the *argument* stage with the filing and serving of the *written briefs*. The appellant's initial brief asks the court to reverse or modify the judgment of the district court and sets out the legal bases for the request. The respondent's brief responds to appellant's arguments and also sets forth affirmative arguments as to why the district court ruled correctly in the respondent's favor. The appellant may file a reply brief, which addresses any unexpected points in the respondent's brief that merit rebuttal.

Following the exchange of briefs, the parties may engage in *oral arguments* before the court. Oral arguments are mandatory before some courts, rare before others; the practice of most courts falls somewhere in between. The oral argument is counsel's last chance to convince the court, but it certainly does not take the place of well-written briefs. Oral argument is discussed in detail in Chapter 19.

Some appeals involve participation by an *amicus curiae*—"friend of the court." An amicus brief is written by a non-party with a strong stake in the outcome of the case; the amicus typically is an organization with an important perspective on the public policy aspects of the case. The appellate court decides whether to let amici participate in the case, based on whether they will contribute a viewpoint or argument that the parties are not likely to present.

As you prepare an appeal, you should research the appellate rules of your jurisdiction—and prepare to follow them to the letter. For instance, your failure to file a brief within the prescribed briefing period may deprive your client of the right to oral argument. See Box 18.3 for a case discussing the impact of a late filing.

BOX 18.3

WHAT HAPPENS WHEN YOU MISS THE DEADLINE?

As you read the following case, think about these questions:

1. *Why (do you think) did the lawyer not manage to catch this deadline?*
2. *What would you do to avoid this situation?*
3. *Is the penalty here appropriate? Would you have issued a different penalty?*

Martinelli v. Farm-Rite, Inc.,
785 A.2d 33 (N.J. Super. Ct. App. Div. 2001).

Plaintiff, who operates a farm in Hammonton, New Jersey, claims defendant supplied him with a defective water pump resulting in the loss of his blueberry crop in 1993. Suit was filed on October 30, 1998 and the case was referred to arbitration on May 19, 2000 . . . .

Upon completion of the arbitration proceeding, the arbitrators assessed liability at eighty percent upon defendant and twenty percent upon plaintiff; they awarded plaintiff damages of $150,000. Neither party filed a notice of rejection of the award and demand for a trial *de novo* within thirty days after the arbitration award was filed. See R. 4:21A-6(b)(1). On June 20, 2000, plaintiff filed a motion to confirm the arbitration award, R. 4:21A-6(b)(3), which defense counsel received on June 22, 2000. Upon receipt of the motion defense counsel reviewed his file. He discovered that due to an apparent system failure, his computerized diary had not alerted him to file a demand for a trial *de novo* within the thirty-day time period as required by R. 4:21A-6(b)(1).

Defense counsel's office was in the end stage of converting from an Alpha-Micro Mainframe Computer System to a local area network (LAN) PC Service System. Counsel relied on the computer "markup" system to diary statutes of limitations and other deadlines, including a diary notation to alert him when to file a demand for a trial *de novo*. Counsel had no backup diary system. Without dispute, counsel had no reason to suspect, in advance of the incident, that the system would not operate correctly. Not until counsel received the motion to confirm the arbitrators' award did the system failure become known and was the loss of the diary notation discovered.

At oral argument defense counsel acknowledged that he was unaware of any other circumstance in which the system failed. Although the reason for the system failure has not been conclusively determined, counsel suspects it was a malfunction of the system's software . . . .

A fact-sensitive analysis is necessary in each case to determine what constitutes an extraordinary circumstance [justifying a late filing]. *Hartsfield*, 149 N.J. at 618, 695 A.2d 259. In *Hartsfield*, the attorney's failure to supervise his secretary and review his diary was not considered an extraordinary circumstance. *Id.* at 619, 695 A.2d 259 . . . .

We agree that a computer malfunction is not sufficient justification for late submission of documents to the court, whether required by statute, court rule or court order. One does not need to be an expert to recognize that computers do not always work. It is not uncommon for previously accessible data to suddenly disappear. There can be any number of reasons why a computer system fails. There can be human errors inputting and accessing the data, electrical failures, power surges, and computer viruses. Not all programs are as dependable as others. Quite simply, systems fail regularly and do not always perform to their specifications. Such an occurrence is neither exceptional, unusual, nor without precedent . . . .

Computer failures, not unlike human failures, must be anticipated. Just as with a manual diary system, where it is commonplace to have at least one backup system available in anticipation of mistakes which are bound to be made by attorneys and other office staff, the same should hold true when a diary system is computerized. In today's environment a computer failure, which results in the late filing of a demand for trial *de novo*, must be treated the same as a wrong date marked on a calendar or the failure of an attorney to properly supervise staff. It is an occurrence that can be anticipated and guarded against . . . .

An attorney is compelled to determine the appropriate method to assure compliance with the thirty-day rule. To permit a computer failure to constitute an excuse to file late is contrary to the underlying goals of the arbitration process—to bring about an inexpensive, expeditious adjudication of disputes and to help ease the caseload of the courts. *Bum*, 286 N.J. Super. at 573-74, 670 A.2d 40 . . . .

[Thus, the lower court's ruling that there was no excuse was affirmed, and the case was dismissed.]

4. Appellate Strategy and Ethics

The appeal of a case may be handled by the lawyer who handled the case in the district court, or the case may pass to a new lawyer for the appeal. Although the original lawyer knows the case very well, a new lawyer may be more objective or have new insights, and the new lawyer will see the case as the appellate court will see it—through the record. Furthermore, litigation in the district court involves rather different skills than appellate practice; indeed, some lawyers specialize in appellate practice.

The process of choosing *whether to appeal* a case, and on which grounds, entails several steps. First, you must review the record to ascertain what did in fact occur in the district court. You should identify exactly what the witnesses said, which motions were made, and so on.

Second, you must apply the substantive and procedural law to the court's rulings; this analysis has several layers. Not only must you identify any errors, you also must determine that those errors fit within the rules on the scope of appellate review (e.g., the reversible error rule). Then you must evaluate each error according to the applicable standard of appellate review to decide whether, as a practical matter, your client has a strong enough argument to merit the appeal. You should set aside errors that could not overcome the applicable standard of review or could not do so without a stretch that the court is unlikely to make.

Third, once you have thus discerned the potential bases for appeal, you should explore the scope of the appeal with your client. Your client may not want to pursue one or more points, or your client may have a strong desire to pursue a particular point.

Once you have decided to appeal and the grounds for appeal, you should carefully consider *which arguments to make*. Few briefs contain more than three or four major arguments. Including more reduces the space for, and dilutes the effectiveness of, the stronger arguments. On occasion, you may make a large number of small arguments, in hopes of casting doubt on the overall fairness of the district court proceedings; this tactic is common in the appellant's brief for a losing criminal defendant.

BOX 18.4

HOW DO APPELLATE COURTS REACT TO MERITLESS APPEALS?

As you read the following case, think about these questions:

1. *Why (do you think) did the lawyer bring this appeal?*
2. *What would you do to avoid this situation?*
3. *Is the penalty here appropriate? Would you have issued a different penalty?*

Federated Mutual Insurance Co. v. Anderson,
920 P.2d 97 (Mont. 1996).

[Jones Equipment leased a feller buncher machine to Brent Anderson, doing business as Conifer Logging. The machine was delivered to Conifer on June 17, 1991, and it was destroyed by fire on July 17, 1991. Conifer notified its insurer, John Deere, of the loss on July 18, 1991. The insurance contract between John Deere and Conifer provided automatic coverage for new equipment provided that Conifer reported the acquisition and paid a new premium within thirty days of the acquisition.

Federated Mutual insured Jones Equipment and paid Jones for its loss. Federated then sought to recover from Conifer, which filed a third-party complaint against John Deere. The trial court denied John Deere's motion for summary judgment and granted Conifer summary judgment. John Deere appealed.]

As a final matter, Conifer requests that this Court sanction John Deere pursuant to Rule 32, M.R. App. P. Sanctions on appeal are appropriate when this Court "is satisfied from the record and the presentation of the appeal in a civil case that the same was taken without substantial or reasonable grounds." Rule 32, M.R. App. P.

This Court does not readily impose sanctions upon parties for filing frivolous appeals. However, given the inconsistent and conflicting positions John Deere has taken throughout this matter, its inaccurate citations to authority, and the lack of support for its claims on appeal, we conclude that sanctions are necessary and appropriate in this case.

John Deere's . . . argument . . . is that no automatic coverage existed because the feller buncher was destroyed thirty-one days after Conifer acquired it. According to John Deere, the day that the feller buncher was delivered must be counted in calculating the thirty-day period of automatic coverage. John Deere's argument, however, is contrary to the universal rule that, unless a contrary intent is clearly manifested, the first day or the day upon which the act was done or the event occurred is generally excluded in computing periods of time. Even more troubling is the fact that, as part of its effort to urge this Court to adopt a different method of calculation, John Deere cites four cases in support of its position; however, three of those cases actually cite the general rule that the first day should be excluded in calculating the thirty-day grace period in insurance contracts and the fourth case was effectively overruled more than 120 years ago. For example, John Deere cites *American National Bank v. Service Lift Insurance Co.* (7th Cir. 1941), 120 F.2d 579, 582, *cert. denied* (1941), 314 U.S. 654 . . . to further its argument; however, on the same page to which John Deere cites, the court states: "[W]e think the weight of authority supports the rule of excluding the first day and including the last where no other or different method has been indicated by the parties."

. . .

Finally, John Deere's sincerity on appeal must be questioned in light of its inconsistent theories for denial of coverage which have culminated in this meritless appeal. For example, on July 18, 1991, John Deere's insurance agent wrote on the property loss notice that the policy's "30 day coverage extension should apply." On August 21, 1991, however, one of John Deere's insurance adjusters notified Conifer that John Deere was denying coverage because the thirty-day "waiting period" would not have been satisfied until July 24, 1991.

Because of John Deere's meritless appeal, Conifer has incurred unnecessary and substantial legal fees to obtain the coverage to which the District Court determined it was entitled under each of its theories. In addition, Conifer has been caused unnecessary delay during the pendency of this appeal. As we stated in *Reilly v. Farm Credit Bank of Spokane* (1993), 261 Mont. 532, 535, 863 P.2d 420, 422: "When an appeal is entirely unfounded and causes delay, the respondent is entitled to reasonable costs and attorney's fees."

Therefore, on the basis of the inconsistent and conflicting positions John Deere has taken throughout this matter, its baseless claims on appeal, and its inaccurate citations in its appellate brief, we assess sanctions against John Deere pursuant to Rule 32, M.R. App. P., and order it to pay Conifer's reasonable costs and attorney fees incurred in defending this appeal.

Your choice of arguments should reflect your *theory of the case*, as discussed in Chapter 16. Appellate courts seek a coherent and compelling understanding of your case to rule in your favor. Thus, your theory should mesh the facts, substantive law, procedural law, and policy; the procedural components should weave in the appellate court's standard of review, along with the procedure from the district court. For example, if the jury favored your client, stress the deference appellate courts afford juries.

The *respondent's task* is to respond to the grounds for appeal selected by the appellant. If the appellant does not raise an anticipated issue, you need not address it. If, as respondent's counsel, you are considering a cross-appeal, you would follow the process just described. Whether shaping a cross-appeal or deciding which arguments to make on an issue raised by your opponent, you should develop your theory of the case as just discussed.

In selecting grounds for appeal, as well as points to cover in the brief, both appellant's and respondent's counsel must comply with the ethical principles regarding legal advocacy. Those rules, detailed in Chapter 16, preclude pursuing frivolous claims or defenses, knowingly presenting false statements of fact, and knowingly failing to disclose known and adverse precedent not disclosed by opposing counsel. These rules are specific expressions of the lawyer's general duty to the legal system, as well as to the client, to act with candor and with respect for the law. See Box 18.4 for a case discussing a meritless appeal.

As an example, the appellant in the *B.H.* case chose to appeal the only ruling of the district court: granting the plaintiffs-students' motion for a preliminary injunction to keep the defendant-school district from enforcing the restrictions on the bracelets that they sought to wear. That ruling involves the intersection of the substantive law on free speech and the procedural law of preliminary injunctions. Both parties elected to discuss the same two strands of free speech case law and all four elements of the preliminary injunction test. However, their respective theories of the case differ significantly. See Box 18.5.

BOX 18.5

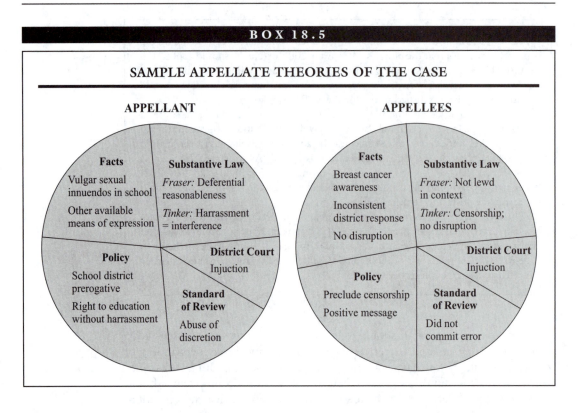

SAMPLE APPELLATE THEORIES OF THE CASE

APPELLANT

Facts
Vulgar sexual innuendos in school

Other available means of expression

Substantive Law
Fraser: Deferential reasonableness

Tinker: Harrassment = interference

District Court
Injuction

Standard of Review
Abuse of discretion

Policy
School district prerogative

Right to education without harrassment

APPELLEES

Facts
Breast cancer awareness

Inconsistent district response

No disruption

Substantive Law
Fraser: Not lewd in context

Tinker: Censorship; no disruption

District Court
Injuction

Standard of Review
Did not commit error

Policy
Preclude censorship

Positive message

C. THE APPELLATE BRIEF

1. Audience and Purpose

The primary *audience* of an appellate brief is, of course, the court: the judges and their clerks. The primary purpose of the appellate brief is, of course, to persuade the court to rule in your client's favor and to do so based on sound legal and factual bases. To persuade the court, you must fully inform these readers about your client's situation, educate those who know little about the area of law involved, and demonstrate the justness of your client's position to those who are skeptical. See Box 18.6 for several appellate judges' statements of what they seek in appellate briefs.

Your brief also will be read by opposing counsel and your client. The brief should convince opposing counsel of the strengths of your case, thereby enhancing the chances of settlement, if that possibility still exists at such a late stage. For your client, your brief should demonstrate your continuing commitment to the case.

2. Overview of the Principal Brief

Every court has its own governing *rules* as to appellate brief format, so you should always read and follow the rules of the court to which you are submitting your brief, which may include both a main set of rules of appellate procedure and a set of local rules. If either set of rules has an appendix of forms, be sure to consult these forms as well. Rules pertaining to the sample briefs, Exhibits 18A and 18B,

BOX 18.6

WHAT DO APPELLATE JUDGES SEEK IN APPELLATE BRIEFS?[6]

A brief will be most helpful to the judge, and net the brief-writer the greatest gain, if the judge can use the brief to compose an opinion in the brief-writer's favor. A kitchen-sink presentation may confound and annoy the reader more than it enlightens her. In busy courts, judges work under the pressure of a relentless clock. If a brief runs too long, the judge may not read beyond the summary of the argument. The same fate may attend a brief that makes arguments a judge cannot reasonably be expected to buy. Of prime importance, a brief should be trustworthy. If authorities are not accurately described, the judge will lose confidence in the reliability of the brief and its author; if the judge reads on at all, she will do so with a skeptical eye.

   —Hon. Ruth Bader Ginsburg, Supreme Court of the United States

A judge, when writing an opinion, strives to craft precise and well-formulated legal holdings that derive from careful analysis of the facts, the procedural posture of the case, interpretation of relevant documents and application of relevant authority. A brief must adhere to those same standards of precision and care.

   —Hon. E. Norman Veasey, Chief Justice, Supreme Court of Delaware

The purpose of the brief is to persuade me that the outcome the writer wants the court to reach is the correct outcome, and the path to that outcome is the correct one. Careful, cogent thought, clearly and cogently expressed, is what convinces me. The brief-writer is most helpful to me when she tells me not only what decision to reach but how to get there.

   Never loosely speculate about what the judge might think is important. Brief-writers should make it so clear that the judge will instantly know what is important and why. Discuss that and little else.

   —Hon. John M Duhé Jr., U.S. Court of Appeals for the Fifth Circuit

---

appear in Exhibit 18C. Please look over those rules now. As you will notice from reading these rules, an appellate brief is a formal document with quite a few components and various technical requirements. Even so, it has parallels to the analytical office memo and the motion practice memorandum, as shown in Box 18.7

The following text discusses the components that are standard to most appellate brief formats, in the order that they appear to the reader. Of course, you need not write them in this order; indeed, you should save the various tables until last. In broad strokes, most brief formats may be divided into four parts:

- A set of technical components opens the brief.
- Next come several introductory components.
- The main component of the brief is the argument, which may be preceded by an introductory component.
- The brief concludes with additional technical components.

---

6. *Judges on Briefing: A National Survey* 6, 17, 4 (Bryan A. Garner comp., 2001).

BOX 18.7

COMPARISON OF APPELLATE BRIEF TO MOTION PRACTICE MEMORANDUM AND ANALYTICAL OFFICE MEMO

Appellate Brief	Motion Practice Memorandum	Analytical Office Memo
OPENING TECHNICAL COMPONENTS		
Cover page	Caption	Caption
Tables of contents and authorities		
Jurisdictional statement		
FOUNDATIONAL COMPONENTS		
Statement of issues	Introduction, summary, or issues	Issues and short answers
Statement of case • Procedure • Facts	Facts, procedure	Facts
ARGUMENT		
Introductory components • Summary of argument • Standard of review		
Argument	Argument	Discussion
CLOSING TECHNICAL COMPONENTS		
Conclusion with signature	Conclusion with signature	Closing
Certifications		
Appendices		

3. Opening Technical Components

Cover page. The typical brief begins with a *cover page* containing specified information, including the name of the appeals court; the case name and docket number; the court appealed from; the title of the document, such as "Appellant's Brief"; and the names, attorney numbers, firms, and contact information of the lawyers. The plaintiff typically is listed first, and both parties' roles in the district court, as well as on appeal, are noted. The title page may be color-coded by the identity of the party.

Table of contents. The *table of contents* lists the brief components, including the major and minor point headings within the argument (described below) and starting pages for each item listed. The table of contents may be the first page that the reader consults, so if the point headings are written well, the reader will have a concise and persuasive overview of the argument just by reading the table of contents.

Table of authorities. The *table of authorities* lists cases, statutes, rules, and other authorities cited in the brief. The table also lists the pages on which each source is cited; "passim" may be used after an initial page number for a very frequently cited source. Generally, authorities are grouped by type and presented in alphabetical or numerical order within groups. As the rules permit, you may be able to order or group authorities so as to emphasize certain types of authorities, thereby driving home a particular theory of the case. For example, you may choose not to break out mandatory and persuasive precedent if you are seeking a change in the law and thus relying heavily on persuasive precedent.

An alternative to the separate tables of contents and authorities is the table of points and authorities. This single table lists the major components of the brief, including the point headings from the argument, along with page numbers. Each point heading is followed by a list of several or all of the authorities cited under that point heading.

Statement of jurisdiction. The *statement of jurisdiction*, required in some brief formats, is typically a compact statement explaining the procedural nature of the case and establishing that the case is properly before the appellate court. The statement of jurisdiction should cite mandatory authority, whether statutory or case law.

As an example, both Exhibits 18A and 18B begin with a title page and the two tables. Only Exhibit 18A, the appellant's brief, includes the jurisdictional statement, which contains citations to a federal statute and federal cases.

4. Foundational Components

The foundational components vary from format to format. Most begin with a statement of the issues presented on appeal. The other foundational components vary, but the content to be covered is generally the same.

Issues. The *issues* (or, in some formats, "questions presented") frame the topics for the court to address. The issues thus are closely related to the major points in the argument (and thus parallel the point headings, discussed below) and appear in the order the points appear in the argument. In a complicated brief, you may include sub-issues.

Most issues combine law and facts; the law may be substantive or procedural or both. The issues usually should be a complete question, although in some areas of practice, the convention is to begin the issue with "whether." By tradition, an issue should be answerable by "yes" or "no." The issue should be written to favor your client; if a court rule requires neutral phrasing, frame the issue as a court ruling in your client's favor would frame it. A classic principle of advocacy is that you can win a case if you can get the court to ask the question your way. See Box 18.8 for parallel issues from Exhibits 18A and 18B.

SAMPLE ISSUES FROM APPELLANT'S AND APPELLEES' BRIEFS

The Two Issues Relating to *Tinker*: Substantial Disruption Rule

Appellant's: Whether the District Court erred in concluding that the use of vulgar sexual innuendos in the public school cannot create a forecast for substantial disruption when Title IX[7] provides that students in the public school have a right to an atmosphere free from sexual harassment.

Appellees': Did the District Court commit error when it applied this Court's precedents to a careful review of the record and concluded that the District failed to justify its censorship under *Tinker*?

The Two Issues Relating to *Fraser*: Lewd Content Rule

Appellant's: Whether the District Court erred in finding that "I [heart] Boobies!" could not reasonably be deemed "vulgar" or "lewd" when the phrase contains sexual connotations.

Appellees': Did the District Court commit error when it considered the context of the Plaintiffs' speech and the school officials' inconsistent reaction to the speech over a two-month period and concluded that the District failed to show that it reasonably characterized Plaintiffs' speech as lewd under *Fraser*?

In some brief formats, an issue is followed by the district court ruling or by a short list of the most pertinent primary authorities. Another option is to follow an issue by a suggested answer.

Statement of the case. In some brief formats, the *statement of the case* encompasses the procedural history of the case and the real-world facts of the dispute that gave rise to the litigation, with the procedural history leading off. In others, this statement encompasses only the procedural history, and a separate component presents states the facts of the dispute. A final variation is to present the procedural history after the facts.

The appellant writes the *procedural history*; the respondent may opt not to cover this topic. This history should recount the main procedural events from the outset of the case to the appeal, with a focus on the rulings that are being appealed. The appellant should make clear that the proper motions or objections were made to preserve the right to appeal the pertinent issues. This statement should have supporting citations to the record. The respondent would write a procedural history if it disagreed with or wanted to supplement the statement of the appellant.

---

7. Title IX is a well-known federal statute addressing sexual harassment in public schools.

Both parties generally write *statements of the facts*, with the appellant writing the initial one and the respondent writing its version in response. The *coverages* of the two facts statements generally overlap substantially but not entirely. The facts statement must include the facts discussed in the argument because these facts are relevant. In addition, background facts needed to make the client's situation understandable to the court should be included. You may include persuasive residual facts, so long as you do so judiciously; an appellate court is unlikely to be swayed by too much extraneous information. Ethical and tactical considerations clearly dictate that unfavorable facts be presented.

The brief is on firmest ground when stating facts that are plainly stated in the record. However, inferences are permissible if firmly supported, and the fact statement may note the absence of a critical fact. Argumentative statements and legal conclusions should be avoided in the statement of the case. For example, it is improper to characterize an act as "negligent."

The facts should be *organized* so as to prompt the court see the events from your client's perspective. For example, although the classic presentation is chronological, you may open with a paragraph that recounts the critical event from your client's perspective, even if it did not occur first. Alternatively, you may use a topical presentation so that you can stack evidence on important topics. Or you may use a perceptual presentation to tell the story in the way your client experienced it and then present the perspectives of others.

Throughout the facts statement, you must refer the court to the *record* where a fact is supported, whether in the testimony of a witness at trial, a deposition, or a document admitted at trial. These references generally are to the transcript from the district court or to the appendix filed with the brief.

As an example, Exhibit 18A, the appellant's brief in the *B.H.* case, presents the procedural statement of the case, beginning with a concise description of the dispute, and then summarizing the various events in the litigation from the complaint to the appeal. Exhibit 18B, the appellees' brief, includes a brief procedural history at the end of its facts statement. Both briefs contain lengthy statements of fact, which in some respects cover the same territory. However, the main messages that they seek to convey differ greatly, as seen in the contrast in their opening topics: the appellant's brief focuses primarily on the dress code and maintaining order, whereas the appellees' brief focuses on the positive message behind the bracelets.

5. Argument

The bulk of the appellate brief is set of components presenting the party's legal arguments. Appellate arguments can be lengthy and complex, so in some formats, the argument must be preceded by a summary, a component stating the standard of review, or indeed both of these. Furthermore, point headings throughout the argument flag the major and minor assertions and guide the reader through the argument.

Summary of argument. More than any other component of the brief, the *summary of the argument* is written to capture the attention of the reader. One to three paragraphs long, it signals what is really at stake, presents your theory of the case, and provides an overview of the argument to come, which should appear sensible and straightforward. The tone of the summary should be affirmative; even for the respondent, it should not be framed as a rebuttal.

Jurisdictions differ on whether a summary is required. Even if it is not required, you often will want to include this material, whether in a separate component so labeled or at the outset of the argument, before the first point heading.

As examples, both Exhibits 18A and 18B include summary of argument components. In both summaries, the main legal arguments are previewed. Both summaries establish the theories of the cases for their respective briefs, using key facts and varied allies (another federal court and Congress for the appellant, as opposed to the district court for the appellees). The tones of these summaries are among the most emphatic in both briefs.

Standard of review. Some brief formats require a separately labeled component in which the *standard of review* applicable to the issues on appeal is stated. If the appeal involves various types of rulings, more than one standard would need to be covered. Some standards of review are stated in various ways in different cases; if so, you should state a formulation that benefits your client. Your propositions should be fully cited to mandatory authority.

This material must be included even if a brief format does not require this component. One option is to include it in the summary. Another option is to include it as the first topic in the argument or at the outset of each topic if the various topics involve different standards of review.

As examples, both of the briefs in the *B.H.* case include standard of review components. They state the same basic standard; Exhibit 18B, the appellees' brief, adds a paragraph discussing the standard as applied in free speech cases.

Argument text. The *argument* explains why the court should rule for your client. The appellant concentrates on undermining the district court's rulings and reasoning, while the respondent uses the district court as its ally. That is, the appellant's brief tries to demonstrate reversible error, while the respondent's brief tries to maintain the status quo. Appellate advocacy is *four-dimensional* involving the facts, substantive law, public policy, and procedural law. See Box 18.9, which depicts the four dimensions of Exhibit 18A, the appellant's brief.

Legal advocacy entails convincingly demonstrating how to *apply substantive legal rules to the facts* of the case so as to favor your client. To do this, you must cite to and explain pertinent mandatory authority; you may cite helpful persuasive authority and may discuss unfavorable persuasive authority. You must reason deductively from the law to the facts, and you should bolster your deductive reasoning with reasoning by example where appropriate. In many cases, the argument also discusses *public policy*, especially when a case in the jurisdiction's high court challenges the current state of the law and argues for a new rule of law. Even in a routine case briefed for an intermediate appellate court, policy can be important; intermediate appellate courts sometimes create precedent and seek to do so based on solid policy grounds. Furthermore, you should directly or indirectly rebut the competing arguments of your opponent, whether they pertain to what the law is or how to apply the law to the facts.

In addition, at the appellate level *procedural law* plays a major role. First, the appellate court is always cognizant of the procedural posture at which the district court issued the rulings under review. Second, the brief should incorporate the applicable standard of review, especially if it is favorable to your client.

BOX 18.9

SAMPLE FOUR-DIMENSION DEPICTION OF APPELLANT'S ARGUMENT

Typeface key: procedural law, *substantive law*, **factual points**, POLICIES.

   I. Likelihood of success on the merits
        Fraser deferential reasonableness test: **"I [heart] Boobies!"** is lewd
        Tinker substantial interference test: **Sexual harassment** interferes
        with every student's right to education
  II. No irreparable harm to Plaintiffs
        **Multiple alternative channels to communicate breast cancer
        awareness**
 III. Harm to District is greater
        District could not exercise its statutory obligations
 IV. Public will be harmed
        DIMINISHMENT OF DISTRICT AUTHORITY AND OBLIGA-
        TION TO REGULATE *MANNER* OF STUDENT SPEECH

Of course, all legal propositions (whether matters of substantive or procedural law) must be fully and accurately cited. The traditional location for these citations is in the text, immediately after the legal propositions. Some lawyers choose to provide citations in footnotes. In a brief with citations in footnotes, the argument itself is easier to read, but the reader sees the authority for a proposition more immediately in a brief with citations in the text. Neither approach is obviously better.

Generally, you need not provide citations to the record as you refer to facts within the argument, because the citations in the facts statement suffice. However, you should provide appropriate citations to the record if you quote from the record, provide more detail than in the facts statement, or want to highlight a particular passage.

Footnotes are routinely used to present content, whether legal or factual, that is tangential to the main text. A footnote may convey information that is needed to make the brief more complete, yet would interrupt the argument's flow if it were in the main discussion. The reader should not lose any essential meaning by not reading a footnote.

Point headings. *Point headings* in appellate briefs present the main assertions that the court must accept (in whole or in part) to rule in the client's favor. Read as a set, the point headings should provide a clear and logical outline of the brief, showing the order of and relationships among the arguments. They also should convey the theory of the case and incline the reader to view the case through a legal prism that favors the client over the other party. As already noted, the point headings appear in the table of contents as an outline. They also appear at the appropriate places within the argument. Compare the excerpts from the point headings drawn from Exhibits 18A and 18B in Box 18.10.

BOX 18.10

SAMPLE POINT HEADINGS

Appellant's Major Point Headings and Selected Minor Point Headings

  I. The School District has a likelihood of success on the merits of its appeal because the District Court abused its discretion, both in its application of the *Fraser* standard of deferential reasonableness and the *Tinker* standard.

   A. The District Court erroneously failed to apply the *Fraser* standard of deferential reasonableness to affirm the School District's reasonable manner restriction on student in-school speech.

   B. The District Court erroneously held that the School District's restraint on "I ♥ Boobies!" did not meet the *Tinker* standard because an atmosphere of sexual harassment substantially interferes with every student's right to an education.

 II. The District Court erred in its holding that the Plaintiffs would be irreparably harmed by a denial of a preliminary injunction because the Plaintiffs have multiple alternative channels of communicating a concern for breast cancer awareness.

III. The harm to the School District by a preliminary injunction is far greater than the denial of a preliminary injunction to the Plaintiffs, particularly because the School District will be unable to exercise its prerogative granted by *Fraser* and its statutory obligations required by the School Code.

 IV. The public will be harmed via the diminishment of the District's authority to exercise its prerogative and obligation to regulate the manner of student speech pursuant to *Fraser* and the School Code.

Appellees' Major Point Headings and Selected Minor Point Headings

  I. The Supreme Court's student speech cases establish the relevant legal framework and bar the District's novel legal arguments.

 II. The District Court properly interpreted and applied the law when it held that the District failed to justify its censorship under *Tinker*.

III. The District Court properly interpreted and applied the law when it held that the District's censorship of the bracelets was unreasonable under *Fraser*.

   A. The District Court properly held that Plaintiffs' speech must be interpreted in context, not in the abstract, to determine whether it is lewd or vulgar, and that determination is a question of law for the court.

   B. The District Court correctly found that the Plaintiffs' bracelets were not and could not reasonably be considered lewd in this context.

 IV. The District Court properly interpreted and applied the law when it held that Plaintiffs established irreparable harm and that the balance of equities and the public interest favors the issuance of the injunction.

Each point heading should be a single sentence. It should be concise and affirmatively phrased. Generally, a major heading combines legal rules and facts; many major headings reflect procedural as well as substantive law. Minor point headings provide steps of the analysis, policy, or reasons. They need not always be fact-and-law combinations.

You should strive to make your point headings informative. Very general point headings are of little help to the court because they neither focus on a specific legal problem nor arise from the facts of the case. On the other hand, too many facts or legal principles make a point heading too long and hard to grasp. If the reader must read a point heading more than once to understand it, it needs rewriting: rephrase it into multiple major point headings, convert it to a major heading with minor headings, or keep the main point in the heading and leave subordinate points to the text.

Point headings in appellate briefs are framed in classic outline form, preceded by Roman numerals (I, II), capital letters (A, B), and Arabic numerals (1, 2). Take care not to use headings more detailed than these three levels, or you may lose your reader. As in outlining, if there is no "B," you should not use an "A." Furthermore, to set your point headings apart from the text, use the format that is required by the court, if any, or some combination of the following: open lines above and below the heading; indentation; and underlining, boldface, and initial capitals. Some favor all-capital letters, although this style reduces readability.

To promote the flow of your argument, you should include not only point headings but also transitional words or phrases, overviews, and summaries to signal the relationships among the parts of the argument.

6. Closing Technical Components

Conclusion and signature block. The *conclusion* is a concise statement of the relief requested. It need not, but may, restate the argument, although conclusions rarely cite authority and should not raise any new arguments.

A *signature block* follows the conclusion. The closing typically reads "Respectfully submitted," followed by the attorney's signature and information (name, client representation, firm affiliation, contact information, and attorney registration number).

Appendix. Most jurisdictions require an appendix at the end of the appellant's brief that contains pertinent parts of the record. The respondent's brief may include additional appendix material if the needed parts of the record are not in the appellant's appendix. Be sure to read the appellate rules on brief format for details on compiling these materials.

7. Additional Possibilities

One or more of the following components also may be required in a particular jurisdiction:

- a request for (or waiver of) oral argument, if oral argument is not automatically granted;
- a statement certifying that the brief has been served;
- a citation to any published opinions of lower courts;

- a statement certifying the length of the brief; and
- citations to or excerpts of statutes or constitutional provisions.

These components may appear at various locations in the brief.

8. Respondent's Brief and the Reply Brief

In general, the *respondent's brief* follows the same form as the appellant's brief. The statement of the issues and case may be optional, but a savvy advocate usually does not let opposing counsel have the only say on these matters.

The *reply brief* has no particular format, but its purpose is to respond to points in the respondent's brief that are not covered in the appellant's main brief. The most common format includes an introduction, an argument, and a conclusion. It is less common to include issues or a facts statement.

D. REVIEW

Appeals provide an important safeguard against district court error, as well as a mechanism for making law. Various appellate legal rules, such as the final judgment and reversible error rules, preserve the proper roles of the district and appellate courts.

An important step in the appellate process is the preparation of the appellate brief, written to convince the court (as well as opposing counsel and the client) of the justness of the client's position. A typical appellate brief format includes the following components:

(1) The cover page identifies the case, the court, the lawyers, and the document.
(2) The tables orient the reader to the parts of the brief, the points made, and the legal authorities relied on in the brief.
(3) The jurisdictional statement establishes that the appellate court has the power to hear the appeal.
(4) The statement of issues frames the questions to be decided by the appellate court.
(5) The statement of the case informs the court of the facts and the procedural background of the case.
(6) The standard of review sets out the degree of scrutiny that the appeals court applies to the ruling of the district court.
(7) The summary of argument presents the theory of the case and an overview of the legal arguments.
(8) The argument draws together substantive and procedural law, facts, and policy to make the case for the client's desired outcomes, with point headings flagging the main assertions.
(9) The conclusion states the relief desired by the client and includes the lawyer's signature.

The brief should be complete, correct, coherent, comprehensible, and (if written according to the points set out in Chapter 16) convincing.

EXHIBIT 18A UNITED STATES COURT OF APPEALS, THIRD CIRCUIT: BRIEF OF APPELLANT*

B.H. & K.M., et al, Plaintiffs, Appellees,

v.

EASTON AREA SCHOOL DISTRICT, Defendants, Appellants.

No. 11-2067.

June 27, 2011.

On Appeal from the United States District Court for the Eastern District of Pennsylvania No. 5-10-cv-06283; The Honorable Mary A. McLaughlin

BRIEF OF APPELLANT

John E. Freund, III, Esq., Counsel for Appellant, Atty ID: 25390, King Spry Herman Freund & Faul, LLC, One West Broad St., Suite 700, Bethlehem PA 18018, (610) 332-0390.

TABLE OF CONTENTS

---

* This is a real brief filed in a real, highly contested case. We have deleted only a few portions in the interests of brevity. Our sincere thanks go to John E. Freund for his permission to reprint this brief for educational purposes.

EXHIBIT 18A (cont.)

TABLE OF AUTHORITIES [This is omitted for space reasons.]

STATEMENT OF JURISDICTION

This appeal is from a denial of a motion for preliminary injunction; thus this Court's review is limited to preliminary injunctive relief. 28 U.S.C. 1292(a)(1); *Punnett v. Carter,* 621 F.2d 578, 582 (3d Cir. 1980); *Oburn v. Shapp,* 521 F.2d 142, 146-47 (3d. Cir. 1975). While a preliminary injunction is not a final order, this Court has jurisdiction pursuant to 28 U.S.C. 1292 (a)(1), which provides that "the courts of appeals shall have jurisdiction of appeals from [i]nterlocutory orders of the district courts of the United States . . . granting, continuing, modifying, refusing or dissolving injunctions." 28 U.S.C. 1292(a)(1); *see Sypniewski v. Warren Hills Regional Bd. of Educ.,* 307 F.3d 243, 252 n.10 (3d Cir. 2002) (explaining that the Third Circuit Court of Appeals has jurisdiction of appeals from decisions regarding motions for preliminary injunctions). Therefore, this Court has jurisdiction over appeals of orders granting preliminary injunctions, the subject of this appeal.

EXHIBIT 18A (cont.)

STATEMENT OF THE ISSUES

(1) Whether the District Court committed a fundamental error by failing to apply a deferential standard of objective reasonableness to review the Principal's decision regarding the appropriate manner of student speech.

Suggested Answer: Yes.

(2) Whether the District Court erred in finding that "I ❤ Boobies!" could not reasonably be deemed "vulgar" or "lewd" when the phrase contains sexual connotations.

Suggested Answer: Yes.

(3) Whether the District Court erred in concluding that the use of vulgar sexual innuendos in the public school cannot create a forecast for substantial disruption when Title IX provides that students in the public school have a right to an atmosphere free from sexual harassment.

Suggested Answer: Yes.

(4) Whether the District Court erred in concluding that the Plaintiffs will endure irreparable harm as a result of the denial of a preliminary injunction when the School District's ban on "I ❤ Boobies!" bracelets was a reasonable restriction on manner of speech which left open multiple alternative means of expression.

Suggested Answer: Yes

(5) Whether the District Court erred in its balancing of the respective harms when the Plaintiffs may express the viewpoint of breast cancer awareness in multiple ways whereas the School District will lose its prerogative under *Fraser* and be unable to implement its responsibilities under the School Code if a preliminary injunction is granted.

Suggested Answer: Yes.

(6) Whether the District Court erred in holding that the harm to the public will be greater if the students are restrained from wearing "I ❤ Boobies!" bracelets when the message of breast cancer awareness has never been repressed and the Plaintiffs are free to wear "I ❤ Boobies!" bracelets off of the school grounds and outside of school activities.

Suggested Answer: Yes.

STATEMENT OF THE CASE

On October 28, 2010, the Principal of grades 7 and 8 of the Easton Area School District (hereinafter the "School District") suspended the school attendance of 13-year-old B.H. and 12-year-old K.M. for refusing to remove bracelets containing the phrase "I ❤ Boobies!". (App. Vol. II at 72, 99, 105, 206). All suspended students were not permitted to attend the Snowball Dance, which was a reward for students exhibiting positive behavior, pursuant to the Positive Behavioral Support System applicable to all

EXHIBIT 18A (cont.)

students in grades 7 and 8. (App. Vol. II at 205-06; Vol. III at 410-11). Therefore, B.H. and K.M. were similarly prohibited from attending the dance. (App. Vol. II at 123).

On November 15, 2010, B.H., via her mother Jennifer Hawk, and K.M., via her mother Amy Martinez, filed a Complaint in the District Court of the Eastern District of Pennsylvania (hereinafter referred to as the "District Court") against the School District alleging that the School District violated K.M. and B.H.'s First Amendment right to free speech. On November 15, 2010, the Plaintiffs filed a Motion for Preliminary Injunction and request for a Temporary Restraining Order, whereby the Plaintiffs requested that the School District lift its ban on the "I ❤ Boobies!" bracelets and allow the girls to attend the Snowball Dance.

Pursuant to the parties' stipulation, the girls were permitted to attend the Snowball Dance and the School District continued to enforce its ban of the "I ❤ Boobies!" bracelets. On November 18, 2010, due to this agreement, the District Court ordered that the Plaintiffs' Motion for Temporary Restraining Order be denied without prejudice. The parties proceeded to the discovery phase. On December 16, 2010, the District Court held a fact-finding hearing, which included testimony from administrators of the School District, the minor Plaintiffs, and Kimberly McAtee of the Keep-A-Breast Foundation. The District Court heard oral argument regarding the Plaintiffs' Motion for Preliminary Injunction from both parties' attorneys on February 18, 2011.

On April 12, 2011, the District Court issued an Opinion and Order granting the Plaintiffs' Motion for Preliminary Injunction, which enjoined the District from enforcing its restriction on bracelets stating "I ❤ Boobies! Keep-A-Breast." On April 21, 2011, the School District filed a Notice of Appeal to the April 12, 2011 Opinion and Order. Further, on May 19, 2011, the School District filed a Motion to Stay with the District Court asking that the District Court stay its order granting Plaintiffs' motion for Preliminary Injunction, pursuant to Rule 62(c) of the Federal Rules of Civil Procedure and Rule 8(a)(1)(c) of the Federal Rules of Appellate Procedure. The District Court denied said motion on June 21, 2011.

The School District respectfully requests that this Court reverse the judgment of the Eastern District Court of Pennsylvania rendered on April 12, 2011 erroneously granting Plaintiffs' a preliminary injunction. This matter is currently before this Court for disposition.

STATEMENT OF THE FACTS

The School District, located on the border of Pennsylvania and New Jersey, is an urban/suburban school district and serves a student population of about 9,200 students in an area with a population of about 62,000 individuals. (App. Vol. II at 202). Due to the student population, the School District divided its middle school into two buildings: Grades 5 and 6 are contained in one building (hereinafter referred to as the 5/6 Building), and grades 7 and 8 are contained in another building (hereinafter referred to as the 7/8 Building). (App. Vol. II at 203). The 5/6 Building and the 7/8 Building are housed in one

EXHIBIT 18A (cont.)

entire complex but administered separately. (App. Vol. II at 203). Within the framework of School District policies, the administrators of both buildings make autonomous decisions with respect to disciplinary matters. (App. Vol. II at 203-04). One such School District policy is the dress code which provides the following:

> The dress, speech and work habits of the student should in every way possible support the seriousness of the educational enterprise. The following examples are considered to be in poor taste and will merit disciplinary actions: No clothing imprinted with nudity, vulgarity, obscenity, profanity and double entendre pictures or slogans . . .

(App. Vol. II at 98, 392; Vol. III at 131-32). Within the framework of the School District's dress code, both building principals make independent determinations regarding violations. (App. Vol. II at 203-04, 404).

The School District's Board of Directors adopted October 28, 2010 as the district-wide Breast Cancer Awareness Day to observe the national Breast Cancer Awareness Month of October. (App. Vol. II at 208, 357). As part of its ongoing promotion of breast cancer awareness and research, over $3,000 was raised for the School District's annual "Susan G. Komen Passionately Pink for the Cure" drive. (App. Vol. II at 208-09, 357, 359). The message of breast cancer awareness was similarly promoted in the 7/8 Building and included instruction for all students with respect to breast health and breast cancer. (App. Vol. II at 208-09, 235-36, 336-39). To promote breast cancer awareness, the 7/8 Building principals encouraged students and staff to wear pink, T-shirts, and pins, within the parameters of the dress code, on Breast Cancer Awareness Day. (App. Vol. II at 208, 269; Vol. III at 412-13). The administration of the 7/8 Building never stifled the message of awareness of breast cancer and, in fact, supported this message. (App. Vol. II at 238).

The administration of the 7/8 Building is as follows: Angela DiVietro, Principal; Amy Braxmeier, Grade 8 Assistant Principal; and Anthony Viglianti, Grade 7 Assistant Principal. (App. Vol. II at 173, 201, 203, 258). In the 7/8 Building, the classroom teachers are responsible for noticing and reporting dress code violations. (App. Vol. II at 268). Pursuant to the School District-wide dress code, students in the 7/8 Building have been asked to remove apparel with the following double entendres: (1) Hooters restaurant, (2) Big Peckers restaurant, and (3) "Save the ta-tas." (App. Vol. II at 255-56). Any student wearing an item containing a double entendre message or any other dress code violation was asked to remove the item and will receive no disciplinary consequences if compliant with the directive. (App. Vol. II at 267). Therefore, students were only given consequences for defiance, not dress code violations independently. (App. Vol. II at 267, 371-72).

In September 2010, the beginning of the 2010-2011 school year, teachers in the 7/8 Building reported to Mr. Viglianti and Ms. Braxmeier that they were noticing students wearing bracelets containing the phrase "I ❤ Boobies!" and did not believe that the bracelets were appropriate under the school dress code. (App. Vol. II at 228, 260). Further, teachers in the 7/8 Building reported that the bracelets were causing a distraction for students in their classrooms. (App. Vol. III Deposition of A. DiVietro at 20; Vol. II at

EXHIBIT 18A   (cont.)

261, 268). Also, during the September through November 2010 timeframe, there were instances of sexual harassment in the 7/8 Building particularly focused on girls' breasts. (App. Vol. II at 230-31, 314, 360-71). A girl in the 7/8 Building, who was wearing an "I ♥ Boobies!" bracelet, reported to Ms. Braxmeier that boys approached the girls at her lunch table and stated that they "love boobies." (App. Vol. II at 231). Another girl reported to Ms. Braxmeier that, while she was having a conversation with other girls at her lunch table about the "I ♥ Boobies!" bracelets, a boy interrupted them and stated "I love boobies" and, while playing with fireball candies, chanted "boobies, boobies." (App. Vol. II at 231). There were also instances that were not reported to Ms. Braxmeier in which some boys were "immature" regarding the "I ♥ Boobies!" slogan and approached other middle school girls about "boobies." (App. Vol. II at 135; Vol. III at 442). Further, during the same timeframe, there were instances of boys touching girls in an unwanted sexual manner. (App. Vol. II at 230-31).

As of September and October of 2010, the School District as a whole had not officially banned or, aside from the dress code itself, offered any guidance regarding the "I ♥ Boobies!" phrase (App. Vol. II at 230, 238, 260, 346[1]). After meeting with Ms. Braxmeier and Mr. Viglianti, Ms. DiVietro, 7/8 Building Principal, decided that, due to the inherent sexual message, bracelets stating "I ♥ Boobies!" were inappropriate for the 7/8 Building students to wear in school. (App. Vol. II at 228, 238, 260, 268). The Principal and Assistant Principals believed that the phrase "I ♥ Boobies!" conveyed a sexual double entendre which is prohibited by the School District-wide dress code policy. (App. Vol. II at 228, 262, 264). Moreover, the unique age group of the 7/8 Building, which ranged from 11 to 14 years old, was considered in the principals' decisions to ban the "I ♥ Boobies!" phrase, specifically because of the wide variety of sexual and physical development of its student population. (App. Vol. II at 23, 230, 238, 261). Accordingly, Grade 7 Assistant Principal, Anthony Viglianti, sent an email in September of 2010 to the 7/8 Building teachers informing them that "I ♥ Boobies!" bracelets were against the dress code and students seen wearing the bracelets should be individually asked to remove the bracelet. (App. Vol. II at 228, 343). Although the administration never made an official determination with respect to the appropriateness *of keepabreast.org*, the bracelets were not permitted to be turned inside out because students were quickly and easily returning their bracelets back to the "I ♥ Boobies!" side. (App. Vol. II at 280).

Because of the sexual message conveyed via the "I ♥ Boobies!" phrase, on October 27, 2010, the day before Breast Cancer Awareness Day, the 7/8 Building issued a televised morning announcement instructing students not to wear "I ♥ Boobies!" bracelets in school. (App. Vol. II at 268, 344). Also, Mr. Viglianti made another announcement at the end of the day reminding students not to wear "I ♥ Boobies!" bracelets. (App. Vol. II at 268, 344). B.H. and K.M., two students in the 7/8 Building, asked their mothers whether they could wear "I ♥ Boobies!" bracelets in defiance of the ban. (App. Vol. II 81, 116-17; A. Martinez Dep. at 21-22; J. Hawk Dep. at 7-8). Both girls' mothers gave their approval or acquiesced to their daughters wanting to wear "I ♥

EXHIBIT 18A (cont.)

Boobies!'' bracelets. (App. Vol. II at 116; A. Martinez Dep. at 21-22; J. Hawk Dep. at 7-8). Ms. Martinez, K.M.'s mother, and Ms. Hawk, B.H.'s mother, both believe that students in school should be able to use any word to express their viewpoints of cancer awareness. (App. Vol. II J. Hawk Dep. at 11-12; A. Martinez at 17-18).

On October 27, 2010, John Border, School District Security, was informed by a cafeteria worker that B.H. was wearing an "I ❤ Boobies!" bracelet. (App. Vol. II at 220). Mr. Border asked B.H. to remove "I ❤ Boobies!" bracelet, but she would not. (App. Vol. II at 220). After B.H. refused to remove the bracelet, Mr. Border escorted B.H. to Ms. Braxmeier. (App. Vol. II at 220-22). Ms. Braxmeier pleaded with B.H. to remove the bracelet. (App. Vol. II at 221-22). As per the standard dress code violation procedure, Ms. Braxmeier informed B.H. that if she removed the bracelet, she would not issue any disciplinary consequences. (App. Vol. II at 221-22). B.H. stated that it was her "right" to wear the bracelet and that it was her generation, "not [y]our generation." (App. Vol. II at 222). After further discussion, B.H. removed the bracelet with no further disciplinary consequences and returned to the cafeteria. (App. Vol. II at 222).

On October 28, 2010, the 7/8 Building celebrated Breast Cancer Awareness Day. (App. Vol. III at 235-36). On this day, faculty and students wore pink as well as other pins and T-shirts, within the dress code, which demonstrated support for breast cancer awareness. (App. Vol. III at 235-36). On this day, Mr. Border was apprised that B.H. was wearing an "I ❤ Boobies!" bracelet again during lunch period. (App. Vol. II at 222). Mr. Border approached B.H. and asked her to remove her bracelet, but B.H. refused to comply. (App. Vol. II at 222). At that time, K.M. stood up in the cafeteria and stated that she was wearing an "I ❤ Boobies!" bracelet and was not going to take it off. (App. Vol. II at 222). Then, a third girl, R.T., stood up [and] said that she was also wearing an "I ❤ Boobies!" bracelet [and] was not going to take it off. (App. Vol. II at 222). Mr. Border escorted the three girls to Ms. Braxmeier's office. (App. Vol. II at 223-24). On their way to Ms. Braxmeier's office, B.H. and K.M. gave each other a high-five because they were proud of themselves for defying the ban. (App. Vol. II at 118-19, 234). K.M. wanted to be "caught" wearing the bracelet because she believed that students should not be punished for wearing clothing that the student believes is appropriate. (App. Vol. II at 131). Both K.M. and B.H. believe that, when used in the context of cancer awareness, any word for the female breast would be appropriate. (App. Vol. II at 101-02, 131, 138). B.H. believes that the existence of the "keep a breast" phrase on the bracelet negates any possible prurient understanding of "I ❤ Boobies!" (App. Vol. II at 102-03). Both girls knowingly defied the ban. (App. Vol. III Dep. K.M. at 31; Dep. B.H. at 33-34; App. Vol. II at 235).

When B.H., K.M., and R.T. arrived in her office, Ms. Braxmeier spoke with each girl individually about the "I ❤ Boobies!" bracelet. First, Ms. Braxmeier spoke with R.T. (App. Vol. II at 234). R.T. agreed to remove her bracelet. (App. Vol. III A. Braxmeier Dep. at 20). In the course of her discussion with Ms. Braxmeier, R.T. explained that she understood why students should not wear the "I ❤ Boobies" bracelets. (App. Vol. III A. Braxmeier Dep. at 20, 26, 67). Specifically, R.T. stated that some boys were "immature"

EXHIBIT 18A **(cont.)**

and have been approaching girls and commenting "I love your boobies" or "I love boobies." (App. Vol. III A. Braxmeier Dep. at 20, 26, 67). After removing her bracelet, R.T. was free to leave with no disciplinary consequences. (App. Vol. II at 234).

Ms. Braxmeier spoke with K.M individually about whether there was any way within the school dress code that K.M. could express her support for breast cancer awareness. (App. Vol. III at 235). K.M. said there was not. (App. Vol. III at 235). Ms. Braxmeier gave K.M. suggestions about other things she could do such as wearing pink. (App. Vol. III at 235). However, K.M. refused to express herself in any other way aside from wearing an "I ❤ Boobies!" bracelet. (App. Vol. III at 235). After discussing the bracelets with K.M., Ms. Braxmeier spoke with B.H. individually about her "I ❤ Boobies!" bracelet. (App. Vol. II at 237). Ms. Braxmeier asked B.H. if there was a way within the dress code that she could express her support for breast cancer awareness. (App. Vol. II at 237). B.H. stated that there was not and refused to remove her "I ❤ Boobies!" bracelet. (N.T. 12/16/2010 at 238). Because they refused to remove the "I ❤ Boobies!" bracelets when asked, B.H. and K.M. were sent to in-school suspension for the remainder of the day and were also given a full day of in-school suspension. (App. Vol. II at 206, 302-03).[2]

"I ❤ Boobies!" bracelets were a fad in the public school. (App. Vol. II at 72, 92; Vol. III at 442). B.H. first purchased an "I ❤ Boobies!" bracelet because she saw people wearing them "walking around the mall" and she saw "a lot of [her] friends wearing the bracelet." (App. Vol. II at 72). Only subsequent to her decision to purchase an "I ❤ Boobies!" bracelet did B.H. discover that the bracelets were intended to promote breast cancer awareness. (N.T. 12/16/2010 at 22). K.M. first saw the bracelets over the summer and purchased one because she thought "the bracelet was really cool." (App. Vol. III at 442). While K.M.'s proffered intent for wearing the "I ❤ Boobies!" bracelet was also for an awareness message, she acknowledged that "[s]ome friends were wearing [the bracelets] just to wear them . . . " (App. Vol. III at 442).

The "I ❤ Boobies" bracelets worn by the Plaintiffs, B.H. and K.M., included pink, black, green, and white-colored bracelets. (App. Vol. II at 77-78). The pink, black, and green bracelets had a one-inch band. The outside of the bracelet contained the phrase "I ❤ Boobies!" in approximately three quarters of an inch lettering with the phrase "(Keep-A-Breast)" in lettering measuring approximately one quarter of an inch. The web address, keep-a-breast.org, was contained on the inside of the bracelets. (App. Vol. II at 112; Vol. III at 406-07, 409). The white bracelet, which was also worn by both K.M. and B.H., has a band measuring approximately one and three-quarter-inch in width. That bracelet contained the phrase "I❤ Boobies!" in approximately half-inch lettering. (App. Vol. II at 78-79, 96). The white bracelet also contained the phrase "Glamour Kills" in approximately three-quarters-inch lettering. (App. Vol. II at 78, 96, 113). Both K.M. and B.H. acknowledged that "Glamour Kills" is a clothing line, unrelated to breast cancer awareness. (App. Vol. II at 96-97).

EXHIBIT 18A (cont.)

"I ♥ Boobies!" bracelets are marketed and distributed by the Keep-A-Breast Foundation, which is based in Los Angeles, California. (App. Vol. II at 154). The Keep-A-Breast Foundation sells "I ♥ Boobies!" bracelets and other merchandise to retailers, including Zumiez, Tilly's, and the website *loserkids.com,* which are called "lifestyle stores," meaning that the shops are targeted at 13 through 30-year-olds who are interested in action sports and music. (App. Vol. II at 146). Truck stops, 7- Elevens, vending machine companies, and "porn stars" have expressed interest in promoting the "I ♥ Boobies!" bracelets. (App. Vol. II at 151-52, 163). Kimberly McAtee, Peer Marketing Manager of Keep-A-Breast, sees a sexual message in the fact that "porn stars" are interested in the Keep-A-Breast brand. (App. Vol. II at 163). In her management capacities with the Keep-A-Breast Foundation, Ms. McAtee has received "a lot" of emails from teachers and principals requesting more information regarding the organization and its purpose. (App. Vol. II at 155-56). While Ms. McAtee maintained that some school administrators are not bothered by the "I ♥ Boobies!" phrase, she also admitted that she is aware of other school administrators who believe the expression is inappropriate. (App. Vol. II at 165).

The "I ♥ Boobies!" bracelets and message were a vehicle for the commercial advertising. (App. Vol. II at 160-63). In exchange for a donation, Keep-A-Breast allows other businesses to market their commercial products using the "I ♥ Boobies!" slogan. (App. Vol. II at 160-63). This is termed "co-branding" or "cause marketing." (App. Vol. II at 161). Keep-A-Breast does "a lot" of co-branding, according to Ms. McAtee. (App. Vol. II at 160). Because of co-branding, the "I ♥ Boobies!" bracelets were used as a platform for the "Glamour Kills" clothing line to market its products. (Vol. II at 97, 161). On Glamour Kills' press release web site, young women's sexuality is used to market its clothing. (Vol. II at 97, 168). In addition to "Glamour Kills," Keep-A-Breast co-brands with the following businesses: Etnies Kleen Canteen, Etnies shoes, and SJC Snare Drum brand apparel. (App. Vol. II at 161-63; Vol. III K. McAtee Dep. at 44-46). At the time of the fact-finding hearing, the "Plastic Sucks" campaign was forthcoming with the Keep-A-Breast Foundation. (App. Vol. II at 162).

Since the District Court's grant of the Plaintiffs' Motion for Preliminary Injunction on April 12, 2011, the students of the 7/8 Building administration have been testing the administration with dress code violations. In its opinion, the District Court stated that "[n]othing in his decision prevents a school from making a case by case determination that some speech is lewd and vulgar while other speech is not." However, any school district that does not even have the authority to determine that "I ♥ Boobies!" is vulgar and inappropriate for middle school students has lost credibility with its student body and the community to make determinations regarding the manner of student speech. For that reason, the decision of the District Court seriously undermined the School District's prerogative to protect children from sexual messages and teach civility in the public school context. The School District's appeal is now before this Court for disposition.

EXHIBIT 18A (cont.)

STATEMENT OF RELATED CASES AND PROCEEDINGS

There has been no previous appeal in this case and no prior or related proceedings.

STATEMENT OF STANDARD OF REVIEW

In reviewing the District Court's decision to grant Plaintiffs' preliminary injunction, this Court should employ a three-part standard of review: (1) The District Court's legal conclusions are assessed *de novo;* (2) findings of fact are reviewed for a clear error; and (3) the District Court's final decision to grant the preliminary injunction is reviewed for abuse of discretion. *Sypniewski v. Warren Reg'l Bd. of Educ.*, 307 F.3d 243, 252 (3d Cir. 2002). This Court should decide that the District Court abused its discretion if its decision was based upon an erroneous legal conclusion, or a clearly erroneous finding of fact, or an improper application of law to fact. *Pappan Enterprises, Inc. v. Hardee's Food Systems, Inc.,* 143 F.3d 800, 803 (3d Cir. 1998) (quoting *Hofkin v. Provident Live & Accident Ins. Co.,* 81 F.3d 365, 369 (3d Cir. 1996)).

To determine whether the District Court appropriately granted a preliminary injunction, this Court must consider the following four factors: (1) whether Plaintiffs have a likelihood of success on the merits of their claim; (2) whether the Plaintiffs would be irreparably injured by a denial of the injunction; (3) whether there will be greater harm to the School District if the injunction is granted; (4) whether granting the injunction is in the public interest. *Sypniewski,* 307 F.3d at 252 (citing *Highmark, Inc. v. UPMC Health Plan, Inc.,* 276 F.3d 160, 170 (3d Cir. 2001)). When considering the four-listed factors, this Court should overturn the District Court if it finds that the District Court based its decision upon an erroneous legal conclusion, or a clearly erroneous finding of fact, or an improper application of law to fact. *Pappan Enterprises, Inc. v. Hardee's Food Systems, Inc.,* 143 F.3d at 803 (quoting *Hofkin v. Provident Live & Accident Ins. Co.,* 81 F.3d 365, 369 (3d Cir. 1996)).

SUMMARY OF ARGUMENT

The District Court abused its discretion by failing to pay the appropriate deference to the 7/8 Building Principal's determination regarding the manner of speech in their public school. There is no evidence presented in this case that the 7/8 Building administration sought to suppress the viewpoint of concern for breast cancer awareness, only the manner in which that viewpoint was conveyed via the "I ♥ Boobies!" phrase. Accordingly, this case concerns only the principals' authority to regulate the manner of speech displayed on clothes that they reasonably regard as vulgar and inappropriate.

In the case of *Bethel School District v. Fraser,* 478 U.S. 675 (1986), the United States Supreme Court declared that school administrators may enforce reasonable restrictions on vulgar or lewd manners of speech and, therefore, found that a student's speech containing sexual metaphor was not protected by the First Amendment in the public school, even though the speech did not include a single express sexual reference. Subsequently, federal courts have given deference to school principals' objectively reasonable decisions

EXHIBIT 18A (cont.)

regarding vulgarity, particularly because the reasonable sensibilities of the principal, as a duly-delegated agent of the voter-elected school board, reflects the community's standards of decency for its school children.

Here, the District Court failed to apply a standard of deferential objective reasonableness to the vulgarity determination of the 7/8 Building principals. Instead, the District Court found that the principals did not act reasonably because Plaintiffs' intended awareness message could be reasonably understood from the "I ❤ Boobies!" phrase. However, according to the prevailing case law, the fact that the Plaintiffs' intended message could be understood from the "I ❤ Boobies!" phrase, as contained on the Keep-A-Breast bracelets, does not render the manner restriction at issue "unreasonable." The law is clear that school principals are not required to adopt a literal interpretation and/or the interpretation of the students for their choice of manner of speech. Administrators' vulgarity determinations with respect to sexual innuendos have been consistently and without exception deemed objectively reasonable by the Supreme Court of the United States and our nation's federal courts, regardless of the students' intended purpose for the speech. Therefore, the District Court abused its discretion by failing to apply a standard of objective deferential reasonableness.

The District Court abused its discretion by finding as fact that the "I ❤ Boobies!" phrase could not be considered vulgar and inappropriate. The manner of speech does not have to be obscene, unspeakable, or a "four-letter-word" for an administrator's ban to be reasonable. The Second Circuit Court of Appeals held in the case of *Guiles ex rel. Guiles v. Marineau,* 461 F.3d 320 (2d Cir. 2006), that the *Fraser* standard applies to "profanity or sexual innuendo." Proclaiming "love" for a sexual part of the body, particularly when utilizing familiar terms, could be deemed sexual innuendo and vulgar by a reasonable public school administrator, particularly in the context of a public middle school. As will be set forth more clearly below, others outside of the 7/8 Building administration have found sexual innuendo in the "I ❤ Boobies!" phrase; thus it could not be said that the administration's vulgarity determination was "unreasonable. For example, Playboy Magazine, a publication that is notoriously engaged in prurient commerce, printed an article regarding this case and a picture of the "I ❤ Boobies!" bracelets on the same page with articles regarding condom use, HIV, and a pornographic movie. Therefore, a reasonable administrator could also find that the "I ❤ Boobies" phrase is vulgar and offensive. Accordingly, while sexual innuendo is not the only interpretation of the "I ❤ Boobies!" phrase as it is contained on the bracelets, the 7/8 Building administration acted reasonably.

Alternatively, pursuant to the case of *Tinker v. Des Moines Independent Community School District,* 393 U.S. 503 (1969), schools may regulate speech if there is a reason to forecast a substantial disruption, which includes the loss of student rights. Sexually harassing speech substantially interferes with the rights of all students according to Title IX of the Education Amendments of 1972, 20 U.S.C. 1681 *et seq.,* which provides students with the right to an environment free from sexual harassment. The District Court erred in its narrow application of *Tinker* to only include disruptions that are akin to

EXHIBIT 18A (cont.)

mayhem. A loss of rights, including the right to be educated in an environment free from sexual harassment of even one child, constitutes a substantial disruption under *Tinker.* Therefore, the District Court erred in applying the law to the facts and, in so doing, abused its discretion.

ARGUMENT

I. The School District has a likelihood of success on the merits of its appeal because the District Court abused its discretion, both in its application of the Fraser standard of deferential reasonableness and the Tinker standard.

A. The District Court erroneously failed to apply the Fraser standard of deferential reasonableness to affirm the School District's reasonable manner restriction on student in-school speech.

Our Supreme Court declared in the landmark case of *Tinker v. Des Moines Independent Community School District,* 393 U.S. 503 (1969), that schools cannot restrain speech because of "a mere desire to avoid the discomfort and unpleasantness that always accompany an unpopular viewpoint." *Id.* at 509. In *Tinker,* a group of students [was] suspended for wearing of a two-inch-wide plain black armband in protest of America's involvement in the Vietnam War. *Id.* at 514. The defendant school district suspended the students pursuant to its ban on the plain black armbands, which was instituted based upon the belief that the anti-Vietnam War sentiment might create a political disturbance, both inside and outside of the schoolhouse. *Id.* at 509 n.3. The Supreme Court explained that "students may not be regarded as closed-circuit recipients of only that which the State chooses to communicate. They may not be confined to the expression of those sentiments that are officially approved." *Id.* at 511. Ultimately, the Court declared that, to "justify prohibition of a particular expression of opinion, [a school district] must be able to show . . . that engaging in the forbidden conduct would 'materially and substantially interfere with the requirements of appropriate discipline in the operation of the school.'" *Id.* at 509 (quoting *Burnside v. Byars,* 363 F.2d 744, 749 (5th Cir. 1966)).

Nearly 20 years later, the Supreme Court, via the case of *Bethel School District No. 403 v. Fraser,* 478 U.S. 675 (1986), declared that deference should be paid to the reasonable manner-of-speech restrictions set by public school administrators. *Id.* at 683. In *Fraser,* one student, Matthew Fraser, for the purpose of nominating his choice candidate in a way that developed "rapport" with his fellow students, delivered a speech containing sexual metaphors.[3] *Id.* at 677-78; *see also Fraser v. Bethel Sch. Dist. No. 403,* 755 F.2d 1356, 1363 (9th Cir. 1985) (explaining that Matthew Fraser's stated reason for utilizing sexual metaphor was to develop "rapport" with his classmates), *overruled by Bethel Sch. Dist. No. 403 v. Fraser,* 478 U.S. 675 (1986). The defendant school district responded by giving Matthew a three-day suspension due to the lewd manner in which he spoke to the students and faculty at attendance during the school assembly. *Id.* at 678-79. The Supreme Court explained that "[t]he First Amendment guarantees wide freedom in matters of adult public discourse . . . It does not follow, however, that simply because the

EXHIBIT 18A (cont.)

use of an offensive form of expression may not be prohibited to adults making what the speaker considers a political point, the same latitude must be permitted to children in the public school." *Id.* at 682. After distinguishing the viewpoint preclusion in *Tinker* from the manner restriction applied to Matthew's speech, the Supreme Court declared that "[t]he First Amendment does not prevent the school officials from determining that to permit a vulgar and lewd speech such as respondent's would undermine the school's basic educational mission." *Id.* at 685; *but cf. Morse v. Frederick,* 551 U.S. 393, 408 (2007) (clarifying that the *Fraser* standard does not apply to public school instituted viewpoint restrictions that would "undermine the school's basic educational mission," such as religious or political viewpoints). Therefore, while schools are not generally permitted to ban offensive viewpoints absent substantial disruption, the Supreme Court has granted school administrators, who are duly-delegated agents of the school board, discretion to implement reasonable manner restrictions when a vulgar medium is used to convey students' viewpoints. *See e.g. Fraser,* 478 U.S. at 683 ("The determination of what *manner* of speech in the classroom [or] in the school assembly is inappropriate properly rests with the school board.")

While this Court has yet to address a manner restriction pursuant to *Fraser,*[4] in the case of *Saxe v. State College Area School District,* 240 F.3d 200 (3d Cir. 2001), this Court provided the following guidance with respect to the type of reasonable manner restriction permitted by the Supreme Court in *Fraser*: "*Fraser* permits a school to prohibit words that 'offend for the same reasons that obscenity offends'—a dichotomy neatly illustrated by the comparison between Cohen's jacket and Tinker's armband." *Id.* at 213 (quoting *FCC v. Pacifica Found.,* 438 U.S. 726, 746 (1978)).[5] The Second Circuit Court of Appeals in the case of *Guiles ex rel. Guiles v. Marineau,* 461 F.3d 320 (2d Cir. 2006), reasoned that the *Fraser* standard applies to "speech that is something less than obscene but related to that concept, that is to say, speech containing sexual innuendo or profanity." *Id.* at 327. As clarified by subsequent case law, student speech that appeals to the prurient interest is generally regarded as proscribable under *Fraser.* In *Broussard ex rel. Lord v. School Board of Norfolk,* 801 F. Supp. 1526 (D. Va. 1992), for example, the defendant school punished Kimberly Ann Broussard for wearing a shirt containing the phrase "Drugs Suck!" At trial, Kimberly Ann testified that "the shirt's message was that it is 'not right to use drugs,' a message that she wanted to convey to others. She intended the shirt to be provocative in its anti-drug message." *Id.* at 1533. Because the use of the word "suck" in its meaning of "disapproval" has sexual connotations, the court held that the school district reasonably banned Kimberly Ann's "Drugs Suck!" shirt due to the vulgarity of its mode of expressing her anti-drug sentiment. *Id.* at 1536-37. [Other case synopses are omitted.] Finally, in *Pyle v. South Hadley School Committee,* 861 F. Supp. 157 (D. Mass. 1994),[6] the court held that high school students could not wear a shirt that contained the phrase "See Dick Drink. See Dick Drive. See Dick Die. Don't be a Dick." The plaintiffs in *Pyle* argued that the court should be responsible for weighing administrators' decisions on its own scale of offensiveness and conclude that the T-shirts were not vulgar. *Id.* at 159. The court explained as follows:

> The question becomes, who decides what is "vulgar"? The question in most cases is easy: *assuming general reasonableness, the citizens of the community,*

EXHIBIT 18A (cont.)

through their elected representatives on the school board and the school administrators appointed by them, make the decision. On questions of coarseness or ribaldry in school, federal courts do not decide how far is too far.

This is because people will always differ on the level of crudity required before a school administrator should react. The T-shirts in question here may strike people variously as humorous, innocuous, stupid or indecent. In assessing the acceptability of various forms of vulgar expression in the secondary school, however, the limits are to be debated and decided within the community; the rules may even vary from one school district to another as the diversity of the culture dictates. *The administrator here acted within reason, and the court's inquiry need go no further.*

Id. (emphasis added).

. . .

i. The District Court committed a fundamental error because it failed to apply the deferential standard of objective reasonableness set forth in *Fraser.*

The 7/8 Building Principal and Assistant Principals restricted the "I ❤ Boobies!" manner in which the minor Plaintiffs conveyed their breast cancer awareness message, not the message of breast cancer awareness itself.[8] Therefore, this case involves only the authority of school officials to regulate language worn by students that the administration considers to be inappropriate and offensive in the context of its school. "Reasonable and nondiscriminatory regulations on time, place, and manner are permissible restrictions on expression." *Broussard,* 801 F. Supp. at 1534; *C.H. ex rel. Z.H. v. Oliva,* 226 F.3d 198, 211-12 (3d Cir. 2000) (explaining that public school teachers may institute reasonable time, place, and manner restrictions).

Deference to school principals' judgment when carrying out the daily work of their schools is firmly established by case law and statute. In *Fraser,* the Supreme Court clarified that lessons of civility and decency in student expression is the "work of the schools;" thus, school boards should be afforded discretion in instances of manner-only speech restraints. *Fraser,* 478 U.S. at 683 ("The determination of what *manner* of speech in the classroom or in school assembly is inappropriate properly rests with the school board."); *but cf. Tinker,* 393 U.S. at 508-09 (explaining that the control of student *viewpoints* is not the work of the schools and should only be done when the expression of student viewpoints substantially interferes with the work of the schools). *See also Morse,* 551 U.S. at 401(giving deference to the principal's reasonable pro-drug-use interpretation of Frederick's banner while there were other possible interpretations); *Fraser,* 478 U.S. at 683 ("The inculcation of these values is truly the 'work of the schools' . . . The determination of what manner of speech is inappropriate properly rests with the school board."); *Poling v. Murphy,* 872 F.2d 757, 762 (6th Cir. 1989) ("Local control over the public schools, after all, is one of this nation's most deeply rooted and cherished traditions."); *Quarterman v. Byrd,* 453 F.2d 54, 56-57 (4th Cir. 1971) ("In prescribing general conduct within the school, the school authorities must have a wide latitude of discretion, subject only to a standard of reasonableness."). Therefore, because regulating

EXHIBIT 18A (cont.)

and eliminating vulgarity from the manner of student speech is the daily "work of the schools," administrators' reasonable determinations regarding vulgarity should be afforded deference.[9]

Moreover, this Court's definition of "vulgarity" in the context of public schools requires deference to schools administrators' judgment as [to] the community standard. As set forth [most] clearly, in *Saxe*, 240 F.3d at 213, this Court clarified that "*Fraser* permits a school to prohibit words that offend *for the same reasons that obscenity offends*" (emphasis added). The way that "obscenity offends" is community dependent. *See e.g. FCC v. Pacifica Foundation*, 438 U.S. 726 (1978) (defining "indecent" by the "contemporary *community standards* for the broadcast medium . . . "). For the community of the Easton Area Middle School, particularly the 7/8 Building, the views of decency held by the 12 and 13-year-old Plaintiffs, their mothers, and the Keep-A-Breast Foundation[10] did not and cannot represent the locally accepted standards of decency. While the two minor Plaintiffs of this case and their mothers believe that any word may be used provided it is being used to raise cancer awareness,[11] it is the 7/8 Building administration, as duly delegated agents of the elected members of the School Board, who is ultimately answerable to the Easton voting community and, therefore, is in the best position to represent the community standard of decency, particularly in the middle school context. *See Fraser*, 478 U.S. at 696 (Stevens, J., dissenting) (explaining that the Court applies contemporary *community standards* in evaluating speech with sexual connotations); *see also Pyle*, 861 F. Supp. at 170 ("the school board . . . is in the best position to weigh the strengths and vulnerabilities of the town's 785 high school students."); *and see Broussard*, 801 F. Supp. at 1536 ("school boards, school administrators, principals, and teachers must be permitted to govern schools attended by children."). Therefore, the community standard for appropriate communication must be vested with the administration, mitigated by a standard of deferential reasonableness.

The distinction between the application of the *Tinker* and *Fraser* standards supports the deferential nature of the *Fraser* standard. To meet the *Tinker* standard, a school must show that the speech would materially and substantially interfere with the "work of the school" or the rights of others. *Sypeniewski*, 307 F.3d at 257. The disruption must be more than hypothetical: There must be a reasonably foreseeable disruption. *Id.* Although it has been termed a "general rule," the *Tinker* standard, particularly post-*Fraser* and *Morse*, is applied when a school district seeks to restrain "pure speech" targeted for its viewpoint or speech that occurs outside of school. See the cases cited and text accompanying note 4. In both of those types of instances, a school district must have an exceptionally high interest in restraining the speech in order to pass constitutional muster. The "water-mark" of this standard is much higher than the standard set for speech that restrains pursuant to manner, as defined by *Fraser*. In *Fraser*, the Supreme Court made clear that teaching values regarding manner of speech is the "work of the schools," thus the school board can restrain vulgar and offensive speech without the showing of a substantial disruption. *Fraser*, 478 U.S. at 683. Because it is a "highly appropriate function of public school education to prohibit the use of vulgar and offensive terms in public discourse,'' when schools seek to restrain on-campus speech due to its vulgar manner, as opposed to offensive viewpoint, the *Fraser* standard permits such a restriction, mitigated by a standard of reasonableness. *Fraser,* 478 U.S. at 683 (''The determination of what manner of speech in the classroom or in school assembly is inappropriate properly rests with the school board.'').

Also, when in-school speech was banned by district administrations due exclusively to its vulgar manner, particularly when sexuality is involved, there has not been a single court in this country, aside from the District Court in the instant case, which has refused to defer to the reasonable sensibilities of a school principal. [The brief then discusses eight cases.] Accordingly, while this Court and others have been reluctant to grant school districts latitude in their ''forecasts for disruption,'' similar scrutiny has not been paid to a school district's decisions to regulate the mode of students' communication, particularly in the case of sexual innuendo.

. . . [The] question is whether a reasonable school administrator could determine that the bracelets were vulgar. As such, the District Court abused its discretion in applying the law to the facts. [But the] District Court failed to apply a standard of deferential reasonableness to the administration's vulgarity determination and, instead, deferred to the minor Plaintiffs' intentions. When applying the law to the facts, the District Court should have first determined whether ''boobies,'' from the expression ''I ❤ Boobies!'', *could* be understood as a familiar term for the female breast.[13] Then, the next inquiry should have been whether expressing a love for the female breast *could* be understood as prurient.[14] The District Court explained that the inclusion of the Keep-A-Breast Foundation name on the bracelet, along with the *keepabreast.org* URL inscription on the inside, renders a finding of vulgarity for the ''I ❤ Boobies!'' message unreasonable. (App. Vol. I at 31) (''[T]he phrase 'I ❤ Boobies!' in the context of these bracelets cannot reasonably be deemed vulgar. 'I ❤ Boobies!' is presented in the context of a national breast cancer awareness campaign. The phrase 'I ❤ Boobies!' is always accompanied by the Foundation's name 'Keep A Breast'.''). This is an incorrect application of the law to the facts. Under a deferential, objective standard of reasonableness, the issue is whether a reasonable administrator, viewing the ''I ❤ Boobies!'' phrase next to the Keep-A-Breast Foundation name, *could* believe that that ''I ❤ Boobies!'' manner of communicating the Keep-A-Breast message appeals to a prurient interest in the female breast. The District Court's analysis inverts this standard and, instead, asks the question of whether a reasonable person could believe that the ''I ❤ Boobies!'' phrase communicates a message of breast cancer awareness in the context of the Keep-A-Breast Foundation's campaign. Applying a standard of deferential reasonableness to children's choice [of] manners of speech effectively surrenders control of the public schools from the teachers, administrators, and elected officials to the public school students, which is an effect specifically derided by the Supreme Court. *Fraser,* 478 U.S. at 686 (favorably quoting Tinker, 393 U.S. at 526 (Black, J., dissenting) (''I wish therefore, . . . to disclaim any purpose . . . to hold that the Federal Constitution compels the teacher, parents, and elected school officials to surrender control of the American public school system to

EXHIBIT 18A (cont.)

public school students.''). Accordingly, the standard of deference that the District Court paid to the students' interpretations of the "I ❤ Boobies!" message is an erroneous application of law to fact. As such, the District Court abused its discretion.

Not only is the District Court's application of the law erroneous, but the precedent set by the District Court's decision promotes inefficiency for the courts and impotence for principals and elected school officials. Local communities elect school board officials who will best represent the policy concerns of the community. School administrators, appointed by those local officials as their duly delegated agents, are chosen to effect the policies set by the elected school board officials. Any time students wear new expressions produced as part of an awareness raising campaign, the administration will have to either allow the choice language of that campaign, even if it is an aberration of the community standards of decency, or the courts will be tasked with determining whether the item was vulgar under the *Fraser* standard. The District Court's analysis provides, in its effect, an exception to the *Fraser* standard when the students and their parents can prove that the speech at issue was used to enhance the message of an awareness raising campaign. (App. Vol. I at 5) ("This Court concludes that these bracelets cannot reasonably be considered lewd or vulgar under the standard of *Fraser*. The bracelets are intended to be and they can reasonably be viewed as speech designed to raise awareness of breast cancer and to reduce the stigma associated with openly discussing breast health."). [Given] the adolescent imagination, particularly in middle school, it is not out of the question to conceive of multiple possibilities for language that could be used as an "awareness raising tool." Therefore, the District Court's decision has set the stage for ineffective school administrators and inefficient courts.

According to all of the above, the District Court erroneously applied a standard of subjectivity and deference to students when the law provides an objective standard of deference to public school administrators. As such, the District Court abused its discretion.

ii. The District Court's finding that "I ❤ Boobies!" could not reasonably be considered vulgar is clearly erroneous [and] thus manifests an abuse of discretion.

. . .

As set forth more clearly, the Principal's decision regarding student manners of speech should be reviewed under the following standard of objective reasonableness: whether a reasonable administrator could consider the phrase "I ❤ Boobies!" vulgar in the context of the public school. This standard is not one of unfettered discretion. For example, it could not be argued that the wearing of a plain black armband is "vulgar." There was no evidence at trial or in depositions that the School District banned "I ❤ Boobies!" bracelets as a pretext to discriminate against the viewpoint of breast cancer awareness— regardless of the 7/8 Building administration's perceived lack of credibility for vigorousness of belief that the bracelets were vulgar, there was never any evidence or accusation that the School District precluded the breast cancer awareness message.

EXHIBIT 18A **(cont.)**

Moreover, the expressive right of students to utilize sexuality to enhance the communication of their viewpoints is not co-extensive with the rights of adults to utilize sexual expression. *See Kuhlmeier,* 484 U.S. at 266 (quoting *Tinker,* 393 U.S. at 506) (explaining that First Amendment rights must be applied "in light of the special circumstances of the school environment"); *see also Fraser,* 478 U.S. at 682 (explaining that the First Amendment rights of students in the public schools "are not automatically coextensive with the rights of adults in other settings"). In *Fraser,* the Supreme Court gave particular consideration to the fact that Matthew Fraser's speech contained sexual innuendo and his audience included children "only 14 years old and on the threshold of awareness of human sexuality." *Fraser,* 478 U.S. at 683.[15] In so doing, the Supreme Court noted that its First Amendment jurisprudence "has acknowledged limitations on the otherwise absolute interest of the speaker in reaching an unlimited audience where the speech is sexually explicit and the audience may include children." *Id.* at 684. Post-*Fraser,* federal courts have defined the *Fraser* manner restriction with specific regard to sexual innuendo. *See Saxe,* 240 F.3d at 213 (explaining that "*Fraser* permits a school to prohibit words that 'offend for the same reasons that obscenity offends'");[16] *Guiles ex rel. Guiles,* 461 F.3d at 327 (reasoning that the *Fraser* standard applies "speech that is something less than obscene but related to that concept, that is to say, speech containing *sexual innuendo* or profanity") [references to lower-court cases omitted].

The District Court abused its discretion by focusing on the Plaintiffs' stated intentions for wearing "I ❤ Boobies!" because the United States Supreme Court has made clear that students' stated intentions for their speech do not negate a school principal's reasonable determination to the contrary. In the case of *Morse v. Frederick,* 551 U.S. 393 (2007), the Supreme Court analyzed whether the speech, BONG HiTS 4 JESUS, could reasonably be understood as advocacy for illegal drug use. The student in the case stated that it was meant to be "gibberish," while the school principal understood the speech to be advocating drug use. The Supreme Court of the United States reasoned that "[g]ibberish is surely a possible interpretation of the words on the banner, but it is not the only one, and dismissing the banner as meaningless denies its undeniable reference to illegal drugs." *Morse,* 551 U.S. at 402.[17] The dissenting judges in *Morse* credited Joseph Frederick's alleged motivation of simply wanting a television appearance. *Id.* at 444-45, (Stevens, J., dissenting). The majority singled out this specific point for admonishment and stated as follows: "[Frederick's motive] is not an interpretation of what the banner says." *Id.* at 402; *see also Fraser v. Bethel Sch. Dist. No. 403,* 755 F.2d 1356, 1363 (9th Cir. 1985) (explaining that Matthew Fraser utilized sexual metaphor in his speech to develop a rapport with his classmates to enhance the effectiveness of his speech), *overruled by* 478 U.S. 675 (1986). Therefore, in its analysis of the reasonableness of an administration's speech interpretation, the United States Supreme Court focused specifically on the words, not the motivation of the speaker. Moreover, the administration does not have to adopt the literal meaning or the students' meaning of their chosen manner of expression. *See also Fraser,* 478 U.S. at 677-78.

EXHIBIT 18A (cont.)

When determining whether a manner restriction was reasonable, federal courts have also considered student intent to be irrelevant. [Discussion of lower-court cases [is] omitted.] Therefore, the District Court in the instant case erred in its focus on the Plaintiffs' motivations in rendering a finding regarding the vulgarity of the "I ♥ Boobies!" message. Accordingly, the District Court's factual finding with respect to the reasonableness of the School District's interpretation of the "I ♥ Boobies!" phrase is clearly erroneous. Furthermore, the District Court's misapplication of the law to the facts manifests an abuse of discretion.

In conducting an objective analysis of whether "I ♥ Boobies!" could reasonably be deemed vulgar, this Court should consider whether the phrase could be interpreted to convey sexual connotations, even in the context of the Keep-A-Breast Foundation's awareness campaign. The "I ♥ Boobies!" phrase, utilized as part of a breast cancer awareness campaign could and has been considered by many to convey the double entendre of a prurient interest in the female breast. As will be explained clearly by the following list, the 7/8 Building administrators and the School District were not alone in their belief that the bracelets conveyed a vulgar sexual double entendre:

(1) Playboy Magazine, a publication regularly engaged in the marketing of prurient commerce, believed that this case would be of interest to its readers. In the February 2011 issue of Playboy Magazine, a picture of the "I ♥ Boobies!" bracelets and an article about this case was featured on page 131 of the magazine, along with other articles on the topics of condom use, HIV, and a pornographic movie.

(2) Truck stops, convenience stores, vending machine owners, and "porn stars" were interested in marketing the "I ♥ Boobies!" bracelets created by the Keep-A-Breast Foundation. (App. Vol. II at 151-52, 163; see also Vol. I at 10). The interest of prurient commerce in the "I ♥ Boobies!" bracelets supports the reasonableness of the School District's belief that the "I ♥ Boobies!" bracelets were an inappropriate medium for communication by children in the public school.[18]

(3) Media commentators, most notably Peggy Orenstein of the New York Times, have noted the sexual connotation of the "I ♥ Boobies!" bracelets. (App. Vol. II at 326-27). On November 12, 2010, the New York Times Magazine published an article by Peggy Orenstein, New York Times best selling author and breast cancer survivor, which states the following regarding the "I ♥ Boobies!" bracelets: "That rubber bracelet is part of a newer trend: the sexualization of breast cancer. Hot breast cancer. Saucy breast cancer. Titillating breast cancer!" (App. Vol. II at 328). Moreover, Ms. Ornstein addressed the "I ♥ Boobies!" message as part of the problem as follows: "today's fetishing of breasts comes at the expense of the bodies, heart, and minds attached to them." (App. Vol. II at 328; see also App. Vol. I at 33 (noting the Peggy Ornstein article as criticizing 'sexy cancer' awareness, but noting that Ms. Ornstein acknowledged that the irreverence is utilized with the purpose of combating fatigue)).[19]

EXHIBIT 18A (cont.)

(4) The "I ❤ Boobies!" phrase has been utilized by T-shirt companies that sell T-shirts and other paraphernalia that are vulgar, offensive, and particularly debasing to women and girls. *See* www.foulmouthshirts.com and www.sikworld.com.

(5) In September 2010, the beginning of the 2010/2011 school year, teachers of the 7/8 Building began noticing the "I ❤ Boobies!" bracelets and made inquiries regarding their appropriateness under the school dress code which prohibits the wearing of double entendre expressions. The students also deciphered a sexual message from the bracelets and made comments expressing "love" for "boobies." Therefore, both teachers and students recognized a prurient interpretation of the "I ❤ Boobies!" phrase, even within the Keep-A-Breast Foundation context.

(6) K.M.'s mother, Amy Martinez, saw an inappropriate meaning in the words of the "I ❤ Boobies!" bracelets. (Vol. III Deposition of A. Martinez at 12, lines 13-17) ("When I initially bought the bracelet for my daughter, the very first one, yes, I absolutely was a parent who said, Oh, my God, boobies is on a bracelet; is that appropriate for a child of 12 in middle school.") According to all of the above responses to the "I ❤ Boobies!" phrase contained specifically on the bracelets of the Keep-A-Breast Foundation, a reasonable administrator could find that the "I ❤ Boobies!" phrase, even in the context of the Keep-A-Breast Foundation's cancer awareness campaign, conveys a sexual double entendre and is, therefore, vulgar and inappropriate in the public school context.

The District Court erred in applying *Fraser* narrowly to only exclude unspeakable profanity from First Amendment protection in the public school. Specifically, the District Court noted that the 7/8 Building administrators have comfortably spoken the phrase in court for this case and over the morning announcements to inform students of the ban on the "I ❤ Boobies!" bracelets. (App. Vol. I at 36). Also, the District Court noted that numerous magazines, newspapers, and internet publications have utilized the "I ❤ Boobies!" phrase when reporting on the Keep-A-Breast bracelets and this case. (App. Vol. I at 33). Nowhere in the *Fraser* opinion does the Supreme Court state that speech must be a "four-letter word" or outright unspeakable profanity to be restrained in the public school for its manner of communication. In fact, Matthew Fraser's speech did not contain a single overt sexual reference, mention of a sexual body part, or actual expletive that could not bear repeating. The manner of language does not have to be unspeakable or explicitly sexual to meet the standard set forth by the United States Supreme Court in *Fraser*. *See Fraser,* 478 U.S. at 683 (explaining that vulgar and offensive manners of communicating may be excluded from school to teach concrete lessons of civility and giving discretion to the school board to determine what is appropriate); *Guiles ex rel. Guiles,* 461 F.3d at 327 (reasoning that the *Fraser* standard applies to "speech that is something less than obscene but related to that concept, that is to say, speech containing *sexual innuendo* or profanity.").

Further, the District Court erred in analyzing the veracity of the 7/8 Building administrators' belief that the "I ❤ Boobies!" phrase was vulgar because the *Fraser* standard, particularly as it was interpreted subsequently by federal courts, is based upon a standard of objective reasonableness. As has been stated earlier, the appropriate standard

EXHIBIT 18A (cont.)

that should be applied is whether a reasonable school administrator *could* believe that "I ❤ Boobies!" conveys a double entendre and is vulgar in the context of the public school. *See Broussard,* 801 F. Supp. at 1534 ("The Court finds that a reasonable middle school administrator *could* find that the word 'suck,' even as used on the shirt, may be interpreted to have a sexual connotation."). In this case, the District Court assessed the 7/8 Building administrators' credibility by noting their use of the "I ❤ Boobies!" phrase when informing students of the ban and when testifying in court. Also the District Court emphasized the immediacy of the 7/8 Building Principal in completely banning the "I ❤ Boobies!" phrase, particularly in comparison with the immediacy of the Bethel School District's response to Matthew Fraser's speech. (App. Vol. I at 37-38). This comparison is factually erroneous and ultimately led to a legally erroneous conclusion by the District Court. The reaction of the 7/8 Building administration was congruent with the speech at issue. Matthew Fraser's speech was announced to the student body at an assembly via spoken word and created an instant school sensation; the "I ❤ Boobies!" speech was delivered on an individual basis via written expression and was viewed by administration as a dress code violation. (*See* App. Vol. II at 228, 260). Therefore, the reaction of the administration was appropriately congruent with the type of speech at issue. Moreover, the District Court's focus on the immediacy of the School District's reaction as a factor weighing against the administrators' credibility is a legally erroneous application of an objective standard of reasonableness [and] thus an abuse of discretion.

The "I ❤ Boobies!" phrase contained on the Keep-A-Breast bracelets has been interpreted by its readers in multiple ways. To some, the phrase was construed to convey [a] sexual double entendre which, couched as a breast cancer awareness message, suggested a prurient attraction to the female breast. Probably to some the bracelets were purely sophomoric. The Plaintiffs in this case claimed that they wore the bracelets for a breast cancer awareness message meant to appeal to their peers. But the 7/8 Building administration, and, ultimately, the School District interpreted the phrase as a sexual innuendo and, therefore, an inappropriate and offensive medium for school children to communicate. That interpretation is plainly reasonable according to the above-listed facts. Therefore, by a standard of objective reasonableness, a reasonable administrator could believe that the "I ❤ Boobies!" phrase is vulgar and offensive. *See Morse,* 551 U.S. at 401.[20] As such, the District Court erred in applying the law to the facts. Further, the District Court made a clearly erroneous factual finding regarding the reasonableness of the administration's interpretation of the bracelets. Accordingly, the District Court abused its discretion.

B. The District Court erroneously held that the School District's restraint on "I ❤ Boobies!" did not meet the Tinker standard because an atmosphere of sexual harassment substantially interferes with every student's right to an education.

The School District demonstrated a reasonable forecast of disruption due to the atmosphere of sexual harassment created by the "I ❤ Boobies!" phrase. "I ❤ Boobies!" has sexual connotations and, particularly in the mind of students in the middle school, creates a sexually charged environment which is disruptive to the public school education. Therefore, under the *Tinker* standard of disruption, the School District did not violate the Plaintiffs' First Amendment rights by proscribing the "I ❤ Boobies!" bracelets. Accordingly, the District Court's conclusions regarding *Tinker* were legally erroneous and constitute an abuse of discretion. *See Broussard,* 801 F. Supp. at 1537 (opining in dicta that the sexual meaning of "Drugs Suck" creates a reasonable forecast of disruption).

Under the standard set forth in *Tinker,* a school may "forecast" a disruption and take preemptive action. *Tinker,* 393 U.S. at 509. No circuit court in this nation has required the administration to wait for an actual disruption before acting. In *Tinker,* the Court upheld students' right to wear plain black armbands in protest of the United States' participation in the Vietnam War because the school showed "no evidence whatever of petitioners' interference, actual or nascent, with the schools' work or of collision with the rights of other students . . . " *Tinker,* 393 U.S. at 508. Under the facts of this case, the "rights of other students" are set forth under Title IX of the Education Amendments of 1972, 20 U.S.C. 1681 *et seq.,* which prohibits "student-on-student" sexual harassment in the public schools. *See e.g. Davis ex rel. LaShonda D. v. Monroe County Bd. of Educ.,* 516 U.S. 629 (1999). Under Title IX, a private cause of action exists for students when a school "acts with deliberate indifference to known acts of harassment in its programs or activities . . . [S]uch an action will lie only for harassment that is so severe, pervasive, and objectively offensive that it effectively bars the victim's access to an educational opportunity or benefit." *Id.* at 633. Whether sexual harassment rises to the level of actionable "harassment" under Title IX depends upon the surrounding circumstances including the ages of the harasser, the victim, and the number of individuals involved. *Id.* at 651 (citing *Oncale v. Sundowner Offshore Services, Inc.,* 523 U.S. 75, 82 (1998). In this case, the "I ❤ Boobies!" phrase was deemed inappropriate for school due to the likelihood of a resultant increase in student-on-student sexual harassment. Students in middle school are at various stages of sexual development and are particularly vulnerable to prurient expressions, especially when said phrases are utilized in school where students are also easily distracted.[21]

In *Saxe,* this Court considered the constitutionality of a public school's harassment policy which completely excluded speech that offended an individual due to gender, race, religion, color, national origin, sexual orientation, disability, or other personal characteristics. *Saxe,* 240 F.3d at 202-03. In striking down the policy, this Court criticized the Middle District Court for naming a categorical "harassment exception" to the free speech guarantees of the First Amendment. *Id.* at 204. Also, this Court cautioned against "[l]oosely worded anti-harassment laws" which "may regulate deeply offensive and potentially disruptive categories of speech based, at least in part, on subject matter and viewpoint." *Id.* at 207. However, in *Saxe,* this Court also qualified that "[w]e do not suggest, of course, that no application of anti-harassment law to express speech can survive First Amendment scrutiny. Certainly, preventing discrimination in the workplace and in the schools is not only a legitimate, but a compelling, governmental interest." *Id.*

at 209-10 (citing *Bd. of Dirs. of Rotary Int'l v. Rotary Club of Duarte,* 481 U.S. 537, 549 (1987)). The policy of the school district in *Saxe* was deemed unconstitutional because, *inter alia,* it included the expression of offensive viewpoints. *Saxe,* 240 F.3d at 215 (citing *Tinker,* 393 U.S. at 509). Also, this Court explained that offensiveness to the listener is not sufficient to "intrude upon . . . the rights of students" as is required and articulated by the Supreme Court in *Tinker. Saxe,* 240 F.3d at 217 (quoting *Tinker,* 393 U.S. at 504). To exclude core political and religious speech, there must be a showing of "severity of pervasiveness" of harassment. *Saxe,* 240 F.3d at 217. Therefore, this Court held that the policy [covered] substantially more speech than could be proscribed under *Tinker*'s substantial disruption test. Accordingly, for a sexual harassment policy or proscription to pass constitutional muster under this Court's understanding of *Tinker,* the proscription may not be targeted at "pure speech."

In this case, the 7/8 Building administration prohibited the "I ❤ Boobies!" bracelets from school due to its dress code proscription of double entendre phrases. Unlike the policy in *Saxe,* which would prohibit students from speaking out against same-sex partnerships, the "I ❤ Boobies!" ban only prohibits the use of that specific phrase which was deemed vulgar and offensive by the 7/8 Building Principal. It does not prohibit students from communicating a concern for breast cancer, and it does not prohibit students from any other "pure speech," targeted only for its expressive content.

Particularly in the context of a public middle school, administrators must be mindful of the fact that sexual harassment is damaging to its sexually developing population of students. While some students are comfortable with reporting sexual harassment to the administration, at the middle school level, most do not. The school maintains its dress code as a proactive measure to curb the sexual harassment that is particularly problematic in its middle school context. Further, the administration acted preemptively in banning the bracelets to avoid the result of sexual harassment which, based upon the experience of all of the administrators, was inevitable. At no point was a viewpoint ever prohibited. Moreover, the target speech was the specific preclusion of one phrase due to its sexual meaning, not all speech pertaining to breast cancer awareness or all speech that could be offensive. Accordingly, the District Court erred in applying too narrow a standard of "substantial disruption" that did not include an analysis of students' Title IX right to an atmosphere free of sexual harassment. Therefore, the District Court abused its discretion.

II. The District Court erred in its holding that the Plaintiffs would be irreparably harmed by a denial of a preliminary injunction because the Plaintiffs have multiple alternative channels of communicating a concern for breast cancer awareness.

The District Court erroneously held that the Plaintiffs would be irreparably harmed by denial of the preliminary injunction because of "the loss of First Amendment freedoms." (App. Vol. I at 41). The Plaintiffs did not lose any "First Amendment freedoms" because the "I ❤ Boobies!" bracelets were banned pursuant to a reasonable manner restriction. Therefore, the District Court abused its discretion.

EXHIBIT 18A **(cont.)**

The United States Supreme Court has consistently declared the following with respect to time, place, and manner restrictions:

> [E]ven in a public forum the government may impose reasonable restrictions on the time, place, or manner of protected speech, provided the restrictions 'are justified without reference to the content of the regulated speech, that they are narrowly tailored to serve a significant governmental interest and they leave open ample alternative channels for communication of the information.'

Ward v. Rock Against Racism, 491 U.S. 781, 791 (1989) (quoting *Clark v. Community for Creative Non-Violence,* 468 U.S. 288, 293 (1984)). The justification for the ban on the "I ❤ Boobies!" bracelets was pursuant to a manner restriction applied because of the School District's significant interest in prohibiting vulgar and offensive terms from the school campus. *See Fraser,* 478 U.S. at 683. With the restraint being "narrowly tailored" only to cover the specific "I ❤ Boobies!" phrase, the School District has left open a plethora of other ways for the Plaintiffs' communication of their concern for breast cancer awareness, including the "Check Yourself bracelets that are also marketed by the Keep-A-Breast Foundation as part of its breast cancer awareness campaign. Therefore, the School District's ban on the "I ❤ Boobies!" bracelets constitutes a reasonable restriction on manner of speech.

In the context of a public school, children do not have a First Amendment interest in the use of vulgar expression. *See Fraser,* 478 U.S. at 682 ("The First Amendment guarantees wide freedom in matters of adult public discourse . . . It does not follow, however, that simply because the use of an offensive form of expression may not be prohibited to adults making what the speaker considers a political point, the same latitude must be permitted to children in the public school.") Provided that school districts do not categorically exclude a viewpoint, it is entirely the prerogative of the public school to categorically exclude vulgar or lewd manners of expression. *Saxe,* 240 F.3d at 214. Therefore, because the "I ❤ Boobies!" phrase was removed from the School District pursuant to a reasonable manner restriction, the Plaintiffs have not been deprived of any First Amendment guarantees. Accordingly, the District Court erred in its application of the law to the facts and, as such, abused its discretion.

III. The harm to the School District by a preliminary injunction is far greater than the denial of a preliminary injunction to the Plaintiffs, particularly because the School District will be unable to exercise its prerogative granted by Fraser and its statutory obligations required by the School Code.

The District has certain statutory responsibilities under the School Code regarding the maintenance of safety and order in the public school. In relevant part, those obligations and/or objectives are set forth in the following provisions of the Pennsylvania School Code:

1. 24 P.S. 13-1317.3 ("The board of directors in any school entity may impose limitations on dress and may require pupils to wear standard dress or uniforms.");

EXHIBIT 18A (cont.)

2. 24 P.S. 5-510 ("The board of directors in any school district may adopt and enforce such reasonable rules and regulations as it may deem necessary and proper . . . regarding the conduct and deportment of all pupils.");

3. 24 P.S. 13-1317 ("Every teacher, vice principal, and principal in the public schools shall have the right to exercise the same authority as to conduct and behavior over pupils attending his school . . . as the parents, guardians, or persons in parental relation to such pupils may exercise.");

4. 24 P.S. 13-1318 ("Every principal or teacher in charge of a public school may temporarily suspend any pupil on account of disobedience or misconduct . . . ").

At this time, the School District is revising its dress code for the 2011-2012 school year and has no clear guidance on how it should proceed. According to the District Court's holding, if students choose to wear an item containing a sexual double entendre as an awareness raising tool, the School District loses its authority under *Fraser* to disassociate itself from the language itself and require the students to use another mode of communication. This leaves the School District without any certainty with respect to its dress code specifically regarding sexually provocative or suggestive messages, vulgarity, and double entendres. By failing to recognize the deference due school authority to determine the manner of expression appropriate to the school community, school board, and its duly delegated agents, the Principal and Vice-Principals, have been prevented from performing one of their basic functions, that of regulating the deportment and conduct of students.

IV. The public will be harmed via the diminishment of the District's authority, exercise its prerogative and obligation to regulate the manner of student speech pursuant to Fraser and the School Code.

The public will be substantially harmed by the loss of school authority to manage its student population, particularly in an urban/suburban district. Without reasonable authority in the schools to regulate students' manners of speech, much of the purpose of obtaining a public education will be lost, particularly with respect to students' transition from school to work.

CONCLUSION

The daily operations of the school, including the manner of student speech, should rest with school principals, the duly delegated agents of the voter-elected school board, who are ultimately answerable to the voting community. In this case, the students were only subject to a speech manner restriction—at no point was the viewpoint of breast cancer awareness restrained, and in fact, it was an openly encouraged viewpoint. Therefore, the appropriate standard to review the principal's decision should be one of deferential reasonableness: whether a reasonable middle school administrator could believe that the "I ❤ Boobies!" phrase was vulgar. A declaration of love for a sexual part of the human anatomy, even if intended to be benign, could be interpreted as sexual innuendo, particularly in the context of a public school. Further, in addition to the opinions of the principal and vice-principals of the 7/8 Building, the "I ❤ Boobies!" phrase was interpreted to convey sexual innuendo by school teachers, students, media, "porn stars," vending machine companies, truck stops, and Playboy Magazine. Therefore, it is reasonable that the 7/8 Building principals would believe that the "I ❤ Boobies!" phrase conveys sexual innuendo and is inappropriate for its 11-14 year-old students. The District Court abused its discretion by paying deference to the students' interpretations of their communication, as opposed to the reasonable interpretation of the 7/8 Building administration. This release of authority from the principal to the students is not only poor public policy, [but] completely inconsistent with current First Amendment jurisprudence.

Alternatively, due to the atmosphere of sexual harassment created by the wearing of double entendre expressions, the 7/8 Building Principal could reasonably anticipate a substantial disruption created by a loss of students' rights to an atmosphere free [of] sexual harassment in the public schools, particularly because the administration was apprised of multiple incidents of sexual harassment precipitated by the bracelets. Accordingly, the "I ❤ Boobies!" bracelets were appropriately banned by the 7/8 Building administration. As such, the District Court committed a fundamental error and abused its discretion.

WHEREFORE, the School District respectfully requests that this Court reverse the judgment of the Eastern District Court of Pennsylvania rendered on April 12, 2011 erroneously granting Plaintiffs a preliminary injunction.

Endnotes

[For space reasons, we have retained only illustrative footnotes.]

[2]   Unlike out-of-school-suspension which is considered a more serious punishment, B.H. and K.M. were permitted to stay in school and complete their school work to avoid getting behind in their classes.

[4]   This Court has heard the following four cases, all of which were addressed under the standard set forth in *Tinker: J.S. v. Blue Mountain Sch. Dist.,* No. 08-4138 (3d Cir. June 13, 2011) (explaining that *Fraser* does not and cannot apply to a MySpace page created outside of school on a home computer); *see also Layschock v. Hermitage Area Sch. Dist.,* 07-4465 (3d Cir. June 13, 2011) (explaining that *Fraser* does not and cannot apply to a MySpace page created outside of school on a home computer); *Sypniewski v. Warren Hills Reg'l Bd. of Educ.,* 307 F.3d 243 (3d Cir. 2002) (challenging a district's ban on a T-shirts which were targeted due to the school district's belief that the written content of the T-shirts expressed racist sentiments via the term "redneck"); *Saxe v. State College Area School District,* 240 F.3d 200 (3d Cir. 2001) (challenging a school harassment policy because students could not express their anti-gay religious beliefs under the policy).

EXHIBIT 18A (cont.)

---

[6] The First Circuit Court of Appeals vacated the District Court of Massachusetts' decision relevant to *state law only* and deferred in its ruling of the state law issue pending the resolution of the Pyles' rights with the Massachusetts Supreme Court. *See Pyle v. South Hadley School District,* 55 F.3d 20 (1st Cir. 1995). The District Court of Massachusetts' decision with respect to the First Amendment of the United States Constitution has not been appealed, certified for appeal, or disturbed in anyway.

[8] As stated, the 7/8 Building participated in the School District's celebration of Breast Cancer Awareness Day for both students and staff as part of the School District's recognition of the national Breast Cancer Awareness Month. Not only does the 7/8 Building address breast health and breast cancer awareness in its health curriculum, but it also annually raises funding for the Susan G. Komen for the Cure Foundation, which is an internationally recognized breast cancer awareness and research organization. While the School District did not and does not support the "I ❤ Boobies!" statement, many breast cancer awareness raising tools, such as the "Check Yourself" bracelet also marketed by the Keep-A-Breast Foundation, are permitted and encouraged by the 7/8 Building administration.

[9] Pennsylvania School Law also firmly establishes that the daily administration of the school and its curriculum is best left up to the reasonable judgments of school administrators. *See, e.g.,* 24 P.S. 5-510 ("The board of directors in any school district may adopt and enforce such reasonable rules and regulations as it may deem necessary and proper . . . regarding the conduct and deportment of all pupils."); 24 P.S. 13-1317 ("Every teacher, vice principal, and principal in the public schools shall have the right to exercise the same authority as to conduct and behavior over pupils attending his school . . . as the parents, guardians, or persons in parental relation to such pupils may exercise."); 24 P.S. 13-1317.3 ("The board of directors in any school entity may impose limitations on dress and may require pupils to wear standard dress or uniforms.").

UNITED STATES COURT OF APPEALS, THIRD CIRCUIT: BRIEF OF APPELLEES*

B.H., a minor, by and through her mother, Jennifer Hawk, and K.M., a minor, by and through her mother, Amy McDonald-Martinez, Plaintiffs-Appellees,

v.

EASTON AREA SCHOOL DISTRICT, Defendant-Appellant.

No. 11-2067.
August 26, 2011.

On Appeal From The Order Granting Preliminary Injunction Of The United States District Court for The Eastern District of Pennsylvania Dated April 12, 2011, At Civil Action No. 5:10-cv-6823

BRIEF OF APPELLEES

Mary Catherine Roper, American Civil Liberties, Foundation Of Pennsylvania, P.O. Box 40008, Philadelphia, PA 19106, Telephone: (215) 592-1513 ext. 116, MRoper@aclupa.org.

Witold J. Walczak, American Civil Liberties Foundation of Pennsylvania, 313 Atwood Street, Pittsburgh, PA 15213, Telephone: (412) 681-7736, VWalczak @aclupa.org.

Molly Tack-Hooper, Berger & Montague, P.C., 1622 Locust Street, Philadelphia, PA 19103, Telephone: (215) 875-5814, MTack-Hooper@bm.net.

Seth F. Kreimer, 3400 Chestnut St., Philadelphia, PA 19104, Telephone: (215) 898-7447, Fax: (215) 573-2025, skreimer@law.upenn.edu, Counsel for Appellees.

TABLE OF CONTENTS

---

* This is a real brief filed in a real, highly contested case. We have deleted only a few portions in the interests of brevity. Our sincere thanks go to Mary Catherine Roper for her permission to reprint this brief for educational purposes.

EXHIBIT 18B (cont.)

TABLE OF AUTHORITIES

[This table is truncated for space reasons.]

STATEMENT OF ISSUES PRESENTED FOR REVIEW ON APPEAL

I. Did the District Court commit error when it applied this Court's precedents to a careful review of the record and concluded that the District failed to justify its censorship under *Tinker?*

II. Did the District Court commit error when it considered the context of the Plaintiffs' speech and the school officials' inconsistent reaction to the speech over a two-month period and concluded that the District failed to show that it reasonably characterized Plaintiffs' speech as lewd under *Fraser?*

III. Did the District Court commit error or abuse its discretion when it held that the Plaintiffs' loss of First Amendment freedoms constituted irreparable harm and that absence of any evidence of harm to the Defendant tipped the balance of equities in favor of an injunction?

Suggested answer to all: No.

SCOPE AND STANDARD OF REVIEW

On appeal from the grant of a preliminary injunction, this Court reviews the district court's legal conclusions *de novo,* its findings of fact for clear error, and its ultimate balancing of the relevant factors for abuse of discretion. *Sypniewski v. Warren Hills Reg. Bd. of Educ.,* 307 F.3d 243, 252 (3d Cir. 2002) (citing *Highmark, Inc. v. UPMC Health Plan, Inc.,* 276 F.3d 160, 170 (3d Cir. 2001)); *see also Oddi v. Ford Motor Co.,* 234 F.3d 136, 146 (3d Cir. 2000) ("An abuse of discretion can . . . occur when no reasonable person would adopt the district court's view. We will not interfere with the district court's exercise of discretion unless there is a definite and firm conviction that the court below committed a clear error of judgment in the conclusion it reached upon a weighing of the relevant factors.").

The fact that this case concerns First Amendment rights does not change this standard of review. The Supreme Court, in *Bose Corp. v. Consumers Union of United States, Inc.,* 466 U.S. 485 (1984), directed appellate courts to engage in an independent factual review of the full record in certain First Amendment cases to ensure "that the [district court] judgment does not constitute a forbidden intrusion on the field of free expression." *Id.* at 499. Where, as here, the district court judgment protects free expression, the rationale for applying the *Bose* heightened factual review is absent. *Cf., Pittsburgh League of Young Voters Educ. Fund v. Port Auth.,* Nos. 09-3352, 09-3563, 2011 WL 3375651, at *3 (3d Cir. Aug. 5, 2011) (noting that "*Bose*'s . . . speaker-protection purpose is triggered only in cases where the speaker lost at the trial level" but declining to decide whether the *Bose* standard applies where the decision below limited the government rather than the speaker).

COUNTERSTATEMENT OF FACTS

In the fall of 2010, B.H. was a thirteen-year-old eighth grader and K.M. a twelve-year-old seventh grader at Easton Area Middle School ("EAMS" or "the Middle School") in

EXHIBIT 18B (cont.)

the Easton Area School District ("School District" or "the District"). J.A. 7. Easton Area Middle School is a large complex that holds two separate schools. J.A. 7. The fifth and sixth grade school has a separate entrance, separate classrooms, separate lunchrooms, and is administered separately from the seventh and eighth grade school. J.A. 7. Plaintiffs attended classes in the EAMS 7-8 Building, which houses student from twelve to fourteen years of age. J.A. 7; J.A. 488 (DiVietro Dep. 16:9-11).

The Keep a Breast Bracelets

The bracelets at issue are bands of colored rubber that bear the slogans "i ❤ boobies! (KEEP A BREAST)," "check y❤ur self!! (KEEP A BREAST)," or an amalgam of similar slogans ("KEEP A BREAST," "KAB," "Glamour Kills," and "boobies!"). J.A. 7-8 & n.2.[1] The web address for the Keep a Breast Foundation, which distributes these bracelets, is keep-a-breast.org and is printed on the inside of all of the bracelets. J.A. 8.

The Foundation's mission is to help eradicate breast cancer by educating young people on methods of prevention, early detection, and support, and it operates many different breast cancer education programs and campaigns oriented towards girls and women up to thirty years of age. J.A. 8-9. The Foundation prides itself on the fact that its programming reaches "a demographic that other breast cancer non-profits do not touch." J.A. 155:21-23; *see also* J.A. 157:4-11 ("we're a youth-based nonprofit so we always want to interact with young people, people [whose] voices might not be heard by other breast cancer foundations"). Among other goals, the Foundation seeks to empower young women to take charge of their breast health and to be able to discuss their breast health with their doctors. J.A. 9. The Foundation encourages young women to establish a baseline knowledge of how their breasts feel in order to improve their ability to detect potentially deadly changes in their breasts. J.A. 9.

The Foundation believes that negative body images among young women pose a barrier to achieving these goals, and that many young women feel that a stigma is associated with touching, looking at, or talking about their breasts. J.A. 9. The Foundation's "i ❤ boobies!" campaign seeks to reduce this stigma and help women talk openly and without shame or embarrassment about their breasts. J.A. 9. The campaign is designed to reach young people by employing commonplace language that young people will find natural and non-threatening. *See* J.A. 150:13-19 ("boobies" is a "commonplace" word); J.A. 166:2 (describing "i ❤ boobies!" as a "very young sounding campaign"); J.A. 150:17 (explaining that "boobies" is a word that people are comfortable using to describe breasts to babies); J.A. 166:1-8 (same). The campaign uses the heart graphic because that is a common symbol for "love," and the theme of loving one's own body is an important part of the Foundation's message. J.A. 148:9-15, 149:16-20. The Keep A Breast Foundation did not intend for the phrase "i ❤ boobies!" to be sexual. J.A. 150:9-12, 151:15-23, 163:17-164:3. Rather, by associating "boobies" with the concept of love, the language of the "i ❤ boobies!" campaign takes aim at negative body images and taboos about self-touching and encourages young women to appreciate and actively care for their breasts. J.A. 148:9-149:1, 149:4-22, 170:16-171:2.

EXHIBIT 18B (cont.)

The "i ❤ boobies!" bracelets serve as an awareness and fundraising tool. J.A. 8-9. The Foundation carefully controls the distribution of the bracelets to reach its target demographic and to ensure that wherever the bracelets are sold, the campaign's message and educational materials will be properly communicated to the purchaser and the [wearer]. J.A. 10; J.A. 146:4-20, 151:24-152:6, 152:14-153:13. The Foundation has rejected requests from truck stops, convenience stores, and vending machine companies to sell the bracelets because of the difficulty of ensuring communication of its message in those venues. J.A. 152:1-6 (McAtee testifying); *see also* J.A. 10. The Foundation also has refused to allow "porn stars" and others to promote or sell the bracelets, J.A. 10, because they would be "inappropriate for our audience". J.A. 151:18-152:13 (The Foundation "absolutely" did not market the bracelets as "sexy," and declined to associate with porn stars or other people who "might have just wanted to use [the 'i [heart] boobies!' campaign] in a different way.").

In addition, the Foundation raises awareness through the slogans on the bracelets themselves, which encourage the wearer to learn about breast cancer and breast health. J.A. 159:21-160:11. The web address printed on every bracelet directs the wearer to a wealth of information about breast cancer, prevention, and detection. J.A. 159:25-160:1; *see also* J.A. 339; J.A. 340; J.A. 341; J.A. 146:24-147:7.

The bracelets are intended to start conversations among young people—not only to facilitate the sharing of information about breast cancer, but to help overcome the fear and taboo associated with discussing breast health. J.A. 9; *see also* J.A. 9-10 n.3 ("The Court finds . . . that the bracelets are intended to be . . . speech designed to raise awareness of breast cancer and reduce stigma associated with openly discussing breast health.").

Plaintiffs' Purchase of the Bracelets
B.H. purchased her first "i ❤ boobies!" bracelet before the beginning of the 2010-2011 school year. J.A. 10. . . .

K.M. first learned about the "i ❤ boobies!" bracelets over the summer of 2010 from B.H. J.A. 11. . . .

After purchasing the bracelets, both B.H. and K.M. sought out and acquired more information about breast cancer. J.A. 11. B.H. learned about the Keep a Breast Foundation through in-store displays and the Foundation's website. J.A. 11. K.M. learned that the youngest girl diagnosed with breast cancer was only ten years old. J.A. 11. She also learned about breast cancer risk factors, the effects of breast cancer, and how to check one's self for lumps. J.A. 11. She learned about her great aunt who had breast cancer and that breast cancer "can run in the family." J.A. 11. K.M. testified that she would not have learned this information about breast cancer if she hadn't purchased the "i ❤ boobies!" bracelets. J.A. 141:22-142:6.

K.M. wanted to wear the bracelets to draw attention to the issue of breast cancer, to demonstrate her own concern about the issue, to promote education about breast cancer, and to honor the memory of her deceased great aunt, who had breast cancer. J.A. 106:9-108:9;

127:2-10. She believes that an understanding of breast cancer issues is important for people of "any age." J.A. 127:10.

Neither B.H. nor K.M. considers "boobies" to be an offensive or vulgar term. J.A. 528 (B.H. Dep. 45:13-15); J.A. 131:11-12; J.A. 561 (K.M. Dep. 31:24- 32:1); *cf.* J.A. 138:6-10 (K.M. testifying that there may be different synonyms for breasts that are "gross" and that she would not want used to refer to her breasts). B.H. and K.M. and their peers and families—including a friend of B.H.'s grandmother who suffered from breast cancer—commonly use the term "boobies" to refer to their own and other women's breasts. J.A. 35; J.A. 75:21-25, 76:19-77:1, 111:2-9; *see also* J.A. 137:14-21. Neither B.H. nor K.M. interprets the phrase "i ❤ boobies!" as a sexual double entendre or believes that the bracelets could be construed to have any sexual meaning. See J.A. 90:8-10, 99:25-1000:19, 133:16-24; J.A. 528 (45:21-23), 532 (64:9-15), 535 (75:7-21) (B.H. Dep.). B.H. explained that the text on the bracelets that says "KEEP A BREAST," a reference to breast cancer awareness and to the Keep A Breast Foundation, makes the breast cancer awareness context of the bracelets clear. J.A. 99:25-100:19; J.A. 528 (45:21-23), J.A. 535 (75:7-21) (B.H. Dep.).

Both B.H. and K.M. believe that the "i ❤ boobies! (KEEP A BREAST)" bracelets raise awareness of breast cancer more effectively than wearing the color pink as a symbol of support for breast cancer awareness. J.A. 11. . . .

EASD's Ban on the Bracelets

The "i ❤ boobies!" bracelets have been popular among Easton Area middle schoolers since the beginning of the 2010-2011 school year, which began on August 30, 2010. J.A. 12. B.H.'s "i ❤ boobies!" bracelets have caused people to ask her about the purpose of the bracelets, but they have not provoked any offensive or negative comments or inappropriate jokes about "boobies." J.A. 76:11-18; J.A. 527 (B.H. Dep. 44:4-7). K.M. also testified that many people asked her about the bracelets and that the bracelets drew the attention of "most of the students in [her] school[.]" J.A. 115:4-24. By wearing the "i ❤ boobies!" bracelets, B.H. has learned of more people—including teachers and friends at school—who have lost family members to breast cancer, because wearing the bracelets leads to conversation about the disease. J.A. 89:4-90:7.

In the EAMS 7-8 building, teachers are responsible for identifying dress code violations and reporting them to the principals. Appellant's Br. at 7. The building has three principals: Mr. Viglianti, the seventh grade assistant principal; Ms. Braxmeier, the eighth grade assistant principal; and Ms. DiVietro, the head principal of the 7-8 building. J.A. 203:9-18. In mid- to late-September, four or five of the 120 teachers in the EAMS 7-8 building spoke to Ms. Braxmeier about the "i ❤ boobies!" bracelets, seeking instruction on how they should be handled. J.A. 12. On or before September 23, 2010, Mr. Viglianti, Ms. Braxmeier, and Ms. DiVietro conferred and agreed that the bracelets should be prohibited. J.A. 12.

At the time of their decision to ban the bracelets, neither Mr. Viglianti, Ms. Braxmeier, nor Ms. DiVietro had heard any reports of disruption or student misbehavior linked to the bracelets. J.A. 13.[3] Nor had any of the principals then heard reports of inappropriate comments about "boobies." J.A. 13.[4]

Enforcement of the Ban

The principals did not announce the bracelet ban to the students at the time of this decision. J.A. 12. Instead, on September 23, 2010, Mr. Viglianti sent an email to the staff of the 7-8 building that stated: "If students are wearing any wristbands that have the word 'boobie' written on them please ask them to remove the band and keep it at home. They can instead wear pink on October 28th when the entire district will be wearing pink to recogniz[e] Breast Cancer Awareness Month." J.A. 12; J.A. 342.

Students continued wearing the bracelets after September 23, 2010. At the request of teachers tired of "constantly asking students to remove the 'I Love Boobie Bracelets!'", the school finally announced the ban to students in the 7-8 building on the afternoon of October 27, approximately two months into the school year. *See* J.A. 351; J.A. 13. Toward the end of that school day, at Ms. DiVietro's request, Mr. Viglianti read a prepared statement over the PA system describing the ban. *See* J.A. 13; J.A. 268:6-9; J.A. 756 (Viglianti Dep. 66:13-22); J.A. 345. The next day during the morning announcements on the school's TV station, a student delivered a statement written by the administration reiterating the ban. J.A. 13. The TV announcement contained the word "boobies." J.A. 13.

That day after school, B.H. told her mother that the "i ❤ boobies!" bracelets had been banned and asked permission to wear her bracelets despite the ban. J.A. 16. Her mother agreed. J.A. 16. That day, K.M. also obtained her mother's permission to wear her bracelets on the school's Breast Cancer Awareness Day in spite of the school's ban. J.A. 16.

EASD's Breast Cancer Awareness Day

Thursday, October 28, 2010 was Breast Cancer Awareness Day in the Easton Area School District. J.A. 16. . . .

B.H. and K.M. wore their "i ❤ boobies!" bracelets to school on Breast Cancer Awareness Day. J.A. 82:20-25 (B.H. testifying); J.A. 116:16-117:16 (K.M. testifying). Neither the girls nor their "i ❤ boobies!" bracelets disrupted any school activities that day. *See* J.A. 17, 223:10-18, 82:20-83:7, 83:22-85:6, 85:10-21, 117:14-119:10, 189:12-190:1, 223:10-18, 224:6-8, 225:9-13.

During the lunch period, a cafeteria monitor observed that B.H. and K.M. were wearing the bracelets and summoned a security guard, Mr. Border. J.A. 16. Mr. Border asked B.H. whether she was wearing a bracelet, and B.H. admitted that she was, as did K.M. and another girl, R.T. J.A. 16-17. The girls declined to remove the bracelets. J.A. 16-17. Mr. Border allowed the girls to finish eating their lunches, then took them to Ms. Braxmeier's office. J.A. 17.

Ms. Braxmeier spoke with each girl separately in her office. *See* J.A. 17-18. R.T. agreed to remove her bracelet and was allowed to return to class without punishment. *See* J.A. 17. B.H. and K.M. each refused to remove her "i ❤ boobies!" bracelets. J.A. 18.

B.H. explained to Ms. Braxmeier that the bracelet was " 'for breast cancer and people in [her] family have been affected by breast cancer,' " and that "it was her freedom of speech to wear the bracelet." J.A. 18. K.M. explained to Ms. Braxmeier that she wanted to wear the bracelets because it was Breast Cancer Awareness Day. J.A. 120:13-18. Ms. Braxmeier conferred with Mr. Viglianti and Ms. DiVietro, and they agreed that B.H. and K.M. would be punished with an in-school suspension for the remainder of that day and for all of the following day, and [they] could not attend the upcoming school dance. J.A. 18. The Plaintiffs' families each received a letter notifying them of the girls' suspensions and stating that the suspensions [were] due to "disrespect," "defiance," and "disruption." J.A. 301; J.A. 302. The principals have conceded, however, that Plaintiffs' only offense was refusing to remove the bracelets. See J.A. 454-55 (Braxmeier Dep. 43:14-46:21); J.A. 189:12-190:1.

The District's Justifications for the Ban

The District's justifications for the ban have changed over time. Initially, in its November 9, 2010 letter to Plaintiffs' counsel, the District claimed that it banned the bracelets because some middle school students are uncomfortable with discussion of the human body; some male middle school students had made embarrassing comments to female students about their breasts; the students who defied the ban were then observed "high-fiving" each other in the cafeteria; and some EAMS teachers believe the bracelets trivialize the subject of breast cancer and are personally offended by the bracelets' "cutesy" message. J.A. 15 n.5 (citing Compl. ¶ 29; Answer ¶ 29).

After litigation commenced, however, the three principals offered several different reasons for their decision in September to ban the bracelets. J.A. 13. Mr. Viglianti testified that their decision was based on the term "boobies," which was "not appropriate." J.A. 13. He thought some middle school students were not mature enough "to understand and see that [as] appropriate," and he was concerned that the use of the word "boobies" in the bracelets would cause students "to start using the word just in communication with other students, talking with other students." J.A. 13-14. At his deposition, Mr. Viglianti testified that it would be similarly inappropriate for either the word "breast" or the phrases "keep-a-breast.org" or "breast cancer awareness" to be displayed on clothing in the middle school. J.A. 14; see also J.A. 748 (35:2—23),759 (81:2-4) (Viglianti Dep.); J.A. 174:18-175:7. Nine days later, during the evidentiary hearing, he changed his mind and testified that a bracelet bearing only the phrase "keep-a-breast.org" would be permissible. J.A. 14.

Ms. Braxmeier and Ms. DiVietro agreed with Mr. Viglianti that the word "boobies" is vulgar and inappropriate for use in the middle school. J.A. 446 (Braxmeier Dep. 11:22-12:10); J.A. 497 (DiVietro Dep. 51:10-12); see also J.A. 489 (20:1-12), 490 (25:1-4) (DiVietro Dep.). Ms. DiVietro also equivocated as to whether the words "breast cancer awareness" or "keep-a-breast.org" would be inappropriate on student clothing. At her deposition, she testified that the words "keep-a-breast.org" are offensive, vulgar, and "not acceptable" for middle schoolers because the word "breast" "can be construed as a sexual connotation." J.A. 14; see also J.A. 490 (23:4-25), 497 (51:24-52:2) (DiVietro Dep.). At the evidentiary hearing, however, she testified that she would not deem the

EXHIBIT 18B (cont.)

words "breast cancer awareness" or a bracelet that simply said "keep-a-breast.org" to be vulgar in the middle school context. J.A. 14.

Ms. Braxmeier and Ms. DiVietro testified that the bracelets violate the Middle School dress code because the phrase "i ❤ boobies!" is an impermissible "double entendre" referring to a sexual attraction to breasts. *See* J.A. 14-15; J.A. 488 (16:5-7, 16:14-16), 489 (19:22-24) (DiVietro Dep.); J.A. 466-67 (Braxmeier Dep. 93:15-94:2); J.A. 229:15-22 (Braxmeier testifying). They emphasized that the bracelets were particularly susceptible to interpretation as having a sexual meaning in the middle school context, given the age and relative immaturity of the students. *See* J.A. 238:22-239:2 (Braxmeier testifying); J.A. 260:21-261:23, 264:12-24 (DiVietro testifying); J.A. 446 (Braxmeier Dep. 10:7-14, 12:12-15).

Indeed, all of the principals expressed concern that the bracelets might cause other students to make offensive remarks about breasts or inappropriately touch female students. All three principals admit, however, that inappropriate sexual statements and touching are unfortunate but common behavior by middle school boys. *See* J.A. 195:24-196:7, 233:9-11, 243:8-22; J.A. 496 (DiVietro Dep. 46:6-19). Ms. Braxmeier acknowledged that sexualizing words is common among middle school students. J.A. 457 (Braxmeier Dep. 56:4-17). Ms. DiVietro agreed. J.A. 284:9-10 ("I'm not surprised. The students are middle school students. You know, it could happen before, it could happen after and it can still happen even though the ban is in effect.").

Additionally, Ms. DiVietro, the ultimate decision maker regarding the ban, testified that her decision was motivated by a belief that the bracelets sent students the wrong message regarding socially "acceptable" and "appropriate" behavior and statements.[7] She added that while the school administrators "don't have the right to say what [students] can or cannot wear" outside of school, "inside the school we have to regulate these types of things." J.A. 276:1-4. Ms. DiVietro also noted that one teacher found the bracelets offensive because they did not treat the issue of breast cancer sufficiently "seriously." J.A. 272:7-14.

Finally, Ms. DiVietro testified that allowing students to wear the Keep A Breast Foundation's "i ❤ boobies!" bracelets would diminish her authority to prevent students from wearing clothing with other statements that the administrators deemed inappropriate. J.A. 15. She explained that banning the "i ❤ boobies!" bracelets " 'makes a statement that we as a school district have the right to have discretionary decisions on what types of things are appropriate and inappropriate for our school children.' " J.A. 15.

The District also argued that the bracelets had caused "disruption." In late October and mid-November, 2010, well after the administrators of the EAMS 7-8 building decided to ban the bracelets, the administrators received two reports of boys making inappropriate remarks about "boobies." First, during Ms. Braxmeier's October 28, 2010 conversation with R.T. about removing her "i ❤ boobies!" bracelets, R.T. told her that she believed "some boys" had acted "immature" and made remarks to girls about their "boobies." J.A. 17. On November 15, 2010 (after receiving the Plaintiffs' November 4 letter demanding that the school lift the ban), the school elicited a written incident report from R.T. in which she alternately described the incident as involving multiple boys and just one boy, and stated that she did not know the student's name. J.A. 17-18. Second, on or about November 16, 2010, the middle school administrators received a report that two female students were discussing the "i ❤ boobies!" bracelets when a boy sitting with them at lunch interrupted them and made statements such as "I want boobies" and made suggestive gestures with two spherical fireball candies. J.A. 19. The administrators spoke with the boy, who admitted that he had said "something rude," and he was suspended for a day. J.A. 19; *see also* J.A. 447 (Braxmeier Dep. 14:24-15:3, 16:9-17:5).

Ms. Braxmeier also testified regarding two unrelated incidents in October of inappropriate touching by middle school boys of eighth grade girls. J.A. 19. There is no evidence that either incident was caused by Plaintiffs' "i ❤ boobies!" bracelets. J.A. 19. Ms. Braxmeier's only reason for identifying these incidents in connection with the bracelets is that they occurred at the same time the bracelets were on campus. *See* J.A. 242:18-243:1-5; J.A. 449 (Braxmeier Dep. 25:1-11).

Procedural History

On November 15, 2010, B.H. and K.M., by and through their mothers, Jennifer Hawk and Amy McDonald-Martinez, filed suit in the Eastern District of Pennsylvania, seeking a temporary restraining order and preliminary injunction to enjoin Defendant Easton Area School District from enforcing its ban on the "i ❤ boobies! (KEEP A BREAST)" bracelets. J.A. 4, 5. During a telephone conference, the court urged the school to allow Plaintiffs to attend the winter dance from which they had been barred, while reserving the right to impose comparable punishment if the Court upheld the ban as constitutional, and the District acquiesced. J.A. 6. The court thus denied Plaintiffs' TRO motion without prejudice. J.A. 6. After a day-long evidentiary hearing, submission of proposed findings of fact and conclusions of law by each party and additional oral argument, on April 12, 2011, the district court granted Plaintiffs' motion for preliminary injunction. J.A. 3. The School District subsequently filed a notice of appeal, and a motion to stay the preliminary injunction pending appeal. The district court denied the motion for a stay on June 21, 2011. The District has not sought a stay from this Court, thereby leaving the injunction in effect.

SUMMARY OF ARGUMENT

This case illustrates why the government bears the burden of proving that restrictions on speech are justified in First Amendment cases. Until the commencement of litigation, the District was describing the Plaintiffs' bracelets as "inappropriate," potentially "embarrassing" to some and "offensive" to others because of their "cutesy" presentation.

After suit commenced, the District changed its tune and argued that the Plaintiffs' bracelets could be prohibited either on the ground that they caused "substantial and material disruption," or as lewd and indecent speech. The bracelets, however, caused no disruption, and neither Plaintiffs, their classmates, nor the school administration treated the bracelets as a sexual message until suit was filed.

EXHIBIT 18B (cont.)

In light of this, the court below correctly concluded that the District's *post hoc* reasons for the ban were not credible, reflecting, instead, a bare desire to exercise plenary authority over student expression: "It appears to the Court that the Middle School has used lewdness and vulgarity as a post-hoc justification for its decision to ban the bracelets. Ms. Braxmeier testified that banning these bracelets 'makes a statement that we as a school district have the right to have discretionary decisions on what types of things are appropriate and inappropriate for our school children.'" J.A. 36-37 (citation omitted).

The record does not support either the contention that these bracelets caused substantial and material disruption or the assertion that they are lewd. The court properly found the Plaintiffs likely to prevail on their First Amendment claims and preliminarily enjoined the School District from enforcing its ban on the bracelets.

ARGUMENT

I. THE SUPREME COURT'S STUDENT SPEECH CASES ESTABLISH THE RELEVANT LEGAL FRAMEWORK AND BAR THE DISTRICT'S NOVEL LEGAL ARGUMENTS.

Public school students do not "shed their constitutional rights to freedom of speech or expression at the schoolhouse gate." *Tinker v. Des Moines Independent Cmty. Sch. Dist.,* 393 U.S. 503, 506 (1969). Rather, "[t]he vigilant protection of constitutional freedoms is nowhere more vital than in the community of American schools." *Id.* at 512 (quoting *Shelton v. Tucker,* 364 U.S. 479, 487 (1960)).[8] Just this term, the Supreme Court reiterated that: "'Speech is neither obscene as to youths nor subject to some other legitimate proscription cannot be suppressed solely to protect the young from ideas or images that a legislative body thinks unsuitable for them.'" *Brown v. Entm't Merchs. Ass'n,* 131 S. Ct. 2729, 2736 (June 27, 2011) (quoting *Erznoznik v. City of Jacksonville,* 422 U.S. 205, 213-14 (1975)).

With respect to minors, then, as with adults, the burden is on the government censor to demonstrate that there is a reason to suppress speech—including the speech of school students—beyond concern for the "tender ears" of youth. "In order for the State . . . to justify prohibition of a particular expression of opinion, it must be able to show that its action was caused by something more than a mere desire to avoid the discomfort and unpleasantness that always accompany an unpopular viewpoint." *Tinker,* 393 U.S. at 509; *see also United States v. Playboy Entm't Group,* 529 U.S. 803, 816-17 (2000) ("When the Government restricts speech, the Government bears the burden of proving the constitutionality of its actions.") (citing, *inter alia, Tinker,* 393 U.S. at 509); *accord Phillips v. Borough of Keyport,* 107 F.3d 164, 172-73 (3d Cir. 1997) (en banc).

The Supreme Court has delineated the limited circumstances that justify censorship "in light of the special characteristics of the school environment." *Tinker,* 393 U.S. at 506. The Supreme Court's decision in *Tinker* established the general rule that, to justify a ban on particular student speech, public school officials must demonstrate that the forbidden speech would materially and substantially interfere with the operation of the school. *Id.* at 509; *J.S. v. Blue Mountain Sch. Dist.,* No. 08-4138, 2011 WL 2305973, *7-8 (3d Cir. June 13, 2011) (en banc).

Since *Tinker,* the Court has identified three categories of speech that fall outside of this analysis and, because of their unique effect on the school environment, may be punished or prohibited without regard to whether they cause disruption: speech that is offensively lewd and indecent, *Bethel School District No. 403 v. Fraser,* 478 U.S. 675 (1986); school-sponsored speech, *Hazelwood School District v. Kuhlmeier,* 484 U.S. 260 (1988); and speech that advocates illegal drug use, *Morse v. Frederick,* 551 U.S. 393 (2007). "Speech falling outside of these categories is subject to *Tinker*'s general rule: it may be regulated only if it would substantially disrupt school operations or interfere with the right of others." *Saxe v. State Coll. Area Sch. Dist.,* 240 F.3d 200, 214 (3d Cir. 2001) (Alito, J.). The Supreme Court has made clear that school districts do not have the power, under *Fraser* or otherwise, to disallow speech in public schools simply because it is deemed "offensive" or "inappropriate." In *Morse,* Chief Justice Roberts explicitly rejected the school district's attempt to expand *Fraser* in this manner:

> Petitioners urge us to adopt the broader rule that Frederick's speech is proscribable because it is plainly "offensive" as that term is used in *Fraser.* See Reply Brief for Petitioners 14-15. We think this stretches *Fraser* too far; that case should not be read to encompass any speech that could fit under some definition of "offensive." After all, much political and religious speech might be perceived as offensive to some.

Morse, 551 U.S. at 409. And Justice Alito, joined by Justice Kennedy, wrote separately to emphasize that his concurrence was conditioned on the majority's rejection of the idea that schools may regulate speech as they see fit:

> The opinion of the Court does not endorse the broad argument advanced by petitioners and the United States that the First Amendment permits public school officials to censor any student speech that interferes with a school's "educational mission." See Brief for Petitioners 21; Brief for United States as *Amicus Curiae* 6. This argument can easily be manipulated in dangerous ways, and I would reject it before such abuse occurs.

Morse, 551 U.S. at 423 (Alito, J., concurring); *see also Tinker,* 393 U.S. at 509 (school may not prohibit speech based on the "mere desire to avoid the discomfort and unpleasantness that always accompany an unpopular viewpoint").

As the district court found, the Easton Area School District offered quickly shifting positions on the bracelets at issue in this case—at first they were "inappropriate"; then, after Plaintiffs' counsel demanded the District lift the ban, the District said they were potentially "embarrassing" to some and "offensive" to others because of their "cutesy" presentation, and finally, after suit was filed, described them as disruptive, lewd and vulgar. This compels the conclusion that the school officials had no basis for the ban,

EXHIBIT 18B (cont.)

beyond "discomfort and unpleasantness" (or perhaps their preference for another breast cancer awareness message). "It appears to the Court that the Middle School has used lewdness and vulgarity as a post-hoc justification for its decision to ban the bracelets." J.A. 36.

The District thus runs afoul of a fundamental principle of First Amendment law: the government's *post hoc* rationalizations can never justify censorship. *See Pittsburgh League of Young Voters Educ. Fund,* 2011 WL 3375651, at *5. . . . [9] Allowing government officials to rely on "post hoc rationalizations . . . mak[es] it difficult for courts to determine in any particular case whether the [government] is permitting favorable, and suppressing unfavorable, expression." *City of Lakewood v. Plain Dealer Pub. Co.,* 486 U.S. 750, 758 (1988).

If the District's post hoc rationalizations are analyzed on the merits, they fare no better. The record does not support either the contention that these bracelets caused substantial and material disruption or that they were lewd.

II. THE DISTRICT COURT PROPERLY INTERPRETED AND APPLIED THE LAW WHEN IT HELD THAT THE DISTRICT FAILED TO JUSTIFY ITS CENSORSHIP UNDER *TINKER.*

A. The District Court Understood And Followed *Tinker.*

School officials may only proscribe speech on the basis of its anticipated disruptive effect if they establish that their expectation of substantial, material disruption is "well-founded." *Sypniewski v. Warren Hills Reg. Bd. of Educ.,* 307 F.3d 243 (3d Cir. 2002) (quoting *Saxe v. State Coll. Area Sch. Dist.,* 240 F.3d 200, 214 (3d Cir. 2001)); *see also Sypniewski,* 307 F.3d at 253 (*"Tinker* requires a specific and significant fear of disruption, not just some remote apprehension of disturbance."); *see also J.S.,* 2011 WL 2305973, at *7 (quoting *Saxe,* 240 F.3d at 211 (*"Tinker* requires a specific and significant fear of disruption, not just some remote apprehension of disturbance.")). Meeting this burden generally requires identifying specific historical evidence that supports the school's expectation of disruption, such as past materially disruptive incidents arising out of similar speech. *Sypniewski,* 307 F.3d at 254-55 & n.11 (citing *Saxe,* 240 F.3d at 212); *see also Tinker,* 393 U.S. at 514 (concluding that nothing in the record could reasonably have led school authorities to forecast the kind of substantial, material disruption of school activities that is required to justify banning speech). Evidence that a student has worn a particular piece of expressive clothing "several times without incident . . . speaks strongly against a finding of likelihood of disruption. . . . " *Sypniewski,* 307 F.3d at 254.

Rather than applying the fact-specific standard set forth in these cases, the School District attempts to re-write *Tinker,* asserting: (1) that *Tinker* requires a court to presume that any speech that could be interpreted as sexual innuendo will cause substantial disruption in the form of sexual harassment, no matter what the historical record;[10] and (2) that *Tinker* applies only to restrictions on student speech that discriminate on the basis of viewpoint and that the School District's decision was not discriminatory.[11] These arguments are specious.

1. The Record Demonstrates that Plaintiffs' Bracelets Caused No Disruption and that the District Lacked Any Reasonable Basis for Anticipating that the Bracelets Would Cause a Substantial, Material Disruption to School Activities.

The District Court correctly found that "[a]t the time that the ban initially went into effect, September 23, 2010, none of the three principals had heard any reports of disruption or student misbehavior linked to the bracelets. Nor had any of the principals heard reports of inappropriate comments about 'boobies.' " J.A. 13. It also found that, at the time of the ban, the bracelets had been on campus for at least two weeks without incident, J.A. 39-40, which undermined any expectation of disruption. *Id.; see also Sypniewski,* 307 F.3d at 254 (evidence that banned T-shirt was worn several times without incident "speaks strongly against a finding of likelihood of disruption"). The Court concluded that, at the time of the ban, "the School had at most a general fear of disruption." J.A. 40.

The district court also correctly rejected the School District's reliance on two incidents that occurred after the ban was enacted: one in which a student stated that she thought one or possibly more boys had made comments to girls about their "boobies" in connection with the bracelets and one in which a boy interrupted two girls' discussion of the bracelets with statements such as "I want boobies" and inappropriate gestures with two spherical candies. J.A. 40. The district court suggested that it need not consider incidents after the enactment of the ban in determining whether the ban was justified under *Tinker* and held that, at any rate, neither of the incidents caused a disruption to the school's learning environment; rather, they were "well within a school's ability to maintain discipline and order[.]" J.A. 40-41.

The School District does not challenge any of the district court's findings of fact about disruption; it challenges only the district court's refusal to credit the District's unsupported claims of an impending wave of sexual harassment, arguing that no risk of sexual harassment is acceptable. But the nature of the feared disruption cannot, alone, determine whether a school's censorship is justified under *Tinker*; the school must always establish some likelihood that the feared disruption actually will follow tolerance of the student speech at issue. A presumption of disruption reverses the constitutionally mandated burden of proof.

This Court's decision in *Sypniewski* makes this clear. In *Sypniewski,* school officials took a number of actions to quell a devastating period of racial intimidation and violence, much of it perpetrated by a gang of white students who called themselves the "Hicks." 307 F.3d at 246-49. During this period, the District banned a shirt that recited jokes about "rednecks," fearing that the term "redneck" would be associated with the bigotry and violence of the "Hicks." *Id.* at 249-51. This Court, however, held that the school officials had failed to show any evidence that the student body equated "redneck" with the

EXHIBIT 18B (cont.)

dreaded "Hicks" or with racial intimidation, and that the absence of any evidence connecting the censored shirt with the feared disruption precluded a finding that the school officials had a "well founded" fear of future disruption that would satisfy *Tinker*. *Id.* at 254-58. *Sypniewski* bars the District's "inevitable" sexual harassment argument.

Moreover, the District's proposed reading of *Tinker* would allow a school to use the lack of self-control on the part of unruly students as an excuse to ban speech by other students that could conceivably be misconstrued and "cause" misbehavior. The District's reading of *Tinker* is incompatible with a long line of cases in which the federal courts have consistently rejected the idea, known as a "heckler's veto," that speech may be restricted because of the likelihood that a speaker will be harassed by listeners or spark other misconduct by listeners. *See, e.g., United States v. Marcavage,* 609 F.3d 264, 282 (3d Cir. 2010) ("[T]he Supreme Court and the courts of appeals have consistently held unconstitutional regulations based on the reaction of the speaker's audience to the content of expressive activity."). This principle applies equally in public schools, and prevents school administrators from banning student speech on the basis of the anticipated reaction to the speech except where the anticipated reaction would be beyond the school's ability to control.[12] In other words, school officials may not "sacrifice freedom upon the [altar] of order, and allow the scope of our liberty to be dictated by the inclinations of the unlawful mob." *Holloman v. Harland,* 370 F.3d 1252, 1276 (11th Cir. 2004) (holding that "Even if [a teacher] were correct in fearing that other students may react inappropriately or illegally, such reactions do not justify suppression of [students'] expression"). Contrary to the School District's assertion, the *Tinker* Court in no way suggested that a school could ban speech that might incite other students to interfere with their classmates' rights; rather, the Court merely distinguished the Tinkers' silent, passive demonstration from more obtrusive forms of speech such as group demonstrations or other expressive conduct that, by its nature, might impinge on the rights of other students. *See Tinker,* 393 U.S. at 508. . . . [13]

The "special circumstances of the school environment" do not justify disciplining young women who seek to engage their peers on important health issues in order to prevent misbehavior by immature classmates who might hear them. Under *Tinker,* the school's responsibility is to discipline misbehavior, not to silence student speech.

2. Tinker Is Not Limited to Viewpoint-Discriminatory Restrictions on Speech, But the School District's Rules Regarding Breast Cancer Awareness Speech Do Constitute Viewpoint Discrimination.

The District also argues that the *Tinker* standard applies only when a school seeks to silence a particular viewpoint, apparently suggesting that in the absence of viewpoint discrimination there are no limits on a school's authority to censor student speech that falls outside of the exceptions outlined in *Fraser, Kuhlmeier,* and *Morse. Tinker* and the other cases cited by the District reflect a special concern about viewpoint discrimination because "[v]iewpoint discrimination is "anathema to free expression." *Pittsburgh League of Young Voters Educ. Fund,* 2011 WL 3375651, at *5. But there is no support, in any case cited by the District, for the proposition that in the absence of such discrimination there is no protection for student speech.

Even on the erroneous premise that *Tinker* only prohibits "viewpoint discrimination," there is ample evidence in the record that the District did engage in viewpoint discrimination. The District explicitly endorsed "wearing pink" as the only acceptable way for students and faculty to express their support for breast cancer awareness: "the color pink is the way to show support for the . . . cause". J.A. 744 (Viglianti Dep. 20:20-21).[14] The District also made available to teachers merchandise bearing various Susan G. Komen Foundation breast cancer awareness slogans that do not contain any references to breasts.[15] In contrast, both before and after the commencement of this litigation, District officials and their counsel criticized the Keep a Breast Foundation as being "commercialized"[16] and maligned the Keep a Breast Foundation's body-affirming "i ❤ boobies! (KEEP A BREAST)" breast cancer awareness campaign as inappropriate,[17] distasteful,[18] trivializing,[19] uncivil,[20] and as touting "sexy breast cancer."[21]

It is of no moment that the District did not enact a ban on all breast cancer awareness messages. As this Court very recently explained, viewpoint discrimination occurs when the government "targets not subject matter, but particular views taken by speakers on a subject," suppressing certain speech on a topic because "the underlying ideology or perspective that the speech expresses" is disfavored or unpopular. *Pittsburgh League of Young Voters Educ. Fund,* 2011 WL 3375651, at *5 (citing *Rosenberger v. Rector & Visitors of Univ. of Va.,* 515 U.S. 819, 829 (1995); *Ridley v. Mass. Bay Transp. Auth.,* 390 F.3d 65, 82 (1st Cir. 2004)).

Not all breast cancer awareness campaigns embody the same perspective on breast cancer. While Susan G. Komen's "Real Rovers" campaign employs a slogan that focuses on survivors of breast cancer and its "Pink for the Cure" slogan focuses on cancer treatment, the Keep a Breast Foundation's "i ❤ boobies! (KEEP A BREAST)" slogan focuses on fostering positive associations with breasts and breast cancer awareness among young people. "REAL ROVERS WEAR PINK TO SUPPORT THE FIGHTERS, ADMIRE THE SURVIVORS, HONOR THE TAKEN, AND NEVER GIVE UP HOPE" does not communicate the same perspective as "i ❤ boobies! (KEEP A BREAST)." The record reflects the School District's clear preference for the former type of breast cancer awareness and distaste for the latter.

What the record does not reflect is any evidence that the Plaintiffs' bracelets caused any disruption or were likely to. The District cannot justify its censorship under *Tinker*.

III. THE DISTRICT COURT PROPERLY INTERPRETED AND APPLIED THE LAW WHEN IT HELD THAT THE DISTRICT'S CENSORSHIP OF THE BRACELETS WAS UNREASONABLE UNDER *FRASER*.

. . . The court below erred, says the District, when it did not "defer to the reasonable sensibilities of a school principal." Appellant's Br. at 34.

EXHIBIT 18B (cont.)

The District's argument boils down to the proposition that *Fraser* allows it to censor any statement that can be taken out of context and misinterpreted as lewd—whether or not it is understood that way. Such a rule would be contrary to both common sense[22] and the First Amendment, as is clear from the Supreme Court's analysis in *Morse* and the approach that this Court took in *Sypniewski*.

A. The District Court Properly Held That Plaintiffs' Speech Must Be Interpreted In Context, Not In The Abstract, To Determine Whether It Is Lewd or Vulgar, And That Determination Is a Question of Law For The Court.

Fraser announced the principle that "the First Amendment gives a high school student the classroom right to wear Tinker's armband, but not Cohen's jacket." *Fraser*, 478 U.S. at 682-83 (quoting *Thomas v. Bd. of Educ., Granville Cen. Sch. Dist.*, 607 F.2d 1043, 1057 (2d Cir. 1979)). In *Fraser,* the Supreme Court upheld discipline against a student who, at a mandatory school assembly, delivered a speech that was heavily and deliberately laden with "elaborate, graphic, and explicit sexual metaphor." *Fraser,* 478 U.S. at 678. The speech at issue in *Fraser* was not merely sexual and not age-appropriate for the entire audience—it was "obscene," *id.* at 679, "vulgar," *id.* at 684, "offensively lewd and indecent," *id.* at 685, and "plainly offensive to both teachers and students—indeed to any mature person." *Id.* at 683. "According to *Fraser,* then, there is no First Amendment protection for 'lewd,' 'vulgar,' 'indecent,' and 'plainly offensive' speech in school. *Fraser* permits a school to prohibit words that 'offend for the same reasons that obscenity offends'—a dichotomy neatly illustrated by the comparison between Cohen's jacket and Tinker's armband." *Saxe,* 240 F.3d at 213 (Alito, J.); *cf. Morse,* 551 U.S. at 422-23 (Alito, J. concurring) ("[*Fraser*] permits the regulation of speech that is delivered in a lewd or vulgar manner as part of a middle school program.").

The *Fraser* Court did not discuss whether it was reasonable for the Bethel High School principal to have understood Matthew Fraser's speech as a sexual metaphor—the lewdness of that speech was beyond question and was admitted and, indeed, intended by the student. *Fraser,* 478 U.S. at 681, 684. And the speech in *Fraser* had precisely the impact on the audience that one would expect from the presentation of a graphic sexual metaphor in a school:

> During Fraser's delivery of the speech ... [s]ome students hooted and yelled; some by gestures graphically simulated the sexual activities pointedly alluded to in respondent's speech. Other students appeared to be bewildered and embarrassed by the speech. One teacher reported that on the day following the speech, she found it necessary to forgo a portion of the scheduled class lesson in order to discuss the speech with the class.

Fraser, 478 U.S. at 678. Because the speech was clearly lewd and vulgar, the Court in *Fraser* did not discuss how to evaluate speech that could be lewd in some contexts, but not in others. For that, the district court properly turned to the Supreme Court's most recent student speech case, *Morse v. Frederick.*

1. The District Court Properly Held That Applying *Fraser* To Speech With Multiple Possible Meanings Requires That The Speech Be Viewed In Context.

. . . [In] *Morse v. Frederick* the Court makes clear that a school's interpretation of student speech must be reasonable in the context in which the speech was uttered.

As in *Fraser,* the *Morse* Court carved out a narrow and specific category of speech that can be censored without evidence of a disruptive effect, because the nature of the speech is inimical to the "special characteristics" of the school environment. *Morse,* 551 U.S. at 406-08 (pro-drug speech "poses a particular challenge for school officials working to protect those entrusted to their care from the dangers of drug abuse"). Unlike in *Fraser,* however, the *Morse* Court had before it an ambiguous statement: "BONG HiTS 4 JESUS [.]" *Id.* at 401 ("The message on Frederick's banner is cryptic."). Principal Morse read the banner as promoting or celebrating illegal drug use, while Joe Frederick claimed it was simply gibberish intended to catch the attention of television crews. *Id.* at 401-02.

The Court did not simply "defer" to the principal's reading of the banner, but weighed the "plausibility" of the competing interpretations. [Quotation omitted.] Faced with a choice between the principal's cogent interpretation of the banner [to refer to smoking marijuana] and Frederick's unadorned assertion that it meant nothing at all, the Court held that the principal's interpretation was a reasonable one under the circumstances and therefore justified Frederick's suspension under the drug promotion exception to *Tinker* announced by the Court's decision. *Id.*

The lesson of *Morse* is that where the speech at issue is capable of multiple meanings, courts should not simply defer to any position articulated by the school. Instead, courts should consider the context of the speech and the evidence supporting the different interpretations, including how the speech is understood by the school community and whether it "can plausibly be interpreted as commenting on any political or social issue." *Morse,* 551 U.S. at 422 (Alito, J., concurring). . . . This does not mean that the school's interpretation must be the only reasonable interpretation of the speech, but that it must be reasonable in the context in which the speech occurs. If the weight of the evidence cuts against the school's interpretation of the speech, that interpretation is not reasonable within the meaning of *Morse.*[23]

This is the same approach applied by this Court—*albeit* under a *Tinker,* not a *Fraser,* analysis—in *Sypniewski v. Warren Hills Regional Board of Education,* 307 F.3d 243 (3d Cir. 2002). In *Sypniewski,* this Court rejected the argument of Warren Hills that because "redneck" is sometimes synonymous with "hick," a t-shirt reciting "redneck" jokes should be treated as a reference to the white racist gang called the Hicks that had terrorized the Warren Hills schools. *Sypniewski,* 307 F.3d at 256-57. Instead of crediting

EXHIBIT 18B (cont.)

Warren Hills' narrow focus on dictionary definitions, *cf.,* Appellants' Br. at 37 n.13, this Court held that the proper analysis had to deal with the realities of the school environment, and that there was no evidence that, in that context, the word "redneck" was associated with the schools' history of racial violence. *Id.* at 257.

In this case, the District's only justification for employing an entirely different approach to analyzing student speech under *Fraser* than is employed under *Morse* or *Tinker* is the *Fraser* Court's statement that "[t]he determination of what manner of speech in the classroom or in school assembly is inappropriate properly rests with the school board." *Fraser,* 478 U.S. at 684. But that cannot be read as a delegation to schools of authority to interpret the First Amendment.

2. Courts Do Not "Defer" To A School Official's Decision Whether Speech Is Protected.

The District argues—and cites some cases that suggest—that school officials have the final say over whether student speech is lewd and profane and therefore outside First Amendment protection.[24] *See* J.A. 276:1-4 (explaining that while the school administrators "don't have the right to say what [students] can or cannot wear" outside of school, "inside the school we have to regulate these types of things").

The District's use of these cases is inconsistent with the discussions above from *Morse* and *Sypniewski.* But, more fundamentally, the District misstates the principle of "deference" to school administrators.

As this Court recently reiterated. the question whether speech is proscribable under *Fraser* is a question of First Amendment law: "In *Saxe v. State College Area School District,* 240 F.3d 200, 213 (3d Cir. 2001), we interpreted *Fraser* as establishing that 'there is no First Amendment protection for [']lewd,' 'vulgar,' 'indecent,' and 'plainly offensive' speech in school." *Layshock v. Hermitage School Dist.,* No. 07-4465, 2011 WL 2305970, at *5 n.12 (3d Cir. Feb. 4, 2011). And the Supreme Court has explained that the deference due school officials—at any level of schooling—relates to school policy and operations, not to the determination of rights under the First Amendment:

> Our inquiry is shaped by the educational context in which it arises: "First Amendment rights," we have observed, "must be analyzed in light of the special characteristics of the school environment." *Widmar,* 454 U.S., at 268, n.5 (internal quotation marks omitted). This Court is the final arbiter of the question whether a public university has exceeded constitutional constraints, and we owe no deference to universities when we consider that question. *Cf. Pell v. Procunier,* 417 U.S. 817, 827 (1974) ("Courts cannot, of course, abdicate their constitutional responsibility to delineate and protect fundamental liberties.").[25]

EXHIBIT 18B (cont.)

Christian Legal Soc. Chapter of Univ. of Hastings Coll. of Law v. Martinez, 130 S. Ct. 2971, 2988, 2989 n.16 (2010) (parallel citations omitted) (emphasis added). School administrators, even the most careful and honest, are not infallible, and have no special expertise in interpreting the law. It is the courts that make legal decisions, and they "owe no deference" to the administrators' views in that regard.

B. The District Court Correctly Found That The Plaintiffs' Bracelets Were Not And Could Not Reasonably Be Considered Lewd In This Context.

The "i ❤ boobies!" bracelets are not the equivalent of Cohen's jacket. They are also, as the district court found, not reasonably seen as the equivalent of Matthew Fraser's assembly speech. They are not the sort of speech that can be censored under *Fraser.*

The district court properly asked whether, in the context of the Plaintiffs' presentation and the realities of the Easton Area Middle School, the District's interpretation of the bracelets is a reasonable one and properly held that it is not.[26]

1. The District Court properly found that neither the word "boobies" nor the phrase "i ❤ boobies!" is—like Cohen's jacket—inherently lewd or profane.

Plaintiffs' bracelets are not patently sexual speech: "words that offend for the same reasons that obscenity offends." *Saxe,* 240 F.3d at 213. Plaintiffs' bracelets undeniably express a message of positive body image and support for breast cancer awareness. J.A. 9 & n.3; J.A. 148:9-15; J.A. 149:16-20. They seek to save lives. But they also, says the District, refer to a "sexual part" of women's bodies (the word "boobies") and express sexual attraction to women's breasts (the phrase "i ❤ boobies!").[27]

The district court flatly rejected the School District's position that all references to women's breasts are "inherently sexual," and so should this Court. There is nothing sexual, much less lewd or patently offensive, about talking about breasts and breast health, even in a middle school context. *See, e.g.,* J.A. 336-39 (EAMS health curriculum). Nor is the word "boobie"—an informal term for "breast"—inherently sexual. As the district court found, it is a common informality used by adults and children alike. J.A. 35, 75:21-25, 76:29-77:1, 111:2-9; *see also* J.A. 128:14-21.

This analysis highlights why the *Fraser* standard cannot be rewritten to permit censorship of any speech that offends the "sensibilities of a school principal." Appellant's Br. at 19, 34. In this case, deference to "the reasonable sensibilities of a school principal" could well have resulted in a ban of the word "breast" at EAMS. *See* J.A. 14; J.A. 748 (35:2-23), 759 (81:2-4) (Viglianti Dep.); J.A. 490 (23:4-25), 497 (DiVietro Dep. 51:24-52:2); J.A. 174:18-175:7; Appellant's Br. at 37 n. 13 ("In the context of 'I ❤ Boobies!', a reasonable interpretation is the slang term for a female breast. . . . Under the *Fraser* standard of deferential reasonableness, the inquiry should go no further.").[28] The District's position that Plaintiffs' life-affirming—and potentially life-saving—speech is lewd because it discusses the female anatomy is manifestly unreasonable (and offensive).

EXHIBIT 18B   (cont.)

2. The District Court properly found that neither "boobies" nor "i ❤ boobies!" could, in the context of the bracelets worn by Plaintiffs at EAMS, reasonably be considered the equivalent of Matthew Fraser's assembly speech.

The District argues that Plaintiffs' bracelets should be judged according to the dictionary and adult contexts outside the school and, as in the Wizard of Oz, that the Court should pay no attention to the actions of the people who actually pulled the levers—its own school principals. But the district court properly held that the question is not whether one can find any lewd reference to "boobies" in this world, or whether the phrase "I love boobies" can ever be used lewdly, but whether the use of "boobies" or "i ❤ boobies!" in this context could reasonably be viewed as lewd. J.A. 34 ("If the phrase 'I ❤ Boobies!' appeared in isolation and not within the context of a legitimate, national breast cancer awareness campaign, the School District would have a much stronger argument that the bracelets fall within *Fraser*.").[29]

The court below exhaustively reviewed the context surrounding the wearing of the bracelets at EAMS and found nothing to suggest that they communicated anything lewd in that context. There was no evidence that the Plaintiffs presented the bracelets in a sexual manner,[30] and the testimony was that their peers—with two exceptions—did not understand or react to the bracelets as lewd or sexy.

And the evidence supports the district court's conclusion that even the EAMS administrators did not consider the bracelets lewd—at least, not until suit was filed. The principals "banned" the bracelets in late September but did not tell the students that they were prohibited. And when they did announce a ban to the students in late October, it was inspired, apparently, by the teachers' frustration with having to enforce a rule that the students didn't know, rather than any new concerns with the bracelets. Finally, the official school announcement of the ban included the word "boobies" and, until the commencement of litigation, the District was describing the bracelets as "inappropriate," potentially "embarrassing" to some and "offensive" to others because of their "cutesy" presentation. In light of all of this, the court below correctly concluded that the District's *post hoc* reliance upon *Fraser* was not credible.[31]

The District itself best explains why these facts are important. In contending that it was "factually erroneous" for the district court to compare the reactions of the EASD administrators to the reactions of the Bethel School District, the District argues that Fraser's speech and the bracelets are very different speech, and that the EASD administrators reacted appropriately by treating the bracelets as a mere dress code violation. Appellant's Br. at 51. If even the District concedes that the bracelets were not the equivalent of Fraser's speech, then its argument is truly no more than that it should be able to "make[] a statement that we as a school district have the right to have discretionary decisions on what types of things are appropriate and inappropriate for our school children.' " J.A. 15.

IV. THE DISTRICT COURT PROPERLY INTERPRETED AND APPLIED THE LAW WHEN IT HELD THAT PLAINTIFFS ESTABLISHED IRREPARABLE HARM AND THAT THE BALANCE OF EQUITIES AND THE PUBLIC INTEREST FAVORS THE ISSUANCE OF THE INJUNCTION.

The district court properly applied the legal presumption of irreparable harm upon finding a First Amendment violation: "The loss of First Amendment freedoms, for even minimal periods of time, unquestionably constitutes irreparable injury." *Elrod v. Burns,* 427 U.S. 347, 373 (1976); *see also American Civil Liberties Union v. Reno,* 217 F.3d 162, 180 (3d Cir. 2000) (generally, in First Amendment challenges, Plaintiffs who meet the merits prong of the test for a preliminary injunction "will almost certainly meet the second, since irreparable injury normally arises out of the deprivation of speech rights."). And the courts have long recognized that "the public's interest favors the protection of constitutional rights in the absence of legitimate countervailing concerns." *Council of Alternative Political Parties v. Hooks,* 121 F.3d 876, 884 (3d Cir. 1997).

The District argues that because the Plaintiffs could express their support for breast cancer awareness in other ways, the bracelet ban did not infringe upon their rights. There are undoubtedly many different ways to communicate a concern for breast cancer awareness. However, these many means of communicating a similar message are not fungible. As discussed above, the Keep a Breast bracelets worn by Plaintiffs embody a different perspective from the breast cancer slogans preferred by the School District. The District Court found that the particular means chosen by Plaintiffs and the Keep a Breast Foundation to express their message of cancer awareness was not gratuitous. J.A. 34. Rather, the words on the bracelets "were chosen to enhance the effectiveness of the communication to the target audience." *Id.; see also id.* at 8-10 (findings of fact regarding the goals of the Keep a Breast Foundation and its "i [heart] boobies!" campaign). The District Court correctly concluded that Plaintiffs will be irreparably harmed absent a preliminary injunction preventing the School District from punishing them for their chosen means of protected expression. The "First Amendment protects [Plaintiffs'] right not only to advocate their cause but also to select what they believe to be the most effective means for doing so." *Meyer v. Grant,* 486 U.S. 414, 424 (1988).

In this case, there are no countervailing concerns to tip the balance of harms in the District's favor. The District asserts that it cannot, while the preliminary injunction remains in effect, meet its statutory obligation to maintain order in the schools, Appellant's Br. at 59-60, but the District neither explains nor supports this remarkable assertion. The district court did not prohibit the District from enforcing its ban on lewd and vulgar language and apparel or changing its dress code, but held [it] that it was unconstitutional for the District to ban the Plaintiffs' bracelets under such rules. Indeed, the district court went out of its way to explain that its ruling in no way compromised Defendant's ability to discipline students for truly vulgar or lewd speech:

EXHIBIT 18B (cont.)

The School has expressed concern that if the ban is lifted, then students will try to test the permissible boundaries with other clothing. Nothing in this decision prevents a school from making a case by case determination that some speech is lewd and vulgar while other speech is not. It should be clear, however, that a school must consider the contours of the First Amendment before it decides to censor student speech.

J.A. 42. In the absence of any threat of harm to the District or the public, the equities clearly support the preliminary injunction issued by the district court.

CONCLUSION

The District's arguments boil down to an assertion that a court should never draw different conclusions than school administrators. But the First Amendment does not provide such "deference" to a government censor. The district court's order should be affirmed.

[For purposes of brevity, the footnotes are omitted.]

EXHIBIT 18C **FEDERAL RULES PERTAINING TO APPELLATE BRIEFS**

QUESTIONS TO CONSIDER AS YOU READ THESE RULES:

1. List the components that an appellant is to include in its brief under Federal Rule 28.
2. List the components that an appellee is to include in its brief under Federal Rule 28.
3. List any additional components required by Third Circuit Rule 28.
4. Look up the following details in the two rules, and provide a specific citation to the source of the answer to each question:
   a. What colors are the covers to be?
   b. What fonts, what size type, and what spacing are required?
   c. How long may a brief be?
   d. How are cases to be cited?
   e. How are the facts to be cited?
   f. How are the parties to be labeled?
   g. How is the brief to be signed?

FEDERAL RULE OF APPELLATE PROCEDURE 28

Rule 28. Briefs

(a) Appellant's Brief. The appellant's brief must contain, under appropriate headings and in the order indicated:

(1) a corporate disclosure statement if required by Rule 26.1;

(2) a table of contents, with page references;

(3) a table of authorities—cases (alphabetically arranged), statutes, and other authorities—with references to the pages of the brief where they are cited;

(4) a jurisdictional statement, including:

(A) the basis for the district court's or agency's subject-matter jurisdiction, with citations to applicable statutory provisions and stating relevant facts establishing jurisdiction;

(B) the basis for the court of appeals' jurisdiction, with citations to applicable statutory provisions and stating relevant facts establishing jurisdiction;

(C) the filing dates establishing the timeliness of the appeal or petition for review; and

(D) an assertion that the appeal is from a final order or judgment that disposes of all parties' claims, or information establishing the court of appeals' jurisdiction on some other basis;

(5) a statement of the issues presented for review;

(6) a concise statement of the case setting out the facts relevant to the issues submitted for review, describing the relevant procedural history, and identifying the rulings presented for review, with appropriate references to the record (see Rule 28(e));

EXHIBIT 18C (cont.)

(7) a summary of the argument, which must contain a succinct, clear, and accurate statement of the arguments made in the body of the brief, and which must not merely repeat the argument headings;

(8) the argument, which must contain:

(A) appellant's contentions and the reasons for them, with citations to the authorities and parts of the record on which the appellant relies; and

(B) for each issue, a concise statement of the applicable standard of review (which may appear in the discussion of the issue or under a separate heading placed before the discussion of the issues);

(9) a short conclusion stating the precise relief sought; and

(10) the certificate of compliance, if required by Rule 32(a)(7).

(b) Appellee's Brief. The appellee's brief must conform to the requirements of Rule 28(a)(1)–(8) and (10), except that none of the following need appear unless the appellee is dissatisfied with the appellant's statement:

(1) the jurisdictional statement;

(2) the statement of the issues;

(3) the statement of the case; and

(4) the statement of the standard of review.

(c) Reply Brief. The appellant may file a brief in reply to the appellee's brief. Unless the court permits, no further briefs may be filed. A reply brief must contain a table of contents, with page references, and a table of authorities—cases (alphabetically arranged), statutes, and other authorities—with references to the pages of the reply brief where they are cited.

(d) References to Parties. In briefs and at oral argument, counsel should minimize use of the terms "appellant" and "appellee." To make briefs clear, counsel should use the parties' actual names or the designations used in the lower court or agency proceeding, or such descriptive terms as "the employee," "the injured person," "the taxpayer," "the ship," "the stevedore."

(e) References to the Record. References to the parts of the record contained in the appendix filed with the appellant's brief must be to the pages of the appendix. If the appendix is prepared after the briefs are filed, a party referring to the record must follow one of the methods detailed in Rule 30(c). If the original record is used under Rule 30(f) and is not consecutively paginated, or if the brief refers to an unreproduced part of the record, any reference must be to the page of the original document. For example:

* Answer p. 7;
* Motion for Judgment p. 2;
* Transcript p. 231.

Only clear abbreviations may be used. A party referring to evidence whose admissibility is in controversy must cite the pages of the appendix or of the transcript at which the evidence was identified, offered, and received or rejected.

EXHIBIT 18C (cont.)

(f) Reproduction of Statutes, Rules, Regulations, etc. If the court's determination of the issues presented requires the study of statutes, rules, regulations, etc., the relevant parts must be set out in the brief or in an addendum at the end, or may be supplied to the court in pamphlet form.

FEDERAL RULE OF APPELLATE PROCEDURE 32

Rule 32. Form of Briefs, Appendices, and Other Papers

(a) Form of a Brief.

(1) *Reproduction.*

(A) A brief may be reproduced by any process that yields a clear black image on light paper. The paper must be opaque and unglazed. Only one side of the paper may be used.

(B) Text must be reproduced with a clarity that equals or exceeds the output of a laser printer.

(C) Photographs, illustrations, and tables may be reproduced by any method that results in a good copy of the original; a glossy finish is acceptable if the original is glossy.

(2) *Cover.* Except for filings by unrepresented parties, the cover of the appellant's brief must be blue; the appellee's, red; an intervenor's or amicus curiae's, green; any reply brief, gray; and any supplemental brief, tan. The front cover of a brief must contain:

(A) the number of the case centered at the top;

(B) the name of the court;

(C) the title of the case (see Rule 12(a));

(D) the nature of the proceeding (e.g., Appeal, Petition for Review) and the name of the court, agency, or board below;

(E) the title of the brief, identifying the party or parties for whom the brief is filed; and

(F) the name, office address, and telephone number of counsel representing the party for whom the brief is filed.

(3) *Binding.* The brief must be bound in any manner that is secure, does not obscure the text, and permits the brief to lie reasonably flat when open.

(4) *Paper Size, Line Spacing, and Margins.* The brief must be on 8 1/2 by 11 inch paper. The text must be double-spaced, but quotations more than two lines long may be indented and single-spaced. Headings and footnotes may be single-spaced. Margins must be at least one inch on all four sides. Page numbers may be placed in the margins, but no text may appear there.

(5) *Typeface.* Either a proportionally spaced or a monospaced face may be used.

(A) A proportionally spaced face must include serifs, but sans-serif type may be used in headings and captions. A proportionally spaced face must be 14-point or larger.

(B) A monospaced face may not contain more than 10 1/2 characters per inch.

EXHIBIT 18C (cont.)

(6) *Type Styles.* A brief must be set in a plain, roman style, although italics or boldface may be used for emphasis. Case names must be italicized or underlined.

(7) *Length.*

(A) *Page Limitation.* A principal brief may not exceed 30 pages, or a reply brief 15 pages, unless it complies with Rule 32(a)(7)(B) and (C).

(B) *Type-Volume Limitation.*

(i) A principal brief is acceptable if:

* it contains no more than 14,000 words; or
* it uses a monospaced face and contains no more than 1,300 lines of text.

(ii) A reply brief is acceptable if it contains no more than half of the type volume specified in Rule 32(a)(7)(B)(i).

(iii) Headings, footnotes, and quotations count toward the word and line limitations. The corporate disclosure statement, table of contents, table of citations, statement with respect to oral argument, any addendum containing statutes, rules or regulations, and any certificates of counsel do not count toward the limitation.

(C) *Certificate of Compliance.*

(i) A brief submitted under Rules 28.1(e)(2) or 32(a)(7)(B) must include a certificate by the attorney, or an unrepresented party, that the brief complies with the type-volume limitation. The person preparing the certificate may rely on the word or line count of the word-processing system used to prepare the brief. The certificate must state either:

* the number of words in the brief; or
* the number of lines of monospaced type in the brief.

(ii) Form 6 in the Appendix of Forms is a suggested form of a certificate of compliance. Use of Form 6 must be regarded as sufficient to meet the requirements of Rules 28.1(e)(3) and 32(a)(7)(C)(i).

(b) Signature. Every brief, motion, or other paper filed with the court must be signed by the party filing the paper or, if the party is represented, by one of the party's attorneys.

(c) Local Variation. Every court of appeals must accept documents that comply with the form requirements of this rule. By local rule or order in a particular case a court of appeals may accept documents that do not meet all of the form requirements of this rule.

THIRD CIRCUIT LOCAL APPELLATE RULE 28

L.A.R. 28.0   BRIEFS

28.1   Brief of the Appellant

(a) The brief of appellant/petitioner must include, in addition to the sections enumerated in FRAP 28, the following:

EXHIBIT 18C (cont.)

(1) in the statement of the issues presented for review required by FRAP 28(a)(5), a designation by reference to specific pages of the appendix or place in the proceedings at which each issue on appeal was raised, objected to, and ruled upon;

(2) after the statement of issues for review, a statement of related cases and proceedings, stating whether this case or proceeding has been before this court previously, and whether the party is aware of any other case or proceeding that is in any way related, completed, pending or about to be presented before this court or any other court or agency, state or federal. If the party is aware of any previous or pending appeals before this court arising out of the same case or proceeding, the statement should identify each such case; and

(b) The following statements should appear under a separate heading placed before the discussion of the issue: the statement of the standard or scope of review for each issue on appeal, *i.e.*, whether the trial court abused its discretion; whether its fact findings are clearly erroneous; whether it erred in formulating or applying a legal precept, in which case review is plenary; whether, on appeal or petition for review of an agency action, there is substantial evidence in the record as a whole to support the order or decision, or whether the agency's action, findings and conclusions should be held unlawful and set aside for the reasons set forth in 5 U.S.C. §706(2). . . .

(d) The court expects counsel to exercise appropriate professional behavior in all briefs and to refrain from making *ad hominem* attacks on opposing counsel or parties.

28.2 Brief of the Appellee

The brief of the appellee or respondent must conform to the requirements of FRAP 28(b) and 3d Cir. L.A.R. 28.1 (a)(2), (b) and (c). If the appellee is also a cross-appellant, the appellee's brief must also comply with rules 28.1(a)(1) and (a)(3). The brief of an appellee who has been permitted to file one brief in consolidated appeals must contain an appropriate cross reference index which clearly identifies and relates appellee's answering contentions to the specific contentions of the various appellants. The index must contain an appropriate reference by appellee to the question raised and the page in the brief of each appellant.

28.3 Citation Form; Certification

(a) In the argument section of the brief required by FRAP 28(a)(9), citations to federal opinions that have been reported must be to the United States Reports, the Federal Reporter, the Federal Supplement or the Federal Rules Decisions, and must identify the judicial circuit or district, and year of decision. Citations to the United States Supreme Court opinions that have not yet appeared in the official reports may be to the Supreme Court Reporter, the Lawyer's Edition or United States Law Week in that order of preference. Citations to United States Law Week must include the month, day and year of the decision. Citations to federal decisions that have not been

EXHIBIT 18C (cont.)

formally reported must identify the court, docket number and date, and refer to the electronically transmitted decision. Citations to services and topical reports, whether permanent or looseleaf, and to electronic citation systems, must not be used if the text of the case cited has been reported in the United States Reports, the Federal Reporter, the Federal Supplement, or the Federal Rules Decisions. Citations to state court decisions should include the West Reporter system whenever possible, with an identification of the state court. Hyperlinks to decisions may be used, but are not required, as provided in L.A.R. Misc. 113.13. If hyperlinks are used, citation to a reporter, looseleaf service, or other paper document must be included, if available. If a hyperlink to a paper document is not available, the internet address of the document cited must be included.

(b) For each legal proposition supported by citations in the argument, counsel must cite to any opposing authority if such authority is binding on this court, e.g., U.S. Supreme Court decisions, published decisions of this court, or, in diversity cases, decisions of the highest state court.

(c) All assertions of fact in briefs must be supported by a specific reference to the record. All references to portions of the record contained in the appendix must be supported by a citation to the appendix, followed by a parenthetical description of the document referred to, unless otherwise apparent from context. Hyperlinks to the

electronic appendix may be added to the brief. If hyperlinks are used, the brief must also contain immediately preceding the hyperlink a reference to the paper appendix page. Hyperlinks to testimony must be to a transcript. A motion must be filed and granted seeking permission to hyperlink to an audio or video file before such links may be included in the brief or appendix. Hyperlinks may not be used to link to sealed or restricted documents.

(d) Except as otherwise authorized by law, each party must include a certification in the initial brief filed by that party with the court that at least one of the attorneys whose names appear on the brief is a member of the bar of this court, or has filed an application for admission pursuant to 3d Cir. L.A.R. 46.1.

28.4 Signing the Brief

All briefs must be signed in accordance with the provision of L.A.R. 46.4. Electronic briefs may be signed with either an electronically generated signature or "s/ typed name" in the signature location. Counsel's state Bar number, if any, and address and phone number must be included with the signature.

TEST YOUR UNDERSTANDING

1. Assume that you are representing Bower's Bounty in its litigation with Sarah Nicholson. The lawyers were not able to reach a settlement, and the case entered litigation. Bower's Bounty moved for summary judgment on the grounds that its statement was protected by a qualified privilege; the court ruled that no privilege applied and, in the alternative, that any such privilege was overcome by Bower's Bounty's reckless disregard for the truth. The case went to a jury trial, the jury found in favor of Ms. Nicholson, and the judge, denying Bower's Bounty's post-trial motions, entered judgment on the verdict. What is the benefit of adding an appeal to these legal proceedings?

2. How does the appeals process differ from the trial process in terms of how a case is presented?

3. Kansas has a two-tier appellate structure. Identify which level is more associated with each term in the following pairs and what the terms mean:
   a. Appeal as of right versus discretionary review
   b. Error-correcting court versus law-making court
   c. En banc consideration versus panel consideration

4. Explain whether Bower's Bounty is positioned well to appeal its loss on the qualified privilege topic under the following principles:
   a. Final judgment rule
   b. Bar on new facts or issues
   c. Reversible error rule
   d. Standard of review

5. What are the main steps that set up an appeal, before the briefing?

6. As for the basic structure of the appeal:
   a. What would be the designation of Bower's Bounty and its brief(s)?
   b. What would be the designation of Ms. Nicholson and her brief?
   c. What outcomes would each of the two parties be seeking?

7. Which types of rules govern the writing of an appellate brief?

8. Who is the audience for the brief that you would write on behalf of Bower's Bounty?

9. What are the four elements of an appellate theory of the case?

10. For each of the opening technical components, identify its role and at least two items of information it contains.

11. What do the issues parallel, and in what way?

12. As for the statement of the case:
    a. Which party typically writes the procedural history, and what is included?
    b. Which types of facts should be included in the statement of facts?
    c. What are the possible organizational options for the statement of facts?
    d. Are the facts cited in the statement of facts?

13. State the roles of the following components related to the argument:
    a. Standard of review
    b. Summary of argument
    c. Point headings

14. As for the argument itself:
    a. What types of reasoning and argumentation should you use?
    b. What types of propositions are cited?
    c. For what purposes are footnotes typically used?

15. What are the standard two closing components?

16. What are the typical components of a reply brief?

TEST YOUR UNDERSTANDING ANSWERS

1. Appeals provide two main benefits: they serve as a check on the district court, and they provide a mechanism for making law.

2. At trial, facts are presented through witnesses, documents, and other items. The appeals court learns about the case through a transcript, so the facts are fixed.

3. As for Kansas's two-tier appellate structure:
   a. Litigants have the right to appeal to the court of appeals; the supreme court has discretion as to which cases it accepts.
   b. The court of appeals focuses on correcting district court errors, whereas the supreme court focuses on making law.
   c. The court of appeals hears most cases in panels (sub-groups), whereas the entire supreme court hears its cases (i.e., en banc).

4. Bower's Bounty is positioned well to appeal its loss based on the following principles:
   a. Final judgment rule—the case has been completely adjudicated in the district court.
   b. Bar on new facts or issues—the issue was raised in the summary judgment motion.
   c. Reversible error rule—if the summary judgment ruling is erroneous, it could have an impact on the outcome.
   d. Standard of review—there is a realistic chance of reversal of a primarily legal summary judgment ruling.

5. The main steps that set up an appeal are taking the right steps during the trial court litigation, the notice of appeal, compilation of the record, and perhaps a pre-hearing conference.

6. As for the basic structure of the appeal:
   a. Bower's Bounty would be the appellant, filing appellant's brief and possibly a reply brief.
   b. Ms. Nicholson would be the respondent or appellee and file only the respondent's or appellee's brief.
   c. Bower's Bounty would seek a reversal (with possibly a remand), and Ms. Nicholson would seek affirmance.

7. The main rules of appellate procedure, likely also rules of the court, along with their forms, govern the writing of an appellate brief.

8. The audience for a brief is comprised of the judges, their clerks, opposing counsel, and your client.

9. An appellate theory of the case encompasses the facts, the substantive law, the procedure in the district court along with the standard of appellate review, and policy.

10. The cover page identifies the case and includes information about the case, the court, the lawyers, and the document. The table of contents and the table of authorities orient the reader to the parts of the brief, the points made, and the legal authorities relied on in the brief. The jurisdictional statement establishes that the appellate court has the power to hear the appeal, by stating what that basis is and citing to legal authorities.

11. The issues parallel the major points in the argument in number, content, and sequence.

12. As for the statement of the case:
    a. The appellant typically writes the procedural history, which covers the main procedural events from the outset of the case to the appeal. The respondent may supplement the statement.
    b. The facts statement includes relevant and background facts, both favorable and unfavorable, as well as a limited number of favorable residual facts.
    c. The organizational options are chronological, topical, and perceptual presentations.
    d. The facts must be cited to the record, whether the transcript or appendix.

13. State the roles of the following components related to the argument:
    a. Standard of review—the standard of review sets out the degree of scrutiny that the appeals court applies to the ruling of the district court.
    b. Summary of argument—the summary of argument presents the theory of the case and an overview of the legal arguments.
    c. Point headings—the point headings flag the major and minor assertions in the argument and appear throughout the argument.

14. As for the argument itself:
    a. You should include deductive reasoning and generally augment it with policy analysis and reasoning by example. Rebutting your opponent's arguments directly or indirectly is also important.
    b. Citations to the law are required. You should cite to factual points that are quoted or especially important.
    c. Footnotes are used for tangential factual or legal content. Some lawyers use footnotes for citations.

15. The standard closing components are the conclusion, with the relief requested and an optional restatement of the argument, and a signature block.

16. The typical reply brief has an introduction, argument, and conclusion.

ORAL ADVOCACY

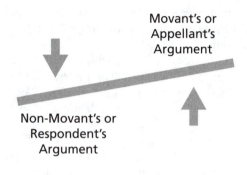

Movant's or
Appellant's
Argument

Non-Movant's or
Respondent's
Argument

Proceed. You have my biased attention.
—Learned Hand,
speaking to a counsel who sought to reargue a motion, quoted in
M. Frances McNamara, *2000 Famous Legal Quotations* (1967)

A. INTRODUCTION

After the memoranda or briefs have been filed and served, the lawyers may have a chance to present *oral arguments* to the court. Oral arguments occur in both district courts and appellate courts. Oral argument is the conversation that many people think of when they envision a lawyer talking.

This chapter first addresses what should be an obvious question: why do courts have oral argument if the parties have already submitted memoranda or briefs? The chapter then generally discusses the somewhat different practices in district and appellate courts surrounding oral argument. The rest of the chapter covers the practice of oral argument: preparing, anticipating and answering questions, and delivering the argument.

For an example, this chapter refers to the *B.H. v. Easton Area School District* case. In that case, public middle school students wore "I [heart-symbol] Boobies!" bracelets to school, which was forbidden. The students sought and obtained a preliminary injunction in federal district court on the grounds that the school district's action violated their free speech rights.[1] The school

---

1. That ruling is reported at 827 F. Supp. 2d 392.

district appealed, and the Third Circuit affirmed, en banc in a split decision.[2] Some of the discussion of this litigation is actual fact, some by way of example.

B. THE FUNCTION OF ORAL ARGUMENT

An oral argument is a *conversation with the court*, not a speech to the court. You should welcome it as a chance to talk with the judge or judges about the arguments in your memorandum or brief, to find out the court's concerns, and to dispel them. Rather than give a book report, you should take advantage of the dialogue, fully and truthfully answering the judges' questions and focusing on the interests of the court.

Your attitude should be one of "respectful intellectual equality" toward the court.[3] Try to think of the court not as an adversary but rather as being an individual or individuals who remain to be convinced of the correctness of your arguments. Your goal is to convince them to adopt your reasoning as their own.

Similarly, you have an ethical duty to show respect for opposing counsel. Opposing counsel has a duty to raise arguments that counter yours. Your dialogue is with the court, not opposing counsel, and should focus on the facts and the law of the case, not on undermining opposing counsel.

Oral arguments help judges to *clarify facets of the case*—its facts, law, and policies—especially in close cases. U.S. Supreme Court justices have found oral arguments to be most effective when characterized by clarity, adaptability, and strategy. Clarity derives from effective organization, language usage, and delivery. Adaptability is counsel's ability to respond to points raised in questions by the court. Strategy is how well the argument can withstand tough questioning from the court and attacks by opposing counsel.[4]

The potential *scope of an oral argument* is the material covered in the parties' briefs. Either party can raise any point or authority covered in any of the briefs, but no new material can be added in oral argument. Courts strongly discourage surprises in oral argument. On rare occasions, newly discovered material may be presented in a supplemental brief if the court allows it.

Rarely will you present the full content of a brief in oral argument. Instead, the oral argument usually focuses on the highly contested issues, i.e., the points of clash. U.S. Supreme Court Chief Justice Rehnquist commented:

> Many litigators . . . mistakenly approach the two instruments of appellate advocacy, the brief and the oral argument, "as the functional equivalent of one another." Many counsel, the justice contends, view an oral argument as no more than a "brief with gestures." . . . Rather, like the preview of a movie that consists of "dramatic or interesting scenes

---

2. That ruling is reported at 725 F.3d 293.
3. Fredrick Wiener, *Briefing and Arguing Federal Appeals* § 101 (1967).
4. Nicholas M. Cripe, *Fundamentals of Persuasive Oral Argument*, 20 Forum 342 (1985).

HOW INFLUENTIAL IS ORAL ARGUMENT?

In two studies, oral arguments were helpful to the judges in 80 percent to 82 percent of argued cases. Moreover, oral arguments influenced the judges' eventual outcomes in 22 percent to 31 percent of the cases heard.[5]

that are apt to catch the interest of the viewer and make him want to see that entire movie," oral argument should have "flesh and blood . . . insert[ed] into it."[6]

Furthermore, oral argument gives you a chance to bring the case to life for the court—to *humanize the case* through the in-person spoken medium. The court naturally assesses the lawyer's commitment to the arguments being raised. Furthermore, you can use voice inflection, gestures, body stance, and other means to impart meaning and conviction that the written word alone cannot convey.

At the same time, the spoken medium carries with it some *challenges* because it occurs in the moment. Thus, the listener must learn the structure of the presentation from oral roadmaps and signposts, changes in inflection, gestures, and pauses. And the ideas must be presented in terms that the listener can process as quickly as the oral advocate presents them.

Another challenge of oral argument is that the oral advocate does not control the argument—in sharp contrast to the nearly complete control of the writer over the written brief. With its questions, the court can almost entirely set the direction and coverage of the argument.

C. ORAL ARGUMENT PROCEDURES

1. Motion Argument

In the district court, an oral argument is presented to a single judge. It may occur any time a motion is pending or the judge is about to make a ruling (for instance, on an evidentiary matter). It may come up on the motion calendar, or it may arise during trial. In many jurisdictions, dispositive pre-trial motions, such as summary judgment or dismissal, are argued both in writing and orally, whereas less crucial motions are submitted only in writing. In other settings, the judge has the discretion whether to hear oral arguments. In yet others, the practice is to permit oral arguments on all motions.

---

5. Myron H. Bright & Richard S. Arnold, *Oral Argument? It May Be Crucial!*, A.B.A. J. 68, 70 (Sept. 1984).
6. *Justice Rehnquist Emphasizes Importance of Oral Argument*, The Third Branch, Dec. 1983, at 1, 2, 4 (quoting excerpts from two speeches by Chief Justice Rehnquist in October 1983).

BOX 19.2

COMPARISON OF MOTION PRACTICE MEMORANDUM AND ORAL ARGUMENT

Motion Practice Memorandum	Oral Argument
Caption	Introduction (who I am and whom I represent)
Introduction, summary, issues	Theory of case; roadmap of issues or arguments
Facts and procedure	Facts (with or without procedure)
Argument	Argument (more selective)
Conclusion	Conclusion

Oral argument procedures in district courts vary considerably. The oral argument may be heard by the motion calendar judge, who may not be familiar with the case, or it may be heard by a judge who has worked on the case for some time. The amount of time may range from only a few minutes to an hour. Some oral arguments occur in the courtroom; others occur in the less formal setting of the judge's chambers, with counsel seated before the judge's desk.

In *formal motion arguments*, the movant speaks first, followed by the non-movant; sometimes the movant is allowed a rebuttal argument as well. The format of these oral arguments is highly variable, although tradition and logic dictate that the issues and the relevant facts be stated near the beginning of the oral argument. *Less formal motion arguments* resemble a discussion, with the judge asking questions and the lawyers responding to those questions and to each other. See Box 19.2, which compares the motion practice memorandum to oral argument.

Before your motion argument, you should study the rules on oral argument before the court hearing your case. You also may want to consult the clerk of the court and local attorneys to learn of any unwritten traditions.

As an example, as recounted in the appellees' brief in the *B.H.* case, the district judge held both an evidentiary hearing and oral argument on the preliminary injunction motion.[7]

2. Appellate Argument

In some appellate courts, all cases are granted oral argument. However, because of increasing caseloads, the trend is toward restricting oral arguments. In some

---

7. Previously, the judge held a telephone conference on a temporary restraining order.

appellate courts, counsel must request and justify oral argument, and the court has discretion to grant or deny that request.

Appellate oral arguments take place in an appellate courtroom; a bench with seats for all of the judges faces a lectern for counsel. The argument may be heard by the full court (en banc) or a smaller panel (typically three judges). The proceeding generally is amplified and audiotaped. Most appellate courts set a fixed time limit for all but the most unusual cases; these limits usually range from fifteen to thirty-five minutes per side. The time limit may or may not include questions by the court and counsel's answers.

In some appellate courts, before the oral argument, the chief or presiding judge tentatively assigns a judge to write the opinion; thus, one judge may be extremely well prepared, while others may have done little preparation. In other courts, the assignment is not made until after the oral argument. Lawyers describe a highly prepared panel of judges as a "hot bench" and a less prepared panel as a "cold bench."[8]

Appellant's argument-in-chief: The *appellant's argument* begins with an *introduction*. You may begin with the formal opening, "May it please the court," or you may bypass the formal phrase and directly introduce yourself and your client. You should state right away how much time you want to reserve for rebuttal. Then introduce the case by stating your theory of the case and providing a roadmap of the issues or arguments that you plan to cover and in what order.

It is customary for the appellant to then *state the case*—that is, the facts and procedural posture. This statement should be whittled down to minimal length and emphasize facts pertinent to the issues being addressed in the oral argument. A longer fact statement is appropriate when the case pivots on a factual dispute or the client's case is strong on the facts and weak on the law. The statement should be fairly balanced, for both ethical and strategic reasons.

Most of your time will be spent discussing the *legal arguments*, discussed in detail in the rest of this chapter.

The *conclusion* should be very brief, with any recapping limited to only a few sentences, if that. You should conclude with the disposition you want the court to grant, e.g., reversal, remand, modification.

Respondent's argument: The *respondent's argument* generally follows the same sequence. You may choose to give your view of the facts and the procedural posture; most respondents' advocates state additional or reframed facts near the beginning of the argument. Otherwise, you will open with your theory of the case and a roadmap of the issues or arguments and then proceed directly to the legal arguments. Your conclusion will be a request for affirmance (unless you have brought a cross-appeal).

Rebuttal: The appellant is allowed to end the oral argument. *Rebuttal* is the appellant's chance at the end of the oral argument to refute respondent's arguments and to present the final conclusion. You should not raise new arguments in

---

8. Myron H. Bright, *How to Win on Appeal: The New Ten Commandments of Oral Argument*, Trial, July 1996, at 68, 69.

BOX 19.3

COMPARISON OF APPELLATE BRIEF AND ORAL ARGUMENT

Appellate Brief	Oral Argument
Cover page	Introduction (who I am and whom I represent)
Statement of issues; also summary of argument	Theory of case; roadmap of issues or arguments
Statement of case	Statement of case: facts and procedure (albeit briefer)
Argument	Argument (more selective)
Conclusion	Conclusion

Some components in the appellate brief are not paralleled in oral argument.

---

a rebuttal. You need not answer all of the respondent's points and, indeed, should not address more than two or three topics. For example, you should address topics you did not cover in your argument-in-chief and point out the respondent's omissions. Alternatively, you could select one or two major topics on which the appellant has strong counterarguments. You should conclude by reiterating the relief that your client seeks from the court.

The time devoted to rebuttal should be proportional to the length of the argument. Two or three minutes is the norm, but five minutes is appropriate if the argument is long and contains many issues. If you fail to reserve rebuttal time, some courts treat rebuttal as waived.

The contrast between oral argument and the appellate brief is demonstrated in Box 19.3. The brief has many components and technical requirements; oral argument is more compact and flexible.

As an example, the *B.H.* case was argued on appeal in the Third Circuit Court of Appeals. Under Federal Rule of Appellate Procedure 34, oral argument is allowed unless a panel of three judges decides that it is not needed. The comments indicate that the majority of circuits generally limit oral argument to thirty minutes per side. The *B.H.* case was so close that it was argued twice, once before a panel and again before the full court.

D. PREPARING FOR THE ORAL ARGUMENT

Although oral argument is a conversation, not a speech, you nonetheless should prepare carefully for it. You should have a plan for what you hope to accomplish, even though you will not be able to control the course of the argument and must defer to the court's direction.

1. Selecting Arguments to Present

Experts suggest presenting one or two, not more than three, major arguments. The court does not expect the oral argument to cover all topics covered in the briefs. In *selecting arguments* for oral presentation, you should consider various factors:

- Focus on points of clash—the issues on which the parties' positions conflict and which pose the greatest challenge to the court. You will most assist the court by dealing with adverse precedent and troublesome arguments raised by opposing counsel.
- Present a coherent picture of your client's case; your arguments should draw on your theory of the case.
- Choose your strongest arguments; if you cannot win on the strongest argument, you are not likely to win on the weakest.
- Emphasize arguments that are well suited for oral presentation—generally policy, factual, or equitable arguments, not technical or complex legal questions.
- Carefully examine arguments in the alternative to see whether you can omit one or more of the alternatives.

As an example, the parties in the *B.H.* case had many issues to choose among: both parties briefed two doctrines of Supreme Court case law on the free speech issue; the preliminary injunction standard has four factors, one of which ties back to the merits of the parties' legal claim. Planning to discuss all of these topics would not be wise under standard time limits. Because the law on preliminary injunctions is well settled and free speech issues are far from settled, it would make sense to focus on the latter. Actually, it would make sense to focus on both doctrines because the two doctrines are related. Finally, both sides constructed clashing theories of the case, zeroing in on the free speech case law: the appellant focused on the school district's prerogative to curtail lewd speech to protect students' right to an education without harassment; the appellees focused on the school district's censorship of a positive message in the absence of any disruption.

2. Setting the Pitch of the Argument

You generally will not know how prepared your judges will be, which raises the issue of how to *pitch* your argument. Thus, you should frame your arguments so that you can educate the judge or judges. Consider covering the basics initially, then elevating the level of discussion as soon as you are reasonably certain that the judges will be able to follow the more complicated aspects of the case.

In the appellate setting, resist the temptation to pitch the entire argument to the apparently least prepared judge. You may thereby limit the depth of your argument and its effectiveness for the more informed judges. On the other hand, you do not want to converse exclusively with the judge who seems to understand the case best. This tactic may result in only a muddled understanding among the members of the court who did not follow your argument and, perhaps, a spirited dissent from the judge with whom you conversed at length.

As an example, the parties in the *B.H.* case could easily assume that the court would be well versed in the law of temporary injunctions and the basic principles of free speech law. On the other hand, the nuances of the pertinent Supreme Court cases—the specific facts, the exact wording of the rules, and the application of the cases to the facts—would be necessary to delineate for the court, as would any pertinent lower court cases.

3. Allocating Time

Just as you should analyze your memoranda and briefs for allocation of space to various components and topics, so too you should plan how to *allocate your oral argument time* to particular components and topics.

In preparing for your argument, time the statement of the case that you plan to deliver. In a fifteen-minute motion argument, the case statement may need to be only a few minutes long. In a thirty-minute appellate argument, the case statement ordinarily should run only five to seven minutes. To fit within these limits, consider the following:

- Condense facts that do not need to be presented in detail.
- Omit facts pertaining to topics that you do not intend to argue orally.
- Present general facts in your case statement, and save the more detailed facts for the body of the argument, when they will mean more to the court and make the legal argument more understandable.
- Limit the procedural history to the rulings that are relevant to the legal issues covered in your oral argument.

In planning the body of your argument, reserve approximately a third of your time for responses to the court's questions, or allocate that time to a less important argument that can be omitted if need be. Of the remaining time, determine how much time to devote to each argument, based on its relative importance and controversy. You may be able to cover some arguments in a few sentences; other arguments may require discussion of several elements, lengthy discussion of a key case, or extensive development of public policy. For each argument, you must judge how much time you need to make the argument clearly and persuasively, so you can decide whether to attempt the argument if time is running out.

As an example, given that the parties in the *B.H.* case had two Supreme Court doctrines to discuss, an important decision would be which to emphasize. They would be equally important to the outcome. One of the two doctrines entailed more legal complexity and arguably more factual complexity as well,[9] whereas both involved interesting issues of public policy.

4. Planning for Flexibility

Of course, you never should count on being able to proceed through your argument without adapting it to respond to the judges' questions and concerns. Furthermore, you will want to account for the arguments made by your

---

9. The more complex issue pertains to the content of the speech; the less complex issue is its interference with the operation of the school. The Third Circuit opinion indicates that the court was most focused on the content issue.

opponent. As the argument unfolds, you may need to switch the order of topics, drastically expand or condense the coverage of a particular topic, or even change which briefed topics you cover.

In planning for flexibility, you should decide which topics and which arguments on each topic you want to cover, at a bare minimum, if you receive many questions. You also should plan how to make transitions between arguments if you are forced to cover the arguments in less-than-optimal order. As for responsiveness to the arguments of your opponent, you must master the authorities and arguments in his or her memorandum or brief, be prepared to answer questions about them, and connect those responses back to affirmative points favoring your client.

As an example, the *B.H.* case, as noted above, involved two main Supreme Court doctrines. Each party had a preference for which to raise first, as revealed in the briefs, and these preferences (not surprisingly) were the opposite of each other. Neither lawyer should expect the court to follow his or her lead or, indeed, to be able to cover one doctrine completely before turning to the other. Furthermore, although the parties cited ten cases in common, the appellant cited thirteen additional cases, as well as federal and state statutes, and the appellees cited twenty-seven additional cases. As another example, consider the opposing policy arguments in the two theories of the cases: the appellant emphasized avoiding sexual harassment, whereas the appellees stressed promoting breast cancer awareness. The lawyers needed to prepare to meet these valid points made by opposing counsel.

5. Preparing Written Materials

Few people can effectively deliver an oral argument without some *written materials* at hand. A written script is not advisable because your presentation will be stilted and you may fail to respond well to questions. Nor are note cards advisable because you will find it difficult to adjust your organization or see the entire argument at a glance, and you may distract the court if you nervously shuffle your cards.

Rather, you should prepare a bare-bones outline of the major issues and arguments, as well as abstracts of the leading cases or statutes, quotations from the important legal rules, and notes of the key facts or policies. One option is a manila folder. Print the outline on one side. On the other side, tape a flip-card index of key authorities, both favorable and unfavorable. Each card has the citation on the bottom of the card and the important facts, quotations, and reasoning on the rest. See Box 19.4.

Most lawyers also assemble a notebook containing an outline of the argument, followed by tabbed sections containing the record and important authorities. This notebook is useful should the court ask you a detailed question about a particular page in the record or authority.

BOX 19.4

FLIP-CARD AND OUTLINE

Facts of case; outcome; key reasoning	I represent ...., the Appellant in this matter.

Facts of case; outcome; key reasoning

Tinker v. Des Moines S. Ct. 1969

Fraser (Bethel Sch. Dist.) S. Ct. 1986

Morse v. Frederick S. Ct. 2007

Sypniewski v. Warren Hills 3d Cir. 2002

Saxe v. State College 3d Cir. 2001

Title IX

Penn. School Code

I represent ...., the Appellant in this matter.

I request three minutes for rebuttal.

My argument today will cover these topics: (1) ....

(2) ....

(3) ....

The key facts are: ....

....

....

....

Point (1) ....

Legal principle = ...

Application here = ...

....

Point (2) ....

Legal principle = ...

Application here = ...

....

Point (3) ....

Legal principle = ...

Application here = ...

Therefore Appellant requests reversal and remand.

---

6. Practicing

Write out and *memorize your introduction and your conclusion*, so that you can open and close the argument cleanly and with confidence. For example:

- Appellant's introduction: "May it please the court. My name is _____, and I represent the Appellant, _____. I wish to reserve _____ minutes for rebuttal. This case is about _____. I will be addressing the following issues in my argument:_____."
- Respondent's conclusion: "In conclusion, both of Appellant's arguments are unsupported by law. I urge the court to affirm the district court and rule in favor of _____. Thank you."

Then *practice talking about the case*. First, present your entire oral argument without interruptions, perhaps recording it once or twice. Practice presenting your arguments in differing orders. You also should rehearse for the possibility that the court will ask you to skip the statement of the case and proceed to the body of the argument.[10] Time your case statement and each argument, and examine those times for conformance to your desired time allocations, as discussed above. Try to discern how easy or difficult it is to follow your presentation.

Next, find someone to *quiz you* on the case. Ask your colleagues to ask tough questions and help you figure out how best to handle the tougher questions. Work on connecting your answers to the arguments that you want to make.

If possible, *tape your presentation*; then review your performance. Watch for distracting nervous mannerisms, such as jingling coins in your pocket, and listen for distracting verbal tics. Also evaluate your posture, general demeanor, and body language. Do you appear forthright and confident in your client's case at all times?

If possible, *visit the courtroom* in which you will be arguing. Evaluate the distance between yourself and the judges; the adequacy of the lighting; the sightlines of each of the judges; and the range of the microphone, if there is one.

E. ANTICIPATING AND ANSWERING QUESTIONS

Because oral argument is a conversation in which the court poses questions, preparing for questions is crucial. So, of course, is answering them well. You should not treat the court's questions as interruptions. Rather, as an accomplished appellate advocate exhorted, "Rejoice when the court asks questions."[11] Questions can be of great assistance to a well-prepared advocate; like weather vanes, they tell you which way the wind is blowing. Without questions from the court, you are left delivering a speech that may not address the court's real concerns.

1. Court Etiquette

Court etiquette dictates that you stop your presentation whenever a member of the court begins a question, even if you are in mid-sentence. Do not interrupt the judge; listen to the entire question; give yourself time to think. Then answer the question, even if the topic is out of the order in which you planned to present your arguments. It is not acceptable to delay the answer to a question unless the judge asking the question signals that you may do so.

Some questions require only a few words in response. Others call for a potentially lengthy response. Once you have answered, you need not wait for the court for a sign of permission to proceed. Rather, you should maintain eye contact with the judge; if he or she seems to have followed your initial response, conclude the answer, and move on. However, if he or she seems puzzled, you might want to

---

10. This practice is especially common in arguments delivered in law school.
11. John Davis, *The Argument of an Appeal*, 26 A.B.A. J. 897 (1940).

elaborate on your initial answer. If the reaction is one of skepticism, you might decide to move to an alternative argument or even another topic that the court may view more favorably. When you move back to your prepared comments, try to link your answer to the argument that you are about to make.

Above all, do not take tough questions personally. A seemingly hostile judge may in fact favor your client and may take a devil's advocate stance, so that your argument is put to its toughest test. At worst, tough questioning represents criticism of your legal arguments, not you personally. The members of the court are usually trying out the reasoning that you are proposing to see whether they are comfortable enough with it to adopt it.

2. Categories of Questions

Questions tend to fall into the categories discussed below. During the argument, discern the type of question the judge has asked, and answer accordingly. Indeed, as you prepare, try to generate and answer various types of questions. See Box 19.5 for questions that could be asked in the *B.H.* case, organized by the categories discussed below.

Questions about the facts. Judges ask *questions about the facts,* primarily to lock in their understanding of the dispute that they are asked to resolve. The judge may not remember a key fact and may simply seek a reminder from you. Or the judge may ask you to clarify or synthesize evidence that is muddled or conflicting; your answer must be supported by the record and should be as favorable to your client as it can be. Or the judge may ask you about a fact that is not in the record; you must respond that the fact is not in the record, and you may draw a favorable inference from the fact if the inference is a strong one based on facts in the record. As much as possible, follow up your answer with a comment about the significance of the fact to the legal analysis or equities of the case.

Questions about the law. Judges ask *questions about the law* as they seek to resolve an ambiguity about the legal rule or its application to the facts of the case. In response, you first should state what the law says, as viewed from your client's perspective and within the confines of ethical principles regarding candor with the court. You may need to disagree respectfully with a judge who does not see the law your way; if so, provide a clear rationale for your viewpoint, whether a succinct quotation or policy argument or later legal development. Next, be sure to draw a connection between the law as you have stated it and the facts of your case. In many instances, the law is not clear in the abstract but becomes so when applied to a specific situation.

Questions about public policy. Especially at the highest court, judges ask *questions about the public policy* implications of possible rulings. Your response should show why the ruling would promote justice in your client's case and how a ruling in your favor will lead to positive outcomes for similar disputes. Often, a case involves conflicting public policies, so your response should show that any concerns about adverse effects are either founded on speculation or outweighed by the positive outcomes.

Questions about hypothetical situations. Under stare decisis, judges must write decisions that will work well in the future, lead to just and predictable outcomes, and avoid undue administrative burdens. Thus, judges are concerned

BOX 19.5

SAMPLE QUESTIONS

QUESTIONS FOR APPELLANT	QUESTIONS FOR APPELLEES
About the Facts	**About the Facts**
How many incidents of sexual comments or conduct occurred due to the wearing of the bracelets?	When did school district administrators first use terminology that captures the lewdness concept, and why does this timing matter?
About the Law	**About the Law**
Has the Supreme Court ever used the phrase "deferential reasonableness"?	Does the view of social commentators condemning the use of the term "boobies" matter under the free speech cases?
About Public Policy	**About Public Policy**
Isn't the school's own Breast Cancer Awareness Day an acknowledgment of the positive message behind the bracelets?	What is the impact of Title IX on this case?
About a Hypothetical	**About a Hypothetical**
Would this case be any different if there were no dress code to be enforced?	Would this case be any different if the bracelets were not part of a national foundation's health-oriented campaign?
Seeking a Concession	**Seeking a Concession**
Doesn't the length of time that passed between the first sighting of the bracelets and their banning establish that there was insufficient disruption under the *Tinker* test?	Given that the school district sponsored a Breast Cancer Awareness Day, which was the point of the bracelets, there really is no viewpoint discrimination here, is there?
About the Opponent's Argument	**About the Opponent's Argument**
Appellees contend that the case entails discrimination among different messages about breast cancer; if so, how does that alter the analysis?	Appellant argues that the school district is charged with the call on whether the bracelet's language is lewd; why, in view of the conflicting evidence on the merits of its phrasing, is that not a strong argument?

with, and ask about, *hypothetical situations*. Answers to hypotheticals help the judges foresee the future operation of the holding in your case.

Hypothetical questions are challenging because they often involve facts, law, and policy in a situation that you may not have fully contemplated while preparing for oral argument. The key to a good answer is to take time to think, so that you can provide not only a conclusion, but also an analysis of why the hypothetical would and should be resolved a particular way in light of the elements of the rule and its policy. If you deem the hypothetical a close call, you should phrase your answer tentatively or provide more than one response and rationale.

If the court asks multiple hypotheticals or engages you in an extended discussion of a single hypothetical, you may feel that your actual case has become lost in the fray and that you are on unsure ground. If so, you may want to observe that your client's case does not raise the problem in the hypothetical, and then show how the court could rule so as to avoid the problem in the hypothetical.

Questions seeking concessions. A judge may signal that one of your assertions or arguments is not credible and thereby exert pressure on you to concede that point. Your response to a *question seeking a concession* can take various forms.

One option is, indeed, to concede. An example is to say, "That's correct, your honor. We no longer are basing our case on that argument." This response may improve your credibility with the court and thereby strengthen the court's support for your other arguments. For instance, as a defendant, you may be able to concede that the plaintiff has a good case on one element of a conjunctive rule, so long as you maintain that another element can be defeated. You should generally minimize the impact of any concessions by pairing the concession with a strong positive assertion.

Another option is to "concede" a point for purposes of the argument: "Even if I were to concede that point for the purpose of argument today, my client still prevails because . . . ."

However, in every case, there are points you cannot concede without sacrificing your client's case. If the court presses you to concede such a point, you must gracefully convey that you disagree with the court and state or restate your most persuasive reasons.

Questions about your opponent's argument. Judges naturally ask counsel to *respond to the opponent's argument*. Your three basic options are to present your client's approach to the topic; to show the fallacies or weaknesses in the opposing argument; or, less commonly, to make a concession. When you do discuss your opponent's argument, you must convey respect for opposing counsel and his or her client by responding to the argument, not addressing the people.

Nudging questions. A question may amount to a *direction to move on*. Often these questions are so-called "soft pitches"—that is, a question in which the judge makes a point favorable to your client and thereby encourages you to discuss that point. Resist the cynic's temptation to look for a trap in the question. Rather, to continue the baseball analogy, you should hit the ball out of the ballpark by first concurring with the judge and then developing the point further by citing authority, referring to relevant facts, or both.

Unclear, irrelevant, or unanswerable questions. If the court asks an *unclear question*, politely tell the court that you are not sure what point the court means to raise and that you need a clarification. For instance: "Your honor, could you rephrase that question? I'm not sure that I understand it."

If the court asks an *irrelevant question*, consider asking the judge to repeat the question so you can be sure you have not misunderstood it. Then answer briefly, or tactfully explain what the more relevant question is, and answer it.

If the court asks a *question you cannot answer*, say so candidly, and offer to submit a supplemental brief on the point. For instance: "I'm sorry, your honor; I'm not familiar with that statute. I would be glad to research it and submit a supplemental brief on it, if that would be helpful." Of course, this approach is appropriate only if you are truly unprepared to answer the question. This response likely will decrease your credibility with the court, but it is better to candidly admit lack of knowledge than to risk an erroneous or ill-considered response.

F. DELIVERING THE ARGUMENT

1. Making Spoken Communication Clear

A judge listening to an oral argument cannot re-listen to a portion that occurred some minutes ago or stop the argument to consider a statement just made. Thus, it is your responsibility to *make your communication clear*.

To help the judges assimilate what is being said, use short to medium-length sentences. Speak at a medium tempo, with occasional pauses. These pauses provide you and the judges with time to think and serve as aural cues equivalent to punctuation and paragraph breaks in written communication. You should pause briefly between sentences and a bit longer between paragraphs.

In addition to tempo and pauses, use roadmaps to alert the court to what you are planning to say and signposts to track your progress. These semantic roadmaps and signposts can be emphasized by inflections, pauses, and gestures.

Generally, quotations are difficult for a listener to process. You are unlikely to read a quotation as naturally as you speak in your own words, and the listener must adjust to the style of the quotation and then back to your speaking style. Many legal texts are complex in syntax or semantics. So if the point you want to make can be made equally well by paraphrasing, do so. Nonetheless, some material may be so important that it merits a direct quotation (for example, the key phrase of a statute in a statutory interpretation case or the telling statement of a key witness). Above all, be sure that you state the quotation accurately. Formally introduce the quotation by indicating its source, and be sure to indicate "end quote."

Sometimes visual aids, such as a timeline, map, or diagram, may be helpful to the court. You should ask the clerk whether the court permits visual aids and, if so, in what form. You may choose to present the material in an appendix to the brief, on an easel, or through a document projection system. Of course, the actual information must have appeared in the briefs or record in some form and must be within the scope of the court's review.

2. Creating a Good Impression

Like it or not, first impressions matter. The court's impression of you will carry over to your client. So you should do what you can to *create a good impression*.

You should dress neatly and appropriately, so that your appearance does not distract from your argument. Consult with a lawyer who argues often before the particular court as to its dress conventions.

Bring to the courtroom the transcript, record, all briefs, your notes, and any other materials to which you may need to refer. You need not bring all these materials to the lectern, but you should have them on the counsel's table, where you can retrieve them if you need them.

Arrive early to scout out the courtroom, if it is unfamiliar to you. You will want to note the acoustics, the height of the lectern, and the timing system. Check with the bailiff or clerk for hints as to the procedures of the particular court and the preferences of the judge(s). The timing system may consist of a conventional countdown timer or a set of lights—green for go, yellow for x number of minutes remaining, and red for stop. Or you and the court may keep track of the time yourselves. You should bring an easy-to-read timepiece and place it on the lectern.

Rise when the court enters and leaves, as well as when you address the court. Wait for the presiding judge to give you permission to begin your argument. Refer to the judge as "your honor," "judge," or "justice" (if you are before the high court of the jurisdiction).

To achieve your goal of a conversation, maintain eye contact as much as possible. Do not read your memorandum or brief; do not read citations unless asked for them. Avoid distracting conduct, such as playing with a pen, covering your mouth, or flipping pages over the front edge of the lectern.

Courtroom demeanor varies considerably from lawyer to lawyer. Some lawyers are fairly passionate and demonstrative; others are more reserved and moderate. To a great extent, your courtroom demeanor will be a matter of your personal style. You also may consider matching your demeanor to the situation, as determined by the nature of the case, the type of argument you that are making (with equitable arguments calling for more passion than technical legal arguments), and the temperament of the court.

In all cases, of course, you must convey respect for the court, opposing counsel, and the law. Address judges with deference, never familiarity. You may disagree with the merits of opposing counsel's arguments, but as stated previously, you should never convey personal disdain for opposing counsel. Furthermore, oral argument is not an occasion for emotional appeals, pejoratives, abstract speeches about justice, or irrelevant (or irreverent) humor. Nor is it an occasion for stating your personal views of the client's case or the state of the law. Indeed, most experts caution against first-person references ("I believe . . .").

You should convey both credibility and a commitment to the client's cause. Ideally, you actually will believe your client's arguments, and this belief will come through naturally. To maximize the appearance of credibility and commitment during the argument, take care in framing your points so that you neither overreach nor understate matters. As much as possible, focus on the material that you personally find most compelling. Answer questions honestly; do not try to bluster through awkward situations. Rather than acting according to your image of a lawyer, be yourself.

According to the recency principle, the last words said carry particular weight, so it is important to conclude well. You need not use all your allotted time.

Courts do appreciate brevity and may be impressed with the simplicity of a short argument. If you finish early, ask the court if it has any more questions, and, if not, conclude and sit down. If you represent the appellant, you may be able to add your leftover time to your reserved rebuttal time. On the other hand, if you run out of time, you should conclude your current sentence in very brief form, then ask the court if you may have an additional thirty to sixty seconds in which to deliver a very brief conclusion. If the court grants the extension, take care not to exceed the time given. If the court refuses the request, thank the court for its attention and sit down.

G. REVIEW

Oral argument is not a speech or book report, but rather a conversation with the court in which your primary goal is to address the court's concerns. Oral argument procedures vary across courts, and you should research the rules and practices of a court before arguing before it.

The movant or appellant argues first. Although oral argument is less fixed than written advocacy, most arguments follow a sequence that bears a loose resemblance to memoranda or briefs: introductory material, facts and procedure, the legal argument, and conclusion. Counsel for the party opposing the motion or appeal speaks next, responding to the points made by opposing counsel and stating his or her own view of the case. The movant or appellant may conclude the argument with a brief rebuttal.

To prepare for an oral argument, you must select the arguments you want to present—typically your strongest arguments, the areas of sharpest conflict between the parties, and arguments that can be stated easily aloud. In addition, you should think through the pitch of your argument, the allocation of time among your various topics, and ways to maintain flexibility during the argument. It is important to prepare written materials to have at the lectern and to practice.

When you deliver your argument, analyze the questions you receive by type (for example, as hypotheticals or policy questions); respond accordingly and fully; then move back into your argument as smoothly as possible. Speak clearly, and use pauses and signals so that the court can easily understand your arguments and follow your organization. Finally, be sure to follow court etiquette so that you make a good impression.

Your argument will be complete if it addresses what the court wants to know. It will be comprehensible if the court can follow your introduction, case statement, and argument. It will be correct and coherent if the facts, law, and policy are accurately stated and mesh into a coherent whole. Lastly, your argument will be convincing if you advocate your client's position with confidence.

Test Your Understanding

1. Assume that you are representing Bower's Bounty in its litigation with Sarah Nicholson. She has claimed defamation against Bower's Bounty based on statements made in a posting in the employee lounge by management after her termination. Explain the role of oral argument as follows:
   a. Its role from the standpoint of the court
   b. The scope of the argument
   c. The opportunity that it provides to you
   d. The challenges of oral argument

2. You could be delivering an argument in district court on a motion. What are some of the ways in which district court arguments vary from court to court, and how would you determine the practices in your particular court?

3. Assume instead that you are to deliver an appellate oral argument.
   a. Describe the typical physical setting of an appellate argument.
   b. Explain the difference between a hot bench and a cold bench.
   c. If Bower's Bounty is the appellant, how many times would you argue, and what would be the basic outline of your arguments?
   d. If Bower's Bounty is the respondent, how many times would you argue, and what would be the basic outline of your arguments?

4. As you prepare for an oral argument:
   a. What principles should guide your selection of topics to cover?
   b. How can you prepare for being flexible during the argument?
   c. What type of written materials should you prepare?
   d. What types of practice should you engage in?

5. As you answer questions:
   a. What does court etiquette call for?
   b. What is a good strategy for answering each of the following types of questions?
      • Questions about the facts
      • Questions about the law
      • Questions about public policy
      • Questions about a hypothetical situation
      • Questions seeking concessions
      • Questions about your opponent's argument

6. As you deliver your argument, what are some speaking practices to engage in and to avoid?

7. What are some non-speaking practices to engage in and to avoid?

TEST YOUR UNDERSTANDING ANSWERS

1. The role of oral argument is as follows:
   a. For the court, oral argument is a conversation in which it obtains clarification of the facts, law, and policies in the case.
   b. The scope of the argument is confined to the material covered in the briefs.
   c. Oral argument provides the lawyer the opportunity to humanize the case and address the court's concerns.
   d. The challenges of oral argument are that it occurs in the moment (so it is harder to follow) and the lawyer does not control it.

2. District court arguments vary from court to court in whether they are granted at all as well as their length, their setting, the method of assigning the judge to hear them, and their formality. Rules on oral argument, the court clerk, and local lawyers can provide this information.

3. As for appellate oral argument:
   a. The typical physical setting is a courtroom with counsel at a lectern (with a timer) and a panel of judges behind the bench.
   b. A hot bench consists of well prepared judges and a cold bench of less prepared judges.
   c. An appellant begins the argument with an introduction, the statement of the case, its legal argument, and a conclusion. The appellant generally also rebuts with two or three points in response to the respondent's argument.
   d. The respondent goes after the appellant and argues only once, stating an introduction, a limited statement of the case, its legal argument, and a conclusion.

4. As you prepare for an oral argument:
   a. Principles guiding the selection of topics to cover include focusing on the points of clash and theory of the case, choosing the strongest arguments, and choosing arguments that can easily be discussed aloud.
   b. Preparing for flexibility includes knowing which arguments are most important, how to move between arguments, and how to respond to the opponent's arguments and authorities.
   c. An outline with key authorities sketched out is the best type of written material to have at the lectern, along with the case file available at counsel's table.
   d. Practices to engage in are memorizing the opening and closing, practicing talking about various parts of the case, being quizzed on the case, and reviewing your taped presentation.

5. As you answer questions:
   a. Court etiquette calls for ceasing talking when a judge begins to talk, answering a question when asked, not interrupting a judge, and moving on without waiting for permission to do so.
   b. Good strategies for answering the following types of questions are:
      • Questions about the facts—accurately answer, and comment on the significance of the facts.
      • Questions about the law—state the law, and draw a favorable connection to your case.
      • Questions about public policy—note how public policy favors your preferred outcome or (if the policy cuts against your client) note how the policy impacts are speculative.
      • Questions about a hypothetical situation—think first; then answer, along with giving your reasoning,
      • Questions seeking concessions—concede only if doing so will not harm your client's case; otherwise, hold firm.
      • Questions about your opponent's argument—focus on the argument rather than on the opponent or counsel personally.

6. As you deliver your argument, use short to medium-length sentences, speak at a medium tempo, pause regularly, and employ inflection. Avoid lengthy quotations, use of the first-person, and improper language.

7. Dress appropriately, stand when the court enters, wait for permission to begin speaking, and maintain eye contact. Avoid distracting conduct, such as playing with a pen or flipping pages over the lectern.

PART FIVE

EXERCISES

The exercises in this part afford you the opportunity to engage in the skills discussed throughout the book. They all relate to an area of law, not addressed elsewhere in the book, that is governed both by the common law and by statute and that raises important and difficult issues of public policy: the liability of a seller of liquor to a person who is injured by a drunk driver to whom the liquor seller provided alcohol.

The exercises call upon you to work through the analytical steps described in the text and to write out the product of your analysis. For some exercises, you will critique draft passages. For other exercises, you will outline what you would write or indeed will write brief passages. For yet other exercises, you will plan how to approach a conversation with a client, opposing counsel, or the court.

The opening pages of this part provide the facts of the two situations you will work on: the Gary Masters situation and the Jody Harrison situation. Those two situations are followed by your law library, which consists of one case printed in full, four additional case briefs, a statute, and a set of statutory interpretation points for that statute. The exercises follow, with each covering the situations and authorities noted in the chart below.

Chapter	Client Situation	Authorities
2. Reading Legal Rules	Neither	Case law rules
3. Reading Cases	Neither	Common law
4. Reading Codes	Gary Masters	Statute
5. Reading Commentary	Neither	Restatement materials provided in exercise

Chapter	Client Situation	Authorities
6. Legal Reasoning	Gary Masters	Common law and statute
7. Writing Legal Analysis	Gary Masters	Common law and statute
8. The Analytical Office Memo	Gary Masters and Jody Harrison	Common law and statute
9. The Advice Letter	Gary Masters	Statute
10. Interviewing the Client	Gary Masters	Common law and statute
11. Counseling the Client	Jody Harrison	Common law and statute
12. The Demand Letter	Gary Masters	Common law
13. Contracts	Gary Masters	None explicitly
14. Pleadings	Gary Masters	Common law and statute
15. Negotiating with Opposing Counsel	Gary Masters	Common law and statute
16 and 17. Legal Advocacy and the Motion Practice Memorandum	Jody Harrison	Common law
16 and 18. Legal Advocacy and the Appellate Brief	Gary Masters	Common law and statute
19. Oral Argument	Gary Masters	Common law and statute

TWO SITUATIONS

Some of the exercises pertain to the Gary Masters situation, others to the Jody Harrison situation, both of which are stated below. Before you do any of the exercises, you might want to think about the legal rules that you would construct for this situation.

Gary Masters Situation

One evening in Stamford, Connecticut, Gary Masters visited two bars over the course of four to six hours. He drank three shots of tequila and six bottles of beer at the first bar. When he arrived at the second bar, the smell of liquor was on his breath. He kept to himself and appeared sullen and withdrawn. He paid for and drank three more shots and six more bottles of beer at the second bar. Shortly after leaving the second bar, he drove his car across the highway into oncoming traffic. He struck a car carrying a child, who was killed.

Jody Harrison Situation

The police report:

(1) A car driven by Marsha Lewis (age 26) crashed going around a bend on Highway 56 near the Simpson farm at about 3:30 p.m.
(2) The car was going approximately 80 mph.
(3) The weather and road conditions were fine.
(4) There was no oncoming traffic.
(5) Both Lewis and passenger Jody Harrison (age 24) were severely injured and taken to the county hospital by ambulance.
(6) Both Lewis and Harrison smelled of alcohol.
(7) A search of the car revealed no valid driver's license for Lewis.

Statement of Marsha Lewis:

(8) My car spun out near the Simpson farm when it hit a wet spot in the road.
(9) The car's speed was approximately 40 mph.
(10) Jody was hurt so badly because she wasn't wearing her seat belt.
(11) Jody and I each drank about four beers during the early afternoon, over two hours, stopping at 3:00 p.m.
(12) We drank them at Hillside Country Club after finishing a round of golf; we also ate lunch.
(13) One bartender, Mark Johnson, served us the first two beers; a second, Gary Martinez, served us the second two.
(14) We were never drunk, neither of us (maybe tipsy).

Statement of bartender Gary Martinez:

(15) I served both Harrison and Lewis two beers between 2:30 and 3:15 p.m., along with an order of nachos.

(16) They were eating, but not drinking, when I arrived on shift.

(17) Harrison was becoming loud and boisterous, so I told her I had decided not to serve her more if she was driving, which she said she was not.

(18) Shortly after, Lewis and Harrison left angrily.

(19) Lewis showed no signs of being drunk.

Statement of Andrew Harrison (Jody's husband):

(20) Doctors say Jody has suffered long-term memory loss and diminished concentration, although her abdominal injuries have healed.

(21) Our marriage is showing signs of strain due to Jody's disability and reduced earning capacity.

(22) Jody and Marsha often drank, Marsha heavily, after golf on Saturdays, so Jody generally drove.

(23) Marsha drove that Saturday because our car was being fixed.

Laboratory report:

(24) Lewis's blood alcohol level was .10.

(25) Harrison's blood alcohol level was .08.

YOUR LAW LIBRARY

The materials in this library are real legal materials from Connecticut on this topic, but they are not exhaustive or current. Rather, we have selected them for their utility in supporting a workable and interesting set of exercises. You will be directed which materials to read for each exercise. The library is as follows:

Case Law. We have provided one case in full, *Moore v. Bunk*, decided by the Connecticut Supreme Court in 1967. We have briefed the remaining cases: *Ely v. Murphy, Kowal v. Hofher, Nelson v. Steffens,* and *Nolan v. Morelli,* all decided by the Connecticut Supreme Court from 1967 to 1988. These cases involve claims that the defendants acted negligently. Negligence is a common law claim involving failure to act as someone of ordinary prudence would under the same circumstances. Negligence per se arises when the duty of care involves a statute, so negligence per se cases include references to statutes. To establish negligence, the plaintiff also must show that the defendant's acts "proximately caused" the plaintiff's injury—that is, that the defendant's conduct "created the risk of a particular harm and was a substantial factor in causing that harm." *Quinnett v. Newman*, 568 A.2d 786, 790 (Conn. 1990).

Statutory Law. We also have reprinted the Connecticut Dram Shop Act, specifically providing for recovery against sellers of liquor in certain situations. That reprint is followed by a set of interpretive materials.

154 Conn. 644
Supreme Court of Connecticut.
Milton MOORE, Administrator (ESTATE of John H. MOORE)
v.
Bradford E. BUNK et al.
March 23, 1967.

Action for death of plaintiffs' decedent allegedly caused by defendants' furnishing alcoholic liquor to him. The Superior Court, New Haven County at Waterbury, Benjamin M. Leipner, J., sustained demurrers by defendants and plaintiff
having failed to plead over rendered judgment for defendants, and plaintiff
appealed. The Supreme Court, King, C.J., held that 16-year-old minor who
consumes liquor is presumed to have done so voluntarily and minor's consumption of liquor and not the furnishing of the liquor was proximate cause of intoxication and resulting injuries and death.

No error.

***

Attorneys and Law Firms

*645 **511 Joseph H. Sylvester, Shelton, with whom was David B.
Cohen, Derby, for appellant (plaintiff).

Alan H. W. Shiff, New Haven, with whom, on the brief, was Philip R. Shiff,
New Haven, for appellees (defendants Bunk et al.).

John H. Cassidy, Jr., Watertown, for appellee (defendant Zalenski).

Thomas J. Hagarty, Hartford, with whom, on the brief, was Joseph T. Swee-
ney, Hartford, for appellee (defendant Smith).

Before ***644** KING, C.J., and ALCORN, HOUSE, THIM and RYAN, JJ.

Opinion

KING, Chief Justice.

This action was brought by the administrator of the estate of John H. Moore
to recover damages for his death. The first count runs against the defendants
Bradford E. Bunk and St. Stanislawa Benefits and Mutual Society, Inc., hereinafter referred to as Society, as permittee and backer, respectively, of Society's club
liquor permit. The second count runs against the defendants Joseph Zaleski,
George Smith, and George Morey.

The complant alleges that on July 18, 1964, the decedent, a minor sixteen
years of age, while he was on Society's club premises, was given, and consumed,
intoxicating liquors in such quantity that he became intoxicated and, as a consequence of that ***646** intoxication, so operated a motor vehicle as to cause it to
collide with some trees, which resulted in the injuries from which he died.

The second count alleges that Zalenski, Smith, and Morey gave the liquor to
the decedent, or permitted him to consume it, and that these acts were violations

of General Statutes §§ 30-77 and 30-86 and constituted a proximate cause of his intoxication.

The first count alleges that Society and Bunk rented to the defendant Zalenski, who was not a member of Society, a portion of the club premises, knowing, or chargeable with knowledge, that intoxicating liquors would therein be dispensed to minors. It is further alleged that the decedent's intoxication, injuries, and death were proximately caused by Society and Bunk in that they rented the club premises to a nonmember, failed to obtain the signatures of the guests in a guest book, and failed to seal off the club barroom from the rented portion of the premises, all in violation of regulations of the liquor control commission; in that they allowed minors to loiter on the premises in violation of General Statutes § 30-90; in that they gave intoxicating liquor or allowed it to be given to a minor on the club premises; and in that they knew or should have known that minors were on the premises and were being given intoxicating liquor, but they failed or neglected to prevent such action from taking place.

**512 All defendants demurred to the complaint, and, upon the sustaining of the demurrers, the plaintiff declined to plead over. From the judgment rendered for the defendants, the plaintiff appealed.

The plaintiff's primary claims are based on alleged violations of various general statutes and of *647 regulations of the liquor control commission claimed to have been enacted for the benefit and protection of persons in the general circumstances of this plaintiff's decedent. Although it is not stated with the precision desirable in pleadings, it appears that the plaintiff is claiming that the violations of these statutes and regulations constituted negligence per se.

[1] [2] The crucial allegations of the complaint are that these violations were the proximate cause of the decedent's intoxication. It is, however, the general common-law rule that the proximate cause of intoxication is the voluntary consumption, rather than the furnishing, of intoxicating liquor. Nolan v. Morelli, 154 Conn. 432, 436, 226 A.2d 383. Thus, the furnishing of intoxicating liquor was not the proximate cause of intoxication or of any damage proximately resulting from such intoxication, whether sustained by the intoxicated person himself or by another. The common-law rule as to proximate cause, of course, applies in any common-law action of negligence, even though that action includes, as specifications of negligence, one or more alleged violations of applicable statutes. This would include, of course, General Statutes § 30-86, which prohibits the furnishing of intoxicating liquor to minors, whether gratuitously or by sale.

The complaint alleges that the decedent consumed the liquor furnished, or permitted to be furnished, by the defendants. The voluntariness of that consumption, while not expressly alleged, is in nowise negated, as it must be to avoid the common-law rule.

There remains for consideration the question whether the portion of § 30-86 which prohibits, with certain exceptions not applicable to the present case, the furnishing of intoxicating liquor to minors, *648 whether gratuitously or by sale, amounts to a legislative declaration that minors are legally incapable of consenting to the consumption of liquor and thus preclude their action in drinking the liquor from being voluntarily within the meaning of the common-law rule.

[3] Although a minor is subject to a legal disability in the management of his property and in his contractual obligations, he nevertheless is permitted to make a will at the age of eighteen (General Statutes § 45-160), and he may be licensed to operate a motor vehicle after he becomes sixteen. General Statutes § 14-36. A minor may be held criminally responsible for his violations of law at age sixteen. General Statutes §§ 17-53, 17-65, 17-72. Under General Statutes s § 52-217, in actions for recovery of damages for injury to person or property, a minor under sixteen is entitled to have the trier of fact determine whether his violation of a statutory duty was negligence, while one sixteen years of age or older is subject to the general rule that the violations of an applicable statute is negligence per se. Santor v. Balnis, 151 Conn. 434, 436, 199 A.2d 2; Bevins v. Brewer, 146 Conn. 10, 15, 147 A.2d 189. Thus, a minor aged sixteen or over is presumed to have the capacity to decide whether or not to violate the law. As a sixteen-year-old minor may be held accountable for violating § 14-227a by operating a motor vehicle while he is intoxicated, he may certainly be held accountable for deciding to consume intoxicating liquor in the first place. Furthermore, § 30-89 provides a criminal penalty for any minor who purchases or attempts to purchase intoxicating liquor. Thus, at least in the case of a minor aged sixteen or over, he may be presumed, if he consumes liquor, to have done so voluntarily.

*649 [4] [5] Since here the decedent's consumption of intoxicating liquor was voluntary, his consumption, rather than any **513 violation, by any of the defendants, of § 30-86 or of other statutes or liquor control commission regulations, was, under the common-law rule, the proximate cause of his intoxication and of the injuries and death claimed to have resulted therefrom. Of course, negligence, whether common-law or statutory, must be proved to have been a proximate cause of the injuries complained of if it is to constitute actionable negligence. Nolan v. Morelli, 154 Conn. 432, 443, 226 A.2d 383.

[6] [7] It is true that the complaint specifically alleges that the giving of liquor to the decedent was a proximate cause of his intoxication, injuries and death. But allegations of legal conclusions are not admitted by demurrer. Rossignol v. Danbury School of Aeronautics, Inc., 154 Conn. -, 227 A.2d 418; McAdam v. Sheldon, 153 Conn. 278, 282, 216 A.2d 193; Barnes v. Viering, 152 Conn. 243, 244, 206 A.2d 112. Consequently, the allegations of proximate cause are ineffective to negate the common-law rule that the voluntary consumption, rather than the furnishing, of the liquor was the proximate cause of the intoxication and the resulting injuries and death.

[8] Finally, we consider briefly certain other allegations of duty appearing in the complaint. As to Zalenski, Smith, and Morey, the complaint alleges that, having allowed the decedent to become intoxicated, they neglected and failed to exercise any degree of care or control to prevent his injury and death at a time

when they were under a duty so to do. But the allegation of the existence of such a duty is merely a legal conclusion. Neither any specific duty nor any facts giving rise to any duty *650 are alleged. The demurrers, therefore, did not admit the existence of any such duty. Rossignol v. Danbury School of Aeronautics, Inc., supra; McAdam v. Sheldon, supra; see Nolan v. Morelli, supra.

[9] As to Bunk and Society, the complaint, construed favorably to the plaintiff, alleges a duty to prevent others on the permit premises from giving or delivering intoxicating liquor to the decedent as a minor. But if such a duty exists, as to the minor decedent in the present case, under the common-law rule any violation of that duty was not a proximate cause of intoxication resulting from the decedent's voluntary consumption of that liquor or of any injuries resulting from such intoxication.

There is no error.

In this opinion the other judges concurred.

All Citations

154 Conn. 644, 228 A.2d 510

BRIEFS OF FOUR ADDITIONAL CASES[1]

Ely v. Murphy, Connecticut Supreme Court 1988

FACTS: Ds hosted high school graduation party involving youth drinking all night. Legal drinking age is 19. No bartenders or security staff; no one monitored drinking. Ds said they took car keys of drunk partygoers. 18-year-old guest became very drunk, said keys were in car, and Ds never got keys, left early in morning, drove into another guest, killing him.

PROCEDURE AND OUTCOME: Among other claims, father of killed guest sued Ds for common law neg in serving liquor. Court granted motion to strike neg count re serving liquor. P appeals. Reversed and remanded.

ISSUE: Is there neg cause of action where social host provides liquor to minor, minor becomes drunk, drives, and fatally injures third party?

HOLDING: Social host may be liable in neg for serving liquor to minor who thereafter becomes drunk and injures third party; proximate cause is not lacking.

REASONING: Old rule is: general rule at common law is no neg cause of action agst person who by sale or gift serves liquor to person who becomes intox'd and then injures self or another, bcz proximate cause of intox'n is consumption, not furnishing of liquor. Rule assumes knowing and intelligent exercise of choice to drink. But statutes on drinking by minors and public attitudes indicate that minors are incompetent by reason of youth and inexperience to deal with liquor. Thus, new rule is consumption of liquor by youth is not

---

1. The cases may be found as follows: *Ely* at 540 A.2d 54, *Kowal* at 436 A.2d 1, *Moore* at 228 A.2d 510, *Nelson* at 365 A.2d 1174, and *Nolan* at 226 A.2d 383.

intervening act necessary to break proximate cause chain. *Moore* and *Nelson* are overruled. Persuasive precedent supports new rule. Proximate cause in minor case is now question of fact.

Kowal v. Hofher, Connecticut Supreme Court 1980

FACTS: According to complaint, D restaurant owner served liquor to already intox'd person, who then negligently drove into car in which decedent was riding.

PROCEDURE AND OUTCOME: Admin of estate sued D for neg and reckless conduct. D moved to strike those counts; ct granted motion. P appeals. Affirmed in part; reversed and remanded in part.

ISSUES: Are there (1) neg or (2) reckless conduct causes of action where commercial seller of liquor serves intox'd person who drives into third party's car, killing him?

HOLDING: Where seller of liquor serves intox'd person who then injures third party, (1) there is no neg cause of action, but (2) there may be reckless conduct cause of action.

REASONING: Old rule (continues): no neg cause of action agst person who by sale or gift serves liquor to person who becomes intox'd and then injures self or another, bcz proximate cause of intox'n is consumption, not furnishing of liquor. This rule covers neg claim.

New rule: where, however, conduct is not neg but wanton and reckless, i.e., in reckless disregard of another's safety, there may be proximate cause. One must bear greater responsibility for injuries due to reckless conduct. Therefore there may be proximate cause in this case as to recklessness claim. Cites persuasive precedent and Restatement of Torts.

CONCURRENCE WITHOUT OPINION: One justice.

CONCURRENCE/DISSENT: Majority is correct as to reckless conduct; should hold similarly as to neg as well. (One justice.)

DISSENT: Decision affronts court's precedent that there is no tort cause of action on these facts. Difference bet neg and reckless conduct is only theoretical and unwise; in any event, distinction pertains not to causation but to degree of care. Distinguishes majority's persuasive precedent. (One justice.)

Nelson v. Steffens, Connecticut Supreme Court 1976

FACTS: D sold liquor to already intox'd minor who then drove with two other boys in car. Car went out of control. One passenger was killed; the other injured.

PROCEDURE AND OUTCOME: Mother of dead/injured boys sued D. D demurred. Ct sustained demurrer. P appeals. Affirmed.

ISSUE: Is there neg cause of action where commercial seller of liquor furnishes liquor to intox'd minor who then drives car so as to injure/kill passengers?

HOLDING: There is no neg cause of action agst commercial seller who furnishes liquor to minor who thereafter injures passengers in car wreck.

RULE OF LAW: There is no neg cause of action agst person who by sale or gift serves liquor to person who becomes intox'd and then injures self or another.

REASONING: Proximate cause of intox'n is consumption, not furnishing of liquor. This is rule suggested in earlier decisions in CT and majority rule elsewhere. P does not cite any reason not to follow this rule.

CONCURRENCE WITHOUT OPINION: Three justices.

DISSENT: Conduct alleged is neg conduct: failure to conform to duty set by statute (here, statute prohibiting service of liquor to minor) or duty to exercise reasonable care. Rule adopted by majority is antiquated. Seller should foresee situation that occurred here, so that minor driver's conduct does not break chain of causation. Proximate cause should be jury judgment.

Nolan v. Morelli, Connecticut Supreme Court 1967

FACTS: D restaurants served adult liquor. He became intox'd, drove car into tree, was injured, and died.

PROCEDURE AND OUTCOME: Driver's wife sued D for neg (among other claims). Ds demurred, ct sustained demurrer. P appeals. Affirmed.

ISSUE: Is there neg cause of action (common law or neg per se) agst commercial seller of liquor for furnishing liquor to adult who became intox'd and killed self in car wreck?

HOLDING: There is no cause of action agst commercial seller of liquor for furnishing liquor to adult who then killed himself when driving while intox'd.

RULE OF LAW: There is no neg cause of action agst person who by sale or gift serves liquor to person who becomes intox'd and then injures self or another.

REASONING: Proximate cause of intox'n is consumption, not furnishing of liquor. This rule has been followed by lower ct in CT. To provide compensation to intox'd person for overindulgence might encourage, rather than discourage, intox'n. Intox'n is voluntary act that is superseding act bet sale and injury. This reasoning covers both common law neg and neg per se.

THE CONNECTICUT DRAM SHOP ACT[2]

§ 30-102. Dram shop act; liquor seller liable for damage by intoxicated person

If any person, by himself or his agent, sells any alcoholic liquor to an intoxicated person, and such purchaser, in consequence of such intoxication, thereafter injures the person or property of another, such seller shall pay just damages to the person injured, up to the amount of twenty thousand dollars, or to persons

---

2. Reprinted from West's *Connecticut General Statutes Annotated* (1990).

injured in consequence of such intoxication up to an aggregate amount of fifty thousand dollars, to be recovered in an action under this section, provided the aggrieved person or persons shall give written notice to such seller within sixty days of the occurrence of such injury to person or property of his or their intention to bring an action under this section. In computing such sixty-day period, the time between the death or incapacity of any aggrieved person and the appointment of an executor, administrator, conservator, or guardian of his estate shall be excluded, except that the time so excluded shall not exceed one hundred twenty days. Such notice shall specify the time, the date, and the person to whom such sale was made, the name and address of the person injured or whose property was damaged, and the time, date and place where the injury to person or property occurred. No action under the provisions of this section shall be brought but within one year from the date of the act or omission complained of.

(1949 Rev., § 4307; 1955, Supp. § 2172d; 1957, P.A. 306; 1959, P.A. 631, § 1, eff. July 1, 1959; 1961, P.A. 432; 1974, P.A. 74-144, § 1, eff. May 8, 1974; 1986, P.A. 86-338, § 7, eff. Oct. 1, 1986; 1987, P.A. 87-227, § 11.)

STATUTORY INTERPRETATION POINTS FOR THE DRAM SHOP ACT[3]

A. A 1985 case decided by the Connecticut Supreme Court holds that a person may be found to be intoxicated when the following symptoms are manifest to an observer: the person's walk or conversation is abnormal, judgment is disturbed, or willpower is temporarily suspended.

B. The prior version of the statute required that the plaintiff establish a causal connection between the provision of the liquor by the defendant and the injury suffered by the plaintiff.

C. According to a 1957 decision by the Connecticut Supreme Court, the legislature was concerned about the danger to public health, safety, and morals from liquor sales and, more specifically, about drunk driving.

D. Under the state's criminal code, "intoxication" is "a substantial disturbance of mental or physical capacities resulting from the introduction of substances into the body."

E. Several decisions by the Connecticut Supreme Court indicate that the Dram Shop Act does not alter one's ability to sue under the common law or the common law cause of action, but rather it provides a statutory claim for limited damages in specified circumstances.

F. In 1957, the Connecticut Supreme Court upheld the statute against the argument that it was unconstitutional in providing a penalty against the seller even though there was no causal connection between the sale and the injury.

---

3. The points listed above are drawn directly or indirectly from the following cases: *Sanders v. Officers Club of Connecticut Inc.*, 493 A.2d 184 (Conn. 1985); *Kowal v. Hofher*, 436 A.2d 1 (Conn. 1980); *Nelson v. Steffens*, 365 A.2d 1174 (Conn. 1976); *Nolan v. Morelli*, 226 A.2d 383 (Conn. 1967); *Pierce v. Albanese*, 129 A.2d 606 (Conn. 1957); *Kelehear v. Larcon, Inc.*, 577 A.2d 746 (Conn. Ct. App. 1990).

The court noted that the statute was a proper exercise of the legislature's broad power to regulate liquor.

G. The Connecticut Supreme Court held in 1957 that a jury could properly infer that two individuals who drank two beers in a bar were sold the beers at the bar; there need not be direct proof of the sale (such as the bartender's testimony).

H. In various cases, the Connecticut Supreme Court has identified three elements of a dram shop case: (1) a sale of intoxicating liquor; (2) to an intoxicated person; (3) who, in consequence of such intoxication, causes injury to the person or property of another.

I. In a 1967 decision by the Connecticut Supreme Court, the court ruled that the Dram Shop Act does not provide recovery where the intoxicated buyer is the injured party.

J. In a 1990 case decided by the Appellate Court of Connecticut, the court accepted the seller's evidence that the buyer was shut off when he became obnoxious, found that evidence that the buyer was seen with a beer can thereafter would not establish a sale, and yet ruled that the jury could find an illegal sale based on sales before the buyer was shut off.

EXERCISES FOR CHAPTER 2

READING LEGAL RULES

Consider the following rules:

RULE #1

"Two conditions [ ] must coexist before statutory negligence can be actionable. First, the plaintiff must be within the class of persons protected by the statute. Second, the injury must be of the type which the statute was intended to protect." *Wright v. Brown*, 356 A.2d 176, 179 (Conn. 1975).

RULE #2

"Failure to exercise due care is negligence, and whether there is such a failure must depend on the circumstances of a particular case. Generally, in the absence of some rule of conduct specifically prescribed by legislation, the standard of due care is that of the ordinary prudent person under the circumstances." *Burritt v. Plate*, 481 A.2d 425, 427 (Conn. Super. Ct. 1984).

RULE #3

"The inquiry whether, in a particular case, a party conducted himself with ordinary care always involves the consideration of the difficulties and obstacles to be encountered, his knowledge of their existence, and his means and power to overcome them. And if men of ordinary prudence would regard the ability of the party insufficient for the purpose, without hazard, there is want of ordinary care in making the attempt." *Fox v. Town of Glastonbury*, 29 Conn. 204, 208-09 (1860).

1. Restate each of the above rules in if/then form; use letters or numbers to set off the various elements and legal consequences. Identify the relationships among the elements as conjunctive, disjunctive, aggregate, balancing, or a combination. Finally, note whether the consequence is a label or an outcome.

2. Select one of these rules, and depict it in a chart.

3. Write your own rule about the liability of a bar for injuries caused by a customer who consumed liquor at the bar and afterward injured a third party in a car accident. Try to state an outcome, not just a label, in the then-clause. Present your rule in if/then form, and identify how the elements are related to each other, including any exceptions to your rule.

EXERCISES FOR CHAPTER 3

READING CASES

Read the explanation of negligence and *Moore v. Bunk* (on page 465).

1. Label the case according to the components of the case brief presented in Chapter 3 (e.g., facts, issue, and reasoning).

2. Read the following three sample briefs of *Moore*, and critique them according to the criteria in Chapter 3. For example, are all relevant facts presented? Does the issue link facts and law in question form? Is the rule of law true to the case?

SAMPLE #1

Moore v. Bunk, Connecticut Supreme Court 1967

FACTS: 16 year old P drank too much liquor provided by Ds. P drove car, collided with trees, died as result of injuries.

PROCEDURE AND OUTCOME: P sued; Ds demurred; trial ct sustained demurrers. P appeals demurrer. Affirmed.

ISSUE: Does absence of proximate cause bar lawsuit against liquor seller for death of minor?

HOLDING: Yes, proximate cause bars suit, bcz minor caused own injuries.

REASONING: Rule: "It is the general common-law rule that the proximate cause of intoxication is the voluntary consumption, rather than the furnishing, of intoxicating liquor." This rule applies to minors. Minors voluntarily consume liquor, as they make other legal decisions voluntarily.

SAMPLE #2

Moore v. Bunk, Connecticut Supreme Court 1967

FACTS: Minor person drank liquor on premises of one D, where another had liquor permit, and 3 other Ds were there giving liquor to minor. Minor then became drunk, drove, killed himself by running into tree. Two counts were agst permittee, backer, 3 other Ds. Ds won at trial court (they are respondents).

ISSUE: Was it error to sustain demurrers agst P's cause of action?

HOLDING: There is no error.

RULE: There must be proximate cause for neg claim.

REASONING: This is neg per se lawsuit, based on violations of liquor laws re minors drinking. Ds did not cause minor to drink. Minors can choose to drink, just as they can choose to make wills, drive, commit crimes. Therefore, Ds did not violate statutes. Nor did Ds fail to control minor when they had duty to do so.

SAMPLE #3

Moore v. Bunk, Connecticut Supreme Court 1967

FACTS: Administrator of John H. Moore estate brought action to recover damages for his death. First count against Bradford Bunk & St. Stanislawa Benefits & Mutual Society (Society). Second count against Joseph Zalenski, George Smith, George Morey.

July 18, 1964, Moore became intox'd on Society's premises and then operated motor vehicle so as to cause it to collide with trees, which resulted in injuries, from which he died.

Violations of statutes 30-77, 30-86, 30-90 alleged (renting to nonmember, failing to obtain signatures in book, failing to seal off barroom, allowing minors to loiter, etc.).

PROCEDURE AND OUTCOME: Admin. of estate sued Bunk, Society, Zalenski, Smith, Morey. All Ds demurred. Trial ct sustained demurrers. P did not re-plead. P appeals jmt rendered for Ds. Affirmed.

ISSUE: Is Society neg where minor Moore becomes intox'd after defendants Zalenski etc. give him liquor on Society premises, Moore drives and wrecks car, and therefore dies?

HOLDING: No, defendants aren't neg where minor Moore becomes intox'd after defendants Zalenski etc. give him liquor on Society premises, Moore drives and wrecks car, and therefore dies.

REASONING: Claims are not well pleaded but basically allege neg per se. There must be proximate cause. Rule of law: There is no proximate cause where furnishing liquor doesn't cause injury, whether sustained by intox'd person or another, whether minor buys or is given liquor. Minors can make many legally binding decisions: will at 18, drive at 16, criminal acts at 16, neg per se at 16, driving while intox'd at 16, etc. So their decision to drink and drive should preclude suits agst liquor sellers. This goes for suit agst Zalenski, Smith, Morey for letting Moore drink.

3. Write your own brief of *Moore*.

4. *Moore* does not include concurrences or dissents. Imagine that you are a concurring justice: what outcome would you urge, and what might your reasoning be? Now imagine that you are a dissenting justice: what outcome would you urge, and what might your reasoning be? Do you personally agree with the actual decision, your concurrence, or your dissent?

5. Which state and federal courts would be bound by the decision in *Moore*, and under what circumstances? Which state and federal courts might use the decision as persuasive precedent, and under what circumstances?

Read the briefs of the four additional cases (on page 468).

6. Construct a hierarchical array and a timeline of the five cases (including *Moore*).

7. Construct a features chart of the five cases in order to discern the pattern of the decisions.

8. Work on a rule fusion of the five cases. Is it possible to fuse a single rule out of the cases? Explain.

9. State your fused rule (or one of them if you derived more than one) in if/then form, and identify the relationship among the elements and the type of consequence.

10. Are you certain about your fusion of the cases, or are there uncertain aspects? If so, what is uncertain?

11. Does your fusion of these cases express your view of what the law should be? Why, or why not?

EXERCISES FOR CHAPTER 4

READING CODES

Read the Gary Masters situation (on page 463) and the Connecticut Dram Shop Act (on page 470).

1. Determine whether any language is *not* pertinent to the Masters situation and cross out that language. Then label the language of the statute that is pertinent to the situation according to the statutory components presented in Chapter 4 (e.g., definitions, general rule, exceptions, and consequences).

2. Read the following three sample briefs. Then critique each brief according to the criteria in Chapter 4. For example, is the statutory language presented accurately? Is all pertinent information presented? Are related ideas presented together?

SAMPLE #1

TITLE: Dram Shop Act

DEFINITIONS: None

SCOPE: None

GENERAL RULES: Illegal for any person:

to sell alcohol to intoxicated person
where purchaser injures another person.

EXCEPTIONS: Injured person does not:

give notice within 60 days of intent to sue
and sue within one year.

CONSEQUENCES/ENFORCEMENT: Just damages paid in action brought by injured person.

SAMPLE #2

IF   any person sells alcoholic liquor to intoxicated person who as consequence injures another person or property
THEN   seller pays $20,000–$50,000 to injured persons.
IF   aggrieved person(s) does not give written notice to seller within 60 days (or up to 120 days in case of death) of injury of intent to bring action—which includes information re sale, injured person, injury
THEN   seller is not liable.
IF   suit is not brought within one year of injury
THEN   seller is not liable.

SAMPLE #3

GENERAL RULE: If any person by himself or agent sells any alcoholic liquor to an intoxicated person, and the purchaser in consequence of intoxication thereafter injures person or property of another, seller pays just damages.

EXCEPTIONS: None.

CONSEQUENCES/ENFORCEMENT: Damages are $20,000 to person injured, up to aggregate of $50,000 to persons injured.

Aggrieved person(s) shall give written notice to seller within 60 days of occurrence of injury to person or property of intention to sue within this statute; time between death or incapacity of injured person and appointment of executor, administrator, conservator, guardian is excluded up to 120 days; notice must include time/date/person to whom sale occurred; name/address of injured person/property; time/date/place of injury to person/property.

No action unless within one year of date of act or omission complained of.

3. Write your own components-based brief of section 30-102.

4. Write your own if/then brief of section 30-102, first in outline style, then in chart form.

5. Read the sample brief set out below:

IF   any person or his/her agent (seller)
          sells
          alcoholic liquor
          to intoxicated person (purchaser)
          and purchaser
          in consequence of intoxication
          injures person/property of third party
          and third party
          gives written notice of intent to sue to seller
                stating time and date of sale; purchaser; name and address of
                third party; time, date, place of injury
                within 60 days of injury (excluding time [up to 120 days]
                between death or incapacity of third party and appointment of
                executor)
                and suit is brought within one year of act/omission
THEN   seller pays to third party just damages
          up to $20,000 per person, $50,000 aggregate.

Do you see any ambiguities in this rule as it relates to the Masters situation? If so, what is ambiguous?

Read the statutory interpretation points (on page 471).

6. Rank the points by how authoritative they are. Explain your rankings.

7. To which phrase of the statute does each point pertain? Incorporate these points into your if/then brief.

8. How might you use canons of construction to enable you to interpret the statute?

9. Is there any ambiguity remaining in the statute, even after these points are used to interpret it? Explain.

10. Does the statute as interpreted express your view of what the law should be? Explain.

EXERCISES FOR CHAPTER 5

READING COMMENTARY

Read the following excerpt from the Restatement (3d) of Torts.

1. If you read this material for the primary purpose of better understanding the law governing the liability of liquor sellers, what have you learned? Draw a bracket beside the key passages.

2. Take notes on both the rule and all pertinent supporting materials, as shown in Box 5.3.

3. How authoritative is this material, as compared to other types of commentary?

4. This material is called a "Restatement of the Law." Can a Restatement section actually constitute the law? Explain.

Restatement (Third) of Torts: Phys. & Emot. Harm § 7 (2010)

Restatement of the Law—Torts
June 2016 update
Restatement (Third) of Torts: Liability for Physical and Emotional Harm
Chapter 3. The Negligence Doctrine and
Negligence Liability

§ 7 Duty

(a) **An actor ordinarily has a duty to exercise reasonable care when the actor's conduct creates a risk of physical harm.**
(b) **In exceptional cases, when an articulated countervailing principle or policy warrants denying or limiting liability in a particular class of cases, a court may decide that the defendant has no duty or that the ordinary duty of reasonable care requires modification.**

Comment:

a. The proper role for duty. As explained in § 6, Comment *f*, actors engaging in conduct that creates risks to others have a duty to exercise reasonable care to avoid causing physical harm. In most cases, courts can rely directly on §6 and need not refer to duty on a case-by-case basis. Nevertheless, in some categories of cases, reasons of principle or policy dictate that liability should not be imposed. In these cases, courts use the rubric of duty to apply general categorical rules withholding liability. For example, a number of modern cases involve efforts to impose liability on social hosts for serving alcohol to their guests. A jury might plausibly find the social host negligent in providing alcohol to a guest who will depart in an automobile. Nevertheless, imposing liability is potentially problematic because of its impact on a substantial slice of social relations. Courts appropriately address whether such liability should be permitted as a matter of duty. Courts may also, for the same reasons, determine that modification of the ordinary duty of reasonable care is required. Thus, courts generally impose on sellers of products that are not defective at the time of sale the limited duty to warn of newly discovered risks, rather than the more general duty of reasonable care, which a jury might find includes a duty to recall and retrofit the product so as to eliminate the risk. Similarly, some courts have modified the general duty of reasonable care for those engaging in competitive sports to a more limited duty to refrain from recklessly dangerous conduct.

There are two different legal doctrines for withholding liability: no-duty rules and scope-of-liability doctrines (often called "proximate cause"). An important difference between them is that no-duty rules are matters of law decided by the courts, while the defendant's scope of liability is a question of fact for the factfinder. When liability depends on factors specific to an individual case, the appropriate rubric is scope of liability. On the other hand, when liability depends on factors applicable to categories of actors or patterns of conduct, the appropriate rubric is duty. No-duty rules are appropriate only when a court can promulgate relatively clear, categorical, bright-line rules of law applicable to a general class of cases.

When addressing duty, courts sometimes are influenced by the relationship between the actor and the person harmed. Thus, courts hold that landowners are free of negligence liability to some trespassers. See Chapter 9. In a different vein, courts have been cautious about imposing liability on physicians when their care for patients causes harm to third parties. At other times, courts focus on particular claims of negligence, forbidding some but preserving others. Thus, a court might hold that a landlord has no duty to provide security for rented space in a building, but has a duty of reasonable care in providing security for common areas in the building. See Chapter 9. Courts also sometimes hold that an actor has a more limited duty than reasonable care, such as an obligation to avoid engaging in reckless conduct that causes physical harm. A number of the factors relevant to these no-duty and modified-duty determinations are explained in Comments *c-g*.

The principle or policy that is the basis for modifying or eliminating the ordinary duty of care contained in § 7(a) may be reflected in longstanding precedent and need not be restated each time it is invoked. Thus, the modified duty applicable to medical professionals, which employs customary rather than reasonable care, reflects concerns that a lay jury will not understand what constitutes reasonable care in the complex setting of providing medical care and the special expertise possessed by professionals. At the same time, new concerns may arise that have not previously been the basis for modification of the duty of reasonable care and, when those are invoked, they should be identified and explained.

　　＊＊＊

c. Conflicts with social norms about responsibility. In deciding whether to adopt a no-duty rule, courts often rely on general social norms of responsibility. For example, many courts have held that commercial establishments that serve alcoholic beverages have a duty to use reasonable care to avoid injury to others who might be injured by an intoxicated customer, but that social hosts do not have a similar duty to those who might be injured by their guests. Courts often justify this distinction by referring to commonly held social norms about responsibility. The rule stated in this Section does not endorse or reject this particular set of rules. It does support a court's deciding this issue as a categorical matter under the rubric of duty, and a court's articulating general social norms of responsibility as the basis for this determination.

***

j. The proper role for foreseeability. Foreseeable risk is an element in the determination of negligence. In order to determine whether appropriate care was exercised, the factfinder must assess the foreseeable risk at the time of the defendant's alleged negligence. The extent of foreseeable risk depends on the specific facts of the case and cannot be usefully assessed for a category of cases; small changes in the facts may make a dramatic change in how much risk is foreseeable. Thus, for reasons explained in Comment *i*, courts should leave such determinations to juries unless no reasonable person could differ on the matter.

A no-duty ruling represents a determination, a purely legal question, that no liability should be imposed on actors in a category of cases. Such a ruling should be explained and justified based on articulated policies or principles that justify exempting these actors from liability or modifying the ordinary duty of reasonable care. These reasons of policy and principle do not depend on the foreseeability of harm based on the specific facts of a case. They should be articulated directly without obscuring references to foreseeability.

Courts do appropriately rule that the defendant has not breached a duty of reasonable care when reasonable minds cannot differ on that question. See Comment *i*. These determinations are based on the specific facts of the case, are applicable only to that case, and are appropriately cognizant of the role of the jury in factual determinations. A lack of foreseeable risk in a specific case may be a basis for a no-breach determination, but such a ruling is not a no-duty determination. Rather, it is a determination that no reasonable person could find that the defendant has breached the duty of reasonable care.

Despite widespread use of foreseeability in no-duty determinations, this Restatement disapproves that practice and limits no-duty rulings to articulated policy or principle in order to facilitate more transparent explanations of the reasons for a no-duty ruling and to protect the traditional function of the jury as factfinder.

***

o. Conduct creating risk. An actor's conduct creates a risk when the actor's conduct or course of conduct results in greater risk to another than the other would have faced absent the conduct. Conduct may create risk by exposing another to natural hazards, as, for example, when a pilot of an airplane flies the plane into an area of thunderstorms. Conduct may also create risk by exposing another to the improper conduct of third parties. See § 19; see also § 37, Comment *c*.

Reporters' Note

Comment a. The proper role for duty. Dean Prosser reports that the concept of duty did not develop until negligence emerged as a separate theory of liability in the 19th century and then was employed in order to confine the scope of liability. William Prosser, Palsgraf *Revisited*, 52 MICH. L. REV. 1, 12-13 (1953). The concept of duty remains confined to claims based on negligence. An early acknowledgment of the ordinary duty to exercise reasonable care was provided in Heaven v. Pender, (1883) 11 Q.B.D. 503, 509:

> The proposition which these recognized cases suggest, and which is, therefore, to be deduced from them, is that whenever one person is by circumstances placed in such a position with regard to another that everyone of ordinary sense who did think would at once recognize that if he did not use ordinary care and skill in his own conduct with regard to those circumstances he would cause danger of injury to the person or property of the other, a duty arises to use ordinary care and skill to avoid such danger.

Edward White plants the principle expressed in § 7(a) deep in the roots of tort history with his observation that the development of a duty of reasonable care owed to all was critical to the emergence of tort as a discrete subject of law in the 19th century. See G. EDWARD WHITE, TORT LAW IN AMERICA 18 (expanded ed. 2003). White relies on the well-known dictum by Holmes that tort law involves duties "of all the world to all the world." Oliver Wendell Holmes, Jr., *The Theory of Torts*, 7 AM. L. REV. 652, 662 (1873) (article has no author attribution but Holmes is widely credited as the author).

For more modern recognition of the "general rule" of negligence liability— along with the acknowledgment that the "judicial power to modify" this general rule "is reserved for very limited situations"—see Stagl v. Delta Airlines, Inc., 52 F.3d 463, 469 (2d Cir. 1995) (Calabresi, J.) (applying New York law); see also Restatement Second, Torts § 302, Comment *a* ("In general, anyone who does an affirmative act is under a duty to others to exercise the care of a reasonable man to protect them against an unreasonable risk of harm to them arising out of the act."). For affirmation of the general duty requiring persons to exercise ordinary care to prevent injury, with departures permitted in particular cases based largely on public-policy considerations, see Vazquez-Filippetti v. Banco Popular de P.R., 504 F.3d 43, 49 (1st Cir. 2007) (applying Puerto Rico law) ("In most cases the duty is defined by the general rule that one must act as would a prudent and reasonable person under the circumstances."); McMellon v. United States, 338 F.3d 287, 298 (4th Cir. 2003) ("Broadly speaking, the general maritime law imposes a duty to exercise reasonable or ordinary care under the circum- stances . . . ."), rev'd en banc on rehearing and vacated, 387 F.3d 329 (4th Cir. 2004); River Prod. Co. v. Baker Hughes Prod. Tools, Inc., 98 F.3d 857, 859 (5th Cir. 1996) (applying Mississippi law) ("Whenever a person does some act, the law imposes a duty upon that person to take reasonable care in perform- ing that act."); Hamilton v. Cannon, 80 F.3d 1525, 1529 & n.4 (11th Cir.

1996) (federal civil-rights law); Taylor v. Smith, 892 So.2d 887, 893 (Ala. 2004) ("[E]very person owes every other person a duty imposed by law to be careful not to hurt him." (quoting Se. Greyhound Lines v. Callahan, 13 So.2d 660, 663 (Ala. 1943))); Div. of Corr. v. Neakok, 721 P.2d 1121, 1125-1126 (Alaska 1986) ("The general rule of negligence law is that a defendant owes a duty of care 'to all persons who are foreseeably endangered by his conduct, with respect to all risks which make the conduct unreasonably dangerous.'" (quoting Rodriguez v. Bethlehem Steel Corp., 525 P.2d 669, 680 (Cal. 1974))); Zelig v. County of Los Angeles, 45 P.3d 1171, 1182 (Cal. 2002); Vasquez v. Residential Invs., Inc., 12 Cal.Rptr.3d 846, 852 (Ct. App. 2004) ("[E]very [negligence] case is governed by the rule of general application that all persons are required to use ordinary care to prevent others from being injured as the result of their conduct." (quoting Weirum v. RKO Gen., Inc., 539 P.2d 36 (Cal. 1975))); Gazo v. City of Stamford, 765 A.2d 505, 509 (Conn. 2001) (stating the general rule that "every person has a duty to use reasonable care not to cause injury to those whom he reasonably could foresee to be injured by his negligent conduct, whether that conduct consists of acts of commission or omission"); United States v. Stevens, 994 So.2d 1062 (Fla. 2008); Union Park Mem'l Chapel v. Hutt, 670 So.2d 64, 67 (Fla. 1996) ("In every situation where a man undertakes to act, . . . he is under an implied legal obligation or duty to act with reasonable care, to the end that the person or property of others may not be injured." (quoting Banfield v. Addington, 140 So. 893, 896 (Fla. 1932))); Bradley Ctr., Inc. v. Wessner, 296 S.E.2d 693 (Ga. 1982); Turpen v. Granieri, 985 P.2d 669 (Idaho 1999) ("Every person, in the conduct of his business, has a duty to exercise ordinary care to 'prevent unreasonable, foreseeable risks of harm to others.'" (quoting Sharp v. W.H. Moore, Inc., 796 P.2d 506, 509 (Idaho 1990))); Karas v. Strevell, 884 N.E.2d 122 (Ill. 2008) ("In general, every person owes a duty of ordinary care to guard against injuries to others."); Davis v. Witt, 851 So.2d 1119, 1128 (La. 2003) ("Generally, there is an almost universal legal duty on the part of a defendant in a negligence case to conform to the standard of conduct of a reasonable person in like circumstances."); Jupin v. Kask, 849 N.E.2d 829, 835 (Mass. 2006) ("[a]s a general principle of tort law, every actor has a duty to exercise reasonable care to avoid physical harm to others." (quoting Remy v. MacDonald, 801 N.E.2d 260, 262-263 (Mass. 2004))); Bundy v. Holmquist, 669 N.W.2d 627, 632 (Minn. Ct. App. 2003) ("[e]very person in the conduct of his affairs is under a legal duty to act with care and forethought; and, if injury results to another from his failure so to do, he may be held accountable in an action at law." (quoting Roadman v. C.E. Johnson Motor Sales, 297 N.W. 166, 169 (Minn. 1941))); Fisher v. Swift Transp. Co., 181 P.3d 601 (Mont. 2008) ("At the most basic level, we all share the common law duty to exercise the level of care that a reasonable and prudent person would under the same circumstances."); Dieter v. Hand, 333 N.W.2d 772, 774 (Neb. 1983) ("common-law duty of every person to use due care so that he does not act or use that which he controls so as to negligently injure another person"); Remsburg v. Docusearch, Inc., 816 A.2d 1001, 1006 (N.H. 2003); Hart v. Ivey, 420 S.E.2d 174, 178 (N.C. 1992) ("[T]he law imposes upon every person who enters upon an active course of conduct the positive duty to exercise ordinary care to protect others from harm, and calls a violation of that duty negligence." (quoting Council v. Dickerson's, Inc., 64 S.E.2d 551, 553 (N.C. 1951)));

Wofford v. E. State Hosp., 795 P.2d 516, 519 (Okla. 1990) ("As a general rule a 'defendant owes a duty of care to all persons who are foreseeably endangered by his conduct with respect to all risks which make the conduct unreasonably dangerous.'" (quoting Tarasoff v. Regents of Univ. of Cal., 551 P.2d 334, 342 (Cal. 1976))); Fazzolari v. Portland Sch. Dist. No. 1J, 734 P.2d 1326, 1336 (Or. 1987) ("In short, unless the parties invoke a status, a relationship, or a particular standard of conduct that creates, defines, or limits the defendant's duty, the issue of liability for harm actually resulting from defendant's conduct properly depends on whether that conduct unreasonably created a foreseeable risk to a protected interest of the kind of harm that befell the plaintiff."); Zanine v. Gallagher, 497 A.2d 1332, 1334 (Pa. Super. Ct. 1985) (identifying "the general duty imposed on all persons not to place others at risk of harm through their actions"); Satterfield v. Breeding Insulation Co., 266 S.W.3d 347 (Tenn. 2008) ("As a general rule, persons have a duty to others to refrain from engaging in affirmative acts that a reasonable person 'should recognize as involving an unreasonable risk of causing an invasion of an interest of another' or acts 'which involve[ ] an unreasonable risk of harm to another.'"); Rochon v. Saberhagen Holdings, Inc., 140 Wash.App. 1008 (Wash. Ct. App. 2007) ("*In general, anyone who does an affirmative act is under a duty to others to exercise the care of a reasonable man to protect them against an unreasonable risk of harm to them arising out of the act*") (emphasis in original); Miller v. Whitworth, 455 S.E.2d 821 (W. Va. 1995); Smaxwell v. Bayard, 682 N.W.2d 923 (Wis. 2004); Coffey v. City of Milwaukee, 247 N.W.2d 132, 138 (Wis. 1976); Andersen v. Two Dot Ranch, Inc., 49 P.3d 1011, 1014 (Wyo. 2002) ("the common law of negligence creates a general duty 'to exercise the degree of care required of a reasonable person in light of all the circumstances.'" (quoting Hill v. Park County, 856 P.2d 456, 459 (Wyo. 1993))); see also DAN B. DOBBS, THE LAW OF TORTS § 227, at 578 (2000) ("Among strangers . . . the default rule is that everyone owes a duty of reasonable care to others to avoid physical harms.") (footnote omitted); 3 FOWLER V. HARPER, FLEMING JAMES, JR. & OSCAR S. GRAY, HARPER, JAMES AND GRAY ON TORTS § 18.6, at 862 (3d ed. 2007) ("By and large, then, people owe a duty to use care in connection with their affirmative conduct, and they owe it to all who may foreseeably be injured if that conduct is negligently carried out."); Fleming James, Jr., *Scope of Duty in Negligence Cases*, 47 NW. U. L. REV. 778, 800 (1953); Oliver Wendell Holmes, Jr., *The Theory of Torts*, 7 AM. L. REV. 652, 662 (1873) (explaining the emergence of negligence as the default standard of care owed by "all the world to all the world") (Holmes is not identified as the author, but is widely credited as having been the author); Jean Elting Rowe & Theodore Silver, *The Jurisprudence of Action and Inaction in the Law of Tort: Solving the Puzzle of Nonfeasance and Misfeasance from the Fifteenth Through the Twentieth Centuries*, 33 DUQ. L. REV. 807, 850-851 (1995) (unless the plaintiff would have suffered the harm in the absence of defendant's existence, a duty of reasonable care exists). But see Williams v. Cingular Wireless, 809 N.E.2d 473, 476 (Ind. Ct. App. 2004) ("A duty of reasonable care is 'not, of course, owed to the world at large,' but arises out of a relationship between the parties." (quoting Webb v. Jarvis, 575 N.E.2d 992, 997 (Ind. 1991))).

***

Comment c. Conflicts with social norms about responsibility. Among the cases imposing liability on commercial dispensers of liquor are Ontiveros v. Borak, 667 P.2d 200 (Ariz. 1983); Mason v. Roberts, 294 N.E.2d 884 (Ohio 1973); Sorensen v. Jarvis, 350 N.W.2d 108 (Wis. 1984).

Among the cases denying the liability of a social host are Settlemyer v. Wilmington Veterans Post No. 49 Am. Legion Inc., 464 N.E.2d 521 (Ohio 1984); Ferreira v. Strack, 652 A.2d 965 (R.I. 1995); Overbaugh v. McCutcheon, 396 S.E.2d 153 (W. Va. 1990).

***

Reliance on foreseeability in finding that no duty exists can also lead courts astray from the real issue that requires confrontation. Thus, in Chavez v. Desert Eagle Distribution Co., 151 P.3d 77 (N.M. Ct. App. 2006), plaintiff was injured by a drunk driver who had been served at an Indian casino that, celebrating its opening, served alcohol continuously for 24 hours. Plaintiff sued the casino and several wholesalers who sold alcohol to the casino. After concluding that sales by the casino, which had settled with plaintiffs, were consistent with state law, the court struggled for a rationale to support holding that the wholesalers were not liable:

> Given the prevalence of drunk driving in our state, it is reasonable for distributors of alcohol to believe that some of the alcohol they sell may be misused and that such misuse may result in alcohol-related accidents and deaths. However, as the district court aptly noted during the hearing below, such risks are the foreseeable consequences of permitting the use and sale of alcohol in our society. We do not believe, nor do Plaintiffs suggest, that this general recognition that alcohol consumption results in injuries and death is sufficient to meet the foreseeability requirement of duty in the present case; otherwise, the legitimate sale of alcohol would create strict liability for all sellers. Rather, we believe that something more is required.

Id. at 84. Had the court eschewed foreseeability as a rationale and instead recognized that the wholesalers were not negligent as a matter of law for refusing to sell alcohol to a licensed retailer who was going to sell it legally, it could have avoided the awkwardness of acknowledging that the risk was foreseeable but relying on foreseeability to conclude the defendants owed no duty to the plaintiffs.

***

Comment j. The proper role for foreseeability.

***

EXERCISES FOR CHAPTER 6

LEGAL REASONING

Read the Gary Masters situation (on page 463) and the following brief of the Dram Shop Act:

IF   A. any person or his/her agent (seller) sells alcoholic liquor to intoxicated person (purchaser)

B. and purchaser in consequence of intoxication injures person/property of third party

C. and third party gives proper notice . . .

D. and suit is brought within one year of act/omission

THEN seller pays to third party just damages up to $20,000 per person, $50,000 aggregate.

1. Assume that elements C and D would be met; focus on elements A and B. Identify which of the classic journalist questions—who, what, when, where, why, and how—are involved in these two elements. Use deductive reasoning to apply the rule formed by A and B to the Masters situation. If you need additional facts, make appropriate assumptions, and proceed. You may want to use a column chart. State your conclusion.

2. If Masters injured himself, could he recover under the Dram Shop Act? Why, or why not?

3. Perform a policy analysis of the Dram Shop Act. You may want to incorporate the statement in a 1957 Connecticut Supreme Court case that the legislature was concerned about the danger to public health, safety, and morals from liquor sales as well as drunk driving. Determine the various stakeholders, their interests, and their desired rules; then state the policy or policies served by the statute. You may want to use a hub-and-spokes diagram.

4. How would a rule read if it favored only the liquor seller's interest? How would a rule read if it favored only the injured party's interest?

5. Apply the statutory policy or policies that you have developed to the Masters situation. Would your analysis vary depending on whether Masters is a minor or adult?

Read the following case law rules:

IF	A. commercial seller of liquor	IF	A. commercial seller of liquor
	B. *negligently* furnishes liquor to		B. *recklessly* furnishes liquor to
	C. adult		C. intoxicated person
	D. who then injures		D. who then injures
	1. self or		1. self or
	2. other		2. other
THEN	no proximate cause; therefore, no cause of action for negligence against seller.	THEN	potential cause of action for recklessness against seller.

6. Identify which of the six classic journalist questions—who, what, when, where, why, and how—each element involves. Apply each rule to the Masters situation. If you need additional facts, make appropriate assumptions, and proceed. You may want to use a column chart. State your conclusion.

Review *Moore v. Bunk* (on page 465) and the four case briefs (on page 468).

7. Select a case that you would use for reasoning by example if Masters is thirty-six years old, and explain why you chose that case. Compare that case to the Masters situation. If you need additional facts, make all appropriate assumptions, and proceed. You may want to use a checkerboard chart. Indicate whether the Masters situation is analogous to or distinguishable from the case that you chose.

8. Now select a case that you would use for reasoning by example if Masters is sixteen years old, and explain why you chose that case. Compare that case to the Masters situation. If you need additional facts, make appropriate assumptions, and proceed. You may want to use a checkerboard chart. Indicate whether the Masters situation is analogous to or distinguishable from the case that you chose.

EXERCISES FOR CHAPTER 7

WRITING LEGAL ANALYSIS

Read the Gary Masters situation (on page 463), the Dram Shop Act and its statutory interpretation points (at page 470), and the brief of *Kowal v. Hofher* (on page 469).

1. Read the following paragraph and label the sentences I, R, A, and C. (Citations are omitted.)

____ The second statutory element is that the individual was intoxicated when he was served by the defendant commercial seller.

____ Witnesses will testify that he had trouble walking and was using foul language when he entered Joe's and for a while thereafter.

____ This was no doubt because Mr. Masters had consumed three shots of tequila and six beers at the first bar before being served at Joe's.

____ This case is thus reminiscent of a 1990 Connecticut Court of Appeals case where the bar was held liable under the statute for serving beer to an obnoxious individual.

____ Therefore, this element is met.

____ Furthermore, the facts meet the definition of a 1985 Connecticut Supreme Court decision indicating that someone is intoxicated when an observer perceives that the drinker's walk or conversation is abnormal, judgment is disturbed, and will power is temporarily suspended.

____ Mr. Masters's ability to play pool well while at Joe's is not significant in light of the other aspects of his behavior.

2. Does the paragraph follow IRAC well? How so, or how not? How might you improve the paragraph?

3. Write an IRAC paragraph on the statutory requirement that the second bar "sell" Masters "alcoholic liquor." You need not include proper citations but should provide simple references to the law. Label your sentences I, R, A, or C.

4 Assume that Masters is an adult. Write an IRAC on the *Kowal* rule, which should include an argument and counter-argument. You need not include proper citations but should provide simple references to the law. Label your sentences I, R, A, or C.

EXERCISES FOR CHAPTER 8

THE ANALYTICAL OFFICE MEMO

Read the Gary Masters situation (on page 463), the Dram Shop Act brief and the two case law rules printed below, and the brief of *Ely v. Murphy* (on page 468). Unless otherwise stated, assume that you do not know the age of Gary Masters. Your client is the second bar.

Case Law Rules

IF	A. commercial seller of liquor	IF	A. commercial seller of liquor
	B. *negligently* furnishes liquor to		B. *recklessly* furnishes liquor to
	C. adult		C. intoxicated person
	D. who then injures		D. who then injures
	1. self or		1. self or
	2. other		2. other
THEN	no proximate cause; therefore, no cause of action for negligence against seller.	THEN	potential cause of action for recklessness against seller.

Dram Shop Act Brief

IF   A. any person or his/her agent (seller) sells alcoholic liquor to intoxicated person (purchaser)

B. and purchaser in consequence of intoxication injures person/property of third party

C. and third party gives proper notice . . .

D. and suit is brought within one year of act/omission

THEN   seller pays to third party just damages up to $20,000 per person, $50,000 aggregate.

    1. Read the following sample issues and short answers. Critique each pair according to the criteria developed in Chapter 8.

SAMPLE #1

ISSUE: Is our client liable under the Connecticut Dram Shop Act to the child killed by Gary Masters?

SHORT ANSWER: Our client clearly is liable under the Dram Shop Act.

SAMPLE #2

ISSUE: Under the Connecticut Dram Shop Act, is a bar liable to a child killed when a drunk driver drives across oncoming traffic and into the car carrying the child after the driver consumed three shots of tequila and six beers at the bar and, prior to that, also consumed three shots of tequila and six beers at a different bar?

SHORT ANSWER: The bar is most likely liable under these facts because the driver was intoxicated.

SAMPLE #3

ISSUE: When is a bar liable under the Connecticut Dram Shop Act to a third party injured by a drunk driver?

SHORT ANSWER: A bar is liable under the Dram Shop Act when the bar serves liquor to an intoxicated person who, as a consequence of intoxication, injures another.

2. Assume that Masters is thirty-six years old. Write your own issue(s) and short answer(s) for the two case law rules.

3. Prepare an outline, a box chart, or a set of the first sentences of each paragraph of the discussion component of a memo. Explain how you determined your sequence of topics.

4. Do any topics appear twice? How would you handle any such topics?

5. Does the analysis of this situation involve any branchpoints? If so, state the type of branchpoints: ambiguous rules, unsettled rules, unknown or disputed facts, or interlocking rules.

6. Assume that Masters is sixteen years old. Write a roadmap paragraph for your discussion.

7. Frame a draft closing for an office memo. First, write a sentence or two summarizing your answers to the legal issues. Then sketch out your recommendations as to options in full sentences or a decision tree.

8. In advising your client, the bar, would you factor in any non-legal considerations? Explain.

To work on drafting a fact statement, read the Jody Harrison situation (on page 463). Your client is Jody Harrison, who is considering a suit against Hillside Country Club.

9. Construct a factual matrix chart and a timeline to weave the facts together.

10. Did you discern any discrepancies in these facts? Identify two, and explain how you would deal with each.

11. In light of the Dram Shop Act and the two case law rules, list the legally relevant, background, and residual facts from each source. Which facts would you include or exclude from your fact statement? Why?

12. Write an introductory paragraph to set the stage for the rest of the fact statement.

13. What organization would you use for the remaining facts? List your main topics, in the order that you would present them.

14. Critique the following sentence: "After drinking heavily and annoying the bartender, Lewis and Harrison left Hillside." Revise the sentence so that it is more appropriately worded for an office memo.

15. Are there additional facts you would like to know? If so, list up to three questions you have.

EXERCISES FOR CHAPTER 9

THE ADVICE LETTER

Read the Gary Masters situation (on page 463) and the Dram Shop Act along with the statutory interpretation points (on page 470).

1. Read the following sample introduction; then critique it according to the principles set forth in Chapter 9.

Dear Client:

This letter presents our analysis of the facts you recounted last Friday in light of the pertinent statute. That statute provides for liability on the part of any person ("seller") who sells alcoholic liquor to an intoxicated person ("purchaser") where that purchaser then injures a third party ("victim"), the victim's injury/death being a consequence of the purchaser's intoxication. On the assumption that the procedural requirements of the statute are met, such liability most probably follows in your situation. The victim's recovery would be capped at $20,000.

This letter is current as of the date of this writing and is based on the following facts as you have recounted them to this office.

2. Assume that your client is the second bar, a regular client. Rewrite the introduction presented above.

3. Now assume that your client, a first-time client, is the father of the killed child. Rewrite the introduction presented above.

4. Assume that the bar is your client. Write two sentences covering the facts pertinent to Masters's intoxication for the facts summary. Would these sentences differ at all if the father were your client? Explain.

5. Assume again that the bar is your client. Write a paragraph for the explanation component on the issue of whether Masters was "intoxicated" under the Connecticut Dram Shop Act. Would this paragraph differ at all if the father were your client? Explain.

6. Assume that you have concluded that your client, the bar, probably would be ordered to pay $20,000 under the Dram Shop Act if the procedural requirements were met by the father. Assume further that the father sent a notice to the bar, but it was three days late. Write your advice section, beginning with a summary of your legal analysis.

7. Which model of lawyering—hired gun, godfather, guru, or friend—would you employ if you represented the bar? Which model would you use if you represented the father? Are there more facts you would want to know before making this choice in either situation? Explain.

EXERCISES FOR CHAPTER 10

INTERVIEWING THE CLIENT

Read the Gary Masters situation (on page 463), as well as the Dram Shop Act brief and the two case law rules printed below.

Your client is the second bar, which has received a letter from an attorney for the father of the child. The letter recounts the basic facts stated in the Gary Masters situation and asks for "significant damages and non-monetary relief."

Case Law Rules

IF	A. commercial seller of liquor		IF	A. commercial seller of liquor	
	B. *negligently* furnishes liquor to			B. *recklessly* furnishes liquor to	
	C. adult			C. intoxicated person	
	D. who then injures			D. who then injures	
		1. self or			1. self or
		2. other			2. other
THEN	no proximate cause; therefore, no cause of action for negligence against seller.		THEN	potential cause of action for recklessness against seller.	

Dram Shop Act Brief

IF   A. any person or his/her agent (seller) sells alcoholic liquor to intoxicated person (purchaser)

          B. and purchaser in consequence of intoxication injures person/ property of third party

          C. and third party gives proper notice . . .

          D. and suit is brought within one year of act/omission

THEN seller pays to third party just damages up to $20,000 per person, $50,000 aggregate.

1. Assume that you have not worked with this potential client before, so you are meeting with the bar's owner for the first time. Write out three statements that you would make to encourage him to speak honestly and openly with you.

2. Write two questions that you could use to begin the narration cycle.

3. List at least four main topics relating to the bar's factual context to explore during the exposition cycle.

4. One topic to explore is the bar's standard practices around ceasing to serve patrons who seem to be intoxicated. Write five probing questions on that topic.

5. Another topic to explore is the serving of Masters. Write five probing questions on that topic.

6. Write two questions that you should *not* ask during the exposition cycle: one that is leading and one that uses loaded language.

7. Write out the last question that you would ask (or request that you would make) as you conclude the discussion of the bar's factual context.

8. Write out four questions that you would use to prompt the bar owner to discuss his interests and goals, including an open-ended question and three probing questions.

9. A potential client in this situation might want to shade the facts. To guard against the possibility that the bar owner might not be straightforward with you at some point, what are some strategies that you might employ?

10. If you were to take on the representation of the bar, what would be a probable attorney fee structure?

EXERCISES FOR CHAPTER 11

COUNSELING THE CLIENT

Read the Jody Harrison situation (on page 463), as well as the Dram Shop Act brief and the two case law rules printed below. However, disregard the facts stated in the bartender's report, which would not be known at this point.

Your client is Jody Harrison, who has come to you about bringing a claim against Hillside Country Club. You will be meeting with both Jody and Andrew Harrison. He is a chef with technical training. She was an accountant earning about $80,000 annually, but she has been out of work due to her diminished capacity since the crash, and her return to work is uncertain.

Case Law Rules

IF	A. commercial seller of liquor
	B. *negligently* furnishes liquor to
	C. adult
	D. who then injures
	  1. self or
	  2. other
		IF	A. commercial seller of liquor
			B. *recklessly* furnishes liquor to
			C. intoxicated person
			D. who then injures
			  1. self or
			  2. other

THEN	no proximate cause; therefore, no cause of action for negligence against seller.	THEN	potential cause of action for recklessness against seller.

Dram Shop Act Brief

IF   A. any person or his/her agent (seller) sells alcoholic liquor to intoxicated person (purchaser)
           B. and purchaser in consequence of intoxication injures person/property of third party
           C. and third party gives proper notice . . .
           D. and suit is brought within one year of act/omission
THEN seller pays to third party just damages
          up to $20,000 per person, $50,000 aggregate.

1. What would you be seeking to accomplish in the preparation stage of the counseling session?

2. Write out how you would explain the various legal standards for potentially holding the club liable to the Harrisons.[4]

---

4. Andrew Harrison may have a separate claim as Jody's spouse, for loss of consortium.

3. Write out how you would frame your legal conclusion as to the club's liability under each standard.

4. Identify specific factors in the Harrisons' situation that you would consider favorable in valuing their claims. Identify factors that you would consider unfavorable in valuing their claims. Do you consider the common law or the Dram Shop Act to be the better basis for recovery?

5. What would be the most likely type of attorney fees in this case?

6. Describe four different methods for resolving the dispute with the club for the Harrisons to consider, which may be inconsistent with each other or a series of steps. For each method, write out a sentence explaining what it entails, and list two advantages and two disadvantages for each one.

7. Assume that you and the Harrisons decide to pursue the claim to some extent. Write out at least three points that you would discuss in determining the remedies that you would seek.

8. Write out at least three process points that you would explore with the Harrisons in order to discern their preferred method of resolving the claim.

9. Imagine that, as the counseling session approaches the point of decision, the Harrisons seem frustrated and ask you to decide what they should do, based on your experience. How would you respond?

EXERCISES FOR CHAPTER 12

THE DEMAND LETTER

Read the Gary Masters situation (on page 463) and the briefs of *Ely v. Murphy* (on page 468) and *Kowal v. Hofher* (on page 469). Assume that you represent the father of the killed child.

1. Critique the following opening paragraph according to the principles set forth in Chapter 12:

Dear Bar Owner:

I am writing to alert you to the potential claim for a substantial remedy by the next of kin of Joseph Fairchild, who tragically died at the hands of Gary Masters, to whom your bar recklessly served alcohol well past the point of intoxication. You may find it wise to hire an attorney to represent you in this manner.

2. Which facts would you lead with in your statement of your client's situation? How would you organize the rest of the fact statement?

3. Assume that Masters is sixteen years old. Write your statement of the rule of *Ely v. Murphy* as you would frame it in your statement of your client's legal position.

4. Assume that Masters is thirty-six years old. Write your statement of the rule of *Kowal v. Hofher* as you would frame it in your statement of your client's legal position.

5. Assume that the highest recent verdict for a killed child of the same age in Connecticut, in a case involving a hunting accident, is $800,000. What figure would you state for a monetary recovery? (Assume that your client supports the approach that you favor.)

6. What non-monetary remedy or remedies might you seek? (Assume that your client supports the approach that you favor.)

7. How might you frame your demands to make them appealing to the bar?

EXERCISES FOR CHAPTER 13

CONTRACTS

Read the Gary Masters situation (on page 463).

The lawyers for the second bar (your client) and the father of the killed child are on the verge of settling the case. One term calls for the bar "to contribute significant support to the activities of a local organization that works to reduce drunk driving, for ten years following the execution of this settlement agreement, as provided in a separate contract incorporated by reference."

You are to draft this contract. The parties did not intend that the support would necessarily be monetary. The father may provide suggestions if he so desires, but he is not required to. You have identified a local branch of Mothers Against Drunk Driving (MADD); visit the MADD website to learn about that organization's activities.

1. Draft definitions of the bar, which is legally known as the Good Apple Bar and Grill LLC, and the organization to receive the support. Identify the label that you would use for each of these entities in the rest of the contract, and explain why you chose those labels.

2. Explain how your definitions reflect foresight.

3. Draft the term setting out the bar's duty under the contract. Depending on your approach, you may need to also draft a definition to connect to this term.

4. Explain how the term that you drafted for question 3 uses the concept of promise. Did you include any conditions? Explain.

5. Explain how the term that you drafted for question 3 is both realistic and practical.

6. Draft a term providing for a privilege on the part of the father.

7. Draft the term stating the duration of the contract. Assume that the contract begins on the date that you are writing your answer.

8. Draft a term providing for a process to resolve any disputes that may arise under the contract.[5]

---

5. You may want to consult the description of dispute resolution processes given in Box 11.3.

EXERCISES FOR CHAPTER 14

PLEADINGS

Read the Gary Masters situation (on page 463), the Dram Shop Act along with the statutory interpretation points (on page 470), the brief of the *Kowal v. Hofher* case (on page 469), and the excerpted sample complaint on the following pages (for general reference).

Assume first that you are representing Joseph Fairchild, the father of the killed child, against the second bar, the Good Apple Bar and Grill LLC, owned by Jason Appleton. Assume that Gary Masters is thirty-six years old. The events occurred on March 5 of the current year. For locations, use street, city, and county names pertinent to your law school.

1. Create a caption for your complaint.

2. Write a set of factual allegations.

3. In what ways did you aim to write persuasively?

4. Write the allegations supporting a count under the Connecticut Dram Shop Act.

5. Write the allegations supporting a count under *Kowal v. Hofher*.

6. Write your request for relief and signature block.

Assume now that you are representing the defendant, Good Apple Bar and Grill, LLC.

7. Review the complaint that you wrote from the perspective of the defendant. Which allegations would you probably admit? Which would you probably deny? As to which would you indicate that you lack sufficient information or belief?

8. Would you likely assert any affirmative defenses? Is there information you do not have that would help you better answer this question?

9. Would you bring any counterclaims against Joseph Fairchild?

16 Conn. Prac., Elements of an Action §5:8

Connecticut Practice Series TM
Elements of an Action
October 2016 Update

Thomas B. Merritt

Chapter 5. Dram Shop Liability
II. Forms

§ 5:8. Sample trial court documents—Sample complaint

2011 WL 6937020 (Conn.Super.) (Trial Pleading)
Superior Court of Connecticut,
J. D. of Waterbury.

New Haven County

Varese LARUE,

v.

BARLEYCORN, LLC dba the Barleycorn Irish Café and Edward D. Bergin.

No. UWY-CV-09-5014639-S.

June 23, 2011.

Amended Complaint

***

SECOND COUNT **Dram Shop claim vs. Barleycorn, LLC dba The Barleycorn Irish Café and its permittee Edward D. Bergin**

1. On the evening of October 10, 2008 to the early morning of October 11, 2008, the plaintiff, Varese LaRue, was an invitee and lawfully at the Barleycorn Irish Café (hereinafter referred to as "Barleycorn") that is located at 92 Store Avenue in Waterbury, Connecticut.

2. Barleycorn is owned and operated by the defendant Barleycorn, LLC and Edward D. Bergin.

3. While at Barleycorn, there was a group of male patrons who were intoxicated, loud and threatening to the plaintiff and other patrons.

4. An initial altercation occurred inside the Barleycorn.

5. Following the initial altercation, the defendants, Barleycorn and Edward D. Bergin and their agents, servants or employees failed to provide medical or other services to Mr. LaRue and instead forced Mr. LaRue and the assailants outside in the parking lot without protection where the assailants continued to attack Mr. LaRue.

6. The plaintiff was stabbed multiple times in the chest and body.

7. As a result of the service of alcohol in violation of Connecticut General Statutes § 30-102a and the violent altercation inside Barleycorn and on the sidewalk in front of the Barleycorn and in the parking lot of Barleycorn, the plaintiff, Varese LaRue, sustained painful injuries, some or all of which are, or may be permanent in nature, which have caused and will continue to cause pain and suffering as follows:

a. Severe shock to his nervous system;
b. Mental and physical pain and suffering;
c. A chest injury;
d. A collapsed lung;
e. Lacerated muscles around his heart and chest;
f. Scarring;
g. Breathing difficulties;
h. Multiple stab wounds.

8. As a further result of said injuries and the effects thereof, the plaintiff, Varese LaRue, was forced to expend considerable sums for medical service, hospital care, x-rays, surgery, medicine and medical care, and the plaintiff will be obliged to expend further sums for such items in the future.

9. As a further result of said injuries and the effects thereof, the plaintiff, Varese LaRue's ability to enjoy life's activities has been severely impaired.

10. On that date and prior to the injury, the assailants were sold alcoholic liquor while they were intoxicated and while they were a customer or a patron at the defendant, Barleycorn.

11. On the aforesaid date the defendant, Edward D. Bergin (hereinafter referred to as "permittee"), was the permittee of the liquor outlet, and the assailants, while intoxicated, were sold and/or served alcoholic liquor by the defendant permittee and/or his agents, servants, and/or employees.

12. The injuries, consequential loss and expense sustained by the plaintiff, Varese LaRue, were in consequence of the intoxication of the assailants, who were sold and/or served alcoholic liquor by the defendant permittee and/or his agents, servants, and/or employees.

13. The plaintiff, Varese LaRue's, injuries and losses were in consequence of the assailants, as herein before set forth and the aforesaid defendants' sale and/or service of alcoholic beverages to the assailants, in violation of Connecticut General Statutes § 30-102. Accordingly, the plaintiff, Varese LaRue, seeks to recover damages for such injuries and losses pursuant to Connecticut General Statutes § 30-102.

14. Written notice as required was given to the defendant, Barleycorn's permittee within the time allowed by law of the occurrence of the plaintiff, Varese LaRue's injuries and losses. A copy of such notice is annexed hereto and marked Exhibit A.

THIRD COUNT—Recklessness

1. On the evening of October 10, 2008 to the early morning of October 11, 2008, the plaintiff, Varese LaRue, was an invitee and lawfully at the Barleycorn Irish Café (hereinafter referred to as "Barleycorn") that is located at 92 Store Avenue in Waterbury, Connecticut.

2. Barleycorn is owned and operated by the defendant Barleycorn, LLC and Edward D. Bergin.

3. While at Barleycorn, there was a group of male patrons who were intoxicated, loud and threatening to the plaintiff and other patrons.

4. An initial altercation occurred inside the Barleycorn.

5. Following the initial altercation, the defendants, Barleycorn and Edward D. Bergin and their agents, servants or employees failed to provide medical or other services to Mr. LaRue and instead forced Mr. LaRue and the assailants outside in the parking lot without protection where the assailants continued to attack Mr. LaRue.

6. The plaintiff was stabbed multiple times in the chest and body.

7. As a result of this violent altercation inside Barleycorn and in the parking lot of Barleycorn, the plaintiff, Varese LaRue, sustained painful injuries, some or all of which are, or may be permanent in nature, which have caused and will continue to cause pain and suffering as follows:

a. Severe shock to his nervous system;
b. Mental and physical pain and suffering;
c. A chest injury;
d. A collapsed lung;
e. Lacerated muscles around his heart and chest;
f. Scarring;
g. Breathing difficulties;
h. Multiple stab wounds.

8. As a further result of said injuries and the effects thereof, the plaintiff, Varese LaRue, was forced to expend considerable sums for medical service, hospital care, x-rays, surgery, medicine and medical care, and the plaintiff will be obliged to expend further sums for such items in the future.

9. As a further result of said injuries and the effects thereof, the plaintiff, Varese LaRue's ability to enjoy life's activities has been severely impaired.

10. On that date and prior to the injury, the assailants were sold alcoholic liquor while they were intoxicated and while they were a customer or a patron at the defendant, Barleycorn.

11. On that date and prior to the injury, the defendant, Edward Bergin, was responsible for and in charge of security at the Barleycorn on that date and the defendant was drinking alcohol and was under the influence of alcohol.

12. On the aforesaid date the defendant, Edward D. Bergin (hereinafter referred to as "permittee"), was the permittee of the liquor outlet, and the assailants, while obviously intoxicated, were sold and/or served alcoholic liquor by the defendant permittee and/or his agents, servants, and/or employees.

13. The injuries, consequential loss and expense sustained by the plaintiff, Varese LaRue, were in consequence of the assailants, while obviously intoxicated, being sold and/or served alcoholic liquor by the defendant permittee and/or his agents, servants, and/or employees and in consequence of Edward Bergin's intoxication while in charge of security.

14. The plaintiff, Varese LaRue's, injuries and losses were a direct result of the defendants, Barleycorn and Edward D. Bergin's reckless service of alcohol to the assailants who were obviously intoxicated and demonstrated signs of violent behavior and as a result of Edward Bergin's consumption of alcohol, his intoxication and his reckless disregard for his duties as head of security at the Barleycorn on October 10, 2008 and October 11, 2008.

WHEREFORE, the plaintiff claims:

1. Money damages;
2. Court costs;
3. Punitive damages and/or treble damages and/or attorney's fees as to Count 3;
4. Damages pursuant to Connecticut General Statutes § 30-102 et seq.;
5. Such other relief as may be fair and equitable.

Dated at Waterbury, Connecticut, this 23rd day of June, 201 1.

«signature»

David J. Scully

Commissioner of the Superior Court

EXERCISES FOR CHAPTER 15

NEGOTIATING WITH OPPOSING COUNSEL

Read the Gary Masters situation (on page 463), as well as the Dram Shop Act brief and the two case law rules printed below.

The attorney for Joseph Fairchild, the father of the killed child, and the attorney for Jason Appleton, who owns the Good Apple Bar and Grill, have investigated the facts and agree about the statement on page #. Furthermore, the police report shows that Gary Masters's blood alcohol level was well above the legal limit and that his intoxication caused the crash leading to the death of Joseph's son. Masters was twenty at the time of the crash.

The boy, Jacob, was ten at the time of the crash. Joseph (a high school teacher and single father) has suffered significant emotional distress and loss of income as a result of his son's death, although he was not in the car at the time of the crash.

Jason Appleton is a small business owner with three bars, all operating under the same name but in different towns. This is the only such situation he has been involved in during his fifteen years in the business.

In a recent case, a jury awarded parents $800,000 based on reckless conduct leading to the death of a child (in a case involving a hunting accident).

You may select either party to represent as you work these exercises, or work them once for each party.

Case Law Rules

IF	A. commercial seller of liquor	IF	A. commercial seller of liquor	
	B. *negligently* furnishes liquor to		B. *recklessly* furnishes liquor to	
	C. adult		C. intoxicated person	
	D. who then injures		D. who then injures	
	1. self or		1. self or	
	2. other		2. other	
THEN	no proximate cause; therefore, no cause of action for negligence against seller.	THEN	potential cause of action for recklessness against seller.	

Dram Shop Act Brief

IF   A. any person or his/her agent (seller) sells alcoholic liquor to intoxicated person (purchaser)

          B. and purchaser in consequence of intoxication injures person/property of third party

          C. and third party gives proper notice . . .

          D. and suit is brought within one year of act/omission

THEN   seller pays to third party just damages up to $20,000 per person, $50,000 aggregate.

1. What are the most important legally relevant facts for your client?

2. Write two or three sentences that concisely state your client's legal position.

3. What might you infer about your client's broader context that could influence the parties' relative power in the negotiation? Or what would you want to know more about, to better answer this question?

4. What would you infer to be your client's interests and possible goals for the negotiation? Or what you would want to know more about, to better answer this question?

5. Develop a list of five terms to be discussed during the negotiations. Keep in mind that a claimant may seek not only money, but also non-monetary remedies; that a settlement often covers when and how any monetary recovery will be paid out; and that a settlement also often covers topics such as whether the respondent admits guilt and whether the terms are to be kept confidential.

6. For each of your five terms, develop your best alternative to a negotiated agreement (BATNA), aspirational positions, and two probable settlement positions. Use either reasonable assumptions about the authority that your client has provided or information that your professor has provided.

7. From this preparation, develop a theory of your negotiation.

8. Identify three factual topics that you would choose to reveal during the negotiation.

9. Identify three factual topics about which you would question opposing counsel during the negotiation.

10. Write your opening proposal on the terms that you have identified for negotiation.

11. Assume that you want to take a problem-solving approach to the negotiation. What mutual interests could you emphasize here?

12. If you have a key proposal for a non-monetary topic that you sense may be unappealing, how can you make it palatable?

13. More likely than not, you will need to make concessions on the monetary topic. How can you make any such concessions in the strongest way?

14. If, after extended discussions, you sensed that there is no positive bargaining zone on the monetary topic, what would you do?

15. Imagine that your opposing counsel is becoming angry, what would you do?

EXERCISES FOR CHAPTERS 16 AND 17

LEGAL ADVOCACY AND
THE MOTION PRACTICE MEMORANDUM

Note: This set of exercises draws on Chapters 16 and 17, asking you to use the methods discussed in Chapter 16 in the motion practice setting.

Read the Jody Harrison situation (on page 463) and all case law materials (on page 465).

Ms. Harrison has sued Hillside Country Club in three counts: two under Connecticut common law, one for negligence and a second for recklessness, and a third count under the Connecticut Dram Shop Act. The liquor seller is moving for summary judgment on the common law counts (not the Dram Shop count). Assume that Connecticut law requires the movant to establish (1) that there is no genuine issue of material fact and (2) that the movant is entitled to judgment as a matter of law.

1. Assume that the Connecticut trial courts operate on a block system. As counsel for Defendant Hillside, would you bring this motion? Why or why not? As counsel for Plaintiff Harrison, would you defend against the motion? Why, or why not?

2. If you did not have to follow a particular format, and you represented Hillside, which of the following components would you present first: introduction, summary, or issues? Explain your choice. What if you represented Ms. Harrison?

3. Read the following sample issues. Critique each sample according to the criteria developed in Chapter 17.

SAMPLE #1

A. Are there genuine issues of material fact precluding summary judgment on the common law claims?
B. Is Defendant entitled to judgment as a matter of law on the common law claims?

SAMPLE #2

Is a commercial seller of alcoholic beverages liable under the common law where an adult purchased and consumed beverages at the seller's establishment and then injured the Plaintiff by driving recklessly?

SAMPLE #3

Is a country club entitled to summary judgment under the common law where the Plaintiff was injured by the reckless driving of a patron, that patron drank several beers at the club over the course of several hours and ate food as well, the Plaintiff also ate and drank at the club, the Plaintiff but not the patron appeared drunk to the club's bartenders, and the patron's blood alcohol level was .10?

SAMPLE #4

Where a club served an adult golfer and friend four drinks over two hours and also served the golfer food, the golfer did not become loud or obnoxious (although her friend did), the golfer and her friend left, the golfer then drove recklessly and crashed, and the friend was injured:

   A. are there genuine issues of material fact, and
   B. is the club entitled to judgment as a matter of law where the law permits recovery in cases where a commercial seller of liquor acts recklessly but not negligently?

4. Write an introduction or summary on behalf of Hillside or Harrison.

5. (a) If you represented Hillside, which facts would you include in your fact statement? List them by number. Are any of them residual facts that you would not have included in an office memorandum? Explain.

   (b) Draft the opening paragraph of your fact statement.
   (c) Which organization would you use for the body of your fact statement: topical, chronological, perceptual, or a combination? Why?
   (d) Draft the closing paragraph of your fact statement; assume that you have not included a procedure component.

6. (a) If you represented Harrison, would you write a fact statement? If so, which facts would you emphasize?

   (b) Draft the opening paragraph of your fact statement.

7. Identify and explain two conflicts in the record as to important facts. Explain how you would handle the fact if you represented Hillside and again if you represented Harrison.

8. (a) Review the procedural rule on summary judgment. What type of rule is it: conjunctive, disjunctive, aggregate, or balancing?

   (b) Review the substantive rule on liability of liquor sellers, as developed in the common law. What type of rule is it: conjunctive, disjunctive, aggregate, or balancing?
   (c) As Hillside's counsel, what must or may you do to succeed in your motion?
   (d) As Harrison's counsel, what must or may you do to defend successfully against the motion?

9. (a) If you represented Hillside, would any of your potential arguments be alternatives to each other? If so, explain.

(b) If you represented Harrison, would any of your potential arguments be alternatives to each other? If so, explain.

10. List in a T-chart the main assertions that Hillside is likely to make and the probable responses of Harrison. Highlight the points of clash.

11. (a) If you represented Hillside, would you consider your case to be strong on facts, law, or policy (or some combination)? What is its overall weakness? Explain.

(b) Identify a case that you would emphasize. Why did you choose that case, and how would you emphasize it?

(c) Is there any unfavorable case that you are ethically bound to raise even if opposing counsel does not? Explain. How would you handle that case?

(d) Would you seek to emphasize or de-emphasize the procedural rule? Explain.

(e) Which facts would you emphasize? Why? How would you emphasize those facts?

(f) Which facts would you de-emphasize? Why? How would you de-emphasize those facts?

(g) Is there any policy that you would seek to emphasize? Explain.

(h) Is there any policy that you would seek to de-emphasize? Explain.

(i) Write out your theory of the case, depict it in a pie chart, or do both.

13. (a) If you represented Harrison, would you consider your case to be strong on facts, law, or policy (or some combination)? What is its overall weakness? Explain.

(b) Identify a case that you would emphasize. Why did you choose that case, and how would you emphasize it?

(c) Is there any unfavorable case that you are ethically bound to raise even if opposing counsel does not? Explain. How would you handle that case?

(d) Would you seek to emphasize or de-emphasize the procedural rule? Explain.

(e) Which facts would you emphasize? Why? How would you emphasize those facts?

(f) Which facts would you de-emphasize? Why? How would you de-emphasize those facts?

(g) Is there any policy that you would seek to emphasize? Explain.

(h) Is there any policy that you would seek to de-emphasize? Explain.

(i) Write out your theory of the case, depict it in a pie chart, or do both.

14. Read the following sample point headings. Critique each sample according to the criteria developed in Chapter 17.

SAMPLE #1

The club is not liable because it did not act recklessly when it served a patron several drinks over a period of two hours and the patron showed no signs of intoxication.

SAMPLE #2

A. There is no genuine issue of material fact because the testimony of all witnesses on the relevant facts is in accord.
B. The club is entitled to judgment as a matter of law, where the law affords recovery only when a liquor seller acts recklessly, because the club acted at most negligently in serving several drinks during an afternoon to a patron who was not intoxicated in the eyes of anyone present.

SAMPLE #3

Summary judgment is not appropriate where there is a genuine issue of material fact and the moving party is not entitled to judgment as a matter of law.

A. There are fact issues because the testimony of some parties conflict.
B. Defendant is not entitled to judgment as a matter of law because the law does afford a cause of action for recklessness.

SAMPLE #4

The club is liable because it did act recklessly when it served an apparently drunk patron several drinks over two hours.

A. Entitlement to judgment as a matter of law
B. Genuine issues of material fact

15. Write improved point headings on behalf of Hillside or Harrison. If you wrote on behalf of Hillside for question 4, write on behalf of Harrison for this question, or vice versa.

EXERCISES FOR CHAPTERS 16 AND 18

LEGAL ADVOCACY AND THE APPELLATE BRIEF

Note: This set of exercises draws on Chapters 16 and 18, asking you to use the methods discussed in Chapter 16 in the appellate setting.

Read the Gary Masters situation (on page 463) and the entire law library (on page 464).

Joseph Fairchild sued the second bar, the Good Apple Bar and Grill, LLC, on two common law counts. The district court directed a verdict for the defendant on the negligence count, concluding that there was no cause of action for selling alcohol to an adult (Masters was an adult) who thereafter injures another by reason of his intoxication. The issue of recklessness was submitted to the jury, which found for the defendant. The district denied the motion to set aside the verdicts and thus rendered judgment for the defendants.

Assume that the Connecticut Appellate Court affirmed, Fairchild has appealed to the Connecticut Supreme Court, and that court has granted review. Also assume that the following procedural law and standards of review apply:

> In reviewing a trial court decision to direct a verdict for the defendant, the appeals court considers the evidence in the light most favorable to the plaintiff and then determines whether the jury reasonably and legally could have reached a conclusion other than in the defendant's favor.

> A jury verdict is entitled to acceptance unless the reviewing court can say as a matter of law that the jury's conclusions were such that reasoning minds could not reasonably have reached them.

> The trial court has broad discretion in deciding a motion to set aside the verdict on the grounds it is contrary to law and the evidence; that decision will not be disturbed in the absence of clear abuse.

1. Assume that the Connecticut Supreme Court uses the factors stated in Chapter 18 in deciding whether to grant discretionary review. Why might it grant review in this case?

2. If the Plaintiff were to appeal his losses on both counts, would the appeal fall within the scope of appellate review? Explain your answer by applying the following rules:

(a) Final judgment rule
(b) Rule prohibiting new facts or theories on appeal
(c) Reversible error rule

3. What legal points must the plaintiff show to win on appeal as to each claim (negligence and recklessness)? Your statement should reflect the intersection

between the substantive law, the nature of the disposition in the district court, and the standard of review on each of the two claims. Which issue (if either) is the plaintiff more likely to win? Why?

For the remaining questions, assume that you represent either Joseph Fairchild, the appellant, or the Good Apple Bar and Grill, the respondent. (Or answer these questions twice, once for each side.)

4. Develop a theory of your case, linking its legal, policy, and factual dimensions. Remember that the legal dimension is both substantive and procedural. Draw a pie chart, write out your theory, or do both.

5. Here are two neutral, broad ways of phrasing the issues that could be raised on appeal:

> Does a cause of action in negligence exist against a commercial vendor who sells intoxicating liquor to an adult who thereafter, due to his intoxication, injures another?

> On the facts of this case, could the jury find that the commercial vendor did not act recklessly?

Rephrase the two issues so as to subtly suggest an answer favoring your client. You may introduce sub-issues.

6. Write a paragraph setting forth the procedural history of the case from your client's perspective.

7. (a) The facts stated in the Gary Masters situation are presented as a court would phrase them. Would you exclude any of the stated facts in your statement of the case? Explain.

   (b) On the assumption that the record contained the information stated below, would you include any of the following facts? Explain.

      (1) The physical or emotional effects of the loss suffered by Joseph Fairchild
      (2) Information about the decedent, Jacob, such as his age, personality, and talents
      (3) The events prompting Masters to drink that day
      (4) The condition of Masters's car or of the road at the time of the crash
      (5) The economic state of the Good Apple
   (c) Write the introductory paragraph of your fact statement.
   (d) List the order of topics that you would discuss after your introductory paragraph.
   (e) Write the topic sentence for the paragraph discussing the serving of liquor to Masters.

8. Write a summary for your argument. Aim for one to three concise paragraphs. Circle up to ten words that you hope your reader will remember best from your summary and from the argument.

9. Sketch out the main topics to be covered in your argument. By percentages, allocate how much space to allot to the topics and within each argument to law, facts, and policy.

10. Write a set of point headings for your argument. You may write more minor headings as well as major headings.

11. The *Kowal* case has two holdings and various opinions, so there is material favoring both parties.

   (a) Would you concede any point to your opponent? Explain.
   (b) Is there a *Kowal* point that your opponent would make that you should rebut? If so, what is it, and how would you rebut it?

12. Masters drank a total of eighteen drinks at two bars. How would you work with this fact on behalf of your client?

13. The Connecticut Supreme Court has declared in a Dram Shop Act case that it is a policy of that statute to address the danger to public health, safety, and morals from liquor sales and, more specifically, drunk driving. How would you work with that policy on behalf of your client?

14. Write a sentence using one or more of the following rhetorical devices: juxtaposition, allusion, aphorism, anaphora, epistrophe, alliteration, and rhetorical question.

Assume for the remaining questions that you are a member of the Connecticut Supreme Court.

15. How would you respond to the following sentences if they appeared in the parties' briefs? If you believe that any sentence needs editing, write in your changes.

   (a) Moments after leaving the Good Apple Bar and Grill, Masters slaughtered an innocent and unsuspecting child.
   (b) This Court's opinion in *Kowal* disregards the legitimate interests of the driving public in favor of the interests of commercial establishments that place drunk drivers on our state's roads.
   (c) Counsel for Appellant has shown little regard for the principle of stare decisis in her argument on the negligence cause of action.
   (d) How many more children must die before the rule of *Nolan v. Morelli* is finally overruled?
   (e) Appellant's counsel would have us believe that it is law-abiding establishments, such as the restaurant sued in this case, that cause the regrettable injuries in cases of this sort. But, as this Court knows, it is clear that the culprits are the Gary Masterses of this world, who are unable to control their deadly impulses.

16. If you were to rule in favor of Joseph Fairchild on the negligence cause of action and thereby change the law, how would you construct your opinion? More specifically, address the following factors:

(a) Current case law
(b) The equities of the new rule
(c) The fairness of applying the new rule to the present case
(d) The limits of the new rule (situations falling within and outside its scope)
(e) The public policies favoring the new rule
(f) The role of the Dram Shop Act

17. If you were to rule in favor of the Good Apple Bar and Grill and thereby adhere to current law, how would you construct your opinion? More specifically, address the following factors:

(a) The equities of the current rule
(b) The public policies favoring the current rule
(c) The role of the Dram Shop Act

EXERCISES FOR CHAPTER 19

ORAL ARGUMENT

Read the Gary Masters situation (on page 463) and the entire law library (on page 464). Joseph Fairchild sued the second bar, the Good Apple Bar and Grill, LLC, on two common law counts. The district court directed a verdict for the defendant on the negligence count, concluding that there was no cause of action for selling alcohol to an adult (Masters was an adult) who thereafter injures another by reason of his intoxication. The issue of recklessness was submitted to the jury, which found for the defendant. The district denied the motion to set aside the verdicts and thus rendered judgment for the defendants.

Assume that the Connecticut Appellate Court affirmed, Fairchild has appealed to the Connecticut Supreme Court, and that court has granted review. Also assume that the following procedural law and standards of review apply:

> In reviewing a trial court decision to direct a verdict for the defendant, the appeals court considers the evidence in the light most favorable to the plaintiff and then determines whether the jury reasonably and legally could have reached a conclusion other than in the defendant's favor.

> A jury verdict is entitled to acceptance unless the reviewing court can say as a matter of law that the jury's conclusions were such that reasoning minds could not reasonably have reached them.

> The trial court has broad discretion in deciding a motion to set aside the verdict on the grounds it is contrary to law and the evidence; that decision will not be disturbed in the absence of clear abuse.

For the following questions, assume that you represent either Joseph Fairchild, the appellant, or the Good Apple Bar and Grill, the respondent. (Or answer these questions twice, once for each side.)

1. Write out the introduction to your oral argument before the Connecticut Supreme Court. Include your theory of the case and a roadmap, summarizing the issues or arguments that you plan to discuss. Practice reciting it until you are pleased with how it sounds. Note: If you have chosen to represent Fairchild, your introduction should include an additional element; what is it?

2. List the key facts in the order in which you would state them. Then talk through those facts, and time yourself. How long does it take you to state these facts? Note: If you have chosen to represent the Good Apple, your statement should be especially concise; why?

3. Write out and recite the procedural posture of the case. Time yourself. How long does it take you to state the procedural posture? Note: If you have chosen to represent the Good Apple, you might choose to omit this portion of your presentation altogether; why?

4. Prepare an outline of your planned argument. Try to note your points in brief terms rather than in lengthy sentences, and be sure to include transitions. Assume you have thirty minutes to argue; allocate fifteen minutes to the assertions that you have identified. Mark stars next to the most important material to convey.

5. Write out the conclusion to your oral argument. Practice reciting it until you are pleased with how it sounds.

6. Select the three sources that you consider the most likely to be discussed extensively in an oral argument. Write out index cards for each of these three sources, with the name of the source and its most important points.

7. Write out questions that you think a court would ask you and sketch out good answers. Try to cover each of the following categories:

(a) Question about the facts
(b) Question about the law
(c) Question about public policy
(d) Question about a hypothetical situation
(e) Question seeking concession
(f) Question about your opponent's argument

POSTSCRIPT

In *Quinnett v. Newman*, 568 A.2d 786 (Conn. 1990), the case on which the Gary Masters situation is based, the Connecticut Supreme Court noted its long-standing rule that there is no proximate cause in a negligence case involving an adult drinker and a commercial seller, as well as the "limited exception" of *Ely v. Murphy*, 540 A.2d 54 (1988), that there is proximate cause when the drinker is a minor and the provider is a social host. *Quinnett*, 568 A.2d at 787. In *Quinnett*, the court declined to expand the *Ely* exception. Instead, the court noted that the legislature had provided a remedy for cases such as this (unlike the situation in *Ely*) in the Dram Shop Act, albeit with a limitation on the amount of recovery. *Quinnett*, 568 A.2d at 788. The majority also found no error in the trial court's denial of Mr. Quinnett's motion to set aside the jury verdicts, *id.* at 787, and declined to recognize a claim for public nuisance, *id.* at 788-89.

Chief Justice Peters and Justice Hull dissented. *Id.* at 789-91. "The continued existence of the present law is a blot on the social conscience and will, sooner or later, be corrected by this court. Why not now?" *Id.* at 791 (Hull, J., dissenting).

In February 2003, the Connecticut Supreme Court decided *Craig v. Driscoll*, 813 A.2d 1003 (Conn. 2003). There, the court ruled that a person who serves alcohol to an obviously intoxicated person and knows or has reason to know that the person plans to drive may be liable in negligence.

However, in June 2003, the Connecticut General Assembly amended the amount recoverable under the Dram Shop Act to $250,000 and added the following sentence: "Such injured person shall have no cause of action against such seller for negligence in the sale of alcoholic liquor to a person twenty-one years of age or older."

In *O'Dell v. Kozee*, 53 A.3d 178 (Conn. 2012), the Connecticut Supreme Court discussed these developments and also the meaning of "intoxication under the Dram Shop Act." After a thorough review of the case law and possible interpretations, the court determined that a plaintiff must have "proof of visible or otherwise perceivable intoxication." *Id.* at 182.

APPENDIX I

THE WRITING PROCESS

Inventor Stage

Architect Stage

Costume-Maker Stage

Critic Stage

Finished Paper

The writing process actually is a sequence of processes. To write well, you must succeed in all of the following stages, each symbolized by a non-legal profession:

- You must first figure out what to say—the *inventor* stage.
- Then you design the paper—the *architect* stage.
- Next you craft the first draft—the *costume-maker* stage.
- Finally you refine the paper—the *critic* stage.[1]

---

1. *See* Betty S. Flowers, *Madman, Architect, Carpenter, Judge: Roles and the Writing Process*, 44 Proceedings of the Conference of College Teachers of English 7-10 (1979) (cited and discussed in Bryan A. Garner, *Legal Writing in Plain English: A Text with Exercises* 5-10 (2001)).

A. THE INVENTOR STAGE

In this early stage, you figure out what to say. As an inventor, you understand and analyze the raw materials available to you (the law and the facts), consider what you are trying to accomplish (serve your client's interests, as well as the audience and purpose of your paper), and conceive a viable and creative solution in the form of a legal analysis.

One key to being a successful inventor is fully understanding the raw materials available to you. In the practice of law, this entails reading, briefing, and fusing cases; reading, briefing, and interpreting statutes; reading and taking notes on commentary; and assembling and understanding your client's facts. Another key to being a successful inventor is combining your raw materials systematically. In law, this entails reasoning deductively, employing policy analysis, and reasoning by example; in advisory contexts, developing and assessing options for the client to consider; and in advocacy contexts, developing a theory of the case. Yet another key to being a successful inventor is considering what you are trying to accomplish. In law, this entails consideration of the audience and purpose of your paper.

Inventors are not only systematic and thorough thinkers; they also are creative thinkers. Here are some strategies that may be useful as you build your capacity for creativity in the legal context:

- When you first learn of a client's situation (that is, before you research and analyze it), mull it over a bit, decide what you would do if you were in charge of making the law, and write out what you believe the legal outcome should be.
- If you are handling a dispute, consider: Which facts are truly compelling? What are the equities in favor of each side?
- If you are handling a transaction, consider: What is most important to my client? What are the risks that should be addressed? What would make the deal fair to both sides?
- Leave behind everything you have in writing or on your computer, take a walk (run, ride your bike, etc.), and let yourself think loosely about the situation and your legal analysis.
- Engage in a continuous writing exercise. Take pen in hand or turn on your computer, set a timer, and write for five solid minutes, uncritically and without stopping.
- Within the bounds of professional responsibility rules, talk with someone about the client's situation. Although most of us enjoy and benefit from talking to another person about a problem, legal rules about confidentiality of client information will ordinarily prohibit you from talking to persons outside your office. In any event, you can talk to the mirror or your voice recorder; you may find that you think more creatively when you speak than when you write.
- Keep a small notepad or electronic device with you. You may find that an idea pops into your head when you least expect it (e.g., when you are shopping for groceries or commuting). Be sure to capture those ideas for your file.

B. THE ARCHITECT STAGE

In this stage, you design the paper. You organize the many factual and legal points to be made into a set of logical and effective structures: one for the paper as a whole, some for each component of the paper, and yet more for each part.

The overall structure of your paper generally will be set by standard conventions of legal writing or, indeed, by format requirements of the courts. Within each major component, you often will have considerable latitude in structuring the material. Standard approaches include chronological, topical, and perceptual approaches to organizing the facts; the IRAC template; principles such as claims/defenses and substantive/procedural rules for organizing the discussion of the office memo; and strategic organizing principles, such as leading with your strong suit, for advocacy writing.

Depending on whether you are a big-picture or detail-oriented thinker, you may prefer to develop your structures and fit your points into them, or you may prefer to organize your points into clusters that give rise to the structures. Here are some strategies that may be useful:

- Label each source (whether factual or legal) with the main topics from your structures (again, whether factual or legal) covered therein. Many sources address more than one topic.
- Create file folders (on paper or in your computer) for the main topics, and file your sources and ideas within them.
- Assign several highlighting colors to your main topics, and highlight key passages accordingly.
- Make piles of your ideas, and lay them out in a logical sequence or set of piles of related thoughts.
- Try out more than one organizing principle, especially if you are having difficulty coming up with a perfectly logical approach.

You most likely will have some material that does not seem to fit well into your structure. Do not discard that material; simply set it aside for consideration at a later stage of the writing process.

Regardless of which component you are writing, be sure that you fully develop each point that you plan to make. Ask two questions: Does this point presuppose any other point? What is the implication of this point? Unless each point is preceded and followed by its logical linking points, the structure is not yet working.

Try various ways of depicting the organization of your material. Different components lend themselves to different depictions: the facts to a timeline, a legal discussion to an outline, a set of recommendations to a decision tree, and so on.

C. THE COSTUME-MAKER STAGE

In this stage, you create the first draft. As a costume-maker executes with care the design drawn by the costume's designer, so you will follow the design developed in the second stage. And as a costume-maker makes adjustments as needed in the design, so you may find as you write the first draft that revisions in the initial design are warranted.

For people who love to write, this is the most exhilarating stage. But for many writers, this is the most difficult step. You may find it hard to get started. Or you may be exasperated by the time that it takes to create a first draft of even the smallest component of the paper. You probably will become aware of omissions or mistakes in your work to date and begin to lose confidence. You may tire out well before you reach the last component. Here are some suggestions that may ease the burden of this third stage:

- Most important, be sure that you take the time and put in the effort to accomplish the first two stages well.
- Almost as important, trust that you will be able to improve your draft later; do not require perfection in your first draft.
- Think about how you prefer to generate text. The obvious choice is to start writing on your computer. Less obvious approaches are to write a few pages longhand, to talk into a voice recorder, and to type with your monitor off (so you are not drawn into fussing too much over each sentence).
- There are three standard approaches to choosing where to start. First, start at the beginning of the paper. Second, start with whichever component seems the most achievable, even if that component does not come first. Third, start with the most challenging or core material, even if that material does not come first. Any of these can work.
- Do not try to resolve all your minor questions along the way. Rather, put a pad of paper beside you on which to note minor concerns or questions to address later. Or drop these questions into a footnote or comment bubble in your electronic document.
- On the other hand, if you encounter a major concern or question, put your draft aside, write out the question, take a brief break, and try to solve the question before you go on. You will not want to continue too far down a perilous road.
- Plan to spend several sessions writing the paper, even if it is short. Develop a plan for how much you hope to accomplish during each session. In other words, pace yourself.
- Stop working when fatigue sets in. You will lose confidence and probably generate inferior text if you push yourself too long.

D. THE CRITIC STAGE

In this last stage, you refine the paper. Like a movie or music critic, you approach the paper as a work of art, seeking to discern its strengths and weaknesses, fundamental and minute. But unlike the critic, you act on your observations to refine, if not perfect, the paper.

This stage is generally called "editing." To edit your own work effectively, you must both distance yourself from your draft and immerse yourself thoroughly in it. This is an apparent but not actual paradox. You must distance yourself emotionally from your draft so that you are able to review it dispassion-ately. Then you must immerse yourself in it intellectually, reviewing every aspect of the draft and reforming what needs improvement.[2]

1. Distancing Yourself from Your Draft

Editing your own work generally is much more difficult than editing someone else's work. It is difficult to see your work as someone else sees it; it is difficult to tell whether you have made your point clearly for your reader, because you wrote it and know what you meant. It is difficult to delete or revise a passage on which you expended significant time and effort. An excellent means of gaining the necessary perspective on your work is, of course, to ask an intelligent and careful reader to review your draft and give you suggestions. If your situation does not permit this assistance—or even if it does—you may want to try the following strategies:

- Leave your draft for a few days. It will seem less familiar, less a part of you when you return to it, and some good ideas may come to you during your respite.
- Edit a printed copy of your draft. Reading on a screen does not replicate the effectiveness of reading on a screen,[3] so you are likely to perceive your text more accurately if you read it on paper.
- Try editing the draft somewhere other than where you wrote it.
- Reread the assignment, and think again about your various audiences and their needs in reading the paper. As you turn to the draft, imagine that you are a member of each audience.
- Imagine an intelligent and interested but uninformed reader looking over your shoulder: What questions would he or she ask? What problems would he or she see?
- When you begin your editing, read your draft aloud.

2. Immersing Yourself in Your Draft

It almost always helps to work through a draft several times, with a specific task for each run-through. Different people begin and end with different tasks. Some are big-picture tasks that fall within the category of revising; others are detail-oriented tasks that fall within the category of polishing. See Box I.1.[4] Presented in the order that generally is the most efficient, the tasks are:

---

2. For further editing suggestions, *see* Mary Barnard Ray & Jill J. Ramsfield, *Legal Writing: Getting It Right and Getting It Written* 122-27 (4th ed. 2005).

3. Ferris Jabr summarized studies from various disciplines on this topic in an online article, *The Reading Brain in the Digital Age: The Science of Paper Versus Screens*, Sci. Am. (Apr. 11, 2013), http://www.scientificamerican.com/article/reading-paper-screens (last visited Dec. 8, 2015).

4. Adapted from Brooke E. Bowman, *Learning the Art of Rewriting and Editing—A Perspective*, 15(1) Perspectives: Teaching Legal Research and Writing 54 (Fall 2006).

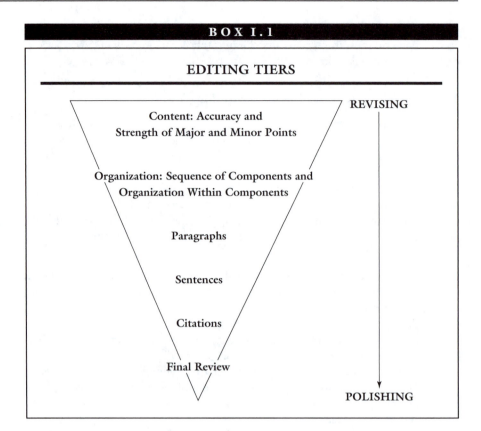

BOX I.1

EDITING TIERS

Content: Accuracy and
Strength of Major and Minor Points

REVISING

Organization: Sequence of Components and
Organization Within Components

Paragraphs

Sentences

Citations

Final Review

POLISHING

Verify—and improve, as needed—the accuracy of your assertions. Look over the factual material on which the paper is based and review your legal research. Then you should compare your draft to the content of these materials. If you have any doubt about the accuracy of a factual or legal point, you should look it up.

Affirm—or rework—your major and minor points. Read the draft fairly quickly, put it aside, and then jot down the major and minor points that you can remember. Then think about whether the points make sense:

- Do they fit the facts, conform to the law, and lead to a just and sensible result?
- Do they relate to each other in a logical and consistent way? For example, if your points are in the alternative, they should be discernible as alternatives.
- Can you proceed through the analysis without wondering "why" or "how" for more than a short time?

If any answer is "no," the next step is to rethink and rework your analysis so that all answers are "yes."

Review—and revise—the organization. To edit carefully, you should consider each organizational level in a separate step of the editing process. So first check the draft against the format requirements for the paper, making sure that you have written all necessary components and that each component conforms to the requirements of the format.

Then make a retrospective outline (or flowchart or other depiction) of the longer sections, typically the component presenting your legal analysis and perhaps also the facts. You might work through the paper, highlighting major topics in yellow, minor ones in pink, and so on. Another preparatory step is to label portions of the draft in the margin. You then can write a traditional outline, or you can extract the topic or thesis sentences from each paragraph. Then review the retrospective outline:

- Is there a sensible overall organizing scheme? For example, does the fact statement flow chronologically or topically? In the discussion, do the topics appear in a logical sequence?
- Is each sub-topic assigned to its corresponding topic?
- Are there excessive cross-references or redundancies?

You may well find that your organization needs adjustment. In general, it is more efficient to reorganize the outline first and then proceed to make changes in the draft itself.

Next, examine the headings; make sure that they clearly convey how each topic relates to what is coming and what has come before. Also examine whether the facts and legal discussions have adequate opening and closing paragraphs.

Refine your paragraphs. Review each paragraph against the guidelines of Appendix II:

- Does the paragraph have a distinct point or topic? Does all material pertain to this point or topic?
- Where is the thesis or topic sentence? Is it clear?
- Do the sentences providing development or support proceed logically?
- Are there clear transitions linking this paragraph to the preceding and following paragraphs?

To sharpen your focus on individual paragraphs, you may find it helpful to work on them out of order.

Refine your sentences. Check each sentence against the guidelines of Appendix II. Look especially carefully at long sentences, where the risks of grammar errors and low readability rise. As you gain practice in editing your own work, make note of the grammatical rules and guidelines that you are prone to violate; focus on them. At this stage, you also should review your spelling and typing. If you edit initially on paper, the standard editing symbols set out in Box I.2 may be useful. As with paragraphs, you may find that working on sentences out of order helps you to focus on the details of each sentence.

Refine your citations. Although you should include rough citations in your first draft, you should wait to perfect your citations until your paper is nearly finished. Some citation aspects (such as long versus short forms and signals) may change as the text evolves. Once your text is in close-to-final form, you should verify that you have provided citations for your factual and legal points and have done so properly.

Computer-assisted editing. You most likely will have available to you various computer-assisted programs to check your spelling, composition, or citation. You should run your text through these programs (especially a spell-check program), but remember that they are neither infallible nor as intelligent as you are. For example, a spell-check program may not correct the following sentence,

---

BOX I.2

EDITING SYMBOLS

red	insert word, letter, punctuation mark
reade	delete word, letter, punctuation mark
raed	invert order of letters or words
court	capitalize
Court	lower case
court	close space
itand	insert space

---

because the words are all spelled right, but it does not understand context: "The trail court red the case narrowly."

3. Your Final Responsibility

You may be required to submit a hard copy of your paper. Remember that technology can fail: computers and printers can delete text and adjust margins; photocopiers can skip pages. Your paper is not done until you have checked over the final product carefully. You, and only you, are responsible for the quality of your written work.

Finally, store your work in more than one truly reliable location, as any responsible lawyer would do. It is no longer acceptable in law school or law practice to say that your computer has malfunctioned and your paper is inaccessible; you should be able to obtain access to it and work on it in more than one reliable way.

APPENDIX II

PARAGRAPHS, SENTENCES, PUNCTUATION, AND WORDS

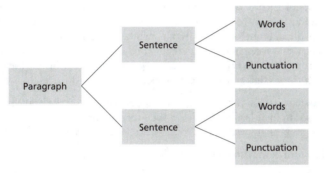

A. INTRODUCTION

It is often said, "Words are a lawyer's stock-in-trade." As a lawyer, you will be a professional writer; you should take pride in your writing skill. Indeed, as shown by the case discussed in Box II.1, failure to write at some level of competence is a breach of professional ethics.

Furthermore, you should write well because you are in a profession where your readers' expectations are high. All readers have some expectations about grammar, punctuation, and word usage. The more formal the prose, the higher the expectations; legal writing is formal prose. Furthermore, legal readers are well educated, with high and particular expectations. If your prose is grammatically correct and easy to read, your reader will think highly of your legal analysis. The opposite is also true; the weaker your composition, the more skeptical your reader will be towards your analysis.[1]

Reader expectations can be requirements or preferences. Requirements are grammar rules embedded in the structure of English. Writing that does not meet

---

1. This is due to the halo effect: if we judge a person positively or negatively on one aspect of a performance, we have a tendency to judge that person similarly on other aspects.

BOX II.1

HOW DO COURTS RESPOND TO WRITING ERRORS?

In re Hawkins,
502 N.W.2d 770 (Minn. 1993).

Hawkins' repeated disregard of the Local Bankruptcy Rules, coupled with the incomprehensibility of his correspondence and documentation, constitutes a violation of Rule 1.1, Minnesota Rules of Professional Conduct. Although it is quite true that the deficiencies in the documents submitted to the bankruptcy court did not, as the referee concluded, cause harm to Hawkins' clients, the lack of harm is fortuitous . . . .

Moreover, harm has occurred: even though Hawkins' clients have not been harmed, administration of the law and the legal profession have been negatively affected by his conduct. Public confidence in the legal system is shaken when lawyers disregard the rules of court and when a lawyer's correspondence and legal documents are so filled with spelling, grammatical, and typographical errors that they are virtually incomprehensible . . . .

Respondent Patrick W. Hawkins is hereby publicly reprimanded for unprofessional conduct. He is ordered to pay costs and disbursements incurred in this proceeding in the amount of $250. Within two years after issuance of this opinion respondent shall successfully complete the following described CLE or other educational programs and shall report quarterly to the Director his progress in complying with these educational requirements:

(1) A program on bankruptcy rules, or if none is available, on the law of bankruptcy;
(2) A program of at least 10 hours in legal writing; and
(3) A program of at least 5 hours on law office management.

Public reprimand with conditions imposed.

Rule 1.1, Minnesota Rules of Professional Conduct, provides as follows: A lawyer shall provide competent representation to a client. Competent representation requires the legal knowledge, skill, thoroughness, and preparation reasonably necessary for the representation.

---

these requirements jars the reader, prompts the reader to reread some material, and causes a major break in the reader's progress. For example, read the following sentence:

A reader expect that a singular verb will follow a singular noun.

Was your attention deflected at some point? What is the defect in the sentence? (A plural verb—"expect"—follows a singular noun—"reader.")

Other reader expectations are merely preferences. Writing that does not conform to these preferences may slow down the reader, who then devotes mental energy to figuring out the sentence's structure and loses focuses on the meaning of the sentence. For example, read the following sentence:

Although the validity of the covenant not-to-compete is debatable because its restraints are so broad, it is doubtful that it will be declined enforcement entirely because Minnesota, unlike many other states, permits blue-penciling of covenants deemed overbroad.

Did your attempt to decipher the structure distract your attention from the meaning?

This appendix covers both requirements and preferences. It first discusses the biggest unit of text: the paragraph. It then works through issues of sentence structure, punctuation, and word usage that frequently pose problems for legal writers.[2]

B. PARAGRAPHS

Within the components of the various documents covered in this book are paragraphs. Just as in other forms of writing, each paragraph should fully develop a topic through one or more related sentences, and each sentence should contain a complete thought. To craft strong paragraphs, you should attend to three features of paragraph design: cohesion among the sentences, paragraph length, and links between paragraphs. The discussion in this part draws on the sample paragraphs in Box II.2.

BOX II.2

SAMPLE PARAGRAPHS

First

I enjoyed talking with you last week and learning about your business. Until our conversation, I had not heard of businesses such as yours. I can see why yours is a growth industry.

Second

All-Day Wellness employees work as consultants to organizations, such as companies and nonprofit organizations, to assist their employees in improving their overall health. All-Day Wellness consultants perform an assessment of the client's workforce, suggest programs tailored to the particular workforce, and implement the program desired by the client, whether through direct service or contracting with another provider. As an example, you noted that a consultant may conduct a nutrition assessment of food available on site, make arrangements for regular yoga classes, and conduct smoking-cessation classes.

Third

Second, the covenant not-to-compete must protect a legitimate interest of the employer. One such interest is the loss of customers who follow the departing employee, when the employer has created the connection between the employee and the customers. In your situation, the experience in Washington demonstrates the risk of loss of customers. Thus, a court asked to enforce a covenant likely would find this requirement met.

---

2. For additional help with grammar, consult a college-level text or a grammar text written for lawyers, e.g., Linda Bahrych & Marjorie Dick Rombauer, *Legal Writing in a Nutshell* (4th ed. 2009); Richard Wydick, *Plain English for Lawyers* (5th ed. 2005).

1. Cohesion Among Sentences

Every paragraph should have a purpose, whether it is covering a topic, support-ing an assertion, or guiding the reader through the document. Compare the paragraphs reprinted in Box II.2: the first paragraph of the All-Day Wellness advice letter is intended to establish rapport with the client, the second paragraph from the summary of facts describes the services that All-Day Wellness provides, and the third paragraph analyzes one of the legal requirements applicable to a covenant not-to-compete that the company is considering implementing.

Every sentence in a paragraph should further its purpose; sentences that diverge from the paragraph's purpose are likely to distract and may confuse the reader. Before you write a paragraph, decide what you are trying to accom-plish and sketch out what is necessary for that task. After you have written a paragraph, go through it, checking all sentences against that purpose.

Paragraph cohesion also is a function of the order of the sentences within the paragraph. The classic paragraph design is TEC: topic, elaboration, and conclu-sion. A TEC paragraph begins with a sentence announcing the topic, several sentences elaborating on that topic follow, and the paragraph concludes with a wrap-up sentence. Indeed, the classic legal mnemonic, IRAC, is a variation on TEC, as shown in the third sample paragraph.

Some paragraphs can be cohesive without following TEC. When the paragraph is fairly short and its organizing scheme is readily apparent, you may be able to dispense with the T or C elements or both. For example, the first sample paragraph, which simply seeks to establish a connection between the lawyer and the reader, has neither a T nor a C sentence, and the second has a T but not a C sentence.

Finally, paragraph cohesion is furthered by links between sentences, includ-ing repeated words or concepts and transitional words or phrases. For example, the third sample paragraph in Box II.2 uses the transition words "one such inter-est" and "thus" and repeats "loss of customers."

2. Paragraph Length

A paragraph should be as long as it needs to be to accomplish its purpose. Because some purposes are easy and others difficult to accomplish, you should expect to see paragraphs of varying length in the same document. Indeed, a one-sentence paragraph is acceptable, so long as it accomplishes its purpose. On the other hand, if a paragraph is overly long, it will tax the reader, even if all of the sentences are related. When you have written a very long paragraph, consider whether you can subdivide its purpose and the paragraph as well. If this is not possible, be sure that the paragraph's cohesion is very strong: it has strong topic and conclusion sentences, and the flow from sentence to sentence is clear.

A study of paragraph length in significant legal treatises and articles of the last fifty years found that the averages ranged from 74 to 153 words.[3] (By way of comparison, the paragraphs in Box II.2 run 33, 84, and 66 words.)

---

3. Bryan A. Garner, *Legal Writing in Plain English: A Text with Exercises* 72-73 (2001).

3. Links Between Paragraphs

No matter how cohesive a paragraph is, if the reader cannot discern its connection to the discussion at hand, the reader will be puzzled. Every paragraph under a heading or sub-heading should, of course, obviously deliver what the heading or sub-heading promises.

Equally important is the connection between one paragraph and the next—the flow of a discussion. There are various ways to link a new paragraph to the preceding paragraph, including a transitional word or phrase and repetition of a key word or phrase from the last sentence of the preceding paragraph. For example, the second sample paragraph in Box II.2 is followed in the advice letter by a paragraph beginning "One of the advantages of the services provided by All-Day Wellness . . . " The third sample paragraph in Box II.2 is the second of three containing the words "first," "second," and "third."

C. Sentences

1. Subjects and Verbs

The core of a sentence is the subject and its verb. A reader starts to read a sentence by looking for these: a subject, because it usually tells who or what is performing an action, and a verb, because it usually tells what is happening. Everything else in the sentence is secondary.

a. Subject-Verb Agreement

Rules of grammar require that a plural verb be used with a plural subject and that a singular verb be used with a singular subject. Subject-verb disagreement most often occurs when many words intrude between subject and verb. For example:

> The posting, which was drafted by Molinaro after discussion with only one employee and read by Nicholson's co-workers, were defamatory.

The easiest way to catch this error is to find the core of the sentence and then match subject to verb. In the example, the true subject is "posting," not "co-workers." Thus, the verb should be "was."

b. Subject-Verb Proximity

Readers prefer the subject and verb of a sentence to be close together, so their connection is clear. If too many words appear between the subject and verb, the reader probably will skim over the intervening words. For example:

> The posting, which was drafted by Molinaro after discussion with only one employee and read by Nicholson's co-workers, was defamatory.

The subject and its verb—"posting was defamatory"—are separated by a lengthy intervening clause that seems like a parenthetical remark but actually is important.

Sentences with many words between subject and verb can be revised in various ways: You can reduce the number of words between subject and verb.

You can move the intervening words elsewhere in the sentence. Or you can break the sentence into two sentences and add an appropriate connector. One revision of the example above is:

> Molinaro talked with one employee and then drafted the posting, which Nicholson's co-workers read. This posting was defamatory.

c. Active and Passive Voice

Each core sentence follows one of five patterns, as shown in Box II.3. When the sentence is phrased in the active voice, the subject noun is doing the action in the sentence. Active-voice sentences are straightforward; they are short and easy to understand. Hence, readers prefer the active voice.

Some sentences can be phrased in passive voice. See the far right column in Box II.3. In a passive-voice sentence, the subject noun is being acted upon rather than doing the action; hence, these sentences are counterintuitive. Passive-voice sentences run long and can be complex because they require some form of the "to-be" verb and a past participle ("written" and "deemed" in Box II.3) and often include the prepositional phrase "by [noun]," explaining who is actually acting. Passive-voice sentences tend to be unwieldy. Again, readers prefer the active voice.

BOX II.3

ACTIVE- AND PASSIVE-VOICE SENTENCE PATTERNS

Sentence Type	Active Voice Version	Passive Voice Version
Subject + intransitive verb	The client agreed.	
Subject + linking verb + subject complement.	The client is satisfied.	
Subject + transitive verb + direct object.	The lawyer wrote a contract.	The contract was written by a lawyer.
Subject + transitive verb + indirect object + direct object.	The lawyer wrote the client a letter.	The letter was written to the client by the lawyer.
Subject + transitive verb + direct object + object complement.	The lawyer deems the contract enforceable.	The contract is deemed enforceable by the lawyer.

You can discern the voice of a sentence by checking whether the verb is in the form of a "to-be" verb plus a past participle of the main verb. However, a "to-be" verb without a past participle is not a passive-voice construction. For example:

Not passive: The three-part test is applicable.
Passive: The three-part test is applied by the courts.

Another way to discern the voice of a sentence is to locate the subject noun in the sentence and then determine whether it is doing the action (active voice) or being acted upon (passive voice).

You may indeed want to use the passive voice on occasion, but only for a good reason. First, use passive voice when the actor is unknown. For example:

The complaint was served on Bower's Bounty.

Second, use passive voice when, for persuasive reasons, you want to de-emphasize the actor or action. For example:

The memo to employees was posted (versus "Mr. Molinaro posted the memo.").

Third, use passive voice when you want to emphasize the object in the sentence rather than the subject. For example:

The qualified privilege defense can be raised only by a speaker acting in good faith.

Fourth, use passive voice to avoid misplacing a modifier. For example:

Having been drafted in haste, the memo was read by the employees with great surprise.

Fifth, use passive voice so that you can use one subject for two verbs. For example:

The posting was not expected and prompted widespread conversation.

d. Postponed Subjects

Some sentences resemble passive voice because the true actor is not in the subject position. Instead, the main clause contains words such as "there is" or "it is [adjective] that." The remainder of the sentence contains the true actor and its action. This type of construction is called a "postponed subject." For example:

There is a California statute that addresses driving while using a cell phone.
It is possible that an exception for driving on private property applies.

It is preferable to avoid postponed subjects because the opening clause has little or no meaning and burdens the reader unnecessarily. The solution is to delete the weak opening and rewrite the remainder. For example:

A California statute addresses driving while using a cell phone. Or simply state the statutory rule and provide a proper citation.
An exception for driving on private property may apply.

2. Verbs

Verbs are the most powerful words in the English language and hence have considerable impact on readers. Legal readers expect legal writing to follow both general conventions for verb usage and the specific conventions of the legal profession.

a. Verb Tenses

Failure to properly anchor an event in time is one of the most disconcerting types of confusion that a writer can induce. Thus, readers expect both proper use of verb tenses and consistency in verb tense, so that a particular event is discussed in the same tense throughout the paper. These expectations are requirements.

The English language provides a wide range of tenses, going well beyond the basic notions of past, present, and future. You may also use the perfect tenses, which show completion of an action before a particular time, and the progressive tenses, which show that an action continues over a particular time period. Box II.4 shows these verb tenses, ordered from distant past to future. Note that transition words, such as "at that time," make your gradations of time even clearer to the reader.

BOX II.4

VERB TENSES

Tense	Examples	Timing
Past Tenses		
Past perfect	had held	Action completed in the past before another action
Past perfect progressive	had been holding	Action continuing and completed in the past before another past action
Past progressive	was holding	Continuing action in the past
Simple past	held	Past action
Present Tenses		
Present perfect	has held	Action that began in the past and is linked to the present
Present perfect progressive	has been holding	Action that began in the past and is continuing in the present
Present progressive	is holding	Continuing action in the present
Simple present	holds	Present action
Future Tenses		
Future perfect	will have held	Action that will be completed before another future action
Future perfect progressive	will have been holding	Action that will be continuing and completed before another future action
Future progressive	will be holding	Continuing action in the future
Simple future	will hold	Future action

Legal readers also expect that certain legal conventions will be followed as to verb tense. One set of conventions addresses the tenses to use for events that occur in the real world. A different set of conventions addresses tenses to use when you state the law and the making of the law. The latter may not seem natural to you at first, but using them properly will help your text read well to a lawyer. See Box II.5. For example, the two passages below show proper factual and legal tense usages:

> Facts: Ms. Collins drove out of the parking lot as she consulted her cell phone to get directions to Starbucks. She had just bought doughnuts for her co-workers. A crash occurred; the police came and cited her for driving while using a cell phone. Fortunately, Ms. Collins is fine, but the other driver has ongoing medical issues, and Ms. Collins is concerned that he will have even more medical bills.
>
> Law: In 1998, the California legislature considered various versions of a cell-phone driving bill. Ultimately, the legislature enacted the present section 123. Section 123 provides for a modest base fine of $20. However, under legislation passed last year, the penalty will rise to $50 next year.[4]

BOX II.5

LEGAL VERB-TENSE CONVENTIONS

Real-World Facts
Past events: Various past tenses
Present events: Various present tenses
Future events: Various future tenses

Rules of Law and Reasoning
Former (repealed, overturned): Various past tenses
Current (in force, in use, valid): Various present tenses
Future (not yet in effect, proposed): Various future tenses

Actions of Courts and Legislatures
Past actions: Various past tenses
Pending actions: Various present tenses
Future actions: Various future tenses

---

b. Verb Moods

A verb's mood gives additional information beyond its tense. The three verb moods are indicative, imperative, and subjunctive, as illustrated in Box II.6. In general, framing verbs in the proper mood is a requirement.

---

4. This example is constructed to show how tenses work, not to reflect actual legal developments.

The one exception is the hypothetical condition contrary to fact, which may or may not be stated in subjunctive mood. A hypothetical sounds more likely when stated in indicative mood and less likely when stated in subjunctive mood, as shown below:

Indicative: If a consultant leaves, the court likely will enforce the covenant not-to-compete.
Subjunctive: If a consultant were to leave, the court likely would enforce the covenant not-to-compete.

Either statement is correct, so your choice of mood for hypotheticals depends on how likely or unlikely you want the hypothetical to sound, with the latter sounding less likely.

BOX II.6

VERB MOODS

Mood	Attitude	Example
Indicative	Facts, opinion, or question	The contract is valid. Is the contract valid?
Imperative	Command or direction	Ignore irrelevancies. Be unbiased.
Subjunctive	Suggestion, desire, requirement, possibility, or hypothetical condition contrary to fact	We suggest that the client develop new policies . . . The law requires that contracts be in writing . . . Had she used a hands-free phone, . . .

---

c. Verb Phrases

Generally, a verb phrase can be interrupted with a single-word adverb without disrupting the sentence. For example:

Ms. Collins had slowly backed out into the street when the crash happened.

However, lengthier interruptions generally dilute the power of the verb and read awkwardly. For example:

Ms. Collins had, while talking into her cell phone, backed out into the street.

The solution is to move the interruption elsewhere in the sentence:

While talking into her cell phone, Ms. Collins had backed out into the street.

The same problem occurs with infinitives, which are verbs preceded by the word "to." A split infinitive occurs when one or more words appear between "to" and the verb. Split infinitives regularly occur in spoken English, but some readers consider them improper. They are acceptable under modern grammar rules when the interruption is small and the result is not awkward.[5] For example:

> To safely drive a car, drivers should not use a cell phone.

Larger interruptions should be avoided. For example:

> Problematic: A driver using a cell phone may find it difficult to, no matter what the traffic conditions are, drive safely.
> Better: A driver using a cell phone may find it difficult to drive safely, no matter what the traffic conditions are.

3. Nouns and Pronouns

Nouns are words that name people, places, things, and concepts. A pronoun, such as "it" or "they," takes the place of a nearby noun. The word to which a pronoun refers is called its "antecedent."

a. Noun-Pronoun Agreement

A pronoun must agree with its antecedent noun in number, person, and gender. Number is whether the pronoun is singular or plural; person is whether the pronoun is in first-, second-, or third-person (such as "I," "you," and "she"); gender is whether a third-person pronoun is feminine, masculine, or neuter. Proper noun-pronoun agreement is required.

Two or more antecedents joined by "and" generally take a plural pronoun, regardless of the number of either antecedent. For example:

> When All-Day Wellness and its consultants signed the contracts, they believed them to be enforceable.

However, when two or more antecedents are joined by "or" or "nor," the pronoun agrees with the antecedent nearer to the pronoun. For example:

> Neither the employer nor its employees believed that their contract was void.

b. Collective Nouns

Legal writing contains many collective nouns that are singular because the group represented by the collective noun functions as a single entity. See Box II.7. Once you know whether you are discussing the group or the persons in the

---

5. *See* H. W. Fowler, *A Dictionary of Modern English Usage* 429, 579-82 (2d ed. Ernest Gowers ed., 1965) (out of the frying pan, split infinitives); Maxine Hairston & John J. Ruskiewicz, *The Scott, Foresman Handbook for Writers* 316-17 (4th ed. 1996).

group, you can write the verbs, pronouns, and the rest of the sentence correctly. Proper treatment of collective nouns is required. For example:

All-Day Wellness (a corporation) offers its clients the services of its consultants.

The supreme court has upheld covenants not-to-compete, but several justices have written concurring opinions to express their concern about the policy implications of doing so.

BOX II.7

COLLECTIVE NOUNS

Singular Collective Noun	Noun Representing Group Members (Plural)
jury	jurors
court	judges or justices
legislature	legislators
board	board members
commission	commissioners
corporation	shareholders
partnership	partners

---

c. Indefinite Pronouns

Indefinite pronouns do not refer to a specific person or thing. Although grammar books differ as to which are singular and which are plural, Box II.8 reflects formal usage.[6] The rest of the sentence, especially the verb, must align with the indefinite pronoun. The following examples are correct:

Either of the employees is willing to use covenants not-to-compete.
None of the employees are willing to use covenants not-to-compete.
Each of the clients was satisfied with the services provided.

---

6. Maxine Hairston & John J. Ruskiewicz, *supra* note 5, at 343.

BOX II.8

INDEFINITE PRONOUNS

Singular	Either (Singular or Plural)	Plural
any-body, -one, -thing	all	few
each	any	many
every-body, -one, -thing	either	several
no-body, -one, -thing	more	
some-body, -one, -thing	most	
	neither	
	none	
	some	

d. Implied Antecedents

When "this" and "that" are used as freestanding pronouns, they often result in unclear implied antecedents. Because the reader has to surmise the unnamed antecedent of the pronoun, readers prefer greater clarity. In the example below, "this" could refer to the covenant, a blue-penciled version, or a non-enforcement order.

> If too broadly drafted, the covenant not-to-compete may be blue-penciled or not enforced at all. This may lead to problematic relationships with employees.

The solution to such implied antecedents is to place the appropriate noun after the word "this." You also may need to reword the preceding sentence to make the connection clearer.

4. Clauses and Phrases

This part discusses how clauses are joined with each other and how their structure affects the meaning of the sentence.

a. One Point per Sentence

A short sentence is more readable than a long sentence because the reader does not have to work so hard to locate the subject and verb. A reader who is confronted with a long, bulky sentence may slow down to process the sentence, or the reader may just move on to the next sentence. Consider the following sentence, which is grammatically correct but bulky:

> Many drivers talk on cell phones, yet few are cited, which is because police are more concerned with actual crashes or other driving violations, such as driving beyond the posted speed limit and running stop signs.

This sentence is trying to get across two points and would work better as two sentences (the material before and after "which").

Sometimes this reader preference must be disobeyed to meet a format requirement. For instance, a point heading in a brief to the court may be required to be a single sentence, which may run long to include all necessary content.

b. Short Introductory Clauses

Short introductory clauses can be very effective. However, long introductory clauses keep the reader from easily locating the core of the sentence and may be skimmed or skipped. To accord with the reader preference against long introductory clauses, you can use various editing strategies. You can delete unnecessary words from an overlong clause. You can move the clause to the end of the sentence. You can make the long clause the main clause and turn the former main clause into a dependent clause. And you can break the sentence into two sentences. Consider the following sentence and its revisions:

> If the covenant is drafted so as not to unduly restrain the employees once they leave All-Day Wellness, the court likely will enforce the covenant.

- The court likely will enforce the covenant if it is drafted so as not to unduly restrain the employees once they leave All-Day Wellness.
- The covenant should be drafted so as not to unduly restrain the employees once they leave All-Day Wellness, and the court likely will enforce the covenant.
- The covenant should be drafted so as not to unduly restrain the employees once they leave All-Day Wellness. Then the court likely will enforce the covenant.

c. "That," "Which," and "Who"

"That" and "which" are relative pronouns; they introduce clauses modifying nouns. The choice between the two depends on whether the clause narrows the modified noun or describes it. Restrictive clauses narrow the modified noun, begin with "that," and are not set off from the rest of the sentence with commas. Nonrestrictive clauses describe but do not narrow the modified noun, begin with "which," and are set off from the rest of the sentence with commas. Using these clauses properly is required. The following examples are correct:

> The clause that imposed the constraint appeared at the end of the contract.

> The covenant not-to-compete, which was in boldface, appeared at the end of the contract.

"Who" is used to introduce a dependent clause that modifies a noun describing a person. "Who" can be restrictive or nonrestrictive. For example:

> The employee who was hired yesterday was not pleased with the covenant not-to-compete.

In this example, "who" is not set off from the rest of the sentence with commas because it is restrictive; it specifies which employee was not pleased.

d. Misplaced and Dangling Modifiers

The reader usually links a modifying word or phrase to the nearest word that could be modified. When the word seemingly modified is the wrong one, the modifier is misplaced; the solution is to re-structure the sentence to place the modifier by the word it modifies. Proper use of modifiers is required. For example:

> Misplaced: The associate drafted the contract for the client using a form book. (Is the client using the form book?)
> Correct: Using a form book, the associate drafted the contract for the client.

Limiting modifiers frequently are misplaced. They should appear immediately before the word or phrase being modified. The major limiting modifier is "only." In the three correct sentences below, the placement of "only" changes meaning:

> Only the associates drafted the contract. (No one other than associates drafted the contract.)
> The associates only drafted the contract in the first month. (The only thing they did was draft.)
> The associates drafted only the contract in the first month. (They did not draft anything else.)
> The associates drafted the contract only in the first month. (After the first month, they did not draft the contract.)

A common instance of a misplaced modifier involves a verb phrase. The implied subject of an introductory verb phrase is the subject of the sentence. If it is not, the phrase is misplaced. For example:

> Misplaced: Trying not to give legal advice, the new hire was referred by her manager to human resources to discuss the matter.
> Correct: Trying not to give legal advice, the manager referred the new hire to human resources.

When a modifier does not seem to modify anything in the sentence, the modifier is dangling, rather than misplaced. Often, passive voice is involved. For example:

> Dangling: Wondering whether the covenant not-to-compete would be valid, counsel was hired to research the question.

Correct: Wondering whether the covenant not-to-compete would be valid, All-Day Wellness's president hired counsel to research the question.

e. Parallel Structure

When a sentence has a compound element, it contains two or more of the same elements, e.g., two verbs, two adverb phrases. Compound elements must follow the same grammatical form. When parallel structure is missing, the result is awkward, jarring, or confusing. For example:

The covenant not-to-compete must be supported by consideration, protect the employer's interest, narrowly tailored, or it may be blue-penciled.

This requirement of parallel structure applies to series. A series is a collection of two or more items joined by one of the coordinating conjunctions: "and," "or, "but," "nor," and "yet." The following examples are correct:

The contract was clear, concise, and enforceable. (series of three adjectives)
The attorney drafted the contract and met with the client to make sure it was accurate. (series of two verbs, both in same tense)
The manager approached the termination hastily and recklessly. (series of two adverbs)

Most lists are series and therefore should be in parallel structure. For example:

The statute has four parts: (1) purpose, (2) definitions, (3) general prohibition, and (4) damages and penalties. (all nouns)

However, the following enumerated sentence does not contain compound elements joined by a conjunction, so it is not required to be in parallel structure:

Ms. Collins was (1) driving (2) while using a non-hands-free cell phone (3) not for an emergency purpose (4) and entering traffic.

Parallel structure also is required for items joined by correlative conjunctions, such as "either/or" and "not only/but also." The following examples are correct:

The employee will receive either a bonus or a promotion upon signing the covenant not-to-compete.
The contract not only was signed by the employee upon hiring but also was reviewed on an annual basis.

Similarly, parallel structure is required between items being compared or contrasted. The following example is correct:

Ms. Collins's risky driving would be remedied more effectively by a safe-driving course than by a small fine.

D. PUNCTUATION

Punctuation marks are compact signals, each conveying a specific message to the reader about the connections among words. If you use a punctuation mark incorrectly, you will send the wrong signal. Not surprisingly, proper use of punctuation is required.

1. Choosing Among Stops: Periods, Semicolons, Commas, Dashes, Parentheses, and Colons

Stops are the punctuation marks that signal a pause; they are periods, semicolons, commas, dashes, parentheses, and colons. In several situations, you may exercise judgment as to how much of a pause you want the reader to take. The situations are summarized in Box II.9.

BOX II.9

CHOICES AMONG STOPS

Purpose	Stops, Listed from Smallest to Largest Stop
Joining two or more main clauses	• Comma (with coordinating conjunction) • Semicolon • Period
Setting apart an aside	• Parentheses • Commas • Dashes
Introducing quote, list, or similar material	• No stop • Comma • Colon

---

a. Joining Main Clauses

One choice among stops occurs when you want to join two or more main clauses. You can use a period, a semicolon, or a comma for this task. Your choice should reflect how closely you want to link the two clauses. If you want to link the two clauses very closely, you should use a comma and a coordinating conjunction (e.g., "and," "but"). For example:

> The covenants not-to-compete likely will be valid, but the employees will not like them.

If you want to link the two clauses less closely yet still show their connection to each other, you should use a semicolon without a coordinating conjunction. You might also include some other connecting word or phrase:

> The covenants not-to-compete likely will be valid; however, the employees will not like them.[7]

---

7. Note that a comma is needed after this use of "however." By contrast, no comma is needed in the following sentence: However you tried to contact me, it did not work.

If you want a distinct break between the clauses, you should use a period to create two separate sentences. Again, you might include a connecting word or phrase:

> The covenants not-to-compete likely will be valid. On the other hand, the employees will not like them.

Generally, two short sentences are more readable than one longer sentence, so you should opt for one long sentence with two clauses only if both clauses are fairly short.

When two clauses that could otherwise be sentences are joined incorrectly, the result is known as a "run-on sentence" or "fused sentence." For example:

> The covenants not-to-compete likely will be valid, the employees will not like them.

Avoiding run-on sentences not only is a requirement; as just noted, it is also easy to do.

b. Setting Apart an Aside

Another choice among stops occurs when an aside—a few words of commentary—needs to be set apart from the rest of the sentence by a pause on either side. For this task, you can use parentheses, a pair of commas, or a pair of dashes. Your choice should reflect how much you want the reader to focus on the interrupting word or phrase. If you want to de-emphasize the aside, use parentheses. If you want more attention paid to the aside, set it off with commas on either side (known as "parenthetical commas"). If you want maximum emphasis, use dashes on either side. For example:

> The covenant not-to-compete (which ran forty words) was easy to understand.
> The covenant not-to-compete, which the company's attorney drafted, passed legal muster.
> The covenant not-to-compete—which the company took verbatim from a form book—was denied enforcement.

A dash can be made with two hyphens if your word processing program or printer will not generate a dash. Dashes are typed flush against adjacent text with no open spaces on either side.

c. Introducing Quotes, Lists, and Similar Material

Yet another choice among stops occurs at the beginning of a quotation, a list, or similar introduced material. You may precede this material with no stop at all, a comma, or a colon. Your choice should reflect how much of a connection you want between the preceding text and the introduced material.

Sometimes you want the introduced material to flow smoothly into the sentence. For this effect, do not use any stop, and do not capitalize the initial letter of the introduced material. For example:

> The three factors are (1) consideration, (2) reasonableness, and (3) . . . .
> The court ruled that "[s]uch covenants are enforceable if they are not overly restrictive."

In the second example, "[s]" shows that "such" had an initial capital letter in the original source, but the writer changed that capitalization to make the quotation fit the rules of this punctuation format.

If you want a medium pause to set a quotation that is a complete sentence apart from the text, precede the quote with a comma and a signaling verb. For example:

> The court ruled, "Such covenants are enforceable if they are not overly restrictive."

Note that the quotation begins with a capital letter.

If you want an emphatic break before the set-apart material, use a more formal introduction, followed by a colon. For example:

> The three factors are firmly established: (1) consideration, (2), reasonableness, and (3) . . .
> The president of All-Day Wellness clearly expressed her concern: "We need to do all we can to protect our competitive position."

In the second example, note that the quotation begins with a capital letter.

When a colon is not followed by a quoted sentence, whether to capitalize the first word after the colon depends on what follows the colon. If what follows is a complete sentence, the first word may or may not be capitalized. If what follows is not a complete sentence, the first letter should not be capitalized (unless, for example, the word is a proper noun).

d. Other Comma Uses

Use a comma after an introductory phrase or word at the beginning of a sentence.

Commas are often, but not always, used in series. A series has three or more items that are similar grammatically (e.g., four nouns, three verb phrases). In a simple series, no item in the series has punctuation within it. Then commas are used to set off the items from each other: commas after all but the second-to-last are required, and a comma after the second-to-last item is preferred for clarity. For example:

> Sarah Nicholson received two raises, five bonuses, and four employee-of-the-month awards.

However, if any item in a series contains a comma, it is a complex series, and semicolons (rather than commas) should appear after all but the last item. For example:

> Sarah Nicholson received two raises, both for the largest amount possible; five bonuses; and four employee-of-the-month awards.

On the other hand, it is erroneous to place a comma between the subject and verb of the same clause or between a verb and its object, unless some other usage requires the comma. For example:

> Incorrect: The regional manager and Dan Molinaro, met to discuss termination procedures.

Correct: The regional manager and Dan Molinaro met to discuss termination procedures.

Incorrect: All-Day Wellness reassessed its concerns underlying the non-compete covenant, and wrote to its attorney to delete it.

Correct: All-Day Wellness reassessed its concerns underlying the covenant not-to-compete and wrote to its attorney to delete it.

Finally, use a comma on either side of the year when it follows the month and the day (in that order). These are preferred usages. For example:

According to her personnel file, Sarah Nicholson was hired on July 1, 2007, and received her last promotion in June 2012.

2. Hyphens

Hyphens are used[8] for words that are hyphenated in the dictionary; this usage is required. Hyphens also have a preferred usage: between two or more words that together create an adjective that precedes a noun. This usage is desirable because it removes ambiguity. For example:

In 2010, Sarah Nicholson received the employee-of-the-month award.

Grammarians disagree about whether to hyphenate when one of the words preceding the noun is an adverb, but the majority rule is not to hyphenate. For example:

This award is a highly cherished honor.

The adverb "highly" could never modify the noun "honor," so the adverb need not be attached to the adjective "cherished" with a hyphen.

However, some legal terms are almost never hyphenated under this rule. These terms are very common legal phrases, the names of legal rules and doctrines, the names of statutes, and foreign terms, such as "common law rule" and "prima facie case."

3. Apostrophes

Apostrophes are required in contractions, such as "can't" and "don't." However, contractions should rarely be used in legal writing. It is generally appropriate to use them only in direct quotations. Note that the contraction "it's" does contain an apostrophe, but the possessive pronoun "its" does not contain an apostrophe. Likewise, the contraction "who's" does contain an apostrophe, but the possessive pronoun "whose" does not contain an apostrophe.

Apostrophes also are required for the possessive form of nouns. Add an apostrophe and the letter "s" to form the possessive of most singular nouns, plural nouns not ending in the letter "s" or "z," and indefinite pronouns. For example:

employee's review
women's employment

---

8. Hyphens are also used in print when a word is split between two lines of text (which is not commonly done these days).

everyone's safety

If a singular noun does end in "s" or "z," the majority rule is to form the possessive by adding an apostrophe and "s" unless the resulting pronunciation is difficult; in that case, add only an apostrophe. For example:

Dr. Ferris's opinion
for goodness' sake

The possessive form of a plural noun ending in "s" or "z" is formed by adding an apostrophe to the noun. For example:

consultants' services

4. Quotation Marks

Quotation marks appear on either side of quoted text or a new term that is to be defined. A quote within a quote is bounded by single quotation marks. For example:

Mr. Molinaro reported, "One of her co-workers told me that 'Sarah is stealing produce.'"

A comma or period at the end of quoted matter goes inside the final quotation mark, regardless of whether it was part of the quote. All other punctuation at the end of quoted matter goes outside the final quotation mark, unless it appeared in the original text from which the quote was taken.

Legal style rules governing quotations appear in *ALWD Guide to Legal Citation* and *The Bluebook: A Uniform System of Citation*. These rules are requirements and differ somewhat from style rules outside the legal profession.

E. Word Usage

The following material first addresses word choices that yield effective text, then word choices that are to be avoided because they yield problematic text.

1. Effective Word Choices

a. Consistent and Distinct Words

In some fields, elegant variation in writing is prized. However, in legal writing, if you use different words to mean the same thing, the result is usually ambiguity. Thus, in legal writing, you should always use the same word for a concept, and you should use different words for different concepts. In the following example, "arrangement" and "contract" may or may not refer to the same thing; one word should be used if there is only one agreement.

The arrangement that All-Day Wellness had with its consultant involved entering into a written contract upon hire.

b. Precise Words

Some words have several meanings, while other words carry but one meaning. Legal readers prefer that, when you have a choice between synonyms, you choose the word with the single meaning so that the reader will not have to decide which of two meanings you intended.

"Because," "since," and "as" are sometimes are used interchangeably. "Because" shows causation: that something happened by reason of or on account of something else. "Since" and "as" can also show causation, or they can have other meanings (a temporal relationship for "since," and sameness for "as"). Thus, when you want to show a causal relationship, you should use "because."

Likewise, "although" and "while" sometimes are used interchangeably. "Although" shows a contrary relationship in the same manner as "in spite of the fact that." "While" can show a contrary relationship, or it can show a concurrent temporal relationship. When you want to show a contrary relationship, you should use "although." When you want to show a concurrent temporal relationship, you should use "while."

An overlapping pair of words is "whether" and "if." "Whether" shows an alternative relationship between two upcoming items. "If" can show a condition ("in the event that"), or it can show an alternative relationship. Thus, when you want to show an alternative relationship, you should use "whether."

"Among" and "between" are not synonyms. "Between" is used to connect two items; "among" is used to connect three or more items.

c. Gender-Neutral Wording

Formerly, legal writers used masculine pronouns when the gender was not specified. However, during the past several decades, the convention has shifted, so gender-neutral wording is preferred. Gender-neutral wording presents your client's message in the most effective light for a wide audience.

The first step in gender-neutral wording is to replace gender-biased words, such as those listed in Box II.10.

BOX II.10

GENDER-NEUTRAL NOUNS

Former Usage	Replacement
chairman	chairperson, chair
fireman	firefighter
policeman	police officer
manpower	resources
reasonable man	reasonable person

The second step is to use gender-appropriate pronouns. Most obviously, figure out the gender of any known person being discussed, and use the appropriate gender-specific pronoun for that person. In discussing a hypothetical situation, you can generate names for the hypothetical characters and then use the appropriate gender-specific pronouns for those characters. Balance the genders of your hypothetical characters by having nearly equal numbers of male and female characters, and take care to avoid gender stereotypes.

The third step is to omit as many gender-specific pronouns in your general text references as possible. Various strategies are possible depending on your document: You can repeat the noun instead of using the pronoun. You can change the discussion to the plural, so that you may use "they," or to the second person, so that you may use "you." You can change the person being discussed to an indefinite pronoun, such as "anyone" or "someone." You can omit a pronoun; for example, "his or her contract" becomes "the contract," and "he or she" becomes "the employee." You can change the sentence to passive voice and eliminate the actor entirely.

Sometimes you will have no choice but to use a singular pronoun for an unknown gender. Box II.11 presents the alternatives with their disadvantages. Weigh the disadvantages in light of the audience and purpose of your document. "He or she" is probably the most commonly chosen alternative.

BOX II.11

GENDER-NEUTRAL PRONOUNS

Option			Disadvantages
Subject	*Object*	*Possessive*	
he/she	him/her	his/her	Too colloquial for formal writing; still has masculine pronoun first
he or she	him or her	his or her	Bulky but often workable; favors masculine pronoun by placing it first
she or he	her or him	her or his	Bulky and somewhat unexpected by the reader, but often workable; favors feminine pronoun by placing it first

---

2. Problematic Word Choices

a. Nominalizations

Some nouns are converted verbs, formed by the addition of "tion," "ment," "ence," or other suffixes. These nouns are called "nominalizations." Although nominalizations are not ungrammatical, readers prefer the action of the sentence to be expressed in verbs, not nouns. Also, readers prefer short sentences; nominalizations generally appear in wordy constructions, such as a verb + noun phrase or a prepositional phrase. To reduce your use of nominalizations, look for nouns that are made out of verbs and decide whether a straightforward verb would work better. For example:

> Nominalizations: In the event of a refusal by a consultant to the inclusion of the covenant not-to-compete, Bower's Bounty may not make an agreement with the consultant.
>
> Better: If the consultant refuses to include the covenant not-to-compete, Bower's Bounty may not agree with the consultant.

b. Unneeded Adverbs

Adverbs are relatively weak parts of speech compared to nouns and verbs. Some add little or no meaning; some convey meaning that a better chosen verb would convey. These adverbs violate a preference that each word carries some useful meaning. In particular, the words "very," "somewhat," and "rather" often can be deleted with no loss in meaning. For example:

> The covenant not-to-compete is [very] enforceable.

c. Multiple Negatives

When two or more negative expressions occur in the same sentence, they often slow down the reader and obscure meaning. Thus, readers prefer not to see multiple negatives. To revise such a sentence, cancel out the pair of negatives and then assess whether the resulting sentence accurately captures the meaning of the original. For example:

> Multiple negatives: It is not unlawful for a company to not enforce a covenant when an employee leaves.
>
> A company may forego enforcing a covenant when an employee leaves.

d. Surplus Words

Readers prefer lean text because short sentences are easier to read and understand. Eliminate redundant legal phrases, such as "cease and desist" and "null and void." By and large, the words in these phrases are synonyms; select and use the better word. Similarly, eliminate legalisms that generally add nothing but syllables, such as "hereinafter" and "aforementioned." Finally, avoid bulky constructions, typically the prepositional phrases presented in Box II.12.

BOX II.12

BULKY PHRASES AND ALTERNATIVES

Bulky	Simplified
at that point in time	then
prior to	before
subsequent to	after
during the time that	during, while
for the period of	for
until such time as	until
by means of	by
in accordance with	by, under
for the purpose of	to
in order to	to
inasmuch as	because
because of the fact that	because
in connection with	with, about, concerning
in relation to	about, concerning
with reference to	about, concerning
in favor of	for
in the event that	if
despite the fact that	although, even though
in some instances	sometimes
in many cases	often
insofar as _____ is concerned	regarding
there was a situation in which	there
there is no doubt but that	doubtless, no doubt

APPENDIX III

CITATION

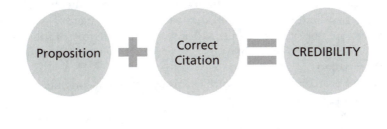

A. INTRODUCTION

Citation is the practice of providing references to sources for propositions stated in a legal document. The most obvious function served by a citation is to permit the reader to locate the source and verify that it says what the document asserts that it says. A proper citation thus establishes the credibility of the proposition; this is critical to legal writing, which is deeply grounded in authority.

Various citation systems exist, including the venerable *The Bluebook: A Uniform System of Citation;* the more recent *ALWD Guide to Legal Citation* (from the Association of Legal Writing Directors); and court citation protocols. All have very detailed rules, such as abbreviating party names in cases and typefaces to use for statutes. Indeed, as you learn it, citation may seem to be unduly detailed.

A better view is that citation rules are justified by three principles. First, the required forms include the information that a legal reader needs to identify, assess, and locate a source. Second, most forms are efficient in calling for compact presentation of the information needed. Third, when a citation is presented in the exact format that your reader expects, he or she can easily process it. This permits your reader to focus on the propositions that you are making rather than their source. In other words, citation functions much as grammar does—just as, for instance, a reader knows to prepare for a new idea upon encountering a period.

Furthermore, proper citation reveals the writer's craft. To a great extent, a citation either does or does not comply with the governing rule. Proper citation, thus, is a hallmark of the writer's attention to detail and professionalism. If a paper has correct citation, the reader is likely to respect its research and analysis as well.

Rather than provide a guide to any particular citation manual or citation forms, this appendix provides a bird's-eye view of how to approach citation strategically.

B. Learn How to Use Your Citation Manual

Most documents that you write will be governed by rules set by a court or by a specified citation manual. The rules of a court tend to be fairly short and cover only certain matters, such as the publications to cite for cases from that court.

On the other hand, the two major citation manuals are large and complicated books. They cover many types of sources, many facets of citations, and various situations in which citations are used. They are not meant to be read cover to cover, but rather to be used as reference tools. The authors recognize this and have provided various user's tools:

- Acquaint yourself with the overall design of the manual. For example, the current *Bluebook* has (1) blue pages with rules that introduce citation and also apply specifically to practice documents; (2) white pages that flesh out the blue pages, beginning with matters common to many types of citations and then covering each category of sources; and (3) tables for such matters as jurisdictional information and abbreviations.
- Learn how to locate pertinent rules through tables of contents, the index, or sample citation pages.
- Once you have found a pertinent rule, work through it carefully, and pursue the cross-references provided in that rule.
- Study as well the many examples provided in the manual. A rule may be unclear, but you may be able to create a citation by analogy to an example.

C. Approach Citation as a Series of Steps

Most legal writers should not craft their citations during the writing of the first draft of a document. Rather, citation should be accomplished both before and after that stage.

During your research, you should engage in pre-citation. As you identify a source you may want to use, record all the information that you will need to cite it properly. This step requires attention to detail. For example, proper citation requires pinpoint citations, such as the page number in a case or the specific statutory section where a proposition appears; record this information as you research. As another example, nearly every citation form requires some type of date; record these dates as you research.

As you write, insert placeholder citations. These citations need not be in proper form but should include the main pieces of information, such as a case's name and page number, that will permit you to develop a complete citation at the next stage. Using placeholder citations is wise for two reasons. First, for most people, developing a proper citation takes time and energy; thus, it detracts from the writing of the analysis or argument. Second, until the document is in nearly final form, it will not be clear in what order the citations will appear; sequence of citations is a key determinant of citation form.

Once the document is in nearly final form, it is time to craft the proper citations. One strategy is to work through the paper, tackling each citation as it comes. Another is to tackle the citations source by source. Either can work.

D. DEVELOP EACH CITATION METHODICALLY

As you craft each citation, a standard approach is to read through the rule governing that particular category of source, then weave in what additional rules may call for. As an example, an overarching question is the typeface in which to present a citation; this may be covered in a general rule rather than in the rule specific to your source. Furthermore, for a good number of sources, you will need to weave in information from a table, such as a table of abbreviations or a jurisdictional table. In other words:

(1) Work through the main rule for the source.
(2) Draw in additional points from general rules (e.g., typeface).
(3) Consult any pertinent tables (e.g., abbreviations, jurisdictions).

One of the intricacies—but also one of the efficiencies—of legal citation is the use of long and short forms. The first time that a source is cited in a stretch of text, the long form must include all required information. When you re-cite a source, much of the information may be excluded and a short form used. The amount that may be excluded depends on whether the current citation immediately follows a citation to that source or whether some other intervening source cited. If the re-citation immediately follows a citation to the same source, the word *id.* is used to tell the reader to refer back to the immediately preceding citation. When a citation to some other source intervenes so that *id.* is not appropriate, some information is needed to help the reader recall the citation. See Box III.1.

BOX III.1

LONG AND SHORT FORMS

	Case	Statute
Long citation form Used for initial citation	*Abraham v. Brooks*, 123 N.W.2d 456 (Minn. 2013).	Minn. Stat. § 123 (2014).
Shortest form Used when the immediately preceding citation is the same source	*Id.* at 458.	*Id.*
Short form Used when a source has been cited in full and some other source has intervened	*Abraham*, 123 N.W.2d at 457.	§ 123

Furthermore, citation format varies somewhat depending on how much you feature your citation in your text. In some situations, you may want to call the source to the reader's attention; this is known as an "in-text reference." In other situations, you may simply state the proposition in text, conclude your sentence, and place the citation at the end in its own grammatical sentence; this is known as a "citation." In general, an in-text reference uses fewer abbreviations than a traditional citation. For example:

- In-text reference: Minnesota Statutes section 123 (2016) requires that a buyer do *x, y,* and *z.*
- Citation: In Minnesota, a buyer must do *x, y,* and *z.* Minn. Stat. § 123 (2016).

E. COMBINE CITATIONS PROPERLY

Not infrequently, it makes sense to include more than one source in support of a legal proposition. A classic example is a rule derived from a statute as interpreted by a court. Combining more than one citation into a string cite is governed by several citation rules. One rule calls for reflecting the hierarchy of the sources, so that, for example, Supreme Court cases precede court of appeals cases and binding precedents precede persuasive precedents. Furthermore, phrases are used to tell the reader how two sources that rely on each other are linked. For example, a citation could indicate that a case interprets a statute.

Some students believe that a string cite is always advisable, on the theory that more is better. Rarely will a legal reader be impressed by the quantity of citations; the more important question is whether the cited material adequately supports the citation. An exception is the rare situation when you are writing to persuade a court to alter its law to match the law of many other jurisdictions.

F. USE CITATION HONESTLY AND PERSUASIVELY

Regardless of the document, whether it is an objective analytical memo or an appellate brief to the highest court, legal propositions must be properly supported by their citations. Much of the time a source will say precisely what is needed. Other times, a source will suggest a proposition. Sometimes a proposition arises from the comparison of two related cases but is not stated in either one.

Indeed, in the advocacy setting, you may find yourself arguing for a position that is somewhat at odds with the law. You may argue for an interpretation of the law that is not the only one supported by current law, or your client may be seeking a change in the law.

One option in these complex situations is to explain in your text how you derived your proposition from the source. Another more graceful option provided by legal citation is the signal: a word that tells the reader what the connection is. Signals fall on a spectrum, as shown in Box III.2. Note that once you progress much beyond the *see* signal, you should provide an explanation, which typically is a phrase at the end of the citation.

BOX III.2

SIGNALS CONTINUUM

[None]	See	See generally	Compare	Cf.	But cf.	But see	Contra

Strongest support ← — — — — — — — — — — — — — — — → Strongest contradiction

---

TABLE OF AUTHORITIES